CORPORATE RESPONSIBILITY FOR HUMAN RIGHTS IMPACTS

NEW EXPECTATIONS AND PARADIGMS

LARA BLECHER

NANCY KAYMAR STAFFORD

GRETCHEN C. BELLAMY

18 17 16 15 14 5 4 3 2 1

Library of Congress Cataloging-in-Publication Data

Corporate responsibility for human rights impacts : new expectations and paradigms / Lara Blecher, Nancy Kaymar Stafford, Gretchen Bellamy, editors.
  pages cm
  ISBN 978-1-62722-391-1 (alk. paper)
  1. Human rights. 2. Social responsibility of business. 3. Corporate governance--Law and legislation. 4. Tort liability of corporations. I. Blecher, Lara Jill, editor of compilation. II. Stafford, Nancy Kaymar, editor of compilation. III. Bellamy, Gretchen, editor of compilation.
  K3240.C668 2014
  341.4'8--dc23

                                                                    2013041938

About the Editors

Lara Blecher

Lara has worked in the area of business and human rights for the last thirteen years. As a Research Fellow in Business and Human Rights at the British Institute of International and Comparative Law, she has contributed to research on the UN Guiding Principles on Business and Human Rights, transnational litigation against businesses for their role in human rights abuses committed abroad, and climate change-related forced migration. Lara also worked for many years on ethical supply chain management, with a particular focus on labor rights. She is a New York-qualified lawyer with a law degree from King's College London. In addition, she holds a Master of Regional Planning degree from Cornell University and a Bachelor of Arts degree from the University of Michigan - Ann Arbor.

Nancy Kaymar Stafford

Nancy is Division Chair for the Africa/Eurasia Division of the American Bar Association Section of International Law ("ABA-SIL"). She is also a consultant with King and Spalding LLP in Atlanta, GA and owner of the Cliffside Inn in Newport, RI. Ms. Stafford started her career as an associate with Piper, Marbury, Rudnick & Wolfe LLP and has worked for women's rights issues in Africa with several organizations. She is the author of numerous articles and book chapters on rights based topics. Ms. Stafford received a J.D. from DePaul University College of Law and an LL.M., in international and comparative law, from Georgetown University Law Center.

Gretchen C. Bellamy

Gretchen is an Assistant General Counsel for Wal-Mart Stores, Inc. From 2011 – 2013, she served as the Diversity Officer for the American Bar Association Section of International Law ("ABA-SIL"), planning CLE programming related to corporate accountability diversity in the legal profession, among other topics. She was a member of the eight-person delegation sent by the American Bar Association to the first Forum on Business and Human Rights in 2012. Ms. Bellamy received a J.D. and LL.M. in international and comparative law from Duke University School of Law. Prior to assuming her role at Wal-Mart, she served as the Director of International Public Interest and Pro Bono Programs at the University of Miami School of Law. She also worked as an associate in the corporate law department of Smith, Anderson, Blount, Dorsett, Mitchell & Jernigan, LLP in Raleigh,

NC and as a summer associate at Shearman & Sterling, LLP in New York, NY. She is a Returned Peace Corps Volunteer (Cameroon 2001).

Contents

Chapter 5
Trade and Investment Arrangements and Labor Rights   121
Jeffrey S. Vogt

Chapter 10
The UK Context for Business and Human Rights

Rachel Chambers and Katherine Tyler

Chapter 11
Current Trends and Future Effects in Transnational Litigation against Corporations in the United Kingdom

Shubhaa Srinivasan

Part III
Looking to the Future   355

Chapter 12
Foreign Direct-Liability Litigation   357
Peter Muchlinski and Virginie Rouas
School of Law, SOAS, University of London

Chapter 13
Labour Rights in the World Economy   393
Sheldon Leader

Chapter 14
Financial Institutions and Human Rights

Dr. Mary Dowell-Jones

Chapter 15
B Corporations: Redefining Success in Business

Andrew Kassoy and Nathan Gilbert

Author Acknowledgments

Robert McCorquodale

My thanks to Lara Blecher for her research assistance for Chapter 3 and to Camilla Wee for her research on the development of the Guiding Principles.

Penelope Simons

Chapter 4 was previously published in volume 3 of the *Journal of Human Rights and the Environment* (2012) and is reproduced here with permission. Earlier drafts of this chapter were presented at the British Institute of International and Comparative Law Annual Meeting: Business and International Law, London, UK, June 5, 2009; the 4th Biennial Conference of the European Society of International Law, Cambridge, UK, September 24, 2010; and at the conference Re-engineering the Corporation: Human Rights, the Corporation, and the Environment, School of Law, Queen's University Belfast, June 28–29, 2011. I would like to thank Karyn Keenan, Don Hubert, Robert McCorquodale, Audrey Macklin, and Sara Seck, as well as the reviewers and editors of the *Journal of Human Rights and the Environment* and the editors of this volume for their very helpful comments and suggestions. I would also like to thank Jordana Laporte, Jon Khan, Gregg Erauw, Heather Curran, and Caitlin Maxwell for their excellent research assistance.

Paul Hoffman

I would like to thank Beth Stephens, Ralph Steinhardt, Rebecca Graham, Catherine Sweetser, and Marco Simons for their insightful comments on drafts of Chapter 7.

Neil Popović

I would like to thank Givelle Lamano, JD, Golden Gate University Law School, for her research.

Erika George

Thanks to Lara Blecher, Joan MacLeod Heminway, Stefan Padfield, and John Plimpton for their comments; to Laurie Evans Abbott, Felicity Murphy, Oriene Shin, Irene Berkey, and Pegeen Bassett for research assistance; and to Spencer Lewis and Becky Dustin for reference review.

Rachel Chambers

I would like to acknowledge Richard Hermer, QC, for his assistance with Chapter 10.

Katherine Tyler

I would like to thank Stuart Biggs and Richard Hermer for their help with Chapter 10.

Peter Muchlinski and Virginie Rouas

This chapter draws upon, updates and revises material previously published in Peter T. Muchlinski, The Provision of Private Law Remedies against Multinational Enterprises: a Comparative Law Perspective, 4 J. Comp. L. 148 (2009). Our thanks to Wildy, Simmonds and Hill Publishing for permission to use this material in this chapter. Also, we thank Ebbe Rogge and Michael Wiebush for providing help in the translation of the Dutch case-law.

Sheldon Leader

This chapter originally appeared in Antoine Lyon-Caen and AdalbertoPerulli, Evaluate Labour Law (Cedam 2010). I would like to thank A. Lyon-Caen and A. Perulli, editors of *Evaluate Labour Law* (CEDAM: Milan 2010).

Andrew Kassoy and Nathan Gilbert

This paper benefits and quotes extensively from William H. Clark Jr. & Larry Vranka, The Need and Rationale for the Benefit Corporation (Benefit Corp., 2013), http://benefitcorp .net/for-attorneys/benefit-corp-white-paper (a piece to which the authors contributed substantially). We would like to acknowledge William H. Clark Jr. and Larry Vranka, who worked together with B Lab to write "The Need and Rationale for the Benefit Corporation," on which Chapter 15 is based.

Sarah Altschuller

Segments of the chapter were previously published as Distinctions with Differences: The Attorney's Role in Distinguishing CSR and Corporate Philanthropy, International Law News (Winter 2010) & Proactive Management of Legal Risk, CSR Journal (A.B.A. Section of International Law, 2008).

Editor Acknowledgments

Huge thanks to all the book authors for their contributions.

Sincere thanks to Robert McCorquodale and the British Institute of International and Comparative Law for providing guidance and support during the editing process.

Many thanks to the student volunteers who gave their time to fact-check and format footnotes. These volunteers are Danielle Falarz, Cassandra A. Castellano, Gudrun Juffer,

Aretha Chakraborti, Benjamin Menker, Erik Johnson, Gina Pham, James Miller, Tarik Hansen, Thomas Worger, Sheila Chen, Hannah Perrin Flamm, and Michelle Ferguson.

Particular thanks to Aretha Chakraborti for *Bluebook*ing multiple chapters and to Paul Hoffman for arranging to have his students check and format footnotes.

Thanks to the American Bar Association, in particular Bill Mock and Rick Paszkiet, for agreeing to publish this book.

Author Biographies

Justine Nolan

Justine Nolan is a senior lecturer in the Faculty of Law at the University of North South Wales and the Deputy Director of the Australian Human Rights Centre. Justine is most recently a co-author of an international human rights textbook titled *The Law of International Human Rights*, OUP, 2011. Prior to joining UNSW in 2004, she worked as the director of the Business and Human Rights Program at the Lawyers Committee for Human Rights (now Human Rights First) in the United States. Justine is a member of the Australian Department of Foreign Affairs and Trade and Ausaid's Human Rights Grants (HRSGS) Scheme Expert Panel, which provides practical financial support for small, community-based projects to promote and protect human rights in developing countries. She is also a member of NSW Legal Aid's Human Rights Panel and an editor of the *Australian Journal of Human Rights*.

Ralph G. Steinhardt

Ralph G. Steinhardt is the Arthur Selwyn Miller Research Professor of Law and International Relations at George Washington University Law School in Washington, D.C. For thirty years Professor Steinhardt has been active in the domestic litigation of international law in U.S. courts, specializing in the representation *pro bono* of various human rights organizations, as well as individual human rights victims, before all levels of the federal judiciary, including the U.S. Supreme Court. He has also served as an expert witness in a variety of cases involving the extraterritorial reach of U.S. law and the civil liability of multinational corporations for their alleged complicity in human rights violations. He has on multiple occasions represented international law scholars *amicus curiae* in litigation under the Alien Tort Statute, including most recently *Kiobel v. Royal Dutch Shell*. He served on the International Commission of Jurists' Expert Legal Panel on Corporate Complicity in International Crimes. He is the cofounder of the Programme in International Human Rights Law at New College, Oxford University, and the founding chairman of the board of directors of the Center for Justice and Accountability, an anti-impunity organization that specializes in litigation under the Alien Tort Statute.

Robert McCorquodale

Professor Robert McCorquodale is the Director of the British Institute of International and Comparative Law in London. He is also Professor of international law and human rights and former Head of the School of Law at the University of Nottingham. He is also a barrister at Brick Court Chambers, London.

Previously he was a Fellow and Lecturer in law at St. John's College, University of Cambridge, and at the Australian National University in Canberra. Before embarking on an academic career, he worked as a qualified lawyer in commercial litigation with leading law firms in Sydney and London.

Robert's research and teaching interests are in the areas of public international law and human rights law. He has published widely on these subjects and has provided advice to governments, corporations, international organizations, nongovernmental organizations, and individuals concerning international law and human rights issues, including advising on the drafting of new constitutions and conducting human rights training courses.

Penelope Simons

Penelope Simons has a PhD in international law from the University of Cambridge and is an associate professor at the Faculty of Law (Common Law Section), University of Ottawa, Canada. She has been engaged in research on corporate human rights accountability since December 1999, when she participated in the Canadian Assessment Mission to Sudan (Harker Mission), appointed by Canada's minister of foreign affairs and international trade, to investigate allegations of slavery as well as links between oil development in Sudan and violations of human rights. Her current research is focused on the human rights implications of domestic and extraterritorial corporate activity as well as state responsibility for corporate complicity in human rights. She is a co-author of the monograph *The Governance Gap: Extractive Industries, Human Rights and the Home State Advantage*, which examines the human rights implications of extractive company activities in zones of weak governance and argues for home state regulation. In addition, she is a co-author of *Integrating Sustainable Development into International Investment Agreements: A Guide for Developing Country Negotiators*. The book was commissioned by the Commonwealth Secretariat and provides guidance for developing countries negotiating international investment agreements on ways to preserve policy space and to support their efforts to regulate foreign investors in a manner that contributes to sustainable development, including the protection of human rights. Penelope teaches international human rights law, business organizations, public international law, and a course on the intersections between human rights, transnational corporate activity, and international economic law.

Jeffrey S. Vogt

Jeff Vogt is the deputy director and legal advisor to the Human and Trade Union Rights Department of the International Trade Union Confederation (ITUC), a global organization that represents 175 million workers in 153 countries and territories. In that capacity, he coordinates the organization's labor standards advocacy before the International Labour

Organization and advises trade unions on international labor law and labor law reform, among other matters. Before joining the ITUC in 2011, he was the global economic policy specialist for the American Federation of Labor and Congress of Industrial Organizations (AFL-CIO) and later the deputy director of its International Department. Previously, he represented domestic and foreign trade unions in litigation in state and federal courts. He is a graduate of Cornell Law School, where he earned his JD and LLM in International and Comparative Law. He further studied international law at the University of Paris 1, Sorbonne.

Beth Stephens

Beth Stephens is a professor of law at Rutgers-Camden Law School. She has published a variety of articles on the relationship between international and domestic law, focusing on the enforcement of international human rights norms through domestic courts and the incorporation of international law into U.S. law. Professor Stephens has written extensively on the historical origins and modern application of the Alien Tort Statute (ATS) and on ATS litigation against corporations. As a cooperating attorney with the Center for Constitutional Rights and a former member of the board of directors of the Center for Justice and Accountability, Professor Stephens continues to litigate human rights cases, including the Supreme Court case *Samantar v. Yousuf*, which held that foreign officials are not protected by the Foreign Sovereign Immunities Act. Her publications include a co-authored book titled *International Human Rights Litigation in U.S. Courts* (Martinus Nijhoff Publishers, second edition, 2008).

Paul Hoffman

Paul Hoffman is a partner in the Venice, California, law firm of Schonbron DeSimone Seplow Harris & Hoffman LLP, where he specializes in civil and human rights litigation. He argued *Kiobel v. Royal Dutch Petroleum* twice in the U.S. Supreme Court and before that argued *Sosa v. Alvarez-Machain*, also in the Supreme Court. He has litigated numerous international human rights cases over the last thirty-five years. Mr. Hoffman was previously the Legal Director of the ACLU Foundation of Southern California and the Chair of the International Executive Committee of Amnesty International and Chair of the Board of Amnesty International-U.S.A. He has taught international human rights law at University of California at Irvine, UCLA, U.S.C, Loyola, and Southwestern law schools as well as at Oxford University. He has written extensively on civil and human rights issues and is the co-author of a treatise on international human rights litigation and a casebook on human rights lawyering.

Neil A. F. Popović

Neil A. F. Popović is a litigation partner at Sheppard Mullin Richter & Hampton LLP in San Francisco, where he chairs the firm's International Arbitration Practice. He is also a lecturer at the University of California, Berkeley, Law School (Boalt Hall), where he has taught international environmental law and international litigation and arbitration. Mr. Popović received his law degree from Boalt Hall and a master's degree from the Fletcher School of Law and Diplomacy at Tufts University, where he was a Ford Foundation Fellow in Public International Law. Mr. Popović served as an appointed law clerk for United States District Judge Alicemarie H. Stotler and a judicial extern for California Supreme Court Justice Joseph R. Grodin. In 1994, while working as an international project attorney for the Sierra Club Legal Defense Fund (now Earthjustice), Mr. Popović served as corapporteur for the UN Meeting of Experts on Human Rights and the Environment that produced the Draft Declaration of Principles on Human Rights and the Environment.

Erika R. George

Erika R. George is professor of law at the University of Utah's S. J. Quinney College of Law, where she teaches constitutional law, international human rights law, international environmental law, civil procedure, and a seminar course on corporations and human rights. She earned her BA with honors at the University of Chicago and her JD at Harvard Law School, where she served as articles editor of the *Harvard Civil Rights-Civil Liberties Law Review*. She also holds an MA in International Relations from the University of Chicago. Her current research explores the responsibilities of multinational corporations to respect international human rights and various efforts to hold corporations accountable for alleged rights violations. She is the author of *Incorporating Rights*, forthcoming from Oxford University Press. Prior to entering the legal academy, Professor George was a corporate litigation associate with the law firms Jenner & Block in Chicago and Coudert Brothers LLP in New York City. She also served as a fellow with Human Rights Watch, conducting human rights investigations. Professor George has testified before international human rights treaty bodies and foreign governments, and she has briefed the international media on international human rights law, racial discrimination, and gender equality and sexual violence. The BBC, the *Economist*, NBC News, CNN, and the *Christian Science Monitor*, among other media outlets, have reported on her human rights investigations.

Rachel Chambers

Rachel Chambers is a barrister specializing in employment law, with a particular emphasis on discrimination and human rights. She previously worked at the International Business Leaders Forum and Amnesty International, and as an academic researcher on the subject of business and human rights at Monash University, Melbourne. Rachel has had a number of articles published on subjects such as corporate complicity in human rights violations, the UN norms on the Responsibilities of Transnational Corporations and Other Business Enterprises with Regard to Human Rights, and litigating in home states against multinational corporations. She co-authored *Human Rights Translated: A Business Reference*

Guide, published by the UN Office of the High Commissioner on Human Rights, and others. She holds an MA in law from Oxford University and an LLM by research, a 40,000-word thesis written under the supervision of Professor Peter Muchlinski, now of the School of Oriental and African Studies (SOAS), University of London.

Katherine Tyler

Katherine Tyler, LLM (international law and human rights), is a barrister practicing in public, regulatory, and criminal law. Katherine has worked with a number of high-profile NGOs and law firms on issues of international corporate responsibility and liability, and she is involved in complementary work in the area of corporate risk. Katherine's published articles consider subjects including the regulation of the extractive industries, the UN norms on the Responsibilities of Transnational Corporations and Other Business Enterprises with Regard to Human Rights, the Organization for Economic Cooperation and Development (OECD) National Contact Point, and other grievance mechanisms. She is speaking in a series of seminars on non-financial regulation of companies, the role of lawyers in the regulation of corporate abuse abroad, and UK liability for human rights abuses.

Shubhaa Srinivasan

Shubhaa is a partner at Leigh Day, a firm that has been at the forefront of group litigation for more than a decade and virtually the only law firm in the United Kingdom to specialize in business and human rights cases involving actions against British multinational corporations.

Shubhaa is a qualified barrister and has an LLM from School of Oriental and African Studies (SOAS), University of London. She has litigated group actions involving personal injury and environmental claims against private British corporations and state entities. In 2007 - 2008 she represented a number of Iraqi torture victims against the UK government. She currently represents UK military service personnel in claims against the UK Ministry of Defense alleging inadequate provision of military equipment during the Iraq war.

Shubhaa has developed an expertise in mass tort litigation involving environmental claims and is currently acting for more than seventy Colombian farmers in an environmental claim against a BP company, the first of its kind to go through the UK courts when it was commenced in 2008.

Professor Peter T. Muchlinski

Peter Muchlinski is professor in international commercial law at the School of Oriental and African Studies (SOAS), University of London. Prior to joining SOAS he was professor of law and international business at Kent Law School, University of Kent (2001–2005). He has taught at the London School of Economics (1983–1998) and was the Drapers' Professor of Law in the Law Department of Queen Mary and Westfield College, University of London, from 1998 to 2001. He specializes in international and European business law, international investment law, law and development, and commercial regulation, in which fields he has authored numerous papers and articles. His more recent published work concentrates on the social dimension of the regulation of international business, with emphasis on human rights and multinational enterprises and on the rebalancing of rights and obligations of host and home countries and investors in international investment agreements. He also has an interest in the relationship between international and comparative legal methodology and the process of globalization, focusing in particular on international and comparative corporate law. He is the author of *Multinational Enterprises and the Law* (second edition, Oxford University Press, 2007) and (with Julia Black and Paul Walker) editor of *Commercial Regulation and Judicial Review* (Hart Publishing, 1998). He is coeditor (with Dr. Federico Ortino and Professor Christoph Schreuer) of the *Oxford Handbook of International Investment Law* (Oxford University Press, 2008). In 1990 he qualified as a barrister in the field of commercial and European law and is a door tenant at Brick Court Chambers, London. He acts as a principal adviser on investment issues to the United Nations Conference on Trade and Development (UNCTAD). During the period of June to October 2003, he was on leave of absence from Kent Law School and worked at UNCTAD in Geneva as a senior legal expert in the Division on Investment Technology and Enterprise Development. He was, until its dissolution in August 2008, corapporteur to the International Law Association Committee on the International Law on Foreign Investment.

Virginie Rouas

Virginie Rouas is currently a PhD candidate in law at the School of Oriental and African Studies (SOAS), University of London. Her research focuses on transnational litigation against multinational enterprises in Europe. She is also coordinating a project led by Frank Bold and the European Coalition for Corporate Justice on civil justice within the EU in the context of transnational business activities and human rights. Over the past years, she has worked for several organizations, including the United Nations Programme Environment (UNEP), the International Union for Conservation of Nature (IUCN), the Centre for International Sustainable Development Law (CISDL), and Global Witness. Virginie holds an LLM in environmental law from the University of Strasbourg (France) and an MSc in political science from Lille II University (France).

Sheldon Leader

Sheldon Leader is Professor of Law at the University of Essex (UK). A graduate of Yale and Oxford Universities, he works in the area of economic relations and human rights, as well as in legal theory. He has been legal advisor to Amnesty International (UK) and has provided analyses of the human rights impacts of investment agreements for civil society organizations and for governments. He is founder and director of the Essex Business and Human Rights Project, a body that carries out research and advice to academic and non-academic bodies. He formulated the basic principles for the *Human Rights Undertaking* governing the BTC pipeline, the first legally binding human rights commitment incorporated into an international investment contract. Among his publications are *Human Rights on the Line*, (Amnesty International UK: 2003) (with Andrea Shemberg); "Human Rights, Risks, and New Strategies for Global Investment" 9 *Journal of International Economic Law* 657 (2006); "The Place of Labour Rights in Foreign Direct Investment" in *Global Labor and Employment Law* eds A. Morris and S. Estreicher, (Kluwer 2010); "Risk Management, Project Finance, and Rights Based Development" in *Global Project Finance, Human Rights, and Sustainable Development*, Sheldon Leader, David Ong (eds.) (Cambridge University Press: 2011); and "Corporate Accountability", in M. Bovens, et al (eds.), *The Oxford Handbook on Public Accountability*, Oxford University Press (2014).

Mary Dowell-Jones

Mary Dowell-Jones is a Research Fellow in the School of Law at the University of New South Wales, Sydney, and a Fellow of the Human Rights Law Centre at Nottingham University, UK. Her research focuses on legal responses to financial crises and the use of law in managing systemic instability in the financial markets. She also researches and writes on the ethical responsibilities of the financial sector and how human rights can be applied effectively to the operations of global financial markets. This includes the areas of bond markets, derivatives, risk management, audit and corporate governance. She has advised various organizations on the financial crisis of 2007 and its global human rights impacts, financial regulation and human rights, and financial institutions and the UN Guiding Principles on Business and Human Rights.

She has a background in both international human rights law and international finance. Her Ph.D. in public international law from Nottingham University analyzed the institutional and policy challenges to realizing the International Covenant on Economic, Social and Cultural Rights in the context of globalization. She has also worked in corporate and investment banking in London and South Africa, including as part of a team implementing the Basel II capital adequacy regulations. She is currently a member of a local government Standards Committee in the UK, which upholds the Code of Conduct for elected officials, and a member of the Audit Committee for one of the UK's police forces.

Andrew Kassoy

Andrew is cofounder of B Lab, a nonprofit dedicated to harnessing the power of business to solve social and environmental problems. He created B Lab with longtime friends Bart Houlahan and Jay Coen Gilbert. Before leaving the private sector to form B Lab, Andrew spent sixteen years in the private equity business, most recently as a partner at MSD Real

Estate Capital, an affiliate of MSD Capital, the $12 billion investment vehicle for Michael Dell. He is a board member of the Freelancers Union and the Freelancers Union Insurance Company and a board member of Echoing Green, a nonprofit venture fund that provides seed capital to emerging social entrepreneurs.

Nathan Gilbert

Nathan Gilbert is the program associate for B Lab, a nonprofit dedicated to creating a new sector of the economy that uses the power of business to solve social and environmental problems. Nathan is supporting B Lab's international partnership development to make the B-Corp certification available to entrepreneurs across the world and build a global community of social entrepreneurs. Nathan earned a BA in ethnomusicology from Indiana University and an MS in nonprofit management from Milano, the New School of Management and Urban Policy. After five years of working with civil society development organizations in Eastern Europe, Nathan pursued his interests in working with nonprofits to develop program-related earned income strategies to becoming self-sufficient. He later became more involved with the for-profit social enterprise sector and went to work with B Lab. Nathan has worked with the NYC Department of Youth and Community Development, the Institute of International Education, and in the Balkans with the Institute for Sustainable Communities. Prior to graduate school, he served in Ukraine as a Peace Corps volunteer.

Sarah Altschuller

Sarah Altschuller has been a member of Foley Hoag's Corporate Social Responsibility (CSR) practice since 2003. In this role, she advises multinational companies regarding the development and implementation of CSR strategies, policies, and procedures, as well as compliance with emerging legal and regulatory requirements. Sarah provides counsel regarding engagements with socially responsible investors, government policymakers, local communities, nongovernmental organizations, and other key stakeholders. She also conducts site-level human rights and labor rights impact assessments as well as due diligence efforts. Sarah is a leading contributor to the firm's Corporate Social Responsibility and the Law blog.

Sarah's in-depth practical experience includes post–law school studies at North South University in Dhaka, Bangladesh (2002–2003), where she conducted research on working conditions in the garment sector. Before entering law school, Sarah conducted social research on publicly traded domestic and international companies at KLD Research & Analytics, a socially responsible investment firm, currently part of MSCI, Inc.

Introduction

This book has been three years in the making and was only possible through the incredible generosity of the authors. It is a testament to the kindness, dedication, and conviction of the business and human rights community that these authors, all of whom are extremely busy and in high demand in their field, did not think twice about contributing chapters to this publication. This commitment involved donating their precious time and resources, which all of them did patiently and without complaint. It also involved negotiating moving deadlines as a result of protracted U.S. Supreme Court cases. The result of this kindness, patience, and generosity is a fascinating collection of perspectives on the key developments and trends in business and human rights law.

Part I sets the international legal context of the business and human rights arena, with Justine Nolan and Ralph Steinhardt trading opposing arguments on the direct applicability of international law to corporations. Robert McCorquodale then offers a critique of the United Nations Framework and Guiding Principles on business and human rights, explaining some of the dilemmas raised by each of the three pillars of the framework. Penelope Simons applies a Third World Approach to International Law (TWAIL) analysis along with feminist critiques of international law to assess the approach of the UN special representative on business and human rights in the development of his Policy Framework and Guiding Principles, and the importance of international law as part of an overall strategy for regulating the human rights impacts of transnational corporations. Jeffrey Vogt concludes the section by describing how trade and investment treaties have developed in their attempts to address the labor violations stemming from multinational business practices in a globalizing economy.

Part II explores domestic policy, legislation, and litigation in the United States and United Kingdom focusing on corporate accountability for human rights. Beth Stephens begins this section with a historical look at the U.S. Alien Tort Statute (ATS) and how it has developed into a tool for corporate accountability. Paul Hoffman and Neil Popović then describe the trajectory of case law against corporations under the ATS, including the recently concluded *Kiobel* litigation, and other relevant U.S. statutes, focusing, respectively, on social and environmental aspects of the cases. Erika George concludes an overview of the U.S. context with an account of developments in U.S. legislation, such as the conflict minerals provision of the Dodd-Frank Act and the California Supply Chain Transparency Act, and likely trends resulting from these developments. By way of comparison, Rachel

Chambers and Katherine Tyler present the UK policy, legislation, and litigation trends in corporate accountability for human rights, flagging the concern of imminent procedural changes in the United Kingdom that could severely curtail further case law in this area. Shubhaa Srinivasan then elaborates on the development of litigation in the United Kingdom against corporations for human rights abuses abroad and challenges typically faced by victim litigants in bringing legal action.

Part III of the book anticipates future developments in corporate accountability for human rights. In building on the analysis of the prior six authors, Peter Muchlinski and Virginie Rouas question whether civil or common law systems are better disposed to accommodate business and human rights litigation by comparing U.S., English, and developing European and Indian case law. Sheldon Leader goes on to suggest that lawyers can better balance different areas of law when performing legal analyses. Mary Dowell-Jones presents a practical example of this balance of laws argument with an analysis of how the financial industry impacts human rights and what the financial crisis suggests about necessary regulatory reform in this industry. Andrew Kassoy and Nathan Gilbert then present a further example of how a better legal balance might be struck with a case study of their organization's initiative to reform corporate law to better align social and environmental considerations with the incentives set by financial markets, or as they put it, to "bake social and environmental considerations into the DNA of a company." Finally, Sarah Altschuller explains how to integrate human rights into legal practice by distinguishing corporate social responsibility (CSR) from corporate philanthropy and explaining why and how CSR is an important tool for attorneys in advising clients.

Despite this eclectic array of perspectives, certain themes and questions emerge. For instance: How will lawyers and courts deal with the thorny issue of extraterritoriality in transnational litigation brought against companies for human rights abuses abroad? The *Kiobel* case in the United States, addressed in so many chapters, has stipulated a "presumption against extraterritoriality" in Alien Tort Statute cases, but clarification of a sufficient nexus with the United States has yet to be determined. As this book went to press, the Supreme Court issued a decision that clarifies limitations on the exercise of personal jurisdiction over foreign parent corporations sued in U.S. courts for extraterritorial torts, although it is too soon to know the full implications of the decision. (*Daimler AG. v. Bauman et al.*, 571 U.S. ___ (2014).) As Justice Sotomayor stated in her concurring opinion in that case, the process chosen by the Court's approach may "shift the risk of loss from multinational corporations to the individuals harmed by their actions." (Slip op. at p. 18.) The UN Guiding Principles, which are also discussed in many of the chapters, offer a noncommittal voice on extraterritoriality but are rapidly developing into a soft law reference, cited in established international standards such as the Organization of Economic Cooperation and Development (OECD) Guidelines for Multinational Enterprises and the updated International Finance Corporation (IFC)

Performance Standards. The European Union has also cited the UN Guiding Principles in its latest CSR strategy, and many national governments are recognizing the need to regulate in the area of business and human rights, as a number of the authors have shown through their analyses of recent policy and statutory developments in the United States, United Kingdom, and European Union.

Inevitably, certain choices must be made in compiling a volume such as this. Though examples of legal developments in corporate accountability for human rights in developing countries are discussed in many chapters, the focus of the book is clearly on developments in the United States and United Kingdom. This decision does not mean to suggest that significant developments are absent in other countries; it merely reflects that the bulk of developments in this area of law to date have occurred in the United States and United Kingdom. This concentration of efforts will surely shift and disperse in the coming years, as suggested in Muchlinski and Rouas's chapter. We would like to emphasize that we hope this book will inspire discussions involving a variety of perspectives, and though the emphasis of this book may be on human rights, we encourage authors with alternative specialties to respond loudly and prolifically to the contents of this volume.

Regardless of one's perspective, this book demonstrates that business and human rights law is a dynamic, rich field that is prompting both legal and business innovations in the pursuit of human rights. We look forward to tracking these developments and hope that this collection of writings will allow a variety of readers to do the same.

Lara Blecher
Nancy Kaymar Stafford
Gretchen Bellamy
January 2014

Part I

Legal Context

Chapter 1

All Care, No Responsibility?
Why Corporations Have Limited Responsibility and No Direct Accountability for Human Rights Violations under International Law

Justine Nolan

Introduction

International law, particularly international human rights law, has been slow to react to the role played in this globalized world by nonstate actors such as corporations. Corporations play a fundamental role in domestic and international economies, and the presence or absence of business can impact human rights both positively and negatively. Corporations can positively affect the economy and broader community in a variety of ways: jobs and wages are made available, goods and services are provided, and taxes are paid, enabling governments to provide further goods and services. Thereby, directly or indirectly, a vast array of human rights may be supported, from the right to work, welfare, food and shelter, and health and education to freedom of speech, association, and movement. Corporations are not only central to the provision of many things that make human life more tolerable, enjoyable, and fulfilling, but corporate enterprise also brings to all communities work and wages, which are key elements to the establishment and maintenance of individual human dignity, which is the end human rights strive to meet.

However, the influence of corporations on human rights is not all benign, and the growth and spread of transnational corporations (TNCs) around the globe has been paralleled by attempts to establish responsibility and/or accountability for the deleterious impacts on human rights from the ever-increasing number of companies whose corporate tentacles stretch across national boundaries and beyond the reach of traditional (domestic) corporate control mechanisms. Corporations, both local and transnational, have been and continue to be minor and major abusers of human rights. The corporate responsibility movement has been spurred on by consistent examples of corporate irresponsibility. Particularly since the early 1990s, various brand names have become synonymous with human rights, some in a positive sense and some more negatively. Some corporations are guilty of treating workers badly in terms of pay and working conditions and environments; some pollute the environment in ways that have dramatic and serious effects far beyond their immediate surroundings; some discriminate against indigenous peoples, certain ethnic or religious groups, women, people with disabilities, or on grounds of sexuality; and some work alongside (or inside) governments that perpetrate gross human rights abuses.[1]

In the human rights sphere, a variety of nonstate actors are playing an increasingly predominant role in both applying relevant human rights standards and enforcing them (through, for example, mechanisms such as reporting and monitoring) in attempts to curb corporate rights violations. Traditionally, international human rights law focuses on the state as both the primary protector and abuser of human rights and has been reluctant to consider whether it is appropriate to define a complementary role for nonstate actors, whether in terms of assigning duties or the enforcement of rights. In the last forty years, attempts to regulate the impact of business activities on human rights have multiplied, employing a range of diverse tactics, such as developing codes of conduct and international guidelines, litigation, and domestic legislation applied extraterritorially. A few earlier attempts to work within the United Nations (UN) system and develop an international legal framework to impose human rights duties on corporations have largely failed.[2] Predominantly, there has been a reliance on "soft law" to link business with human rights internationally, but neither industry-based initiatives, such as corporate codes, nor multilateral initiatives, such as the United Nations Global Compact, involve the kind of concrete obligations that some human rights, labor, and other advocates believe are necessary to effectively restrain corporate misbehavior. To the dismay of activists and the satisfaction of some TNCs, some argue that a proliferation of codes, networks, and standards has been helping to improve corporate reputations while effectively keeping any discussion of potential international "hard law" measures off the agenda. Litigation conducted against corporations for human rights violations has been relatively high profile but largely restricted to the use of the U.S. Alien Torts Claims Act[3] and has touched only a relatively small number of companies. The appointment of Dr. John Ruggie as UN

---

1.   David Kinley & Justine Nolan, *Trading and Aiding Human Rights: Corporations in the Global Economy*, 25 NORDIC J. HUM. RTS. 353, 358 (2008).

2.   See discussion below in Section II.

3.   Alien Tort Claims Act, 28 U.S.C. § 1350. This avenue of accountability has likely now been severely restricted by the U.S. Supreme Court decision in Kiobel v. Royal Dutch Petroleum, 621 F.3d 111 (2013). See Section III for further discussion.

Special Representative of the Secretary-General (SRSG) on business and human rights in 2005 sparked renewed efforts by the UN to engage in these issues and clarify the responsibilities attributable to both states and nonstate actors in respecting, protecting, and fulfilling the human rights of individuals around the world.

Over the last three to four decades, attitudes toward and interest in issues of corporate responsibility have waxed and waned. *Corporate responsibility*, *corporate social responsibility*, *corporate accountability*, and *corporate citizenship* are all terms that have been used to describe a corporation's relationship with human rights. The lack of clarity around the terminology is indicative of the confusion and lack of consensus about how, why, and when corporations might assume some level of responsibility for human rights. The difference in semantics may seem trivial, and both *responsibility* and *accountability* can be similarly defined with perhaps very little difference to a nonlegal observer. *Corporate responsibility* has, however, been used as a softer term, referring to something that should be done, because it is seen as the right thing to do, with a basis more in morality than in legality. *Corporate accountability* has tended to imply a more stringent standard, involving a legal obligation that imposes a duty that must be fulfilled. The 2011 endorsement by the UN Human Rights Council of the SRSG's Guiding Principles on Business and Human Rights[4] entrenches the concept of an international corporate responsibility for human rights that is driven by the parameters of social expectations and stands apart (and alongside) any (domestic) legal obligations that might attach to a corporation's activities. Those looking to the UN to embrace proactively an opportunity for international human rights law to move beyond its traditional state-centric focus may have been disappointed with its most recent endorsement of a nonlegal corporate responsibility standard.

International human rights law does not attribute any direct responsibility to corporations for human rights, and the mechanisms for holding corporations to account have largely arisen by default and not design. This chapter considers the limited avenues for holding corporations to account in the international arena, whether by *hard* or *soft* law. The first section considers the hard law international framework for attributing indirect responsibility for human rights to corporations. The second section then examines the soft law mechanisms that have developed to imbue corporations with a sense of responsibility and perhaps accountability for rights, starting with the most recent developments within the UN, which stem from the work of the SRSG in proposing a framework of corporate responsibility for human rights that entrenches a nonlegal basis for this concept. Section II concludes with a discussion of the cacophony of codes developed at an international

---

4.   Special Representative of the Secretary-General, *Guiding Principles on Business and Human Rights: Implementing the United Nations "Protect, Respect and Remedy" Framework: Report of the Special Representative of the Secretary-General on the Issue of Human Rights and Transnational Corporations and Other Business Enterprises*, UN Doc. A/HRC/17/31 (2011) [hereinafter *Guiding Principles* (by John Ruggie)].

level that preceded the SRSG's framework. The third section then briefly comments on the use of the courtroom, whether to apply domestic litigation that is applicable extraterritorially or to use the International Criminal Court. Either can be alternative methods to reign in corporations, given the paucity of direct international human rights legal obligations that attach to companies.

The State (Not Nonstate) Duty to Protect Human Rights

International instruments that enunciate human rights obligations are primarily directed toward states. Accordingly, the multilateral human rights instruments that establish the benchmarks for human rights standards are not generally interpreted as establishing direct human rights obligations for nonstate actors.[5] On that view, the legal source of human rights obligations for corporations are found elsewhere, including national laws, contracts, or other corporate undertakings, although international human rights law may define the content of human rights standards imposed by these means. Thus a contract or domestic law that includes a requirement to respect human rights may refer to international human rights law for a meaningful interpretation of that requirement. However, it has also been suggested that international law can extend international legal obligations to corporations in relation to human rights, or at least that there is no conceptual barrier to doing so.[6] One commentator argues that human rights obligations can attach to nonstate parties through the medium of the state that has control or jurisdiction over that nonstate party.[7] This circular obligation could be characterized as an indirect imposition of duties on the corporation because it is only realized by a state first assuming its direct obligation to protect human rights. Even if one accepts the view that corporations can indirectly assume human rights obligations, the capacity to enforce those standards remains at the domestic level. Although international human rights law has developed mechanisms for enforcing human rights obligations against states, it is left to states to

---

5.   Special Reprentative of the Secretary General, *Interim Report of the Special Representative of the Secretary General on the Issue of Human Rights and Transnational Corporations and Other Business Enterprises*, UN Doc. E/CN 4/2006/97 (2006) (by John Ruggie) [herienafter *Interim Report*] (especially ¶ 60). *Cf.* UN Sub-Comm'n on the Promotion and Prot. of Human Rights, *Norms on the Responsibilities of Transnational Corporations and Other Business Enterprises with Regard to Human Rights*, UN Doc. E/CN.4/Sub.2/2003/12/Rev.2 (2003) (the "Norms"). The preamble recites: "Realizing that transnational corporations and other business enterprises, their officers and persons working for them are also obligated to respect generally recognized responsibilities and norms contained in United Nations treaties and other international instruments."

6.   INT'L COUNCIL ON HUMAN RIGHTS POLICY, BEYOND VOLUNTARISM: HUMAN RIGHTS AND THE DEVELOPING INTERNATIONAL LEGAL OBLIGATIONS OF COMPANIES 55–76 (2002).

7.   David Bilchitz, "A chasm between 'is' and 'ought'? A critique of the normative foundations of the SRSG's framework and Guiding Principles" in Human Rights Obligations of Business: Beyond the Corporate Responsibility to Respect (Deva S. & Bilchitz D (eds)), Cambridge, 2013 (111–12).

develop their own enforcement mechanisms against nonstate actors, including corporations. This type of argument advocates that corporations are capable of attracting *hard*, albeit indirect, human rights obligations that are grounded in international law, rather than *soft* responsibilities that are based on social expectations.

There are a number of sources one might use to form the basis of an international legal obligation, the first being the Universal Declaration of Human Rights (UDHR),[8] along with others stemming from human rights treaties. The UDHR lists thirty substantive human rights that are promulgated as a common standard of achievement for all peoples and all nations: every "individual and organ of society."[9] The UDHR is expressed entirely in terms of entitlements for individuals and peoples rather than obligations for states or other entities. As a declaration of the UN General Assembly, it does not create legal obligations in itself. Nevertheless, the UDHR is frequently cited as the source of human rights obligations that corporations are urged to follow. One explanation is that some of the rights contained in the UDHR have crystallized as customary international law, such that the conduct by states necessary to secure these rights will be legally binding on states. Defining rights as custom is complex because custom does not crystallize or harden at a particular moment but develops gradually over time. Rules obliging states to observe particular rights may gradually emerge but remain focused on the state and not the nonstate actor.

Another view is that the expression "every individual"[10] in the UDHR includes juridical persons. Thus "every individual and organ of society" excludes no one, including corporations, and the UDHR applies to them all.[11] Furthermore, the phrase "every organ of society" indicates that the human rights in the UDHR are to be respected, protected, and promoted not only by states but by all social entities capable of affecting the enjoyment of human rights, including corporations.[12] Extending the moral, if not legal, authority of the UDHR to corporations relies on Article 29, which acknowledges that *everyone* has *duties* to the community, and Article 30, which prohibits any *group* from engaging in any activity or performing any act aimed at destroying any of the rights and freedoms in the

---

8. Universal Declaration of Human Rights, G.A. Res. 217 (III) A, UN Doc. A/Res/217A (Dec. 10, 1948).

9. The arguments presented in this section relating to the link between human rights treaties and corporations draw on the work of Adam McBeth & Justine Nolan, *The International Protection of Human Rights and Fundamental Freedoms*, in INTERNATIONAL CORPORATE LEGAL RESPONSIBILITY 180–186 (Stephen Tully ed., 2012).

10. Declaration of Human Rights, *supra* note 8 (see *Preamble* and accompanying text).

11. *See generally* Jeffrey Dunoff, *The Universal Declaration at 50 and the Challenge of Global Markets*, 25 BROOK. J. INT'L L. 125 (1999).

12. Peter Muchlinski, *The Development of Human Rights Responsibilities for Multinational Enterprises*, in BUSINESS AND HUMAN RIGHTS: DILEMMAS AND SOLUTIONS 39 (Rory Sullivan ed., 2003). *See also* UN Secretary-General, *Implementation of the Declaration on the Right and Responsibility of Individuals, Groups and Organs of Society to Promote and Protect Universally Recognized Human Rights and Fundamental Freedoms: Rep. of the Secretary-General*, UN Doc E/CN.4/2000/95 (Jan. 13, 2000).

UDHR. Ultimately, it can be concluded that the UDHR's provisions, rather than directly imposing any binding legal obligation, express no more than a desire that corporations *strive* to promote respect for human rights.[13]

Human rights treaties clearly impose obligations on states to ensure that the rights they contain are both respected and protected. As part of this duty, states are required to ensure that the rights of individuals are not violated by third parties (such as corporations); this is an essential component of the uncontroversial state duty to protect that the SRSG embraces as the first pillar of his framework. Human rights treaties, in particular the International Covenant on Civil and Political Rights[14] and the International Covenant on Economic, Social and Cultural Rights,[15] make all the rights in the UDHR (other than the right to property) obligations of states, and though these treaties, and many that follow, continue to remain partially blind to the opportunity to speak more directly to influential nonstate actors, including corporations, more recent treaties, and occasionally treaty bodies, have begun to refer more directly to the role of states in specifically preventing human rights abuses by corporations.

For example, the Convention on the Rights of Persons with Disabilities provides that states have an obligation to take all appropriate measures to eliminate discrimination on the basis of disability by any person, organization, or private enterprise.[16] Article 2(e) of the Convention on the Elimination of Discrimination Against Women[17] provides that, under general international law and specific human rights covenants, states may be responsible for private acts if they fail to act with due diligence to prevent violations of rights or to investigate and punish acts of violence, and for providing compensation to victims of discrimination. States must therefore protect women against discrimination by private enterprises in both the public and private spheres.[18] A number of UN Treaty Body comments issued in the last decade acknowledge the important role potentially played by nonstate actors in the international human rights rubric. In 2004 the UN Human Rights Committee (HRC), when commenting on the nature of a state's obligations under the International Covenant on Civil and Political Rights (ICCPR), affirmed

---

13.   D. Kinley & J. Tadaki, *From Talk to Walk: The Emergence of Human Rights Responsibilities for Corporations at International Law*, 44 Va. J. Int'l L. 931, 948 (2003–04).

14.   International Covenant on Civil and Political Rights, Dec. 16, 1966, S. Treaty Doc. No. 95-20, 6 I.L.M. 368 (1967), 999 UNT.S. 171.

15.   International Covenant on Economic, Social and Cultural Rights, S. Treaty Doc. No. 95-19, 6 I.L.M. 360 (1967), 993 UNT.S. 3.

16.   Convention on the Rights of Persons with Disabilities, at art. 4(e), G.A. Res. 61/106, UN Doc. A/61/49 (Dec. 13, 2006).

17.   Convention on the Elimination of Discrimination Against Women, UN Doc. A/RES/2263 (Nov. 7, 1967).

18.   UN Committee on the Elimination of Discrimination Against Women, *CEDAW General Recommendation 25: Article 4, paragraph 1, of the Convention (Temporary Special Measures)*, ¶¶ 7, 29, 31, 32 (2004).

that the obligation is only discharged if individuals are protected by the state not just against human rights violations by its agents but also against acts committed by private persons or entities.[19] The HRC thus acknowledges the growing need to include corporations within the framework of human rights protection, although its interpretation of the obligation retains the primacy of states in protecting against the abuse of human rights by nonstate actors, at least where protective action is required within its borders. Although in most jurisdictions national law regulates corporate activities that affect human rights—including labor rights, antidiscrimination law, environmental protection, and criminal law—domestic legislation typically does not apply extraterritorially. In General Comment No. 14 concerning the right to health, the Committee on Economic, Social, and Cultural Rights considered that

> to comply with their international obligations in relation to Article 12, States parties have to respect the enjoyment of the right in health in other countries, and to prevent third parties from violating the right in other countries, if they are able to influence these third parties by way of legal or political means, in accordance with the Charter of the United Nations and applicable international law.[20]

With regard to the right to water, the same committee called on states "to prevent their own citizens and companies from violating the right to water of individuals and communities in other countries [w]here States parties can take steps to influence other third parties to respect the right, through legal or political means."[21] Some treaty bodies have directly referred to the need to ensure corporations act consistently with the legal standards set out in various human rights treaties. The Committee on the Elimination of Racial Discrimination has singled out UK and Australian corporations to ensure their activities are consistent with the rights contained in the treaty and do not negatively impact the rights of indigenous communities affected by their operations.[22]

---

19. Human Rights Committee, *General Comment 31: The Nature of the General Legal Obligation on States Parties to the Covenant*, ¶ 8, UN Doc. CCPR/C/21/Rev.1.Add.13 (2004).

20. Committee on Economic, Social and Cultural Rights (CESCR), *CESCR General Comment 14: The Right to the Highest Attainable Standard of Health (Art. 12)*, ¶ 39, UN Doc E/C.12/2000/4 (Aug. 11, 2000).

21. CESCR, *General Comment 15: The Right to Water*, ¶ 31, UN Doc. E/C.12/2002/11 (Feb. 20, 2003).

22. With regard to the United Kingdom, *Concluding Observations of Committee on the Elimination of Racial Discrimination: United Kingdom of Great Britain and Northern Ireland*, ¶ 29, UN Doc. CERD/C/GBR/CO/18-20 (Sept. 14, 2011). With regard to Australia, the Committee on the Elimination of Racial Discrimination noted "with concern the absence of a legal framework regulating the obligation of Australian corporations at home and overseas whose activities, notably in the extractive sector, when carried out on the traditional territories of Indigenous peoples, have had a negative impact on Indigenous peoples' rights to land, health, living environment and livelihoods." CERD, *Concluding Observations: Australia*, ¶ 13, UN Doc. CERD/C/AU.S./CO/15-17 (Sept. 13, 2010).

One clear nexus between state and corporate responsibility becomes evident when a corporation's actions that violate human rights are carried out in its capacity as a state agent or under state authority or control. An entity, including a corporation, that exercises elements of governmental authority in place of state organs will attract the responsibility of the state for a wrongful act.[23] When a state has privatized or contracted out traditionally governmental functions to a private entity, the state can be held responsible under international law for any human rights violations or other violations of international law committed by that private entity.[24] Private entities are therefore capable of committing direct violations of international law that are in turn imputed to a state. However, international law continues to rely on states to take the necessary remedial action against such entities rather than providing an international enforcement mechanism for direct recourse against private perpetrators.[25]

This discussion demonstrates the convoluted and complex nature of the relationship between international law and corporations, and it also demonstrates that the interplay between national and international law is crucial for establishing both a legal basis and a mechanism for holding corporations accountable for human rights violations. Though it is uncontested that corporations should obey the law in the jurisdictions where they operate, when the content of rights in such jurisdictions does not meet the standards of international law, there is a failure in the legal governance regime for protecting human rights. The steady evolution of a global social expectation that companies should respect international human rights standards, combined with the slow integration of international human rights laws and standards into national law, is changing the nature and possibility of developing a firmer basis for corporate legal accountability for human rights. But it is not yet sufficient to declare that companies can or will be held accountable for rights violations in all jurisdictions in which they operate. As such, soft law mechanisms have grown and deepened around the theme of corporate responsibility partly in recognition of the failure of legal regulation, both internationally and domestically, to hold corporations accountable.

---

23.   International Law Commission, *Report of the 53rd Session*, UN Doc. A/56/10, Commentary to the Draft Articles, Article 5(1).

24.   ANDREW CLAPHAM, HUMAN RIGHTS OBLIGATIONS OF NONSTATE ACTORS 242 (2006).

25.   The European Court of Human Rights has held that a State cannot absolve itself of responsibility by delegating its obligations to private bodies or individuals: Costello-Roberts v. United Kingdom, 247 Eur. Ct. H.R. (ser. A), ¶ 27 (1993).

Corporate Responsibility (Not *Necessarily* Accountability) for Human Rights: Soft Law Getting Softer?

In 2011 the UN Human Rights Council endorsed the SRSG's Guiding Principles on Business and Human Rights. The Guiding Principles build on his earlier three-pronged "Protect, Respect, Remedy" Framework, which demarcates a state's duty to protect human rights from a corporation's responsibility to respect rights. The path to the Guiding Principles began formally within the UN in 2004 (although this was not the UN's first foray into this field), when the UN Commission on Human Rights asked the Office of the High Commissioner on Human Rights to compile a report on the potential human rights responsibilities of TNCs. Following up on this report, in April 2005 the UN Commission on Human Rights called on the UN secretary-general to appoint a special representative (SRSG) on the issue of human rights and transnational corporations and other business enterprises to investigate the legal responsibilities of businesses for social and environmental issues. The resolution[26] provided the SRSG with a mandate to clarify the standards of corporate responsibility and elaborate on the role of states in regulating business. On July 28, 2005, the UN secretary-general appointed Dr. Ruggie as the special representative. During his initial three-year term, the SRSG spent time mapping both the plethora of mechanisms used to attempt to prevent corporate rights violations as well as the rights violations themselves. His early annual reports[27] to the UN Human Rights Council (which were drafted after extensive consultations with large and small stakeholders) framed the problem and examined existing responses, but it was not until 2008 that his framework for the way forward was revealed. In 2008 the SRSG presented to the UN Human Rights Council a "conceptual and policy framework" that he suggested would "anchor the business and human rights debate and . . . help guide all relevant actors."[28] The Framework rests on three pillars: "the State duty to protect against human rights abuses by third parties, including business; the corporate responsibility to respect human rights; and the need for more effective access to remedies."[29] The SRSG's term was extended in 2008 for another

---

26. UN Comm'n on Human Rights, *Human Rights Resolution 2005/69: Human Rights and Transnational Corporations and Other Business Enterprises*, UN ESCOR, 61st Sess., UN Doc. E/CN.4/RES/2005/69 (Apr. 20, 2005).

27. *See, e.g.*, Ruggie, *Interim Report, supra* note 5; Special Representative of the Secretary-General, *Business and Human Rights: Mapping International Standards of Responsibility and Accountability for Corporate Acts: Report of the Special Representative of the Secretary-General on the Issue of Human Rights and Transnational Corporations and Other Business Enterprises*, UN Doc. A/HRC/4/35 (Feb. 9, 2007) [hereinafter Business and Human Rights] (by John Ruggie); and Special Representative of the Secretary-General, *Protect, Respect and Remedy: A Framework for Business and Human Rights: Report of the Special Representative of the Secretary-General on the Issue of Human Rights and Transnational Corporations and Other Business Enterprises*, UN Doc. A/HRC/8/5 (Apr. 7, 2008) [hereinafter *Protect, Respect and Remedy*] (by John Ruggie).

28. *See generally* Ruggie, *Protect, Respect and Remedy, supra* note 27.

29. Ruggie, *Protect, Respect and Remedy, supra* note 27.

three years, and in 2011, with his final report to the UN Human Rights Council, the SRSG endeavored to *operationalize* the framework and proposed the Guiding Principles. In July 2011 the UN Human Rights Council endorsed the Guiding Principles and announced the formation of a Working Group "to promote the effective and comprehensive dissemination and implementation of the Guiding Principles."[30]

The decision of the SRSG to distinguish the state duty to protect rights from the corporate responsibility to respect rights was a deliberate one, discriminating between a legal obligation and a moral responsibility. The first prong of the SRSG's 2008 framework is uncontroversial and somewhat narrowly framed to identify the state duty expressly as having territorial and jurisdictional limits. It is articulated in the Guiding Principles by noting that "States must protect against human rights abuse within their territory and/or jurisdiction by third parties, including business enterprises. This requires taking appropriate steps to prevent, investigate, punish and redress such abuse through effective policies, legislation, regulations and adjudication."[31] The commentary attached to Guiding Principle 2 further elaborates on the territorial/jurisdictional limit by noting the possibilities open to states to broaden and deepen the scope of the duty to protect, but not obliging states to act in this regard:

> At present States are not generally required under international human rights law to regulate the extraterritorial activities of businesses domiciled in their territory and/or jurisdiction. Nor are they generally prohibited from doing so, provided there is a recognized jurisdictional basis. Within these parameters some human rights treaty bodies recommend that home States take steps to prevent abuse abroad by business enterprises within their jurisdiction.
>
> There are strong policy reasons for home States to set out clearly the expectation that businesses respect human rights abroad, especially where the State itself is involved in or supports those businesses. The reasons include ensuring predictability for business enterprises by providing coherent and consistent messages, and preserving the State's own reputation.[32]

The SRSG's nondeterminative stance in recognizing but not requiring states to regulate companies extraterritorially continues the gentle and disengaged approach of international

---

30. Human Rights Council, *Promotion and Protection of All Human Rights, Civil, Political, Economic, Social and Cultural Rights, Including the Right to Development,* ¶ 6(a), UN Doc. A/HRC/RES/17/4 (July 6, 2011), http://www.business-humanrights.org/media/documents/un-human-rights-council-resolut ion-re-human-rights-transnational-corps-eng-6-jul-2011.pdf.

31. John Ruggie, *Report of the Special Representative of the Secretary-General on the Issue of Human Rights and Transnational Corporations and Other Business Enterprises; Guiding Principles, supra* note 4, at ¶ A1.

32. Ruggie, *Guiding Principles, supra* note 4, Sec. I, ¶ A2.

human rights law toward business. Other commentators point to "the need for the adoption of a new international instrument aimed at clarifying, and where necessary at extending, the obligations of States to protect human rights against any violations of . . . rights originating in the activities of transnational corporations. . . . While this would build on current developments in the international law of human rights, it would also go beyond them in obliging the home State to exercise a form of extraterritorial jurisdiction over the corporations which have its nationality for their operations overseas."[33]

The corporate responsibility to respect is defined in the Guiding Principles as meaning business "should avoid infringing on the human rights of others and should address adverse human rights impacts with which they are involved."[34] The explanatory commentary accompanying the principles states that "the responsibility to respect human rights is a global standard of expected conduct for all business enterprises wherever they operate" and that this responsibility "exists independently of States' abilities and/or willingness to fulfill their own human rights obligations, and does not diminish those obligations."[35] The commentary attached to Guiding Principle 12 (as to what rights should be respected) is defined by reference to a litany of *hard* international human rights laws, but its source of obligation is more inchoate and softer. It is grounded in social expectation, not legal obligation, and it is the *courts of public opinion*[36] that are relied on to *enforce* such expectations. The decision to frame it as *not-law* elevated the odds of achieving governmental consensus and business backing but is a sticking point for many NGOs.[37] The concept of due diligence (Guiding Principle 17) is introduced as a mechanism by which companies might discharge their responsibility to respect rights and reflects the continued reliance on self-regulation to curb corporate human rights violations.

The language used in the Guiding Principles when framing the corporate responsibility to respect human rights is generally nonauthoritative and in itself unlikely to provoke a binding, normative response.[38] Some stakeholders may welcome the ambiguity of the language because it allows for specific idiosyncratic tailoring of responses at an industry

---

33. Olivier De Schutter, *Extraterritorial Jurisdiction as a Tool for Improving the Human Rights Accountability of Transnational Corporations* (2006), http://www.reports-and-materials.org/Olivier-de-Schutter-report-for-SRSG-re-extraterritorial-jurisdiction-Dec-2006.pdf.

34. Ruggie, *Report: Human Rights & Transnational Corporations*, *supra* note 31; *Guiding Principles*, *supra* note 4, Section II ¶ A11.

35. *Id.*

36. Ruggie, *Protect, Respect and Remedy*, *supra* note 27, at ¶ 54.

37. *See, e.g.*, Joint Civil Society, *Statement On the Draft Guiding Principles on Business and Human Rights* (Jan. 2011), http://raid-uk.org/docs/HR/JointCSOStatement_GPs_13Jan.pdf.

38. For example, Guiding Principle 11 states "Business enterprise . . . should address adverse human rights impacts . . . "; or Guiding Principle 13 "The responsibility to respect human rights requires that business enterprises: . . . (b) Seek to prevent or mitigate adverse human rights impacts"; or Guiding Principle 23 "In all contexts, business enterprises should: . . . (b) Seek ways to honour the principles of internationally recognized human rights when faced with conflicting requirements"; or Guiding Principle 24 "business enterprises should first seek to prevent."; Ruggie, *supra* note 4.

and state level. On the other hand, the looseness of the language can invite inaction and a business-as-usual approach from companies that remain hesitant about their responsibility to act. In short, the 2011 version of the corporate responsibility to respect rights is of a nonlegal character. The commitment of corporations to discharge their responsibility depends on the voluntary uptake of the Guiding Principles, and the *enforcement* of this part of the principles is left largely to market forces, including peer pressure and NGO and consumer activism.

Fundamentally, the Framework and Guiding Principles stay true to the traditional approach of international human rights law in demarcating duties as belonging primarily to states. No legal duties are directly imposed on corporations, which as nonstate actors remain outside the international legal framework. The development of the Framework and Guiding Principles does not seem to overcome one of the recurring critiques of earlier attempts to regulate corporations with respect to human rights, that of the need to articulate enforceable responsibilities, mechanisms of accountability, and remedies for business. Rather the Framework and Guiding Principles build on the soft law that preceded them, albeit this time with a little more punch by incorporating the endorsement of the UN Human Rights Council.

To fully understand the SRSG's approach, one needs to consider it in the context of his appointment and the debates that preceded it. A key part of the SRSG's methodology was focused on overcoming the failure of agreement triggered by the introduction of the UN Norms in 2003, and his approach was characterized by a focus on building broader unanimity among the various stakeholders. From the outset, it was clear that the SRSG was looking to overcome the turbulence of the UN Norms and develop a plan based on consensus and pragmatism. He wanted to move ahead with "an unflinching commitment to the principle of strengthening the promotion and protection of human rights as it relates to business, coupled with a pragmatic attachment to what works best in creating change where it matters most—in the daily lives of people."[39]

The Guiding Principles emerged from decades-long reliance on soft measures to prevent and police corporate human rights violations that were primarily designed to guide corporate behavior but not necessarily legally bind it. There appears to be little consensus among commentators in agreeing on indicators that might determine whether a particular instrument, guideline, declaration, or code might be branded as law, soft law, quasi-law, pre-law, or simply not-law, whether in this field or any other. What is clear, particularly in the field of business and human rights, is that reliance on what is defined below as soft law is and has been the predominant method of regulating the impact on human rights by businesses in recent decades, and this soft law's evolution has involved both state and nonstate actors. Reliance on soft law has not emerged simply because there is a lack of

---

39. Ruggie, *Interim Report, supra* note 5, at ¶ 81.

anything better, though that is a significant part of it. The use of soft law can be more attractive (in this case particularly to businesses and governments) because it often contains inspirational goals and aspirations that aim for the best possible scenario with few constraints if such goals are not met, and thus consensus is easier to achieve. Attempts to define a soft instrument even loosely as law or not-law are more often obfuscatory than definitive, and definitions vary.[40] For the purposes of this discussion, *soft law* is seen to include all those international instruments described variously as codes, guidelines, or principles, excluding treaties (even in their soft form), and also incorporates codes of conduct developed not only at an international level but also at a micro-level, such as by individual corporations, NGOs, or multi-stakeholder groups.

The cacophony of codes and guidelines that preceded the SRSG's work on business and human rights was reflected in his oft-repeated statement that there is no *silver bullet* that will provide a systemic solution to reducing the incidence of business-related human rights abuses.[41] For much of the recent decades that preceded the SRSG's appointment, a plethora of tactics were adopted in attempts to regulate or at least reduce the negative impact businesses can have on human rights, with varying levels of success. More than a decade ago, Peter Muchlinski argued that "a climate of expectation as to proper corporate conduct should be built up through both 'soft law' and 'hard law' options [and] [d]evelopments in 'soft law' through corporate and NGO codes of conduct are already creating a climate in which it might be expected that the management of MNEs [multinational enterprises] includes a conscious assessment of . . . human rights implications."[42] However, what has been apparent since Muchlinski wrote this in 2001 is that while developments in the soft law regulation of corporations with respect to human rights have continued to expand and build on this climate of expectation, the development of hard law has lagged behind.

Codes of conduct are part of a soft law paradigm for protecting human rights. Their *normative*[43] effect (that is, the development of broadly accepted standards for corporate

---

40.   Dinah Shelton, *Normative Hierarchy in International Law*, 100 AM. J. INT'L. L. 291, 319 (2006) (defining soft law as generally referring "to any international instrument other than a treaty that contains principles, norms, standards or other statements of expected behaviour."); Contrast Chinkin, who notes some argue for a broader classification with soft law being defined as ranging "from treaties, but which include only soft obligations, to non-binding or voluntary resolutions and codes of conduct formulated and accepted by international and regional organisation, to statements prepared by individuals in a non-government capacity, but which purport to lay down international principles." C.M. Chinkin, *The Challenge of Soft Law: Development and Change in International Law*, 38 INT'L & COMP. L.Q. 850, 851 (1989); *see also* Stephen Freeland, *For Better or For Worse? The Use of 'Soft Law' Within the International Legal Regulation of Outer Space*, 36 ANNALS AIR & SPACE L. 409 (2011).

41.   Ruggie, *Protect, Respect and Remedy, supra* note 27, at ¶ 7.

42.   Peter Muchlinkski, *Human Rights and Multinationals: Is There a Problem?* 77 INT'L. AFF. 31, 31 (2001).

43.   Bilchitz, *supra* note 7, at 2 (distinguishing between "binding normativity" (where an obligation stems from a legitimate source in international (or domestic) law that justifies recognizing and enforcing such obligations) and 'moral normativity' (involving questions about what morally "ought" to be the case even if no legal obligation is attached to it)).

conduct through the aggregation of individual codes of conduct) might transform into legal effects. For example, the standards enumerated in a code may be incorporated into employment, supplier, or agency contracts, but in and of itself, the code is not generally regarded as legally binding.[44] Codes of conduct and their enforcement through nongovernmental monitoring have taken root within international business over the last forty years, although the concept remains severely limited. Contemporary efforts are marked by inconsistency, duplication, or inefficiency and reflect ad hoc decision-making rather than systems-based approaches.[45] The UN has dived in and out of this process and has been somewhat schizophrenic in its application of international human rights law to the issue. In 1973 the UN Economic and Social Council charged a "Group of Eminent Persons" to advise on matters related to TNCs and their impact on the development process.[46] In 1974 the UN established the Centre on Transnational Corporations, which by 1977 was coordinating the negotiation of a Draft Code of Conduct on Transnational Corporations (Draft Code). Negotiations lingered until the early 1990s, but no final agreement was concluded. The Draft Code was never officially adopted and its legal nature was never established. There were proponents of both a universally applicable, legally binding code and a voluntary code. If binding, the code would have served as a convention with both national and international implementation mechanisms. If voluntary, it would merely have been a set of broad guidelines to be observed by participating parties.

Both the Organization for Economic Cooperation and Development (OECD) and the International Labour Organization (ILO) have produced soft law instruments to guide corporate behavior with respect to human rights. The OECD Guidelines for Multinational Enterprises[47] are recommendations addressed by governments to multinational enterprises (MNEs) and continue the traditional paradigm of addressing corporate behavior through the medium of states. The OECD guidelines are a statement of the standards expected by home governments of their corporations operating abroad. The guidelines are voluntary. MNEs are invited to adopt the guidelines in their management systems and incorporate the principles into corporate operations. The guidelines address several issues, including labor and environmental standards, corruption, consumer protection, technology transfer, competition, and taxation. They also require MNEs to respect the internationally recognized human rights of those affected by their activities.[48] The revised (2011) OECD guidelines

---

44. Halina Ward, Legal Issues in Corporate Citizenship: Report prepared for the Swedish Partnership for Global Responsibility 6–7 (2003).

45. See generally Helle Bank Jørgensen, et al., Strengthening Implementation of Corporate Social Responsibility in Global Supply Chains, Report of the Corporate Social Responsibility Practice in the Investment Climate Department, World Bank (2003).

46. The arguments presented in this section relating to the development of soft law draw on the work of McBeth & Nolan, supra note 9, at 188–199.

47. OECD, OECD Guidelines for Multinational Enterprises, Recommendations for Responsible Business Conduct in a Global Context (May 25, 2011).

48. Id. ¶ A(2).

draw on the "Protect, Respect and Remedy" Framework developed by the SRSG and the ensuing Guiding Principles. Respect for human rights is stated to be the global standard of expected conduct for MNEs in the OECD guidelines, independent of states' ability or willingness to fulfill their human rights obligations; states' degree of willingness or ability does not diminish those obligations. Decisions cannot be enforced directly against corporations, and the power to compel behavioral change depends on the political will and ability of national governments.[49]

During the same period when the OECD guidelines were originally drafted, the ILO adopted a Tripartite Declaration of Principles Concerning Multinational Enterprises and Social Policy (ILO Declaration).[50] The ILO declaration was adopted in response to the growing role and influence of TNCs during the 1960s and 1970s. The declaration encourages member governments to support the positive contributions of MNEs to economic and social progress and to minimize and resolve the difficulties their operations may cause. The ILO declaration offers a set of core principles and guidelines for corporations with respect to employment, training, working conditions, and industrial relations. The instrument is voluntary.

In 2000 the UN reinvigorated its efforts to involve business in the business of respecting human rights and established the Global Compact.[51] Former UN Secretary-General Kofi Annan called on corporations to voluntarily embrace and enact in their corporate practices a set of then nine (currently ten) principles relating to human rights, labor rights, environmental protection, and corruption. The Global Compact reflects norms found in international law, including the UDHR and human rights treaties, ILO conventions, the Rio Declaration on the Environment and Development,[52] and the Convention against Corruption,[53] but it does not draw on them to imply any legal obligation that might attach to corporations with respect to human rights. The Global Compact has been criticized for lacking meaningful enforcement power.[54] It is also undermined by a lack of clarity in the content and scope of its principles, the limited notions of accountability and transparency

---

49. INT'L COUNCIL ON HUMAN RIGHTS POLICY, BEYOND VOLUNTARISM: HUMAN RIGHTS AND THE DEVELOPING INTERNATIONAL LEGAL OBLIGATIONS OF COMPANIES, MAIN REPORT 99–102 (2002).

50. Int'l Labour Org., Tripartite Declaration of Principles Concerning Multinational Enterprises and Social Policy, adopted by the Governing Body of the International Labour Office at its 204th Session (Geneva, Nov. 1977) as amended at its 279th (Nov. 2000) and 295th Session (Mar. 2006).

51. See generally THE GLOBAL COMPACT OFFICE/OHCHR, EMBEDDING HUMAN RIGHTS PRINCIPLES IN BUSINESS PRACTICE (2004).

52. Declaration on the Environment and Development, Report of the UN Conference on Environment and Development, UN Doc. A/CONF.151/5/Rev.1 (1992), Annex 1.

53. United Nations Convention Against Corruption, G.A. Res. 58/4 (2003).

54. See, e.g., Justine Nolan, The United Nations' Compact with Business: Hindering or Helping the Protection of Human rights? 24 U. QUEENSLAND L.J. 445, 445 (2005); Surya Deva, Global Compact: A Critique of UN's Public-Private Partnership for Promoting Corporate Citizenship 34 SYRACUSE J. INT'L L. & COM., 107, 107–51 (2006); Jennifer Anne Bremer, How Global is the Global Compact? 17 BUS. ETHICS 227 (2008).

employed (although there have been some revisions in this regard),[55] and an overemphasis on (very soft) voluntary approaches to improving corporate behavior.

At the same time, within the UN a parallel process stemming from an initiative of the UN Sub-Commission on the Promotion and Protection of Human Rights was also focused on examining the activities of TNCs. Beginning in 1998, a working group was established to draft norms on the responsibilities of TNCs and other business enterprises with regard to human rights.[56] In 2003 the UN Sub-Commission on the Promotion and Protection of Human Rights unanimously adopted a comprehensive set of international norms specifically applying to TNCs and other businesses (thereby applying to any business entity regardless of international or domestic nature),[57] but the document went no further. The norms controversially drew together the human rights guarantees from various human rights instruments relevant to corporations and expressed them in a form suitable for application to them. In that sense, the norms claimed to be a restatement of existing legal obligations rather than the creation of new obligations; however, the norms controversially supported both states and corporations as having complementary duties to protect and respect human rights grounded in international law. The norms have no formal legal status, and in 2005 the UN Commission on Human Rights took note of the *code* but, in its recommendations to the UN Economic and Social Council, affirmed that the code had not been requested by the commission and, as a draft proposal, had no legal standing. The UN High Commissioner on Human Rights has also expressed the view that the norms have no legal standing.[58] The SRSG has been patently critical of some aspects of

---

55. In 2004 the UN Global Compact introduced new "Integrity Measures" following a comprehensive review of the Compact's governance system. In accordance with the Integrity Measures, companies are required to communicate annually to their stakeholders on progress made in implementing the ten principles of the UN Global Compact. Failure to meet the Communication on Progress (COP) deadline results in a company being listed as "non-communicating" on the Global Compact Web site. The delisting policy was first implemented in January 2008, when 394 companies were removed from the participant list.

56. Sub-Comm'n on the Promotion and Protection of Human Rights, *The Relationship Between the Enjoyment of Economic, Social and Cultural Rights and the Right to Development, and the Working Methods and Activities of Transnational Corporations*, UN Doc. E/CN.4/Sub.2/Res/1998/8 (1998). Meetings were held over five years, with comments received from nongovernmental observers and other organisations. *See* Report of the Sessional Working Group on the Working Methods and Activities of Transnational Corporations on its Second Session, UN Doc. E/CN.4/Sub.2/2000/12 (2000); Report from the Third Session, UN Doc. E/CN.4/Sub.2/2001/9 (2001); Report from the Fourth Session, UN Doc. E/CN.4/Sub.2/2002/13 (2002).

57. Adopted by the Sub-Comm'n on the Promotion and Protection of Human Rights, Resolution 2003/16, at 53, UN Doc. E/CN.4/Sub.2/2003/L.11 (2003). *See also* Sub-Commission on the Promotion and Protection of Human Rights, *The Norms on the Responsibilities of Transnational Corporations and Other Business Enterprises with Regard to Human Rights*, UN Doc. E/CN.4/Sub.2/2003/12 (2003) and the Accompanying Commentary, UN Doc. E/CN.4/Sub.2/2003/38/Rev.2 (2003); Sub-Comm'n on the Promotion and Protection of Human Rights, *Working Group, Draft Resolution: Responsibilities of Transnational Corporations and Other Business Enterprises with Regard to Human Rights*, UN Doc. E/CN.4/Sub.2/2003/L.8 (2003).

58. Sub-Comm'n on the Promotion and Protection of Human Rights, *Report of the United Nations*

the norms, viewing the initiative as "engulfed by its own doctrinal excesses" and creating "confusion and doubt" through "exaggerated legal claims and conceptual ambiguities." The SRSG has argued that the norms should be abandoned rather than pursued.[59]

Corporate lobby groups criticized the norms as an inappropriate effort to privatize vague human rights standards in a manner that invites subjective, politicized claims. They observed that the binding and legalistic approach favored by the norms will not meet the diverse needs and circumstances of corporations and will limit the innovation and creativity shown by them in addressing human rights issues in the context of finding practical and workable solutions to corporate responsibility challenges.[60] In 2008 these same organizations endorsed the SRSG's three-pronged framework, which differentiates a state's legal duty to protect human rights from a corporation's responsibility to respect rights.[61]

The intense debate initially triggered by the introduction of the norms reveals a variety of approaches and attitudes (both before and after the norms) toward the role of both states and corporations in respecting and protecting human rights. What distinguishes the current Framework and Guiding Principles from the norms (and the earlier efforts of the UN in the 1970s) is a deliberate move away from pursuing an explicit legal connection between international human rights law and corporations. As a result, the ensuing corporate responsibility to respect rights is framed in a soft form with an amorphous basis in, and link to, human rights law. Responsibility is distinguished from accountability, and corporations will take their cue largely from human rights embodied in soft law formats, whereas states will continue to look to international law to divine their legal duties. Any accountability corporations might face under this current framework is limited to actions taken by states in *hardening* the application of the Guiding Principles to corporations via domestic law or a corporation's own voluntary commitment to assume a responsibility to respect human rights.

High Commissioner on Human Rights on the Responsibilities of Transnational Corporations and Related Business Enterprises with Regard to Human Rights, UN ESCOR, 61st Sess., 59th mtg., Item 16 of the Provisional Agenda, UN Doc. E/CN.4/2005/91 (Feb. 15, 2005).

59. Ruggie, *Interim Report*, *supra* note 5, at 57–59.

60. Int'l Chamber of Commerce, *Joint Views of the IOE and ICC on the Draft Norms on the Responsibilities of Transnational Corporations and Other Business Enterprises with Regard to Human Rights*, UN Doc. E/CN.4/Sub.2/2003/NGO/44; 66th sess. (July 29, 2003).

61. INT'L ORG. OF EMPLOYERS/INT'L CHAMBER OF COMMERCE/BUSINESS AND INDUS. ADVISORY COUNCIL TO THE OECD, JOINT INITIAL VIEWS TO THE EIGHTH SESSION OF THE HUMAN RIGHTS COUNCIL ON THE THIRD REPORT OF THE SPECIAL REPRESENTATIVE OF THE UN SECRETARY-GENERAL ON BUSINESS AND HUMAN RIGHTS (2008).

Grasping at Straws? Alternative Mechanisms to Protect Human Rights[62]

Violations of human rights standards that have been incorporated into a state's domestic law—whether in criminal law, labor law, tort law, or company law—will of course expose the violator to the enforcement process and sanctions prescribed by that law.[63] In the absence of a global legal framework for holding corporations accountable for human rights violations, and in frustration with the selective nature of soft law mechanisms, innovative human rights activists have employed a variety of litigious techniques to seek that illusory concept of accountability for corporations via the mechanism of domestic laws applied extraterritorially. As discussed, international law, to the extent that it is considered by some to impose (indirectly) human rights obligations on corporations, does not have any such enforcement mechanisms that can be imposed directly on corporations. In the absence of such specific measures, a sense of creativity has been employed to the application of domestic tort law, in particular to address human rights violations. "Human rights standards and liability in domestic tort share a common purpose: to protect people from harm by deterring others from certain conduct."[64] The overlap between human rights violations and tortious liability is currently a matter of debate in cases brought under the Alien Tort Claims Act of 1789 (ATCA).[65] The fact that the ATCA draws directly on international legal norms differentiates it from other avenues of domestic law, such as negligence principles, which can also be used when appropriate to hold corporations liable for conduct that violates human rights.

Since 1980 the ATCA has provided a link between international obligations and domestic enforcement by characterizing a "violation of the law of nations" as a tort under U.S. federal law and thus allowing a plaintiff (who is not a resident of the United States) to sue a defendant over whom a U.S. court has personal jurisdiction for a violation of the law of nations, even if the event in question had no connection to U.S. territory. These parameters have now changed with the 2013 decision of the U.S. Supreme Court in *Kiobel v. Royal Dutch Petroleum*.[66] Before this decision, a number of U.S. cases had proceeded on the assumption that corporations can be liable under the ATCA for breaches of international customary law. Significant cases include *Doe v. Unocal, The Presbyterian Church of Sudan v. Talisman Energy*, and *Wiwa v. Royal Dutch Petroleum*.[67] The U.S. Supreme

---

62. The arguments presented in this section relating to litigious techniques draws on the work of McBeth & Nolan, *supra* note 9, at 241–45.

63. SARAH JOSEPH, CORPORATIONS AND TRANSNATIONAL HUMAN RIGHTS LITIGATION 8–16 (2004).

64. S. McMurray & S. Rice, *Lifting the Veil: Human Rights Violations and Tort Law in Australia*, 70 PRECEDENT 27 (2005).

65. 28 U.S.C. § 1350.

66. 621 F.3d 111 (2013).

67. Doe I v. Unocal Corp., 963 F. Supp. 880 (C.D. Cal. 1997) (denying the defendants' motion to

Court revisited the question of whether human rights violations constitute a violation of the law of nations in the 2004 case of *Sosa v. Alvarez Machain*.[68]

In September 2010, the assumption of corporate liability under the ATCA was directly addressed by the Second Circuit Court of Appeals decision in *Kiobel v. Royal Dutch Petroleum*.[69] The plaintiffs alleged that the defendants were complicit in human rights breaches by the Nigerian government in the Ogoni region, including procuring the Nigerian military to suppress the local human rights and environmental activists as well as providing support to the Nigerian military, including transport, food, and compensation. The majority (two to one) held that because corporations are not liable under the customary international law of human rights, they cannot be subject to liability under the ATCA. The majority recognized that although states are the primary subjects of international law, in a limited number of circumstances individuals can be held liable for certain crimes, such as crimes against humanity, war crimes, and torture. However, the liability of individuals related to actual persons, not *juridical* persons such as corporations. The minority opinion delivered by Circuit Judge Leval was critical of this reasoning.[70]

The case was appealed to the U.S. Supreme Court, and on April 17, 2013, the court ruled unanimously that the Kiobel plaintiffs' claims fell beyond the scope of jurisdiction offered by the statute. Though the initial question before the court was whether corporations are excluded from liability under the ATCA for violations of the law of nations, on March 5, 2012, the Supreme Court took the unexpected step of issuing an order asking the parties to submit supplemental briefs on whether the ATCA allows U.S. courts to consider lawsuits alleging violations of international law occurring outside the United States. The court's decision focused exclusively on that question, leaving the issue of corporate liability undecided. The justices split five to four in their reasoning, with the majority relying on the presumption against extraterritoriality, arguing that nothing in the wording, logic, or history of the ATCA showed that Congress necessarily meant to sweep into U.S. courts wholly non-U.S. claims involving non-U.S. parties. Justice Breyer, however, in a concurrence joined by three others, rejected that the presumption against extraterritoriality applied to the statute and instead advocated an analysis "guided in part by principles and

---

dismiss the complaint); Presbyterian Church of Sudan v. Talisman Energy, 582 F.3d 244, 261 n.12 (2d Cir. 2009); Wiwa v. Royal Dutch Petroleum, 226 F.3d 88 (2d Cir. 2000).

68. Sosa v. Alvarez Machain, 542 U.S. 692 (2004).

69. Kiobel v. Royal Dutch Petroleum Co., 621 F.3d 111 (2d Cir. 2010).

70. *Id.* at 51. Judge Leval stated, "The majority opinion deals a substantial blow to international law and its undertaking to protect fundamental human rights. According to the rule my colleagues have created, one who earns profits by commercial exploitation of abuse of fundamental human rights can successfully shield those profits from victims' claims for compensation simply by taking the precaution of conducting the heinous operation in the corporate form." The dissent of Judge Leval is reflected in two more recent decisions. *See* Flomo v. Firestone Natural Rubber Co., No. 10-3675, 2011 WL 2675924 (7th Cir. July 11, 2011) (Judge Posner); Doe v. Exxon, No. 09-7125, 2011 WL 2652384 (D.C. Cir. July 8, 2011) (Judge Rogers).

practices of foreign relations law" to determine whether an ATCA plaintiff's allegations involved "sufficient ties" to the United States to trigger jurisdiction. Here, with non-U.S. plaintiffs, defendants, and conduct surrounding the claims, it was deemed insufficient to trigger such potential jurisdiction.

No case brought against a corporation under the ATCA for violation of human rights has yet resulted in a merits decision in favor of the plaintiff. Nevertheless, the potential for a corporation to be considered capable of violating the law of nations and thus liable under the ATCA has led to considerable emphasis on this piece of legislation in the literature on corporate responsibility for human rights violations,[71] but the future and capability of the law to hold corporations to account remains in flux. The Supreme Court's *Kiobel* decision leaves open a number of significant questions regarding the reach and interpretation of ATCA. The attention given to this piece of legislation has been disproportionate to the number of companies sued under it. It is a mechanism whereby the principles of international human rights law can be directly tied to corporate practices and includes a *hard* mechanism for enforcing that link. However, the category of rights violations that falls within the law of nations is relatively narrow,[72] and the plaintiffs' allegations must at a minimum involve sufficient ties to the United States to trigger the jurisdiction of a U.S. court. Not every human rights violation is liable for suit under the ATCA, nor is every company. Arguably the statute's potential impact has been overplayed in academic literature, and its reach has now been significantly narrowed.

Leaving litigation under the ATCA aside, tort-based litigation claims have also been brought against several companies in a variety of jurisdictions, including both home (where the company is incorporated) and host (where the company is operating) states. The common denominator for all jurisdictions that permit the direct application of international law in national courts is the relative underutilization of that route. The challenge in those jurisdictions is to demonstrate that treaty-based or customary norms of international human rights law give rise to obligations for corporations and that those obligations are self-executing and sufficiently precise. Because existing human rights treaties are addressed toward states, a conclusion that those treaties contain self-executing obligations for corporations is, as discussed above, somewhat problematic.

---

71.   A small sample of some of the more recent literature includes Julian Ku, *The Curious Case of Corporate Liability Under the Alien Tort Statute: A Flawed System of Judicial Lawmaking*, 51(2) Vir. J. Int'l. L. 353 (2011); David L. Wallach, *The Alien Tort Statute and the Limits of Individual Accountability in International Law*, 46 Stan. J. Int'l. L. 121 (2010); Paul Hoffman & Adrienne Quarry, *The Alien Tort Statute: An Introduction for Civil Rights Lawyers*, 2 L.A. Pub. Int. L.J. 129 (2009); Bama Athreya & Julie Su, *The Perils and Promise of the Alien Tort Statute in Practice: A Comment on "The Alien Tort Statute: An Introduction for Civil Rights Lawyers" by Paul Hoffman & Adrienne Quarry*, 2 L.A. Pub. Int. L.J. 203 (2009).

72.   Sosa v. Alvarez Machain, 542 U.S. at 692 (2004).

One of the additional challenges is the choice of fora for tort-based litigation. Corporations are obliged to comply with laws enacted by host states in the discharge of the obligations those states have assumed under international law. However, power differentials and problems inherent in enforcing domestic laws against corporations hinder host states in enforcing those standards against corporations. Poor prospects for recovering compensation from the local subsidiary may also be a factor. An alternative and more controversial approach is to litigate in the home state of a corporation for harm inflicted in states where litigation by victims may prove fruitless. Transnational cases based on harm caused to communities in developing states by multinational mining and chemical companies have recently been litigated in several home states. Although framed under tort law, these cases involved significant human rights issues, as well as the right to health, compensation for land, and other rights. In most cases there will be significant obstacles to exercising jurisdiction over transnational corporations, particularly where the entity consists of multiple, separately incorporated corporations and harm was suffered in a state other than the one where the case is brought. The extraterritorial application of national law is a particular concern for national courts. Those obstacles can be overcome if the wrongful act is characterized as a decision made or order given at the corporate headquarters, or where there is failure to supervise operations overseas properly, provided plaintiffs can establish an obligation to do so. Such an approach was applied to decisions made in the head offices of English multinational enterprises that led to harm suffered in developing states.[73] In *Lubbe v. Cape plc*, the English parent company was sued for failing to take measures to reduce the exposure of workers employed by its foreign subsidiaries to asbestos. After the House of Lords held that the English courts had proper jurisdiction to hear the case, it settled out of court. Nonetheless, none of these cases led to a merits decision, thereby negating their value as formal precedents. Holding home states responsible under human rights law for the extraterritorial actions of their corporations is, as evidenced by the laissez faire approach to extraterritoriality of the SRSG, still considered by some as a *radical step* that requires further international legal development.[74]

Another litigious technique that has been tested is an attempt to harden or give legal effect to the voluntary soft human rights standards espoused by a company in its code of conduct or its announcements and operations more generally; however, this has only been used in a very limited sense to date. For example, litigation was commenced in California under consumer protection legislation whereby Nike was accused of misleading and

---

73. Connelly v. RTZ, [1998] AC 854; Sithole v. Thor Chemical Holdings, [1999]; EWCA Civ. 706; Lubbe v. Cape P.L.C., [2000] 4 All ER 268; R. Meeran, The Unveiling of Transnational Corporations—A Direct Approach, in HUMAN RIGHTS STANDARDS AND THE RESPONSIBILITY OF TRANSNATIONAL CORPORATIONS (M. Addo ed.)) 164-9 (1999). Also, for a U.S. example, *see* Martinez v. Dow Chemicals, 219 F. Supp. 2d 719 (E.D. La. 2002).

74. Sarah Joseph, *An Overview of the Human Rights Accountability of Multinational Enterprises*, in LIABILITY OF MULTINATIONAL CORPORATIONS UNDER INTERNATIONAL LAW 85–87 (Menno Kamminga and Saman Zia-Zarifi eds., 2000).

deceptive practices by denying human rights abuses committed within its supply chains.[75] Although the case settled, the precedent demonstrates the potential for how codes might be used to prevent misleading conduct by corporations with respect to specific standards. Conversely, it highlights the danger for corporations to subscribe to a code on labor standards if its commitments do not match the reality of its commercial practice.

Each of the techniques discussed above rely on the application of domestic law extraterritorially, and the challenges that imposes are clear. At the global level, the reach of the International Criminal Court (ICC) provides, in certain circumstances, the opportunity to hold individuals within companies accountable for egregious human rights abuses. Since 1998, some 122 countries have ratified the Rome Statute of the International Criminal Court. The ICC has jurisdiction only over natural persons,[76] because a proposal for jurisdiction over corporations was rejected at the conference that drafted the court's statute. However, as individuals, officials of corporations can be held accountable before the ICC for directly or indirectly facilitating conduct that leads to violations of international law. For example, if a company that trades natural resources pays money to a government that then uses the money to fund soldiers who commit war crimes, such a company may have facilitated a war crime and its relevant officers could be prosecuted.

The ICC has jurisdiction to try cases of genocide, crimes against humanity, and war crimes when the state with domestic criminal jurisdiction is unable or unwilling to carry out a criminal investigation. If the operations of a transnational corporation reach the level of these international crimes or aid and abet the perpetration of such crimes by others, international criminal law can be used to prosecute the individuals involved if there is unwillingness to prosecute or if practical obstacles at the municipal level are standing in the way of prosecution. In legislating to give domestic effect to the crimes covered by the ICC, many states have created extraterritorial jurisdiction for the prosecution of their nationals for those crimes.[77] Other international criminal tribunals have prosecuted and convicted individuals for commercial operations that amounted to international crimes, although the corporations themselves have not been prosecuted as independent legal persons. In the *IG Farben* case, twelve out of the twenty-three accused were officers of a corporation that procured and used slave labor from Auschwitz concentration camps and were convicted by the U.S. Military Tribunal at Nuremberg.[78] More recently, in *Prosecutor v. Musema*,[79] the International Criminal Tribunal for Rwanda held Alfred Musema, the

---

75.   Nike Inc. v. Kasky, 539 U.S. 654 (2003).
76.   *Rome Statute of the International Criminal Court*, opened for signature July 17, 1998, 2187 UNT.S. 90 (entered into force July 1, 2002) art. 25(1).
77.   For example, Australia's *Criminal Code Act 1995* (Cth), Division 268, inserted in 2002, gives effect to Australia's ratification of the ICC statute.
78.   *In re* Krauch and Others (IG Farben Trial), 15 I.L.R. 668 (1948).
79.   Prosecutor Alfred Musema (Judgment and Sentence) (International Criminal Tribunal for Rwanda, Trial Chamber, Case No ICTR-96-13-T, Jan. 27, 2000).

director of a tea factory, accountable for the acts of his employees in massacring Tutsis. He was convicted of genocide and the crime against humanity of extermination on the basis of command responsibility and also on the basis of ordering and aiding and abetting.

The effect and reach of the Rome Statute has globalized criminal law protections against the worst forms of human rights abuse via domestic jurisdictions, and though it continues to restrict accountability to individuals, the statute can potentially impact a company's operations and the corporate culture[80] instilled in that company with respect to human rights, although once again, the number of companies and violations that are likely to fall within the ambit of the ICC are severely limited.

Conclusion

The chain connecting corporations with international human rights law seems to be missing several crucial links. A system that has developed focusing almost exclusively on the role of states (and consequently excluding nonstate actors) is outdated and in need of adaptation. Soft law can work alongside hard law (both domestic and international) to ensure corporations adhere to human rights standards, but corporate responsibilities need to be grounded in and linked directly to international legal human rights standards and not be dependent on a society's ever-changing expectations. Though there is an increasing recognition that corporations have a responsibility to respect (if not protect) human rights within their everyday operations, the precise legal basis of that responsibility and possible mechanisms for enforcing human rights standards are lacking. For the time being, it is necessary to extrapolate from international human rights law obligations that were written with states in mind, to rely on voluntary measures, or to invoke domestic laws from other fields that cover certain aspects of corporate impact on human rights, such as criminal law or tort law. Respecting human rights should not be optional or dependent on the whim of society. The current patchwork-quilt system of human rights protection provides the foundation for developing a stronger link between international human rights law and corporations. What is missing in the international arena is the political courage to connect legal obligations with corporate responsibilities.

---

80. For a discussion on corporate culture, *see* ALLENS ARTHUR ROBINSON, CORPORATE CULTURE AS A BASIS FOR THE CRIMINAL LIABILITY OF CORPORATIONS: REPORT PREPARED FOR THE UNITED NATIONS SPECIAL REPRESENTATIVE OF THE SECRETARY-GENERAL ON HUMAN RIGHTS AND BUSINESS (2008), http://198.170.85.29/Allens-Arthur-Robinson-Corporate-Culture-paper-for-Ruggie-Feb-2008.pdf.

Chapter 2

Multinational Corporations and Their Responsibilities under International Law

Ralph G. Steinhardt

The George Washington University Law School

Introduction

Cutting-edge controversies about what international law requires have typically turned on more abstract questions about what international law really is and how its content is determined. Few other fields of law have this existential puzzle at their core. Tax lawyers do not generally feel compelled to return to first principles and establish the reality of tax law in order to determine what a client's lawful deductions are. Securities lawyers rarely agonize in public over the theoretical status of the Securities Exchange Act of 1934. By contrast, international lawyers, especially when trying to describe what they see as a development in the law, face a unique burden of justification: not only must they determine the content of international norms, they must also be prepared to defend the reality of international law and its processes. In other words, the substantive argument—whatever it is—often rests on implicit assumptions about international legal process. As a consequence, to ask whether international law defines and imposes obligations for multinational corporations is to confront the problem of how international law comes into being in the first place and how it works, if at all.

The question of whether a multinational corporation can be liable under international law has arisen sharply in American courts under the Alien Tort Statute of 1789 (ATS or Act)[1]—especially in the *Kiobel* litigation and its precursors—but the issue is hardly limited to that setting. On the contrary, the issue of corporate liability under international law

---

1.   28 U.S.C. § 1350 (2012). In its modern form, the statute provides that "the district courts shall

long predates and survives *Kiobel*.[2] Nor is it new that litigants in ATS litigation typically confront broader issues of international law. Ever since 1980, when the Second Circuit Court of Appeals decided *Filártiga v. Peña-Irala*,[3] litigation under the ATS has repeatedly, even characteristically, offered fresh context for resolving ancient and recurring questions of law, including: What is the content of customary international law? What is the relationship between domestic law and the law of nations? What is the proper constitutional role of U.S. courts in interpreting and applying international standards? And in what circumstances might the exercise of jurisdiction to provide a remedy under the ATS for a tort in violation of international law be itself a violation of international standards?

In this chapter, I broaden focus beyond the ATS and the *Kiobel* litigation. I argue that multinational corporations are not immune from international law and that every primary form of international law—treaties, customary international law, and general principles of law—recognizes or defines the legal responsibilities of juridical entities. None exempts the corporation from any and all liability. The corporation in short can bear a responsibility that is distinct from the responsibility of the human beings who run it, own it, or work for it. In addition, I argue that the contrary position rests on (a) certain anachronistic assumptions about personality under international law, (b) a rigid and unrealistic division between international law and domestic law, and (c) the highly theoretical and misleading distinction between public and private international law. Admittedly, under international law the exact contours of corporate liability, like the exact contours of government liability, are highly fact dependent, but corporations do not operate in an

---

have original jurisdiction of any civil action by an alien for a tort only, committed in violation of the law of nations or a treaty of the United States."

2.   After oral argument on the issue of corporate liability under international law and the Act, the Supreme Court required the parties to brief the question "[w]hether and under what circumstances the Alien Tort Statute . . . allows courts to recognize a cause of action for violations of the law of nations occurring within the territory of a sovereign other than the United States." After reargument, the Supreme Court addressed only the extraterritorial application of the ATS and completely ignored the question of whether multinational corporations could in principle bear responsibilities under international law. The judgment of the Court of Appeals dismissing the case was affirmed, but the lower court's lengthy analysis of international law— as well as the extensive briefing on that issue by the parties and dozens of *amici*—was ignored.

By its terms, of course, the ATS does not distinguish among types of defendants, and the framing generation would certainly have been familiar with corporate responsibility for transitory torts and violations of international law. Over a century ago, the attorney general of the United States concluded that corporations are in principle capable of violating the law of nations or a treaty of the United States for purposes of the Alien Tort Statute. 26 Op. Att'y Gen. 250 (1907) (concluding that aliens injured by a private company's diversion of water in violation of a bilateral treaty between Mexico and the United States could sue under the ATS). *See generally* MICHAEL KOEBELE, CORPORATE RESPONSIBILITY UNDER THE ALIEN TORT STATUTE: ENFORCEMENT OF INTERNATIONAL LAW THROUGH U.S. TORTS LAW (2009).

3.   630 F.2d 876 (2d Cir. 1980). *Filártiga* clarified that the statute could be used to advance human rights claims in U.S. courts, even if the abuse occurred abroad and involved exclusively non-American citizens, so long as the defendant was within the personal jurisdiction of the court.

international-law–free zone; indeed (and somewhat paradoxically), they would be both disadvantaged and perversely empowered if they did.

Clearing the Decks: Ask the Right Legal Question, Then Allocate the Burden of Answering It

In its simplest form, the argument that corporations are immune from international legal standards runs along the following lines. By definition, international law regulates the relations among states and, with a few exceptions such as piracy and war crimes, it binds governments, not human beings, and certainly not the abstraction of a corporation. Aside from those well-rehearsed exceptions (none of which explicitly applies to corporations), violations of international law require some measure of state action as an element of the offense.[4] The corporation by contrast is quintessentially a creature of domestic law: there is no such thing as an internationally chartered corporation, and the regulation, or not, of the corporation's activities lies within the domestic jurisdiction of the state in which the company is incorporated and the state(s) in which the company conducts its business. Of course in the exercise of their sovereignty, governments can by treaty create specific rights and obligations for human beings and corporations, but those obligations must be translated into and enforced through domestic law; therefore, in those circumstances, it is domestic law that reaches corporations, not international law. The other dominant form of international law, namely customary international law, requires a universal state practice combined with the conviction that the conduct is required by law (*opinio juris*). But there is no universal practice among states imposing or enforcing civil or criminal liability on corporations for violations of international law, and therefore there can be no customary norm of corporate responsibility. It is true that international criminal law shows that individuals can bear some human-rights–related obligations, but the international criminal tribunals that have been established to enforce those standards—such as the Nuremberg Tribunal and the Yugoslavian War Crimes Tribunal—were not given jurisdiction over corporations; therefore, even those most basic international legal obligations do not apply

---

4. *See, e.g.*, the definition of *torture* in the United Nations Convention Against Torture and Other Cruel, Inhuman, or Degrading Treatment or Punishment:

> [T]orture means any act by which severe pain or suffering, whether physical or mental, is intentionally inflicted on a person for such purposes as obtaining from him or a third person information or a confession, punishing him for an act he or a third person has committed or is suspected of having committed, or intimidating or coercing him or a third person, or for any reason based on discrimination of any kind, *when such pain or suffering is inflicted by or at the instigation of or with the consent or acquiescence of a public official or other person acting in an official capacity.*

Convention Against Torture and Other Cruel, Inhuman or Degrading Treatment or Punishment, Dec. 10, 1984, 1465 UNT.S. 85, art. 1(1) (entered into force June 26, 1987) (emphasis added).

to companies. It is also true that some international human rights courts have held that governments are obligated under international law to provide a remedy for human rights abuses, including those committed by private actors, but that remedial obligation amounts to an obligation of governments with respect to their own domestic law and institutions. It does not even purport to create a direct obligation for corporate entities.

Whatever plausibility and appeal this argument may have in the abstract, each step in the analysis is wrong.

Is it true that international law is limited to regulating the relations among governments?

No. It is anachronistic to treat international law as though it deals exclusively with the legal obligations of governments in their dealings among themselves. Traditionally, only states could be the subjects of international law, that is, only states could have rights and obligations cognizable at international law. Only states could create and assume treaty relations. Only states' behavior could give rise to customary international law. It made sense from that perspective to conclude, virtually with the force of axiom, that "[i]nternational law governs relations between independent States."[5]

One of the substantive consequences of state exclusivity in international lawmaking was that international law preserved more power for states than it constrained: intergovernmental organizations with broad lawmaking authority were nonexistent, universal treaties began to appear only in the twentieth century, and sovereignty rested on an expansive right of states to be left alone. As a consequence, international law was more likely to protect governments' discretion than to regulate it, and problems that crossed international borders were more likely to be tackled (when they were tackled at all) in one state at a time rather than in some international institution. The law was primarily a matter of jurisdictional line drawing, "a negative code of rules of abstentions"[6] and immunities. In effect, the law built and policed fences between states and protected their legal right to be left alone.

But contemporary international law is less about fences and more about bridges. International law has been transformed from the *negative code* into a more affirmative code of obligations of states to cooperate in the solution of problems perceived to be communal. Consider, for example, the rise of intergovernmental institutions to address issues of common concern by promoting international communication, protecting health and the environment, fighting international crimes, setting capital requirements for banks, developing harmonized standards for wills and trusts, or gathering evidence in transnational litigation. These developments affect the daily work and conduct of nonstate actors, and those actors have increasingly played a role in the articulation of international standards: multinational corporations, the International Chamber of Commerce, and thousands of

---

5.   S. S. Lotus (Fr. v. Turk.), 1927 P.C.I.J. (ser. A) No. 10, at 18 (Sept. 7).
6.   WOLFGANG FRIEDMANN, THE CHANGING STRUCTURE OF INTERNATIONAL LAW 62 (1964).

other nongovernmental organizations have contributed to the evolution of law in such fields as international trade, transportation, human rights, and commercial transactions, even as they have operated under the law that emerges from the process. In other words, states can no longer claim to be the exclusive subjects of international law, and the legal component of relations among states can no longer adequately describe the content of international law. As noted by Sir Robert Jennings in his account of the transformation in international law,

> [p]erhaps the most important change is that the old, classical orthodoxy that international law was concerned only with the relations of States, and by its very nature, could not be concerned with individuals or even with corporations, has simply disappeared. . . . Nowadays, treaty-law affects the everyday life of people, and the more advanced the country, the more likely are people to find themselves subjected to international law in a myriad ways.[7]

It is doubtless true that governments retain primacy under international law—primacy in lawmaking, primacy in responsibility—but it does not follow from that premise that all others are immune, especially where the primary forms of international law cut in precisely the opposite direction.[8]

Does each state's "exclusive domestic jurisdiction," recognized and protected by the Charter of the United Nations and customary international law, imply that the regulation of multinational corporations must be left to each government, without international legal scrutiny?

No. The concept of an exclusive domestic jurisdiction refers to no unchanging or inert set of state competencies. The history of international law over the last century proves that matters that may at one time lie within a state's exclusive domestic jurisdiction do not necessarily remain there. And that is because the line between domestic and international concern is a

---

7.   Robert Y. Jennings, *Universal International Law in a Multicultural World, in* LIBER AMERICO-RUM FOR THE RT. HON. LORD WILBERFORCE, 39 (Bos & Brownlie eds., 1987); *see also* Joel Paul, *Holding Multinational Corporations Responsible Under International Law*, 24 HASTINGS INT'L & COMP. L. REV. 285 (2001).

8.   *See infra* pp. 39–49. For this reason, the International Law Commission's Articles on State Responsibility do not undermine the conclusion that international law— in the form of treaties, general principles, and custom—recognizes corporate liability for the violation of at least some international norms; indeed, the Articles are not directly relevant to the issue of corporate accountability at all. As the title suggests, these Articles, drafted by scholars and jurists in their private capacities rather than by government representatives, offer principles governing the responsibility of states for internationally wrongful acts. They were never intended to and do not offer a comprehensive and exclusive restatement of all forms of responsibility under international law. As shown below, for example, it is well-established that individuals, whether acting under color of authority or not, can be liable for violations of international law, and yet these and the other examples of individual responsibility are explicitly *not* the subject of the ILC Articles.

function of diplomatic history, not transcendent principle: states, by their conduct and following their interests, define what is and what is not within their exclusive domestic jurisdiction. As noted in the *Tunis-Morocco Nationality Cases*, by the Permanent Court of International Justice (precursor to the modern International Court of Justice), "The question whether a certain matter is or is not solely within the jurisdiction of a State is an essentially relative question. It depends on the development of international relations."[9] It follows that the right legal question is not whether corporations are *ex ante* within a state's exclusive domestic jurisdiction. It is whether governments and intergovernmental organizations have actually made the multinational corporation a matter of international concern. This they have clearly done,[10] removing the regulation of multinational corporations from individual states' exclusive legal preserve.

Does the international law of human rights govern the conduct of governments exclusively?

No. The relevant distinction at international law is not simply between governments (or government actors) and corporations. It is between conduct that the law considers a violation only when committed by or under the auspices of a state (such as torture under the Torture Convention, discussed below), and conduct that violates international law even when committed without state action or participation (such as piracy and genocide, discussed below). In other words, certain egregious conduct violates international human rights standards, whether committed by state or nonstate actors. Thus, both juristic and natural individuals violate international law if they engage in activity that does not require state action to be wrongful *or* if they are, by analogy to the antidiscrimination laws of the United States, a "willful participant in joint action with the State or its agents" or were otherwise acting "under color of law." [11]

The correct analysis under international law is exemplified by *Kadic v. Karadzic*,[12] in which the Second Circuit Court of Appeals rightly concluded that conventional and customary international law imposes human rights obligations on a variety of persons who are not *State actors*. Specifically, the court ruled that

> the law of nations as understood in the modern era [does not] confine its reach to state action. Instead, certain forms of conduct violate the law of nations whether undertaken by those acting under the auspices of a state or only as private individuals.[13]

---

9.   Nationality Decrees Issued in Tunis and Morocco (Fr. v. Gr. Brit.), 1923 P.C.I.J. (ser. B) No. 4, at 24 (Feb. 7).

10.   *See infra* pp. 3949. *See generally* ANDREW CLAPHAM, HUMAN RIGHTS IN THE PRIVATE SPHERE 89–133 (1993); Steven Ratner, *Corporations and Human Rights: A Theory of Legal Responsibility*, 111 YALE L.J. 443 (2001); MICHAEL KERR, RICHARD JANDA, & CHIP PITTS, CORPORATE SOCIAL RESPONSIBILITY: A LEGAL ANALYSIS (2009).

11.   *See* Dennis v. Sparks, 449 U.S. 24, 27 (1980).

12.   70 F.3d 232 (2d Cir. 1995), cited with approval by the Supreme Court in *Sosa*, 542 U.S. at 748.

13.   *Id.* at 236.

The *Karadzic* court articulated two separate circumstances under which a nominally private actor might bear international responsibility: the first is when the individual commits one of a narrow class of wrongs identified by treaty and custom as not requiring state action to be considered wrongful, and the second is when the offensive conduct is sufficiently infused with state action to engage international standards. In both cases, it is the nature of the conduct, not the nature of the actor, that matters.

The first category, which I call "*per se* wrongs," comprises conduct that is internationally wrongful even in the absence of state action. For at least two hundred years it has been recognized that there are acts or omissions for which international law imposes responsibility on individuals and for which punishment may be imposed, either by international tribunals or by national courts.[14] For example, as shown more fully below, the Genocide Convention requires that persons committing genocide be punished, "whether they are constitutionally responsible rulers, public officials or *private individuals.*"[15] Certain aspects of the war crimes regime of the Geneva Conventions of 1949, especially Common Article 3, similarly apply to nonstate actors, including militia groups, when they are parties to an armed conflict.[16] The antislavery regime is similar in not prohibiting exclusively state-run slavery rings.[17] Crucially, these regimes do not explicitly distinguish between natural and juridical individuals, and it is implausible that international law would not reach a corporation that engaged in the slave trade, acted as a front for piracy on the

---

14. Indeed, the *least* controversial aspect of the Alien Tort Statute is that private individuals who commit torts in the course of violating international law fall squarely within its jurisdictional reach. Pirates, the exemplars of intended defendants under § 1350, were not always or necessarily considered "state actors," and there was never any question that their depredations were in violation of the law of nations. One of the earliest exercises of jurisdiction under the Act involved an unlawful seizure of property by a nonstate actor. Bolchos v. Darrel, 3 F. Cas. 810 (D.S.C. 1795). Nor was there any doubt that private citizens who infringed the rights of ambassadors or diplomats could be sued under § 1350, and that statute clearly provided jurisdiction over a child custody dispute that involved a breach of the law of nations. Adra v. Clift, 195 F. Supp. 857 (D. Md. 1961).

15. Convention on the Prevention and Punishment of the Crime of Genocide, Dec. 9, 1948, 78 UNT.S. 277 (emphasis supplied).

16. *See, e.g.*, Convention for the Amelioration of the Condition of the Wounded and Sick in Armed Forces in the Field, Feb. 2, 1956, 6 U.S.T. 3114, 75 UNT.S. 31; Convention for the Amelioration of the Condition of the Wounded, Sick, and Shipwrecked Members of Armed Forces at Sea, Feb. 2, 1956, 6 U.S.T. 3217, 75 UNT.S. 85; Convention Relative to the Treatment of Prisoners of War, Feb. 2, 1956, 6 U.T.S. 3316, 75 UNT.S. 135; Convention Relative to the Protection of Civilian Persons in Time of War, Feb. 2, 1956, 6 U.S.T. 3516, 75 UNT.S. 287.

17. *See, e.g.*, Slavery, Servitude, Forced Labour, and Similar Institutions and Practices Convention of 1926, Sept. 25, 1926, 60 L.N.T.S. 253; Convention Concerning Forced or Compulsory Labour, June 28, 1930, 39 UNT.S. 55. As Professor Ratner has noted:

> The slave trade represented, in a sense, the worst form of private enterprise abuse of human rights. To end it, abolitionists eschewed sole reliance on state responsibility, both because traders operated on the high seas and because many states tolerated the practice. Instead, they convinced governments to conclude a series of treaties that allowed states to seize vessels and required them to punish slave traders. Thus the first true example of international human rights law was a response to commercially oriented violations of rights.

Ratner, *supra* note 10, at 465 (footnote omitted).

high seas, or produced the contemporary equivalent of Zyklon B for the destruction of Jews in concentration camps.

The second category of nonstate liability according to the *Karadzic* court, which I will refer to as "contextual wrongs," refers to conduct that is internationally wrongful by virtue of the private actor's relationship with a state, and is entirely consistent with precedent and principle. International law recognizes the possibility that a private entity might become a state actor in fact or deed, as for example when the private entity acts on behalf of the government or exercises governmental authority in the absence of official authorities.[18] In *Karadzic*, the plaintiffs were entitled to prove their allegations that Karadzic acted in concert with Yugoslav officials or with significant Yugoslavian aid. A substantial degree of cooperative action between private actor defendants and government officials can trigger the application of international standards.

These categories of liability hardly erase the distinction between state and nonstate actors altogether, but they are sufficiently well established to support the *Karadzic* court's more modest conclusion that "certain forms of conduct violate the law of nations whether undertaken by those acting under the auspices of a State or only as private individuals." Under international law, there can be no prophylactic rule against private obligations under international law, especially for egregious violations of human rights law. If there were, states could as a matter of law privatize their way around international obligations to protect human rights.

Does the fact that international law is characteristically implemented through domestic law imply that corporations are immune from international legal standards?

One strategy for immunizing the corporation from international standards rests on a radical demarcation between international law and domestic law. In treaties purportedly imposing standards on private actors, for example, the treaty obligation is typically on a state party to criminalize or otherwise prohibit the conduct in question. Each state then uses the instrument of its domestic law to implement the treaty. A formalist might conclude on that basis that the private actor's obligation is a function of domestic, not international, law and that international law itself cannot reach the private actor.

The argument proves both too much and too little. It proves too much because international law almost never defines the means of its domestic implementation, leaving a sovereign wide berth in assuring that internationally agreed-upon standards are respected and enforced in accordance with its own law and traditions.[19] If implementation through

---

18. *See, e.g.,* Yeager v. Islamic Republic of Iran, 17 Iran-U.S. Cl. Trib. Rep. 92, 103-04 (1987). Professor Clapham helpfully refers to these contextual wrongs as "complicity crimes." Andrew Clapham, *On Complicity, in* Le droit pénal à l'épreuve de l'internationalisation, 241-75 (M. M. Henzelin & R. Roth eds., 2002).

19. *See* Philip Trimble, *International Law, World Order, and Critical Legal Studies*, 42 Stan. L. Rev. 811, 835 (1990). "Instead of being seen as a single, unitary system applicable across the 'world

domestic law were proof of a limit on the reach of international law, we would be left with the absurdity that the great bulk of international law, because it is dependent on domestic implementation, is not really international law at all.

The formalist argument also proves too little: the systemic preference for domestic law and proceedings in the implementation of international law says nothing about whether a substantive international norm, such as international legal standards for corporate behavior, exists or not. That the individual state is traditionally the agent for implementing international norms does not mean that the standard around which the domestic laws harmonize is not international law after all. For an analogy, recall John Chipman Gray's famous observation on behalf of legal realists everywhere that "all . . . law is judge-made law."[20] As a way of emphasizing the role of judicial interpretation in giving content to law, the aphorism, like all caricatures, tells a certain limited truth. But caricature is not portrait, and a literal understanding of Gray mistakes the part for the whole, utterly dismissing the roles of the legislature and the executive in *making* the law. A similar mistake occurs if someone concluded that there are no drug laws except those enforced by the police. Whatever element of truth or cynicism is captured in the observation, it is outweighed by the reality that the drug laws are actually made by the legislature and then enforced by the police. So too in international law: reliance on domestic law at the point of implementation cannot in principle and does not in fact negate the existence of an international standard. Complementarity arises specifically when there is agreement around a substantive international standard in the first place. In short, the corporation is not immunized from whatever international standards exist just because implementation is through domestic instrumentalities.

If there were no domestic judicial decisions imposing civil or criminal liability on corporations under international law, would that imply that businesses are free from all regulation under international law?

No. The Permanent Court of International Justice established that international norms could not be inferred from the absence of domestic proceedings:

Even if the rarity of the judicial decisions to be found among the reported cases were sufficient to prove the circumstance alleged by the French government, it would merely show that States had often, in practice, abstained from instituting criminal proceedings, and not that they recognized themselves as being obliged to do so. [21]

---

community,' public international law should be imagined as a series of parallel systems, more or less convergent depending on the subject, separately applicable within the various nations of the world.".

20.   John Chipman Gray, The Nature and Sources of the Law 125 (2d ed. 1927).

21.   S. S. Lotus (Fr. v. Turk.), *supra* note 5, at 28.

If it were otherwise, *Filártiga v. Peña-Irala*—the fountainhead of ATS jurisprudence for a generation and now a globally respected advance in the development of human rights standards—would have been wrongly decided. Prior to that case, internationally defined state-sponsored torture, though common, had never grounded an award of civil damages from the torturer to the victim in the domestic courts of that state, let alone some other country.

As an objection to corporate liability under international law, the argument also founders on the facts. There have been multiple proceedings against corporations for their complicity in international law violations, both criminally and civilly, and in a variety of jurisdictions.[22]

Does the orthodox distinction between "public international law" and "private international law" imply that multinational corporations are exempt from international obligations, especially with respect to human rights norms?

No. First, there are multiple ambiguities in the term *private international law*.[23] In jurisdictions other than the United States, it generally refers to the conflicts of law, including choice of law doctrine, jurisdiction, and the recognition and enforcement of foreign judgments.[24] Violations of private international law in this sense, unlike violations of public international law, allegedly do not trigger a state's responsibility as that term is understood in the law of nations. A state could violate this private international law without engaging the obligation to make reparations and without justifying a resort to war. In the United States, by contrast, *private international law* has a very different meaning and typically refers to international business transactions and transnational family law. This would include, among other things, the international law of sales, international trade, banking,

---

22.   In the United Kingdom, for example, several cases have been brought successfully against multinational corporations by communities in the developing world. *See, e.g.*, Lubbe & Ors v. Cape PLC, [2000] 1 W.L.R. 1545 (H.L.) (assessing the company's liability for harm to South African miners caused by exposure to asbestos dust); Motto & Ors v. Trafigura [2011] EWCA (Civ) 1150 (London-based international commodities trader settles a case brought by Ivorian citizens injured by toxic waste dumped in Côte d'Ivoire in 2006); Mario Alberto et al. v. Monterrico Metals PLC [2009] EWHC (QB) 2475 (injunction issued against Monterrico Metals PLC, pending resolution of claims that the company and its Peruvian subsidiary participated in the torture and arbitrary detention of a group of indigenous Peruvians protesting the company's copper mine); Chandler v. Cape PLC, [2012] EWCA (Civ) 525 (adopting the theory of "direct foreign liability," which defines the circumstances under which a parent company involved in the operations of a subsidiary owes a duty of care to its employees or anyone affected by those operations).

23.   *See* Ralph G. Steinhardt, *The Privatization of Public International Law*, 25 Geo. Wash. J. Int'l L. & Econ. 523 (1991).

24.   *Cf.* Philip Marshall Brown, *Private Versus Public International Law*, 36 Am. J. Int'l L. 448, 449 (1942) ("The *raison d'être* of private international law is to provide the territorial sovereign with a uniform norm of judicial procedure in matters affecting the rights of aliens."), *with* W. E. Beckett, *What Is Private International Law*, 7 Brit. Y.B. Int'l L. 73, 94 (1926) ("Private International Law consists of principles of private law which determine (a) in what circumstances the courts of a country have jurisdiction to pronounce judgment; and (b) the law which they have jurisdiction to pronounce, and of *nothing else*.") (emphasis supplied).

adoption, and dispute settlement between nonstate actors. It includes broad freedoms of contract and the ability of private actors to specify the applicable law.

A rigid application of the orthodox distinction between *private* and *public* international law locates rights in a *public* realm, binding only on governments in their dealings with individuals, and corporate conduct in a *private* realm, governed only by the rules of the marketplace. But the argument fails. Over the last two decades, prominent transnational companies have adopted codes of conduct that make the protection of at least some human rights an explicit corporate objective.[25] Coalitions in apparel, textiles, and footwear have adopted standards industrywide to govern international labor practices.[26] Various global standards for social accountability have been created to guide and assess corporate compliance with international human rights norms across industrial and geographical boundaries.[27] Many companies now advertise their international human rights policies. Corporate officers periodically gather at human rights roundtables and affirm the strategic value of a public commitment to such rights, even as a self-styled *progressive* stream of corporate and management scholarship offers a theoretical foundation for understanding the economic self-interest of corporate social responsibility. The consequence is that there are now transnational marketplace mechanisms for enforcing human rights undertakings by companies and industry groups.[28]

The orthodox distinction has also been undermined by the established obligation of governments to provide a remedy for human rights violations no matter who commits the wrong.[29] In *Velasquez-Rodriguez v. Honduras*, the Inter-American Court of Human Rights found Honduras responsible for the disappearances at issue, even in the absence of any direct evidence implicating the Honduran government. Instead, the government's responsibility lay in its failure to exercise due diligence in the investigation of the allegations that persons acting under color of its authority had kidnapped and killed Velasquez. The case was considered revolutionary at the time because it suggested that a government might be liable if it systematically failed to investigate and prosecute violations of the law in the *private* realm. Post-*Velasquez*, a government's systemic failure to prosecute domestic

---

25. See, for example, those of Reebok, Levis, and Wal-Mart.

26. See, for example, the Fair Labor Association (FLA) and the Global Social Compliance Program (GSCP).

27. See, for example, SA 8000 and ISO 26000.

28. Ralph G. Steinhardt, *Soft Law, Hard Markets: Competitive Self-Interest and the Emergence of Human Rights Responsibilities for Multinational Corporations*, 33 BROOK. J. INT'L L. 933 (2008). In many respects, the most promising means of enforcing these otherwise aspirational codes is the incorporation of human rights clauses in private and public contracts, which can create legal obligations under a variety of legal regimes. *See generally* Laura A. Dickinson, *Public Law Values in a Privatized World*, YALE J. INT'L L. 383, 401–22 (2006).

29. Velásquez-Rodríguez v. Honduras, Judgement, Inter-Am. Ct. H.R. (ser. C) No. 4 (July 29, 1988). *See also* Osman v. United Kingdom, in which the European Court of Human Rights held that state authorities have a "positive obligation . . . to take preventive operational measures to protect an individual whose life is at risk from the criminal acts of another individual." 1998-VIII Eur. Ct. H.R. 3124.

violence and other forms of gender violence would constitute a violation of its obligation to protect the human rights of the victims and survivors.[30]

In short, nothing in the concept or content of *private international law* amounts to an exemption of corporations from the operation of international standards.

Does the fact that international criminal tribunals generally do not have jurisdiction over corporate entities imply that corporations are free from all regulation under international law?

No. Although it is true that the instruments defining the jurisdiction of international criminal tribunals distinguish between natural and juristic persons *for purposes of criminal prosecution at the international level*, these instruments and the tribunals generally do not limit the conduct that violates international law;[31] instead, they simply provide an extraordinary means of enforcement against individual human beings. Nothing in international law or the charters of the international criminal tribunals precludes the imposition of civil or tort liability for corporate misconduct, which of course is common in legal systems around the world. The right legal question is therefore not whether human rights treaties explicitly impose liability on corporations, or whether the international criminal tribunals have jurisdiction over corporations, or even whether other states have universally imposed criminal or civil liability for violations of international law. It is whether those treaties, the charters of the criminal tribunals, and the practice of states affirmatively distinguish between juristic and natural individuals in a way that exempts the former from all responsibility for violations of international law. As shown in Part III below, they clearly do not.

Allocating the burden of persuasion. At a minimum, governments are clearly not foreclosed from remedying violations of international standards committed by juridical entities within their jurisdiction. This follows from the permissive nature of international law, under which limitations on state action must be proved and not merely presumed. Thus, if U.S. courts allow corporations to be sued under the Alien Tort Statute or Congress amends the statute to make that possible, that is not a violation of international law. The question of principle, whether nonstate actors bear obligations under international law, is somewhat harder, and who bears the burden of persuasion: Those who argue that corporations are exempt from international legal regimes, or those who argue that juridical individuals

---

30.   *See* Comm. on the Elimination of Discrimination Against Women, General Recommendation 19, UN Doc. No. A/47/38 (Jan. 29, 1992), at ¶ 9.

31.   *See, e.g.*, Rome Statute of the International Criminal Court, July 17, 1998, 2187 UNT.S. 90, art. 10 (Rome Statute) ("Nothing in this Part shall be interpreted as limiting or prejudicing in any way existing or developing rules of international law for purposes other than this Statute."). As noted by the chairman of the Rome Statute's Drafting Committee, "all positions now accept in some form or another the principle that a legal entity, private or public, can, through its policies or actions, transgress a norm for which the law, whether national or international, provides, at the very least damages . . . and other remedies such as seizure and forfeiture of assets." M. CHERIF BASSIOUNI, CRIMES AGAINST HUMANITY IN INTERNATIONAL CRIMINAL LAW 379 (2d rev. ed. 1999).

are presumptively treated like other nonstate actors? The analysis above suggests that old definitions or conceptions of *international law* are not helpful given (a) the reduced state-centeredness of contemporary international law, (b) the transformation in the range of conduct that international law addresses, (c) the interpenetration of international and domestic law (rather than their separation), and (d) the two categories of nonstate actor liability. If it can be demonstrated that a company facilitated egregious violations of human rights, entered into business agreements with the intent and the understanding that human rights would be violated for profit, or committed international wrongs that by definition do not require state action, then the burden of persuasion must rest on those who would carve out an exemption for creatures of the state. That burden cannot be met because, as shown next, international law neither creates nor allows a law-free zone for corporations.

International Law Recognizes the Legal Responsibilities of Multinational Corporations

Each of the three primary types of international law[32]—treaties, general principles, and customary international law—establishes independently that corporations are not immune from responsibility under international standards. In the argument that follows, I draw first on *treaties* to establish that corporate behavior, long internationalized as a commercial matter, has been internationalized as a legal matter: governments have repeatedly used international agreements to impose specific legal obligations on corporations. That these obligations are typically enforced through the instrumentalities of domestic law proves only that corporate responsibility is like other international legal obligations and does not amount to a justification for treating corporations differently from human beings. Second, *general principles of law recognized by civilized nations* recognize corporate personality and the legal responsibility of companies, as the International Court of Justice recognized in the *Barcelona Traction* case. Third, for at least two hundred years, *customary international law* has recognized the legitimacy of holding nonhuman entities accountable for egregious violations of international norms. Taken together, these three dominant sources

---

32. Article 38(1) of the Statute of the International Court of Justice, June 26, 1945, 59 Stat. 1055, 33 UNT.S. 993, is generally treated as the authoritative catalogue of the sources of international law:
> The Court, whose function is to decide in accordance with international law such disputes as are submitted to it, shall apply: (a) international conventions, whether general or particular, establishing rules expressly recognized by the contesting states; (b) international custom, as evidence of a general practice accepted as law; (c) the general principles of law recognized by civilized nations; (d) . . . judicial decisions and the teachings of the most highly qualified publicists of the various nations, as subsidiary means for the determination of rules of law.

The text of this provision distinguishes between implicitly primary sources (¶¶ 1(a)-(c)) and "subsidiary means" (¶ 1(d)) for determining the rules of international law.

of international law flatly contradict the argument that corporations occupy some ersatz legal space devoid of international standards.

Treaties. Across time and subject matters, a variety of treaties has defined acts or omissions for which international law imposes responsibility on individuals and for which punishment may be imposed, generally though not exclusively through national institutions. These particular treaty-based wrongs do not include state action as an element of the offense and do not apply exclusively to state actors. Nor do the legal regimes governing these wrongs distinguish between natural and juridical individuals in such a way as to immunize the latter from all responsibility. Outside the context of human rights law, a diverse array of treaties—dealing with, among other things, terrorism, environmental protection, and bribery—reveals the international consensus that corporations can have international obligations, specified by treaty and implemented (as usual) through the various instrumentalities of domestic law.[33]

The same is true of numerous human rights treaties.[34] Consider, for example, Article IV of the Genocide Convention, which requires that persons committing genocide be punished, "whether they are constitutionally responsible rulers, public officials or private individuals."[35] Nothing in the text or the *travaux préparatoires* of the Genocide Convention suggests that the phrase "private individuals" refers exclusively to human beings, and it would be inconsistent with the remedial purpose of the convention if the only type of entity exempt from its reach would be a juridical creation of the state itself. Certain aspects of the war crimes regime of the Geneva Conventions of 1949,

---

33. *See, e.g.,* European Convention on the Prevention of Terrorism, art. 10(1), May 16, 2005, C.E.T.S. No. 196 ("Each Party shall adopt such measures as may be necessary, in accordance with its legal principles, to establish the *liability of legal entities* for participation in the offences set forth in Articles 5 to 7 and 9 of this Convention."); Convention Against Transnational Organized Crime, art. 10(1), Nov. 15, 2000, 2225 UNT.S. 209 ("Each State Party shall adopt such measures as may be necessary, consistent with its legal principles, to establish the *liability of legal persons* for participation in serious crimes involving an organized criminal group and for the offences established in accordance with Articles 5, 6, 8 and 23 of this Convention."); Convention on Combating Bribery of Foreign Public Officials in International Business Transactions, art. 2, Dec. 17, 1997, S. Treaty Doc. No. 105-43 ("Each Party shall take such measures as may be necessary, in accordance with its legal principles, to establish the *liability of legal persons* for the bribery of a foreign public official."); Basel Convention on the Control of Transboundary Movements of Hazardous Wastes and Their Disposal, Mar. 22, 1989, 1673 UNT.S. 57; International Convention on the Suppression and Punishment of the Crime of Apartheid, art. I(2), Nov. 3, 1973, 1015 UNT.S. 243 ("The States Parties to the present Convention declare criminal those *organizations, institutions, and individuals* committing the crime of apartheid."); International Convention on Civil Liability for Oil Pollution Damage, Nov. 29, 1969, 973 UNT.S. 3; Convention on Third Party Liability in the Field of Nuclear Energy, July 29, 1960, 956 UNT.S. 251; Convention Concerning Occupational Safety and Health and the Working Environment, art. 16(1), June 22, 1981, 1331 UNT.S. 279 ("*Employers* shall be required to ensure that, so far as is reasonably practicable, the workplaces, machinery, equipment and processes under their control are safe and without risk to health.") (emphasis supplied in all cases).

34. *See generally* Beth Stephens, *The Amorality of Profit: Transnational Corporations and Human Rights*, 20 BERKELEY J. INT'L L. 69 (2002).

35. Convention on the Prevention and Punishment of the Crime of Genocide, Dec. 9, 1948, 78 UNT.S. 277.

especially Common Article 3,[36] similarly bind nonstate actors when they are parties to an armed conflict. The antislavery regime is similar in not requiring state action, and contemporary forms of slavery, such as forced labor and child labor, are internationally wrongful whether committed by governments or nonstate actors. The International Covenant on Civil and Political Rights confirms that the primacy of state responsibility in the human rights regime does not implicitly exempt *groups* and *persons* from human rights obligations.[37] More indirect but still real *per se* obligations are imposed on private parties, including corporations, in virtually all of the arms limitation agreements, which oblige state parties to translate the international prohibitions into domestic law binding on the private sector. Thus, for example, a corporation is not free to traffic in anti-personnel landmines in a country that is a party to the Ottawa Convention on the Prohibition of the Use, Stockpiling, Production and Transfer of Anti-personnel Mines and Their Destruction.[38]

Treaties also establish the potential liability of corporations for their contextual wrongs, not just the *per se* wrongs that do not require state action as an element of the offense. There is no rule in international law that corporations, regardless of their relationship with a government, enjoy immunity from treaty-based norms when they engage in state-like or state-related activities, such as when they interrogate detainees, provide public security, work weapons systems in armed conflict, or run prisons. As noted by the UN Special Representative to the Secretary-General in his summary of international legal principles as applicable to business enterprises, the corporate responsibility to respect human rights includes avoiding complicity, which has been most clearly elucidated "in the area of aiding and abetting international crimes, *i.e.* knowingly providing practical assistance or encouragement that has a substantial effect on the commission of a crime."[39]

---

36.   *See supra* note 15.

37.   Article 5(1) of the International Covenant on Civil and Political Rights, Dec. 16, 1966, S. Exec. Doc. E, 95-2 (1978), 999 UNT.S. 171, provides:

> [n]othing in the present Covenant may be interpreted as implying for any State, group or person any right to engage in any activity or perform any act aimed at the destruction of any of the rights and freedoms recognized herein or at their limitation to a greater extent than is provided for in the present Covenant.

Article 5(1) of the International Covenant on Economic, Social and Cultural Rights, Dec. 16, 1966, 993 UNT.S. 3, is identical. Given the breadth of this language and the protective and remedial purpose of the Covenants, the burden rests on those arguing against corporate responsibility under international law to explain why corporations are specially treated.

38.   Article 9 of the Convention on the Prohibition of the Use, Stockpiling, Production and Transfer of Anti-Personnel Mines and on Their Destruction, Sept. 18, 1997, 2056 UNT.S. 241, provides:

> Each State Party shall take all appropriate legal, administrative and other measures, including the imposition of penal sanctions, to prevent and suppress any activity prohibited to a State Party under this Convention undertaken by persons or on territory under its jurisdiction or control.

39.   *Report of the Special Representative of the Secretary-General on the Issue of Human Rights and Transnational Corporations and Other Business Enterprises*, ¶¶ 73-74, UN Doc. A/HRC/8/5 (Apr. 7, 2008).

The clear application of these treaties to corporate actors is established by the work of the international bodies established under the treaties themselves. For example, the Human Rights Committee, which oversees states' compliance with the International Covenant on Civil and Political Rights, has ruled that states must "redress the harm caused by such acts by private persons *or entities*."[40] Though phrased in terms of the obligation of governments to provide remedies, the committee's statement would be nonsense-on-stilts if corporations were in principle exempt from the covenant's standards altogether. Admittedly, as noted above, some of the covenant's norms require state action to be wrongful (such as torture), and others do not require state action to be wrongful (such as slavery), which means that the precise contours of a corporation's liability—the settings in which liability, if any, will be appropriate—must vary with the facts presented and the norm involved. But the pure position that corporations are beyond the reach of international law cannot be squared with the committee's authoritative interpretation of the treaty itself. Similarly, the Convention on the Elimination of All Forms of Racial Discrimination obliges states to remedy "any acts of racial discrimination," and the Race Committee, which was established under the convention, has consistently ruled that this provision includes the acts of corporations.[41] Thus, whether the corporation commits one of the wrongs that do not require state action or is enmeshed with the state itself in the commission of violations that do require state action, the companies potentially face liability.

General Principles of Law Recognized by Civilized Nations. As a general principle of law recognized by civilized nations, the obligation of corporations to make reparation for their egregious wrongs—typically designated *torts* in common law or *delicts* in civil law terminology—qualifies as international law, even if treaties did not explicitly address the question.[42] Arguments from general principles require a demonstration that a particular legal norm or maxim recurs in the domestic legal systems of representative jurisdictions worldwide.[43] International law is routinely established through this systematic exercise in

---

40.   UN Human Rights Comm., Gen. Comment No. 31, Nature of the General Legal Obligation Imposed on States Parties to the Covenant, ¶ 8, UN Doc. CCPR/C/21/Rev.1/Add.13 (Mar. 29, 2004) (emphasis supplied).

41.   UN Comm. on the Elimination of Racial Discrimination (CERD), *Consideration of Reports Submitted by States Parties under Article 9 of the Convention: International Convention on the Elimination of All Forms of Racial Discrimination Concluding Observations of the Committee on the Elimination of Racial Discrimination: United States of America,* ¶ 30, CERD/C/U.S.A/CO/6 (May 8, 2008).

42.   *See* Statute of the International Court of Justice, *supra* note 31, at art. 38(1)(c). Section 102(1)(c) of the Restatement (Third) of U.S. Foreign Relations Law (1987) similarly provides that "[a] rule of international law is one that has been accepted as such by the international community of states . . . by derivation from general principles common to the major legal systems of the world." General principles encompass maxims that are "accepted by all nations *in foro domestico.*" Permanent Ct. of Int'l Justice, Advisory Comm. of Jurists, *Procès Verbaux of the Proceedings of the Committee,* July 16–24, 1920, with Annexes (the Hague 1920) at 335 (quoting Lord Phillimore, the proponent of the general principles clause).

43.   *See* BIN CHENG, GENERAL PRINCIPLES OF LAW AS APPLIED BY INTERNATIONAL COURTS 390, 392 (2006) (noting that general principles encompass "the fundamental principles of every legal system"

comparative law.[44] For our purposes, the uniform recognition of corporate personality and liability in domestic legal systems around the world demonstrates, independently of treaties or customary international law, that legal responsibility accompanies legal personality.

In the *Barcelona Traction Case*, for example, the International Court of Justice (ICJ) explicitly recognized corporate personhood—meaning, among other things, the ability to sue and be sued—as a general principle of law, based on the "wealth of practice already accumulated on the subject in municipal law."[45] The ICJ reaffirmed the connection between international law and domestic law, especially with respect to corporate personality, in the case of *Ahmadou Sadio Diallo (Guinea v. Dem. Rep. Congo)*:

---

and that they "belong to no particular system of law but are common to them all"). *Jus gentium* was the precursor to what the eighteenth century Anglo-American lawyers called "the law of nations," and it consisted essentially of general principles among civilized nations that the Roman praetors would consider in resolving *transnational* cases. It was by no means limited to state responsibility norms, because it would apply whenever the case involved two aliens (*i.e.*, non-Roman citizens) in what we would today characterize as a transitory torts or contracts case.

44. This is true in both international and domestic tribunals. *See, e.g.*, Barcelona Traction, Light & Power Co., 1970 I.C.J. 3, 38–39 (Feb. 20); Factory at Chorzow (Ger. v. Pol.), 1928 P.C.I.J. (ser. A) No. 17, at 29 (Sept. 13) ("[I]t is a general conception of law that every violation of an engagement involves an obligation to make reparation."); Prosecutor v. Kunarac, et al., Case No. IT-96-23-T & IT-96-23/1-T, Trial Judgment, ¶¶ 439–460 (Int'l Crim. Trib. for the Former Yugoslavia Feb. 22, 2001) (relying on general principles of law in the definition of rape as reflected in the basic principles contained in and common to most legal systems). In the United States, the Supreme Court has repeatedly used general principles to determine the content of international law. *See, e.g.*, United States v. Smith, 18 U.S. 153, 163–80 (1820); Factor v. Laubenheimer, 290 U.S. 276, 287–88 (1933); First Nat'l City Bank v. Banco Para el Comercio Exterior de Cuba, 462 U.S. 611, 623, 633 (1983).

The Second Circuit's decision in Kiobel v. Royal Dutch Petroleum was especially misguided on the issue of general principles, categorically misunderstanding the proof, the status, and the use of general principles as a source of international legal principles. The existence of general principles does not depend on the proof of *opinio juris*, as the panel majority thought. 621 F.3d 111, 141 n.43 (2d Cir. 2010). *Opinio juris*—the conviction that a sovereign's conformity to some general practice of states is a matter of legal obligation—is a constituent element of customary international law, not general principles. *See* Statute of the International Court of Justice (ICJ), *supra* note 32, at art. 38(1)(b). Nor are general principles a *secondary* source of international law, as the majority of the panel believed. *Kiobel*, 621 F.3d at 141 n.43. Under Article 38(1)(c) of the ICJ Statute, treaties in subparagraph (a), custom in subparagraph (b), and general principles in subparagraph (c) are equally valid *primary* sources of international law. Only the sources outlined in subparagraph (d)—including "judicial decisions and the writings of the most highly qualified publicists of the various nations"—are designated "secondary." Most important, indeed fatal to the *Kiobel* majority's approach to general principles is the fact that the majority inexplicably limited its consideration to principles of criminal liability when the pertinent inquiry in the case is civil liability. The civil liability of corporations for their torts (and, in civil law jurisdictions, their delicts) plainly qualifies as a general principle of law recognized by civilized nations.

In affirming the Second Circuit's disposition of *Kiobel*, the Supreme Court relied exclusively on the presumption against extraterritoriality and said nothing in support of the lower court's analysis of international law or its zone of immunity for coprorations.

45. Barcelona Traction, Light & Power Co., *supra* note 44, at 38–39; *cf.* First Nat'l City Bank (FNCB) v. Banco Para el Comercio Exterior de Cuba, 462 U.S. 611, 628–29 & n.20 (holding that under international law "the legal status of private corporations . . . is not to be regarded as legally separate from its owners in all circumstances") (emphasis removed).

In determining whether a company possesses independent and distinct legal person-ality, *international law looks to the rules of the relevant domestic law.*[46]

The laws of the various nations do not necessarily use the terminology of international human rights law in detailing the scope of liability that attaches to corporate personal-ity, but it is the substance and not the label that counts in the discernment of general principles. Every national jurisdiction protects interests such as life, liberty, dignity, and physical and mental integrity when these are threatened by corporate action. Each includes remedial mechanisms that mirror the reparations required by international law for the suffering inflicted by abuse. Certainly no legal system exempts corporations alto-gether from the obligation to compensate those it injures. "Legal systems throughout the world recognize that corporate legal responsibility is part and parcel of the privilege of corporate personhood."[47]

It is readily demonstrated that corporate liability for serious harms is a universal feature of the world's legal systems and therefore qualifies as a general principle of law. Articulated as a rule of positive liability, virtually every legal system around the world encompasses some form of tort law (or delicts) that applies to corporations. In some legal systems, this can take the form of actual criminal or quasi-criminal liability in addition to civil liability or administrative sanction.[48] Articulated instead as a general principle of nonimmunity, there is no domestic jurisdiction that completely exempts corporations from all liability for their civil wrongs, although there is variation in the principles of attribution and remedy.

Over the last decade, every comprehensive survey of domestic law on corporate liability has confirmed that corporate liability is the rule, with only isolated and peculiar exceptions. In 2008, for example, the International Commission of Jurists Panel of Legal Experts[49] undertook a global inventory of domestic law addressing corporate criminality—a more contested issue than corporate civil liability or administrative sanctions against compa-nies—and determined that general principles of accountability exist, even if the precise details of liability vary from jurisdiction to jurisdiction.[50] The International Federation for

---

46. Ahmadou Sadio Diallo (Guinea v. Dem. Rep. Congo), Preliminary Objections, 2007 I.C.J. 190, 194 (May 24) (emphasis added).

47. Doe v. Exxon Mobil Corp., 654 F.3d 11, 53–54 (D.C. Cir. 2011) (emphasis supplied).

48. *See* Robert C. Thompson, Anita Ramasastry & Mark B. Taylor, *Translating* Unocal: *The Expand-ing Web of Liability for Business Entities Implicated in International Crimes*, 40 GEO. WASH. INT'L L. REV. 841, 886 (2009) (discussing the *action civile* in Argentina, Belgium, France, Japan, the Netherlands, and Spain, under which a victim of a crime may seek civil damages against a criminal defendant). *See also* ALLENS ARTHUR ROBINSON, "CORPORATE CULTURE" AS A BASIS FOR THE CRIMINAL LIABILITY OF CORPORATIONS (Feb. 2008), http://www.reports-and-materials.org/Allens-Arthur-Robinson-Corporate-Culture-paper-for-Ruggie-Feb-2008.pdf.

49. The author of this chapter served as a member of the ICJ's Expert Legal Panel.

50. *See* INT'L COMM'N OF JURISTS, BUSINESS AND HUMAN RIGHTS—ACCESS TO JUSTICE: COUN-TRY REPORTS (20102013), http://www.icj.org/category/publications/access-to-justice-human-rights-ab uses-involving-corporations/ (discussing corporate accountability in representative jurisdictions). *See*

Human Rights has also published a guidebook on corporate accountability for human rights abuses, which demonstrates that domestic legal principles, especially in Europe and the United States, allow for the imposition of civil liability on corporations for their participation in human rights abuses.[51] The Fafo Institute for Applied International Studies undertook a small but representative sampling of jurisdictions, limited to grave breaches of international law, and found overwhelming consistency in the principle that corporations could be liable for such violations, though the form of liability varied:

> The survey illustrates a potential web of liability created by the integration of [international criminal law/international humanitarian law] provisions to a wide range of domestic legal systems containing provisions for the prosecution of legal persons, including business entities, as well as extraterritoriality and universality provisions which extend jurisdiction abroad.[52]

The burden shifts to those arguing for corporate immunity from international law that the common denominator of accountability either does not exist in fact or does not qualify as a general principle recognized by civilized nations.

Customary International Law. Customary international law has long recognized the authority of domestic courts to enforce claims against nonhuman and nonstate entities for violations of the law of nations. Under the maritime law (an ancient and specialized subspecies of customary international law), ships, like modern corporations, were the entities through which business owners and managers engaged in commercial transactions across borders. The exposure of these nonhuman entities to liability under international standards was routinely recognized through the instrument of civil *in rem* jurisdiction or its equivalent. For example, in the United States, as in other jurisdictions around the world, the international violation of piracy was enforced against not only the individual pirate but also the vessel he used. In other words, legal responsibility for this archetypal violation of customary international law was not limited to natural persons. "The vessel

---

generally Int'l Comm'n of Jurists, Report of the Expert Legal Panel on Corporate Complicity in International Crimes (2008), http://www.icj.org/report-of-the-international-commission-of-jurists-expert-legal-panel-on-corporate-complicity-in-international-crimes/ (last visited Nov. 24, 2013).

51. Int'l Fed'n for Human Rights, Corporate Accountability for Human Rights Abuses: A Guide for Victims and NGOs on Recourse Mechanisms (2010), http://www.fidh.org/Corporate-Accountability-for-Human-Rights-Abuses. *See also Business and Human Rights: European Cases Database*, European Ctr. for Constitutional and Human Rights (ECCHR), http://www.ecchr.de/index.php/business_and_human_rights.html (last visited Nov. 24, 2013).

52. Anita Ramasastry & Robert C. Thompson, Commerce, Crime and Conflict: Legal Remedies for Private Sector Liability for Grave Breaches of International Law: A Survey of Sixteen Countries (2006), http://www.fafo.no/pub/rapp/536/536.pdf (examining corporate liability in Argentina, Australia, Belgium, Canada, France, Germany, India, Indonesia, Japan, Norway, the Netherlands, Spain, South Africa, Ukraine, the United Kingdom, and the United States).

which commit[ted] the aggression [wa]s treated as the offender" and was subject to for-feiture.[53] In *The Marianna Flora*, the Supreme Court, per Justice Story, concluded on the basis of international law that "piratical aggression by an armed vessel . . . may be justly subjected to the penalty of confiscation for such a gross breach of the law of nations."[54] Similarly, in *The Palmyra*, the Court clarified that "[t]he thing is here primarily considered the offender, or rather *the offence is attached primarily to the thing*."[55]

Pirates were not the only ones whose *entities* faced sanction under international legal standards: one routine way to enforce the international prohibition on the slave trade was to condemn the vessel involved.[56] In addition to whatever sanctions may have been imposed on the people involved, international law was enforced against the entities involved in the violation. Crucially, no treaty established the right or the obligation of U.S. courts to enforce international law in this way. It was instead a right and obligation of the state under the law of nations.

Over time, the applicable international law broadened from the prohibition of piracy and slave trading to include international humanitarian law. After World War II, the human beings who managed the world's largest chemical company, IG Farben, were placed on trial at Nuremberg, but the corporations through which they committed their crimes were at no point immunized from responsibility. To the contrary, the corporations were sanctioned out of existence before the trials even began, as effectively *seized* as ships engaged in piracy or the slave trade. The legal basis for this administrative action lay initially in Article 9 of the London Charter, which provided the following:

> At the trial of any individual member of any group or organization the Tribunal may declare (in connection with any act of which the individual may be convicted) that the group or organization of which the individual was a member was a criminal organization.[57]

---

53. Harmony v. United States (the Malek Adhel), 43 U.S. (2 How.) 210, 233 (1844).
54. 24 U.S. (11 Wheat.) 1, 40–41 (1825).
55. 25 U.S. (12 Wheat.) 1, 14 (1827) (emphasis supplied). In *The Little Charles*, 26 F. Cas. 979, 982 (No. 15,612) (C.C. Va. 1818), Chief Justice Marshall, sitting on circuit, explained that "it is a proceeding against the vessel, for an offence committed by the vessel."
56. Jenny S. Martinez, *Antislavery Courts and the Dawn of International Human Rights Law*, 117 YALE L.J. 550, 590–91 (2008).
57. There was no doubt that the term *person* covered both human beings and juridical entities. Under Control Council Law No. 5, Vesting and Marshalling of German External Assets (Oct. 30, 1945), *reprinted in* 1 Enactments and Approved Papers of the Control Council and Coordinating Committee 176, http://www.loc.gov/rr/frd/Military_Law/Enactments/Volume-I.pdf, "the term 'person' shall include any natural person or collective person or any juridical person or entity under public or private law having legal capacity to acquire, use, control or dispose of property or interests therein."

In Control Council Law No. 9, adopted even before the tribunal was established, the occupation authority explicitly dissolved Farben and seized its assets:

> All plants, properties and assets of any nature situated in Germany which were, on or after 8 May, 1945, owned or controlled by I.G. Farbenindustrie A.G., are hereby seized and the legal title thereto is vested in the Control Council.[58]

Nor was Farben the only corporation held accountable for Nazi crimes. Insurance companies were directly dissolved and their assets liquidated.[59] Alfried Krupp was sentenced to twelve years imprisonment and ordered to forfeit all his property,[60] but the Krupp business, central to many of the Nazi regime's crimes, was confiscated.[61] In other words, the failure to prosecute corporations criminally creates no immunity from civil or administrative liability for international wrongs. Responsibility under international law can be established in ways having nothing to do with criminal prosecution.

Even in the course of finding individual human beings guilty of international crimes, the Nuremberg tribunals established that juridical entities were bound by customary international standards, including those codified in the Hague Regulations on the Laws and Customs of War of 1907:

> Where a private individual *or a juristic person* becomes a party to unlawful confiscation of public or private property by planning and executing a well-defined design to acquire such property permanently, acquisition under such circumstances subsequent to the confiscation constitutes conduct in violation of [Article 47 of] the Hague Regulations. . . . The result was the enrichment of Farben and the building of its greater chemical empire through the medium of occupancy at the expense of the

---

58. Control Council Law No. 9, Seizure of Property Owned by I. G. Farbenindustrie and the Control Thereof (Nov. 30, 1945), *reprinted in* 1 ENACTMENTS AND APPROVED PAPERS OF THE CONTROL COUNCIL AND COORDINATING COMMITTEE 225, http://www.loc.gov/rr/frd/Military_Law/Enactments/Volume-I.pdf.

59. *See generally* GERALD D. FELDMAN, ALLIANZ AND THE GERMAN INSURANCE BUSINESS 1933–1945, at 497 (2001); Control Council Law No. 57, Dissolution and Liquidation of Insurance Companies Connected with the German Labor Front (Aug. 30, 1947), *reprinted in* 8 ENACTMENTS AND APPROVED PAPER OF THE CONTROL COUNCIL AND COORDINATING COMMITTEE 1, http://www.loc.gov/rr/frd/Military_Law /Enactments/Volume-VIII.pdf. *See also* Military Government Law No. 52, Military Government—Germany, United States Zone, Blocking and Control of Property (May 8, 1945), amended version *reprinted in* U.S. Military Government Gazette, Germany, Issue A, at 24 (June 1, 1946).

60. United States v. Krupp (the Krupp Case), 9 Trials of War Criminals Before the Nuremberg Military Tribunals Under Control Council Law No. 10 1449, 1449—50 (1950).

61. Military Government Law No. 52, and General Order No. 3. Allied Military Government, U.S. Zone, General Order No. 3 (Pursuant to Military Government Law No. 52): Firma Friedrich Krupp [General Order No. 3], Military Government Gazette (June 6, 1946). As noted correctly by Judge Richard Posner, "[a]t the end of the Second World War the allied powers dissolved German corporations that had assisted the Nazi war effort . . . and *did so on the authority of customary international law.*" Flomo v. Firestone Natural Rubber Co., 643 F.3d 1013, 1017 (7th Cir. 2011) (emphasis supplied).

former owners. Such action on the part of Farben constituted a violation of rights of private property, protected by the Laws and Customs of War. . . . [T]he objective of pillage, plunder and spoliation stands out, and there can be no uncertainty as to the actual result. . . . With reference to the charges in the present indictment concerning Farben's activities in Poland, Norway, Alsace Lorraine and France, we find that the proof established beyond a reasonable doubt that offences against property as defined in Control Council Law No. 10 were committed by Farben, and that these offences were connected with, and an inextricable part of the German policy for occupied countries.[62]

Although the tribunal may have lacked the jurisdiction to impose criminal sanctions on corporations, it could not have been clearer that customary international law applied to corporations engaged in egregious violations of humanitarian norms, and that they could be held accountable for it. In our own time, an even broader range of customary international humanitarian law (IHL) has been extended to business enterprises.[63] The International Committee of the Red Cross—by consensus the authoritative interpreter of IHL obligations—has increasingly addressed the complex relationships between state and nonstate actors in times of armed conflict and developed principles that do not recognize some broad-gauged exemption for companies.[64]

It is now common for intergovernmental organizations to address the human rights responsibilities of multinational corporations, even if they have historically failed to adopt a comprehensive code of conduct for companies.[65] For example, in June 2011 the Human Rights Council of the United Nations approved three Guiding Principles proposed by the Special Representative of the Secretary-General on the Issue of Human Rights and Transnational Corporations and Other Business Enterprises. These principles include (a) the duty of the state to protect against human rights abuses by, or involving, transnational corporations and other business enterprises; (b) the corporate responsibility to respect all human rights; and (c) the need for access to effective remedies, including through appropriate judicial or nonjudicial mechanisms.[66] Then in November 2011 the

---

62. United States v. Krauch (the IG Farben Case), VIII Trials of War Criminals Before the Nuremberg Military Tribunals Under Control Council Law No. 10 1131–32, 1140–41 (1952) (emphasis supplied).

63. *See* JEAN-MARIE HENCKAERTS & LOUISE DOSWALD-BECK, CUSTOMARY INTERNATIONAL HUMANITARIAN LAW, VOL. I: RULES 495–98 (2005).

64. *See* INT'L COMM. OF THE RED CROSS, BUSINESS AND INTERNATIONAL HUMANITARIAN LAW: AN INTRODUCTION TO THE RIGHTS AND OBLIGATIONS OF BUSINESS ENTERPRISES UNDER INTERNATIONAL HUMANITARIAN LAW (2006).

65. *See, e.g.*, the abortive UN Draft International Code of Conduct for Transnational Corporations, 23 I.L.M. 626 (1984), which was never adopted despite years of drafting and negotiation within the UN Commission on Transnational Corporations.

66. UN Human Rights Council, *Human Rights and Transnational Corporations and Other Business Enterprises*, UN Doc. A/HRC/RES/17/4 (July 6, 2011).

United Nations described the Guiding Principles as "the global standard of practice that is now expected of all governments *and businesses* with regard to business and human rights."[67] The Interpretive Guide makes it clear that the Guiding Principles, though not legally obligatory themselves, offer an authoritative elaboration on "*existing* standards and practices for States *and businesses*."[68]

The United Nations is not the only intergovernmental organization to articulate and implement the human rights responsibilities of corporations.[69] The Organization for Economic Cooperation and Development (OECD), through its National Contact Points process, now routinely receives and processes complaints that specific corporations have acted inconsistently with the OECD's Guidelines for Multinational Enterprises.[70] In Paragraph 1, those guidelines specifically emphasize the duty of business enterprises to respect the human rights of those affected by their activities. With respect to the human rights of workers, the Declaration on Fundamental Principles and Rights at Work, adopted in 1998 by the International Labour Organization (ILO), requires all ILO member states to implement and enforce the principles contained in the eight so-called "core conventions," each of which governs employment relationships in the private sphere.[71] The ILO instrument is especially significant given the inclusion of corporate representatives in the organization's tripartite governing structure. The law of the European Union can also create obligations for business entities, as established repeatedly by the European Court of Justice.[72]

Taken together, these authorities establish at a minimum that customary international law does not recognize, preserve, or allow an international-law–free zone for corporations. To the contrary, the orthodox separation between states and businesses has been breached, even if it has not been (and could not be) dismantled altogether.

---

67. THE CORPORATE RESPONSIBILITY TO PROTECT HUMAN RIGHTS: AN INTERPRETIVE GUIDE 3 (Nov. 2011) (emphasis supplied).

68. *Id.* (emphasis supplied). Nonbinding interpretations of existing international law by the UN or its agencies can qualify as evidence of custom. *Cf.* I.N.S. v. Cardoza-Fonseca, 480 U.S. 421, 439 (1987) ("In interpreting the Protocol's definition of 'refugee' we are further guided by the analysis set forth in the Office of the United Nations High Commissioner for Refugees, Handbook on Procedures and Criteria for Determining Refugee Status (Geneva, 1979)").

69. *See generally* Ralph Steinhardt, *Corporate Responsibility and the International Law of Human Rights: The New Lex Mercatoria, in* NONSTATE ACTORS AND HUMAN RIGHTS, 205–214 (Philip Alston ed., 2005) (outlining the work of various intergovernmental organizations in the articulation or enforcement of human rights norms for businesses, including the United Nations, the World Bank and International Monetary Fund, the OECD, the ILO, the World Trade Organization, among others).

70. OECD, SPECIFIC INSTANCES CONSIDERED BY NATIONAL CONTACT POINTS (Nov. 22, 2011). *See also* OECD, POLICY BRIEF: THE OECD GUIDELINES FOR MULTINATIONAL ENTERPRISES: A KEY CORPORATE RESPONSIBILITY INSTRUMENT (2003), http://www.oecd.org/dataoecd/52/38/2958609.pdf.

71. Tripartite Declaration of Principles Concerning Multinational Enterprises and Social Policy, adopted by the Governing Board of the International Labour Organization (1977), *reprinted in* 37 I.L.M. 1233 (1998).

72. *See, e.g.,* Case 36/74, Walrave v. Ass'n Union Cycliste Internationale, 1974 E.C.R. 1405; Case 43/75, Defrenne v. Société Anonyme Belge de Navigation Aérienne Sabena, 1976 E.C.R. 455.

Conclusion

The tragedy in 1984 at the Union Carbide chemical plant in Bhopal, India—the worst industrial accident in history—is a potent symbol of the traditional system of international law. The decentralization of international law meant that India, like every other sovereign state, could freely choose what it viewed as the best approaches to economic development, environmental protection, and corporate responsibility. Union Carbide, like every other multinational corporation, could structure its international business (including its foreign subsidiaries) to minimize its exposure to civil and criminal liability, regulation, and taxes; indeed, its legally enforceable obligation to maximize the return on its shareholders' investment required it to do so. And without an international court for the resolution of environmental disputes with transnational elements, it fell to the domestic courts of each state to address whatever corner of the problem fell within its jurisdiction as defined by international law. On the other hand, as shown above, contemporary developments in international law—the emergence of an international economic law, international standards for the protection of the environment, transnational norms of corporate responsibility, the rise of civil society activism, and the use of domestic courts to enforce international standards—suggests that Bhopal is actually a physical representation of the old legal regime in its final days. The multinational corporation is subject to a limited but potent and expanding body of international law.

Chapter 3

International Human Rights Law Perspectives on the UN Framework and Guiding Principles on Business and Human Rights

Robert McCorquodale

Introduction

Human rights are at stake—and so, too, is the social sustainability of enterprises and markets as we know them.[1]

With these words, Professor John Ruggie completed his term as Special Representative of the Secretary-General (SRSG) of the United Nations on the Issue of Human Rights and Transnational Corporations and Other Business Enterprises.[2] Over the six years of his term he had changed the debate about corporations' responsibilities for human rights abuses and provided a framework for analysis (Framework) and guiding principles (Guiding Principles) to put this framework into operation.[3] The main purpose of this chapter is

---

1.   John Ruggie, Special Representative of the Secretary-General on the issue of human rights and transnational corporations and other business enterprises, Statement to the UN Human Rights Council (May 31, 2011).

2.   *See* Commission on Human Rights Res. 2005/69 of 20 April 2005, UN Doc. E/CN.4/2005/L.10/Add.17.

3.   There have been a number of attempts at the national, regional, and international levels to deal with the impacts on human rights of corporate activity through legal regulation. *See, e.g.,* Norms on the Responsibilities of Transnational Corporations and Other Business Enterprises with Regard to Human Rights, UN Doc. E/CN.4/Sub.2/2003/12/Rev.2 (2003); OECD, GUIDELINES FOR MULTINATIONAL ENTERPRISES (2011), http://www.oecd.org/daf/inv/mne/48004323.pdf; Most attempts have not succeeded, largely through lack of political will by states or through strong resistance by business enterprises.

to clarify the Framework and Guiding Principles developed by the SRSG to provide the background to many of the other chapters in this book.

This Framework has three elements (or "pillars"): the state's duty to protect against human rights abuses by corporations; the corporate responsibility to respect human rights; and the need for effective access to remedies. The following is the stated justification for this Framework:

> [There is] the State duty to protect because it lies at the very core of the international human rights regime; the corporate responsibility to respect because it is the basic expectation society has of business; and access to remedy, because even the most concerted efforts cannot prevent all abuse. . . . The three principles form a complementary whole in that each supports the others in achieving sustainable progress.[4]

The SRSG produced other reports that sought to *operationalize*[5] this Framework.[6] Then in 2011 he provided the Guiding Principles,[7] which were adopted by the United Nations Human Rights Council on June 16, 2011.[8] Importantly, the SRSG clarified that corporations (called "business enterprises," the term also used in this chapter to cover a broad range of corporations) can abuse all types of human rights—economic, social, cultural, civil, political, and collective—and that all business enterprises, no matter their size, nature, or location, should be subject to the Framework and Guiding Principles.[9]

Though there are some well-made criticisms of these developments (both conceptually and practically),[10] the Framework and Guiding Principles are generally seen as the cur-

---

4.   Special Representative of the Secretary-General, *Report of the Special Representative of the Secretary-General on the Issue of Human Rights and Transnational Corporations and Other Business Enterprises*, ¶ 9, UN Doc A/HRC/8/5 (Apr. 7, 2008) [hereinafter SRSG Report 2008] 9.

5.   The United Nations Human Rights Council (UNHRC), in extending the mandate of the Special Representative, stated that it "recognizes the need to operationalize this framework." *See* Human Rights Council Res. HRC Resolution, 8th Sess., A/HRC/RES/8/7, Preamble (June 18, 2008).

6.   *See* Special Representative of the Secretary-General, *Business and Human Rights: Towards Operationalizing the "Protect, Respect and Remedy" Framework*, Hum. Rts. Council, UN Doc. A/HRC/11/13 (Apr. 22, 2009), http://www2.ohchr.org/english/bodies/hrcouncil/docs/11session/A.HRC.11.13.pdf [hereinafter SRSG Report 2009]; Special Representative of the Secretary-General on the Issue of Hum. Rts. and Transnat'l Corp. and Other Bus. Enter., *Business and Human Rights: Further Steps Toward the Operationalization of the "Protect, Respect and Remedy" Framework*, Hum. Rts. Council, UN Doc. A/HRC/14/27 (Apr. 9, 2010), http://198.170.85.29/Ruggie-report-2010.pdf [hereinafter SRSG Report 2010].

7.   Special Representative of the Secretary-General on the Issue of Hum. Rts. and Transnat'l Corp. and Other Bus. Enter., *Guiding Principles on Business and Human Rights: Implementing the United Nations "Protect, Respect and Remedy" Framework*, Hum. Rts. Council, UN Doc. A/HRC/17/31 (Mar. 21, 2011) [hereinafter Guiding Principles], http:// www.ohchr.org/Documents/Issues/Business/A-HRC-17-31_AEV .pdf.

8.   Human Rights Council Res., *Human Rights and Transnational Corporations and Other Business Enterprises*, A/HRC/RES/17/4 (Jul. 6, 2011), http://www.unglobalcompact.org/docs/issues_doc/human _rights/A.HRC.17.RES.17.4.pdf.

9.   SRSG Report 2008, *supra* note 4, ¶ 6.

10.   *See, e.g.*, SIEGE OR CAVALRY CHARGE? THE UN MANDATE ON BUSINESS AND HUMAN RIGHTS (Radu Mares ed., 2012).

rent primary way forward.[11] However, as the SRSG has noted, "The Guiding Principles are not intended as a tool kit, simply to be taken off the shelf and plugged in. . . . When it comes to means for implementation, therefore, one size does not fit all."[12] In addition, he has stated that

> "The Guiding Principles" normative contribution lies not in the creation of new international law obligations but in elaborating the implications of existing standards and practices for States and businesses; integrating them within a single, logically coherent and comprehensive template; and identifying where the current regime falls short and how it should be improved.[13]

Therefore, in this chapter I will examine each of the pillars of the Framework and consider the Guiding Principles primarily by reference to their relationship with international human rights law. The pillars are: (1) the state's duty to protect human rights, (2) corporate responsibility to respect, and (3) access to remedy.

The State's Duty to Protect Human Rights

Under international human rights law, each state has a duty or legal obligation to protect against human rights violations. The obligation of a state to protect human rights includes an obligation to protect against violations by state officials. This also includes an obligation to protect against actions by nonstate actors (such as business enterprises) within its territory that violate human rights. These customary international law obligations (being obligations of all states) are essentially restated in the first Guiding Principle:

> States must protect against human rights abuse within their territory and/or jurisdiction by third parties, including business enterprises. This requires taking appropriate steps to prevent, investigate, punish and redress such abuse through effective policies, legislation, regulations and adjudication.[14]

In the applications of these international legal obligations in relation to the activities of business enterprises, states have been found by the human rights treaty bodies to be in

---

11.   *See* Human Rights Council Res. HRC Resolution, *supra* note 5, ¶ 1; *see also* UN HUMAN RIGHTS OFFICE OF THE HIGH COMMISSIONER, THE CORPORATE RESPONSIBILITY TO RESPECT HUMAN RIGHTS, AN INTERPRETIVE GUIDE (2012), http://www.ohchr.org/DocumentsPublications/HR.PUB.12.2_En.pdf [hereinafter Interpretive Guide].
12.   *See* Guiding Principles, *supra* note 7, Principle 15, commentary.
13.   *See* Guiding Principles, *supra* note 7, Principle 14, commentary.
14.   *See* Guiding Principles, *supra* note 7, Principle 1.

breach of their obligations when, for example, employees of business enterprises have been dismissed or victimized for joining a trade union,[15] the activities of business enterprises have polluted air and land,[16] and the state has failed to protect indigenous peoples' land from harm caused by corporate activities or from corporate development.[17] In each of these cases, the state was in breach of its obligations under the relevant human rights treaty because its acts or omissions (including its acquiescence) enabled the business enterprise to act as it did. Therefore, even when a state (or a state official) is not directly responsible for the actual violation of international human rights law, the state can still be held responsible for a lack of positive action in responding to or preventing the violation of human rights by the business enterprise.

In many situations, the government of a state is less economically powerful than the business enterprise.[18] However, even when there is such economic inequality, a state is still responsible for the violations of human rights that occur in its jurisdiction because of the business enterprise. Indeed, a state's obligation to protect human rights extends to situations where there is internal armed conflict and where the actions that violate human rights are committed by paramilitary or armed opposition groups,[19] and even to parts of a state's territory where it is not currently exercising effective control.[20]

Indeed, the abiding message of the SRSG's approach in relation to the state's duty to respect human rights is that inaction by a state in this area is in breach of its international

---

15. *See* Young, James and Webster v. United Kingdom, App. 7601/76, 4 Eur. H.R. Rep. 38; Laval un Partneri Ltd v. Svenska Byggnadsarbetareforbundet and others [2008] IRLR 160 (C-319/05), http://eur-lex .europa.eu/LexUriServ/LexUriServ.do?uri=CELEX:62005J0341:EN:HTML; International Transport Workers' Federation and Finnish Seamen's Union v. Viking Line [2008] IRLR 143 (C-438/05), http://eur-lex .europa.eu/LexUriServ/LexUriServ.do?uri=CELEX:62005J0438:EN:HTML.

16. *See, e.g.*, Soc. and Econ. Rights Action Ctr. for Econ. and Soc. Rights v. Nigeria, Communication No. 155/96, ¶ 59, African Commission on Human and Peoples' Rights (2001) ("[Nigeria is in violation] of local people's rights to . . . health . . . and life [by] breaching its duty to protect the Ogoni people from damaging acts of oil companies"). *See also* Lopez Ostra v. Spain, App. No. 16798/90, 20 Eur. H.R. Rep. 277 (1995); Guerra v. Italy, App. No. 00014967/89, 26 Eur. H.R. Rep. 357 (1998).

17. *See* Yanomami Indians v. Brazil, Inter-Am. C.H.R. 7615, OEA/Ser.L.V/II/66 doc. 10 rev. 1 (1985); Case of the Mayagna (Sumo) Awas Tingni Community v. Nicaragua, Merits, Reparations, and Costs, Judgment, Inter-Am. Ct. H.R. (ser. C) No. 79, ¶ 149 (Jan. 31, 2001); Pueblo Indígena Kichwa De Sarayaku y Sus Miembros v. Ecuador, Request 167/03, Report No. 62/04, Inter-Am. C.H.R., OEA/Ser.L/V/II.122, doc. 5 rev. 1 (2005).

18. For example, BHP, an Australia-based business enterprise, had such a strong influence over the government of Papua New Guinea and its income that the government passed laws to protect BHP from legal challenge over its activities there, even though those activities had a profound negative impact on its own citizens. *See* BHP v. Dagi [1996], 2 VR 117 (Victorian Court of Appeal). This situation is not necessarily limited to economically weaker states. *See, e.g.*, Michael Lewis, Liar's Poker (1990) (describing how traders at the merchant bank, Salomon Brothers, repeatedly succeeded in lobbying the U.S. Congress to relax laws regarding mortgage transactions, which he argues led to windfalls for Salomon Brothers and the financial industry and a dramatic increase in home foreclosures).

19. *See, e.g.*, Ergi v. Turkey, App. No. 23818/94, 32 Eur. H.R. Rep. 388 (1998); Timurtas v. Turkey, App. No. 23531/94 (2003). *See also* Guiding Principles, *supra* note 7, at §I.B ¶ 7.

20. *See* Ilascu v. Moldova and Russia, App. No. 48787/99, 40 Eur. H.R. Rep. 46 (2004).

human rights legal obligations. He goes further, warning that "States should not assume that businesses invariably prefer, or benefit from, State inaction, and they should consider a smart mix of measures—national and international, mandatory and voluntary—to foster business respect for human rights."[21] However, there are two issues of international law that require some clarification in relation to the Framework and Guiding Principles: *extraterritorial jurisdiction* and the *attribution of states* for the actions of business enterprises. These will be discussed in turn.

Extraterritoriality

The SRSG did not firmly conclude that a state's obligation to protect human rights extends to the regulation of the activities of their corporate nationals (that is, those business enterprises incorporated or domiciled in that state) outside the territory of that state.[22] This hesitancy is disappointing because in international human rights law a state's obligation to protect human rights is not normally limited to its territory but does extend to all those within its *jurisdiction*.[23] The difference between *territory* and *jurisdiction* was clarified by the Inter-American Commission on Human Rights, which stated that

> [the Commission] does not believe . . . that the term "jurisdiction" . . . is limited to or merely coextensive with national territory. Rather, the Commission is of the view that a state . . . may be responsible under certain circumstances for the acts and omissions of its agents which produce effects or are undertaken outside that state's territory.[24]

In general, all persons are *within the jurisdiction* of a state acting extraterritorially, whether that (home) state is acting with the consent or acquiescence of the government of the host state (that is, the state on whose territory the activity contrary to human rights is occurring),

---

21. *See* Guiding Principles, *supra* note 7, Principle 3, commentary.

22. *See* Guiding Principles, *supra* note 7, at §I.A ¶ 2, commentary ("At present States are not generally required under international human rights law to regulate the extraterritorial activities of businesses domiciled within their territory and/or jurisdiction. Nor are they generally prohibited from doing so, provided there is a recognized jurisdictional basis.").

23. *See, e.g.*, American Convention on Human Rights, Nov. 22, 1969, 1144 UNT.S. 123, 9 I.L.M. 673 (entered into force July 18, 1978), art. 1; European Convention on Human Rights, Nov. 4, 1950, art. 1.

24. IACommHR, Saldaño v. Argentina, Judgment on Inadmissability, Report No. 38/99, ¶ 17 (Mar. 11, 1999). The same approach has been taken by the European Court of Human Rights, *see* Drozd and Janousek v. France and Spain, Appl. No. 12747/8, 14 EHRR 745, ¶ 91 (2001), and the UN Human Rights Committee; *see* UN OHCHR, Human Rights Comm., General Comment No. 31; The Nature of the General Legal Obligation Imposed on States Parties to the Covenant, ¶ 3, UN Doc. CCPR/C/21/Rev.1/Add.13 (2004).

whether the home state is in effective overall control of a part of the host state's territory, and whether the host state is a party to the relevant human rights treaty.[25]

For example, the Inter-American Commission on Human Rights had to consider this issue in relation to the legal status of the persons detained by the United States at Guantanamo Bay, Cuba.[26] The Commission considered that, although the detainees were outside the territory of the United States, they were subject to its jurisdiction because they were "wholly within the authority and control of the United States government."[27] Though there are limits to the extent to which a state can be held to have jurisdiction and control, including over its own nationals, a state can be found to be in violation of its obligations under international human rights treaties for actions taken by it extraterritorially, in relation to anyone within the power, control, or authority of that state, as well as within an area over which that state exercises effective overall control.[28] In fact, an extensive research project has shown that there is substantial state practice in which national laws have been extended extraterritorially.[29] This includes regulation of the conduct of corporate nationals operating extraterritorially through foreign subsidiaries, in areas such as competition law, shareholder and consumer protection, antibribery and corruption, and tax law. In relation to bribery and corruption, states have concluded treaties imposing obligations on them to regulate extraterritorial conduct of corporate nationals and their subsidiaries.[30]

Because each state has a general duty not to cause harm, such as environmental pollution, outside its territory,[31] there is growing support for the view that "where a state knows that its national's activities will cause, or are causing, harm to other states or peoples, it is

---

25.   Note that the commentary to Guiding Principle 2 could be seen as accepting this type of extraterritoriality as being where there is *a recognized jurisdictional basis. See* Guiding Principles, *supra* note 7, at §I.A ¶ 2.

26.   Inter-American Commission on Human Rights, *Detainees at Guantanamo Bay, Cuba (Precautionary Measures)*, 41 I.L.M. 532 (2002).

27.   *Id.* at 533.

28.   *See* Armed Activities on the Territory of the Congo (Dem. Rep. Congo v. Uganda) 45 I.L.M. 271, ¶ 217 (Int'l Ct. Justice, Dec. 19, 2005) (holding that the African Charter of Human and Peoples' Rights and the Convention on the Rights of the Child applied extraterritorially).

29.   *See* Jennifer A. Zerk, *Extraterritorial Jurisdiction: Lessons for the Business and Human Rights Sphere from Six Regulatory Areas* (Harvard Corporate Social Responsibility Initiative, Working Paper No. 59, 2010), http://www.hks.harvard.edu/m-rcbg/CSRI/publications/workingpaper_ 59_zerk.pdf.

30.   For example, the UN Convention Combating Bribery of Foreign Public Officials in International Business Transactions imposes obligations on states parties to establish laws and criminal sanctions with respect to the bribery of foreign public officials and officials of public international organisations and to extend liability (whether criminal, civil, or administrative) and sanctions to legal persons. UN Convention Combating Bribery of Foreign Public Officials in International Business Transactions 2003, adopted Oct. 31, 2003, 43 I.L.M. 37 (2004) (entered into force Dec. 14, 2005).

31.   *See, e.g.,* Trail Smelter Arbitration (U.S. v. Can.), 3 R.I.A.A. 1905 (1938) (enjoining the Canadian company operating the Trail Smelter from causing further pollution in the State of Washington), *further proceedings at* 3 R.I.A.A. 1938 (1941); The Rainbow Warrior (New Zealand v. France), 82 I.L.R. 449 (1990).

consistent with this [general] duty that it should prevent such harm."[32] Both the European Court of Human Rights and the Human Rights Committee have considered that a state may be responsible "because of acts of their authorities, whether performed within or outside national boundaries, which produce effects outside their own territory,"[33] and for "the extraterritorial consequences of its intra-territorial decisions."[34] It has also been suggested that the obligation on a state to protect under the International Covenant on Economic, Social and Cultural Rights "includes an obligation for the state to ensure that all other bodies subject to its control (such as transnational business enterprises based in that state) respect the enjoyment of rights in other countries."[35]

However, the difficulty with this approach is, that in many instances, business enterprises operate with many subsidiaries and business associates, and those business enterprises are often not incorporated in the state of the parent corporation. As such, at least in international legal theory, they are not within the parent state's jurisdiction and so cannot be subject to that state's laws.[36] However, state practice reflects a variety of approaches for dealing with "the tendency of groups of companies to utilize their legal structure to avoid state regulation."[37] There is a long-standing practice of some national courts to look at the whole operation of a business enterprise, and not just its notionally separate parts, to bring a foreign parent corporation within the jurisdiction of a state.[38] Indeed, the European Union seems to be moving toward locating the *domicile* of the business

---

32.   Muthucumaraswamy Sornarajah, *Linking State Responsibility for Certain Harms Caused by Corporate Nationals Abroad to Civil Recourse in the Legal Systems of Home States, in* TORTURE AS TORT 507 (Craig Scott ed., 2001).

33.   ECHR, Loizidou v. Turkey, Judgment on Preliminary Objections of 23 March 1995, Appl. No. 15318/89, 20 EHRR 99, para. 62; *see also* Guiding Principles, *supra* note 7, at §I.A ¶ 2.

34.   Sarah Joseph, Jenny Schultz, & Melissa Castan, THE INTERNATIONAL COVENANT ON CIVIL AND POLITICAL RIGHTS: CASES, COMMENTARY AND MATERIALS, at 96 (2d ed. 2004).

35.   Fons Coomans, *Some Remarks on the Extraterritorial Application of the International Covenant on Economic, Social and Cultural Rights, in* EXTRATERRITORIAL APPLICATION OF HUMAN RIGHTS TREATIES 192 (Fons Coomans & Menno Kamminga eds., 2004). Note that Guiding Principle 5 appears to consider that if a state function is privatized, that state is ostensibly still responsible for the human rights outcome. *See* Guiding Principles, *supra* note 7, at § I.B ¶ 5.

36.   *See* Frederick A. Mann, *The Doctrine of International Jurisdiction Revisited after Twenty Years, in* COLLECTED COURSES OF THE HAGUE ACADEMY OF INTERNATIONAL LAW 56 (1985) ("[a] subsidiary is a separate legal entity and therefore necessarily distinct from its parent . . . as a matter of international law, parent and subsidiary are each subject to the exclusive jurisdiction of their respective [States]"). *See also* Case Concerning the Barcelona Traction, Light and Power Co Ltd (Second Phase) (Belgium v. Spain), 1970 I.C.J. Reports 3.

37.   *See* Janet Dine, THE GOVERNANCE OF CORPORATE GROUPS 65 (2000). *See generally* Janet Dine, COMPANIES, INTERNATIONAL TRADE AND HUMAN RIGHTS (2005).

38.   *See* Radu Mares, *Responsibility to Respect: Why the Core Company Should Act When Affiliates Infringe Human Rights, in* SIEGE OR CAVALRY CHARGE? THE UN MANDATE ON BUSINESS AND HUMAN RIGHTS 9 (Radu Mares ed., 2011). Mares elaborates on the limits of the Framework and Guiding Principles in addressing the state treatment of business networks. Specifically, the Guiding Principles treat the core business enterprise as the focal point rather than adopting the enterprise model of business relationships. As a consequence, the business relationships are treated as more remote and so issues of control become much more difficult to prove.

enterprise, rather than its state of incorporation, in relation to the application of some areas of European Union law.[39]

Further, a number of national courts have allowed for the possible liability on the parent corporate nationals for the acts of foreign subsidiaries that constitute violations of international human rights law. For example, in the case of *Chandler v. Cape plc*,[40] the English courts considered whether there could be a claim against a UK-based parent corporation for injury suffered by employees of a subsidiary corporation based in southern Africa. In that instance, Mr. Chandler contracted asbestosis as result of exposure to asbestos dust during the course of his employment with a subsidiary, and he sued the parent corporation because the subsidiary had been dissolved and the subsidiary's insurance policy contained an exclusion regarding asbestosis claims. The English Court of Appeal held that in appropriate circumstances, the law may impose on a parent corporation a duty of care in relation to the health and safety of its subsidiary's employees. The court held that the following factors could give rise to such a duty:

> (a) the business of the parent and subsidiary are in a relevant respect the same; (b) the parent has, or ought to have, superior knowledge on some relevant aspect of health and safety in the particular industry; (c) the subsidiary's system of work was unsafe as the parent company knew or ought to have known; and (d) the parent knew or ought to have foreseen that the subsidiary or its employees would rely on its using that superior knowledge for the employees' protection.[41]

In that case, the court found that the Cape *plc* had assumed responsibility for the health and safety of its subsidiary's employees, and that Cape *plc* was responsible for setting specifications of the products manufactured by its subsidiary. In addition, it found that the subsidiary relied on technical know-how from Cape *plc* and followed Cape *plc* working practices; that health and safety specialists employed by Cape *plc* were involved in assessing health risks of asbestos exposure and devising practices to manage those risks; and that Cape *plc* had established group policies regarding health and safety that were to be followed by subsidiaries.[42]

The reasoning in this case suggests that there is an increase in the likelihood that some national courts will consider that a parent corporation incorporated in that state has assumed a duty of care toward third parties affected by the operations of subsidiaries

---

39. European Council Regulation (EC) No. 44/2001 of 22 December 2000 on Jurisdiction and the Recognition and Enforcement of Judgements in Civil and Commercial Matters, 2001 O.J. (L 12) 1, (Brussels 1) http://eurlex.europa.eu/LexUriServ/LexUriServ.do?uri=OJ:L:2001:012:0001:0023:en:PDF.
40. Chandler v. Cape plc [2012] EWCA Civ 525.
41. *Id.* at 80.
42. *Id.* at 72–76.

located elsewhere, at least where there are groupwide policies and practices developed and implemented by the parent corporation. Indeed, many decisions about matters such as human resource policies, marketing and finances, and subcontracting requirements are in reality made by the parent corporation and not by a subsidiary, as part of the parent's business enterprise methodology.

In addition, it is notable that the approach taken by the court in *Chandler* is one that is not dependent on the state of incorporation of the subsidiary and is not directly affected by any apparent jurisdictional limits on the reach of the laws of the state of the parent corporation. It also does not depend on a specific legislative power within the state—compared, for example, to the U.S. position—on which a claimant would have to rely.[43] It thus challenges the rather limited perspective of the state's obligations indicated by the commentary to the Guiding Principles and shows that the obligations on states to respect human rights in relation to the activities of business enterprises can be applied much more widely to the activities of corporate nationals and others operating, including through subsidiaries, outside the territory of the state.

Therefore, it is argued here that the state's obligation to protect human rights goes beyond the hesitant comment in the Guiding Principles and includes an obligation to act in such a way that it has effective laws and practices that protect actions and omissions by state agents[44] and their corporate nationals who violate human rights outside the territory of the state. Indeed, without some form of extraterritorial regulation of corporate nationals, such business enterprises "could easily bypass the mandate of municipal law by transferring or relocating their business operations offshore where human rights obligations are less stringent."[45]

Attribution to a State for Actions of Business Enterprises

This issue of control by a state over a business enterprise's activities is also relevant in a different way. Though the actions by business enterprises (as private bodies) are not usually attributed to a state such that the state is responsible under general international law

---

43. In a similar decision, on January 30, 2013, a Dutch court ruled that Shell Petroleum Development Company of Nigeria (SPDC) must compensate a farmer for property damage caused by a sabotaged well in Nigeria in 2006 and 2007. *See* Akpan & Milieudefensive v. Royal Dutch Shell Plc & Shell Petroleum Development Company of Nigeria Ltd., LJN: BY9854, Rechtbank's-Gravenhage, C/09/337050/HA ZA 09-1580 (2013), http://zoeken.rechtspraak.nl/detailpage.aspx?ljn=BY9854&u_ljn=BY9854. SPDC is a wholly owned subsidiary of Royal Dutch Shell (a Dutch incorporated company) and is the designated operator of a joint venture between several companies in Nigeria. Therefore, the impact of the Kiobel case may not be of much significance on the developing case law outside the United States, *see* Robert McCorquodale, *Waving Not Drowning: Kiobel Outside the United States* 107 AMERICAN J. INT'L L. (2013), p. 846.

44. Note that Guiding Principle 8 requires states to have policy coherence across all government departments, which could prevent a state claiming that it did not know what all its officials were doing. *See* Guiding Principles, *supra* note 7, at § I.B ¶ 8.

45. Surya Deva, *Acting Extraterritorially to Tame Multinational Corporations for Human Rights Violations: Who Should "Bell the Cat"?* 5 MELBOURNE J. INT'L. L. 37, 49 (2004).

for their actions, sometimes those actions can be attributed to a state. Indeed, the commentary to General Principle 4 supports this by stating that "where a business enterprise is controlled by the State or where its acts can be attributed otherwise to the State, an abuse of human rights by the business enterprise may entail a violation of the State's own international law obligations."[46]

The position is set out explicitly by the International Law Commission in its Articles on the Responsibility of States for Internationally Wrongful Acts,[47] which apply generally to international law and not only international human rights law. The commission has identified four key situations in which the acts of nonstate actors such as business enterprises can be attributed to the state, for which the state will incur international responsibility where there is a breach of an international obligation (such as an obligation under a human rights treaty).[48] First, a state would be responsible for the acts of a person or entity where the latter was empowered by law to exercise elements of governmental activity.[49] Second, a state would be responsible for the acts of a person or entity acting under the instructions, direction, or control of the state.[50] Third, a state may incur international responsibility for the acts of a person or entity when the state adopts or acknowledges the act as its own.[51] Fourth, a state may also incur international responsibility when it is complicit in the activity of the nonstate actor or fails to exercise due diligence to prevent the effects of the actions of nonstate actors.[52]

Though a fuller discussion of this issue is beyond the scope of this chapter,[53] one example will illustrate its potential impact in relation to business enterprises and human

---

46. Note that Guiding Principle 4 seems to focus on the proximity of the business to the state in determining responsibility for action. *See* Guiding Principles, *supra* note 7, at § I.B ¶ 4.

47. Int'l Law Comm'n, Articles on the Responsibility of States for Internationally Wrongful Acts, Report of the International Law Commission on the Work of its 53d session, A/56/10, Aug. 2001, UN Doc. A/56/10(SUPP); GAOR, 56th Sess., Supp. No. 10 (2001) [hereinafter ILC Articles]. Not all the ILC Articles can be considered to be customary international law, though most of them—including those relevant to this chapter— have been adopted by international tribunals as reflective of customary international law. *See generally* Helen Duffy, *Towards Global Responsibility for Human Rights Protection: A Sketch of International Developments*, 15 INTERIGHTS BULLETIN 104 (2006).

48. See also *Armed Activities on the Territory of the Congo, supra* note 24, at 55–56, 90.

49. ILC Articles, *supra* note 43, Art. 5.

50. *See* JAMES CRAWFORD, THE INTERNATIONAL LAW COMMISSION'S ARTICLES ON STATE RESPONSIBILITY: INTRODUCTION, TEXT AND COMMENTARIES ¶¶ 91, 121 (2002) [hereinafter ILC Commentaries]. Interestingly, nonstate actors such as business enterprise may wish their actions to be attributable to the state in order to avoid national legal claims and yet at the same time claim that they are private entities.

51. *See* ILC Articles, *supra* note 43, Art. 11. The early global business enterprises, such as the Dutch East India Company and the Newfoundland Company, were granted charters as a delegation of powers by the monarch, and many of their activities were attributable to the state. *See generally* Stephen Bottomley, *From Contractualism to Constitutionalism: A Framework for Corporate Governance*, 19 SYDNEY L. REV. 277 (1997).

52. *See* Case Concerning United States Diplomatic and Consular Staff in Tehran (U.S. v. Iran), ICJ Reports 1980 at 3, ¶¶ 57, 69–71. *See also* Guiding Principles, *supra* note 7, at §I.B ¶ 3 (explaining the need for a state to engage in human rights due diligence).

53. For a fuller discussion, see Robert McCorquodale & Penelope Simons, *Responsibility beyond*

rights. A business enterprise could be acting under the instructions, direction, or control of a state where the business enterprise or its employees are "employed as auxiliaries or are sent as 'volunteers' to neighboring countries, or who are instructed to carry out particular missions abroad."[54] This issue has become more prominent since the beginning of the (illegal) action by the occupying forces in Iraq, where it became clear how many business enterprises were contracted by the states involved to provide a wide variety of services, from providing intelligence to re-creating state infrastructure to support such military action.[55] Indeed, the investigations after the discovery of prisoner abuse in Abu Ghraib in Iraq (and elsewhere) have shown that employees of business enterprises committed some of these abuses.[56] With the increasing use of business enterprises by states in their extraterritorial military activities, as well as in trade and other areas, there is clearly the possibility that the activities of these business enterprises will be attributed to the state.[57] When such activities violate international human rights law, the state will incur international responsibility, including in those situations where the business enterprise contravenes instructions.[58]

The state may also be complicit in a business enterprise's activities that have led to human rights violations. Governments are often very active in their support of their corporate nationals through financing, such as the provision of export credits and political risk insurance; developing essential contacts in other states and participating in government trade missions abroad; and entering into bilateral investment treaties that assist their corporate nationals. This active support can lead to the state being internationally responsible for the consequences of a corporate national's activities.[59] For example, the legal (and financial) structures of the business enterprise (as a consortium) that operate the Baku-Tbilisi-Ceyhan pipeline[60] include agreements between the consortium and the host

---

Borders: State Responsibility for Extraterritorial Violations by Corporations of International Human Rights Law, 70 MOD. L. REV. 598 (2007).

54.   ILC Commentaries, *supra* note 46, ¶ 110. Guiding Principle 6 refers to states' needs to account for human rights considerations when engaging in business contracts. *See* Guiding Principles, *supra* note 7, at § I.B ¶ 6.

55.   *See, e.g.*, Susan S. Gibson, *Lack of Extraterritorial Jurisdiction over Civilians: A New Look at an Old Problem*, 148 MIL. L. REV. 114 (1995); Michael N. Schmitt, *Humanitarian Law and Direct Participation in Hostilities by Private Contractors or Civilian Employees*, 5 CHI. J. INT'L L. 519 (2005).

56.   For example, four Iraqi torture victims have alleged that a private U.S.-based contractor, CACI, tortured them during interrogations at Abu Ghraib prison in Iraq. *See generally* Al Shimari v. CACI Int'l., Inc., No. 1:08-cv-827 (GBL/JFA), 2013 WL 3229720 (E.D.Va. June 25, 2013).

57.   For a discussion in the context of private military firms, *see* Oliver R. Jones, *Implausible Deniability: State Responsibility for the Actions of Private Military Firms*, 24 CONN. J. INT'L L. 249 (2009).

58.   *See* ILC Articles, *supra* note 43, Art. 7.

59.   *See* Guiding Principles, *supra* note 7, at §I.B. ¶ 9 (discussing investment treaties and contracts with other states and businesses).

60.   The consortium members include Amerada Hess, AzBTC, BP, Chevron, ConocoPhillips, Eni, INPEX, Itochu, Statoil, Total, and TPAO. *See Baku-Tbilisi-Ceyhan, Corporate Profile*, AZBTC, http://www.azbtc.com/profile.html#333 (last visited Nov. 28, 2013).

state governments that contain stabilization clauses. These make the host state liable to pay compensation to the consortium when, for example, it makes any regulatory changes that adversely affect the economic equilibrium of the project. These agreements effectively prohibit the host state from applying certain labor standards to the consortium members or from giving an increased human rights protection in that state, even if this is contrary to that state's international human rights obligations.[61] It is of note that BP, the leader of the consortium managing the project, responded to these concerns of NGOs by entering into a Human Rights Undertaking, which prevents the consortium from asserting in legal proceedings an interpretation of the governing agreements that is inconsistent with the regulation by host states of their obligations under human rights treaties.[62]

This example shows that if a home state has provided financial backing or other support for activity by its corporate national outside its territory, that state would be wise to ensure that such undertakings by its corporate nationals (and their subsidiaries) are made to reduce the possibility of the state itself being found complicit in a host state's internationally wrongful act (for example, a violation of its human rights obligations) in relation to the corporate national's activities.[63] It cannot reasonably be argued today that states do not know their corporate nationals may engage in human rights violations in their extraterritorial operations, because there are an increasing number of investor and consumer campaigns in relation to business enterprises' human rights impacts and claims being brought in national courts against business enterprises for violations of human rights.[64]

---

61. Thus, for example, in its Host Government Agreement for the Baku pipeline, the Turkish government is prevented from requiring any consortium members to comply with labour standards "that i) exceed those international labour standards or practices which are customary in international petroleum transportation projects, or ii) are contrary to the goal of promoting an efficient and motivated workforce." *See* AMNESTY INT'L, HUMAN RIGHTS ON THE LINE: THE BAKU-TBILISI-CEYHAN PIPELINE PROJECT (May 2003), http://www.amnesty.org.uk/content.asp?CategoryID=10128. *See also* Terra E. Lawson-Remer, *A Role for the International Finance Corporation in Integrating Environmental and Human Rights Standards into Core Project Covenants: Case Study of the Baku-Tbilisi-Ceyhan Oil Pipeline Project*, in TRANSNATIONAL CORPORATIONS AND HUMAN RIGHTS 410–11 (Olivier De Schutter ed., 2006). In a separate report, Ruggie's team raised concerns about the use of stabilization clauses in investment treaties as possibly leading to a host state contravening its human rights legal obligations. *See* ANDREA SHEMBERG, STABILIZATION CLAUSES AND HUMAN RIGHTS, A RESEARCH PROJECT CONDUCTED FOR IFC AND THE UNITED NATIONS SPECIAL REPRESENTATIVE TO THE SECRETARY GENERAL ON BUSINESS AND HUMAN RIGHTS (Mar. 11, 2008).

62. BTC Human Rights Undertaking (Sep. 2003), http://subsites.bp.com/caspian/Human%20Rights%20Undertaking.pdf.

63. Another example of this issue may be the on-going claims about the UK government's involvement in BAE Systems activities in Saudi Arabia that may have breached human rights. *See, e.g., Q&A: The BAE-Saudi Allegations*, BBC NEWS (Jul. 30, 2008), http://news.bbc.co.uk/1/hi/business/6729489.stm; *BAE Systems: Corporate Crimes*, CORPORATE WATCH (June 2002), http://www.corporatewatch.org/?lid=185.

64. The impact of this approach and the Framework has already been seen in, for example, the announcement of Canada's export credit agency's new Statement on Human Rights. *See New Statement Sets Out EDC's Principles for the Consideration of Human Rights*, CNW (Apr. 30, 2008), http://www.newswire.ca/fr/story/282357/new-statement-sets-out-edc-s-principles-for-the-consideration-of-human-rights. *See*, UK

Therefore, in relation to the first pillar of the Framework and the Guiding Principles, each state does have extensive legal obligations to protect all those within its territory from violations of human rights by both state officials and business enterprises in relation to those human rights for which the state has accepted legal obligations (under both treaty and customary international law). Despite the hesitant approach by the SRSG, it is clear that this obligation extends to activities by a business enterprise outside the territory of the state and requires a state to enact laws and establish practices, including regulation of both corporate nationals and their subsidiaries, to protect against human rights violations.

The extent of the regulation required by states is indicated in Guiding Principles 3 to 7, which clarify the state's regulatory and policy functions, from oversight of commercial transactions to control of state-owned business enterprises, and Guiding Principles 8 to 10, which concern policy coherence by states within their state and in relation to their roles internationally. This policy coherence is not limited to a state's implementation of its own international human rights obligations but extends horizontally as well, as the commentary notes:

> Vertical policy coherence entails States having the necessary policies, laws and processes to implement their international human rights law obligations. Horizontal policy coherence means supporting and equipping departments and agencies, at both the national and subnational levels, that shape business practices—including those responsible for corporate law and securities regulation, investment, export credit and insurance, trade and labor—to be informed of and act in a manner compatible with the Governments' human rights obligations.[65]

Thus states should ensure that they meet their international human rights obligations and not allow investment treaties to restrict their human rights protection activities. States should also ensure that their own engagement with business enterprises—such as in export credit guarantees and public procurement processes—respect human rights, and they should ensure that business enterprise acting in conflict zones, fragile states, and emerging markets are appropriately regulated. If states take these obligations and these approaches

---

Secretary of State for Foreign & Commonwealth Affairs, *Good Business: Implementing the UN Guiding Principles on Business and Human Rights* (Sept. 4, 2013), https://www.gov.uk/government/uploads/system/uploads/attachment_data/file/236901/BHR_Action_Plan_-_final_online_version_1_.pdf (Sept. 2013). The ICJ Report on corporate complicity from 2008 also warns that business complacency in this regard could lead to litigation, since reports of corporate involvement in human rights abuse are now so widely disseminated. 1–3 REPORT OF THE ICJ EXPERT LEGAL PANEL ON CORPORATE COMPLICITY IN INTERNATIONAL CRIMES (2009), http://www.icj.org/report-of-the-international-commission-of-jurists-expert-legal-panel-on-corporate-complicity-in-international-crimes/.

65. Guiding Principles, *supra* note 7, at § I.B ¶ 8, commentary.

seriously, significant steps forward will be made in the protection of the human rights affected by corporate activity.

Corporate Responsibility to Respect

The Framework, as elaborated in the Guiding Principles, has made clear that business enterprises have a responsibility to protect human rights. This responsibility is defined as follows:

> [The corporate] responsibility to respect is defined by social expectations—as part of what is sometimes called a company's social license to operate . . . [and] "doing no harm" is not merely a passive responsibility for firms but may entail positive steps. To discharge the responsibility to respect requires due diligence. This concept describes the steps a company must take to become aware of, prevent and address adverse human rights impacts.[66]

This is a strong and important statement that is then set out in as five foundational principles in Guiding Principles 11 to 15. Two of these reiterate that this responsibility is in relation to all human rights[67] and that it applies to all business enterprises,[68] as discussed above, and the other three are discussed below. In addition, the Guiding Principles make clear that the corporate responsibility to respect human rights "exists independently of states' abilities and/or willingness to fulfill their own human rights obligations [and] . . . over and above compliance with national laws and regulations."[69]

The Framework does not alter the position that under the current international human rights law structure, business enterprises do not have any direct international legal obligations. Accordingly, business enterprises cannot be directly responsible for violations of international law.[70] Yet the SRSG acknowledged that this responsibility is not a *law-free zone* and will be affected by developments in law, especially national law.[71]

The key element of the Framework and Guiding Principles that will be explored here in terms of international human rights law is that of *due diligence*, because it appears to

---

66. SRSG Report 2008, *supra* note 4, ¶¶ 54–61.
67. *See* Guiding Principles, *supra* note 7, at § II.A ¶ 12.
68. *See* Guiding Principles, *supra* note 7, at § II.A ¶ 14.
69. *See* Guiding Principles, *supra* note 7, at § II.A ¶ 11, commentary.
70. This is due to the fact that international human rights law imposes the legal obligations to protect human rights on states alone and has not yet developed so as to regulate directly the activities of business enterprises or other nonstate actors. For a discussion of this, *see generally* Robert McCorquodale & Rebecca La Forgia, *Taking off the Blindfolds: Torture by Nonstate Actors*, 1 HUM. RTS. L. REV. 189 (2001). *See also* J. Nolan's and R. Steinhardt's chapters in this book.
71. *See* SRSG Report 2010, *supra* note 6, ¶ 66.

rely to some extent on international human rights legal ideas. However, before considering this, some clarification is needed about the difference between corporate social responsibility policies and human rights policies, and the concept of *responsibility*.

Corporate Social Responsibility

Many business enterprises and business organizations have supported this second pillar of the Framework.[72] Much of this support comes because many of these business enterprises see their corporate social responsibility (CSR) policies as being the equivalent of a human rights policy and/or as making them compliant with human rights norms.[73] However, having a CSR policy is not the same as providing protection for all human rights. Though there are a variety of definitions of CSR, one that is frequently used is as follows:

> CSR can be defined as a concept whereby companies voluntarily decide to respect and protect the interests of a broad range of stakeholders and to contribute to a cleaner environment and a better society through active interaction with all. CSR is a voluntary commitment by business to manage its role in society in a responsible way.[74]

Broadly, there are two aspects to these definitions of CSR:

> [F]irst, those that focus on outcomes—including outcomes in terms of "business impacts", "commercial success" and wider societal goals; and, second, those that stress the voluntary nature of CSR ("voluntary" in that CSR relates to business activity that is not mandated by legislation).[75]

What is important about all the definitions is essentially that CSR efforts are management-driven and corporate-determined policies designed to assist the business enterprise, including its reputation, even if genuinely aimed for a positive social end.

---

72. The International Organisation of Employers, the International Chamber of Commerce, and the Business and Industry Advisory Committee to the OECD, *Joint Statement on Business and Human Rights to the United Nations Human Rights Council*, May 30, 2011, http://www.iccwbo.org/Advocacy-Codes-and-Rules/Document-centre/2011/Joint-Statement-on-Business-Human-Rights-to-the-United-Nations-Human-Rights-Council (last visited Nov. 28, 2013).

73. *See, e.g.*, Adam McBeth & Sarah Joseph, *Same Words, Different Language: Corporate Perceptions of Human Rights Responsibilities*, 11 AUSTL. J. HUM. RTS. 95 (2005) (presenting survey evidence of business enterprises in relation to human rights).

74. *See generally* Ramón Mullerat, *Corporate Social Responsibility (A Human Face to the Global Economy)* OGEL 5 (2004); CORPORATE SOCIAL RESPONSIBILITY: THE CORPORATE GOVERNANCE OF THE 21ST CENTURY (Ramón Mullerat ed., 2005).

75. *See* Halina Ward, *Corporate Social Responsibility in Law and Policy*, in PERSPECTIVES ON CORPORATE SOCIAL RESPONSIBILITY 10 (Nina Boeger et al. eds., 2008).

In contrast, human rights protections are person-centered and have legitimate compliance mechanisms (even if these are not always very strong). Human rights are not voluntary; they are an expression of human dignity and the right to be protected in that human dignity.[76] In addition, most CSR policies tend to refer to, or focus on, a limited range of human rights, such as the right to privacy or freedom from torture. Though there is now a growing acceptance by many of the major transnational business enterprises that CSR policies need to align with human rights, it is still vital that this distinction between CSR policies and human rights protections is made clearly and unequivocally.

Responsibility

The Framework, as reflected in the Guiding Principles, draws a deliberate distinction between the state's *duty* to protect and the corporate *responsibility* to respect. This is perhaps to sharpen the difference between legal and moral obligations as well as to define the scope of the obligation.[77] This corporate *responsibility* is called a *social expectation* in the SRSG Report 2008, as quoted above. In the SRSG Report 2009, it is called a "social norm" on which a corporation's "social license to operate is based,"[78] and in the SRSG Report 2010 it is seen as a "standard of expected conduct."[79] So there has been a degree of movement and lack of coherence in the definition. In addition, the distinction in terminology between a *duty* of state (which is a legal obligation) and a corporate *responsibility* can be confusing.

Yet the concept of corporate responsibility, as Ruggie himself noted in an earlier report, is "the legal, social or moral *obligations* imposed on companies."[80] That earlier view is consistent with the general understanding that

the concept of corporate responsibility is based on the expectation that private companies should no longer base their actions on the needs of their shareholders alone, but rather have obligations towards the society in which the company operates.[81]

---

76. The literature on human rights is vast. For a useful summary *see* James Nickel & David Reidy, *The Philosophy of Human Rights*, in INTERNATIONAL HUMAN RIGHTS LAW (Daniel Moeckli et al. eds., 2010).

77. In the Introduction to the Guiding Principles there is an attempt to distinguish between *duties* and *responsibilities*. *See* Guiding Principles, *supra* note 7, Introduction ¶ 2, ¶ 6. *See also* Melvin Aron Eisenberg, *The World of Contract and the World of Gift*, 85 CALIF. L. REV. 821 (1997).

78. See SRSG Report 2009, *supra* note 6, ¶ 46.

79. See SRSG Report 2010, *supra* note 6, ¶ 55.

80. Special Representative of the Secretary-General, *Report of the Special Representative of the Secretary-General on the Issue of Human Rights and Transnational Corporations and Other Business Enterprises*, ¶ 6 UN Doc. A/HRC/4/35 (Feb. 19, 2007) (emphasis added).

81. ELISA MORGERA, CORPORATE ACCOUNTABILITY IN INTERNATIONAL ENVIRONMENTAL LAW 18 (2009) (emphasis in the original). She prefers the use of the term *corporate accountability* as it implies that corporations are answerable to others for their actions.

Interestingly, when the Human Rights Council endorsed the Framework in its 2009 Resolution, it used the term *responsibility* for both states and business enterprises.[82]

Further, there is a real difficulty in determining a *social expectation* or a *social norm* in this instance, as there is

> frequently a gap between citizens' expectations and what they perceive to be the reality of business behavior. This gap is caused partly by . . . an insufficient understanding on the part of some enterprises of fast evolving societal expectations, as well as by an insufficient awareness on the part of citizens of the achievements of enterprises and the constraints under which they operate.[83]

Yet even if a *social expectation* can be discerned through empirical evidence, which society is the relevant society for determining the expectation? Is it all the international community or only the industrialized, consumer-active North? Does it include the rural poor in non-industrialized states? Will it affect those business enterprises that produce consumer goods (especially those with a parent corporation in an industrialized state) more than those that do not produce consumer goods? If there is such a *social license* for a business enterprise to operate, then it is highly unlikely that those who are oppressed and those whose human rights are violated by a business enterprise will be in a position to withdraw that social license. Indeed, there is also the concern that these *social expectations* could be defined to serve only some entrenched economic interests or selected social partners.[84] Because there is usually a lack of full and transparent information from business enterprises on these matters, it would be difficult to see if there is really compliance with any human rights by a business enterprise.

To base such an important distinction between the state's and the corporation's human rights obligations on the nebulous idea of a social license to operate and on vague social expectations is unsatisfactory. Though the SRSG was clearly trying to use his consultations and practical experiments to change the expectations of business enterprises and civil society, there is still a gulf between the responsibilities and expectations, and the reality. Thus this is an area that will need to be clarified in the application of the Guiding Principles.

---

82.   Human Rights Council Resolution, *supra* note 5, Preamble.

83.   European Commission, A Renewed EU Strategy 2011-14 for Corporate Social Responsibility COM (2011) 681 final (Oct. 25, 2011), ¶ 4.2, http://eur-lex.europa.eu/LexUriServ/LexUriServ.do?uri=COM :2011:0681:FIN:EN:PDF.

84.   *See* Michael E. Porter & Mark R. Kramer, *Creating Shared Value*, HARV. BUS. REV. (Jan.-Feb. 2011), http://www.waterhealth.com/sites/default/files/Harvard_Buiness_Review_Shared_Value.pdf (arguing that business should espouse social goals to achieve financial objectives, as an example of the potential for business to define human rights standards in such a way as to meet their own objectives).

Due Diligence

The concept of due diligence is used throughout this second pillar, with Guiding Principle 15 being one of the foundational principles, providing the following:

> In order to meet their responsibility to respect human rights, business enterprises should have in place policies and processes appropriate to their size and circumstances, including:
> a. a policy commitment to meet their responsibility to respect human rights;
> b. a human rights due diligence process to identify, prevent, mitigate and account for how they address their impacts on human rights;
> c. processes to enable the remediation of any adverse human rights impacts they cause or to which they contribute.

Guiding Principles 17 to 21, which discuss the practical steps that business enterprises should take to discharge this responsibility, appear under the heading, "Human rights due diligence."[85] These steps include having a human rights policy; assessing human rights impacts of business activities; integrating those values and findings into corporate cultures and management systems; and tracking as well as reporting performance.

This concept of due diligence is defined as follows:

> Such a measure of prudence, activity, or assiduity, as is properly to be expected from, and ordinarily exercised by, a reasonable and prudent [person or enterprise] under the particular circumstances; not measured by any absolute standard, but depending on the relative facts of the special case. In the context of the Guiding Principles, human rights due diligence comprises an ongoing management process that a reasonable and prudent enterprise needs to undertake, in light of its circumstances (including sector, operating context, size and similar factors) to meet its responsibility to respect human rights.[86]

This appears to be an integration of the international human rights legal obligation of due diligence in relation to the actions of nonstate actors (such as business enterprises),[87] and the general voluntary business practice of due diligence.[88] In relation to the general business practice, the SRSG Report 2009 notes the following:

---

85. For a fuller discussion of the issue of due diligence in the Guiding Principles upon which some of this text is based, see Jonathan Bonnitcha & Robert McCorquodale, *Is the Concept of "Due Diligence" in the Guiding Principles Coherent?* (Jan. 29, 2013), http://ssrn.com/abstract=2208588.

86. Interpretive Guide, *supra* note 11, at 4.

87. *See* Velásquez Rodriguez v. Honduras, 28 I.L.M. 294, ¶¶ 172, 176 (1989).

88. *See, e.g.*, Jeffery S. Perry & Thomas J. Herd, *Mergers and Acquisitions: Reducing M&A Risk through Improved Due Diligence*, 32 STRATEGY & LEADERSHIP 12, 12 (2012).

Businesses routinely employ due diligence to assess exposure to risks beyond their control and develop mitigation strategies for them, such as changes in government policy, shifts in consumer preferences, and even weather patterns. Controllable or not, human rights challenges arising from the business context, its impacts and its relationships, can pose material risks to the company and its stakeholders, and generate outright abuses that may be linked to the company in perception or reality. Therefore, they merit a similar level of due diligence as any other risk.[89]

Thus the Framework cleverly aims to use a terminology that is familiar to both human rights law and business management practices. This could be helpful, except that the terminologies are based on different bases.

Under international human rights law, the obligation of due diligence is a positive legal obligation on a state that demands considerable state resources, such as undertaking fact-finding and criminal investigation, and providing redress, even when the original act was by a business enterprise.[90] There is a clear standard established by the human rights treaty bodies to determine if this legal obligation to have due diligence about individuals' and groups' interests has been breached.[91] In contrast, the business practice of due diligence, which is often undertaken as a form of audit, especially during mergers and acquisitions, is a procedural practice to reduce risk in relation to the business enterprise's own interests. Though the reality of management of risk is a vital part of corporate activity, and a poorly conducted due diligence audit can have adverse consequences (especially for the legal and accounting advisors to the business enterprise), it is difficult to establish a clear standard of business due diligence that can be adjudicated by human rights treaty bodies and other dispute settlement bodies.[92] It is therefore puzzling that the SRSG Report 2009 adopts a definition of due diligence that includes a legal aspect:

> Due diligence is commonly defined as "diligence reasonably expected from, and ordinarily exercised by, a person who seeks to satisfy a legal requirement or to discharge an obligation." . . . The special representative uses this term in its broader sense: a comprehensive, proactive attempt to uncover human rights risks, actual and

---

89. SRSG Report 2009, *supra* note 6, ¶ 52.

90. *See, e.g.*, Jordan v. UK, App. No. 24746/94 (2001) (finding the conduct of the investigation, the coroner's inquest, delay, the lack of both legal aid for the victim's family, and the lack of public scrutiny of the reasons of the Director of Public Prosecutions not to prosecute, was a violation of Article 2 of the ECHR). *See also* UN Committee Against Torture, Halimi-Nedzibi v. Austria (8/1991), 1(2) IHRR 190, ¶ 13.5 (1994).

91. *See, e.g.*, INT'L HUMAN RIGHTS AND BUSINESS, THE "STATE OF PLAY" OF HUMAN RIGHTS DUE DILIGENCE (2011), http://www.ihrb.org/pdf/The_State_of_Play_of_Human_Rights_Due_Diligence.pdf.

92. *See* Daria Davitti, *On the Meanings of International Investment Law and International Human Rights Law: The Alternative Narrative of Due Diligence*, 12 HUM. RTS. L. REV. 421 (2012).

potential, over the entire life cycle of a project or business activity, with the aim of avoiding and mitigating those risks.[93]

This confusion is carried through into the Guiding Principles. When the Guiding Principles refer to processes to "identify, prevent, mitigate and account for . . . adverse human rights impacts" (as in Guiding Principle 15(b) above), the term "due diligence" is used in the business-practice sense of the term, being about the subjective means of conduct. In contrast, the general foundational statement in General Principle 11 is as follows:

> Business enterprises should respect human rights. This means that they should avoid infringing on the human rights of others and should address adverse human rights impacts with which they are involved.

This approach uses the term *due diligence* as a standard of conduct and so is used in the human rights law sense of the term. Thus there is some confusion in the application of the term *due diligence* in the Framework and Guiding Principles.

The other aspect of the term *due diligence* that can cause confusion is how it can be applied to different situations. General Principle 17 provides the following:

> In order to identify, prevent, mitigate and account for how they address their adverse human rights impacts, business enterprises should carry out human rights due diligence. The process should include assessing actual and potential human rights impacts, integrating and acting upon the findings, tracking responses, and communicating how impacts are addressed. Human rights due diligence:
> (a) Should cover adverse human rights impacts that the business enterprise may cause or contribute to through its own activities, or which may be directly linked to its operations, products or services by its business relationships;
> (b) Will vary in complexity with the size of the business enterprise, the risk of severe human rights impacts, and the nature and context of its operations;
> (c) Should be ongoing, recognizing that the human rights risks may change over time as the business enterprise's operations and operating context evolve.

General Principle 17(a) continues the distinction drawn in General Principle 13 between human rights due diligence for adverse human rights impacts that the business enterprise may cause or contribute to through its own activities, and human rights due diligence for adverse human rights impacts of third parties. General Principle 13 is as follows:

---

93.   SRSG Report 2009, *supra* note 6, ¶ 71 (internal citations omitted).

The responsibility to respect human rights requires that business enterprises:
(a) Avoid causing or contributing to adverse human rights impacts through their own activities, and address such impacts when they occur;
(b) Seek to prevent or mitigate adverse human rights impacts that are directly linked to their operations, products or services by their business relationships, even if they have not contributed to those impacts.

Thus, a clear distinction is made between the responsibility on a business enterprise to *avoid* causing or contributing to its own human rights impacts (13 (a)) and the responsibility to *seek to prevent or mitigate* impacts by third parties (13 (b)).

This distinction is also seen in the use of the term *leverage* to describe how a business enterprise should respond to actions by third parties. For example, General Principle 19 (b)(ii) provides that appropriate action by a business enterprise will depend on the "extent of [the business enterprise's] leverage in addressing the adverse impact." The commentary to General Principle 19 states the following:

Leverage is considered to exist where the enterprise has the ability to effect change in the wrongful practices of an entity that causes a harm. Where a business enterprise has not contributed to an adverse human rights impact, but that impact is nevertheless directly linked to its operations, products or services by its business relationship with another entity, the situation is more complex. Among the factors that will enter into the determination of the appropriate action in such situations are the enterprise's leverage over the entity concerned, how crucial the relationship is to the enterprise, the severity of the abuse, and whether terminating the relationship with the entity itself would have adverse human rights consequences.[94]

Therefore, two different standards of due diligence are operating in the application of General Principle 13 to a business enterprise: a strict standard of avoiding its own impacts and a leveraged standard for seeking to prevent others' impacts. The former is consistent with the human rights legal obligations on states, which is objective and for which compliance can be determined, and the latter is more consistent with the corporate social responsibilities on business practices, which are more voluntary and based on the business enterprise's own risks.

To be consistent with international human rights law, there would need to be objective legal criteria in regard to the standard of conduct required of a business enterprise in relation to its own impacts. In addition, where the human rights standard of conduct applied, the operation of a business practice standard of due diligence would not be a

---

94. Guiding Principles, *supra* note 7.

legitimate defense by a business enterprise to an action based on the business enterprise's failure to respect human rights. Indeed, those who helped to draft the Framework and Guiding Principles accepted this position.[95] A due diligence standard of conduct could be enforced through an international or national legal compliance mechanism. So although the corporate responsibility to respect human rights was considered voluntary, it is evident that there may be legal aspects to its application.

In any event, the lack of clearer legal obligations on business enterprises in the Framework and Guiding Principles in relation to the violation of human rights makes it very difficult to access or enforce any remedies against them.[96] This is of particular importance because Guiding Principle 22 provides that "where business enterprises identify that they have caused or contributed to adverse impacts, they should provide for or cooperate in their remediation through legitimate processes." This leads to the issue of how to access a remedy, which is the third pillar of the Framework.

Access to Remedy

The third pillar of the framework is the need for access to a remedy. This is expressed in terms that there should be "effective grievance mechanisms" for the actions of both states and business enterprises "where there is a perceived injustice evoking an individual's or a group's sense of entitlement, which may be based on law, explicit or implicit promises, customary practice, or general notions of fairness."[97] The remedies can be judicial and nonjudicial.[98] The Guiding Principles set this out in terms of states' duties and business enterprises' responsibilities in this area, so each will be considered in turn.

States Remedies

A state has an obligation under international human rights law to provide a remedy where there is a violation of human rights.[99] Though there is some discretion in a state as to how

---

95.   John F. Sherman & Amy Lehr, *Human Rights Due Diligence: Is It Too Risky?* 18 (Corp. Soc. Resp. Project, Working Paper No. 55, Feb. 2010) (citing Lucien J. Dhooge, *Due Diligence as a Defence to Corporate Liability Pursuant to the Alien Tort Statute* 22 Emory Int'l. L. Rev. 455 (2008)), http://www.hks.harvard.edu/m-rcbg/CSRI/publications/workingpaper_55_shermanlehr.pdf.

96.   *See e.g.*, the cases against Coca-Cola in Colombia where the company was accused of complicity in the murder of trade union members working at a Coca-Cola bottler, but it was not held liable because the company's involvement was not deemed sufficiently proximate to find legal liability. Sinaltrainal v. Coca-Cola, 578 F.3d 1252 (2009); Mark Thomas, *Colombia: To Die For*, Guardian UK (September 20, 2008); Alison Frankel, *11th Circuit Invokes 'Iqbal' in Affirming Dismissal of Alien Tort Claim Against Coca-Cola and Bottlers*, The American Lawyer (Aug. 13, 2009).

97.   SRSG Report 2010, *supra* note 6, ¶ 90.

98.   SRSG Report 2008, *supra* note 4, ¶¶ 82–103; *see also* Guiding Principles, *supra* note 7, at § III.A ¶ 25 (discussing effective remedies).

99.   *See* Guiding Principles, *supra* note 7, at § I.A ¶ 1.

to provide a remedy, it must be "accessible and effective . . . [with] appropriate judicial and administrative mechanisms for addressing claims of rights violations under domestic law."[100] As shown above, a state's obligation to protect human rights includes an obligation to regulate, through law and practice, the actions of business enterprises that violate human rights. This obligation requires states to regulate their corporate nationals as part of the states' responsibilities under international human rights law.

This obligation is confirmed in Guiding Principle 25, which is the foundational principle of the third pillar:

> As part of their duty to protect against business-related human rights abuse, States must take appropriate steps to ensure, through judicial, administrative, legislative or other appropriate means, that when such abuses occur within their territory and/ or jurisdiction those affected have access to effective remedy.

Interestingly, there is no equivalent foundational principle in the Guiding Principles for access to a remedy in relation to business enterprises.

An appropriate and effective way that states can comply with their obligation to enable access to remedies is to amend their corporate/company law, including in areas such as directors' duties, to regulate the activity of a business enterprise in relation to any of the business enterprise's activities (including extraterritorially and for its subsidiaries) that could adversely impact the protection of human rights. Some states are now doing this,[101] and some states are also extending their criminal law to include corporate activity.[102] This principle could extend beyond corporation/company law to other areas of law as well.[103] As discussed above, laws should also be developed so parent corporations are clearly legally responsible in their home state for the actions of their subsidiaries in other states that occurred due to the subsidiary operating the policies of the parent corporation (for

---

100. OHCHR General Comment 31, at n.20, ¶ 15, *cf.* Guiding Principles, *supra* note 7, at § III.A ¶ 25 (reiterating this standard but also referring to *any* appropriate means). For a fuller discussion *see*, Gwynne Skinner, Robert McCorquodale, Olivier de Schutter and Andie Lambe, *The Third Pillar: Access to Judicial Remedies for Human Rights Violations by Transnational Business* (2013), http://corporate-responsibility.org/wp-content/uploads/2013/12/The-Third-Pillar-Access-to-Judicial-Re medies-for-Human-Rights-Violation....pdf.

101. See, for example, the UK Companies Act 2006 that requires directors to "have regard" to such matters as "the impact of the company's operations on the community and the environment" as part of their duties (§ 172 (1) (d)), and the South African Companies Act 2008 allows the government to pre-scribe social and ethics commitments for companies (§ 72 (4)).

102. *See, e.g.,* Italian statute Decreto Legislativo 231, 2001, and Australian Commonwealth Criminal Code 1995.

103. For example, the UK Agency Worker Regulations (in effect from October 2011) require UK employers to ensure that short-term contract workers (many of whom are non-nationals) have compa-rable employment protections to permanent workers. *Agency Workers: Your Rights*, UK.gov (2013), https://www.gov.uk/agency-workers-your-rights/your-rights-as-a-temporary-agency-worker.

example, on human resource policies, marketing, and finances).[104] This may also be a means to enable appropriate capacity-building support in some economically weaker states.

In addition, states can take international legal actions. For example, the OECD Guidelines on Multinational Enterprises, which were revised to take some account of the Framework,[105] provide for national mechanisms (National Contact Points (NCPs)) to consider breaches of the OECD Guidelines by business enterprises. However, there are no effective compliance mechanisms in the Guidelines to enforce decisions by NCPs. The process relies more on peer pressure of other OECD states or a business enterprise's own willingness to act.[106] These compliance mechanisms need to be stronger and have effective sanctions. These could, for example, link the NCPs more directly into the OECD state's existing national human rights institutions, require the state of the business enterprise in breach not to allow that business enterprise access to government contracts and export credits, or create a distinct OECD Guidelines legal committee with enforcement powers. There is a particular need for these types of powers where business enterprises are operating in conflict zones, fragile states, and regions where governance is weak.[107] Other possible means to ensure increased access to remedies under the current international legal system can be found in areas such as trade, finance, and investment, especially because all these areas facilitate global corporate activity, as discussed elsewhere in this book.[108]

It might be feasible to devise a treaty that would encompass business enterprises' obligations with respect to human rights, in the same way that there are aspects of international law, such as international criminal law and international humanitarian law, that encompass nonstate actors' obligations.[109] Yet this is unlikely to occur without the politi-

---

104. An example is the California Supply Chain Transparency Act 2010, under which companies worth more than a stated amount are required to report whether they are engaged in ethical supply chain management and the extent of this engagement. By setting a volume threshold in capturing companies under the law, foreign companies operating in California are subject to its extraterritorial effect, as foreign companies must report on foreign suppliers linked to California. *See* California Supply Chain Transparency Act 2010, Cal. Civ. Code § 1714.43.

105. OECD, OECD GUIDELINES FOR MULTINATIONAL ENTERPRISES (2011), http://www.oecd.org/daf /inv/mne/oecdguidelinesformultinationalenterprises.htm. *See also* Lahra Liberti, *OECD 50th Anniversary: The Updated OECD Guidelines for Multinational Enterprises and the New OECD Recommendation on Due Diligence Guidance for Conflict-free Mineral Supply Chains*, 13 BUS. L. INT'L. 35, 37 (2012).

106. See the ECCJ, *Fatal Transactions, Cafod, Global Witness, European Office of the Jesuits, IPIS, Briefing for the European Parliament Human Rights Sub-Committee* 5 (Apr. 16, 2009), http://www .europarl.europa.eu/document/activities/cont/200904/20090421ATT54044/20090421ATT54044EN.pdf.

107. *See, eg.*, OECD, OECD RISK AWARENESS TOOLS FOR MULTINATIONAL ENTERPRISES IN WEAK GOVERNANCE ZONES (2006), http://www.oecd.org/daf/inv/mne/weakgovernancezones-riskawarenesstoo lformultinationalenterprises-oecd.htm.

108. *See generally* Andrew Lang, *Trade Agreements, Businesses and Human Rights: The Case of EPZs* (Harvard Corp. Soc. Resp. Initiative, Working Paper No. 57, Apr. 2010). See also chapter 5 on this topic in this book.

109. The SRSG did not preclude or encourage this development. *See* Special Representative of the Secretary-General, OHCHR, *Mandate of the Special Representative of the Secretary-General on the Issue of Human Rights and Transnational Corporations and other Business Enterprises: Recommendations on*

cal will of states—both the host states that gain the investment of business enterprises and the home states that gain the returns on this investment—and the acceptance by the economically powerful lobby of business enterprises that this would be in their interest. Pressure by civil society on states and business enterprises would be relevant in any process. This acceptance is not impossible, though relief on normative action.[110] Though the process of drafting a treaty can be slow, it can be important for allowing many ideas and voices to be heard. It can also operate as part of a pull toward compliance of business enterprises with recognized international human rights legal standards.

Business Enterprises Remedies

In relation to business enterprises' obligations for access to remedies, Guiding Principle 29 provides the following:

> To make it possible for grievances to be addressed early and remediated directly, business enterprises should establish or participate in effective operational-level grievance mechanisms for individuals and communities who may be adversely impacted.

The contrast between this Guiding Principle and Guiding Principle 25 is that the obligation on business enterprises is expressed here as a *should*, whereas that on states is expressed as a *must*. Indeed, though many business enterprises have committed themselves to global, sectoral, or other statements about CSR, some of which include reference to human rights,[111] these are all voluntary commitments, and none of them have any compliance mechanisms with independent dispute settlement bodies. This prevents access to legally effective remedies.[112]

Follow-Up to the Mandate (Feb. 2011), http://www.business-humanrights.org/media/documents/ruggie/ruggie-special-mandate-follow-up-11-feb-2011.pdf.

110. For a fuller discussion *see*, Robert McCorquodale, *Pluralism, Global Law and Human Rights: Strengthening Corporate Accountability for Human Rights Violations*, 2 GLOBAL CONSTITUTIONALISM 287 (2013).

111. *See, e.g., Global Compact*, UNITED NATIONS, http://www.unglobalcompact.org (last visited Nov 28, 2013). The Global Compact includes the following principles that business enterprises should adopt: "World Business should *Principle 1*: support and respect the protection of human rights within their sphere of influence; *Principle 2*: make sure that their own corporations are not complicit in human rights abuses." *See also* the promotion of CSR by the International Council on Mining and Metals. *Sustainable Development Framework*, INTERNATIONAL COUNCIL ON MINING AND METALS (2013), http://www.icmm.com /our-work/sustainable-development-framework. The Equator Principles (http://www.equator-principles .com) and the Extractives Industry Transparency Initiative (http://eiti.org/) are two additional examples.

112. *See, e.g.*, the chemical industry activities discussed in: James H. Colopy, *Poisoning the Developing World: The Exportation of Unregistered and Severely Restricted Pesticides from the United States*, 13 UCLA J. ENVTL L. & POL'Y 167 (1994/1995); Robert Gottlieb et al., *Greening or Greenwashing?: The Evolution of Industry Decision Making*, in REDUCING TOXICS: A NEW APPROACH TO POLICY AND INDUSTRIAL DECISION MAKING (Robert Gottlieb ed., 1995). Regarding the oil and gas industry, *see* Lindsay et al., *supra* note 36, at § 4, Rae Lindsay *et al.*, *Human Rights Responsibilities in the Oil and Gas Sector: Applying the UN Guiding Principles*, 6 J. WORLD ENERGY LAW BUS. 1, 1–65 (2013).

Guiding Principle 31 sets out the effectiveness criteria for business enterprises in relation to access to a remedy (all of which are non-judicial). It provides that these mechanisms should be legitimate, accessible, predictable, equitable, transparent, rights compatible, a source of continuous learning, and based on engagement and dialogue. Though these are very useful and laudable, it can be argued that the due diligence responsibility of business enterprises, especially when related to impacts caused by the business enterprise itself, should, as discussed above, be directly linked to effective, legitimate monitoring and compliance mechanisms regulated by law and not left to regulation by a self-reviewing system.[113] Of course, such independent judicial mechanisms do not exist in some states, especially in conflict zones and fragile states, and so there is also a requirement for the rule of law to be supported.[114]

Indeed it might be argued that most business enterprises respond better to preventive regulation by a state than to reactive litigation, not least because it reduces uncertainty and risk for the business enterprise. Yet when there is reference to legal regulation of business enterprises, it tends to focus on the possibility of criminal sanctions, especially in relation to corporate complicity. Though a discussion of this issue is outside the parameters of this chapter, this issue of corporate criminal responsibility is particularly problematic because of the requirement in criminal law of showing intent.[115] This requirement usually necessitates that there be a specific individual in a business enterprise to whom the obligation would attach.[116] However, the requirement of individual responsibility to enable access to a remedy for a corporate act is not necessary in many areas of civil liability. Business enterprises, as legal entities, have been held civilly legally responsible around the world for actions that violate aspects of human rights, such as in consumer protection areas and environmental damage.[117] There is also the possibility of joint liability at the international level for a state and a business enterprise, in the same way that it can occur within many states' national laws.[118] All these civil liability aspects of a business enterprise's

---

113. There is also likely to be more consistency if international human rights standards are applied than if they are either nationally based or deal with cultural issues in a different way than international human rights law.

114. For a fuller discussion of the importance of the rule of law in this area, see Robert McCorquodale, *Business, the International Rule of Law and Human Rights*, in THE RULE OF LAW IN INTERNATIONAL AND COMPARATIVE LEGAL CONTEXT (Robert McCorquodale ed., 2010). Also Guiding Principle 7 stresses conflict zones as a major concern for corporate complicity in human rights abuses. *See* Guiding Principles, *supra* note 7, § I.B ¶ 7.

115. See the *Talisman* case and how the construction of an intent requirement in civil law may be relevant in corporate complicity in human rights abuse under the Alien Torts Claims Act. Presbyterian Church of Sudan v. Talisman, 582 F.3d 244 (2d Cir., 2009) (discussed in Chapters 6 and 7 of this book).

116. *See generally* REPORT OF THE INTERNATIONAL COMMISSION OF JURISTS, CORPORATE COMPLICITY AND LEGAL ACCOUNTABILITY (2008); David Silver, *Collective Responsibility, Corporate Responsibility and Moral Taint*, 30 MIDWEST STUD. PHIL. 269 (2006).

117. See Sornarajah, *supra* note 28.

118. *See, e.g.*, Morgera, *supra* note 77.

responsibility in relation to access to remedies should be explored to be consistent with international human rights legal developments.

While the last pillar of the Framework is essential, it is built on the other two pillars and it has flaws, not the least of which being whether there can be effective access to a remedy against a business enterprise when there is no legal obligation on that business enterprise to have a legally enforceable grievance mechanism. There also are issues of costs, standing, and access to justice, which will require effective cooperation between and within states.[119]

Conclusion

The Framework created by Ruggie has made a significant change in the debate about the responsibility of business enterprises for violations of human rights, as assisted by his method of active consultation. There is still a great amount of work to be done to ensure that the obligations and standards recommended are not the very minimum but are a platform for dynamic change, and that, as a consequence, there is support for capacity-building initiatives to assist governments and business enterprises around the world toward upholding their responsibilities. The operation of the Guiding Principles requires more research, especially in how they can be applied on an industry-by-industry basis.[120]

Yet the Framework and Guiding Principles do not fully apply current international human rights law, and they do not fully comply with international human rights law. The state duty to protect human rights does extend to activities of business enterprises operating beyond the territory of the state, despite the hesitancy of the Guiding Principles in this regard. A corporation's responsibility to respect human rights is rightly seen as distinct from a business enterprise's CSR policies, but its due diligence requirements are not elaborated sufficiently in terms of the human rights due diligence standard of conduct. Without legally enforceable grievance mechanisms against business enterprises that abuse human rights, the risk remains that access to a remedy for many people affected by the activities of business enterprises will be largely illusory.[121]

Therefore, legal regulation consistent with international human rights law is needed in the application of the Guiding Principles. Indeed, much of the activity of business enterprises is assisted substantially by the operation of a rule of law. A rule of law requires

---

119. *See* Skinner et al, *supra* note 100.

120. This was done in relation to the oil and gas industry. *See* Lindsay et al., *supra* note 36.

121. *See* Susan Aaronson & Ian Higham, *Commentary: Re-Righting Business: John Ruggie and the Struggle to Develop International Human Rights Standards for Transnational Firms* (2011), http://www .business-humanrights.org/Links/Repository/1007044/jump; Penelope Simons, *International Law's Invisible Hand and the Future of Corporate Accountability for Violations of Human Rights*, 3 J. Hum. Rts. & Env't. 5 (2012).

good governance consistent with justice and human rights, that all actors are accountable to the law (including governments and those with power), that all actors can have disputes settled in an independent and accessible way, and that there are compliance-checking mechanisms.[122] Where there is an effective rule of law, business enterprises can conduct their business aware that there is likely to be a large degree of stability, certainty, and recourse, and hence reduce their risks.[123] Therefore, as noted in the opening quotations, it is essential for both the protection of human rights and the integrity of markets to find the best solutions in law and practice.

---

122. Tom Bingham, *The Rule of Law*, 66 CAMBRIDGE L.J. 67 (2007).

123. See the report from the World Bank on the link between the Rule of Law and GDP, DANIEL KAUFMANN, AART KRAAY, & MASSIMO MASTRUZZI, GOVERNANCE MATTERS (2005), http://www.worldbank.org/wbi/governance.

Chapter 4

International Law's Invisible Hand and the Future of Corporate Accountability for Violations of Human Rights

Penelope Simons

Associate Professor, University of Ottawa, Faculty of Law—Common Law Section, Canada

There is no long-term future outside of a radical cultural shift banning the self-serving Western perspective. . . . The beginning is necessary of a process aimed at the development of a legal system that is much less about creating an efficient backbone for an exploitative economy and much more about a vision of civilization, justice and respect.[1]

Those studying globalization must begin to consider the ways in which globalizing processes intersect with and reproduce preexisting forms of exploitation and exclusion.[2]

Introduction

There is something very wrong with our global economic system, which takes little, if any, account of the environmental and human rights costs of business activity. Such costs are neither internalized by markets nor adequately able to restrain market actors as *external*

---

1.   Int'l Univ. College of Turin (IUC) Global Legal Standards Research Grp., *Executive Summary—IUC Independent Policy Report: At the End of History*, 9 GLOBAL JURIST 1, 3 (2009).

2.   Susan Marks, *Empire's Law*, 10 IND. J. GLOBAL LEGAL STUD. 449, 464 (2003).

norms or standards. As Paul Hawken notes, "The single most damaging aspect of the present economic system is that the expense of destroying the earth is largely absent from the prices set in the marketplace."[3] Meanwhile, Upendra Baxi has remarked that "the suffering of impoverished people is irrelevant to the ruling standards of the global capital, which must measure excellence of economic entrepreneurship by standards other than those provided by endless human rights normativity."[4] Moreover, there is a considerable unevenness of treatment between human rights and environmental concerns. Though it may be possible to discern at least a rhetorical willingness among powerful corporate actors to consider binding legal obligations to address some of the environmental impacts of commerce that contribute to climate change, any discussion of binding international human rights obligations still meets with strong resistance, if not vehement opposition.[5] This resistance has characterized the debate on business and human rights for decades. The current iteration of this debate now occupies a central place in global politics and has been focused around the (now completed) mandate of Harvard professor John Ruggie, the UN Special Representative of the Secretary-General (SRSG) on the Issue of Human Rights and Transnational Corporations and Other Business Enterprises.[6] This new UN special procedure emerged out of the ashes of the controversy created by the draft UN Norms on the Responsibility of Transnational Corporations and Other Business Enterprises with Regard to Human Rights (the Norms),[7] which were unanimously adopted in 2003 by the former Sub-Commission on Promotion and Protection of Human Rights. Their submission to the Human Rights Commission (now the Human Rights Council) sparked

---

3.   PAUL HAWKEN, THE ECOLOGY OF COMMERCE: A DECLARATION OF SUSTAINABILITY 13 (rev. ed. 1993).

4.   UPRENDA BAXI, THE FUTURE OF HUMAN RIGHTS 252 (2d ed. 2006).

5.   At the British Institute of International and Comparative Law Annual Conference 2009, Richard Skinner, CEO of Rio Tinto, remarked that the "nudge and wink" approach (referring to voluntary self-regulation by corporate actors) was not sufficient to address the threat of climate change effectively. However, when asked by the author whether he supported binding international human rights obligations for business, he expressed strong concern about the regulatory burden and costs that would be imposed on corporations by such legal norms. See also John G. Ruggie, Reconstituting the Global Public Domain—Issues, Actors and Practices, 10 EUR. J. INT'L REL. 499, 520 (2004), where he notes that "several major oil companies lobbied the U.S. Congress for some form of greenhouse gas limits." On corporate resistance to binding international human rights obligations, see infra notes 14, 15, and 30 and accompanying text.

6.   Scott Jerbi, Business and Human Rights at the UN: What Might Happen Next? 31 HUM. RTS. Q. 299, 300 (2009); see also Rep. of the UN Human Rights Council, Report of the Special Representative of the Secretary-General [SRSG] On the Issue of Human Rights and Transnational Corporations and Other Business Enterprises, Business and Human Rights: Towards Operationalizing the "Protect, Respect and Remedy" Framework, ¶¶ 3–5, UN Doc. A/HRC/11/13 (Apr. 22, 2009) (where the SRSG discusses how the Framework is beginning to be used by governments, business and civil society).

7.   Rep. of the UN Econ. and Soc. Council, Norms on the Responsibilities of Transnational Corporations and Other Business Enterprises with Regard to Human Rights, UN Doc. E/CN 4/Sub 2/2003/12/Rev 2 (Aug. 26, 2003); and Rep. of the UN Econ. Soc. Council, Commentary on the Norms on the Responsibilities of Transnational Corporations and Other Business Enterprises with Regard to Human Rights, UN Doc E/CN 4/Sub 2/2003/38/Rev 2 (Aug. 13, 2003).

a heated controversy and propelled the issue to the forefront of global debate. Unlike other codes of conduct and multi-stakeholder initiatives such as the Global Compact,[8] the OECD Guidelines for Multinational Enterprises,[9] or the Voluntary Principles on Security and Human Rights,[10] the Norms were drafted in mandatory language, were designed as a basis from which a treaty could be negotiated,[11] and if adopted would have imposed binding human rights obligations directly on corporate actors.

There were some problems with the structure and content of the draft Norms.[12] However, as David Kinley and his co-authors point out in their analysis of the politics behind the draft standards, one of the most contested and polarizing characteristics of the Norms was "their apparent attempt to impose obligations directly on companies, in addition to parallel obligations on states."[13] In fact, the earliest critiques by the business community focused primarily on the fact that the Norms contemplated legally binding international obligations for corporate actors. Thus, the Norms were criticized for their "binding and legalistic approach,"[14] and it was argued that "any shift toward mandatory compliance

---

8.   UN GLOBAL COMPACT, www.unglobalcompact.org (last visited Sep.3, 2011).

9.   Org. for Econ. Cooperation and Dev., *The OECD Guidelines for Multinational Enterprises*, in OECD Declaration on International Investment and Multinational Enterprises (May 25, 2011).

10.   *The Voluntary Principles on Security and Human Rights*, BUS. http://www.voluntaryprinciples .org (last visited Sept. 3, 2011).

11.   *See* David Kinley, Justine Nolan, & Natalie Zerial, *The Politics of Corporate Social Responsibility: Reflections on the United Nations Human Rights Norms for Corporations*, 25 COMPANY AND SEC. L.J 30, 34 (2007). Kinley, Nolan, and Zerial make the important point that the "Norms" were never intended to be adopted in their current form; they were rather "explicitly in draft form, and were brought before the international community with the intention that they would be the subject of amendment, debate and reform."

12.   *See, e.g.*, Larry C. Backer, *Multinational Corporations, Transnational Law: The United Nations' Norms on the Responsibilities of Transnational Corporations as a Harbinger of Corporate Social Responsibility in International Law*, 37 COLUM. HUM. RTS. L. REV. 287 (2006); Maurice Mendelson, *In the Matter of the Draft "Norms on the Responsibilities of Transnational Corporations and Other Business Enterprises with Regard to Human Rights": Opinion of Professor Emeritus Maurice Mendelson*, QC (Apr. 4, 2004), http://www.reports-and-materials.org/CBI-Annex-A-Mendelson-opinion.doc (last visited Dec. 6, 2013); and Rebecca Wallace & Olga Martin-Ortega, *The UN Norms: A First Step to Universal Regulation of Transnational Corporations' Responsibilities for Human Rights?* 26 DUBLIN U.L.J. 304 (2004). *See also* David Kinley & Rachel Chambers, *The UN Human Rights Norms for Corporations: The Private Implications of Public International Law*, 6 HUM. RTS. L. REV. 447 (2006).

13.   Kinley et al., *supra* note 11, at 35.

14.   Rep. of the UN Econ. and Soc. Council, *Joint Written Statement Submitted by the International Chamber of Commerce and the International Organization of Employers, Non-Governmental Organizations in General Consultative Status*, at 2, UN Doc. E/CN.4/Sub.2/2003/NGO/44 (July 24, 2003). The ICC and IOE argued that this approach "will not meet the diverse needs and circumstances of companies and will limit the innovation and creativity shown by companies in addressing human rights issues in the context of their efforts to find practical and workable solutions to corporate responsibility challenges. The approach taken by the draft norms is bound to conflict with company policies and practices based on history, culture, philosophy and laws and regulations of the countries in which they operate. To be effective and relevant to a company's specific circumstances, business principles and responsibilities should be developed and implemented by the companies themselves."

would violate accepted international practices."[15] Subsequent critiques of the Norms have focused on more technical issues.[16]

Throughout his tenure as SRSG, Ruggie skillfully avoided the controversy created by the Norms. He made the decision early in his first mandate to leave them behind, dismissing them as a "distraction."[17] Adopting an approach he termed "principled pragmatism,"[18] he trod a careful and strategic path, consulting with a wide range of stakeholders and keeping business and government on the side.

In May 2011, at the end of his second mandate, Ruggie submitted his Guiding Principles on Business and Human Rights.[19] These principles are intended to implement his Protect, Respect, and Remedy policy framework, elaborated in his 2008 report[20] and further developed in his 2009[21] and 2010[22] reports. The policy framework and Guiding Principles focus on addressing the regulatory gaps in relation to the human rights impacts of business activity and, in particular, business activity in so-called "Third World"[23] states.

---

15.   Alan Boyd, *Multinationals and Accountability*, ASIA TIMES ONLINE (Aug. 19, 2003), www.atimes .com/atimes/Global_Economy/EH19Dj01.html.

16.   *See supra* note 12.

17.   Rep. of the UN Econ. and Soc. Council, *Interim Report of the Special Representative of the Secretary-General [SRSG] on the Issue of Human Rights and Transnational Corporations and Other Business Enterprises* , ¶ 69, UN Doc E/CN 4/2006/97 (Feb. 2006). *See* the next section, below.

18.   *Id.* at 81. *See also* Rep. of the UN Human Rights Council, *Report of the Special Representative of the Secretary General [SRSG] On the Issue of Human Rights and Transnational Corporations and Other Business Enterprises, John Ruggie, Business and Human Rights: Further Steps Toward the Operationalization of the "Protect, Respect and Remedy" Framework*, ¶¶ 4–15, UN Doc A/HRC/14/27 (April 9, 2010).

19.   Rep. of the UN Human Rights Council, *Guiding Principles on Business and Human Rights: Implementing the United Nations "Protect, Respect and Remedy" Framework: Report of the Special Representative of the Secretary-General [SRSG] on the Issue of Human Rights and Transnational Corporations and other Business Enterprises*, UN Doc. A/HRC/17/31 (Mar. 21, 2011) (by John Ruggie).

20.   Rep. of the UN Human Rights Council, *Protect, Respect and Remedy: A Framework for Business and Human Rights: Report of the Special Representative of the Secretary-General [SRSG] on the Issue of Human Rights and Transnational Corporations and Other Business Enterprises*, UN Doc. A/ HRC/8/5 (Apr. 7, 2008) (by John Ruggie).

21.   SRSG, 2009 report, *supra* note 6.

22.   SRSG, 2010 report, *supra* note 18.

23.   In this article, I adopt the term *Third World* states as opposed to *developing* states or the *Global South*. The term has been embraced by Third World Approaches to International Law (TWAIL) scholars and is used in both a descriptive and normative sense. *See* Karin Mickelson, *Rhetoric and Rage: Third World Voices in International Legal Discourse*, 16 WIS. INT'L L.J. 353, 360 (1998). Makau Mutua explains that *Third World* "describes a set of geographic, oppositional, and political realities that distinguish it from the West. It is a historical phenomenon that has a dialectic relationship with Europe in particular and the West in general. The Third World is more truly a stream of similar historical experiences across virtually all non-European societies that have given rise to a particular voice, a form of intellectual and political consciousness. The term Third World is different from less-developed, crisis-prone, industrialising, developing, underdeveloped, or the South because it correctly captures the oppositional dialectic between the European and non-European, and identifies the plunder of the latter by the former. It places the state of crisis of the world on the global order that the West has created and dominates." Makau Mutua, *What Is TWAIL?* 94 AM. SOC'Y INT'L L. PROC. 31, 35 (2000). See also Bhupinder S. Chimni, who states that "because legal imagination and technology tend to transcend differences in order to impose uniform global

One cannot dispute the significance of Ruggie's contribution to the global dialogue on corporate accountability. In addition to his articulation of the policy framework and Guiding Principles aimed at the framework's operationalization, the work of the SRSG has been invaluable for the volume of studies commissioned on key issues related to corporate human rights accountability, the comprehensive mapping of current international standards and so-called "governance gaps,"[24] and importantly, the bridges Ruggie has built to bring states and business back to the table.[25]

However, although it was within the scope of his mandates to do so,[26] neither the policy framework nor the Guiding Principles elaborate a role for binding international human rights obligations for business actors. Beyond making a recommendation to the HRC for the establishment of an international process to clarify legal standards relating to egregious violations of human rights that amount to international crimes—which are already widely accepted to be applicable to business entities—Ruggie did not recommend that, going forward, the UN strategy for addressing corporate human rights impunity should include the goal of developing international legal obligations for business entities.

Both the 2008 policy framework and the Guiding Principles were well received by the HRC[27] and the business community.[28] The fact that these documents failed to include a

---

legal regimes, the use of the category 'third world' is particularly appropriate in the world of international law. It is a necessary and effective response to the abstractions that do violence to difference. Its presence is, to put it differently, crucial to organizing and offering collective resistance to hegemonic policies." Bhupinder Chimni, *Third World Approaches to International Law: A Manifesto*, in THE THIRD WORLD AND INTERNATIONAL ORDER: LAW POLITICS AND GLOBALIZATION 49 (Antony Anghie et al. eds., 2003).

24.   This term was first used in this context by Georgette Gagnon, Audrey Macklin, and Penelope Simons, *Deconstructing Engagement: Corporate Self-Regulation in Conflict Zones—Implications for Human Rights and Canadian Public Policy* (U. of Toronto Pub. L. Res. Paper No. 04–07, 2003), http://papers.ssrn.com/sol3/papers.cfm?abstract_id=557002.

25.   SRSG 2010 report, *supra* note 18, at ¶ 15. The SRSG makes reference to this fact in his 2010 Report noting that his approach of "[p]rincipled pragmatism has helped turn a previously divisive debate into constructive dialogues and practical action paths."

26.   *See* Human Rights Council Res. 8/7, *Mandate of the Special Representative of the Secretary-General on the Issue of Human Rights and Transnational Corporations and Other Business Enterprises*, 4(a)-(c), 28th meeting, UN Doc. A/HRC/RES/8/7 (June 18, 2008).

27.   Jerbi points out that "with 28 countries joining the 12 cross-regional co-sponsors of the resolution and passage without a vote, the Human Rights Council's endorsement of the Guiding Principles could not be stronger." *See* Scott Jerbi, *UN Adopts Guiding Principles on Business and Human Rights—What Comes Next?* INST. FOR HUMAN RIGHTS & BUS. (June 17, 2011), www.ihrb.org/commentary/staff /un_adopts_guiding_principles_on_business_and_human_rights.html).

28.   On the Guiding Principles, *see, e.g.*, Int'l Org. of Emp'rs, Address to the UN Human Rights Council, delivered at the Palais des Nations in Geneva, Switzerland (May 31, 2011), webcast.un.org/ ramgen/ondemand/conferences/unhrc/seventeenth/hrc110531am1-eng.rm?start=01:59:04&end=02:02:45, which "[s]upports the approach taken in the principles to elaborate the implications of existing standards and practice into practical guidance rather than seeking to create new international legal obligations or seek to assign legal liability." See also the range of letters from business actors endorsing the Guiding Principles, including Coca-Cola (statement by Edward Potter, personal communication (May 26, 2011), www.global-businessinitiative.org/SRSGpage/files/Guiding%20Principles%20Endorsement%20from %20Coke.pdf); and Total (statement by Peter Herbl, personal communication (May 23, 2011), www .global-business-initiative.org/SRSGpage/files/Total%20S%20A%20letter%20to%20John%20Ruggie

call for the development of new international legal obligations for corporations likely contributed to their favorable reception.[29] Indeed, from the adoption of the UN Norms by the Sub-Commission on the Promotion and Protection of Human Rights to the end of the SRSG's six-year tenure, the business community has consistently opposed the development of such binding standards.[30] On the other hand, the work of the SRSG has been criticized by others (mainly less powerful stakeholders such as NGOs and some Third World states) who would have preferred that the SRSG go further and include some reference to the role of such binding human rights obligations within his overall strategy for addressing corporate human rights impunity.[31]

This chapter will argue that Ruggie's approach to addressing this crucial issue was misconceived and that the product of his two mandates may now allow the HRC and the global business community (six years on) to embrace principles that remain problematic—due

---

.pdf). On the 2008 Framework, *see, e.g.*, Rep. of the Int'l Chamber of Commerce, Int'l Org. of Emp'rs & Bus. and Indus. Advisory Comm. to the OECD, *Joint Initial Views of the International Organisation of Employers (IOE), the International Chamber of Commerce (ICC) and the Business and Industry Advisory Committee to the OECD (BIAC) to the Eighth Session of the Human Rights Council on the Third Report of the Special Representative of the UN Secretary-General on Business and Human Rights*" (May 2008), www.reports-and-materials.org/Letter-IOE-ICC-BIAC-re-Ruggie-report-May-2008.pdf.

29. The International Organization of Employers noted in its statement to the HRC that it supported "the approach taken in the principles to elaborate the implications of existing standards and practice into practical guidance rather than seeking to create new international legal obligations or seek to assign legal liability." *Id. See also* Memorandum from Weil, Gotshal and Manges LLP, Memorandum: Corporate Social Responsibility for Human Rights: Comments on the UN Special Representative's Report Entitled "Protect, Respect and Remedy: A Framework for Business and Human Rights" (May 22, 2008), *www*.reports-andmaterials.org/Weil-Gotshal-legal-commentary-on-Ruggie-report-22-May-2008.pdf. The memorandum states that business should support the "Protect, Respect and Remedy" Framework: "We believe the basic concepts embodied in the Report are sound and should be supported by the business community in the United States for the reasons elaborated in this memorandum. Those reasons can be summarized as follows: . . . [if] taken seriously by foreign governments and foreign companies, it will benefit U.S. corporations by leveling the playing field in placing on foreign boards and management the responsibilities to adhere to many of the same fiduciary and binding legal obligations presently applicable to U.S. companies. U.S. companies will find no new legal obligations advocated by the Report."

30. *See supra* notes 14 and 15 and accompanying text. *See, e.g.*, Comments on the Mandate for the Special Representative of the Secretary-General on the Issue of Human Rights and Transnational Corporations and Other Business Enterprises, in letter dated Dec. 20, 2010, from John Cyr, Partner, Hogan Lovells LLP addressed to John Ruggie, Special Representative of the Secretary-General (Dec. 2010), *www*.business-humanrights.org/media/documents/talisman-comments-on-guiding-principles-dec-2010.pdf.

31. *See* Mauricio Montalvo (Ecuador), Address to the UN Human Rights Council, delivered at the Palais des Nations in Geneva, Switzerland (June 16, 2011), webcast.un.org/ramgen/ondemand/conferences/unhrc/seventeenth/hrc110616pm3-eng.rm?start=00:13:33&end=00:16:32; and the comments of the South African representative. Information release, UN Human Rights Council, Council Holds Dialogue with Experts on Summary Executions, Independence of Judges and Lawyers, Transnational Corporations (May 30, 2011), *www*.ohchr.org/EN/NewsEvents/Pages/DisplayNews.aspx?NewsID=11082&LangID=E; *see also* Amnesty Int'l, Submission to the Special Representative of the Secretary-General on the Issue of Human Rights and Transnational Corporations and Other Business Enterprises (July 2008), *www*.business-humanrights.org/Documents/RuggieHRC2008; Joint NGO Statement to the Eighth Session of the Human Rights Council: Third Report of the Special Representative of the Secretary-General on Human Rights and Transnational Corporations and Other Business Enterprises (May 19, 2008), www.hrw.org/en/news/2008/05/19/joint-ngo-statement-eighth-session-human-rights-council.

to their inadequate standards and the lack of oversight mechanisms[32]—without having to take any real steps toward effectively dealing with corporate accountability. According to Ruggie, "The root cause of the business and human rights predicament today lies in the governance gaps created by globalization—between the scope and impact of economic forces and actors, and the capacity of societies to manage their adverse consequences." These gaps, he has argued, create a "permissive environment for the wrongful acts by companies of all kinds without adequate sanctioning or reparation."[33] It will be argued here, however, that to address corporate impunity effectively, one cannot simply deal with the governance gaps alone. One must also identify and address the root causes of those gaps.

This chapter contends that corporate human rights impunity is deeply embedded in the international legal system. It begins (in the following section) by assessing the SRSG's approach to binding international legal obligations for business entities. The next section analyses the "Protect, Respect and Remedy" policy framework and the Guiding Principles in light of Ruggie's focus on strengthening host-state governance capacity. Then the sections on Governance Capacity and on Feminist Insights will seek to demonstrate the problems with the SRSG's approach by arguing that, along with the interventions of international financial institutions in the economies of developing states, one of the most significant impediments to corporate human rights accountability is the structure of the international legal system itself. An examination of the critiques of the international legal system by Third World Approaches to International Law (TWAIL) scholars, as well as insights drawn from feminist critiques of international law, will explore the validity of this assertion. It will be contended that powerful states have used international law and international institutions to create a globalized legal environment that protects and facilitates corporate activity. The final section will argue that although the SRSG identified symptoms of this reality during his tenure,[34] he did not examine the deep structural aspects of this problem. As will become clear below, such an examination by the SRSG would have revealed the crucial need for binding international human rights obligations for business entities in any adequate strategy aimed at addressing corporate impunity. The article will conclude with some recommendations for developing such obligations incrementally.

---

32. Press Release, Human Rights Watch, UN Human Rights Council: Weak Stance on Business Standards (June 16, 2011), http://www.hrw.org/news/2011/06/16/un-human-rights-council-weak-stance-business-standards.

33. SRSG, Protect, Respect, and Remedy, *supra* note 20, at ¶ 3.

34. *Id.*

Binding Obligations for Corporate Actors and the Approach of the SRSG

Throughout his mandate, the SRSG implied that binding international obligations for corporate actors might be included in his strategy to address corporate human rights impunity. In his 2006 report to the Human Rights Committee, Ruggie suggested that there might be limited circumstances in which it would be helpful to impose international legal obligations on business actors, particularly in situations where the host state is unable or unwilling to regulate the human rights impacts of these entities.[35] Making reference to the Norms and to his decision that they were unhelpful to the advancement of the mandate,[36] Ruggie maintained that he had not ruled out the possibility that international obligations could have a place in his recommendations:

> Nothing that has been said here should be taken to imply that innovative solutions to the challenges of business and human rights are not necessary or that the further evolution of international and domestic legal principles in relation to corporations will not form part of those solutions.[37]

He also noted that "international instruments may well have a significant role to play in this process, but as carefully crafted precision tools complementing and augmenting existing institutional capacities."[38] His policy framework, he has stated, "offers a platform for generating cumulative and sustainable progress without foreclosing further development of international law."[39] Yet despite his contention that he had not written binding international obligations out of his plan, the final report of the SRSG's first mandate;[40] the first two reports of his second mandate (2009 and 2010),[41] which build on this framework; and the Guiding Principles[42] do not outline any concrete role for international legal obligations for corporations.[43] Admittedly, Ruggie did propose that the HRC establish a process for clarifying "the applicability to business enterprises of international standards

---

35.   SRSG, 2006 report, *supra* note 17, at ¶ 65.

36.   *Id.*at ¶ 69.

37.   *Id.*

38.   John G. Ruggie, *Business and Human Rights: The Evolving International Agenda*, 101 Am. J. Int'l L 819, 839 (2007).

39.   John G. Ruggie, *Treaty Road Not Travelled*, Ethical Corp. 42, 43 (May 2008).

40.   SRSG, Guiding Principles, *supra* note 19.

41.   SRSG, 2009 report, *supra* note 6; SRSG, 2010 report, *supra* note 18.

42.   SRSG, 2010 report *id.*

43.   Prior to his appointment as SRSG in 2005, Ruggie wrote that "there is little chance of transnational firms becoming subject to legally binding regulations at the global level any time soon; the political will or even capacity simply is not there, and much of the corporate world would unite to fight it." John G. Ruggie, *supra* note 5, at 518.

prohibiting gross violations of human rights abuses, potentially amounting to the level of international crimes."[44] One of the three options he put forward was "an intergovernmental process of drafting a new international legal instrument to address the specific challenges posed by this protection gap."[45] However, in his presentation of the Guiding Principles and the recommendations for follow-up on his mandate, Ruggie warned that although

> the law must continue to evolve and keep pace with—indeed to guide—socio-economic changes and normative aspirations . . . any attempt to squeeze all elements of business and human rights into an all-encompassing international legal instrument would quickly take us back to the contentious pre-2005 days, and thus be counterproductive.[46]

Outside the formal UN reports, the SRSG actually pushed back against calls for binding international human rights obligations for corporate actors. He argued that short-term action was needed and that "there are bodies of law and regulation applicable to business that have greater leverage over business practices, and in a shorter span of time, than traditional international human rights law, and that the human rights community needs to take advantage of those opportunities."[47] He focused on measures he saw as both effective and feasible.[48] His justification for not calling for binding obligations was premised on the idea that there was an expectation among civil society organizations and other stakeholders of immediate action on such a treaty. For Ruggie, the slowness of international treaty negotiations, the risk that such a process would undermine shorter-term measures to elevate corporate human rights standards, and the problem of how such obligations would be enforced were important reasons not to recommend the negotiation and adoption of a treaty that would impose international legal obligations on corporate actors.[49] Though there appears to be no international consensus concerning the establishment of such international obligations,[50] this would not have prevented the inclusion of a recommendation

---

44. Rep. of the UN Human Rights Council, *Special Representative of the Secretary-General (SRSG) on the Issue of Human Rights and Transnational Corporations and Other Business Enterprises: Recommendations on Follow-Up to the Mandate*, at 4 (Feb. 11, 2011), *www*.business-humanrights.org/media /documents/ruggie/ruggie-special-mandate-follow-up-11-feb-2011.pdf.

45. *Id.* at 5.

46. Professor John G. Ruggie, *Presentation of Report to United Nations Human Rights Council* (May 30, 2011), http://www.business-humanrights.org/media/documents/ruggie-statement-t-oun-human-rights-council-30-may-2011.pdf.

47. John G. Ruggie, Response, *Response by John Ruggie to Misereor/Global Policy Forum*: "Problematic Pragmatism—The Ruggie Report 2008: Background, Analysis and Perspectives" (2008), www .reports-and-materials.org/Ruggie-response-to-Misereor-GPF-2-Jun-2008.pdf.

48. Remarks by SRSG John Ruggie, for the conference on "Business and Fundamental Rights: The State Duty to Protect and Domestic Legal Reform," at 6, South African Institute for Advanced Constitutional, Public, Human Rights and International Law, Johannesburg (Nov. 3, 2008), *available at* 198.170.85.29/Ruggie-remarks-South-Africa-3-Nov-2008.pdf.

49. Ruggie, Treatie Road, *supra* note 39, at 42.

50. "Legally-binding standards in the form of a comprehensive human rights treaty addressing the

for the future development of binding international human rights obligations as part of an overall strategy to address corporate impunity. Indeed such a recommendation could have helped to develop such consensus.

Ruggie has even urged the international community to move beyond the focus on international corporate human rights obligations.[51] Such responsibilities on their own, he observes, "cannot fix larger imbalances in the system of global governance," which he notes, quoting Iris Marion Young, "are the product of the mediated actions of many."[52] Yet although such obligations are clearly not a panacea, this statement does not adequately explain why a recommendation to develop such obligations in the future did not find a place in his framework or in the recommendations for the follow-up to his mandate. In his critique of the UN Norms, he went so far as to suggest that binding international human rights obligations could themselves undermine the governance capacity of states by weakening "domestic political incentives to make governments more responsive and responsible to their own citizenry,"[53] an argument that has also been made by the business community.[54]

The "Protect, Respect and Remedy" Policy Framework, the Guiding Principles, and Governance Capacity

For Ruggie, an important first step in addressing corporate human rights impunity was the further elucidation and codification of the state *duty to protect*. This exercise, he argued, would help to clarify where direct legal obligations for corporations might be needed.[55] Accordingly, the "Protect, Respect and Remedy" framework aims to provide a coherent approach to addressing governance gaps and overcoming the problems of individual action by states and corporate actors;[56] the framework also aims to provide a means by which to develop the normative content of corporate responsibility for human rights. The framework focuses on three pillars: the further development of the state duty to protect under international human rights law; the clarification of the moral responsibility of

---

obligations of corporate actors seem to be completely off the agenda for the foreseeable future. Most governments still have not publicly indicated their positions on this issue or otherwise signaled that a treaty addressing business responsibilities is of particular urgency." Jerbi, *supra* note 6, at 316.

51. Ruggie, Evolving International Agenda, *supra* note 38, at 839.

52. *Id.*

53. *Id.* at 826, 838.

54. *See* Joint Written Statement of the ICC and IOE, *supra* note 14, at 3: "The IOE and ICC strongly believe that the establishment of the legal framework for protecting human rights and its enforcement is a task for national governments. Indeed, to the extent that the draft norms divert the attention and resources of national governments away from implementing their existing obligations on human rights—obligations intended to protect all citizens not just those doing business with foreign enterprises—they would do more harm than good."

55. Ruggie, Evolving International Agenda, *supra* note 38, at 838–39.

56. SRSG, *supra* note 19, at ¶ 17.

corporate actors to respect human rights; and the development of remedies for victims of corporate violations of human rights.[57] The framework and its further development, or "operationalization" in the 2009 and 2010 reports, along with the Guiding Principles go some way to addressing aspects of the problem of corporate human rights impunity. This includes disentangling and clarifying the respective human rights obligations of states under international human rights law and the moral responsibility of corporations to respect human rights (to do no harm); suggesting a range of important policy areas on which both home and host states should focus to ensure that corporate actors respect human rights in their business activities; providing ideas for grievance mechanisms for victims of human rights abuses; and providing guidance to states and businesses on how to implement these policies.

In the 2010 report, Ruggie developed five core policy areas "through which states should strive to achieve greater policy coherence and effectiveness as part of their duty to protect."[58] These are (a) the safeguarding of state capacity to protect international human rights;[59] (b) human rights considerations for states engaging in business with corporate actors; (c) policies for ensuring a human-rights-sensitive corporate culture; (d) guidance for business activity in conflict zones; and (e) the problem of extraterritorial jurisdiction.[60]

Sections (b) to (d) deal with domestic measures to be taken by states, and section (e) deals with the question of the authority and capacity of states to regulate extraterritorial conduct. It is in section (a) that the SRSG specifically addresses problems for

---

57.   SRSG, Guiding Principles, *supra* note 19, at ¶ 17.

58.   SRSG, 2010 report, *supra* note 18, at ¶ 20.

59.   Under international human rights, states have a three-part obligation to respect, protect, and fulfill human rights. The obligation to protect is an obligation of due diligence, which obliges states to take measures to prevent, regulate, investigate, and prosecute actions by private actors, including business entities that violate the rights of individuals subject to that state's jurisdiction. *See, e.g.*, Velásquez Rodriguez v. Honduras, 28 I.L.M. 294 (1989); Herra Rubio v. Colombia (161/1983), HRC Report, UNGAOR 43rd Session Supp. 40 190 (1988), ¶ 11. *See also* ANDREW CLAPHAM, HUMAN RIGHTS IN THE PRIVATE SPHERE (1993); Andrew Clapham, *Revisiting Human Rights in the Private Sphere: Using the ECHR to Protect the Right of Access to the Civil Court,* in TORTURE AS TORT: COMPARATIVE PERSPECTIVES ON THE DEVELOPMENT OF TRANSNATIONAL HUMAN RIGHTS LITIGATION 513 (Craig Scott ed., 2001).

60.   SRSG, 2010 report, *supra* note 18, at ¶ 19. In his 2008 report, Ruggie notes that he is not advocating "specific legislative or policy actions," but rather pointing to key problems (that "deserve serious consideration") and innovative means addressing them. SRSG, Protect, Respect, and Remedy, *supra* note 20, at para. 28. In response to an NGO critique of the 2008 policy framework, the SRSG stated that his discussion of strategies to address the problem of transnational human rights governance was "illustrative material, intended to throw greater light on what the three foundational principles of the framework mean and imply" and that specific recommendations would follow the HRC's approval of the framework. Ruggie, *supra* note 47 In his 2010 report, *supra* note 18, at ¶ 17, Ruggie notes that the section sets out a variety of "possible" measures for states "to promote corporate respect for human rights and prevent corporate-related abuse." However, it is clear from the wording in paragraph 19 ("The Special Representative has identified five priority areas though which States should strive to achieve greater policy coherence and effectiveness as part of their duty to protect") that Ruggie is clearly advocating particular approaches to addressing governance capacity. At the very least, one could state that certain categories of solutions are being emphasised above others. The wording above supports this view.

human-rights governance capacity associated with international law and the international legal system. The SRSG focuses on bilateral investment treaties (BITs) and host-state government agreements (HGAs). With respect to BITs and free trade agreements (FTAs) with investment chapters, the SRSG endorses the view—widely held among NGOs, international human rights scholars, and some international investment-law scholars—that these agreements, which create strong protections for foreign investors (corporations) in host states, can also impose regulatory constraints on these states.[61] In addition, under these agreements, investors usually have rights to bring host states to binding arbitration for violations of the provision of the treaty.[62] As the SRSG observes, through arbitration or the threat of arbitration, "a foreign investor may be able to insulate its business venture from new laws and regulations, or seek compensation from the Government for the cost of compliance."[63] This, Ruggie notes, creates an imbalance between investor rights and the state *duty to protect* human rights. "Consequently, host States can find it difficult to strengthen domestic social and environmental standards, including those related to human rights, without fear of foreign investor challenge."[64] To address this problem, the SRSG urges states that are in the process of, or considering, reviewing their policy with respect to these agreements "to ensure that the new model BITs combine robust investor protection with adequate allowances for bona fide public interest measures, including human rights, applied in a non-discriminatory manner."[65]

Similarly, a study carried out for the SRSG with the support of the IFC identified the potential for HGAs to constrain host-state governance capacity in the area of human rights.[66] These agreements often include stabilization clauses that impose constraints on host-state regulatory change, either by freezing the law of the host state for the duration of the project or requiring the host state to compensate investors for the cost of compliance

---

61. *See* SRSG, Protect, Respect, and Remedy, *supra* note 20, at ¶¶ 34–36. David Schneiderman, for example, states that the key tenets of these type of agreements can operate to restrict the capacity of host states "to regulate and control the inflow of investment. . . to resist the encroachment of foreign influence and distribute the gains from economic development more evenly across a broader socioeconomic spectrum." David Schneiderman, *Investment Rules and the New Constitutionalism*, 25 L. & Soc. Inquiry 757, 758 (2000); *see also* M. Sornarajah, The International Law on Foreign Investment 261 (2d ed. 2004).

62. J. Anthony VanDuzer, Penelope Simons, and Graham Mayeda, *Modeling International Investment Agreements for Economic Development*, in Veniana Qalo, Bilateralism and Development: Emerging Trade Patterns 389 (2008). *See also* Luke Eric Peterson, Rights & Democracy, Human Rights and Bilateral Investment Treaties: Mapping the Role of Human Rights Law within Investor-State Arbitration 15–17 (2009), http://publications.gc.ca/collections/collection_2012/dd-rd/E84-36-2009-eng.pdf.

63. SRSG, 2009 report, *supra* note 6, at ¶ 30.

64. SRSG, Protect, Respect, and Remedy, *supra* note 20, at ¶ 34.

65. SRSG, 2010 report, *supra* note 18, at ¶ 23.

66. Andrea Shemberg, *Stabilization Clauses and Human Rights: A Research Project Conducted for IFC and the United Nations Special Representative to the Secretary-General on Business and Human Rights*, Int'l Finance Corp. (May 27, 2009), www.ifc.org/ifcext/enviro.nsf/AttachmentsByTitle/p_Stabilization ClausesandHumanRights/$FILE/Stabilization+Paper.pdf.

with any new laws that may adversely affect the "economic equilibrium" of a project.[67] As with BITs, the investor corporations often have the right to take host states to binding international arbitration to seek compensation, even if the impugned regulations are introduced for the purpose of protecting human rights.[68] One of the interesting findings of the SRSG-IFC report, highlighted by Ruggie, is that where contracts between investors and OECD host states contained stabilization clauses, these provisions were "tailored . . . to preserve public interest considerations."[69] Conversely, HGAs signed with non-OECD states had stabilization clauses that were significantly more constraining of the regulatory powers of the host state than those signed with OECD states, and these clauses were applicable to a broader set of laws.[70] Moreover, the most constraining of these types of provisions were found in contracts with sub-Saharan African states.[71]

The SRSG notes that the "imbalance" created by these agreements "is particularly problematic for developing countries . . . [and] it is precisely in developing countries that regulatory development may be most needed."[72] He otherwise makes no comment on the wider significance of these findings. In his 2010 report, he simply concludes that "one important step for States in fulfilling their duty to protect against corporate-related human rights abuses is to avoid unduly and unwittingly constraining their human rights policy freedom when they pursue other policy perspectives."[73] Likewise, Guiding Princi-

---

67. *Id.* at vii. Shemberg identifies three categories of stabilisation clause: freezing clauses, economic equilibrium clauses, and hybrid clauses. The latter, she notes, "share some aspects of both of the other categories [of clauses]" and "require the state to restore the investor to the same position it had prior to changes in law, including, as stated in the contract, by exemptions from new laws."

68. For a short discussion of the human rights implications of these type of agreements, *see* Robert McCorquodale & Penelope Simons, *Responsibility Beyond Borders: State Responsibility for Extraterritorial Violations by Corporations of International Human Rights Law*, 70 M.L.R 598, 612–13 (2007) and accompanying footnotes. *See also* AMNESTY INT'L, HUMAN RIGHTS ON THE LINE: THE BAKU-TBILISI-CEYHAN PIPELINE PROJECT (May 2003), *www*.amnestyusa.org/business/humanrightsontheline.pdf; AMNESTY INT'L, CONTRACTING OUT OF HUMAN RIGHTS: THE CHAD CAMEROON PIPELINE PROJECT, 26 (Sep. 2005), *www*.amnesty.org/en/library/info/POL34/012/2005; and Terra Lawson-Remer, *A Role for the International Finance Corporation in Integrating Environmental and Human Rights Standards into Core Project Covenants: Case Study of the Baku-Tbilisi-Ceyhan Oil Pipeline Project*, in TRANSNATIONAL CORPORATIONS AND HUMAN RIGHTS 393–425 (Olivier De Schutter ed., 2006). *See also* Shemberg, *supra* note 66.

69. SRSG, 2009 report, *supra* note 6, at ¶ 32. *See also* Shemberg, *supra* note 66, at ¶¶ 66–70 and Figure 6.2.

70. *Id.* at ¶ 63; SRSG, *id.* at ¶ 32. Shemberg concludes that based on the data, "the economic equilibrium clauses found in the non-OECD contracts on the whole apply to a broader set of laws (and therefore a broader set of social and environmental laws) than do the large majority of the contracts from OECD countries. This means that the contracts in this study from non-OECD countries are more likely than those from OECD countries to result in exemptions for the investor from new social and environmental laws or to provide compensation to the investor for its compliance with such laws." Shemberg, *supra* note 66, at ¶ 132;. *see also*, Shemberg *supra* note 66 at ¶¶. 136–42 (where Shemberg discusses the relationship between stabilisation clauses and BITs); and SRSG, Guiding Principles, *supra* note 19, at 34–37.

71. SRSG, 2009 report, *supra* note 6, at ¶ 32.

72. SRSG, Protect, Respect, and Remedy, *supra* note 20, at ¶ 36.

73. SRSG, 2010 report, *supra* note 18, at ¶ 25.

ple 9 suggests that states "maintain adequate domestic policy space to meet their human rights obligations when pursuing business-related policy objectives with other States or business enterprises, for instance through investment treaties or contracts."[74]

First, leaving aside how this might be accomplished, or whether in the case of some states it is even feasible, protecting policy space for host states will not fully address the power differential or leverage that investors can have with respect to a Third World host state by virtue of these agreements. Even the most powerful states have been subject to arbitral proceedings or threats of such proceedings with respect to the introduction of public-interest legislation that would allegedly have an impact on investors' protected investments.[75] Traditional BITs and other international investment treaties provide the host state with few if any tools to ensure that the investment will support sustainable development.[76] Host states have no means under these treaties to address investor conduct that has a negative impact on human rights. These agreements include no obligations for investors to comply with human rights standards, and there are no mechanisms to regulate investor behavior. These agreements also provide no means for host states to counterclaim in any arbitral proceedings brought against them in which the investor has committed, or been complicit in, grave violations of human rights.

One means of addressing the power imbalance between host states and investors would be to include in these BITs and HGAs legally binding human rights obligations for investors, along with other targeted provisions, that might address a host state's sustainable development goals.[77] Indeed, a submission to the SRSG from the International Institute for Sustainable Development called for the development of "model language that can be included in [international investment agreements] in order to promote the articulation and implementation of human rights values in international investment."[78] Moreover, at least two model treaties have been drafted that include such language.[79] The negotiation of a BIT creates an

---

74. SRSG, Guiding Principles, *supra* note 19, at ¶ 12. The commentary on this principle is cursory and does not provide further guidance on how this might be accomplished.

75. See, *e.g.*, Dow Agrosciences LLC v. Government of Canada, Notice of Arbitration under the UNCITRAL Arbitration Rules and North American Free Trade Agreement (Mar. 31, 2009), www.naftaclaims.com/Disputes/Canada/Dow/Dow-Canada-NOA.pdf. In its notice of arbitration, Dow Chemical claims that the province of Quebec's pesticide ban is an unfair expropriation of Dow Chemical's pesticide operations.

76. J. ANTHONY VANDUZER, PENELOPE SIMONS, & GRAHAM MAYEDA, INTEGRATING SUSTAINABLE DEVELOPMENT INTO INTERNATIONAL INVESTMENT AGREEMENTS: A GUIDE FOR DEVELOPING COUNTRY NEGOTIATORS (Commonwealth Secretariat, 2013) at 20–23.

77. *See id.* at 294–322. *See also* Howard Mann, *International Investment Agreements, Business and Human Rights: Key Issues and Opportunities*, INT'L INST. FOR SUSTAINABLE DEV. (Feb. 2008), www.oecd.org/dataoecd/45/50/40311282.pdf.

78. Mann, *id.* at 39. *See also* VANDUZER et al., Modelling IIAs *supra* note 62, at 409–10.

79. *See* HOWARD MANN ET AL., INT'L INST. FOR SUSTAINABLE DEV., MODEL INTERNATIONAL AGREEMENT ON INVESTMENT FOR SUSTAINABLE DEVELOPMENT (2005). The Commonwealth Secretariat has also developed a guide with simple treaty provisions that includes such language. VANDUZER et al., Integrating Sustainable Development, *supra* note 76.

opportunity to include provisions that not only address policy space but also proactively enhance host-state governance capacity. VanDuzer, Simons, and Mayeda note that incorporating such obligations for investors into a BIT helps to address some of the difficulties faced by host states in regulating investor conduct since it allows for the use of treaty-based enforcement mechanisms, which can complement those available in domestic law.[80]

Regrettably, the SRSG did not recommend such obligations and missed an opportunity to use the goodwill he had developed during his mandates to address this imbalance. His policy framework and Guiding Principles include only moral or voluntary responsibilities for corporations, except to the extent that certain behavior is required by domestic law.[81]

Second, the SRSG's recommendations with respect to BITs and HGAs appear to ignore or to gloss over the power relations reflected in, and created by, these types of agreements, as well as the long history of exploitation of Third World states and facilitation of foreign corporate activity. For instance, in the 2008 report he suggested that in drafting and negotiating BITs, "states, companies, the institutions supporting investments, and those designing arbitration procedures should work towards developing better means to balance investor interests and the needs of host States to discharge their human rights obligations."[82] This assumes that companies will change their method of operation and support measures that may diminish their leverage with host states and increase the regulatory hold over their activities—something that companies have worked hard to avoid since the end of the colonial period.[83]

In addition, in the 2008 report the SRSG puts forward peer learning as one means of providing guidance and support for host-state regulatory control over foreign investors. In particular, Ruggie suggests that where home and host states have extensive trade and investment links, home states could provide technical or financial assistance to host states on the regulation, compliance monitoring, and enforcement of human rights standards.[84] This fails to address the imbalance of power between many home and host states, and in addition, past practice of technical and financial support to host Third World states (whether through international financial institutions, domestic export credit, or development agencies) has often focused on economic policy and regulatory reform to create an environment more conducive to foreign corporate activity.[85] For such technical assistance

---

80. VanDuzer et al. *id.* at 309.

81. SRSG, 2010 report, *supra* note 18, at ¶¶ 55, 66.

82. SRSG, Guiding Principles, *supra* note 19, at ¶ 38.

83. *See, e.g.,* the following section below, which discusses how early arbitral awards were used to remove the contracts between corporations and Third World states from the purview of domestic law. *See also* Baxi, *supra* note 4, at 258.

84. SRSG, Protect, Respect, and Remedy, *supra* note 20, at ¶¶ 44–45.

85. For example, the Canadian International Development Agency (CIDA) played an integral role in the redrafting of the Colombian Mining Code, providing both financial and technical support to the Colombian government. The new law, passed in 2001, "weakened a number of existing environmental and social safeguards and created significant financial incentives [for foreign investors] including dramatically

to work, it cannot be left to the *goodwill* of home states. Rather, a carefully conceived obligation on the home state would need to be embedded in a BIT along with other mechanisms discussed above.[86]

In any event, BITs and HGAs are only the tip of the iceberg. Reimagining these two types of agreements, although an important step forward, does not address the long history of using international law to facilitate business activity in Third World states. As the following section aims to demonstrate, the human rights governance capacity of many Third World states has been undermined by years of economic intervention by international financial institutions and is deeply embedded in the structure of the international system. The history and current iteration of this process will be examined with reference to the work of Third World Approaches to International Law (TWAIL) scholars.

Governance Capacity: International Law and Institutions

TWAIL scholarship considers and critiques the power relationships entrenched in the structure of international law from the perspective of Third World peoples and states. Though by no means homogeneous in their critiques, TWAIL scholars articulate certain common concerns.[87] According to Okafor, the "TWAIL movement within the discipline of international legal studies is best viewed as a broad dialectic (or large umbrella) of opposition to the generally unequal, unfair, and unjust character of an international legal regime that all-too often (but not always) helps subject the Third World to domination, subordination, and serious disadvantage."[88] For Mutua, TWAIL scholarship

> is driven by three basic, interrelated and purposeful objectives. The first is to understand and deconstruct, and unpack the uses of international law as a medium for the creation and perpetuation of a racialized hierarchy of international norms and institutions that subordinate non-Europeans to Europeans. Second it seeks to construct

---

reduced mining royalty and tax rates." *See* Canadian Network on Corporate Accountability, Dirty Practices, Dirty Business: How the Federal Government Supports Canadian Mining, Oil and Gas Companies Abroad 6.1 (2007), *www*.halifaxinitiative.org/dirtypractices/DirtyPractices.pdf.

86.   VanDuzer et al., Integrating Sustainable Development, *supra* note 76, at 291, 499–507.

87.   *See* Mickelson, *supra* note 23, at 360, who describes TWAIL scholarship as "a chorus of voices that blend, though not always harmoniously, in attempting to make heard a common set of concerns [and to articulate] a fundamental rethinking of international relations." Mickelson notes in a later work that one of the aims of TWAIL scholarship is to provide "a substantive critique of the politics and scholarship of mainstream international law to the extent that it has helped to reproduce structures that marginalize and dominate third world peoples." *See also* Karin Mickelson, *Taking Stock of TWAIL Histories*, 10 Int'l Community L. Rev. 355, 358 (2008) (citing the TWAIL Vision Statement).

88.   *See* O.C. Okafor, *Newness, Imperialism, and International Legal Reform in Our Time: A TWAIL Perspective*, 43 Osgoode Hall L.J. 171, 176 (2005).

and present an alternative normative legal edifice for international governance. Finally, TWAIL seeks through scholarship, policy, and politics to eradicate the conditions of underdevelopment in the Third World.[89]

In an increasingly globalized world, "national governments, even the most powerful among them, face growing difficulty in controlling the activities of business."[90] However, it is the Third World states that face the greatest challenges in this regard. In addition, a significant proportion of corporate violations of human rights or complicity in such abuses takes place within these states.[91] TWAIL scholarship therefore provides an indispensable critical lens for examining the problem of corporate human rights impunity and governance capacity.

The Postcolonial Era and Economic Governance

In his monograph *Imperialism, Sovereignty and the Making of International Law*, Antony Anghie undertakes a historical analysis of colonialism and international law. In doing so, he unpacks and demonstrates the ways in which international law has been used from colonial times to the present to subjugate and suppress the peoples of the Third World. Unsurprisingly, the economic interests of European and other Northern states (and their corporate actors) have played a central role in this history. The desire to gain control of natural resources was the driving force behind the conquest of non-European peoples and the establishment of colonies.[92] International legal rules were developed in relation to colonialism to justify and protect those interests. The underlying purpose of international law that was developed in the context of the colonial and postcolonial eras was precisely the promotion and protection of the economic interests of the North.[93] Thus, as newly independent states emerged from colonial rule as sovereign entities and attempted to assert their sovereignty and establish control over their natural resources, Northern states responded using legal doctrines such as state succession, acquired rights, contracts, and consent to protect the interests of their corporate nationals in these states, and to resist the attempt by these new sovereign actors to establish a new international economic order that included their own sovereignty over their natural resources.[94]

---

89. Mutua, *supra* note 22, at 31.

90. Marks, *supra* note 2, at 461. Marks goes on to say that "the question of the significance of this development for nation-state based systems of power is considered by many to be one of the most important political questions of our age."

91. Rep. of the UN Human Rights Council, *Report of Special Representative of the Secretary-General on the Issue of Human Rights and Transnational Corporations and other Business Enterprises, Addendum: Corporations and Human Rights: A Survey of the Scope and Patterns of Alleged Corporate Related Human Rights Abuse*, fig.2, UN Doc. A/HRC/8/5/Add 2 (2008).

92. ANTONY ANGHIE, IMPERIALISM, SOVEREIGNTY AND THE MAKING OF INTERNATIONAL LAW 211 (2005).

93. *Id.* at 269.

94. *Id.* at 211ff. *See also* Permanent Sovereignty over Natural Resources, G.A. Res. 1803(XVII), UN

Anghie notes, for example, that former colonial powers sought new ways to justify the protection of concession agreements, which had often been acquired through coercion or dubious legal agreements based on the ostensible "consent" of colonial peoples.[95] According to Anghie, this protectionism was accomplished through early arbitral decisions concerning disputes between Third World states and transnational oil and gas corporations. Anghie points to two key decisions—the Abu Dhabi arbitration[96] and the Qatar case[97] —that were among those cases instrumental in developing international law with respect to state contracts. These cases, he states, explicitly demonstrate the techniques used by arbitrators to extend the protections for corporate investors, with the effect of diminishing host-state sovereignty[98] and thereby host-state governance capacity. This was accomplished in a number of ways. First, such contracts were removed from the purview of the domestic law of the host state on the basis that no domestic law existed (as in the case of Abu Dhabi) or that such law that did exist was not sufficient for the purpose of interpreting the investment contract in question (as in the case of Qatar).[99] In these and subsequent cases, arbitrators drew on the doctrine of sources to apply "general principles of law" to extend the laws, legal doctrines, and principles of the home state (including acquired rights and unjust enrichment) to the contract.[100] Second, arbitrators began to treat these agreements as having been "internationalized." This conclusion, Anghie notes, was based on the asserted "unique nature" of such agreements and on the fact that they were governed not by domestic law but by an "international law of contracts" drawn from general principles of law.[101] Thus, Anghie notes, by the time the *Texaco v. Libya* award[102] was decided in the late 1970s, these developments had "enabled the effortless transposition of Western concepts of law that provided for the comprehensive protection of private property."[103]

In disputes over these contracts, international law and legal argumentation were also used to alter the relative bargaining power of the corporate actors involved by bringing them onto the same plane as the sovereign states. Accordingly, the agreements, on the one hand, were held to be "quasi-treaties" between a sovereign state and a private actor. By

---

Doc. A/5217 (Dec. 14, 1962).

95. ANGHIE, *supra* note 92, at 211–12.

96. Petroleum Development Ltd. v. Sheikh of Abu Dhabi (1951)18 I.L.R. 144.

97. Ruler of Qatar v. Int'l Marine Oil Co. (1953) 20 ILR 534.

98. ANGHIE, *supra* note 92, at 236. Anghie notes that although "these decisions have acquired a certain notoriety in the field of arbitration, and are now regarded with a certain embarrassment [they are] significant examples because] they raise, in a very explicit form, the crucial issues raised by this emerging field of transnational law for the sovereignty of new states [and the techniques used] were to some extent obscured by the later, more diplomatically worded arbitration decisions." *Id.*

99. *Id.* at 226–27.

100. *Id.* at 226ff.

101. *Id.* at 229–30.

102. Texaco Overseas Petrol. Co. and Cal. Asiatic Oil Co. v. Gov't of the Libyan Arab Republic, (1977) 53 ILR 389.

103. ANGHIE, *supra* note 92, at 230.

contracting with a private actor, it was argued, the states in these situations elevated the corporate actors to a quasi-sovereign entity. On the other hand, such agreements were characterized as private contracts not between a sovereign state and a private actor but between two private parties, thus negating the sovereign status of the state and removing its bargaining power as a sovereign entity.[104] As Anghie puts it, "Whether a quasi-treaty between a sovereign and a quasi-sovereign entity, or a contract between two private parties, what is common to both characterizations is the real reduction of the powers of the sovereign Third-World state with respect to the Western corporation."[105]

This series of developments, among others, ensured that the economies of these former colonies were kept open for business (by Northern states) as they emerged into the international community as sovereign states. This was accomplished by diminishing the sovereign powers of these states with respect to their dealings with foreign corporations through apparently neutral rules applied by notionally independent arbitrators.

Not only was the Third World attempt to reform international law [through its promotion of the New International Economic Order] largely thwarted, but it had to contend with a new set of rules, the "international law of contracts," that sought to expand the powers of the multinational corporations well beyond the powers those corporations had enjoyed under the traditional law of state responsibility.[106]

What Anghie's research makes clear is that a diminished economic governance capacity has been a reality for Third World states since their emergence as states into the international community. Put another way, these states began their lives as new subjects of international law with significantly less control over foreign investment than their Northern counterparts.

International Financial Institutions and Human Rights Governance

One recurring theme that emerges in the TWAIL scholarship is how this history of Third World states and international law is replicated in the contemporary international legal system. As Okafor notes, "Despite the discontinuities that exist in the exact forms and techniques that were deployed, there is indeed a historical continuity from at least the 16th century onward in international law's tolerance of, if not active support for, the negation and/or erasure of Third World . . . agency."[107]

---

104. *Id.* at 233–35.

105. *Id.* at 235.

106. *Id.* at 235–36.

107. Obiora C. Okafor, *Poverty, Agency and Resistance in the Future of International Law: An African Perspective*, in INTERNATIONAL LAW AND THE THIRD WORLD: RESHAPING JUSTICE 100–101 (Richard Falk, Balakrishnan Rajagopal & Jacquelin Stevens eds., 2008). *See also* ANGHIE, *supra* note 92, at 243–44, who states: "colonialism reconstructed itself through new techniques . . . even while reproducing the fundamental structure of the civilizing mission. In this sense, the colonial encounter has ineluctably

For Chimni, what distinguishes more recent developments in international law from the colonial period are the means and manner through which this is accomplished:

> The colonial period saw the complete and open negation of the autonomy of the colonized countries. In the era of globalization, the reality of dominance is best conceptualized as a more stealthy, complex and cumulative process. A growing assemblage of international laws, institutions and practices coalesce to erode the independence of third world countries in favor of transnational capital and powerful States. The ruling elite of the third world, on the other hand, has been unable and/or unwilling to devise, deploy, and sustain effective political and legal strategies to protect the interests of third world peoples.[108]

This assemblage of international laws, institutions, and practices that has transformed the relationship between Third World states and international law, refers to, among other things, the lending practices and policies of the World Bank and the IMF, as well as the growth of international trade and investment rules over the past two decades. Both of these have had significant implications with respect to Third World states' authority and ability to comply with their international human rights obligations.

It is well known that recipient states of IMF and World Bank loans are required by these institutions to implement a particular set of economic policies to restructure their economies and reduce government intervention. The voting structure in these institutions, as Chimni observes, has given Northern states "a dominant voice in the decision-making process, with the result that third world countries and peoples [have been] unable to influence in any way the content of conditionalities imposed upon them."[109] These conditionalities required, among other things, the liberalization of domestic markets (including the lowering of tariffs, the deregulation of labor markets, privatization, and deregulation of business activity) on the basis that such measures would stabilize their economies and enhance economic growth. In addition, the IMF and the World Bank often provided the technical support to reform legal regimes in a manner that would accomplish these objectives.

---

shaped the fundamental doctrines of international law—sources and sovereignty. Further, it has created an international law which, even when it innovates, follows the familiar pattern of the colonial encounter, the division between civilized and uncivilized, the developed and the developing, a division that international law seeks to define and maintain using extraordinarily flexible and continuously new techniques." *See also* Chimni, *supra* note 23, at 47, 72, who argues that for Third World states, international law has not been "an instrument for establishing a just world order," but rather "the principal language in which domination is coming to be expressed in the era of globalization."

108. Chimni, *id.* at 72.

109. Bhupinder S. Chimni, *International Institutions Today: An Imperial Global State in the Making*, 15 EUR. J. INT'L L. 1, 20 (2004).

For example, a study undertaken as part of the *Extractive Industries Review* 2003[110] examined the role of structural-reform programs with regard to sustainable development outcomes in Peru, Tanzania, and Indonesia. The study found that the reform measures supported by the World Bank and the IMF in these states

> tended to concentrate on improving policies and institutions in favor of investors, mainly foreign, without commensurately strengthening policies and institutions for the poor and environment and thereby creating an imbalance. For example, new contract models with fixed environmental costs locked in environmental standards for ten to twenty years.[111]

The study also found that the World Bank efforts to address the social and environmental impacts of reform were limited, and that "the biggest constraint to the effectiveness of these programs has been the lack of leverage with governments and/or weak capacity of governments to ensure implementation of World Bank advice."[112] Despite the bank's recognition of state incapacity in this area, the structural-reform programs were put forward on the assumption that increased foreign investment would stimulate wider economic growth and reduce poverty.[113] The report also concluded that "market, policy, and institutional failures that were either left uncorrected or were created by structural adjustment and policy/institutional reforms" were responsible for negative social and environmental impacts.[114] These institutional failures included the privatization of state hydrocarbon and mineral enterprises and assets before states had developed the capacity to regulate private-sector extractive activity.[115]

In Peru, for example, the increased investment in the extractive sector that followed the reforms was met by a significant increase in public protest over the social and environmental impacts of both mining and oil and gas extractive activity.[116]

---

110. Following criticism of the World Bank Group (WBG) policies by civil society organizations at the June 2000 Annual Meeting of the World Bank and IMF, the WBG President, James Wolfensohn, agreed to undertake "a review of the Bank's role in oil, gas, and mining." The Extractive Industries Review was then initiated by IFC-World Bank Mining Department and Oil, Gas and Chemicals Department. THE WORLD BANK GROUP, STRIKING A BETTER BALANCE: THE FINAL REPORT OF THE EXTRACTIVE INDUSTRIES REVIEW 2 (2003).

111. Heike Mainhardt-Gibbs, *The World Bank Extractive Industries Review: The Role of Structural Reform Programs Towards Sustainable Development Outcomes*, in THE WORLD BANK GROUP, STRIKING A BETTER BALANCE: THE FINAL REPORT OF THE EXTRACTIVE INDUSTRIES REVIEW 6 (2003).

112. *Id.*

113. *Id.* at 7.

114. *Id.*

115. *Id.* at 49.

116. *Id.* at 35. In June 2009 indigenous protesters who were engaged in a peaceful blockade near Bagua in Peru's Amazon region were attacked by Peruvian Special Forces. The violence resulted in 25 civilian deaths and 150 injured. The blockade was undertaken in protest of two decrees issued by the Peruvian president to implement the U.S.-Peru Free Trade Agreement. The decrees opened up areas of

Extractive exploration and activity moved into more ecologically sensitive areas and onto aboriginal lands. Although "[t]he structural reform program supported new mining and hydrocarbon legal codes that strengthened the rights and access of investors to extractive resources, . . . [it] did not address conflicting land classification schemes and thus mining and hydrocarbon rights overlap with protected areas and indigenous reserves."[117]

The structural adjustment programs, development policies, and good-governance policies were premised on addressing poverty and the needs of Third World states. TWAIL scholars, among others, have argued that the development and good-governance policies allowed the World Bank to increase its intervention in these states and give the appearance of protecting human rights while continuing the pursuit of their neoliberal policies. Thus, James Gathii observes that:

> The good governance agenda recasts the neo-liberal economic policies of the World Bank in the guise of a new lingo compatible with, rather than opposed to, human rights. This conception gives preference to economic policy over human rights, unless these rights can be conceptualized within this economic logic, such as openness in international trade, finance, commerce, and reduced social spending in education and health, for example. The World Bank has, therefore, tended to support only those rights that fit within its ascendant laissez-faire commitments. Ultimately then, it is civil and political rights—those most compatible with neo-liberal economic reform, such as private property and freedom of contract—that have received the most support in the good governance agenda.[118]

The measures prescribed also served the interests of foreign investors of the states that control the World Bank and the IMF. The effect of these conditionalities was to relocate the economic governance of these Third World states to the international financial institutions, while at the same time weakening or undermining the ability of these states to undertake social reform, including measures to respect, protect, and fulfill the human rights of those subject to their jurisdiction.[119] Moreover, these programs have played a significant role in

---

indigenous lands in the Amazon to private extractive activity, logging and large-scale farming. *See* Gregor MacLennon, *Police Open Fire on Indigenous Blockade in Peruvian—25 Civilians and 9 Police Dead, 150 Injured*, AMAZONWATCH (June 6, 2009), www.amazonwatch.org/newsroom/view_news.php?id=1837. *See also Deadly Clashes in Peru's Amazon*, BBC NEWS (June 5, 2009), news.bbc.co.uk/2/hi/americas/8086595.stm.

117. Mainhardt-Gibbs, *id.* at 43.

118. James T. Gathii, *Good Governance as a Counter Insurgency Agenda to Oppositional and Transformative Social Projects in International Law*, 5 BUFFALO HUM. RTS. L. REV. 107, 121–22 (1999). *See also* BAXI, *supra* note 4, at 262, who observes that "in good governance stands articulated a set of arrangements, including institutional renovation, which primarily privileges and disproportionately benefits the global producers and consumers."

119. Margot E. Salomon, *International Economic Governance and Human Rights Accountability*

increasing poverty in these states[120] and causing violations of human rights. As Salomon observes, "[d]isaggregated into its component parts, poverty reflects a range of violated human rights and the violation of many human rights is, in turn, a cause of poverty."[121]

International Trade and Investment Law: Entrenching Liberalization Measures

International trade and investment laws are also implicated in this de-territorialization of economic governance and the facilitation of corporate activity. An increasingly sophisticated regime of direct and indirect corporate rights has been entrenched under the various free trade agreements, such as the North American Free Trade Agreement (NAFTA),[122] the World Trade Organization (WTO) agreements, and the large number of bilateral free trade agreements and investment treaties between developed and Third World states.[123]

An examination of WTO law, policy, and practice as well as their impact is essential to understanding the current state of human rights governance incapacity, particularly in Third World states. First, the relationship between the WTO, the World Bank, and the IMF is entrenched in the Marrakesh Agreement establishing the WTO. The WTO has an obligation to cooperate with the bank, the IMF, and other related agencies with the aim of "achieving greater coherence in global economic policy-making."[124] Second, these agreements have had much the same effect on governance capacity as the World Bank and IMF interventions have had. As William Tabb observes, "the thrust of international agreements on trade and investment has been almost uniformly to extend TNC freedom to operate with fewer impediments globally. It is the freedom of sovereign states to regulate economic activity which has been restricted."[125] Studies have shown that the liberaliza-

---

10 (London School of Economics, Law, Society and Economy Working Papers 9/2007), *www*.lse.ac.uk /collections/law/wps/wps.htm. Salomon observes: "These measures are often compulsory, despite resistance by recipient states, with human rights-holders left to direct claims to their enfeebled governments as duty-bearers under the relevant human rights treaties." *See also* Antony Anghie, *Civilization and Commerce: The Concept of Governance in Historical Perspective*, 45 VILLANOVA L. REV. 887, 909 (2000).

120. *See* Howard Stein, *Africa and the Making of Adjustment: How Economists Hijacked the Bank's Agenda*, BRETTON WOODS PROJECT (Sept. 29, 2008), www.brettonwoodsproject.org/art-562552. According to Stein, "structural adjustment has been central to the making of Africa, with terrible consequences. The region has seen a marked increase in absolute and relative poverty. Closely associated with this economic deterioration is a dramatic decline in the health of the population. Average life expectancy dropped from 50 to 46 years from 1980 to 2003. No area of the world has done so poorly and no area has been subjected to more conditionality or adjustment." For a full discussion, *see* HOWARD STEIN, BEYOND THE WORLD BANK AGENDA: AN INSTITUTIONAL APPROACH TO DEVELOPMENT (2008).

121. Salomon, *supra* note 119, at 19.

122. North American Free Trade Agreement, U.S.-Can.-Mex., Dec. 17, 1992, 32 I.L.M. 289 (1993).

123. According to UNCTAD, there are currently more than 3,000 bilateral investment treaties and other international investment treaties. *See* UN CONFERENCE ON TRADE AND DEVELOPMENT, WORLD INVESTMENT REPORT 2011: NON-EQUITY MODES OF INTERNATIONAL PRODUCTION AND DEVELOPMENT 100 (2011).

124. Marrakesh Agreement Establishing the World Trade Organization, arts. III (5), adopted Apr. 15, 1994, 1867 UNT.S. 154, cited in Salomon, *supra* note 119, at 16.

125. WILLIAM K. TABB, ECONOMIC GOVERNANCE IN THE AGE OF GLOBALIZATION 272 (2004).

tion requirements imposed by the trade agreements—which WTO member states were required to adopt as a complete package[126] —can and do have an impact on the ability of states to comply with their international human rights obligations.

The WTO Agreement on Agriculture (AoA)[127] is a case in point. Agriculture plays a vital role in the economies of many Third World states. According to the Food and Agriculture Organization (FAO),

> Some 70 per cent of the poor in developing countries live in rural areas and depend on agriculture for their livelihoods, either directly or indirectly. In the poorest of countries, agricultural growth is the driving force of the rural economy. Particularly, in the most food-insecure countries, agriculture is crucial for income and employment generation.[128]

For Third World states, particularly those in the early stages of economic development, state intervention in the agricultural sector is critical to ensuring agricultural growth.[129] Historically, states have protected their agriculture sectors as they move from early to middle stages of economic development.[130] They have done so by using a wide range of policy mechanisms—including state trading and export monopolies, a variety of nontariff barriers, state marketing boards to ensure price stability for both producers and consumers, subsidies for producer inputs, and credit and government investment in rural infrastructure and agricultural research[131]—most of which are now prohibited under the AoA.

The AoA requires WTO members to liberalize their agricultural markets by eliminating farm subsidies (although certain minimum levels are allowed), reducing export subsidies, changing all nontariff barriers to tariffs (a process known as "tariffication"), and reducing their tariffs on agricultural products. Many Third World states had already liberalized their agricultural markets under the structural-reform programs of the World Bank and IMF. Many of them therefore had few, if any, subsidy programs in place and are now prohibited from reintroducing them.[132] At the same time, the AoA rules allowed certain industrialized

---

126. Chimni notes that "strategies such as the concept of a 'package deal' and the 'single undertaking' (as in the case of the WTO) are used to ensure that third world states cannot opt out of legal obligations that are inimical to interests of their people." Chimni, *supra* note 109, at 25.

127. Agreement on Agriculture, adopted Apr. 15, 1994, 1867 UNT.S. 410.

128. FOOD AND AGRICULTURE ORGANISATION OF THE UNITED NATIONS (FAO), THE STATE OF FOOD INSECURITY IN THE WORLD 2006: ERADICATING WORLD HUNGER—TAKING STOCK TEN YEARS AFTER THE WORLD FOOD SUMMIT 28 (2006). See also Harmon Thomas & Jamie Morrison, *Trade Related Reforms and Food Security: A Synthesis of Case Study Findings*, in TRADE REFORMS AND FOOD SECURITY: COUNTRY CASE STUDIES AND SYNTHESIS 56, 64 (Harmon Thomas ed., 2006); and MICHAEL STOCKBRIDGE, OXFAM, AGRICULTURAL TRADE POLICY IN DEVELOPING COUNTRIES DURING TAKE-OFF 7, 10 (2006).

129. Thomas and Morrison, *id.* at 41, state that "there is ample evidence to suggest that the state needs to play a significant role in stimulating the transformation of agriculture."

130. Thomas and Morrison, *id.* at 22.

131. STOCKBRIDGE, *supra* note 128, at 12.

132. *See* Caroline Dommen, *Raising Human Rights Concerns in the World Trade Organisation: Actors,*

states to keep particular subsidy programs intact and, through the tariffication process, to set high initial tariffs on many products crucial to the economies of Third World states "in terms of food supply, employment, economic growth and poverty reduction."[133]

The impact of the AoA rules is compounded by corporate activity in global agricultural markets. These markets are dominated by small groups of corporations that control almost every sector of the agricultural industry, from farm inputs such as seeds, pesticides, and fertilizers to exporting, shipping, processing, and food retailing.[134] There are no provisions in the AoA or in any other WTO agreement to deal with market structure and concentration of corporate power.[135] Nor does the AoA, or any other relevant WTO agreement, adequately regulate the practice of selling goods at below-production costs—a practice known as dumping.[136] Transnational corporate actors, mainly from industrialized states that control the markets, have been able to benefit from, among other things, protected subsidies that allow them to sell on the world market at below the cost of production, with the result that many Third World states have been unable to compete

---

Processes and Possible Strategies, 24 HUM, RTS. Q. 1, 35 (2002); *See also* Food and Agriculture Organization of the United Nations (FAO), *Issues at Stake Relating to Agricultural Development, Trade and Food Security*, FAO CORPORATE DOCUMENT REPOSITORY (Sept. 1999), www.fao.org/docrep/003/x4829e /x4829e04.htm (Paper No. 4 of the FAO Symposium on Agriculture, Trade and Food Security: Issues and Options in the Forthcoming WTO Negotiations from the Perspective of Developing Countries, Geneva, September 23–24, 1999, 14, Table 2). The FAO states that of a selection of 100 developing states, only 12 reported a base Total AMS above de minimus levels, 8 claimed positive base Total AMS but below de minimus levels, and 80 claimed zero or negative base Total AMS. For more on the relationship between SAPs and agricultural trade, *see* JOHH MADELEY, TRADE AND HUNGER: AN OVERVIEW OF CASE STUDIES ON THE IMPACT OF TRADE LIBERALIZATION ON FOOD SECURITY 7 (2000).

133. Food and Agriculture Organization of the United Nations (FAO), *Synthesis of Country Case Studies*, FAO CORPORATE DOCUMENT REPOSITORY (Sept. 1999), www.fao.org/docrep/meeting/X3065E .htm (Paper No. 3 of the FAO Symposium on Agriculture, Trade and Food Security: Issues and Options in the Forthcoming WTO Negotiations from the Perspective of Developing Countries, Geneva, September 23–24, 1999, 19).

134. *See* BILL VORLEY, INT'L INST. FOR ENV'T & DEV., FOOD, INC.: CORPORATE CONCENTRATION FROM FARM TO CONSUMER (2003); UN Conference on Trade and Development, *Tracking the Trend Towards Market Concentration: The Case of the Agricultural Input Industry*, UNCTAD/DITC/COM/2005/16 (Apr. 20, 2006); and William Heffernan, *Report to the National Farmers Union: Consolidation in the Food and Agriculture System* (Feb. 5, 1999).

135. It appears that much of the consolidation of market power has taken place since the end of the Uruguay Round in 1994; *see* Mark Ritchie & Kristin Dawkins, *WTO Food and Agricultural Rules: Sustainable Agricultural and the Human Right to Food*, 9 MINN. J. GLOBAL TRADE 9, 19 (2000). Even if the AoA has not caused or contributed to the current market structure, the fact that it is oligopolistic and thus will affect competition means that it should be addressed within the WTO.

136. This is true despite the fact that the Peace Clause (which prevented states challenging certain AoA subsidies) expired in 2003 and that subsidies can be and are being challenged in the WTO Dispute Settlement Body. For most Third World states, the use of the DSB to challenge subsidies is not a viable means to address the inequalities of the agreement, given the complexity and cost (both financial and political) of such cases and the difficulties of enforcement. *See* SOPHIA MURPHY, CATHOLIC INST. FOR INT'L RELATIONS, TRADE AND FOOD SECURITY: AN ASSESSMENT OF THE URUGUAY ROUND AGREEMENT ON AGRICULTURE 14 (1999); and Karen Halverson Cross, *King Cotton, Developing Countries and the "Peace Clause": The WTO's U.S. Cotton Subsidies Decision*, 9 J. INT'L ECON. L. 149, 192–93 (2006).

globally against such commodities with their exports. Nor have these states been able to prevent cheaper subsidized goods from undercutting the price of locally produced agricultural products in domestic markets. In both cases, the livelihoods of farmers and farm laborers are placed at risk.[137]

In this way, the AoA has contributed to undermining the ability of these states to protect important economic and social rights, including, significantly, the right to food.[138] The FAO has noted that

> opening national agricultural markets to international competition—especially from subsidized competitors—before basic market institutions and infrastructure are in place can undermine the agriculture sector, with long-term negative consequences for poverty and food security.[139]

Thus the AoA not only restricts government capacity to regulate and implement policy measures in the area of agriculture (measures with important implications for human rights), but it also facilitates corporate behavior that contributes to the erosion of human rights governance capacity. As Orford observes, such measures have further "entrenche[d] a relationship between states and transnational corporations that privileges the property interests of those corporations over the human rights of local peoples and communities."[140] The impact of international trade and investment law on human rights governance capacity—and therefore on the ability of these states to comply with the obligation to protect human rights—is layered over the governance inadequacies created or exacerbated by World Bank and IMF structural reforms.

---

137. For a full discussion, see Penelope Simons, *Binding the Hand that Feeds Them: Sovereignty, the Agreement on Agriculture, Transnational Corporations, and the Right to Adequate Food in Developing Countries*, in REDEFINING SOVEREIGNTY IN INTERNATIONAL ECONOMIC LAW (Wenhua Shan, Penelope Simons & Dalvinder Singh eds., 2008); Carmen G. Gonzalez, *Institutionalizing Inequality: The WTO Agreement on Agriculture, Food Security, and Developing Countries*, 27 COLUM. J. ENVTL. L. 433, 454 (2002); and SOPHIA MURPHY, CAFOD POLICY BRIEF: FOOD SECURITY AND THE WTO (September 2001) at *www*.ukfg.org.uk/docs/CAFOD%20Trade%20Food%20security%20and%20the%20WTO.htm.

138. Numerous studies have assessed the impact of the AoA on the right to food. *See, e.g.*, Jamie Morrison & Alexander Sarris, *Determining the Appropriate Level of Import Protection Consistent with Agriculture Led Development in the Advancement of Poverty Reduction and Improved Food Security*, in WTO RULES FOR AGRICULTURE COMPATIBLE WITH DEVELOPMENT (J. Morrison & A. Sarris eds., 2007); Gonzalez, *supra* note 137, at 454; Dommen, *supra* note 132; Murphy, *supra* note 137; FAO, *supra* note 133.

139. FOOD & AGRICULTURE ORG. OF THE UNITED NATIONS (FAO), STATE OF FOOD AND AGRICULTURE 2005: AGRICULTURAL TRADE AND POVERTY—CAN TRADE WORK FOR THE POOR? 6 (2005).

140. Anne Orford, *Contesting Globalization: A Feminist Perspective on the Future of Human Rights*, 8 TRANSNAT'L L. & CONTEMP. PROBS. 171, 183 (1988). *See also* Chimni, *supra* note 109, at 28, who notes that "an unjust globalization process . . . has resulted in the erosion of the autonomy of third world states in taking crucial decisions of national economic and social life."

Feminist Insights: Corporate Actors and the Structure of International Law

The preceding sections illustrate some of the ways that international law and international financial institutions can be understood to have undermined the ability of states to regulate foreign economic activity in compliance with their human rights obligations. This section will engage in a closer study of the structure of international law and its implications for corporate human rights accountability, and it will do so by drawing on feminist insights.

Many of the TWAIL critiques of the international legal system have their analogues in feminist international-law scholarship. For example, feminist scholars explore how international law and legal argumentation have been used in ways that continually re-create or reinforce a patriarchal and/or colonial international legal system.[141]

Feminist structural-bias critiques, in particular, provide a useful approach to exploring the power dynamics and partiality embedded in the structure of international law. These critiques of international law[142] are premised upon the notion that international law protects male interests and that therefore its structure is biased against women.[143] In their monograph *The Boundaries of International Law*,[144] Hilary Charlesworth and Christine Chinkin show how the gendered structure of international law marginalizes or excludes women:

> Permeating all stages of the [examination into the layers of gender bias in international law] is a silence from and exclusion of women. This phenomenon does not emerge as a simple gap or vacuum that weakens the edifice of international law and that might be remedied by some rapid construction work. It is rather an integral part of the structure of the international legal order, a critical element of its stability. The silences of the discipline are as important as its positive rules and rhetorical structures.[145]

International legal discourse, they contend, is founded on dichotomies such as *public/ private, international/domestic, action/passivity, binding/non-binding, independence/ dependence*. These "binary oppositions" are gendered in the sense that the first term represents male or objective or higher-value characteristics, whereas the second represents

---

141. *See, e.g.*, HILARY C. CHARLESWORTH AND CHRISTINE M. CHINKIN, THE BOUNDARIES OF INTERNATIONAL LAW: A FEMINIST ANALYSIS (2000); INTERNATIONAL LAW: MODERN FEMINIST APPROACHES (Doris Buss & Ambreena Manji eds., 2005); Orford, *supra* note 140; Dianne Otto, *Rethinking Universals: Opening Transformative Possibilities in International Human Rights Law*, 18 AUSTRALIAN Y.B. INT'L L. 1.

142. For a full discussion of various forms and critiques of structural bias scholarship, *see* Karen Engle, *International Human Rights and Feminisms: When Discourses Keep Meeting*, in Buss and Manji, *supra* note 141, at 47–66.

143. *Id.* at 52.

144. Charlesworth and Chinkin, *supra* note 141.

145. Charlesworth and Chinkin, *id.* at 49.

female or subjective or lower-value characteristics.[146] Examining these dichotomies is one means of exposing and exploring the silences of international law.[147] Drawing on these insights, it is suggested that this conception of the structure of international law and its silences provides a valuable analytic tool for understanding how international law and the international legal system operate to privilege and protect commercial activity.

Charlesworth and Chinkin observe that "a variety of distinctions, ostensibly between 'public' and 'private', shape international law and that many of them have gendered consequences."[148] For example, although international law "formally removes 'private' concerns from its sphere, the international legal system nevertheless strongly influences them. One form of influence is the fact that 'private' issues are left to national, rather than international, regulation."[149] Certain concerns that may have an impact on women, therefore, may be left to be dealt with by the domestic law of the state, even where this may result in, or allow for, the subjugation of women.[150] Thus, these public/private distinctions, they argue, not only "characterize the reality of the international community, . . . they are also connected with political choices of whether or not to intervene legally."[151]

In a similar way, international law generally leaves the regulation of corporate actors (private capital) to the domestic sphere.[152] International human rights law speaks to the actions of states and does not directly address the activities of nonstate actors.[153] It also imposes no clear obligations on states to regulate the extraterritorial human rights conduct of their corporate nationals. Nor does it clearly require states to deal with corporate groups in a way that protects the human rights of individuals outside the state's jurisdiction. International law itself views transnational corporate actors as disaggregated entities—each parent, subsidiary, and affiliate as a separate legal entity—each subject to the laws of the state within which they are incorporated or operate,[154] even though these

---

146. Charlesworth and Chinkin, *id.* at 49–50.

147. Charlesworth and Chinkin, *id.* at 49.

148. Charlesworth and Chinkin, *id.* at 57.

149. Charlesworth and Chinkin, *id.* at 56.

150. Charlesworth and Chinkin, *id.* at 57.

151. *Id.*

152. An exception might be bribery and corruption, for example.

153. It is now widely accepted, however, that corporate actors can incur international criminal liability for complicity in or commission of violations of human rights that constitute international crimes. *See* Andrew Clapham, *State Responsibility, Corporate Responsibility, and Complicity in Human Rights Violations,* in Responsibility in World Business: Managing Harmful Side-Effects of Corporate Activity 68 (Lene Bomann-Larsen & Odney Wiggen eds., 2004). The SRSG has also recognised such liability, *see* Rep. of the UN Human Rights Council, *Report of the Special Representative of the Secretary-General on the Issue of Human Rights and Transnational Corporations and Other Business Entities: Business and Human Rights: Mapping International Standards of Responsibility and Accountability for Corporate Acts,* 19–32 UN Doc A/HRC/4/35(2007).

154. James Crawford and Simon Olleson, *The Nature and Forms of International Responsibility,* in International Law 453–54 (Malcolm D. Evans ed., 2d ed. 2006).

entities may, and often do, act as an integrated whole. This lack of direct international oversight has an important impact on how the domestic sphere deals with these actors.

Although a number of national legislatures have considered laws to regulate the extra-territorial impacts of their corporate nationals, no state has yet enacted such legislation.[155] State reticence in this regard is likely due to (or at least bolstered by) pressure from powerful domestic and international business lobby groups and arguments that such regulation would disadvantage their corporate nationals in the global marketplace. This was certainly the case in Canada with the defeat of Bill C-300 in October 2010, which, had it been enacted, would have imposed obligations on extractive companies to comply with certain human rights and environmental standards when operating in Third World states. It would also have established a system of sanctions and a complaints mechanism. The lobbying effort against the bill was led by major Canadian mining companies and mining-industry associations, and it was reported that dozens of meetings took place with ministers, MPs, and civil servants.[156]

Moreover, in domestic law the integrated nature of the corporate group generally remains legally unrecognized[157]—a factor that has significant implications for human rights accountability. Under domestic corporate and company laws, corporate actors may legitimately use a subsidiary to shelter the parent company and other members of a corporate group from activities that may attract legal liability.[158] Even in cases where a

---

155. The most recent example is the Canadian Bill C-300, dubbed the "Responsible Mining Bill," which survived to its third reading but was defeated by six votes on October 27, 2010. *See* An Act Respecting the Extraterritorial Activities of Canadian Businesses and Entities, Establishing the Canadian Extraterritorial Activities Review Commission and Making Consequential Amendments to other Acts, 2010–11, Bill [C-438] (Can.).

156. *See* Bill Curry, *Lobbying Blitz Helps Kill Mining Ethics Bill*, GLOBE AND MAIL (Oct. 27, 2010), http://www.theglobeandmail.com/news/politics/ethical-mining-billdefeated-after-fierce-lobbying /article1775529. *See also* Carl Meyer, *Opposition MPs Who Skipped C-300 Vote Were Targeted by Industry Lobby*, EMBASSY (Nov. 3, 2010), http://www.embassynews.ca/news/2010/11/03/ opposition-mps-who-skipped-c-300-vote-were-targeted-by-industry-lobby/39577?absolute=1, who states: "According to the Office of the Commissioner of Lobbying, this effort was led by Barrick Gold, IAM-Gold, Vale Canada, the Mining Association of Canada and the Prospectors and Developers Association of Canada, all of which were vehemently opposed to Bill C-300." See also the testimonies of corporate representatives against the Canadian Bill C-300 (Canada, Standing Committee on Foreign Affairs and International Development, Evidence, 40th Parl., 2d Sess., No. 032 (Oct. 9, 2009) and No. 042 (Nov. 26, 2009)).

157. It should be noted, however, that certain states have long sought to regulate these groups in areas of taxation, competition law, shareholder, and consumer protection. The U.S., for instance, "has developed very broad theories of the unity or integration of the enterprise, of acting as 'alter ego' or whatever other phrases may have been employed to establish that the foreign parent is in fact present, resident or 'found' in the United States." Francis A. Mann, *The Doctrine of International Jurisdiction Revisited After Twenty Years*, in COLLECTED COURSES OF THE HAGUE ACADEMY OF INTERNATIONAL LAW 63 (1985). *See also* JANET DINE, THE GOVERNANCE OF CORPORATE GROUPS 65 (2000), who notes that the European Court of Justice has taken the approach in competition cases of investigating "the parameters of the [corporate] group structure and the reality of the interrelationships within the group."

158. Rachel Nicolson & Emily Howie, *The Impact of the Corporate Form on Corporate Liability for International Crimes: Separate Legal Personality, Limited Liability and the Corporate Veil—An Australian*

subsidiary is found liable for egregious human rights abuses, "the liability will not nec-essarily attach to related companies and therefore it will not necessarily be the case that a successful claimant can access the assets of the corporate group . . . or the assets of its members and directors."[159] Domestic courts are reticent to *pierce the veil* of corporate groups to impose liability on parent companies for the acts of their subsidiaries.[160] This reticence becomes all the more problematic in cases where the subsidiary (that allegedly committed, or was complicit in, the impugned acts in the host state) is held by the parent corporation in the home state through a number of subsidiaries, each one incorporated in a different national jurisdiction.[161]

Feminist theoretical insight suggests that the structure of international law is such that these entities can exploit its silences, remaining on the margins and navigating between two dichotomously constructed regulatory spheres. In this way, corporate entities avoid both international and domestic oversight, while at the same time gaining robust legal protections for their trade and investment activities. Karen Engle draws an interesting comparison in this regard between women and market actors. Both, she argues, inhabit the margins of international law. But unlike women who seek to be included and protected by international law, corporations and other business entities, operating from a position of power, have chosen to remain on the unregulated periphery, seeking precisely to avoid public international law's interference in their activities.[162]

Perspective 11 (2007), http://www.hrlrc.org.au/files/icj-paper-e-howie-and-r-nicolson-final-0207.pdf (paper for the ICJ Expert Legal Panel on Corporate Complicity in International Crimes).

159. *Id.*

160. INTERNATIONAL COMMISSION OF JURISTS, CORPORATE COMPLICITY & LEGAL ACCOUNTABIL-ITY: VOLUME 3—CIVIL REMEDIES: REPORT OF THE INTERNATIONAL COMMISSION OF JURISTS EXPERT LEGAL PANEL ON CORPORATE COMPLICITY IN INTERNATIONAL CRIMES 47 (2008). The jurisprudence of the courts on this issue is uneven, however they will often disregard the separate legal personality in situ-ations where the latter is "being abused to perpetrate fraud or avoid existing legal obligations." *Id.*

161. Talisman Energy's operations in Sudan, for example, were conducted through TGNBV, which was a 25 percent owner of the consortium, Greater Nile Petroleum Operating Company (GNPOC). Talisman Energy held TGNBV through four other subsidiaries incorporated in two other of jurisdictions. TGNBV was a Dutch company, owned by Goal Olie-en-Gasexploratie BV (also a Dutch company), which in turn was owned by two UK companies—Supertest and Igniteserve—both of which were owned by Talisman (UK), a subsidiary of Talisman Energy. In Presbyterian Church of Sudan v. Talisman Energy, Inc., 453 F. Supp. 2d 633 (S.D.N.Y. 2006), the defendant's motion to dismiss was granted and the plaintiffs' motion to amend their complaint was dismissed. The court, however, went on to analyze the amended claim stat-ing, among other things, that the plaintiff had not demonstrated in the case of GNPOC and the various subsidiaries of Talisman Energy Ltd, that it was appropriate for the court to pierce the corporate veil to find Talisman Energy liable for the acts committed by GNPOC or the various members of the consor-tium, including TGNBV. Talisman had been accused of aiding and abetting the government of Sudan to commit genocide, torture, war crimes, and crimes against humanity. These acts included the creation of a cordon sanitaire around GNPOC's oilfields to facilitate the exploration and extraction of oil, forcibly displacing some of the plaintiffs, supplying fuel to and transporting the Sudanese military, and allowing Sudanese forces to use the consortium airstrips for offensive bombing raids.

162. Karen Engle, *Views from the Margins: A Response to David Kennedy*, 1994 UTAH L. REV. 105, 108–9 (1994). Engle draws this comparison with the aim of critiquing the public/private dichotomy and arguing that like market actors, women can seek refuge, or find their power, in the private sphere.

However, contrary to Engle's conclusion that global business actors operate solely in the private or unregulated sphere,[163] it is clear that these powerful actors are able to play on both sides of the public/private fence. Thus, the regulation of trade and investment—which addresses and circumscribes governmental conduct to facilitate and protect the activities of private capital—is deemed an appropriate matter for international law to address.[164] Unlike women, transnational corporate actors are the privileged insiders of the international legal system, playing key roles in the promotion, negotiation, and drafting of these trade and investment regimes[165] and enjoying remarkable success in resisting and avoiding the "imposition of new human rights norms on their structure and operations."[166] The public/private, international/domestic, and regulated/unregulated distinctions are interdependent[167] and operate to facilitate rather than restrain corporate activity.

Charlesworth and Chinkin, as well as Rochette[168] and others, have also pointed to the gendered consequences of the distinction in international law between binding and non-binding obligations. Matters of concern to women such as the environment and human rights are treated as *soft* issues that are deemed appropriately regulated by *soft*, nonbinding instruments. As Charlesworth and Chinkin state,

> States use "soft" law structures for matters that are not regarded as essential to their interests ("soft" issues in international law) or where they are reluctant to incur binding

163. Engle, *id.*, argues that trade and other business activities fall outside the regulatory space of public international law and within the private or unregulated sphere at the margins of the international legal system. Yet, as Buss points out, this view is misconceived: "Far from being unregulated and marginal, however, international trade operates within numerous legal limitations and may exercise influence over aspects of international law. . . . International law in this context is not seen as repressive, but as necessary to the effective conduct of international trade." Doris Buss, *Going Global: Feminist Theory, International Law, and the Public/Private Divide*, in CHALLENGING THE PUBLIC/PRIVATE DIVIDE: FEMINISM, LAW, AND PUBLIC POLICY 372–73 (Susan B. Boyd ed., Univ. of Toronto Press 1997).

164. *Id.*

165. According to the UNDP, for example, the agricultural industry in the U.S. was able to exert significant influence on "national positions in international trade negotiations." UN DEVELOPMENT PROGRAM, HUMAN DEVELOPMENT REPORT 2002: DEEPENING DEMOCRACY IN A FRAGMENTED WORLD 68 (2002). *See also* MURPHY, TRADE AND FOOD SECURITY, *supra* note 136, at 11, who notes that a former vice president of Cargill (which controls about 60 percent of global trade in cereals and 30 percent of the global corn market) acted as the U.S. negotiator on agriculture in the initial stages of the Uruguay Round before returning to work in the grain industry. Chimni (citing Joseph Nye) states that "the transnational corporations and offshore fund managers are playing a larger-than-ever role in establishing rules and standards. Their practices often create de facto governance." Chimni, *supra* note 109, at 35–36.

166. This, Baxi notes, "is clearly manifest in the recent successful efforts excluding multinationals from the jurisdiction of [the] International Criminal Court, and since the 1970s preventing all United Nations-based efforts at a Code of Conduct for Transnationals." BAXI, *supra* note 4, at 258. *See also* Anna Grear, *Challenging Corporate "Humanity": Legal Disembodiment, Embodiment and Human Rights*, 7 HUM. RTS, L, REV. 511, 514 (2007).

167. Buss and Manji, *supra* note 141.

168. Annie Rochette, *Transcending the Conquest of Nature and Women: A Feminist Perspective on International Environmental Law*, in Buss and Manji, *supra* note 141, at 220–22.

obligations. Many of the issues that concern women thus suffer a double marginaliza-
tion in terms of traditional international law-making: they are seen as the "soft" issues
of human rights and are developed through "soft" modalities of law-making that allow
states to appear to accept such principles while minimizing their legal commitments.[169]

A consistent feature of the business and human rights debate has been the insistence by
states and corporations on *soft* or *voluntary* forms of regulation,[170] and this approach has
characterized the work of the SRSG. In the same way, therefore, the human rights of those
subject to corporate abuses (or business complicity in such abuses) are doubly marginalized by being treated as a soft issue and by the regulation of extraterritorial corporate
activity by *soft* law. In the end, this soft-law approach becomes binding in its result on
the victims of human rights abuses.[171]

International Law's Invisible Hand and the Future of Corporate Human Rights Accountability

The preceding sections suggest that the root causes of corporate impunity for violations
of human rights are deeply embedded in the international legal system. International law

---

169. Charlesworth and Chinkin, *supra* note 141, at 66. Baxi makes reference to the hard/soft dichotomy in the context of the effects of economic globalization, which requires both hard and soft states. A
soft state or "progressive" state "is one that is a good host state for global capital . . . that protects global
capital against political instability and market failures . . . [and one] that represents accountability not
so much directly to its people, but one that offers itself, as a good pupil, to the World Bank and International Monetary Fund." Hard states "must be market-efficient in suppressing and de-legitimizing human
rights–based practices of resistance or the pursuit of alternative politics. Rule of law standards and values need to be enforced by the state on behalf, and at the behest, of formations of global economy and
technology. When, to this end, it is necessary for the 'host' state to unleash a reign of terror against its
own people, it must be empowered, locally and globally, to do so." Baxi, *supra* note 4, at 249, 252.

170. *See, e.g.*, Joint Written Statement of the ICC and IOE, *supra* note 14, at 3; Canada, Standing
Committee Evidence No 32, *supra* note 156, at 10, in which the president and CEO of the Mining Association of Canada testified that there already exists "a wide range of international guidelines and standards
that provide appropriate reference points for the CSR-related processes and issues." *See also* Canada,
*Building the Canadian Advantage: A Corporate Social Responsibility (CSR) Strategy for the Canadian
International Extractive Sector* (2009), www.international.gc.ca/trade-agreements-accords-commerciaux
/ds/csr-strategy-rse-stategie.aspx, which puts forward a voluntary self-regulation scheme for Canadian
companies, with no reporting requirements or sanctions. It includes a complaints mechanism. However,
the mechanism allows for investigation into allegations of human rights abuses by a Canadian company
only in cases where the company consents.

171. Baxi puts it another way, saying that the proponents of economic globalization, have pushed
for "the creation of a borderless world for global capital, even though it stands cruelly bordered for the
violated victims subject to practices of the politics of cruelty, even barbaric practices of power. Myanmar
is thus borderless for Unocal though not for Aung San Suu Kyi and the thousands of Burmese people she
symbolizes. India is borderless for Union Carbide and Monsanto but not for the mass disaster-violated
Indian community. Ogoniland is borderless for Shell but becomes the graveyard of human rights and
justice movements led by Ken SaroWiwa." Baxi, *supra* note 4, at 247.

has been used progressively since colonial times to protect and facilitate foreign investment and trade activity while at the same time undermining the ability of Third World
states to control and regulate transnational corporate actors. The policies and practices
of international financial institutions have played a central role in this process. In addition, the structure of international law itself and international law's relationship with
domestic law are also implicated.

During his tenure, the SRSG identified certain aspects of this reality but failed to
examine the deep structural roots of this problem. Ruggie's focus on state governance
capacity, for example, did not lead to any meaningful consideration of the impact of the
policies and practices of the World Bank and IMF, despite their important implications
for human rights governance.[172] His 2010 report alludes only to the human rights obligations of member states of these institutions, among others, and to the need for changes in
the policies of these international organizations.[173] This recommendation is only slightly
further developed in Guiding Principle 10, which states,

> States, when acting as members of multilateral institutions that deal with business-
> related issues, should:
> (1) Seek to ensure that those institutions neither restrain the ability of their member
> States to meet their duty to protect nor hinder business enterprises from respecting
> human rights;
> (2) Encourage those institutions, within their respective mandates and capacities, to
> promote business respect for human rights and, where requested, to help States meet
> their duty to protect against human rights abuse by business enterprises, including
> through technical assistance, capacity-building and awareness-raising;
> (3) Draw on these Guiding Principles to promote shared understanding and advance
> international cooperation in the management of business and human rights challenges.

The commentary to General Principle 10, among other things, reminds states that they
"retain their international human rights obligations when they participate in such institutions" and notes that "collective action" through such international organizations "can
help States level the playing field with regard to business respect for human rights." The
commentary also suggests that "capacity-building and awareness raising through such
institutions can play a vital role in helping all States to fulfill their duty to protect."[174]

---

172. Some civil society organisations called on Ruggie to address this issue. *See* Canadian Network
on Corporate Accountability, *Submission to the UN Secretary General's Special Representative on Business and Human Rights (SRSG)* 4–5 (July 21, 2008), www.halifaxinitiative.org/updir/CNCA_statement
_re_Ruggie_report-July_08.pdf.

173. SRSG, 2010 report, *supra* note 18, at ¶ 52.

174. SRSG, Guiding Principles, *supra* note 19, at 12. *See also* SRSG, 2010 report, *supra* note 18, at
¶ 52.

Yet given the role of the World Bank and IMF in undermining human rights governance capacity, Ruggie's approach to this issue appears misconceived. A significant cultural and structural transformation of these financial institutions would need to occur for these suggestions (and in particular the latter recommendation) to have any credibility.[175]

For example, an ethnographic study of the World Bank's organizational culture by Galit Sarfaty[176] shows that, despite the bank's mandate to address development and poverty reduction, there is a range of obstacles that have kept the issue of human rights marginalized within the organization. These include the decision-making structure and the organizational culture of the bank. The board of executive directors, made up of member states, acts as the policy-making organ of the bank. Decision-making is generally by consensus. When the member-state governments fail to attain consensus, they have to delegate authority to bank officials. Human rights are an issue over which the board has "been deeply divided," and bank officials have consequently been hesitant to propose a human rights agenda.[177] In addition, Sarfaty notes that there are perceived legal constraints in the bank's articles of agreement and that efforts for reform have failed largely due to bureaucratic obstacles.[178] Consensus building has been difficult among bank employees "from different sectors and disciplinary backgrounds, who held divergent views on how to define human rights and interpret them with respect to the Bank's operations."[179] Sarfaty also points to the bank's organizational culture, which is dominated by economists and in which the prospects for promotion are based on "the approval of projects and the size of those projects in terms of money lent."[180] Thus, the bank's safeguard policies (which address some human rights–related concerns) are perceived by many employees "as impediments to lending because they add constraints to the tasks and thereby reduce efficiency and opportunities for promotion."[181]

With respect to international economic law, Ruggie's consideration of the human rights implications of BITs and HGAs has been discussed in detail above. However, it should be noted that the work of the SRSG does not address concerns raised by the international

---

175. Similarly, Ruggie has suggested that there should be policy alignment between a home state's export credit agency and its development agency. Thus, where an export credit agency (ECA) provides support for a particular project that has "a large physical and social footprint" the host-state development agency could provide support to local authorities in managing the project. SRSG, Protect, Respect, and Remedy, *supra* note 20, at ¶ 41. This recommendation raises serious concerns, given the history of ECA support for projects with significant negative human rights and environmental impacts, their inadequate screening methodologies and the fact that national development agencies have a history of supporting a neo-liberal or business friendly form of "development." See CNCA, *supra* note 172, at 3–4.

176. Galit A. Sarfaty, *Why Culture Matters in International Institutions: The Marginality of Human Rights at the World Bank*, 103 AM. J. INT'L L. 647 (2009).

177. *Id.* at 655–56.

178. *Id.* at 658–59.

179. *Id.* at 662.

180. *Id.* at 669.

181. *Id.*

trade regime's impact on human rights governance capacity, despite the fact that Ruggie flagged this as an issue in his 2009 report and stated that he was engaged in extensive consultations with experts "on whether and how the trade regime may constrain or facilitate the State duty to protect."[182] Notwithstanding this, there was no further consideration of international trade law in the 2010 report. The Guiding Principles do not directly discuss international trade law, although they do recommend that states protect policy space "to meet their international human rights obligations when pursuing business-related policy objectives with other States."[183] Although General Principle 10 would apply with respect to the WTO, there is no specific commentary on how states should go about recovering policy space constrained by WTO agreements such as the AoA, discussed above. In his role as the SRSG, Ruggie did not publicly articulate a clear rationale for why he did not investigate the role of international financial institutions (IFIs) and the global trade regime in undermining host-state governance capacity.[184]

In his work to develop and operationalize a framework capable of increasing state governance capacity and addressing corporate impunity, the SRSG pushed back against calls for international legal obligations for business entities and cautioned that we should

> resist succumbing to what . . . Max Weber called a "means-ends reversal," turning the quest for binding legal obligations into an end in itself before sorting out what means—legal and non-legal, different bodies of law, various areas of public and self-regulation—are most promising for which contexts.[185]

Although the state obligation to protect in the SRSG's framework and Guiding Principles is anchored in international human rights law and includes both binding and nonbinding norms, the norms applicable to business actors rely on soft or voluntary forms of regulation at the international level. As noted above, beyond domestic law, Ruggie's framework conceives of a moral or voluntary "responsibility to respect human rights."[186] General Principle 11 states, "Business enterprises should respect human rights. This means that they should avoid infringing on the human rights of others and should address adverse human rights impacts with which they are involved."[187] To fulfill this responsibility, corporations are to develop a corporate policy commitment and self-regulate through corporate-defined

---

182. SRSG, 2009 report, *supra* note 6, at ¶ 37.

183. SRSG, Guiding Principles, *supra* note 19, at 9.

184. Ruggie was certainly aware of some of the implications of international economic law for human rights and governance. *See* Ruggie, *supra* note 5, at 511–12.

185. SRSG, Remarks, *supra* note 48.

186. The responsibility to respect consists of an obligation to do no harm. According to the SRSG this "is not merely a passive responsibility for firms but may entail positive steps." SRSG, *supra* note 20, at ¶ 55.

187. SRSG, Guiding Principles, *supra* note 19, at 13.

due diligence and remediation processes.[188] The key elements of the human rights due diligence process are set out in General Principles 17 through 21. This process is to be ongoing and initiated at the earliest possible opportunity. It should include assessment of actual and potential human rights impacts, corporate integration and action based on the findings, tracking the effectiveness of the corporate response to the impacts, and communicating on action taken to address such impacts.[189] In relation to impacts amounting to egregious violations of human rights, the SRSG recommends that business actors treat this risk "as a legal compliance issue."[190] Beyond voluntary observance of these principles and except where activities violate domestic law, compliance with such responsibilities is to be monitored and enforced by the "courts of public opinion."[191]

Responding to critics, Ruggie has contended that the distinction between mandatory and voluntary obligations is misleading. For example, he asserts that "there is nothing 'voluntary' about conducting due diligence for companies claiming to respect rights, because there simply isn't any other way to demonstrate it. This is not a matter of law," he argues, "but of logic."[192] However, it is difficult to see how, without the complement of international legal obligations, this privatized voluntary process will be significantly more effective than other voluntary self-regulation regimes in regulating and enforcing the compliance of corporations with human rights norms.[193] The articulation of the business responsibility to respect, including the components of human rights due diligence, is an important improvement on what previously existed, in so far as it creates a single universal standard and will likely ensure more universal uptake, but as this argument implies, it is insufficiently progressive. Ruggie himself remarks that the normative contribution of the Guiding Principles "lies not in the creation of new international law obligations but in elaborating the implications of existing standards and practices for States and businesses; integrating them within a single, logically coherent and comprehensive template"[194]—thus implying (or conceding) that there is insufficient movement here beyond *business-as-usual*.

---

188. *Id.* at 15. *See also* SRSG, Protect, Respect, and Remedy, *supra* note 20, at ¶¶ 56–59.

189. SRSG, Guiding Principles *supra* note 19, at 16–20.

190. *Id.* at 21.

191. SRSG, Protect, Respect, and Remedy, *supra* note 20, at ¶ 54. Ruggie notes that the "courts of public opinion [include] employees, communities, consumers, civil society, as well as investors—and occasionally [compliance will be enforced by] charges in actual courts. Whereas governments define the scope of legal compliance, the broader scope of the responsibility to respect is defined by social expectations— as a part of what is sometimes called a company's social licence to operate." *Id.*

192. *See* John G. Ruggie, SRSG, Address in London: Opening Statement to UK Parliament Joint Committee on Human Rights, 2–3 (June 3, 2009), transcript available at *www.*businesshumanrights.org /Documents/Ruggie-statement-UK-3-Jun-2009.pdf.

193. Corporate actors have become very savvy in their CSR reporting. For a discussion of reporting standards and practices and their effectiveness, *see* Penelope Simons, *Corporate Voluntarism and Human Rights: The Adequacy and Effectiveness of Voluntary Self-Regulation Regimes*, 59 RELATIONS INDUSTRI-ELLES/ INDUS. REL. 101 (2004).

194. SRSG, Guiding Principles, *supra* note 19, at ¶ 14.

Indeed, the guidelines and the follow-up mechanism endorsed by the HRC suffer from some of the same shortcomings found in other multi-stakeholder and voluntary initiatives: inadequate standards and lack of effective oversight. In a Joint Civil Society Statement to the HRC, a group of NGOs (including Amnesty International, Human Rights Watch, and the International Commission of Jurists), while welcoming the progress made during the SRSG's mandate, expressed concern that the Guiding Principles were a step back in some respects from the 2008 framework. They also noted that

[though the Guiding Principles do] provide some useful indication of how states and companies can begin to apply the UN Framework, [they] do not adequately reflect or address some core issues including extraterritorial obligations and responsibilities, the need for more effective regulation, . . . the right to remedy and the need for accountability in a manner fully consistent with international human rights standards. Thus the Guiding Principles alone cannot serve as an overarching set of standards to address the full range of business and human rights issues.

We therefore urge that the follow-on mandate assess the implementation of the Framework as a whole with reference to the proposed Guiding Principles where relevant but also to wider standards and issue recommendations accordingly.[195]

The HRC did not heed this advice. In its resolution adopting the Guiding Principles, it established a working group to follow up on the work of the SRSG.[196] The working group's mandate does not include a complaints mechanism or the power to assess the implementation and efficacy of the Guiding Principles. In a strongly worded press release, Human Rights Watch stated that in endorsing the Guiding Principles and their shortcomings and by failing "to put in place a mechanism to ensure that the basic steps to protect human rights set forth in the Guiding Principles are put into practice, . . . the council endorsed the status quo: a world where companies are encouraged, but not obliged, to respect human rights."[197]

It is important to concede that voluntary self-regulatory mechanisms and multi-stakeholder initiatives are, nonetheless, important tools with which to address corporate human rights impunity, and that these softer norms and forms of regulations can offer flexibility

---

195. Amnesty International, et al., *Joint Civil Society Statement to the 17th Session of the Human Rights Council*, HUMAN RIGHTS WATCH (May 30, 2011), www.hrw.org/news/2011/05/30/joint-civil-society-statement-17thsession-human-rights-council. *See also* Press Release, FIAN, Resolution of Human Rights Council on Business and Human Rights Fails Victims of Transnationals (June 17, 2011), *www*.fian.org/news/press-releases/copy_of_resolution-ofhuman-rights-council-on-business-and-human-rights-fails-victims-of-transnationals.

196. Rep. of the UN Human Rights Council, *Human Rights and Transnational Corporations and Other Business Enterprises*, at 1, UN Doc. A/HRC/17/L/17/Rev (June 16, 2011).

197. Press Release, Human Rights Watch, UN Human Rights Council: Weak Stance on Business Standards' Press Release (June 15, 2011), *www*.hrw.org/en/news/2011/06/16/un-human-rights-council-weak-stancebusiness-standards.

that is not available in the development of binding legal obligations. For instance, as Mutua points out, the special representative on internally displaced persons (IDPs) had argued that rather than pursuing a treaty or declaration that could get mired in protracted state negotiations and preclude the possibility of using the international human rights law standards to protect IDPs in the near future, developing guiding principles on IDPs would allow him to develop a normative framework relatively quickly.[198] As noted in the earlier section on Binding Obligations, the SRSG has made similar arguments with respect to the development of binding international obligations for corporate actors.[199] The point here, however, is not to dredge up the voluntary versus mandatory debate[200] and argue for the development of international legal obligations over other nonlegal means of regulation. Rather, the aim of this chapter is to demonstrate that binding legal obligations have an important place alongside voluntary or soft forms of regulation in any comprehensive framework to address corporate human rights impunity and that the consideration of this important fact remains underdeveloped in Ruggie's approach.

Ruggie has also called for pragmatism, "identifying the specific attributes of the different challenges we face, laying out the full array of tools, and then selecting the ones that provide the best mix of effectiveness and feasibility."[201] A truly pragmatic approach, however, must look carefully at the deep structural aspects of the problem. The "Protect, Respect and Remedy" policy framework and the Guiding Principles will go some way in tackling the complex problem of corporate human rights impunity, but, as presently conceived, they fail to take into account Third World states' diminished governance capacity, which is the result of years of intervention by international law and international financial institutions. Legal obligations are necessary to begin to redress the power imbalance created by these developments and to address the structural bias of international law.

Ruggie himself has acknowledged that "it may be desirable in some circumstances for corporations to become direct bearers of international human rights obligations, especially where host Governments cannot or will not enforce their obligations and where the classical international human rights regime, therefore, cannot possibly be expected to function as intended."[202] Indeed, as noted above, he recommended to the Human Rights Council that one means for clarifying the legal obligations applicable to business entities where their acts or complicity in abuses might amount to international crimes would be

---

198. Makau Mutua, *Standard Setting in Human Rights: Critique and Prognosis*, 29 HUM. RTS. Q. 547, 560–61 (2007).

199. Ruggie, *supra* note 39.

200. See SRSG, Opening Statement, *supra* note 192. *See also* MICHAEL KERR, RICHARD JANDA, & CHIP PITTS, CORPORATE SOCIAL RESPONSIBILITY: A LEGAL ANALYSIS 271ff (Chip Pitts ed., 2009), who claim that the distinction between voluntary and mandatory obligations is misconceived.

201. SRSG, Remarks, *supra* note 48, at 6.

202. SRSG, 2006 report, supra note 17, at 65.

the development of an international legal instrument.[203] Though the SRSG in making these suggestions was concerned with business activity in conflict zones, situations of diminished governance capacity, such as those discussed in the preceding sections, mean that many Third World host states may be unable to fulfill their *duty to protect*. It is clear, therefore, that in these latter situations, the current international human rights system is also dysfunctional and requires international legal measures to address this failure.

However, given that international law has been used to create an enabling and protective environment for business activity, even as it has removed governance capacity from Third World states, one might ask whether international law is an appropriate means by which to address this imbalance and to protect individuals effectively from the activities of corporate actors. TWAIL scholars are critical of the way international law has been used as a hegemonic tool[204] and of how international human rights law itself has been co-opted in the service of economic globalization.[205] Indeed, as Sara Seck notes, the work of Balakrishnan Rajagopal and Anthony Anghie suggests that human rights, among other things, "may be viewed as mass resistance that feeds international law and international institutions with a new agenda [that gives] a human face to neo-liberal globalization . . . [but] does not challenge the underlying structure of the system."[206]

Nonetheless, many TWAIL scholars do see the potential of international human rights law to help reconstruct a just legal order. Anghie and Chimni have argued that TWAIL scholars are not in a position to forgo international law, despite the injustices suffered by the Third World. For TWAILers, international law has "transformative potential," and they believe "in the ideal of law as a means of constraining power."[207] In addition, they contend that

> international law has now become an extraordinarily powerful language in which to frame problems, suggest fault and responsibility, propose solutions and remedies. International law rules matter and must be taken seriously. It is not simply a distinctive style of argumentation but has serious consequences for how ordinary people live.[208]

With respect to international human rights law specifically, Chimni has argued elsewhere that "even as [international human rights law] legitimizes the internationalization of property rights and hegemonic interventions, . . . [i]t holds out the hope that the international

---

203. SRSG, Recommendations on Follow-Up, *supra* note 44, at 5.
204. Chimni, *supra* note 23, at 72.
205. *See* Gathii, *supra* note 118; *see also* Baxi, *supra* note 4, at 252ff.
206. Sara Seck, *Unilateral Home State Regulation: Imperialism or Tool for Subaltern Resistance?* 46 Osgoode Hall L.J. 565, 589 (2008).
207. Antony Anghie & B. S. Chimni, *Third World Approaches to International Law and Individual Responsibility in Internal Conflicts*, 2 Chinese J. Int'l L. 77, 101 (2003).
208. *Id.*

legal process can be used to bring a modicum of welfare to long suffering peoples of the third and first worlds."[209]

A small but important step toward addressing the long-standing structural bias discussed above would be to bring transnational corporate actors in from the margins and within the purview of international human rights law. The rights and protections enjoyed by these powerful actors were created by international law and facilitated by the interventions of international financial institutions. These rights are often enforceable in international arbitral tribunals. The creation of international corporate human rights obligations and effective enforcement and compliance mechanisms could go some way toward addressing the structural bias created by these developments and interventions. Properly conceived, enforceable human rights obligations for corporate actors could begin to shift the balance of power from transnational corporate actors to Third World host states and victims of corporate human rights abuses.

Conclusion

Currently, there does not appear to be the requisite consensus among states or business actors for developing a treaty with corporate human rights obligations. However, consensus does not simply appear. It needs to be built and nurtured. Transnational corporate actors and their home states will remain opposed to binding legal obligations as long as they are allowed to be. Ruggie amassed significant goodwill among states and the business community during his tenure. His normative framework was widely endorsed by these two powerful constituencies, but by limiting his recommendations to the clarification of legal norms applicable to businesses when they engage in behavior that violates international criminal law norms, while at the same time cautioning against the adoption of a more general international treaty, Ruggie missed the opportunity to push states and business actors out of their respective comfort zones. At the very least, it would have helped to push the global debate forward if he had issued a statement that the necessary follow-up to his work would be the eventual development of an international instrument (or a range of instruments) imposing binding obligations on corporate actors and requiring home states to regulate their corporate nationals.

There are constituencies in OECD governments that support the idea of developing legal obligations for corporate actors.[210] The UK Joint Committee on Human Rights, for

---

209. Chimni, *supra* note 23, at 73. See also Balakrishnan Rajagopal, *Counter-Hegemonic International Law: Rethinking Human Rights and Development as a Third World Strategy*, in FALK et. al., *supra* note 108, at 71 (stating that human rights discourse "can serve as an important tool in developing and strengthening a counter-hegemonic international law").

210. The Canadian, Australian, UK, and U.S., legislatures have considered regulation of extraterritorial

example, has stated "that an international agreement should be the ultimate aspiration of any debate on business and human rights" and has called on the UK government to work collaboratively both on the regional and global level to this end.[211] In Canada there were five private member's bills before Parliament in 2010 addressing various aspects of corporate human rights accountability,[212] and one of them, Bill C-300 (discussed above), was defeated in its third reading by only six votes.[213] Perhaps most importantly, some Third World members of the HRC spoke of the need for binding human rights obligations. Thus, the South African representative noted that Ruggie's Guiding Principles "were a first and complementary step in the definition of an internationally binding framework that would require States to regulate activities of business enterprises."[214] The Ecuadorean representative stated that his government would "not stand in the way of consensus" on the HRC resolution adopting the Guiding Principles, but "the United Nations must continue to work to establish binding international legal standards to govern the activities of transnational corporations."[215]

The development of binding obligations can be incremental. There is already global recognition that corporate actors have obligations under international law not to commit international crimes and that they can therefore incur international criminal liability for complicity in, or commission of, egregious violations of human rights that amount to such crimes.[216] The SRSG recognized this liability.[217] This could serve as a starting point for an international agreement. Although the HRC did not adopt Ruggie's recommendation on clarifying these legal standards, this does not mean that this goal should not continue to be pursued.

In addition, as discussed above, human rights obligations, as well as treaty-based compliance mechanisms, could be introduced into BITs and other international trade and investment agreements as well as HGAs.[218] Such agreements might include specific

---

corporate human rights impacts.

211. JOINT COMMITTEE ON HUMAN RIGHTS, ANY OF OUR BUSINESS? HUMAN RIGHTS AND THE UK PRIVATE SECTOR, 2009–2010, H.L. 5–1, at 106, www.publications.parliament.uk/pa/jt200910/jtselect/jtrights/5/5i.pdf.

212. See Bill C-300, *supra* note 155; An Act Respecting Corporate Social Responsibility for the Activities of Canadian Mining Corporations in Developing Countries, 2010-11, Bill [C-298] (Can.); An Act Respecting the Extraterritorial Activities of Canadian Businesses and Entities, Establishing the Canadian Extraterritorial Activities Review Commission and Making Consequential Amendments to Other Acts, 2010-11, Bill [C-438] (Can.); An Act Respecting Corporate Practices Relating to the Purchase of Minerals from the Great Lakes Region of Africa, 3rd Sess., 40th Parl., 2010-11, Bill [C-571] (Can.); and An Act to Amend the Federal Courts Act (international promotion and protection of human rights), 2010-11, Bill [C-354] (Can.) (this bill was reinstated from: 2nd Sess., 40th Parl.).

213. October 27, 2010, H.C. Jour. (2010) 88 (Can.).

214. UN Human Rights Council, Information Release, *supra* note 31.

215. Montalvo, *supra* note 31. Montalvo also noted that the lack of independent complaint mechanism for victims of corporate human rights abuse associated with the GPs was problematic.

216. *See supra* note 153.

217. *Id.*

218. These types of provisions in HGAs would obviously be contractual and not based in international

investor human rights obligations—including obligations not to commit or be complicit in human rights violations amounting to international crimes—and might also include labor obligations as well as obligations relating to environmental impact, bribery, and corruption, for example. Compliance mechanisms could include requirements to ensure civil and criminal liability for foreign investors both in the home and host states, as well as a right of the host state to counterclaim in any arbitral proceeding initiated by an investor corporation where that corporation has allegedly violated its obligations under the treaty.[219] These incremental steps would also help to build international consensus for a broader multilateral agreement.

The problem of corporate impunity for extraterritorial human rights violations is deeply complex and needs to be tackled creatively and intelligently at a variety of jurisdictional and normative levels. The SRSG has made significant inroads on a number of fronts. Nevertheless, binding international human rights obligations for transnational human rights actors must form a part of the global strategy going forward. Robert McCorquodale has noted that "there are many methods of regulation . . . [but] regulation without law and legal compliance mechanisms is rarely effective as a means of long-term social, economic or public behavioral change."[220] Without engaging international law as an integral part of the strategy to address corporate human rights impacts and accountability, as well as state governance capacity, there remains the fear that despite some changes in state policy, business policy, due diligence, and reporting, we will more or less continue business as usual.

---

law but would serve the same function of addressing the power imbalance between investors and host states.

219. For a full discussion of the scope and content of these types of provisions, *see* VANDUZER et al., Integrating Sustainable Development, *supra* note 76, at 294ff. In addition to these types of obligations and compliance mechanisms, core investor protection provisions such as those relating to national treatment, most favored nation treatment, and expropriation found in BITs and other international investment agreements can be modified to ensure that they do not preclude the introduction of nondiscriminatory regulatory measures designed to achieve the protection of human rights. *id.* at 110–182.

220. Robert McCorquodale, Corporate Social Responsibility and International Human Rights Law 87 J. BUS. ETHICS 385, 385 (2009).

Chapter 5

Trade and Investment Arrangements and Labor Rights

Jeffrey S. Vogt

Introduction

Increasingly, governments are negotiating commitments on human rights, including labor rights, in their trade and investment arrangements. Such commitments are still largely concentrated in the arrangements adopted or negotiated by the United States, the European Union (and its member states), and Canada. However, countries including Japan, Australia, New Zealand, and Chile are also gradually adopting labor rights criteria in their trade and investment arrangements.[1] The scope of these commitments and the extent to which they may be enforced through dispute-settlement mechanisms continue to evolve and vary significantly.

This chapter surveys the development of labor rights in trade and investment arrangements, principally bilateral and regional trade agreements, unilateral trade preference programs, and bilateral investment treaties. It examines their development by the leading proponents of the trade-labor linkage: the United States, the European Union, and Canada. In addition to tracking the evolution of these labor provisions, this chapter examines the extent to which they have been effective in improving the labor legislation and prevention and enforcement practices of governments, as well as the behavior of enterprises doing

---

1.   Though usually not as comprehensive as those promoted by the U.S., EU, and Canada, labor rights commitments are also found in trade agreements negotiated by countries in Asia, Africa, and Latin America. *See, e.g.*, Franz Ebert & Anne Posthuma, *Labour Provisions in Trade Arrangements, Current Trends and Perspectives* 15–20 (International Labour Organization (ILO) International Insitute for Labour Studies Discussion Paper Series, 2011); *see also Selection of Other Relevant Trade Agreements from Various Countries (Japan, China, Australia, New-Zealand, Chile, Eastern and Southern Africa, Caribbean Region)*, INT'L LABOR ORG. (Oct. 20, 2009), http://www.ilo.org/global/standards/information-resources-and-publications/free-trade-agreements-and-labour-rights/WCMS_115876/lang--en/index.htm.

business in those states. It concludes with thoughts on the role these instruments may play in promoting labor rights in the future. It does not, however, cover the well-trod territory of whether labor rights and trade and investment should be linked in the first place.[2]

The results to date are at best mixed. Trade preference programs, such as the U.S. Generalized System of Preferences (GSP), have secured some important legislative reforms and created opportunities to resolve specific labor violations, though progress has been at best incomplete and uneven. EU trade preferences programs, including the GSP and GSP+, arguably have had a lesser impact than their U.S. counterpart, though GSP+ has been successful in improving the ratification of International Labour Organization (ILO) "core" conventions among its select group of beneficiaries.[3] The United States has placed no emphasis on ILO Convention ratification, no doubt due to its own dubious record in this regard. Trade agreements in the United States have created some leverage to bring about important reforms to labor laws and regulations as well as reforms to labor institutions, such as labor inspection prior to ratification. Complaints filed under the labor chapters of these trade agreements once they have gone into force have so far achieved limited results. Bilateral investment treaties (BITs) appear to have created the least, if any, positive human rights benefits as yet. To the contrary, BITs have in some cases threatened to undermine the exercise of labor rights.

Free Trade Agreements

The United States (2001 to Present)

The North American Agreement on Labor Cooperation (NAALC), the side agreement to the North American Free Trade Agreement (NAFTA), is the usual starting point for any discussion of labor standards in trade agreements. At once innovative and frustratingly limited, the NAALC's example, both positive and negative, continues to inform debates on trade and labor today. Numerous legal articles have been written providing detailed

---

2.   Several books and articles have been written on this subject. At this point, there is a broad acceptance of the trade-labor linkage and labor clauses are appearing with greater regularity in international instruments. There remain disagreements of course on the scope of the obligations and the enforcement mechanisms. For texts reviewing the trade-labor linkage debate, HUMAN RIGHTS, LABOR RIGHTS AND TRADE (Lance Compa & Stephen Diamond eds., 1996); CHRISTIAN BARRY & SANJAY REDDY, INTERNATIONAL TRADE AND LABOR STANDARDS, A PROPOSAL FOR LINKAGE (2008).

3.   GSP is a program first proposed in the 1960s by which industrialized nations would provide duty-reduced or duty-free access to the exports of developing nations. The idea was that the preferential market access would help to attract investment, foment economic growth and thereby spur development. The GSP+ program is an incentive program in the EU in which countries that agree to more stringent conditions on labor, human rights, the environment, and good governance receive even greater preferential market access. The GSP programs are explained more fully in the section titled "Unilateral Trade Preferences."

analysis and pointed criticism of the NAALC since it entered into force in 1994. I will therefore not cover it here and instead focus on its progeny.[4]

In the Americas, the United States has pursued a number of free trade agreements in the past fifteen years. It sought (unsuccessfully) to conclude negotiations for the proposed Free Trade Area of the Americas (FTAA), a hemispheric-wide agreement that traced its origins to the First Summit of the Americas in Miami in 1994. At the same time, the United States pursued a bilateral agreement with Chile and two regional trade pacts, with Central America and the Andean Region, in an effort to build momentum for the hemispheric pact. The Central America Free Trade Agreement (CAFTA), which the Dominican Republic later joined, was ratified by a mere two-vote margin in the U.S. House of Representatives (the House) in 2006, following intense lobbying by the president and suspension of the House rules during the vote.[5] Most of the floor speeches in opposition to the agreement raised serious concerns regarding the labor conditions in the region. The Andean Free Trade Agreement (AFTA) fell apart when Bolivia, and later Ecuador, withdrew, though bilateral trade agreements with Peru and Colombia were eventually concluded and ratified. However, the latter was stalled for several years because of concerns over extreme levels of anti-union violence.

In the Middle East and North Africa, the United States sought to solidify political ties through free trade agreements (FTAs) with *western-leaning* monarchies, including Oman, Bahrain, Morocco, and the United Arab Emirates (UAE). Labor concerns were raised with each of these countries and again were among the reasons cited by those who opposed the agreements. All but the UAE eventually concluded an FTA with the United States.

In Sub-Saharan Africa, U.S. efforts to conclude a trade agreement with the South African Customs Union (SACU, which includes Botswana, Lesotho, Namibia, South Africa,

---

4.   It is notable that new cases continue to be filed under the NAALC. In 2011, the Sindicato Mexicano de Electristas (SME) and the Centro de Derechos de Migrantes (CDM) filed submissions against Mexico and the United States respectively, suggesting that some continue to view the NAALC as a useful, albeit limited, tool to seek redress of labor violations and to build international labor solidarity. The writings of Lance Compa, the first head of the NAFTA Secretariat of the Commission for Labor Cooperation, are particularly informative. *See, e.g.*, COMPA AND DIAMOND, HUMAN RIGHTS, LABOR RIGHTS AND INTERNATIONAL TRADE, (1996); L. Compa, *NAFTA's Labor Side Accord: A Three-Year Accounting*, 3 L. & BUS. REV. AMERICAS 6, 6–23 (1997); L. Compa, *NAFTA's Labor Side Agreement Five Years On: Progress and Prospects for the NAALC*, 7 CANADIAN LABOR & EMP. LAW J. 1 (1999); L. Compa,*NAFTA's Labor Side Agreement and International Labor Solidarity*, in PLACE, SPACE AND THE NEW LABOR INTERNATIONALISMS (P. Waterman & J. Wills eds., 2001). A lengthy bibliography of the articles written on the NAALC during the 1990s is available at the Web site of the Secretariat of the Commission for Labor Cooperation, http://new.naalc.org/index.cfm?page=258. Public comments submitted during the NAALC's four-year review are also http://new.naalc.org/index.cfm?page=256.

5.   Edmund Andrews, *How CAFTA Passed by 2 Votes*, N.Y. TIMES (July 29, 2005), http://www.nytimes.com/2005/07/29/politics/29cafta.html?pagewanted=all.

and Swaziland) stalled due to fundamental differences over the scope of the negotiations.[6] Labor and environmental rules played a role in the agreement's demise.[7]

In the Asia-Pacific region, negotiations with Thailand and Malaysia faltered, whereas bilateral trade agreements with Singapore, Australia, and South Korea were eventually concluded. The Obama Administration, as part of its "Pivot to Asia," is negotiating an ever-expanding regional trade agreement with Asia-Pacific Economic Cooperation (APEC) members, which now include Australia, Brunei Darussalam, Canada, Chile, Japan, Malaysia, Mexico, New Zealand, Peru, Singapore, Vietnam, and the United States.[8]

The Bush Administration Labor Template

The labor chapters of the trade agreements negotiated during the Bush Administration contain four basic commitments. CAFTA is cited here as the exemplar of this model. It requires parties to:

- "reaffirm their obligations as members of the International Labor Organization (ILO) and their commitments under the *ILO Declaration on Fundamental Principles and Rights at Work and its Follow-Up* (1998) (ILO Declaration)" and to "strive to ensure that such labor principles and the internationally recognized labor rights set forth in Article 16.8 are recognized and protected by its law;"[9]
- "strive to ensure that its laws provide for labor standards consistent with the internationally recognized labor rights . . . and shall strive to improve those standards in that light;"[10]
- "not fail to effectively enforce its labor laws, through a sustained or recurring course of action or inaction, in a manner affecting trade between the Parties, after the date of entry into force of this Agreement;"[11]
- "strive to ensure that it does not waive or otherwise derogate from, or offer to waive or otherwise derogate from, such laws in a manner that weakens or reduces adherence to the internationally recognized labor rights . . . as an encouragement for trade with

---

6.   The SACU countries had pushed to exclude intellectual property rights, government procurement, investment, and services from the negotiations, calling on market access commitments to be made first. The United States sought a comprehensive deal that included these issues. Further, the SACU wanted to employ a positive list to its industrial sector rather than a negative list approach where everything was on the table unless specifically excluded.

7.   *See, e.g.*, Danielle Langton, Cong. Research Serv., RS21387, United States-Southern African Customs Union (SACU) Free Trade Agreement Negotiations: Background and Potential Issues (2008).

8.   *See, e.g.*, Mark Manyin *et al.*, Cong. Research Serv., R42448, Pivot to the Pacific? The Obama Administration's "Rebalancing" Toward Asia 22–23 (2012).

9.   Article 16.1.1.

10.   Article 16.1.2.

11.   Article 16.2.1(a).

another Party, or as an encouragement for the establishment, acquisition, expansion, or retention of an investment in its territory."[12]

These trade agreements contain identical dispute-settlement procedures for labor claims, with the Chile and Singapore FTAs being minor exceptions. Again, the CAFTA consists of the following basic steps:

- A party to the agreement may request in writing "cooperative labor consultations" regarding "any matter arising under the chapter."[13]
- If the matter is not resolved by cooperative labor consultations, the party may request in writing that the Labor Affairs Council be convened in order to seek a resolution of the matter.[14]
- If the matter concerns whether a party failed to effectively enforce its own labor laws, and the matter was not resolved through cooperative consultations within sixty days, the complaining party may request consultations or a meeting of the commission under the dispute settlement chapter.[15]
- If a matter is not resolved within thirty days from the establishment of the commission, the complaining party may request in writing the establishment of an arbitration panel.[16]
- If the party complained against fails to implement the final report of the arbitration panel, it may result in an annual monetary assessment of up to $15 million, which is paid into a fund administered by the commission and expended for labor initiatives such as improving or enhancing labor law enforcement.[17]

Trade unions and human and labor rights organizations criticized the CAFTA labor chapter for doing little to improve labor laws and law enforcement or to curb future abuses.[18]

---

12. Article 16.2.2.
13. Article 16.6.1.
14. Article 16.6.4–5.
15. Article 16.6.
16. Article 20.6.1.
17. Article 20.17.
18. For criticism of the CAFTA labor chapter, *see, e.g.,* Report of the Labor Advisory Committee for Trade Negotiations and Trade Policy (LAC), The U.S.-Central America Free Trade Agreement (Mar. 2004), http://ustraderep.gov/assets/Trade_Agreements/Regional/CAFTA/CAFTA _Reports/asset_upload_file63_5935.pdf; Human Rights Watch, CAFTA's Weak Labor Rights Protections: Why the Present Accord Should Be Opposed (Mar. 2004), http://www.hrw.org/legacy /english/ docs/ 2004/03/09/cafta90days.pdf; Bama Athreya, *Testimony Regarding the Central America Free Trade Agreement (CAFTA)*, Int'l Lbor Rights Fund (Apr. 12, 2005), http://ilrf.org/sites/default/files /publications-and-resources/TRADECAFTA.pdf. Identical critiques were made of the other FTAs negotiated at this time. *See, e.g.,* Report of the Labor Advisory Committee for Trade Negotiations and Trade Policy (LAC), U.S.-Oman Free Trade Agreement (Nov. 2005), http://www.ustr.gov/ archive/Trade_Agreements/Bilateral/Oman_FTA/Reports/Section_Index.html; Report of the Labor Advisory Committee for Trade Negotiations and Trade Policy (LAC), The U.S.-Bahrain Free

Critics also argued that it signaled a retreat from the then high-water mark for labor rights established by the U.S.-Jordan Free Trade Agreement.[19] For example, the U.S.-Jordan FTA, subjected all the labor commitments to dispute settlement and was not limited to the commitment to enforce one's own labor laws. Furthermore, labor claims were subject to the same dispute-settlement procedures and remedies as the commercial provisions of the FTA.[20]

One of the central criticisms of the CAFTA was that it did not require a party's labor laws to comply with the international standards established by ILO conventions. Instead, the parties were merely required to "strive to ensure" compliance with these standards and similarly strive not to weaken them to attract trade or investment. A party's breach of these commitments could not be challenged in dispute settlement. Indeed, only one of the chapter's commitments—to enforce one's own labor laws—could be subject to dispute settlement in case of a breach.[21] Because many of these countries maintained laws that fell far short of the international minimum set of rights set forth in the eight fundamental ILO conventions,[22] the requirement merely to enforce those laws was viewed as woefully inadequate and an invitation to continued abuse. Excluding nondiscrimination from the list of rights that a party was required to enforce based on its domestic legislation was

---

TRADE AGREEMENT (July 2004), http://www.ustr.gov/archive/Trade_Agreements/Bilateral/Bahrain_FTA/Reports/Section_Index.html; REPORT OF THE LABOR ADVISORY COMMITTEE FOR TRADE NEGOTIATIONS AND TRADE POLICY (LAC), THE U.S.-AUSTRALIA FREE TRADE AGREEMENT (Mar. 2004), http://www.ustr.gov/archive/Trade_Agreements/Bilateral/Australia_FTA/Reports/Section_Index.html.

19. *See, e.g.,* AFL-CIO, THE REAL RECORD ON WORKERS' RIGHTS IN CENTRAL AMERICA 8–9 (Apr. 2005), http://www.ibew769.com/library/CAFTA.pdf. *But see* U.S.TR, CAFTA IS STRONGER THAN THE JORDAN FTA ON LABOR (2005), http://www.ustr.gov/archive/assets/Trade_Agreements/Regional/CAFTA/Briefing_Book/asset_upload_file100_7719.pdf.

20. This was severely undercut when, in 2001, U.S. Trade Representative (U.S.TR) Robert Zoellick sent a letter to the Jordanian Ambassador to the United States stating, "[M]y Government would not expect or intend to apply the Agreement's dispute settlement procedures to secure its rights under the Agreement in a manner that results in blocking trade. . . . . [M]y Government considers that appropriate measures for resolving any difference that may arise regarding the Agreement would be bilateral consultations and other procedures, particularly alternative mechanisms that will help to secure compliance without recourse to traditional trade sanctions." Side Letter on Labor and Environment from Ambassador Robert B. Zoellick, U.S.TR, to His Excellency Marwan Muasher, Ambassador of the Hashemite Kingdom of Jordan to the United States (July 23, 2001).

21. *See, e.g.,* CAFTA, Chapter 16, Article 16.6.8.

22. These eight conventions are: Convention (No. 87) Concerning Freedom of Association and Protection of the Right to Organise, adopted Aug. 31, 1948, 68 UNT.S. 17 (entered into force July 4, 1950); Convention (No. 98) Concerning the Application of the Principles of the Right to Organise and to Bargain Collectively, adopted Aug. 18, 1949, 96 UNT.S. 257 (entered into force July 18, 1951); Convention Concerning Forced or Compulsory Labour, adopted June 28, 1930, 39 UNT.S. 27 (entered into force May 1, 1932); Convention Concerning the Abolition of Forced Labour, adopted July 4, 1957, 320 UNT.S. 291 (entered into force Jan. 17, 1959); Convention (No. 138) Concerning Minimum Age for Admission to Employment, adopted June 26, 1973, 1015 UNT.S. 298 (entered into force June 19, 1976); Convention (No. 182) Concerning the Prohibition and Immediate Action for the Elimination of the Worst Forms of Child Labor, adopted June 17, 1999, 2133 UNT.S. 161 (entered into force Nov. 19, 2000); Equal Remuneration Convention (No. 100), adopted June 29, 1951, 165 UNT.S. 303 (entered into force May 23, 1953); Convention (No. 111) Concerning Discrimination in Respect of Employment and Occupation, adopted June 25, 1958, 362 UNT.S. 32 (entered into force June 15, 1960).

also a serious flaw, particularly in a region where gender, age, and racial discrimination in employment are common. Moreover, the omission of nondiscrimination is inconsistent with the trade agreement's reference to the ILO's 1998 Declaration on Fundamental Principles and Rights at Work.

Similarly, the dispute-settlement procedures are overly cumbersome and weaker than the procedures established for commercial disputes. In particular, under the rules governing commercial disputes, trade sanctions are supposed to have an "effect equivalent" to that of the disputed measure.[23] The imposition of sanctions can be avoided if the parties negotiate a mutually acceptable compensation. For labor disputes, the amount of an annual monetary assessment is not based on the harm caused by the measure (equivalent effect) but rather considers additional factors that could lessen the assessment.[24] For labor violations, the annual monetary assessment is fixed at a maximum of $15 million, which may be significantly less than the effect of the measure (such as labor violation).[25] In a commercial dispute, a party can suspend the full original amount of trade benefits (equal to the harm caused by the offending measure). The level of trade benefits a party can revoke if a monetary assessment is not paid in a labor dispute is limited to the value of the assessment itself, which again is capped at $15 million.[26] On a more practical level, even if the funds are paid and used for appropriate labor programs, nothing in the agreement guarantees that the funds would not be offset by a party adjusting its budget to account for the funds, leading to no net increase in funds directed to improve labor rights.

The Compromise of May 10, 2007

In November 2006, the Democratic Party claimed both the House and the Senate. Many of the successful candidates ran on economic populist messages, arguing that free trade and outsourcing were responsible for the decline in U.S. manufacturing. Passage of then-pending trade agreements negotiated by the Bush Administration—with Peru, Panama, Colombia, and South Korea—was low on the Democrats' agenda. However, the party was not interested in letting the agreements languish indefinitely either. The search for a Democratic trade template thus began.

By January 2007, trade unions and environmental, family farm, public health, and consumer organizations were at work sketching out a new trade template that, if adopted, would be considered a *fair trade* agreement and thus win their support.[27] The chair of

---

23. Article 20.16.2.
24. Cf. 20.16.2 *with* 20.17.2 (which includes a number of what appear to be mitigating factors that could lessen the amount of the monetary assessment).
25. Article 20.17.2.
26. Cf. 20.16.8 *with* 20.17.5 (which also reminds the parties "to [bear] in mind the Agreement's objective of eliminating barriers to trade and while seeking to avoid unduly affecting parties or interests not party to the dispute.").
27. That work later went on to inform the Trade Reform, Accountability, Development and

the Ways and Means Subcommittee on Trade was Sander Levin, a former labor lawyer and outspoken opponent of previous trade agreements lacking sufficient labor protections, took the lead with Committee Chairman Charles Rangel to devise a new template. By April, discussions for a new trade template had intensified, with new proposals on labor, the environment, investment, government procurement, and pharmaceutical patents taking shape. On May 10, 2007, a press conference was called announcing that a deal between Congress and the White House had been reached. The following day, the U.S. Trade Representative (U.S.TR) and the House Ways and Means Committee each issued outlines of the Bipartisan Agreement on Trade Policy, commonly known as the May 10th Agreement (May 10th).[28]

When the final text was released, the American Federation of Labor and Congress of Industrial Organizations (AFL-CIO)[29] explained that May 10th signaled a significant, if insufficient, advance and a starting point for future reforms.[30] The most important advance was the abandonment of the "enforce your own laws" approach of the earlier model. Instead, the May 10th required each party to both "adopt and maintain in its statutes, regulations, and practices thereunder" the "rights as stated in the ILO Declaration on Fundamental Principles and Rights at Work and its Follow-Up (1998) (ILO Declaration)." It also stated that a party should "not fail to effectively enforce its labor laws . . . through a sustained or recurring course of action or inaction, in a manner affecting trade or investment between the Parties."[31] Additionally, the new template dropped the aspirational language with regard to its waiver and nonderogation provision. Unlike the previous model, all matters arising under the labor chapter could be taken to dispute settlement. Furthermore, responding to a common refrain from organized labor that the previous trade agreements had created a different (and lesser) dispute-settlement mechanism for labor than for commercial disputes, the May 10th template simply applied the commercial dispute-settlement machinery to labor violations.

Because an arbitration panel has not interpreted any of the terms in May 10th, or identical terms in previous trade agreements, several questions still remain. Foremost, the requirement to adopt and maintain in law the rights as stated in the ILO Declaration (and only the ILO Declaration) introduces some uncertainty about the full extent of the obligation. This matter is aggravated by the U.S.TR's inconsistent application of this

---

Employment of 2008, introduced in the House by Michael Michaud and by Sherrod Brown in the Senate.

28.   Available at http://waysandmeans.house.gov/Media/pdf/110/05%2014%2007/05%2014%2007 .pdf.

29.   The AFL-CIO is the national federation of U.S.-based trade unions. It currently has fifty-seven affiliated unions with more than 12 million members throughout the United States. *See* AFL-CIO, www .aflcio.org (last visited Dec. 1, 2013).

30.   *See, e.g.,* Testimony of Thea Mei Lee, Policy Director, AFL-CIO, Before the Senate Finance Committee on the U.S.-Peru Trade Promotion Agreement (Sept. 11, 2007).

31.   *See, e.g.,* Trade Promotion Agreement, U.S.-Peru, ch. 17, Apr. 12, 2006, http://www.ustr.gov/ trade-agreements/free-trade-agreements/peru-tpa/final-text.

objective standard in seeking amendments to the laws of other parties prior to ratification or certification. Furthermore, the wording "sustained or recurring course of action or inaction" calls into question just how much evidence a complainant must provide in order to make and sustain a claim. The requirement not to fail to enforce labor laws effectively "in a manner affecting trade or investment between the Parties" is also ambiguous. So far, petitioners in cases against Guatemala and Honduras, for example, have referred to situations where the government failed to enforce the law in sectors exporting to the United States, such as agricultural goods and garments, as well as trade-related infrastructure such as ports used to ship goods to the United States. It is unclear whether it is sufficient that the unremedied violations have merely occurred in a tradable sector, as appears to be the current U.S. view, or whether a more substantial link will be required, such as a clear impact of the unremedied violation on bilateral trade. It is also unclear how far back into the supply chain of a tradable good the labor provisions of the FTA can reach.

An Obama Labor Template?

As noted above, the Obama Administration is currently negotiating an ambitious regional trade agreement called the Trans-Pacific Partnership (TPP).[32] The labor chapter of the proposed TPP, in addition to superseding the existing labor commitments in several existing bilateral FTAs with the United States, will create a new template with broad geographic coverage and is likely to be a model elsewhere. The United States has tabled a complete proposal on labor, though details are not publicly available because the agreement has been negotiated largely in secret. The trade press reports, however, that the U.S. proposal includes a requirement to have laws related to "acceptable conditions of work" (minimum wages, hours of work, and safety and health) rather than merely a commitment to enforce those laws that a party may have, if any. The proposal purportedly also contains a requirement that countries take affirmative steps to discourage the importation of goods made by forced labor or child labor. It allegedly clarifies that national laws must be applied in export-processing zones and establishes model procedures for filing labor complaints.[33] As of late 2013, technical negotiations on the labor chapter had largely concluded, with the remaining points of disagreement to be resolved at the political level. One significant point of disagreement relates to penalties, with some countries, including Canada, proposing monetary fines while the United States continues to promote the suspension-of-benefits approach found in prior FTAs.[34]

---

32. *See, e.g., Trans-Pacific Partnership (TPP)*, U.S.TR, http://www.ustr.gov/tpp (last visited Dec. 1, 2013).

33. *See Business Wary of U.S. TPP Labor Proposal on Substance and Politics*, INSIDE U.S. TRADE (Jan. 13, 2012).

34. *Labor Negotiators Wrap Up Technical Work, No Plans to Meet in Malaysia*, INSIDE U.S. TRADE (July 3, 2013).

A coalition including most of the trade unions in the TPP countries put forward a labor chapter proposal that builds on the May 10th template on labor.[35] In addition to improving the existing text, the proposal also calls for new rules on labor recruitment meant to prevent trafficking in persons, calls for the establishment of an independent labor secretariat to monitor the implementation of the agreement, and seeks the establishment of an adapted European Works Council model in the TPP countries to foster transnational industrial relations.

What Have These Agreements Accomplished?

In evaluating the efficacy of these chapters, it is important to look at what leverage they have created for reforms prior to the ratification and certification of free trade agreements and what effect they have had once an agreement has entered into force.

Preratification/Certification

Before ratifying a trade agreement, the United States has often sought reforms of the labor laws of the other party to address at least the most serious problems. With May 10th, the United States arguably has had more leverage to seek wider-ranging reforms to the labor laws of Peru, Panama, Colombia, and Korea. However, politics and power played a large role in defining the ambition of the changes sought, the specific terms of the agreement being somewhat less important. Indeed, important amendments were made to the labor laws of Bahrain and Oman, even though the trade agreements with these two countries contained weak labor language. On the other hand, no amendments were demanded of South Korea despite the far stronger labor requirements of the post–May 10th agreement.

Case Study 1: Peru[36]

Efforts to identify needed reforms to Peruvian labor law began in 2006, with trade unions in the United States and Peru providing detailed analysis and examples of violations in practice to congressional staff and the administration of the Peruvian labor legislation. Of particular importance to the unions was the use of repeated short-term contracts and subcontracting arrangements to exploit workers and avoid unions. Indeed, in many industries, such as mining, workforces had been divided into essentially two classes of workers: those directly employed workers who enjoyed better wages and working conditions and the many more who were employed through sham shell companies that provided labor to the employer at wages and working conditions far inferior to those of directly employed workers.

Key members of the U.S. Congress also expressed considerable concern regarding labor rights in Peru, which had been sharply repressed during the Fujimori regime in the 1990s.[37]

---

35. The text of the proposed chapter is available online at http://www.ituc-csi.org.

36. This case study is based on the author's firsthand knowledge of the U.S.-Peru negotiations.

37. *See, e.g.*, Sander Levin, *Remarks of Representative Levin for Discussion on FTAs between the U.S. and Latin America*, Carnegie Endowment for International Peace (Mar. 14, 2006),

Following the 2006 U.S. elections it became clear to the White House that securing labor reforms would be necessary if the agreement were to get an affirmative vote. The Ways and Means Committee then largely assumed responsibility for negotiating directly with the government of Peru on a package of reforms necessary to win Democratic support. In August 2007, a final deal was announced following high-level negotiations between the two governments.[38] The deal included provisions on reigning in the abuse of short-term contracts, limitations on the use of subcontracting, protecting the right of workers to strike, and stronger measures to combat anti-union discrimination. The deal eventually paved the way for the implementing legislation to become law in late 2007.

In January 2009, however, members of the U.S. Congress wrote to the U.S.TR explaining that Peru had failed to meet all of its commitments under the deal, including changing its legal framework to ensure that subcontractors were legitimate employers and not simply shell companies created for the purpose of union avoidance. They urged the administration not to certify the agreement.[39] Nonetheless, the U.S.TR declared that Peru had in fact met all of its obligations and that the FTA would enter into force on February 1, 2009.[40]

Despite these legal reforms, Peruvian workers reported continued obstacles in law and in practice to the exercise of their fundamental labor rights, including anti-union dismissals, following the implementation of the FTA.[41] Unions reported that although labor inspection did improve in Lima, it remained poor in other regions of the country. Further, efforts to crack down on illegal subcontracting and short-term contracts have been insufficient, thus allowing the practice to continue. Of note, ten complaints to the ILO Committee on Freedom of Association have been filed against Peru since 2011.[42]

Case Study 2: Colombia

Colombia had long been recognized as the most dangerous place in the world to be a trade unionist, and anti-union violence still remains at alarming levels. By October 2011, when Congress ratified the U.S.-Colombia trade agreement, twenty-three trade union leaders and activists had been murdered that year alone, according to the Escuela Nacional

---

http://carnegieendowment.org/2006/03/14/remarks-of-representative-levin-for-discussion-on-ftas-betwe en-us-and-latin-america/9pn.

38. *U.S., Peru Reach Labor Deal, Administration Vows to Fight for All FTAs*, INSIDE U.S. TRADE (Aug. 10, 2007).

39. Letter from Representatives Charles Rangel and Sander Levin, to the Honorable Susan C. Schwab (Jan. 14, 2009).

40. U.S.TR Press Release, Statement of U.S. Trade Representative Susan C. Schwab Regarding Entry into Force of the Peru FTA (Jan. 16, 2009), http://www.ustr.gov/about-us/press-office/press-releases/2009 /january/statement-us-trade-representative-susan-c-schwab-r.

41. *See, e.g.*, SOLIDARITY CENTER, PERUVIAN SOCIETY, WORKERS, AND LABOR LAW (Dec. 2009), http://www.solidaritycenter.org/content.asp?pl=422&sl=407&contentid=896.

42. *International Labour Standards Country Profile: Peru*, INT'L LABOUR ORG., http://www.usleap .org/files/ENS%20Report%20on%20Labor%20Action%20Plan_English.pdf (last visited Dec. 1, 2013).

Sindical.[43] The total number of trade unionists murdered since records were first kept in 1986 to October 2011 was at least 2,908.[44] Trade unionists also received hundreds of explicit death threats, with 295 such threats reported from January to October 2011.[45] Those threats have often been effective in chilling freedom of association because trade unionists know that such threats are often carried out. Furthermore, in 2011 the rate of impunity for assassinations remained above 90 percent, according to data from the Colombian Commission of Jurists.[46] Indeed, the 2011 ILO High Level Mission to Colombia confirmed that "impunity has prevailed in Colombia for a long period and has caused immense damage to the country and suffering to its people." It also confirmed that "the great majority of homicide cases remained unresolved." [47]

In the 2008 U.S. presidential campaign, the issue of trade union violence in Colombia became a debate topic. During the third presidential debate, when asked about the Colombia FTA, then-candidate Barack Obama stated, "The history in Colombia right now is that labor leaders have been targeted for assassination on a fairly consistent basis and there have not been prosecutions. . . . We have to stand for human rights and we have to make sure that violence isn't being perpetrated against workers who are just trying to organize for their rights."[48] Despite serious concerns about pursuing a trade agreement with the Colombian government due to the level of human rights violations in Colombia, by late 2010 it was clear that the Obama Administration intended to seek ratification of the agreement. Labor organizations, human rights NGOs, and members of the U.S. Congress all issued benchmarks they hoped would guide negotiations with the Colombian government. All of them called on the Obama Administration to demand a significant reduction in anti-union violence and a sharp increase in arrests and prosecutions of those responsible for human rights violations, as well as significant labor law reforms *prior* to the ratification of the agreement.[49]

---

43. Escuela Nacional Sindical, The Action Plan Related to Labor Rights—A New Frustration?: Evaluation of the First Six Months Since the Implementation of the Action Plan Related to Labor Rights Between the Governments of Colombia and United States 7 (Oct. 2011), http://usleap.org/us-congress-passes-colombia-fta-fight-continues.

44. *Id.*

45. *See* Testimony of ITUC *et. al.* on the Right to Freedom of Association in Colombia, 143rd Sess. of the Inter-American Comm'n on Human Rights (Oct. 27, 2011) (citing ENS statistics) (available online in Spanish at http://www.coljuristas.org/documentos/adicionales/27-10-2011_audiencia_cidh_libertad _sindical.html).

46. *Id* at 9.

47. Int'l Labor Org., Conclusions of the High-Level Tripartite Mission to Colombia 3 (2011).

48. *See Complete Final Debate Transcript: John McCain and Barak Obama*, L.A. Times (Oct. 15, 2008), http://latimesblogs.latimes.com/washington/2008/10/debate-transcri.html.

49. *See, e.g.*, AFL-CIO, Comments Concerning the Pending Free Trade Agreement with Colombia (Sept. 15, 2009); Memo from McGovern *et. al.* to President Obama, Advancing Colombian Labor and Human Rights and Congressional Consideration of the U.S.-Colombia Free Trade Agreement (Mar. 17,

In April 2011, the Obama Administration issued a Colombia Action Plan.[50] The plan did respond to a number of demands by stakeholders and required, among other things:

- the reconstitution of the Ministry of Labor and the hiring of 480 additional labor inspectors;
- legislation criminalizing anti-union acts committed by employers;
- measures banning the use of labor cooperatives to avoid direct employment relationships;
- legal reforms regarding the use of collective pacts with nonunion employees as a means to undercut trade unions;
- expansion of the protection program for trade union leaders to include rank-and-file members, and;
- direction of more resources toward the prosecutor's office in an effort to reduce the rate of impunity.

There were, however, several problems with the plan. First, it did not include any specific commitments to dismantle new, illegal armed groups, which are responsible for much of the continuing anti-union violence in Colombia. Second, the plan committed the government of Colombia to issue new laws and regulations, create new institutions, issue reports, improve processes, and hire additional personnel by certain dates but did not actually require Colombia to establish a meaningful record of enforcement of these commitments prior to the implementation of the FTA. Third, the Labor Action Plan fell short in a number of important substantive areas. The failure to include commitments with regard to collective bargaining in the public sector, collective bargaining above the enterprise level, or collective bargaining over pensions ignored major concerns of both the trade unions and the ILO. Furthermore, the Labor Action Plan contained two provisions with regard to collective pacts and essential public services that are inconsistent with the observations of the ILO.[51] Finally, the plan is not part of the trade agreement and is not subject to any dispute-settlement mechanisms should the government of Colombia fail to fully comply with the plan (especially with regard to those commitments that extend years into the future). In response to these concerns, the Obama Administration was urged to

---

2011), http://www.usleap.org/files/Colombia%202011%20-%20MC%20memo%20to%20President%20Obama.pdf.

50. *See* U.S.TR, Colombia Action Plan Related to Labor Rights (Apr. 7, 2011), http://www.ustr.gov/webfm_send/2787.

51. *See, e.g.*, Testimony Of Jeffrey S. Vogt, Deputy Director, International Department, AFL-CIO, Before The Senate Finance Committee Hearing On The U.S.-Colombia Free Trade Agreement (May 11, 2011), http://www.aflcio.org/issues/jobseconomy/globaleconomy/upload/colombia_senate_testimony.pdf (including a line by line analysis of the Labor Action Plan).

incorporate the action plan into the FTA implementing legislation by members of Congress, but they declined to do so.

Prior to the ratification vote, Colombian trade unions and NGOs reported that the Colombian government failed to meet all of the indicated deadlines.[52] More importantly, abuses continued even with the steps taken by the Colombian government pursuant to the action plan. On September 26, 2011, the AFL-CIO reported that fifteen trade unionists had been murdered just since the Labor Action Plan was issued in April.[53] Though some companies dissolved labor cooperatives and hired their employees directly (as intended by the Labor Action Plan), in many cases workers were hired through new forms that severed the direct relationship with the employer and thereby frustrated the exercise of fundamental rights. Illegal use of collective pacts and temporary service companies also continued, with as yet insufficient enforcement action to put an end to these abuses. Therefore, it was clear that the plan's remedial measures were not up to the task.

On the sidelines of the sixth Summit of the Americas, held in April 2012 in Cartagena, Colombia, President Obama announced that the U.S.-Colombia Trade Promotion Agreement would enter into force on May 15, 2012, based in part on "Colombia's important steps to fulfill the Action Plan Related to Labor Rights."[54] The decision was made over the strong objections of labor and human rights organizations, which noted that although there had been some progress, several points of the action plan had been only partly implemented or not implemented at all.[55]

No doubt Colombia did and continues to take important steps, including reconstituting the Ministry of Labor, hiring additional labor inspectors, directing more resources toward the public prosecutor's office, and reforming laws governing cooperatives. However, many of the same issues identified prior to ratification remain. At the end of 2012, 20 trade unionists had been murdered and 431 had received threats according to the Escuela Nacional Sindical. Though it reflects a downward trend, the number is still extremely high. New

---

52. *See* Testimony, *supra* note 51.

53. *See* Kevin Bogardus, *AFL-CIO President Trumka Sends List of Killed Colombian Labor Leaders to Obama*, The Hill (Sept. 26, 2011), http://thehill.com/business-a-lobbying/183909-afl-cio-sends-list-of-killed-colombian-labor-leaders-to-obama.

54. U.S.TR Press Release, United States, Colombia Set Date for Entry into Force of U.S.-Colombia Trade Agreement (Apr. 2012), http://www.ustr.gov/about-us/press-office/press-releases/2012/april/united-states-colombia-set-date-entry-force-us-colom.

55. For reactions, *see, e.g.*, Tula Connell, *Trumka: Colombia Trade Pact 'Puts Commercial Interests Over Workers'*, AFL-CIO BLOG (Apr. 16, 2012), http://www.aflcio.org/Blog/Global-Action/Trumka-Colombia-Trade-Pact-Puts-Commercial-Interests-Over-Workers; Press Release, Washington Office on Latin America (WOLA), Obama Clears Way for Colombia Free Trade Agreement to Move Forward, WOLA Sees Missed Opportunity to Help Improve Colombian Labor Rights (last visited April 15, 2012), http://www.wola.org/news/ obama_certifies_colombia_free_trade_agreement. For analysis of the implementation of the action plan, see Escuela Nacional Sindical, *Balance del Primer Año de Implementación del Plan de Acción en Derechos Laborales*, http://www.ens.org.co/index.shtml?apc=Na--;12;-;-;&x=20166893 (finding that "of the 37 measures contained in the action plan, at least 9 were not adopted and of the 28 that were adopted, some can be described as parcial or insufficient.") (translation by author).

laws have been enacted to clamp down on labor cooperatives, but unions have reported that many employers have simply reestablished cooperatives as "simplified corporations" (Sociedades por Acciones Simplificadas) and continued as before. In 2013, Law 1610 of 2013 was enacted, providing important new tools to convert illegal, indirect employment schemes to direct employment relationships. As yet, it is too early to assess its efficacy.[56]

Case Study 3: South Korea

Some of the labor issues in South Korea, particularly with regard to subcontracting and irregular contracts, were similar to issues identified with Peru.[57] In Peru it led to the adoption of laws and regulations disciplining these practices at the insistence of the U.S. government. The failure to act on these same issues with South Korea cannot be explained any other way than that the United States, especially after having just extracted a new deal on auto trade, simply did not want to press the Korean government on labor law reform that was certain to face substantial opposition and further delay this economically sizable agreement. Further, the Korean government, unlike others, was more likely to point out that the United States was itself not in compliance with international labor standards and urge it to changes its laws as well. To avoid this potential embarrassment, labor law reform was never made a meaningful demand during negotiations with South Korea or prior to ratification.

Postratification

The first non-NAFTA case was filed against Jordan under the U.S.-Jordan FTA in 2006, following an exposé by the National Labor Committee that revealed serious and widespread labor violations in the Qualified Industrial Zones (QIZs).[58] Since then, four labor

---

56. An October 2013 report by Congressmen George Miller and James McGovern shows that indirect employment schemes remain a serious problem in Colombia. *See* The U.S. Colombia Labor Action Plan: Failing on the Ground, A Staff Report on Behalf of U.S. Representatives George Miller and James McGovern to the Congressional Monitoring Group on Labor Rights in Colombia, October 2013, *available online* at http://democrats.edworkforce.house.gov/sites/democrats.edworkforce .house.gov/files/documents/Colombia%20trip%20report%20-%2010.29.13%20-%20formatted%20- %20FINAL.pdf

57. U.S. Dep't of Labor, Republic of Korea Labour Rights Report (2011), *www*.dol.gov/ilab /map/countries/southkorea.htm.

58. Nat'l Labor Comm., U.S.-Jordan Free Trade Agreement Descends into Human Trafficking and Involuntary Servitude (2006), http://www.globallabourrights.org/admin/documents/ files/Jordan_Report_05_03.pdf. The petition was never formally accepted, because the U.S.-Jordan FTA lacks a formal process for the receipt of complaints. Further, the Bush Administration had issued a letter to the government of Jordan explaining that it would not invoke the labor provisions. However, the news stories and the complaint provoked the government to respond to the public relations nightmare. In 2008, the ILO Better Work project was established in Jordan in an effort to better monitor working conditions in the QIZs. Some of the promised legal reforms have yet to materialize, and the reports of the Better Work program continue to cite frequent violations. *See, e.g.*, Better Work Jordan, Third Compliance Synthesis Report (2012), http://www.betterwork.org/sites/Jordan/English/Pages/index.aspx.

complaints have been filed under CAFTA. In 2008, the AFL-CIO and a coalition of Gua-temalan unions filed the first complaint against Guatemala (detailed below). The AFL-CIO filed a more comprehensive complaint nearly four years later against Honduras in March 2012.[59] That complaint alleged widespread violations of labor rights in the garment, agriculture, and shipping industries, as well as numerous assassinations and attempted assassinations of trade unionists since CAFTA entered into force. The International Long-shore and Warehouse Union and Catholic priest Father Christopher Hartley, respectively, filed complaints against Costa Rica and the Dominican Republic. In 2010, the Sindicato Nacional de Unidad de Trabajadores de SUNAT filed a complaint under the U.S.-Peru FTA. In 2011, the AFL-CIO filed a complaint against Bahrain under a bilateral FTA dur-ing the height of the government's crackdown on demonstrators, urging the United States to serve notice of its intent to withdraw from the pact.

Case Study 1: Guatemala

Although Guatemala made several commitments to reform its laws and improve its labor inspection and judicial system in 2005 in the run-up to the ratification of the CAFTA,[60] and despite millions of U.S. dollars directed toward labor capacity building, the human rights situation in Guatemala continued to deteriorate.[61] Workers were routinely dismissed for exercising their right to associate, and labor administrators and judges did little to ensure that the law was enforced. Furthermore, the assassination of trade unionists increased precipitously following the agreement's passage.

Thus, the AFL-CIO and Guatemalan unions filed a submission under chapter 16 of the CAFTA in April 2008 alleging that the government failed to enforce its labor laws effec-tively. It cited three cases of anti-union dismissals and two assassinations of trade union leaders.[62] The complaint also outlined areas where the government had failed to "strive to ensure that such labor principles and the internationally recognized labor rights . . . are recognized and protected by its law." The U.S. Department of Labor (DOL) accepted the

59. Press Release, AFL-CIO, The AFL-CIO Joins Honduran Trade Unions in Filing a Petition with Department of Labor against Honduran Government for Failing to Enforce Labor Laws under Trade Agreement (Mar. 29, 2012), http://www.aflcio.org/Press-Room/Press-Releases/The-AFL-CIO-Joins-Hon duran-Trade-Unions-in-Filing-a-Petition-with-Department-of-Labor-against-Honduran-Government-for-Failing-to-Enforce-Labor-Laws-under-Trade-Agreement.

60. *See* The Labor Dimension in Central America and the Dominican Republic (White Paper, Apr. 30, 2005), http://www.ilo.org/sanjose/programas-y-proyectos/verificaci%C3%B3n-implementaci%C3%B3n-libro-blanco/WCMS_184287/lang--es/index.htm.

61. For an in depth assessment of U.S.-funded capacity building programs in Central America and their impact on improving respect for worker rights, see Washington Office on Latin America (WOLA), DR-CAFTA and Workers Rights: Moving from Paper to Practice (2009), http://www.wola.org/dr_cafta_and_workers_rights_moving_from_paper_to_practice.

62. AFL-CIO et al., Public Submission to the Office of Trade & Labor Affairs Concerning the Fail-ure of the Government of Guatemala to Effectively Enforce Its Labor Laws (Apr. 23, 2008), http://www.docstoc.com/docs/79799993/CAFTA-complaint---AFL-CIO.

complaint for review in June 2008 and thereafter conducted an investigation into the complaint, including two visits to Guatemala and numerous interviews with workers, employers, and the government.

In each of the five cases detailed in the submission, the DOL's Office of Trade and Labor Affairs (OTLA) sustained both the facts and legal arguments, in whole or in large part, of the petitioners. In some cases, the report contained additional factual findings even more damning than those alleged in the submission. For example, the report provided additional details regarding several repeated failures by the government to act, including (a) failure of labor inspectors to conduct inspections over employers' objections (twelve times); (b) repeated failure of inspectors to use police power to access facilities when companies refused entry; (c) failure of the Labor Ministry to impose or enforce fines for impeding inspections or other violations of the law; and (d) repeated failure of courts to enforce orders, where failure to comply with an order constitutes a criminal violation (eleven times). The OTLA found that in no case had the labor violations been remedied in accordance with the law of Guatemala.

In part due to transitions in the U.S. government, the DOL decided to delay decision on consultations for six month both to allow the new U.S. administration to take up the case and for the government of Guatemala to try to address the issues outlined in the DOL report after submission. There were minor steps forward during that time: a settlement was reached with workers at a frozen vegetable exporter, Inproesa, and labor inspectors conducted inspections at two garment factories named in the complaint, with the result that workers were reinstated and back pay was awarded. However, in the Avandia factory, workers were subjected to retaliation and some were refired. In the Fribo factory the company opted to close down rather than comply fully with the orders of the labor inspector. No apparent effort was made by the Guatemalan government to challenge the legality of the plant closing or to determine whether the factory reopened elsewhere under a new name—a practice all too common in Guatemala.

Despite the ongoing violations and the lack of real progress in the two murder cases, the U.S.TR decided not to proceed to consultations; this decision suggested that the enforcement efforts by the government had weakened the viability of the case.[63] Undeterred, the unions conducted interviews with workers and unionists in numerous sectors and regions and compiled information on several additional cases. The infusion of new cases kept the CAFTA submission going.

In an attempt to prompt the government of Guatemala to take the process more seriously, the DOL and U.S.TR invoked formal consultations in July 2010.[64] The consultations,

---

63. Though never taking a firm position, the U.S. government has treated the assassinations as beyond the scope of the CAFTA labor chapter and thus to be addressed on a separate track.

64. *See* Letter from U.S.TR Kirk and Labor Secretary Solis to Economy Minister Coyoy and Labor

which were to last a minimum of sixty days before moving to the next step, lasted over a year as the United States sought progress, though ultimately with no tangible results. The U.S.TR and DOL announced that they would convene the FTA commission, the last step before a party could request arbitration; this was held in June 2011. The U.S. government attempted to persuade the government of Guatemala to accept a comprehensive action plan, including legal and administrative reforms that would address the matters raised in the complaint (assassinations aside). Several attempts were made to strike a deal, but the Guatemalan government eventually balked at the plan, particularly over provisions that required restoring the ability of labor inspectors to sanction employers who violate the labor law (a power that was previously deemed unconstitutional) and requiring businesses that receive special tax breaks under a law promoting exports to post a bond to cover compensation and benefits to workers in case of closure.

In August 2011, the United States requested the establishment of an arbitral tribunal, as every means to reach a cooperative conclusion had failed by that point. The Guatemalan Economy Minister responded by arguing that the United States had failed to comply with the procedures established under CAFTA.[65] He later suggested another meeting of the Free Trade Commission, this time including the trade ministers of the seven CAFTA countries. That proposal was rejected. The two parties continued negotiations, though a new administration in Guatemala in 2012 slowed down the process. It was nearly another year and a half after the tribunal was requested before the two parties agreed to a plan of action.

In April 2013, the U.S. government announced that a deal had been reached in principle, though the details were still being negotiated.[66] The U.S.TR set forth detailed binding commitments, with short timelines for implementation, that the government agreed to undertake in order to stave off the convention of the arbitration panel.[67] The enforcement plan included several elements, such as police assistance for labor inspectors, enhanced ability for the Ministry of Labor to fine violators, stricter oversight of exporting companies benefiting from tax holidays, and assurance that judicial orders, once awarded, are actually enforced. The AFL-CIO, which filed the complaint, saw the agreement as a "crucial first step" but urged that "more needs to be done to strengthen Guatemala's labor laws, to sanction violators, and to stem the violence against trade unionists."[68]

The conclusion of this agreement was likely assisted by the fact that several workers'

Minister Rodriguez (July 30, 2010), http://www.ustr.gov/trade-agreements/free-trade-agreements/cafta-dr-dominican-republic-central-america-fta/kirk-solis-le.

65. *Guatemala Details Objections to U.S. Panel Request in CAFTA Labor Dispute*, Inside U.S. Trade, Aug. 15, 2011.

66. *See Fact Sheet: Guatemala Agrees to Comprehensive Labor Enforcement Plan*, U.S. Dep't of Labor (Apr. 11, 2013), http://www.ustr.gov/about-us/press-office/fact-sheets/2013/april/guatemala-labor-enforcement.

67. The Labor Rights Enforcement Plan is http://www.ustr.gov/about-us/press-office/blog/2013/april/U.S.-Guatemala-labor-enforcement.

68. Vicki Needham, *U.S., Guatemala Resolve Labor Enforcement Concerns*, The Hill (Apr. 11,

delegates to the ILO's International Labor Conference in 2012 had filed a request for the establishment of a Commission of Inquiry in Guatemala to investigate Guatemala's failure to comply with its obligations under ILO Convention 87 regarding the right to freedom of association and to organize.[69] The delegates raised many of the same concerns cited in the initial CAFTA complaint.

In October 2013, U.S.TR announced that although there were "serious concerns about the enforcement of Guatemala's laws protecting worker rights" and that "significant work remains to ensure that an Enforcement Plan", the U.S.TR again deferred arbitration and gave the government of Guatemala another six months to effectively implement the plan. U.S.TR did make clear that arbitration remained a possibility.[70] On October 22, the petitioners sent a seven-page letter to U.S.TR and DOL detailing how the government of Guatemala had failed to implement the enforcement plan both on paper and in practice and criticized the decision to defer arbitration.[71]

Case Study 2: Bahrain

As the Arab Spring began to unfold in Tunisia and Egypt in early 2011, Bahrain soon followed, with roughly a third to a half of its small population in the streets seeking political freedoms and economic reforms. The result was one of the harshest crackdowns in the region up to that point. With the U.S. Fifth Fleet stationed in Manama, Bahrain, U.S. public criticism of the pro-Western monarchy was markedly muted. As the repression in Bahrain deepened and efforts were underway to dismantle the General Federation of Bahrain Trade Unions (GFBTU) and to punish its leaders, as well as workers who had joined a general strike, trade unions in Bahrain and the United States decided to file a complaint under the FTA on April 21, 2011, in a last-ditch effort to call attention to the human rights violations in Bahrain.

Because of the brutal repression of peaceful protest carried out by the police and armed forces of Bahrain and the Gulf Cooperation Council, labor groups called on the United States to serve notice of its withdrawal from the FTA with the government of Bahrain,

---

2013), http://thehill.com/blogs/on-the-money/1005-trade/293511-us-guatemala-resolve-labor-enforcement-concerns.

69. *See* Complaint under Article 26 of the ILO Constitution against the Government of Guatemala for Non-observance of Convention No. 87 on Freedom of Association and Protection of the Right to Organize, http://www.ituc-csi.org/complaint-under-article-26-of-the.

70. *See*, U.S.TR, UNITED STATES CONTINUES TO PRESS GUATEMALA ON ENFORCEMENT OF WORKER RIGHTS, Oct 2013, *online at* http://www.ustr.gov/about-us/press-office/press-releases/2013/October/U.S .-Guatemala-enforcement-worker-rights

71. AFL-CIO Press Release, *AFL-CIO, Guatemalan Trade Unions Call for Reinstitution of Arbitral Panel After Flawed "Enforcement Plan" Failed to Protect Basic Workers' Rights, available online at* http://www.aflcio.org/Press-Room/Press-Releases/AFL-CIO-Guatemalan-Trade-Unions-Call-for-Reinstitution-of-Arbitral-Panel-After-Flawed-Enforcement-Plan-Failed-to-Protect-Basic-Workers-Rights

pursuant to Article 21.5.2.[72] These groups argued that the United States should not provide preferential trade treatment to a country that had engaged in such well-documented, widespread, and serious violations of human rights of its citizens and residents. Specifically, the limitations on freedom of association and the discriminatory firings experienced by Bahraini workers were alleged to violate Article 15.1, which requires parties to "reaffirm their obligations as members of the International Labor Organization (ILO) and their commitments under the *ILO Declaration on Fundamental Principles and Rights at Work and its Follow-Up* (1998) (ILO Declaration)" and to "strive to ensure that such labor principles and the internationally recognized labor rights set forth in Article 15.7 are recognized and protected by its law." Although a submission filed under that provision could go only as far as consultations, it was seen as the only avenue to provoke at least a public review of what was happening to the labor movement and to the population generally.[73]

The U.S. government quickly dismissed the idea of withdrawing from the agreement, but the DOL did accept the petition for review in June 2011. At roughly the same time, a complaint was filed with the ILO Committee on Freedom of Association, and worker delegates to the ILO International Labor Conference filed a complaint under Article 26 of the ILO Constitution seeking the establishment of a Commission of Inquiry. The Bahraini government immediately hired several lobbyists in an attempt to diffuse criticism in the United States and at the ILO. However, the dismissals, military trials of trade union and human rights activists, and efforts to weaken or dismantle civil society institutions did not cease, and international pressure continued to build. In November 2011, during the meeting of the ILO Governing Body, the government of Bahrain proposed that a tripartite commission review the nearly 3,000 dismissals and suspensions in the public and private sector; this proposal was adopted. The first meeting of this commission took place in mid-December 2011.

Also in November 2011, the Bahrain Independent Commission of Inquiry (BICI) issued a 501-page report regarding the February and March 2011 events in relation to international human rights norms. The report confirmed that the dismissals were undertaken in retaliation for participation in demonstrations and legal strikes, that the government created an environment that encouraged the dismissals and in some cases directly urged companies to fire employees, that the authorities applied the law in a discriminatory manner, and that the vast majority of the firings were illegal under domestic and international law.

A DOL report on the complaint, due in mid-December 2011, but was not issued until a year later, in December 2012. The 41-page report upheld the assertions of the petitioners

---

72.   Article 21.5.2 provides "Either Party may terminate this Agreement on 180-days written notice to the other Party."

73.   As time passed and more information became available, it was clear that the dismissals also violated Bahraini labor law, thus making the case subject to dispute resolution should the case not be resolved prior.

that the government of Bahrain, in its initial response to the protests and subsequent acts, violated principles of the rights to freedom of association, bargaining collectively, and nondiscrimination in employment.[74] The report concluded with a set of recommendations to be taken up during the formal consultations, including enacting substantial labor law reforms, ensuring that workers be unconditionally reinstated with back pay, reviewing all criminal cases against trade unionists and dropping charges where no violence was committed, and refraining from any further activities that would undermine trade unions, including the national trade union center, the GFBTU.

Even before the parties entered into formal consultations in mid-2013, the complaint and the subsequent bilateral engagement it provoked did have an important impact. The complaint immediately seized the attention of the government of Bahrain, which did not foresee the trade consequences of its 2011 crackdown. The FTA complaint arguably contributed to the pressure, together with the complaints lodged at the ILO, that led to the establishment of the tripartite commission on reinstatement. That process returned thousands to work, though according to the GFBTU, some still remain without work, and still others who were reinstated were brought back into inferior positions. The situation in Bahrain remains tense, and trade union activity has stalled in light of the constant threats leveled against the GFBTU. It remains to be seen whether the formal bilateral consultations will lead to any concrete developments.

Labor Rights in FTAs outside of the United States
Canada[75]
In Canada, the evolution of labor rights provisions in trade agreements roughly follows the evolution of those in the United States. Of course, the two countries share a common trade history. Both countries are parties to the NAALC. Today, Canada's most recent labor provisions, such as those found in the Canada-Colombia Agreement on Labor Cooperation (ALC) (a side agreement to the Canada-Colombia FTA), closely resemble the text of May 10th. The ALC does make some improvements to the labor obligations, though it maintains outdated language relating to dispute-settlement procedures.

Article 1 of the Canada-Colombia ALC, for example, calls on each party to "ensure that its statutes and regulations, and practices thereunder, embody and provide protection for

---

74. *See* U.S. DEP'T OF LABOR, PUBLIC REPORT OF REVIEW OF U.S. SUBMISSION 2011-01 (BAHRAIN) (2012), http://www.dol.gov/ilab/programs/otla/20121220Bahrain.pdf.

75. The following free trade agreements are currently in force (as of May 2013): North American Free Trade Agreement (NAFTA), Canada-Israel Free Trade Agreement (CIFTA), Canada-Chile Free Trade Agreement (CCFTA), Canada-Costa Rica Free Trade Agreement (CCRFTA), Canada-European Free Trade Association (EFTA), Canada-Peru Free Trade Agreement, Canada-Colombia Free Trade Agreement, Canada-Jordan Free Trade Agreement, and the Negotiations for a Canada-Honduras Free Trade Agreement have been concluded. See the Web site of Foreign Affairs and International Trade Canada, http://www .international.gc.ca/trade-agreements-accords-commerciaux/agr-acc/index.aspx?view=d.

the following internationally recognized labor principles and rights." The first four of the principles and rights listed include the eight ILO core labor conventions, with an explicit reference to the right to strike; this right is not explicitly mentioned in May 10th but is assumed. The fifth principle incorporates the U.S. FTA concept of acceptable conditions of work. The sixth creates an obligation to "provid[e] migrant workers with the same legal protections as the Party's nationals in respect of working conditions." This protection for migrant workers is a key difference between the U.S. and Canadian labor chapters. Similar language existed under the NAALC, but the protection of migrant workers dropped out of subsequent U.S. FTAs. The nonderogation clause in Article 2 also applies to all six principles and rights, not just the fundamental rights as provided in the May 10th template.

Article 3 expresses the effective enforcement obligation in the affirmative and eliminates any reference to a "sustained or recurring pattern or practice" or a "manner affecting trade or investment between the parties." Thus, unlike in the May 10th model, the failure of a party to enforce laws effectively in a workplace that has no trade or investment nexus with Canada may nonetheless lead to consultation and even ministerial consultations. However, if a party seeks arbitration over labor violations, it must show that "the matter is trade-related" and that there is a "persistent failure to effectively enforce its labor law," or that it failed to bring its statutes and regulations in line with the ILO Declaration. This formulation does appear to preclude arbitration over labor violations linked to an investment rather than trade-related matter, unlike May 10th.

The Canada-Colombia FTA retains the Bush Administration's approach with regard to monetary assessments in case of nonimplementation of the final report. Under that agreement, a party's failure to implement a final report may lead to the levying of a monetary assessment of up to only $15 million annually. Of note, the Canada-Jordan ALC, which entered into force in October 2012, does not set a maximum threshold.[76] The Canada-Panama FTA, which entered into force in April 2013, includes the $15 million cap.[77]

To date, no complaints (other than those filed under the NAALC) have been filed under the labor chapter of a Canadian FTA. There is also no record of demands made on parties to reform legislation in advance of ratification of an FTA. Rather, labor capacity-building programs appear to be the preferred form of engagement.

Of note, trade union and civil society concerns over human and trade-union rights violations in Colombia resulted in an agreement for each party to conduct yearly self-assessments of the human rights implications of the trade agreement. The Canadian Labour Congress, which opposed the deal, said the proposal was "equivalent to 'putting the fox

---

76. Available online at http://www.labour.gc.ca/eng/relations/international/agreements/lca_jordan .shtml.

77. Available online at http://www.labour.gc.ca/eng/relations/international/agreements/lca_panama .shtml.

in charge of the hen house.'"[78] Human rights organizations have blasted the reports, with Amnesty International Canada describing the latest as a "human rights report without human rights."[79]

European Union

The labor provisions in EU trade agreements have recently developed substantially from the rudimentary provisions found in, for example, the EU-South Africa (2000) and EU-Chile (2003) trade agreements.[80] The EU-Chile agreement, for instance, addressed labor rights only as a subject for social cooperation, with no binding commitments or enforcement mechanisms.[81] The current generation of agreements is far more robust, though at once more expansive and more limited than the templates found in the United States and Canada; the EU-Korea FTA (2011) is a case in point.

The labor obligations of that trade agreement are found in chapter 13 of the FTA, on "Trade and Sustainable Development."[82] Each party is required to "seek to ensure that those laws and policies provide for and encourage high levels of . . . labor protection, consistent with the internationally recognized standards or agreements," and "shall strive to continue to improve those laws and policies."[83] In many ways, this text reflects the aspirational language found throughout the NAALC. However, the concept of *labor* in the EU-Korea agreement is quite broad, not limited merely to core labor rights but instead to the ILO Decent Work Agenda, which also contemplates social protection, social dialogue, and job creation.

In Article 13.4 of the EU-Korea FTA, parties "reaffirm the commitment" under the 2006 Ministerial Declaration of the UN Economic and Social Council on Full Employment and Decent Work. Parties also commit, in accordance with their membership in the ILO and the ILO Declaration on Fundamental Principles and Rights at Work, to "respect, promote and realize" in their laws and practices the principles concerning the ILO fundamental

---

78. Press Release, Canadian Labor Congress Statement on Passage of Canada-Colombia Free Trade Agreement (July 12, 2010), http://www.canadianlabor.ca/news-room/statements/canadian-labor-congress-statement-passage-canada-colombia-free-trade-agreement.

79. *See* Press Release, Amnesty International Canada, Canada-Colombia Free Trade: Another Human Rights Report Without Human Rights (June 24, 2013), http://www.amnesty.ca/news/public-statements/canada-colombia-free-trade-another-human-rights-report-without-human-rights.

80. *See, e.g.,* Ebert and Posthuma, *supra* note 1, at 14–15.

81. *See, e.g.,* Trade Agreement, E.U.-Chile, art. 44, Nov. 18, 2002 ("1. The Parties recognise the importance of social development, which must go hand in hand with economic development. They shall give priority to the creation of employment and respect for fundamental social rights, notably by promoting the relevant conventions of the International Labour Organisation covering such topics as the freedom of association, the right to collective bargaining and non-discrimination, the abolition of forced and child labour and equal treatment between men and women.").

82. Free Trade Agreement, E.U.-Republic of Korea, Sept. 16, 2010, http://eur-lex.europa.eu/LexUriServ/LexUriServ.do?uri=OJ:L:2011:127:0006:1343:EN:PDF.

83. Article 13.3.

rights. This provision is not unlike that found in the pre–May 10th FTAs in the United States. Of particular note, and not found in the labor provisions of any U.S. or Canadian FTA, the parties reaffirm their commitment to enforce effectively those conventions that each party has already ratified. In the case of Korea, unfortunately, it has not ratified core conventions such as ILO Convention 87 on freedom of association and the right to organize, or ILO Convention 98 on collective bargaining. The parties do, however, make a commitment to "make efforts" to ratify the fundamental and "up-to-date" conventions.

Like the U.S. FTAs, the EU adopts nearly word for word the May 10th requirements to enforce labor laws and not to waive or derogate from those laws to encourage trade or investment.

The biggest difference between EU and U.S. agreements relates to dispute settlement, where the European Union takes a decidedly less contentious approach. Article 13.10 of the EU-Korea FTA requires, for example, that the parties commit to "reviewing, monitoring and assessing the impact of the implementation" of the agreement. Further, Article 13.13 requires the convention of a civil society forum each year, with representatives drawn from "domestic advisory groups," including labor groups. Under Article 13.14, a party may request consultations with another party on any matter of "mutual interest" arising under the chapter; submissions from the domestic advisory group may form the basis for a request for consultations. The parties are to "make every attempt to arrive at a mutually satisfactory resolution." With regard to labor, the parties must "ensure that the resolution reflects the activities of the ILO . . . so as to promote greater coherence between the work of the Parties" and the ILO. If the party deems that further discussion is necessary, the party may request that the Committee on Trade and Sustainable Development be convened with an aim to agree on a resolution. If that fails, a party may request that a panel of experts be convened to examine the matter. The experts will issue a report with recommendations, the implementation of which will be monitored by the Committee on Trade and Sustainable Development. Unlike the U.S. or Canadian model, there is no fine or sanction of any kind. If the parties cannot resolve their disagreement about the application of the chapter, there is nothing else to be done.[84]

Conclusions

Each model has its own strengths and limitations, as noted above, both with regard to minimum obligations and dispute-settlement procedures. In each case, however, there has been an unmistakable evolution forward. The most serious problem with each is the fact that any decision to seek a party's compliance with the terms of an agreement,

---

84. Of note, the E.U.-CARIFORM trade agreement (2008), a regional pact with the Caribbean Forum of African, Caribbean, and Pacific States, does provide dispute settlement procedures on labor issues though trade-related sanctions are unavailable.

either pre- or postratification, is both a political and legal decision, and thus the agreements will only be as useful as the politicians desire them to be. Governments hostile or indifferent to labor have done little to use FTAs, regardless of the language, to seek strengthening of labor laws, fortify labor institutions, or seek dispute resolution when serious breaches occur. In other cases, foreign policy interests may trump the application and enforcement of the labor obligations. Even when there is political will, labor violations often occur in weak, unstable, or corrupt states with deeply underfunded and/or weak administrative and judicial institutions. Overcoming these and other related problems requires a long-term commitment of time and resources, in which few governments will want to invest to resolve a labor rights petition. Additionally, those parties actually committing most labor violations, namely private employers, are beyond the reach of the trade-agreement dispute mechanisms. Although employers may be held accountable if a country reacts to a petition by enforcing the law against them specifically, or may be affected indirectly if the sector loses orders because a country is seen as a business risk, most employers continue to violate the law knowing that the FTA is unlikely to be vigorously applied or enforced.

Unilateral Trade Preferences

In 1964, Raul Prebish, secretary-general of the United Nations Conference on Trade and Development (UNCTAD), advocated that developed countries grant preferential tariff treatment to developing countries. The Generalized System of Preferences (GSP), adopted at UNCTAD II in New Delhi in 1968, did just that. Today, several countries maintain a GSP scheme, including Australia, Canada, the EU, Japan, New Zealand, Norway, the Russian Federation, Switzerland, and the United States. However, only the U.S. and the EU currently condition eligibility for trade preferences on compliance with international labor standards, though the conditions differ significantly. Although the U.S. and the EU both maintain multiple trade preference programs, this section will focus largely on the U.S. and EU GSP while noting innovations in other recent programs.

The United States
GSP
The Trade Act of 1974 (Trade Act) established the GSP scheme, which entered into force in 1976.[85] In 1984, the statute was amended, in part, by conditioning a country's eligibility for benefits on meeting certain labor criteria. The obligation as stated is simple:

---

85.   19 U.S.C. § 2461 *et seq.*

The President shall not designate any country a beneficiary developing country under this subchapter if . . . [s]uch country has not taken or is not taking steps to afford internationally recognized worker rights to workers in the country (including any designated zone in that country).[86]

"Internationally recognized worker rights" is defined under the Trade Act to include: "(a) the right of association; (b) the right to organize and bargain collectively; (c) a prohibition on the use of any form of forced or compulsory labor; (d) a minimum age for the employment of children; and (e) acceptable conditions of work with respect to minimum wages, hours of work, and occupational safety and health."[87] In 2000, beneficiary countries were also required to implement their commitments "to eliminate the worst forms of child labor" in order to remain eligible.[88]

The 1984 amendment was historic and in the United States it cemented a link between labor and trade that is now taken as a given. However, as subsequent experience with the clause has demonstrated, it has certain limitations.[89] For example, the clause requires no minimum level of compliance. A country has only to improve its labor standards marginally over time. A country with poor labor laws may continue to qualify for these preferences so long as it temporarily and marginally improves them if a country practice petition is filed.[90] The U.S. GSP creates no incentive for countries to improve their laws and practices, unlike the EU GSP+ (described below), except for the potential threat of a country practice petition by a third party, or when the U.S. government undertakes a rare, self-initiated investigation. Many countries currently benefitting from the program have not only failed to take steps to afford internationally recognized worker rights, but some have regressed significantly.

Furthermore, the labor clause falls short of current international minimum standards. In 1998, the members of the ILO agreed on a set of universal minimum labor rights applicable to all members. These rights were enshrined in the ILO Declaration on Fundamental Principles and Rights at Work, committing all members to respect and promote principles

---

86.   19 U.S.C. § 2462(b)(2)(G).

87.   19 U.S.C. § 2467(4).

88.   19 U.S.C § 2462(b)(2)(H).

89.   For a thorough review of the first twenty years' experience with the GSP labor chapter, see Lance Compa & Jeffrey Vogt, *Labor Rights in the Generalized System of Preferences: A 20-Year Review*, 22 Comp. Labor Law & Pol'y J. 199 (2001).

90.   The GSP petition process is set forth at 15 C.F.R. 2007 (Jan. 1, 2008). In short, any person may file a written petition with U.S.TR during a designated period to withdraw, suspend, or limit a beneficiary country's trade preferences on the basis that it has failed to comply with the program's labor eligibility criteria. If the petition is accepted for review, a public hearing before an interagency panel is usually scheduled. The government also undertakes its own fact-finding. The interagency committee will thereafter decide to withdraw, suspend, or limit the preferences, put the country under a continuing review (essentially a probationary period), or close the case.

and rights in four categories: freedom of association and the effective recognition of the right to collective bargaining, the elimination of forced or compulsory labor, the effective abolition of child labor, and the elimination of discrimination in employment and occupation.[91] All ILO members are obliged to respect and promote these principles and rights, regardless of whether they have ratified the relevant underlying fundamental conventions, simply by virtue of their membership.[92]

Despite the adoption of the ILO Declaration nearly fourteen years ago, the GSP and most trade preference programs still refer to "internationally recognized worker rights" (IRWR). There are important differences between IRWR and the ILO fundamental labor rights. For example, IRWR do not include the prohibition on discrimination in employment and occupation contained in the ILO Declaration.[93] In addition, GSP refers to "a minimum age for the employment of children," which is weaker than the ILO formulation of "the effective abolition of child labor." The GSP does, however, call for the elimination of child labor *in its worst forms*, referring to ILO Convention 182, one of the few fundamental conventions that the United States ratified. Finally, because IRWR do not refer to any external source of law, they can and have been invested with the meaning given to them by the U.S.TR rather than the meaning conferred on them by the ILO.[94] IRWR do notably include the concept of *acceptable conditions of work*, which refers to minimum wages, hours of work, and occupational safety and health; this goes beyond the scope of the ILO Declaration.

Procedural issues also limit the effectiveness of the program. The GSP allows for third parties to submit petitions alleging violations of the program's labor eligibility criteria and demand that the program be suspended. The regulations implementing each program limit petitions to only once a year, though the statute imposes no such limitation.[95] Thus, if a major labor rights violation occurs a month after the petition window closes, a petitioner will have to wait nearly an entire year to raise the matter through a formal petition process (though informal pressure remains possible).

---

91.   *See* Int'l Labor Org., ILO Declaration on Fundamental Principles and Rights at Work and its Follow-up (June 18, 1998), http://www.ilo.org/declaration/thedeclaration/textdeclaration/lang--en/index.htm.

92.   See Article 2 of the ILO Declaration.

93.   The proponents of the original GSP labor clause urged the inclusion of nondiscrimination in employment, but it was later stripped out of the draft legislation. For a discussion of its exclusion, see Karen F. Travis, *Women in Global Production and Worker Rights Provisions in U.S. Trade Laws*, 17 YALE J. INT'L L 173 (1992).

94.   An infamous example of this is the so-called "Clatanoff Rule," articulated by former Assistant U.S.TR for Labor, William "Bud" Clatanoff. At a 2003 conference at the National Academy of Sciences regarding monitoring international labor standards, he stated with regard to freedom of association: "If someone tries to form a union, they can't get shot, fired or jailed. I'm sorry. I know there are thousands of pages of ILO jurisprudence I am not going to read, but that's my criteria—shot, fired or jailed, you're not given freedom of association." *See* NATIONAL RESEARCH COUNCIL (U.S.), MONITORING INTERNATIONAL LABOR STANDARDS: NATIONAL LEGAL FRAMEWORKS, SUMMARY OF A WORKSHOP 42 (2003).

95.   *See* 15 C.F.R. § 2007.3.

However, the most problematic issue is the unchecked discretion the United States exercises in applying the statute.[96] Numerous well-supported petitions detailing widespread violations of worker rights have been rejected over the years without any official explanation. In other situations, cases are accepted and then left open for years under a "continuing review"—in essence a probationary period during which the granting government waits to see whether a country is making sufficient progress to retain its eligibility. Though using a continuing review as a means to provoke the improvements necessary to avoid suspension is legitimate, some such reviews have continued for several years while workers' rights continued to be routinely violated. The lack of transparency in the process has frustrated petitioners, because a written statement is never issued about why a petition is or is not accepted for review or why a review, once opened, is subsequently closed. This has left petitioners guessing why a petition was rejected or, once accepted, what actions, if any, the government is taking to press the beneficiary country to address the issues raised in the petition.

The impact of the GSP worker rights clause on raising labor conditions in beneficiary countries is very difficult to quantify. Several reports have found that labor rights provisions have had a positive impact in some cases, though the results are uneven at best.[97] In the best cases, targeted legislative reforms and resolution of specific violations were possible. This often happens because of a combination of sustained political will by the U.S. government, political will by the beneficiary government (which calculates whether it has more to lose economically by failing to comply than by continuing to violate the terms of the statute), and effective campaigning and organizing by unions and NGOs in the beneficiary country. One commentator notes that factors including the degree of democracy, the kind of worker right targeted in the complaint (child labor versus wage and hour violations), and the availability of local resources to address violations are

---

96. A large coalition of trade unions and NGOs, led by the International Labor Rights Fund, filed a federal lawsuit challenging the Bush Administration's failure to apply the workers' rights provisions of the statute. *See* ILRERF v. Bush, 752 F. Supp. 495 (Dist. D.C. 1990), *affirmed*, 954 F.2d 745 (D.C. Cir. 1992). However, the case was ultimately dismissed on questions of justiciability and standing—leaving the agency's application of the worker rights clause effectively unreviewable.

97. For example, see OECD, Trade Employment and Labor Standards: A Study of Core Workers Rights and International Trade (1996); Kimberly Ann Elliott, Institute for International Economics, *Preferences for Workers? Worker Rights and the U.S. Generalized System of Preferences* (1998); Henry Frundt, *Trade Conditions and Labor Rights: U.S. Initiatives, Dominican and Central American Responses* (1998); Lance Compa & Jeffrey Vogt, *Labor Rights in the Generalized System of Preferences: A 20-Year Review*, 22 Comp. Labor Law & Pol'y J. 199 (2001); Kimberly Ann Elliot & Richard Freeman, Institute for International Economics, Can Labor Standards Improve Under Globalization? (2003); Sandra Polaski, Carnegie Endowment for Int'l Peace, Trade and Labor Standards: A Strategy for Developing Countries (2003); Thomas Greven, Social Standards in Bilateral and Regional Trade and Investment Agreements: Instruments, Enforcement, and Policy Options for Trade Unions (2005); Bama Athreya, U.S. Dep't of Labor, Comparative Case Analysis of the Impacts of Trade-Related Labor Provisions on Select U.S. Trade Preference Recipient Countries (2011), http://www.dol.gov/ilab/programs/otla/2010ILRF.pdf.

important in assessing the impact complaints have in improving workers' rights.[98] Still, reforms are rarely deeply structural, and labor violations often continue once the spotlight no longer shines on the country. In the worst cases, as discussed below, the United States has done little even in the face of serious and systematic violations, as enforcement of labor standards takes a back seat to other economic or geopolitical interests (though rarely stated as such).

Case 1: Bangladesh

The government of Bangladesh has been a frequent subject of GSP petitions for violations of internationally recognized worker rights. The first petition called for the withdrawal of preferential treatment because the government had refused to apply its labor laws to the sizeable Export Processing Zones (EPZs).[99] A second petition was filed because the government had failed to meet established deadlines to adopt and enforce workers' rights in the EPZs. In response to the second petition, the government published a notice in its official gazette in January 2001 that provided that all workers "will have their legal rights and related rights in the EPZs and that this will be effective from January 1, 2004."[100]

In December 2004, a third petition was filed highlighting the decision of the Bangladesh Export Processing Zones Authority (BEPZA) to review the performance of the Workers Rights and Welfare Committees in the EPZs prior to permitting the full exercise of free association and collective bargaining; this action was inconsistent with the notice in the Bangladesh *Gazette*. In 2005, a further GSP petition alleged ongoing violations in the EPZs. The most recent petition, still under review, was filed in 2007 following a military coup and the subsequent declaration of a state of emergency by the junta. This declaration restricted the exercise of all civil liberties, expressly inclusive of "trade union activities." The petition also noted several serious labor violations in the garment industry, in the EPZs, and in the growing shrimp-processing industry.

The 2007 petition was accepted for review by U.S.TR. Immediately, there was some progress in the EPZs, which are under the management of a brigadier general. The EPZs held elections for worker associations (what is allowed in the zones in lieu of unions) in the majority of factories, with most workers voting to form an association. The beginning of industrial relations in the zones was making tentative steps forward. Grievance

---

98. *See* KIMBERLY ANN ELLIOT & RICHARD FREEMAN, INSTITUTE FOR INTERNATIONAL ECONOMICS, CAN LABOR STANDARDS IMPROVE UNDER GLOBALIZATION? (2003).

99. EPZs are specially designated zones where inputs are imported and processed or manufactured and then exported. Such goods face no duties so long as they do not enter the market of the country where the EPZ is located. In many cases, EPZs offer tax benefits and other advantages (in some cases, including Bangladesh, weaker labor laws) in order to encourage manufacturers to produce in these zones.

100. For a critique of the effectiveness of the GSP on this case up to this point, see Lisa Clay, *Effectiveness of the Worker Rights Provisions of the Generalized System of Preferences: The Bangladesh Case Study*, 11 Transnat'l L. & Contemp. Probs. 175 (2001).

committees began to form and some disputes were resolved through negotiation. The experience in the Readymade Garment (RMG) sector, however, was the exact opposite. Where the garment exporter associations made numerous promises but failed to follow through on respect for wage and hour and health and safety laws, let alone on respecting the right of workers to form unions. In the shrimp industry, a foundation was established to educate producers and workers on workplace rights, and some wage and workplace safety issues did improve.

The GSP petition was in part responsible for these steps, but the more important factor was the garment industry's hope of taking advantage of a proposed duty-free, quota-free bill in the U.S. Congress: the New Partnership for Development Act. The bill would have granted Bangladesh much greater market access to the United States for its apparel products—its key industry, which is excluded from the GSP. The government of Bangladesh knew that it would not be possible to benefit from the proposed bill if it remained under the GSP review for serious worker rights violations in the very industry that stood to benefit most. Thus, the government and industry launched an intense lobbying campaign in Washington, D.C., to present themselves as having reformed. Few, however, were convinced.

As time moved on, early gains stalled. In the shrimp-processing sector, workers continued to report forced overtime, nonpayment of the minimum wage, and the lack of protective equipment. Nascent unions in this sector were busted. In three cases, employers fired the leadership of the union (and no other workers). In other cases, workers were told that they could return if they renounced their union activity. In the EPZs, little progress was made on collective bargaining. Thus, with no ability to negotiate over the terms and conditions of employment or to resolve collective disputes, the workers' associations became moribund and workers began to lose hope and interest. The RMG sector, as before, remained largely union free.

In 2012, the situation worsened substantially. In April, union leader Aminul Islam, who had been severely beaten by police and national intelligence officers in 2010, was found murdered, apparently for his trade union advocacy.[101] In November, a major fire broke out at the Tazreen Fashions factory in Dhaka, claiming the lives of more than one hundred workers.[102] The pressure on the United States to take action on Bangladesh mounted. In January 2013, U.S.TR issued a Federal Register notice calling for public comments on the potential impact of the withdrawal, suspension, or limitation of trade preference for

---

101. Julfikar Ali Manik & Vikas Bajaj, *Killing of Bangladeshi Labour Organizer Signals an Escalation in Violence*, N.Y. Times (April 9, 2012), http://www.nytimes.com/2012/04/10/world/asia/bangladeshi-labor-organizer-is-found-killed.html.

102. Vikas Bajaj, *Fatal Fire in Bangladesh Highlights the Dangers Facing Garment Workers*, N.Y. Times (Nov. 25, 2012), http://www.nytimes.com/2012/11/26/world/asia/bangladesh-fire-kills-more-than-100-and-injures-many.html.

Bangladesh—a clear sign that it was losing its patience.[103] A public hearing on the GSP petition was held in March 2013.

Just one month later, in April 2013, the nine-story Rana Plaza building collapsed on the outskirts of the capital, claiming over 1,100 lives.[104] The building had housed garment factories that had produced goods for several U.S.- and EU-based retailers.[105] Large cracks in the building had appeared the previous day, alarming local building engineers, but the management of the garment companies insisted that workers nevertheless report to work. This tragedy sent shockwaves through the garment industry, with brands such as Disney pulling its orders out of Bangladesh entirely.[106] Divisions emerged within the U.S. government to determine the next steps. The Department of Labor favored suspension of GSP in light of the lack of progress and the need to maintain the credibility of the labor rights criteria; this suspension could provide leverage to demand progress. The State Department, on the other hand, appeared concerned about potential harm to diplomatic relations and the Bangladesh economy.[107] However, on June 27 the Obama Administration decided to suspend GSP to Bangladesh, sending a strong signal to the government of Bangladesh that business could not continue as usual.[108]

The immediate impact of the decision was the move by the government of Bangladesh to make improvements to labor legislation by establishing a high-level committee to review the amendments.[109] The parliament adopted a new labor code on July 15, 2013, but the new law failed to address many of the key issues raised with regard to freedom of association and collective bargaining.[110] Whether the GSP suspension will be success-

---

103. 78 Fed. Reg. 1300-1301 (Jan. 8, 2013), http://federal.eregulations.us/rulemaking/document/U.S.TR-2012-0036-0001.

104. Associated Press, *Death Toll in Bangladesh Passes 1,100*, N.Y. TIMES (May 11, 2013), http://www.nytimes.com/2013/05/12/world/asia/death-toll-in-bangladesh-collapse.html.

105. Steven Greenhouse, *Retailers Are Pressed on Safety at Factories*, N.Y. TIMES (May 10, 2013), http://www.nytimes.com/2013/05/11/business/global/clothing-retailers-pressed-on-banglad esh-factory-safety.html?ref=asia.

106. Steven Greenhouse, *Some Retailers Rethink Their Role in Bangladesh*, N.Y. TIMES (May 1, 2013), http://www.nytimes.com/2013/05/02/business/some-retailers-rethink-their-role-in-bangladesh.html ?pagewanted=all.

107. Ian Urbina, *Unions Press to End Special Trade Status for Bangladesh*, N.Y. TIMES (May 30, 2013), http://www.nytimes.com/2013/05/31/business/us-pressure-rises-to-end-bangladesh-trade-status .html?smid=fb-share.

108. Steven Greenhouse, *Obama to Suspend Trade Privileges with Bangladesh*, N.Y. TIMES (June 27, 2013), http://www.nytimes.com/2013/06/28/business/us-to-suspend-trade-privileges-w ith-bangladesh-officials-say.html?pagewanted=all. *See also* Proclamation of the President, Technical Trade Proclamation to Congress Regarding Bangladesh (June 27, 2013), http://www.whitehouse.gov/ the-press-office/2013/06/27/technical-trade-proclamation-congress-regarding-bangladesh.

109. *See, e.g., Govt Plans Labour Law Review to Reinstate GSP Facility*, THE INDEPENDENT (July 1, 2013), http://www.theindependentbd.com/index.php?option=com_content&view=article&id=176152 :govt-plans-labour-law-review-to-reinstate-gsp-facility&catid=132:backpage&Itemid=122.

110. *See Editorial: Half-hearted Labor Reform in Bangladesh*, N.Y. TIMES (July 17, 2013), http://www .nytimes.com/2013/07/18/opinion/halfhearted-labor-reform-in-bangladesh.html?_r=0. *See also* ILO

ful in helping to bring about long-term and sustainable reform in Bangladesh, combined with other initiatives, remains to be seen.

Case 2: Uzbekistan

In June 2007, the International Labor Rights Fund filed a GSP complaint against Uzbekistan alleging that the government was engaging in widespread forced labor and forced child labor in the annual cotton harvest.[111] At that time, and in subsequent reports, human and labor rights organizations documented the mobilization of an involuntary army of laborers.[112] These reports provided substantial evidence that orders for this mobilization came from the top of government and were transmitted through governors and regional governors to school administrators, who were responsible for supplying child labor to assigned farms. Government officials and police oversaw the harvest mobilization. Parents who refused to send their children to work in the fields faced sanctions such as the removal of welfare subsidies or shutoff of gas or electricity. Security was employed throughout the cotton region to prevent anyone from observing the harvest and reporting on the widespread abuses. Children and parents were instructed to deny that they were picking cotton.

This work is hazardous, and the death of child workers has been reported during previous harvests. Children have been reported to suffer from exhaustion, malnutrition, and other health problems after weeks or months of arduous labor. Older children and children working on remote cotton farms were often forced to stay in makeshift dormitories with insufficient food and drinking water.

The United States has on many occasions communicated its concerns on forced child labor to the government of Uzbekistan. In addition, in its most recent Global Trafficking in Persons Report, on June 24, 2013, the U.S. State Department downgraded Uzbekistan to "Tier 3"—a designation reserved for those countries that fail to act on forced labor and human trafficking—largely on the basis of continuing reports of forced child labor in

---

Statement on Reform of Bangladesh Labour Law (July 22, 2013), http://www.ilo.org/global/about-the-ilo/media-centre/statements-and-speeches/WCMS_218067/lang--en/index.htm.

111. Original petition available online at http://ilrf.org/sites/default/files/publications-and-resources/GSP%20Uzbekistan%20Petition%20June%202007.pdf.

112. *See, e.g.,* Environmental Justice Foundation's Pick Your Cotton Carefully campaign, http://www.ejfoundation.org/page141.html; Anti-Slavery International's End Cotton Crimes campaign, http://www.antislavery.org/english/campaigns/cottoncrimes/default.aspx; Uzbek-German Forum for Human Rights, uzbekgermanforum.org; and Human Rights Watch, http://www.hrw.org/europecentral-asia/uzbekistan. These and other sources served as the basis for workers' group interventions at the 2011 and 2013 ILO Conference Committee on Application of Standards on Convention 182, http://www.ilo.org/wcmsp5/groups/public/---ed_norm/---relconf/documents/meetingdocument/wcms_157818.pdf. and http://www.ilo.org/ilc/ILCSessions/102/reports/committee-reports/WCMS_216456/lang--en/index.htm. Comments by the IOE and the ITUC are also reflected in the 2012 and 2013 report of ILO Committee of Experts, http://www.ilo.org/wcmsp5/groups/public/---ed_norm/---relconf/documents/meetingdocument/wcms_174843.pdf and http://www.ilo.org/ilc/ILCSessions/102/ reports/reports-submitted/WCMS_205472/lang--en/index.htm.

the cotton industry.[113] However, to date, the United States has declined to suspend trade preferences in response to this situation.

Other U.S. Preference Programs

Most regional trade preference programs incorporate the GSP labor clause or adopt a minor variation thereof.[114] A bilateral trade preference program for Haiti, the Haitian Hemispheric Opportunity through Partnership Encouragement Act of 2008 (HOPE II), discussed in detail below, signaled a substantial departure from the GSP model, requiring higher labor standards and factory registration, as well as participation in an ILO-sponsored Better Work monitoring program.[115] A proposed Reconstruction Opportunity Zone (ROZ) program for Afghanistan and Pakistan included labor criteria based largely on the HOPE II model but was never enacted, in part due to objections to the proposed labor requirements by the apparel, footwear, and retail industry, as well as Senate Republicans.[116] A duty-free, quota-free bill for least-developed countries, initially introduced in 2009, advocated a far more robust approach on labor rights and oversight but was never adopted.[117]

Despite demands from labor, industry, and environmental and development organizations over the years to improve on the program's conditionality, transparency in decision-making, and rules on product coverage,[118] the GSP was simply renewed in its existing form in October 2011 until July 2013. The political moment for substantial progress disappeared after the 2010 elections, when the Democratic Party lost control of the House of Representatives.

Haiti

HOPE II included novel labor protections for a trade preference program. It established a labor ombudsman—a government representative responsible for maintaining a registry of the apparel producers that may seek preferential treatment—and a committee comprising representatives of government agencies, employers, and workers to consult on the implementation of the ILO Program. The ombudsman is also responsible for

---

113. U.S. STATE DEP'T, TRAIFFICKING IN PERSONS REPORT 2013 (2013), http://www.state.gov/j/tip/rls/tiprpt/2013/210551.htm.

114. *See, e.g.,* Andean Trade Preference Act (ATPA) (Dec. 1991), as amended by the Andean Trade Promotion and Drug Eradication Act (ATPDEA) (incorporating by reference worker rights criteria of the GSP); Caribbean Basin Initiative (CBI) (entered into force Oct. 1, 2000) (same); African Growth and Opportunities Act (AGOA) (substituting "making continual progress toward establishing" in place of the "taking steps to afford" approach in GSP).

115. *See* Food, Conservation, and Energy Act of 2008 (P.L. 110–246), Subtitle D, Part I.

116. Afghanistan-Pakistan Security and Prosperity Enhancement Act, H.R. 1318, 111th Cong. (2009).

117. New Partnership for Trade Development Act of 2009, H.R. 4101, 111th Cong. (2009).

118. Views and reform proposals from numerous government, industry, labor, development, and environmental witnesses were debated at a November 2009 Ways and Means Committee hearing on the "Operation, Impact and Future of the U.S. Preference Programs." The written testimony is available online at http://democrats.waysandmeans.house.gov/Hearings/transcript.aspx?NewsID=10412.

receiving comments from interested parties about the labor conditions in the facilities of the registered producers as well as calling for the establishment of an ILO Better Work program.

The ILO program in Haiti has two essential elements: monitoring and capacity building. The central element of the monitoring program is a labor rights assessment of the registered factories. The ILO assesses the compliance of each producer with the core labor standards and the national labor laws of Haiti related to the core labor standards and acceptable conditions of work, such as wages, hours, and safety and health. The assessment consists of conducting unannounced site visits to factories and conducting confidential interviews separately with workers and management. The ILO then provides to management, workers, and unions the results of the assessment and makes specific suggestions for remediating any violations. The ILO also assists the producer to remediate any violations identified in the assessment and conducts follow-up visits to the facilities to assess progress. Further, the ILO provides training to workers and management to promote compliance with the national and international labor laws.

Every six months, the ILO issues a report that covers the preceding six-month period. The report includes the name of each producer listed in the registry that has met the labor conditions and the name of each producer listed in the registry that has violated the labor conditions and has failed to remedy such violations. For each producer that has failed to remedy the violations, the report provides a description of the violations and the specific suggestions for remediating such violations. For each producer that has been identified as a labor violator in a previous report, the report includes a description of the progress made in remediating such violations since the prior report and an assessment of whether any violations still persist.

Under HOPE II, each year the United States determines whether Haiti has established or is making continual progress toward establishing internationally recognized worker rights. The determination is made in part by referring to the six-month assessments produced by the ILO. Every two years, the United States identifies those registered producers that have failed to comply with the core labor standards and tries to assist each producer to come into compliance with core labor standards. If such efforts fail, the United States withdraws, suspends, or limits the application of preferential treatment for that producer. The producer can be reinstated if it demonstrates improved practices and compliance with core labor standards.

However, the program has been beset by many problems from the beginning, and matters became substantially worse after a massive earthquake in January 2010 leveled the capital city of Port-au-Prince. The garment industry has always been characterized by exploitation, with garment factory owners among the wealthiest people in the country and largely beyond the reach of the law. Extremely weak government institutions have meant that the labor law is almost never enforced. The most recent report by ILO Better

Work confirms, for example, that not one garment factory is paying the minimum wage.[119] The report also notes that the only collective agreement in the industry is not being fully respected, that employers in one factory have coerced union activists to resign from the union, and that 140 workers fired for participating in a legal strike the previous year still had not been reinstated.[120]

The European Union[121]

Although the European Union enacted its GSP program in 1971, it was not until 1995 that labor criteria were added as a condition of eligibility. Unlike the United States, whose GSP program has remained relatively unchanged, the EU GSP's labor provisions are regularly modified and have evolved substantially (both substantively and procedurally) since it was first introduced. Over time, the substantive obligations have become more robust, with even higher standards required to apply and remain eligible for the special incentive arrangement (GSP+). The minimum level of compliance necessary to avoid a temporary withdrawal of trade preferences under any scheme has become more rigorous as well. At the same time, procedures have shifted away from a complaints-based mechanism, under which the European Commission (Commission) could receive information from third parties, evaluate the evidence, and draw its own conclusions, to a process whereby the outcomes of ILO supervisory processes largely determine whether the Commission can take action to modify a country's eligibility for trade preferences. A reform that will enter into force in January 2014 attempts to reempower the Commission to seek external sources of information on labor rights to supplement the conclusions of the ILO supervisory system, if any.

Evolution of Substantive Obligations[122]

In January 1995, the EU GSP provided for the first time that trade preferences could be temporarily withdrawn in the case of the "practice of any form of forced labor" and the "export of goods made by prison labor."[123] In January 1998, two special-incentive arrange-

---

119. BETTER WORK HAITI, GARMENT INDUSTRY 6TH BIANNUAL REPORT UNDER THE HOPE II LEGISLATION 18 (2013), http://betterwork.org/global/wp-content/uploads/HOPE-II-Report_April-2013_Final.pdf.

120. *Id.* at 16–17.

121. I do not here discuss the Cotonou Agreement, which provides additional trade preferences to the African-Caribbean-Pacific (ACP) states—most of which were former colonies or territories of Member States. The Cotonou Agreement contains a labor clause, Article 50, unlike its predecessor, the Lome Convention. However, it requires beneficiaries to do little more than "reaffirm their commitment to the internationally recognised core labor standards."

122. For a further useful discussion on the evolution of the E.U. GSP up to 2005, see THOMAS GREVEN, SOCIAL STANDARDS IN BILATERAL AND REGIONAL TRADE AND INVESTMENT AGREEMENTS: INSTRUMENTS, ENFORCEMENT AND POLICY OPTIONS FOR TRADE UNIONS 16–23 (2005).

123. Council Regulation 3281/94, art. 9 (Dec. 19, 1994) (EC).

ments anticipated in the initial 1994 European Council Regulation came into force.[124] Under the special incentive for labor, a country could be eligible to participate if it provided proof that it had "adopted and actually appl[ied] domestic legal provisions incorporating the substance of the standards laid down in ILO Conventions Nos. 87 and 98 concerning freedom of association and protection of the right to organize and the application of the principles of the right to organize and to bargain collectively and Convention 138 concerning minimum age for admission to employment."[125] Like the U.S. GSP, the right of nondiscrimination in employment and occupation was excluded.

In December 1998, the GSP program was amended again, this time by Council Regulation 2820/98. The regulation essentially renewed the labor and environment special-incentive program under the previous regulation[126] but added an additional incentive program for those countries engaged in combatting drug production and export.[127] This new incentive was particularly controversial because it granted additional tariff preferences to Andean and Central American countries, most of which were (and continue to be) notorious labor rights violators, without imposing any labor obligations beyond the prohibitions on forced and prison labor common to all arrangements. The new regulation did establish an extensive application procedure for the labor incentive, including a process by which interested parties could submit information for or against inclusion.[128] The Commission would make a determination based on the evidence before it. A successful country was also required to participate in monitoring and administrative cooperation programs. Furthermore, the regulation provided that the additional preferences under the incentive arrangements could be withdrawn if "sufficient evidence" was presented that a country had not fulfilled its obligations. [129]

In 2001, the special-incentive arrangement for labor was once again amended. It allowed the incentive to be granted to "a country the national legislation of which incorporates the substance of the standards laid down in ILO Conventions No 29 and No 105 on forced labor, No 87 and No 98 on the freedom of association and the right to collective bargaining, No 100 and No 111 on non-discrimination in respect of employment and occupation, and No 138 and No 182 on child labor and which effectively applies that legislation."[130] The incentive for combating drugs also now required the Commission to assess a country's respect for the promotion of the standards in the 1998 ILO Declaration on Fundamental Principles and Rights at Work, taking into account the findings of the

---

124. *Id.* at title II.

125. *Id.* at art. 7.

126. Article 8 of Council Regulation 2820/98 (Dec. 21, 1998) (EC); *See also* Council Regulation No. 1154/98, May 25, 1998 (EC).

127. *Id.* at art. 7.

128. *Id.* at arts. 11–15.

129. *Id.* at art. 20.

130. Council Regulation No. 2501/2001, art. 14 (EC).

ILO.[131] Importantly, the temporary withdrawal of any of the preferential arrangements was now also possible for the "serious and systematic violation of the freedom of association, the right to collective bargaining or the principle of non-discrimination in respect of employment and occupation, or use of child labor," in addition to the forced-labor and prison-made goods provisions in previous iterations. These additions represented a substantial expansion of the obligation applicable to all beneficiaries.[132] Of course, those countries in the incentive program could also have their additional preferences withdrawn for failing to meet the specific criteria of that program.

In 2005, following a legal challenge by India at the World Trade Organization (WTO), the special-incentive arrangements were substantially overhauled.[133] The European Union eliminated the separate social, environmental, and anti-drug schemes and combined them into a "sustainable development and good governance" program.[134] The consolidated special-incentive program now requires beneficiaries to have *ratified and effectively implemented* sixteen human rights conventions, including the eight ILO core conventions and at least seven of eleven conventions on the environment and governance (and undertake to ratify the remainder within three years). The examination of an application takes into account the findings of relevant international organizations and agencies, and it may evaluate the claims based on any other relevant sources. Trade preferences on all or certain products can be temporarily withdrawn if there is a "serious and systematic violation of principles laid down in the [eight ILO conventions], on the basis of the conclusions of the relevant monitoring bodies," or in the case of the export of goods made by prison labor.

The EU GSP regulations in force through 2013 are essentially those issued in July 2008.[135] The 2008 regulations make no noteworthy innovations on the labor provisions established in the 2005 regulations. As discussed below, the regulations will change again in January 2014 in some important respects.

---

131. *Id.* at art. 25.

132. *Id.* at art. 26.

133. In 2002, India requested the establishment of a WTO panel to assess the legality of the new special incentive arrangements, though later limited its challenge to the application of the drugs program. It argued that the program was inconsistent with the Most Favored Nation principle as well as violated the enabling clause, which requires nonreciprocal and nondiscriminatory preferences. The panel found that the program was in fact discriminatory. In 2004, the Appellate Body found that "preference-granting countries can 'respond positively' to 'needs' that are not necessarily common or shared by all developing countries." However, the types of needs to which a response is envisaged are limited to "development, financial and trade needs." Further, the existence of a "development, financial [or] trade need" must be assessed according to an objective standard. WTO, European Communities—Conditions For The Granting Of Tariff Preferences To Developing Countries, AB-2004-1, *Report Of The Appellate Body*, WT/DS246/AB/R, 7 April 2004. The Appellate Body concluded that the E.U. failed to demonstrate that the drug arrangement was based on objective criteria that would allow all developing countries similarly situated to qualify for the preferences. The E.U. was ordered to revise its GSP program.

134. Council Regulation No. 980/2005, articles 8–11 (June 27, 2005) (EC).

135. *See* Council Regulation No. 732/2008 (July 22, 2008), (EC), http://eur-lex.europa.eu/LexUriServ/LexUriServ.do?uri=OJ:L:2008:211:0001:0039:EN:PDF.

Procedural Evolution—Temporary Withdrawal of Preferences[136]

Initially, the GSP regulations provided for a more U.S.-style complaints mechanism. Under the Council Regulation 3281/94, there was a formal process that allowed any person with an interest in the withdrawal of a country from the program to submit information (only about forced labor or export of prison-made goods). The Commission communicated the information to all EU member states. The Commission or any member state could request consultations. If the Commission found that there was sufficient evidence to initiate an investigation, it could do so. Taking at least a year, the Commission could seek additional information, dispatch experts to the field, and hold hearings. If it found that a temporary withdrawal of tariff preferences was necessary in light of the investigation, it could submit a proposal to the Council of the European Union, which would decide on the basis of a qualified majority. The findings of the ILO were not mentioned as a source for making this determination in the regulations. It was under this process that Myanmar was removed from the GSP program in light of extensive use of forced labor within the country.

The process has now been turned on its head. Under the 2008 regulations, the Commission determines whether preferences should be temporarily withdrawn based on the "conclusions of the relevant monitoring bodies."[137] This approach, while arguably more objective, has obvious limitations that allow serious labor rights violators to continue to receive benefits. First, conditioning review on the conclusions of the relevant monitoring bodies easily prevents the EU Commission from ever taking action in a number of cases. For example, if a beneficiary under the general arrangement has failed to ratify a convention (or to report on its compliance with a ratified convention), there simply will be no observations from the ILO Committee of Experts on the Application of Conventions and Recommendations and, consequently, no conclusions from the Conference Committee on the Application of Standards (CAS), which could serve as the basis for the Commission's action. Indeed, only the Committee on Freedom of Association could be used as a potential reference, because that committee can review a country's compliance with principles of freedom of association and collective bargaining even in the absence of ratification.

However, the problem is further complicated. The practice of the Commission is to determine that a serious and systematic violation has occurred if the ILO Governing Body establishes a Commission of Inquiry to investigate a country's failure to secure the effective observance of a convention (a rare occurrence), or if the CAS has reviewed a country for noncompliance with a ratified convention and has decided to put its conclusions in a

---

136. The evolution of the role of the ILO in the Commission's decisionmaking is treated in great detail in Orbie & Tortell, *The New GSP+ Beneficiaries: Ticking the Box or Truly Consistent with ILO Findings*, 14 Eur. Foreign Aff. Rev. 663 (2009).

137. *See* Council Regulation No. 732/2008, art 15.1(a) (EC).

"special paragraph." This has happened on only two occasions.[138] The process of obtaining a special paragraph is also an extremely long one, sometimes taking years even in egregious cases. Even though the decision about which cases are brought before the CAS (the most political of the supervisory mechanisms of the ILO) is the subject of negotiation between workers and employers and there is a limitation of twenty-five cases per year, countries where serious violations are occurring may nevertheless make it on this list. Even if it does, not every case will be referenced in a special paragraph. This situation arises through negotiation and consensus between the workers' and employers' groups.

Nowhere does the regulation require the EU Commission to apply such a limited review of the conclusions of the relevant monitoring bodies. It does, of course, accomplish the goal of setting a bright line with no need for independent analysis of multiple sources or any independent judgments.

In Practice

In many, if not most, of the countries currently receiving tariff preferences under the general arrangement or the special-incentive arrangement, there are frequent and serious violations of the core labor rights. On the whole, EU GSP has been ineffective at improving compliance among its beneficiaries. If anything, it has increased the ratification of core ILO conventions since ratification became a requirement under the special-incentive arrangement.[139] However, there is often little correlation between ratification of a convention and the transposition of its terms into domestic law or the effective enforcement of those laws. A 2010 evaluation of the GSP by the Centre for the Analysis of Regional Integration at Sussex University (CARIS) supports this view. It found that Georgia, Nicaragua, and Peru, the three countries studied for the evaluation, did not effectively transpose conventions 87, 98, and 100 into national legislation after the conventions were ratified.[140] The researchers also concluded "that available data are largely consistent with the hypothesis

---

138. A *special paragraph* is a tool used by the CAS to signal heightened opprobrium for the acts of a particular country. According to the European Commission, it views a special paragraph to signal a serious failure while a second special paragraph would signal that the violation is now also systematic. Note that Orbie and Tortell, *supra* note 133, suggest that only the establishment of a Commission of Inquiry will satisfy the European Commission—a reasonable conclusion based on the date. DG Trade has confirmed that two special paragraphs may also serve the same purpose.

139. Of note, one of the few E.U. investigations on labor rights took place when the Supreme Court of El Salvador declared that several provisions of Convention 87 were incompatible with the constitution. The concern was not so much that the right of freedom of association was routinely violated in practice, but that it was uncertain whether the ILO convention remained in force in the country. Once it was confirmed that the convention remained valid, and a constitutional amendment was undertaken, the investigation was terminated. The Commission's decision is available online at http://trade.ec.europa .eu/doclib/docs/2009/october/tradoc_145209.pdf.

140. *See* CARIS, MID-TERM EVALUATION OF THE E.U.'S GENERALISED SYSTEM OF PREFERENCES 159 (2010).

that the GSP+ scheme and its conditionality has not yet resulted in significant changes in the situation 'on the ground' in beneficiary countries."[141]

Trade unions and other labor rights advocates have also complained for years about the EU's apparent reluctance to invoke GSP's labor conditionality when presented with clear evidence of ongoing serious violations. To date, only two countries have had their trade preferences withdrawn over labor violations: Myanmar/Burma (in 1997, over allegations of forced labor)[142] and Belarus (in 2007, over allegations of violation of freedom of association). In both cases, the countries were brutal dictatorships subject to near universal condemnation. However, the withdrawal of preferences had little discernible effect on behavior, though very recent efforts in Myanmar/Burma to eradicate forced labor may be attributable, in part, to its wish to normalize political and economic relations with Europe.

In 1995, the International Confederation of Free Trade Unions (ICFTU, now ITUC) and the European Trade Union Confederation (ETUC) also filed a submission on the commission of forced child labor in Pakistan, but no formal investigation was ever launched. Instead, the Commission engaged with the government of Pakistan and supported its participation in ILO's International Programme on the Elimination of Child Labour (IPEC), which provided technical assistance to help remove children from the workforce. The implicit threat of an investigation was understood, though the European Union at the same time sought to deepen trade ties under a cooperation agreement signed in 2001. Later that year, with the issues still unresolved, the country received further preferences for textiles and apparel.

In July 2009, the ETUC urged the EU to suspend GSP+ in relation to Honduras following the country's coup and the imposition of a state of emergency earlier that year. Though the EU did temporarily suspend development assistance, trade preferences continued.

In 2011, the ITUC and ETUC jointly urged the Commission to take action in two cases: Uzbekistan and Georgia. In August 2011, Trade Commissioner Karel DeGucht responded to the Uzbekistan submission, stating that although he did not question the allegations, the Commission would not initiate an investigation and instead would use continued dialogue to incentivize the government to eliminate the use of child labor gradually.[143] Staff at the Directorate General for Trade explained that under the regulation, there was nothing they could do unless the ILO established a Commission of Inquiry or the CAS put its conclusions for a second time in a special paragraph of its report.

In June 2011, the ITUC and ETUC also wrote to the Commission requesting an investigation into the Republic of Georgia for violating the terms of the special-incentive

---

141. *Id.* at 166.

142. *See* Council Regulation 552/97. A legislative proposal to repeal the Council Regulation is currently before the European Parliament and is expected to pass.

143. Letter from Commissioner DeGucht to ETUC and ITUC (July 28, 2011) (on file with the author).

arrangement, of which the country was a beneficiary.[144] The petitioners noted numerous legal provisions that were well out of compliance with the ILO core conventions, including the lack of sufficient protections at the time of recruitment and at the time of termination from anti-union discrimination. Indeed, many union activists were being dismissed with no effective legal recourse. The letter contained lengthy citations to various ILO supervisory bodies to support each of the allegations. Indeed, a 2008 EU Commission Staff Report acknowledged that the labor code in Georgia, revised in 2006, "falls short in addressing the obligations of the ILO Conventions on freedom of association and on the right to organize and collectively bargain" and that "the Code is to be revised accordingly if Georgia wants to benefit from the GSP+ scheme in 2009."[145] The labor code was never revised, but Georgia was granted preferences nevertheless. In August 2011, Commissioner DeGucht declined to initiate an investigation despite the clear breach of the terms of the special-incentive arrangement.

In November 2011, the United States announced the initiation of a GSP investigation against Georgia over allegations that the country was not taking steps to afford internationally recognized workers' rights, a far weaker obligation than the GSP+ obligation to ratify and effectively implement the eight ILO core conventions.[146] The European Union, on the other hand, announced that it was pursuing a Deep and Comprehensive Free Trade Area Agreement with Georgia under the scope of an association agreement already under negotiation.[147]

EU GSP Reform

In 2014, a new GSP regulation will enter into force.[148] Regarding the general arrangement, Article 19 of the proposal does not modify the existing labor rights obligation, namely that a beneficiary country must not engage in "serious and systematic" violations of the principles of the conventions listed in part A of annex VIII (which includes the eight core conventions of the ILO) to remain eligible for preferential trade treatment. The proposal does, however, eliminate the clause "on the basis of the conclusions of the relevant monitoring bodies" to address the procedural problems noted above.

Regarding the special-incentive arrangement, Article 9.1 sets forth the labor criteria. A beneficiary country benefits from the reduced- and zero-tariff preferences provided under

---

144. Letter from ETUC and ITUC to Trade Commissioner Karel DeGucht (June 6, 2011), http://www .ituc-csi.org/georgia-s-anti-union-laws-prompt.html.

145. Note 137 *supra* at p. 163, citing European Commission Staff Working Document (SEC (2008) 393).

146. 76 Fed. Reg. 67,530, 67, 530–67,531 (Nov. 1, 2011), http://www.gpo.gov/fdsys/pkg/FR-2011-11-01 /html/2011-28248.htm.

147. For more on the application of the labor provisions of the E.U. GSP, *see* Franz Ebert, *Between Political Goodwill and WTO-Law: Human Rights Conditionality in the Community's New Scheme of Generalised Tariff Preferences (GSP)*, Zentrum für Europäische Rechtspolitik, Universität Bremen (Sept. 2009); Orbie and Tortell, *supra* note 133.

148. *See* Council Regulation (EU) No. 978/2012.

this arrangement if it has ratified all the conventions listed in annex VIII and if the most recent available conclusions of the relevant monitoring bodies do not identify a *serious failure* to implement any of these conventions effectively. The country must also give a binding undertaking to maintain ratification of the conventions and to ensure their effective implementation, accept the reporting requirements imposed by each convention, give a binding undertaking to accept regular monitoring and review of its implementation record, and give a binding undertaking to participate in and cooperate with the program's monitoring procedure.

The major development in the new regulation is the addition of the term "serious failure," a concept apparently at odds with the idea of effective implementation as defined in the proposed regulations. This construction means that flagrant labor rights violators will likely enjoy enhanced trade preferences. By insisting that only the reports of the relevant monitoring bodies be referenced, it may in some cases lead the EU to conclude that there are not serious failures when in fact there are. The regular reports of the ILO Committee of Experts on the Application of Conventions and Recommendations are issued once a year, and reporting on the core conventions—the ones relevant to the GSP+—is now required only every three years, barring other circumstances. In the best cases, these reports provide useful snapshots of major issues in a country but may not necessarily be comprehensive or up to date. Other reports, such as from the Committee on Freedom of Association, are issued only in response to a complaint, in some cases years after the conflict first arose. Under the proposal, one assumes that any country that has not been branded with a special paragraph by the CAS or worse will qualify for GSP+.

The United States versus the European Union

Both the U.S. and EU programs have some advantages. For example, the European Union has more rigorous standards and an incentive-based program that requires, at least on paper, a beneficiary to ratify the core ILO conventions and effectively implement them. In practice, the U.S. GSP appears to be more nimble, accepting third-party complaints and more frequently using the threat of an investigation or withdrawal to achieve some concessions. In each case, however, the program has had only a marginal effect on enhancing enjoyment of labor rights, though the U.S. program appears to have been more successful in achieving limited reforms, in some cases, in response to third-party petitions and external advocacy. The recent case of Bangladesh, where the European Union rattled the GSP saber following the factory collapse,[149] may provide an interesting case with regard

---

149. *See* Joint Statement by HR/VP Catherine Ashton and E.U. Trade Commissioner Karel De Gucht following the recent building collapse in Bangladesh (Apr. 30, 2013), http://europa.eu/rapid/press-release _MEMO-13-395_en.htm.

to how these two programs are employed to bring about meaningful change on labor rights compliance.

Bilateral Investment Treaties

According to the UN Conference on Trade and Development's World Investment Report 2012, there were 2,833 Bilateral Investment Treaties (BITs) in force at the close of 2011.[150] Though there is of course considerable variation among them, most BITs have some common characteristics. In general, they require that investors and their investments be treated as favorably as the host party treats its own investors (national treatment) and their investments or investors and investments from any third country (most-favored nation). They provide a minimum standard of treatment, often expressed as "fair and equitable treatment" and "full protection and security." BITs typically afford these rights for the life of the investment, though in some cases rights extend even before the establishment of an investment. BITs include disciplines on expropriation (direct and indirect) and require payment of prompt, adequate, and effective compensation when expropriation takes place. They also provide for the free movement of investment-related capital into and out of the territory of a party. Some other common features include restrictions on performance requirements meant to boost use of local content, domestic employment, and transfer of technology. Finally, some BITs give investors the right to sue a government over an investment dispute before an international arbitration panel rather than in that country's courts.

As we will see, foreign investors are given extensive protection for their investments under BITs but are assigned few responsibilities. Rather, the state bears the majority of obligations of BITs, and constraints placed on its ability to regulate can have a direct impact on the enjoyment of human rights. Regarding labor specifically, very few BITs include language that requires a state party, let alone an investor, to respect the fundamental labor rights of workers. On the other hand, the investment rules of BITs (and investment agreements) have been or could be used by investors to sue governments over labor-related matters. This section reviews the various approaches taken by governments to incorporate labor protections into BITs (which to date oblige only state parties). It also highlights provisions of BITs that have been or could be used to frustrate the rights of workers.

---

150. *See* UNCTAD, WORLD INVESTMENT REPORT 2012, at XX (2012), http://www.unctad-docs.org /files/UNCTAD-WIR2012-Full-en.pdf

Promoting Workers' Rights[151]

The United States

The United States currently has BITs in force with forty countries.[152] Like other countries, the United States typically negotiates BITs on the basis of a "Model BIT." The model is reviewed and modified from time to time based on input from U.S. businesses and civil society through formal and informal processes.[153] Labor provisions did not appear in the U.S. BITs until the early 1990s, and even then only in the preamble. At first, the text was sparse:

> Recognizing that the development of economic and business ties can contribute to the well-being of workers in both Parties and promote respect for internationally recognized worker rights . . .[154]

In 1994, the labor provision of the Model BIT improved only slightly.[155] Still in the preamble, the text shifted from merely asserting that economic ties contribute to the well-being of workers to identifying the promotion of respect for internationally recognized worker rights as one of the goals of the BIT:

> Foremost is the encouragement and protection of investment. Other goals include economic cooperation on investment issues; the stimulation of economic development; higher living standards; *promotion of respect for internationally-recognized worker rights*; and maintenance of health, safety, and environmental measures. While the Preamble does not impose binding obligations, its statement of goals may assist in interpreting the Treaty and in defining the scope of Party-to-Party consultation procedures pursuant to Article VIII.[156]

---

151. For a general discussion on labor provisions in investment agreements, including BITs, see Bertram Boie, *Labour Related Provisions in International Investment Agreements* (ILO Employment Working Paper No. 126, 2012) (BITs are discussed specifically at 8–19).

152. *See*, *United States Bilateral Investment Treaties*, U.S. State Dep't, http://www.state.gov/e/eb/ifd/bit/117402.htm (last visited Dec. 1, 2013).

153. Formal processes include the State Department's Advisory Committee on International Economic Policy (ACIEP), which maintains a subcommittee on Bilateral Investment Treaties. The most recent report of this subcommittee, which concluded its review of the Model BIT in September 2009, can be found at http://www.state.gov/e/eb/rls/othr/2009/131098.htm. The author was staff to the co-chair of the subcommittee.

154. *See, e.g.*, Bilateral Investment Treaty, U.S.-Khazakstan, May 19, 1992, http://2001-2009.state.gov/documents/organization/43566.pdf. Other BITs in this mold include those with Argentina, Ecuador and Jamaica.

155. United States, Treaty Between the Government of the United States of America and the Government of [Country] Concerning the Encouragement and Reciprocal Protection of Investment (1994 Model BIT) (1994).

156. *See, e.g.*, Bilateral Investment Treaty, U.S.-Albania, Jan. 11, 1995, (emphasis added)

The preamble is explicit in stating that it creates no binding obligations on either party but rather assists in the interpretation. It was not for another ten years, in 2004, that *binding* obligations regarding worker rights were included in the body of a BIT. The impetus for the revision of the 1994 Model BIT came from the U.S. Congress, which passed the 2002 Trade Promotion Authority (TPA). This legislation contained specific mandates on investment.[157] In the context of this revision, the issue of worker rights was also reexamined. Article 13 of the 2004 Model BIT included a nonderogation clause that requires each party to:

> strive to ensure that it does not waive or otherwise derogate from, or offer to waive or otherwise derogate from, such laws in a manner that weakens or reduces adherence to the internationally recognized labor rights . . . as an encouragement for the establishment, acquisition, expansion, or retention of an investment in its territory.[158]

If a party believes that the other party has violated this provision, it may request consultations "with a view to avoiding any such encouragement."

Two U.S. BITs have been concluded since the promulgation of the 2004 Model BIT: with Uruguay in 2005 and Rwanda in 2008. Both BITs contain the above-referenced language; however, the Uruguay BIT also contains an additional subarticle, Article 13.3, which provides, "Nothing in this Treaty shall be construed to prevent a Party from adopting, maintaining, or enforcing any measure otherwise consistent with this Treaty that it considers appropriate to ensure that investment activity in its territory is undertaken in a manner sensitive to labor concerns."[159]

In 2009, the U.S. State Department's Advisory Committee on International Economic Policy (ACIEP) announced that it was ready to take a fresh look at the 2004 Model BIT and convened a subcommittee including representatives of business, labor, and environmental organizations, as well as legal scholars and investment arbitrators, to make recommendations.[160] The labor representatives on the ACIEP had hoped that the 2004 BIT could be substantially improved with respect to labor rights given the recent change

---

http://2001-2009.state.gov/documents/organization/43474.pdf. Other BITs in this mold include ones with Azerbaijan, Bolivia, El Salvador, Georgia, Honduras, Jordan, Mongolia, Mozambique, and Uzbekistan.

157. 19 U.S.C. § 3802(b)(3) (Supp. 2002).

158. U.S. 2004 Model BIT, http://www.state.gov/documents/organization/117601.pdf.

159. *See* Treaty between the United States of America and the Republic of Uruguay Concerning the Encouragement and Reciprocal Protection of Investment, Nov. 4, 2005, http://www.ustr.gov/sites/default/files/uploads/agreements/bit/asset_upload_file748_9005.pdf.

160. *See* DEP'T OF STATE, REPORT OF THE SUBCOMMITTEE ON INVESTMENT OF THE ADVISORY COMMITTEE ON INTERNATIONAL ECONOMIC POLICY REGARDING THE MODEL BILATERAL INVESTMENT TREATY (2009), http://www.state.gov/e/eb/rls/othr/2009/131098.htm. The author served as staff to the labor cochair of the subcommittee.

in the White House and the fact that the United States had already moved well beyond the 2004 language in the context of post–May 10th trade agreements.

The 2004 Model BIT raised several obvious concerns from a rights perspective.[161] First, under Article 13.1, a party does not have an absolute obligation not to waive or derogate from its domestic labor laws (or offer to do so) to encourage investment. It needs only to strive not to do so. Second, Article 13.2 refers to "internationally recognized worker rights," which as mentioned previously is defined to exclude nondiscrimination. Subsequent U.S. trade legislation and international instruments have since referred to "core labor standards" or to the 1998 ILO Declaration on Fundamental Principles and Rights at Work. Third, the Model BIT does not actually require a country to have any labor laws, just not to waive or derogate from those that they have. Therefore, if the existing labor laws in a state party are not strong, the state is not obliged to strengthen them (and might in fact be penalized for doing so in some cases, under certain stabilization clauses; see the next section on limitations of BITs in relation to protecting labor rights). Finally, if a party has encouraged investment by waiving or derogating from country labor laws, the only available remedy is state-to-state consultations. The labor provisions are explicitly excluded from state-to-state dispute resolution (Articles 37.1 and 37.5). If the matter is not resolved in consultations, workers are simply out of luck.

Labor activists considered several alternatives for labor provisions in the new Model BIT. In the end, it was determined that the most feasible approach was be to attempt to graft the substantive obligations of the May 10th FTA template onto the BIT (adapted to investment) and to use the existing state-to-state dispute-resolution provisions available in the BIT. Recognizing that this was a far from perfect solution, particularly the idea of having labor matters settled through lengthy International Centre for the Settlement of Investment Disputes (ICSID) or United Nations Commission on International Trade Law (UNCITRAL) arbitration procedures,[162] it nonetheless would represent a significant improvement over the aspirational nonderogation language in the current BIT. However, this proposal was perceived as a step too far by others in the subcommittee.

---

161. These concerns were raised by several members of the ACIEP subcommittee. *See* DEP'T OF STATE, REPORT OF THE SUBCOMMITTEE ON INVESTMENT OF THE ADVISORY COMMITTEE ON INTERNATIONAL ECONOMIC POLICY REGARDING THE MODEL BILATERAL INVESTMENT TREATY: ANNEXES, Annex B (Sept. 30, 2009), http://www.state.gov/e/eb/rls/othr/2009/131118.htm#1 (a collective statement from Sarah Anderson *et al.*).

162. ICSID, the International Centre for the Settlement of Investment Disputes, "is an autonomous international institution established under the Convention on the Settlement of Investment Disputes between States and Nationals of Other States with over one hundred and forty member States. . . . The primary purpose of ICSID is to provide facilities for conciliation and arbitration of international investment disputes." *See* ICSID, https://icsid.worldbank.org/ICSID/Index.jsp (last visited Dec. 1, 2013). The United Nations Commission on International Trade Law (UNCITRAL) is "the core legal body of the United Nations system in the field of international trade law." *See* http://www.uncitral.org/uncitral/en/about/origin.html.

Business representatives argued that labor obligations would overburden the BIT and make such agreements unappealing to other nations, placing the United States at a disadvantage to those nations that negotiated BITs without such language. Of particular concern was the potential impact of such language on the ability to conclude BIT negotiations with China and India, which had been progressing in fits and starts for years. Labor proponents countered that the idea of a BIT being overburdened by labor provisions was cynical given that business had advocated for and achieved provisions that imposed many serious constraints on governments on a wide range of economic activity. The labor provisions proposed did little more than attempt to make enforceable the commitments that all member states of the ILO had already undertaken by way of the 1998 ILO Declaration, if not through already ratified core conventions. The idea that a party would reject a BIT on the basis of labor provisions also seemed unlikely, and no evidence was provided that this had happened in practice. Proponents further argued that, even if true, it is not in the interest of the United States to further deepen investment relations with a party that cannot respect the agreed-upon global floor on labor standards.

Completion of the review was expected in January 2010. However, the sharp disagreement on the ACIEP Subcommittee on Labor Rights (and environment, though to a lesser degree) created considerable political problems for the new administration and the U.S. Senate (which, under the U.S. Constitution, is the only chamber authorized to vote on BITs). The White House, though sympathetic to business arguments, wanted to avoid the appearance of having its first international economic instrument include labor standards weaker than those the Bush Administration had recently agreed to in the trade agreement context. The Senate Finance Committee also realized that labor discontent over the BIT could jeopardize its chances of passing the then-pending trade agreements and urged the administration to insert the May 10th language in the BIT.[163] Other Senators recommended ways that the Model BIT labor language could be improved, keeping it in line with that of the labor representatives of the ACIEP BIT subcommittee.[164]

In April 2012, the Obama administration finally launched the new Model BIT.[165] Regarding labor rights, the Model BIT made some progress but fell short of expectations. The main advances to Article 13 include the following: (a) hortatory language found in pre-May 10th FTAs that parties "reaffirm" their obligations as members of the ILO and their commitments under the ILO Declaration; (b) an obligation not to waive or otherwise derogate from its labor laws, or offer to waive or derogate, where doing so would be

---

163. *See, e.g, Hormats Says BIT Must Balance Business Needs with Labor, Environment* INSIDE U.S. TRADE (Mar. 12, 2010).

164. *See, e.g.*, Letter of Senators Brown and Stabenow to Secretaries Clinton and Solis and Ambassador Kirk (Jan. 14, 2010).

165. The 2012 U.S. Model Bilateral Investment Treaty is available online at http://www.state.gov/documents/organization/188371.pdf.

inconsistent with the core labor rights (whereas the party previously only had to strive to do so); (c) the definition of *labor laws* now include the elimination of discrimination in employment and occupation; (d) a requirement that parties cannot fail to enforce their labor laws effectively, through a sustained or recurring course of inaction, as an encouragement for the establishment, acquisition, expansion, or retention of an investment in its territory; (e) a provision that if a party requests consultations, the other party must respond in thirty days, and the parties should endeavor to reach a mutually satisfactory resolution; and (f) a provision that parties *may* provide opportunities for public participation regarding matters arising under Article 13.

Though an improvement, the 2012 Model BIT falls short of the labor proposal in two key areas: (1) It does not require a party to bring its laws into line with international labor standards; it only requires that the party not waive or derogate from the labor laws already on the books, or not fail to enforce those laws. (2) It does not provide for dispute settlement but rather the consultations already available under the 2004 Model BIT.

In Practice

Due to the severe limitation of the labor provisions and the lack of dispute settlement, trade unions and labor advocates have not viewed the labor provisions of the U.S. BITs as a tool to promote labor rights. In most cases, the problem is not the waiver of or derogation from a labor law (or the offer to do so) to attract investment, but inadequate legislation and the failure to enforce those laws already on the books. The 2012 Model BIT does include language regarding enforcement of labor laws, though the absence of dispute settlement will likely mean that the 2012 Model BIT will be used as much as the 2004 Model BIT was in relation to labor rights, which is to say not at all. As such, trade-preference programs and bilateral and regional trade agreements, even given their limitations, so far have provided labor advocates with greater potential leverage than those found in a BIT.

European States/European Union

European states have been negotiating BITs since 1959, when Germany entered into such an agreement with Pakistan. Today, all the member states of the EU, with the sole exception of Ireland, have negotiated BITs, collectively amassing about 1,100 such treaties. However, that competency has shifted to the EU level following the entry into force of the Lisbon Treaty in December 2009.[166] The EU will also enter into EU-wide BITs, though

---

166. The Lisbon Treaty modified the Treaty of Rome and the Maastricht Treaty. Now, Article 206 provides that the E.U. shall contribute to the "progressive abolition of restrictions on international trade and foreign direct investment" and Article 207 provides that foreign direct investment is one of the areas covered by the "common commercial policy" of the E.U. and that the common commercial policy is an area of "exclusive competence" under Article 3(1) of the Lisbon Treaty. See the Consolidated Version of the Treaty on the Functioning of the European Union, http://eur-lex.europa.eu/LexUriServ/LexUriServ .do?uri=OJ:C:2010:083:0047:0200:en:PDF.

such instruments will likely be viewed as mixed agreements that require the European Union and members states to conclude agreements together.

Labor rights obligations are not commonly found in BITs negotiated by EU member states, but there are some exceptions. For example, Belgium and Finland each include labor provisions in their respective model BITs. Finland takes a minimalist approach, including in the preamble language that closely follows the text in the 1994 U.S. Model BIT, "recognizing that the development of economic and business ties can promote respect for internationally recognized worker rights."[167]

Were it not for the excision of the text stating that economic and business ties can "contribute to the well-being of workers," the Finnish text would be identical to that of the U.S. BITs of the early 1990s. The preamble of the Finnish BIT also states that a stable investment environment can "improve living standards," and that the objectives of the BIT can be "achieved without relaxing health, safety and environmental measures."

On the other end of the spectrum, the 2002 Belgium-Luxembourg Model BIT[168] is much more robust than the Finnish model. Indeed, the BIT copies nearly verbatim the labor provisions of the U.S.-Jordan Free Trade Agreement, signed in late 2000. Both contain an obligation to "strive to ensure that its laws provide for labor standards consistent with the internationally recognized labor rights" as defined in the instrument and to "strive to improve those standards in that light." Both also contain an obligation to "strive to ensure that such labor principles and the internationally recognized labor rights" as defined therein "are recognized and protected by domestic law." Both also contain similar nonderogation language, with the BIT referring to investment rather than trade. They even have the same peculiar definition of labor law, which excludes the principle of nondiscrimination and includes "acceptable conditions of work." Unlike the U.S.-Jordan FTA, and like most BITs, disputes are limited to consultations. In the case of the Belgium-Luxembourg Model BIT, these are expert consultations.[169]

Of course, the Belgian BIT is limited. Even if a trade union convinced the Belgian government to invoke the BIT and request expert consultations, there appears little else under the BIT that could be done if. That being said, the fact that such consultations could be convened, if widely known by governments and investors, could create the pressure necessary for the consultations to be fruitful.

---

167. OECD, INTERNATIONAL INVESTMENT LAW: UNDERSTANDING CONCEPTS AND TRACKING INNOVATIONS 180 (2008).

168. *Id.* at 175–77. *See also* Boie, *supra* note 151 at 16–17; NATHALIE BERNASCONI-OSTERWALDER & LISE JOHNSON, INTERNATIONAL INSTITUTE FOR SUSTAINABLE DEVELOPMENT (IISD), BELGIUM'S MODEL BILATERAL INVESTMENT TREATY: A REVIEW 23–25 (Mar. 2010).

169. For a discussion of BITs negotiated on the basis of the Belgian-Luxembourg 2002 model BIT, see RAFAEL PEELS, THE INCLUSION OF LABOUR PROVISIONS IN EU'S BILATERAL TRADE AND INVESTMENT AGREEMENTS: WHAT ABOUT DIALOGUE AND DISPUTES? 55–58 (2011), https://hiva.kuleuven.be/resources /pdf/publicaties/R1377_PeelsMay2011.pdf.

A New EU Approach?

Post-Lisbon, competency on the subject of foreign direct investment (FDI) shifted to the European Union. This shift raised the obvious question of what EU investment policy would look like. In 2010, the EU Commission issued the paper *Towards a Comprehensive European International Investment Policy*, which articulated its vision for a new, European international investment policy.[170] In it, the EU Commission specifically recalled that the investment policy of the European Union must be guided by its broader external principles and objectives, including human rights, sustainable development, and a rule of law.[171]

In April 2011, the EU Parliament also issued its Resolution on the Future European International Investment Policy. That resolution reiterated that the "EU's future policy must also promote investment which is sustainable, respects the environment (particularly in the area of extractive industries) and encourages good quality working conditions in the enterprises targeted by the investment; it asks the Commission to include, in all future agreements, a reference to the updated OECD Guidelines for Multinational Enterprises."[172]

The inclusion of a reference to the OECD Guidelines for Multinational Enterprises is an interesting innovation in that a BIT would no longer impose obligations only on state parties but also on corporations in those states. However, it remains unclear what labor obligations states would incur under this new policy, to what extent corporations would be *bound* by otherwise voluntary guidelines, or whether the dispute-resolution machinery of the BIT could be invoked to enforce them.

As in the United States, trade unions put forward an ambitious proposal with regard to EU BIT policy.[173] The key features of the proposal include a requirement that both parties effectively implement the core labor standards and other decent work components, ratify the ILO core conventions, not lower labor standards to attract foreign investment, submit regular reports on progress toward implementing these commitments and sustainable-impact assessments, and invoke a binding complaints mechanism and technical assistance. The OECD Guidelines for Multinational Enterprises are also promoted in the proposal. As with the U.S. BITs, there appears to have been little if any use of these provisions by trade unions and other labor advocates, again likely because of the weakness of those few BITs that include labor language. This deficiency will continue to be the case unless the EU BITs provide meaningful obligations on states and investors with regard to labor rights as well as an effective dispute-settlement mechanism to enforce those obligations.

---

170. Text available online at http://trade.ec.europa.eu/doclib/docs/2011/may/tradoc_147884.pdf.

171. *Id.* at 9.

172. *See* Resolution on the Future of European International Investment Policy, Eur. Parl. Doc. 2010/22-3(INI), ¶ 27 (2011), http://www.europarl.europa.eu/sides/getDoc.do?type=TA&reference=P7-TA-2011-0141&language=EN.

173. ETUC, ETUC Resolution on EU Investment Policy, adopted Mar. 2013, http://www.etuc.org/a/11025.

BITs Used to Frustrate Workers' Rights

There is ample literature on how various provisions of BITs may impact the exercise of human rights. I here focus on three areas that seem most relevant for labor.

Full Protection and Security

One of the common obligations of the state to a foreign investor is to provide full protection and security. The boundaries of this obligation are not entirely clear; however, "[a]t a minimum, this obligation requires that states provide a baseline of police protection for foreign-owned projects; this is not a strict liability obligation but it does mandate a certain level of due diligence on the part of the host country."[174] States must exercise due diligence in protecting investment not only from the actions of state actors but from those of nonstate actors as well. Notably, some arbitrators have also held that the "protection and security standard includes not only the physical protection of foreign-owned investments, but also security from other forms of 'harassment' which pose no physical threat to assets or threat of violence."[175] This requirement can put states in a difficult situation—legally bound to protect foreign investments (to a legally ambiguous degree) while respecting the rights of citizens to express rights they enjoy under national and/or international law—particularly with regard to assembly and association.

In recent years, investors have actually sued states for failure to provide "full protection and security" for their investments when labor unrest has erupted. The jurisprudence in this area is so far quite limited, but it appears possible that an arbitration panel could find a state liable in some limited circumstances for failure to quell labor unrest.

In *Noble Ventures Inc. v. Romania*, for example, the foreign investor sued Romania under the U.S.-Romania BIT, claiming, among other things, that the government had failed to quell frequent strikes and demonstrations by the employees of Combinatul Siderurgic Resita (the claimant's investment) and thus breached its obligation to provide full protection and security. On this point, the tribunal denied the investor's claim, holding, "It seems doubtful whether that provision can be understood as being wider in scope than the general duty to provide for protection and security of foreign nationals found in the customary international law of aliens. The latter is not a strict standard, but one requiring due diligence to be exercised by the State."[176] The tribunal further concluded that the government had not failed to exercise due diligence and, even if it had, the claimant could

---

174. Luke Eric Peterson, *Human Rights and Bilateral Investment Treaties: Mapping the Role of Human Rights Law within Investor-State Arbitration*, RIGHTS AND DEMOCRACY 32 (2009).

175. *Id.*

176. Noble Ventures Inc. v. Romania, ICSID Case No. ARB/01./11, ¶ 164 (Oct. 25, 2005), http://italaw .com/documents/Noble.pdf.

not prove that its alleged injuries and losses could have been prevented if due diligence was exercised.[177]

A similar claim was made in *Plama Consortium Limited v. Republic of Bulgaria*.[178] There, the investor argued that the bankruptcy trustee incited workers to go on strike and to riot unlawfully at the refinery premises, forcing the factory to close. The investor further argued that police had failed to protect the refinery or the management adequately.[179] The government of Bulgaria argued to the contrary that the demonstrations, which were over the nonpayment of wages, were peaceful and did not amount to a riot, that police were present at the refinery, and that in any case the demonstrations were not the cause of the refinery shutdown. The tribunal was eventually unable to determine which of the contradictory sets of facts were true and dismissed the claim because the claimant failed to meet its burden of proof.

Though these claims were ultimately dismissed on the facts, it nevertheless supports the position that it is possible for states, in some cases, to incur liability for strikes, pickets, or similar forms of public protest, especially if they are large, unruly, or continue for a long period of time. It also remains to be seen whether governments will err on the side of caution and limit or terminate popular protests out of fear of facing liability under the full protection and security clauses of a BIT.

Fair and Equitable Treatment and Expropriation

In 2006, European investors in the mining sector invoked BITs from Italy and Luxembourg to challenge South Africa's Black Economic Empowerment program, a set of policies meant to help historically disadvantaged South Africans through affirmative action in employment, preferential access to procurement contracts, and divestment requirements that required some investors to sell shares to the program's beneficiaries.[180] The government argued that these policies were needed to undo the legacy of apartheid and to comply with its international human rights obligations. The claimants argued that the laws breached the fair and equitable treatment and expropriation clauses and alleged suffering of up to $350 million in damages. After years of litigation, the investors dropped this claim, but this case is an example of how investors can and do use BITs to undermine social and environmental initiatives implemented by national governments.

---

177. *Id.* at ¶ 166.
178. Plama Consortium Limited v. Republic of Bulgaria, ICSID Case No. ARB 03/24 (Aug. 27, 2008), http://italaw.com/documents/PlamaBulgariaAward.pdf.
179. *Id.* at ¶ 236.
180. Piero Foresti v. Republic of South Africa, ICSID Case No. ARB(AF)/07/1.

Stabilization Clauses

Found in some BITs,[181] though most common in contracts between investors and host governments, stabilization clauses generally attempt to insulate investors from changes in law or governmental decisions made after the effective date of the agreement. Investment experts have categorized three kinds of stabilization clauses: (1) freezing clauses, which freeze the law of the host state for the life of the investment; (2) economic equilibrium clauses, which provide that the investor comply with new laws but be compensated for doing so; and (3) hybrid clauses, which require that the investor be returned to its position prior to the enactment of the new law and be exempted from such new laws.[182] It is argued that these clauses could be enforced under a BIT referring to (1) an umbrella clause, in which states promise to abide by the contracts of investors of the other party; (2) a "fair and equitable treatment" clause; and (3) an expropriations clause.[183] Research to date has not found cases in which stabilization clauses have in fact been enforced through a BIT, but there have been cases in which arbitrators noted that the absence of a stabilization clause was a relevant factor.[184]

Stabilization clauses potentially could have an impact on all regulation and labor law reform. Legislation making it easier to organize, bargain collectively, or strike, as well as providing stronger health and safety regulations, could be potential targets of such a clause. Most recently, in 2012, Veolia, a French corporation, filed an arbitration claim against Egypt BIT for, inter alia, the decision of the city of Alexandria to increase the minimum wage. The company claimed that the government failed to respect contractual terms, including, apparently, a stabilization clause meant to protect the company from

---

181. *See* STRATOS PAHIS, INTERNATIONAL COMMISSION OF JURISTS, BILATERAL INVESTMENT TREATIES AND INTERNATIONAL HUMAN RIGHTS LAW, HARMONIZATION THROUGH INTERPRETATION 43 (2012) (citing LG&E Energy Corp. v. Argentine Republic, ICSID Case no. ARB/02/1, Decision on Liability, ¶ 125 (Oct. 3, 2006) ("[T]he stability of the legal and business framework in the State is an essential element in the standard for what is fair and equitable treatment. As such, the Tribunal considers this interpretation to be an emerging standard of fair and equitable treatment in international law.")).

182. *See* Andrea Shemberg, *Investment Agreements and Human Rights: The Effects of Stabilization Clauses* (CSR Initiative Working Paper No. 42, Kennedy School of Government, 2008). *See also* HOWARD MANN, INTERNATIONAL INSTITUTE FOR SUSTAINABLE DEVELOPMENT, INTERNATIONAL INVESTMENT AGREEMENTS, BUSINESS AND HUMAN RIGHTS: KEY ISSUES AND OPPORTUNITIES, 32–35 (2008).

183. *Id.* at 37.

184. *See, e.g.*, Methanex Corp. v. United States, Final Award, at 278 (Aug. 3, 2005) ("As a matter of general international law, a non-discriminatory regulation for a public purpose, which is enacted in accordance with due process and, which affects, inter alia, a foreign investor, or investment is not deemed expropriatory and compensable unless specific commitments had been given by the regulating government to the then putative foreign investor contemplating investment that the government would refrain from such regulation."); Parkerings-Compagniet v. Lithuania, Award, ICSID Case No. ARB/05.08, ¶ 332, Sept. 11, 2007 ("It is each state's undeniable right and privilege to exercise its sovereign legislative power. A state has the right to enact, modify or cancel a law at its own discretion. Save for the existence of an agreement, in the form of a stabilization clause or otherwise, there is nothing objectionable to the amendments brought to the regulatory framework existing at the time an investor made its investment.")

such changes.[185] There has been a successful effort to *undo* a stabilization clause, at least in part. The Baku-Tbilisi-Ceyhan (BTC) Pipeline Project was a highly controversial project undertaken by a consortium led by BP, in which two pipelines were designed to stretch from the Caspian Sea and cut through Azerbaijan, Georgia, and Turkey. The BP consortium had signed a Host Government Agreement with the Turkish government that contained a stabilization clause providing that no existing or future law would affect the rights of the investors, and that even if Turkey assumed new international obligations, they would not be applicable to the project. The clause even froze in place judicial interpretations of domestic or international law. In response to a pressure campaign from the human rights community to the radical legal overreach undertaken by the BTC consortium, the project partners entered into a unilateral "human rights undertaking," agreeing that the group would not use the stabilization clause to challenge the acts of the host state to apply international obligations in the areas of human rights (including labor rights), the environment, and health and safety.[186]

The undertaking was an important innovation, but it essentially carves out an exception to the clause, leaving it in place to affect negatively other issues unrelated to human rights. It was also unilateral, raising questions about potential enforceability should BTC have decided to challenge state action related to human rights despite the undertaking. Clearly, should stabilization clauses continue to be included in BITs or investment agreements, broad carve outs for international law, including those pertaining to human rights and the environment, are needed to avoid potential problems whereby a government fails to uphold international rights out of fear of a lawsuit seeking substantial compensation.

Conclusion

As this chapter illustrates, trade- and investment-based mechanisms have been only marginally successful in improving labor rights compliance. The reasons for these limited advances are many. Importantly, each of the mechanisms reviewed requires the state to intervene on behalf of aggrieved workers; workers themselves have no direct access to international dispute-settlement mechanisms. Thus, governments, balancing a range of foreign policy and economic interests, may decide not to act in certain cases where there are compelling countervailing interests. Aggrieved parties will not usually have a legal process available to compel the government to act and thus must rely instead on

---

185. Luke Eric Peterson, French company, Veolia, launches claim against Egypt over terminated waste contract and labor wage stabilization promises, INVESTMENT ARBITRATION REPORTER, vol. 5, No. 12, July 1, 2013.

186. *See* Baku-Tbilisi-Ceyhan Pipeline Company, BTC Human Rights Undertaking (Sept. 22, 2003), http://subsites.bp.com/caspian/Human%20Rights%20Undertaking.pdf.

political pressure and campaigns. In other cases, the instruments themselves create little incentive for compliance and provide little leverage when the conditions are unmet. A country whose exports benefit little from a preference program or that faces minimal or no fines or sanctions under a trade agreement or a BIT will likely determine that the costs of noncompliance are less than any possible losses, though the loss of preferences or the application of sanctions could have a stronger effect as a signal that could deter investors. By now, most countries must know that the chances of being subject to review for labor practices are quite low and that facing sanctions is extremely unlikely.

Even if there is the political will to comply with labor obligations, resource constraints can make this difficult. Unfortunately, there are often few resources made available for labor capacity building. Much of what is available has in the past been directed to awareness campaigns, but without sufficient resources to empower those workers to exercise these rights. Further, millions of dollars have been provided directly to labor ministries with little accountability for how the funds are used. No amount of computers, data management systems, or vehicles will improve labor inspection if there is no will to enforce the law. Furthermore, many national laws need significant improvement to allow trade and investment mechanisms to protect labor rights adequately.

Part II

Domestic Policy, Legislation, and Litigation

Chapter 6

Human Rights Litigation in U.S. Courts against Individuals and Corporations

From 1789 to the Present

Beth Stephens

Introduction

For over thirty years, victims and survivors of human rights abuses have filed civil lawsuits in U.S. federal courts in an effort to hold both individuals and corporations liable for egregious international law violations, including genocide, crimes against humanity, summary execution, and torture. Although plaintiffs have collected damages in only a handful of cases, the litigation has drawn attention to human rights abuses around the world, strengthened international human rights norms, and contributed to efforts to hold perpetrators accountable and provide remedies to victims of abuses.

Most of the U.S. human rights cases rely on the Alien Tort Statute (ATS),[1] an eighteenth-century U.S. statute that has been used successfully against individual defendants since 1980 and against corporations since the mid-1990s. The statute provides that "the district courts shall have original jurisdiction of any civil action by an alien for a tort only, committed in violation of the law of nations." In April 2013, in a much-anticipated decision in *Kiobel v. Royal Dutch Petroleum Co.*, the Supreme Court ruled that the ATS does not permit claims by foreign plaintiffs against a foreign corporation with only a mini-

---

1. 28 U.S.C.A. § 1350 (West 2012). The statute has also been called the Alien Tort Claims Act (ATCA).

For a more detailed discussion of ATS litigation, see Beth Stephens, et al., International Human Rights Litigation in U.S. Courts (2d ed. 2008), which I coauthored with Judith Chomsky, Jennifer Green, Paul Hoffman, and Michael Ratner.

mal presence in the United States, when all of the relevant conduct took place outside of the United States.[2] Although the court did not directly resolve a split in the lower courts about whether other corporate-defendant cases trigger jurisdiction under the ATS, the fact that the court ignored this threshold issue could indicate that a majority of the court concluded that the federal courts do have jurisdiction over such cases. Given the lack of a direct answer from the court, however, the question of whether cases can continue to be litigated against U.S. corporations or foreign corporations with a significant presence in the United States, or when substantial conduct took place in the United States, will have to be addressed by the lower courts and will, most likely, reach the Supreme Court once again.

Given that so few ATS cases have required corporations to compensate plaintiffs, the cases have had a limited economic impact. Nevertheless, the business community has strongly opposed the corporate-defendant cases. The heated battle over the statute may reflect the symbolic resonance of the cases, which usually dwarfs their economic impact. Human rights claims lead governments, activists, and the media to focus on international law abuses by corporations and thereby contribute to an ongoing movement to hold corporations accountable for human rights violations.

This chapter will review the history of the ATS and related statutes and the human rights cases that rest on them; explain the development of corporate-defendant cases; explore the key contentious issues currently pending; evaluate the impact of the cases in the United States and on the global movement for corporate accountability; and conclude with an assessment of the prospects for future litigation seeking to hold corporations liable for international human rights violations.

The Alien Tort Statute: Human Rights Litigation in U.S. Courts

In 1976, Joelito Filártiga, a seventeen-year-old Paraguayan, was tortured to death in Paraguay by a Paraguayan police officer, Americo Norberto Peña-Irala.[3] Despite an international campaign calling for prosecution of the torturer, the Paraguayan government refused to take action. Instead, the government helped Peña-Irala slip out of the country. In 1979, after discovering Peña-Irala living in New York City, the Filártiga family searched for a means to hold him accountable for Joelito's torture and murder. Their search led them to the Center for Constitutional Rights (CCR), a U.S. nongovernmental organization whose mission is the advancement of the rights protected under the U.S. Constitution and the Universal Declaration of Human Rights. CCR lawyers proposed that they sue Peña-Irala under the Alien Tort Statute (ATS).

---

2.   *Kiobel*, 133 S. Ct. 1659, 1669 (2013).

3.   For the facts of this case, *see* Filártiga v. Peña-Irala, 630 F.2d 876, 878–79 (2d Cir. 1980).

The Early History of the ATS

The ATS was enacted in 1789 in the first session of the newly created U.S. Congress as part of the act that created the U.S. federal court system.[4] Although little information about the origins of the ATS has survived, scholars have been able to explain its likely purpose and the jurisprudential background against which it was enacted.[5] As explained by the U.S. Supreme Court in *Sosa v. Alvarez-Machain*,[6] a 2004 case interpreting the ATS, the eighteenth-century framers of the U.S. legal system understood that the new nation had an obligation to comply with international law. More practically, they feared that international law violations could trigger retaliation against the United States by a more powerful state. Their concerns were magnified by a series of torts committed against foreign diplomats that fell within the jurisdiction of the states, not the federal government. The federal government was forced to respond to the diplomatic tensions triggered by these incidents, but lacked the power to ensure that they were properly handled by the courts. The Supreme Court has long included the ATS in a list of statutes "reflecting a concern for uniformity in this country's dealings with foreign nations and . . . a desire to give matters of international significance to the jurisdiction of federal institutions."[7]

Two cases decided in the 1790s recognized that the ATS granted jurisdiction over torts in violation of international law,[8] as did a 1795 opinion by the U.S. attorney general.[9] The attorney general had been asked whether U.S. citizens could face legal repercussions for their involvement in an attack on a British colony in Sierra Leone. In that opinion, he responded as follows:

> There can be no doubt that the company or individuals who have been injured by these acts of hostility have a remedy by a *civil* suit in the courts of the United States; jurisdiction being expressly given to these courts in all cases where an alien sues for a tort only, in violation of the laws of nations, or a treaty of the United States.[10]

Over the next two centuries, fewer than two dozen reported cases invoked jurisdiction under the ATS.[11] The courts sustained jurisdiction in only one, a 1961 international cus-

---

4. Judiciary Act of 1789, ch. 20, § 9, 1 Stat. 73, 77 (codified at 28 U.S.C. § 1350).

5. For an overview of the history of the ATS summarized in this paragraph, *see* Sosa v. Alvarez-Machain, 542 U.S. 692, 710–26 (2004).

6. 542 U.S. 692 (2004).

7. Banco Nacional de Cuba v. Sabbatino, 376 U.S. 398, 427 n.25 (1964).

8. *See* Moxon v. The Fanny, 17 F. Cas. 942, 948 (D. Pa. 1793) (dismissing a claim by shipowners for the seizure of their ship because it involved restitution, not "a tort only"); *see also* Bolchos v. Darrell, 3 F. Cas. 810 (D.S.C. 1795) (finding ATS jurisdiction over a claim for "property" seized in violation of international law). Although the "property" in *Bolchos* was actually three enslaved persons, the opinion made no mention of possible international law issues surrounding slavery.

9. Breach of Neutrality, 1 Op. Att'y. Gen. 57, 59 (1795).

10. *Id.* (emphasis added).

11. Twenty-one cases claimed ATS jurisdiction prior to *Filártiga*. Kenneth C. Randall, *Federal*

tody dispute.[12] Although twelve of those early cases involved corporate defendants, all of them were dismissed, most because their allegations of common law claims such as negligence, theft, or fraud failed to state violations of international law.[13]

The *Filártiga* Case

By the time the Filártigas filed their case in the late 1970s, the post–World War II human rights movement had transformed international law. The 1948 Universal Declaration of Human Rights was followed by wide-ranging human rights agreements adopted by the members of the United Nations and by regional organizations in the Americas and Europe.[14] In the United States, President Jimmy Carter, in office from 1977 to 1981, emphasized the importance of human rights to U.S. foreign policy.

The Filártigas' complaint asserted jurisdiction under the ATS, claiming that the torture of Joelito Filártiga constituted a tort in violation of the law of nations. The district court dismissed the case, relying on earlier Second Circuit decisions holding that international law did not govern a state's treatment of its own citizens within its own territory.[15] On appeal, the Second Circuit reversed the dismissal, finding that modern international law had evolved to prohibit a state's torture of its own citizens: "Deliberate torture perpetrated under color of official authority violates universally accepted norms of the international law of human rights, regardless of the nationality of the parties."[16] The landmark decision held that the ATS authorized a federal court lawsuit against the torturer, provided that the court had personal jurisdiction over the defendant.

To reach its holding, the court relied on three key points: First, international law evolves, and the ATS incorporates current international norms, not those recognized when the statute was enacted in 1789.[17] Second, the applicable international law is defined by applying the "stringent" standard set forth by the Supreme Court in the *Paquete Habana*, which requires "a settled rule of international law" that commands "the general assent of

---

Jurisdiction Over International Law Claims: Inquiries into the Alien Tort Claims Statute, 18 N.Y.U. J. INT'L L. & POL. 1, 4–5 nn.15–17 (1985).

12. Adra v. Clift, 195 F. Supp. 857 (D. Md. 1961). *Adra* upheld ATS jurisdiction over a claim by a Lebanese national that his ex-wife had illegally seized custody of his children, using a false passport to bring the children to the United States. The court cobbled together the tort (wrongful interference with custody) with an international law violation (passport falsification) to find a violation of the ATS. The fact that the plain language of the statute ("a tort in violation of the law of nations") requires that the tort itself constitute a violation of the law of nations was not discussed in the opinion.

13. For a list of corporate-defendant cases as of 2007, *see* Beth Stephens, *Judicial Deference and the Unreasonable Views of the Bush Administration*, 33 BROOK. J. INT'L L. 773, 813 App. B (2008).

14. For an overview of international human rights law after World War II, *see* Jeffrey M. Blum & Ralph G. Steinhardt, *Federal Jurisdiction over International Human Rights Claims: The Alien Tort Claims Act after* Filártiga v. Peña-Irala, 22 HARV. INT'L L.J. 53, 64-75 (1981).

15. Filártiga v. Peña-Irala, Civ. No. 79-917 (E.D.N.Y. May 15, 1979) (citing Dreyfus v. von Finck, 534 F.2d 24, 31 (2d Cir. 1976); IIT v. Vencap, Ltd., 519 F.2d 1001, 1015 (2d Cir. 1975)).

16. Filártiga v. Peña-Irala, 630 F.2d 876, 878, 884-85 (2d Cir. 1980).

17. *Id.* at 881.

civilized nations."[18] Finally, the court applied modern international law norms to conclude that torture by a government official is prohibited by the law of nations.[19]

The Second Circuit requested the views of the U.S. executive branch, which filed a brief that strongly supported the plaintiffs' claims. The brief concluded that "the protection against torture must be considered a fundamental human right" because "torture is universally condemned and incompatible with accepted concepts of human behavior."[20] The executive branch noted that "no state asserts a right to torture its nationals. Rather, nations accused of torture unanimously deny the accusation and make no attempt to justify its use."[21] The executive branch explicitly supported the use of the ATS to bring claims for human rights violations such as torture.[22]

The *Filártiga* opinion closed with a call for the implementation of human rights norms as part of the global struggle to protect against lawless violence:

> In the twentieth century the international community has come to recognize the common danger posed by the flagrant disregard of basic human rights and particularly the right to be free of torture. . . . Among the rights universally proclaimed by all nations . . . is the right to be free of physical torture. Indeed, for purposes of civil liability, the torturer has become like the pirate and slave trader before him *hostis humani generis*, an enemy of all mankind. Our holding today, giving effect to a jurisdictional provision enacted by our First Congress, is a small but important step in the fulfillment of the ageless dream to free all people from brutal violence.[23]

From *Filártiga* to *Sosa*

The *Filártiga* case held liable the person who had physically tortured Joelito Filártiga. Many post-*Filártiga* cases were filed against high officials held liable for violations committed by their subordinates, including, for example, claims against Ferdinand Marcos, the ex-dictator of the Philippines.[24] The *Marcos* case led to a judgment holding him liable for thousands of human rights victims and their families for executions, torture, and forced disappearances committed under his command.

Post-*Filártiga* cases also recognized that additional international law violations triggered ATS jurisdiction, including genocide, crimes against humanity, war crimes, summary execution, and forced disappearance. For example, a 1995 judgment against a Guatemalan

---

18. *Id.* (quoting The Paquete Habana, 175 U.S. 677, 694 (1900)).
19. *Id.* at 884.
20. Brief for the United States as Amici Curiae, Filártiga v. Peña-Irala, 630 F.2d 876 (2d Cir. 1980) (No. 79-6090), 1980 WL 340146 at *15.
21. *Id.* at *16.
22. *Id.* at *20–25.
23. *Filártiga*, 630 F.2d at 890.
24. Hilao v. Estate of Marcos, 103 F.3d 789 (9th Cir. 1996).

general held him liable for torture, summary execution, and forced disappearance committed in the 1980s as part of a brutal campaign against civilians.[25] In another case, a jury found a Chilean military officer liable for extrajudicial killing, torture, crimes against humanity, and cruel, inhuman, and degrading treatment, based on the torture and murder of opponents of the military government.[26] To reach a decision on the issue, all courts adopted *Filártiga*'s application of the ATS to modern human rights abuses.

The U.S. Supreme Court reviewed the doctrine for the first time in 2004, upholding the *Filártiga* interpretation of the ATS in *Sosa v. Alvarez-Machain*.[27] The unusual facts of the *Sosa* case stemmed from the 1985 murder of Enrique Camarena-Salazar, a U.S. drug enforcement agent in Mexico. Agents hired by the U.S. government kidnapped Humberto Alvarez-Machain, a Mexican doctor who was accused of participation in the murder, and forcibly brought him to the United States to face criminal prosecution. After Alvarez-Machain was acquitted of involvement in the murder of Camarena-Salazar, he filed a civil lawsuit against the U.S. government and the individuals involved in the kidnapping. In a 2004 appeal of a judgment in his favor, the Supreme Court held that the ATS grants the federal courts jurisdiction over federal common law claims for violations of modern international law norms. The opinion stressed that courts should be cautious in recognizing ATS claims, limiting them to clearly defined, widely accepted norms. The court stated that the "narrow class" of modern international norms actionable under the ATS includes norms "of international character accepted by the civilized world and defined with a specificity comparable to the features of the 18th-century paradigms" upon which the statute was based.[28] The court overturned the judgment for Alvarez-Machain after holding that he had not alleged an international law violation that met the standard required to trigger ATS jurisdiction.

An Overview of ATS Litigation

From the 1980 *Filártiga* decision through the 2004 decision in *Sosa*, about eighty cases were filed asserting ATS jurisdiction, but only about a dozen led to final judgments in favor of the plaintiffs. Most cases were dismissed for failure to allege a violation of international law. Others were dismissed because the defendant was immune from suit, or through application of standard defenses such as statutes of limitations, *forum non conveniens*, or the political question and act of state doctrines. However, the courts generally upheld claims when plaintiffs alleged cognizable violations of international law against defendants who were subject to the jurisdiction of the U.S. courts.

Case filings increased somewhat after *Sosa* affirmed the validity of the modern application of the statute. Many were dismissed for the same reasons as pre-*Sosa*, most often

---

25.   Xuncax v. Gramajo, 886 F. Supp. 162, 201 (D. Mass. 1995).
26.   Cabello v. Fernández-Larios, 402 F.3d 1148 (11th Cir. 2005).
27.   542 U.S. 692 (2004).
28.   *Id*. at 725, 729.

either a failure to state an international violation or the immunity of the defendant. In response to measures taken by the administration of President George W. Bush in the aftermath of the September 11, 2001, attacks, many ATS cases were filed against U.S. government officials; all of these were dismissed, however, usually based on sovereign immunity or claims that litigation would expose state secrets. Cases filed directly against foreign governments were generally dismissed on the basis of foreign sovereign immunity.[29] Cases against individual defendants, usually former foreign government officials, made up most of the successful cases.

Before turning to corporate-defendant human rights cases, which include approximately half of the post-*Sosa* ATS cases, it will be useful to understand why plaintiffs choose to file ATS claims, even though only a small number have been able to collect money judgments.

The Multifaceted Goals of Human Rights Litigants

U.S. litigation is not a substitute for other enforcement mechanisms. It is far from an ideal means to hold perpetrators accountable and provide redress to victims, given that cases are slow, expensive, and respond to only a small number of human rights violations. However, opportunities to hold accountable those responsible for abuses are rare, and the U.S. cases can play an important role for the plaintiffs and for the human rights movements in their home countries, in the United States, and internationally.

The victims and survivors of human rights abuses who file lawsuits in U.S. courts often emphasize that they chose this path because all other efforts to obtain redress failed. The Filártiga family, for example, sued in the United States only after family members seeking justice in Paraguay were thrown into jail, along with their Paraguayan lawyer, and the perpetrator left the country to evade their efforts to hold him accountable. Plaintiffs in a lawsuit against Royal Dutch Shell alleging abuses in Nigeria filed suit after the leaders of their protest movement were executed by the military government, which worked closely with the oil company to suppress opposition to oil company practices in their region.[30]

Although several cases have produced multimillion-dollar judgments for the plaintiffs, the judgments are difficult to enforce. Human rights plaintiffs were able to seize over $1 million from a Haitian general—money that he had won in the Florida state lottery[31]— and the plaintiffs in a case against two Salvadoran generals collected over $300,000 from

---

29. Pursuant to a statute enacted in 1996, U.S. citizens can file civil claims for torture and extrajudicial execution against a small number of foreign states listed by the U.S. government as "state sponsors of terrorism." 28 U.S.C. § 1605A (formerly codified at 28 U.S.C. § 1605(a)(7)). In 2012, four states were on the list: Cuba, Iran, Sudan and Syria. 22 U.S.C. § 7205(a) (2001).

30. *See* Wiwa v. Royal Dutch Shell, 226 F.3d 88, 92–93 (2nd Cir. 2000) (summarizing plaintiffs' allegations).

31. For details of the victory in *Jean v. Dorelien, see Haiti: The High Command and the Rabotean*

the defendants.[32] A few corporate-defendant cases have settled for tens of millions of dollars, including *Wiwa v. Royal Dutch Shell* and *Doe v. Unocal*.[33] Plaintiffs with uncollected judgments, including the Filártigas, continue to search for means to satisfy their claims.

Plaintiffs in human rights cases often see non-financial aspects of their lawsuits as just as important as collecting a judgment. Filing a lawsuit enables them to obtain a judicial hearing on their allegations and may force a defendant to answer in court or leave the United States. The judicial file creates an official record of the plaintiff's story. In the process, the survivors often feel that, finally, they have been able to fight back against those who harmed them and their families. Dolly Filártiga recounts that on the night of her brother's death, she said to the man who had tortured and murdered him, "Tonight you have power over me, but tomorrow I will tell the world."[34] Her family's lawsuit gave her the opportunity to launch a human rights movement. Carlos Mauricio, plaintiff in a lawsuit against two Salvadoran generals, emphasized the importance of telling his story as part of the "struggle against impunity."[35] "One of the facts from torture," he said, "is that they make you not want to talk about it."[36] Only by telling his story he emphasized, was he "really out of prison."[37] Similarly, the three plaintiffs in a case filed against an Ethiopian torturer found that the process of confronting their torturer in open court contributed to the recovery from their brutal experiences.[38] The parents who sued for the loss of their children in the *Filártiga* and *Todd* cases also took consolation from knowing that they had forced those responsible for the deaths of their sons to flee the United States.[39] In addition, many plaintiffs feel that they are acting as the symbolic representatives of other victims, who take some comfort from a judgment against those who abused them and their family members.

Massacre, THE CENTER FOR JUST. & ACCOUNTABILITY, http://cja.org/article.php?list=type&type=78 (last visited Dec. 2, 2013).

32. For details about this case, *see Case Summary: Romagoza Arce et al. v. Garcia and Vides Casanova*, THE CENTER FOR JUST. & ACCOUNTABILITY, http://cja.org/article.php?list=type&type=82 (last visited Dec. 2, 2013).

33. *See* Ed Pilkington, *Shell Pays Out $15.5m Over Saro-Wiwa Killing*, THE GUARDIAN (June 8, 2009), www.guardian.co.uk/world/2009/jun/08/nigeria-usa; *see* Bloomberg News, *Unocal Settles Rights Suit in Myanmar*, N.Y. TIMES, Dec. 14, 2004, at C6, http://www.nytimes.com/2004/12/14/business/14unocal.html.

34. Dolly Filártiga, Op-Ed., *American Courts, Global Justice*, N.Y. TIMES (Mar. 30, 2004) at A21, http://www.nytimes.com/2004/03/30/opinion/american-courts-global-justice.html.

35. David Gonzalez, *Torture Victims in El Salvador Are Awarded $54 Million*, N.Y. TIMES (July 24, 2002) http://www.cja.org/downloads/Romagoza_NYT_7.24.02.pdf.

36. *Id.*

37. STEPHENS, ET AL., INTERNATIONAL HUMAN RIGHTS LITIGATION IN U.S. COURTS (2d ed. 2008), at xxiv.

38. Abebe-Jira v. Negewo, 72 F.3d 844 (11th Cir. 1996).

39. Filártiga v. Peña-Irala, 630 F.2d 876 (1980); Todd v. Panjaitan, No. 92-12255-PBS, 1994 WL 827111 (D. Mass. Oct. 26, 1994). In *Todd v. Panjaitan*, Helen Todd sued an Indonesia general for the death of her son, who was killed by the Indonesia military in East Timor in a massacre in which hundreds of Timorese were also killed.

U.S. litigation can also trigger human rights progress in the country where the abuses occurred by drawing attention to the human rights abuses, creating a documented historical record, and naming some of those responsible. After a U.S. judgment held Alvaro Rafael Saravia liable for the murder of Archbishop Oscar Romero in El Salvador, for example, Saravia confessed to his role in the killing. His confession helped trigger a new search for those responsible for human rights abuses in that country.[40]

Finally, U.S. litigation contributes to the international movement for accountability, highlighting the absence of other remedies and strengthening international human rights norms. This global impact has been evident in the response to U.S. corporate-defendant cases, the topic of the next section.

Corporate-Defendant Litigation under the Alien Tort Statute

Before 1990, only a handful of ATS cases had been filed against corporate defendants, and all had been dismissed, usually because they alleged domestic tort or contract claims, not violations of international law. Modern corporate-defendant human rights litigation began in the 1990s and accelerated after the *Sosa* decision in 2004.

Recognizing Private-Party Liability under the ATS

A 1995 decision by the Second Circuit in *Kadic v. Karadzic*[41] paved the way for ATS litigation against corporations. The plaintiffs in *Kadic* were victims and survivors of brutal ethnic cleansing in Bosnia-Herzegovina in the early 1990s. They sued Radovan Karadzic, the head of the Bosnian Serb political entity, for torture, summary execution, genocide, war crimes, and crimes against humanity. The district court dismissed the complaint, stating that only state actors could violate international law, and that Karadzic could not be held liable because he was not an official of a recognized state. The Second Circuit reversed, holding that Karadzic could be held liable for genocide and war crimes even without state action, because neither violation requires conduct committed under color of law. The court also recognized that Karadzic could be held liable for international law violations that require state action including torture and summary execution, because he acted in complicity with the government of the former Yugoslavia.[42] The case thus found that the ATS grants jurisdiction over claims against private actors who either commit

---

40. *See* Gerardo Reyes, *End of Silence in 1980 Death of Archbishop*, EL NUEVO HERALD, Mar. 24, 2006, https://www.cja.org/cases/Romero%20Press/Miami%20Herald_3.24.06.pdf.

41. 70 F.3d 232 (2d Cir. 1995).

42. *Id.* at 241–42, 245. The court also held that Karadzic could be found to be acting under color of law as the leader of an illegal, de facto state. *Id.* at 244–45.

international law violations that do not require state action or who act in concert with government officials.

These principles were used in the case holding a private individual liable for the execution of Archbishop Oscar Romero, because the court found that the defendant, a member of a private paramilitary group in El Salvador, had acted under color of law of the Salvadoran government.[43] The same principles applied to permit ATS litigation against corporate defendants.

Corporate-Defendant Litigation, from *Unocal* through *Kiobel*

The recognition that private actors are both bound by international law norms that do not require state action and can be held liable when they act in concert with state actors enabled ATS litigation against corporations. When applied to corporations, these holdings indicate that corporations can be sued for violations that do not require state action, such as genocide, slavery, forced labor, war crimes, and crimes against humanity, and that corporations can be sued for abuses committed in conjunction with state officials.

This theory was first applied in *Doe v. Unocal Corp.*, a case in which Burmese villagers alleged that they were subjected to murder, forced labor, rape, and other forms of torture in connection with Unocal's construction of a gas pipeline through their region.[44] The plaintiffs asserted that Unocal was liable for their damages because the company had hired the Burmese military to provide security, knowing that the military was likely to violate human rights while doing so.

Several dozen corporate cases were filed in the decade after *Doe v. Unocal*. Some alleged that corporate employees directly committed human rights abuses. In *Wiwa v. Royal Dutch Petroleum Co.*,[45] for example, plaintiffs alleged that the defendant's officials had been directly involved in a sham criminal process that led to the conviction and execution of Ken Saro-Wiwa and other leaders of a local movement protesting environmental harms inflicted by multinational oil companies in Nigeria. The *Wiwa* case settled in 2009, on the eve of trial.[46] In another Nigerian case, *Abdullahi v. Pfizer*, which also settled before trial,

---

43.   Doe v. Saravia, 348 F. Supp. 2d 1112, 1149–52 (E.D. Cal. 2004) (finding the defendant responsible for crimes against humanity for his role in the assassination of Archbishop Oscar Romero, who was shot while saying mass in El Salvador in 1980). *See also* Doe v. Constant, Civ. No. 04-10108 (S.D.N.Y. Oct. 24, 2006), http://ccrjustice.org/files/10.24.06%20Finding%20Facts%20and%20Conclusions%20of%20Law.pdf (finding the defendant liable for torture committed by a paramilitary group because the group was "working in concert with the government.").

44.   *See* Doe v. Unocal, 963 F. Supp. 880 (C.D. Cal. 1997) (district court decision denying motion to dismiss claims against the defendant corporation). After extensive litigation, the Doe v. Unocal Corp. litigation was settled under undisclosed terms. *See Unocal Settles Rights Suit in Myanmar*, N.Y. TIMES (Dec. 14, 2004) at C6, http://www.nytimes.com/2004/12/14/business/14unocal.html.

45.   226 F.3d 88 (2d Cir. 2000) (reversing dismissal of case on *forum non conveniens* grounds), remand *to* 2002 WL 819887 at *20–27 (S.D.N.Y. Apr. 19, 2002) (denying the defendants' motion to dismiss for failure to state a claim).

46.   *See* Ed Pilkington, *Shell Pays Out $15.5m Over Saro-Wiwa Killing,* THE GUARDIAN (June 8,

plaintiffs claimed that the pharmaceutical corporation failed to seek informed consent from parents before including their children in a trial of a new drug that caused serious joint and liver damage.[47]

Most corporate-defendant cases relied on secondary liability to hold defendants liable for their assistance in or other formal connection to human rights violations committed by the governments with which they do business. For example, some of the claims in *Wiwa* concerned the Nigerian military's use of violence against civilians who were peacefully protesting oil company operations. Plaintiffs alleged that the oil companies conspired with or aided and abetted the Nigerian military's commission of human rights violations. Similarly, a cluster of cases involved allegations that U.S. corporations operating in Colombia and Guatemala hired private paramilitary groups that violently suppressed labor union activity.[48] The central issue in these cases is how to distinguish actionable corporate complicity in egregious human rights abuses from non-tortious *doing business* in foreign countries. Where a government commits human rights abuses in connection with a corporation's activities, how much knowledge of and involvement in the violation must be shown to find a corporation legally responsible? As discussed below, this issue has divided U.S. courts.

The *Sosa* opinion contained an ambiguous footnote that is the basis for heated dispute about corporate-defendant ATS cases. In the midst of a sentence addressing how to determine whether an international law norm "is sufficiently definite to support a cause of action," the court dropped a footnote that states the following:

> A related consideration is whether international law extends the scope of liability for a violation of a given norm to the perpetrator being sued, if the defendant is a private actor such as a corporation or individual. Compare *Tel-Oren v. Libyan Arab Republic*, 726 F.2d 774, 791–795 (D.C. Cir.1984) (Edwards, J., concurring) (insufficient consensus in 1984 that torture by private actors violates international law), with *Kadic v. Karadzic*, 70 F.3d 232, 239–241 (2d Cir. 1995) (sufficient consensus in 1995 that genocide by private actors violates international law).[49]

2009), http://www.guardian.co.uk/world/2009/jun/08/nigeria-usa.

47.   Abdullahi v. Pfizer, Inc., 562 F.3d 163 (2d Cir. 2009); Joe Stephens, *Pfizer Reaches Settlement Agreement in Notorious Nigerian Drug Trial*, WASH. POST, Apr. 4, 2009, http://www.washingtonpost.com/wp-dyn/content/article/2009/04/03/AR2009040301877.html.

48.   *See* Estate of Rodriguez v. Drummond Co., 256 F. Supp. 2d 1250 (N.D. Ala. 2003) (alleging that Alabama mining company hired paramilitaries to torture, kidnap, and murder union leaders in Colombia); Sinaltrainal v. Coca-Cola, Co., 256 F. Supp. 2d 1345 (S.D. Fla. 2003) (alleging that Coke used paramilitaries to murder, torture, and detain union leaders); Aldana v. Del Monte Fresh Produce, N.A., Inc., 416 F.3d 1242 (11th Cir. 2005) (alleging that Del Monte utilized quasi-governmental security forces to torture union leaders in Guatemala).

49.   Sosa v. Alvarez-Machain, 542 U.S. 692, 732 n.20 (2004).

This footnote has been dissected by all sides in debates over the fundamental question of whether corporate defendants can be sued at all for international law violations, an issue that, as explained in the following section, has split the appellate courts and remains unresolved by the U.S. Supreme Court.

The Unresolved Debates over Alien Tort Statute Liability

Over thirty years after the *Filártiga* decision, and fifteen years after *Unocal*, the first major corporate-defendant ATS case, several fundamental issues remain unresolved. This section first explores two issues that were considered by the Supreme Court in 2013 but not definitively resolved: whether corporations are subject to suit under the ATS and whether the statute applies to conduct that occurs within the territory of another sovereign state. The section then looks at a longstanding issue in corporate-defendant ATS cases: the appropriate standard of liability when a defendant is charged with aiding and abetting an international law violation. Finally, the section explains a fourth pending issue: how to decide whether the United States is the proper forum for ATS litigation—a question that arises both through claims that the plaintiffs must exhaust domestic remedies in the place where the injuries occurred and through *forum non conveniens* motions.

Can Corporations Be Sued under the ATS?

Prior to 2010, corporate-defendant decisions unanimously accepted that corporations were subject to suit under the ATS to the same extent as natural persons. With little or no discussion, the cases assumed that the same liability rules applied to all private defendants, whether they were corporate or natural persons. The consensus was so strong that no majority opinion even addressed the issues.[50] As Judge Katzmann explained, "We have repeatedly treated the issue of whether corporations may be held liable under the AT[S] as indistinguishable from the question of whether private individuals may be."[51] After a 2007 concurring opinion questioned whether corporations could be sued under the ATS,[52] subsequent cases again rejected the suggestion that corporations might be subject to different rules than individual defendants.[53]

---

50. Kiobel v. Royal Dutch Petroleum Co., 621 F.3d 111, 161 (2d Cir. 2010), *aff'd on other grounds*, 133 S. Ct. 1659 (2013) (Leval, J., concurring) (stating that no court had ever dismissed a case on this ground or "discussed such a rule with even vaguely implied approval").

51. Khulumani v. Barclay Nat. Bank Ltd., 504 F. 3d 254, 282 (2d Cir. 2007) (Katzmann, J., concurring).

52. *Id.* at 321 (Korman, J., concurring in part and dissenting in part).

53. Even after Judge Korman's opinion first raised the issue, "[e]very court that has passed on the question has rejected the contention." *Kiobel*, 621 F.3d at 161 (Leval, J., concurring).

In the 2010 opinion in *Kiobel v. Royal Dutch Petroleum Co.*,[54] a sharply divided panel of the Second Circuit held that the ATS does not provide jurisdiction over claims against corporate defendants. The two-judge majority reasoned that international law governs the scope of the violations actionable under the statute, including who can be held liable for those violations, and that international law does not recognize corporate liability for human rights violations. Critics, including the dissenting judge, argued that federal law governed the decision as to which private defendants can be held liable for international law violations because international law leaves implementation of its norms to domestic law. They also argued that even if international law governs, it permits private suits for human rights violations against corporations to the same extent as against natural persons.

Kiobel conflicted with an earlier decision of the Eleventh Circuit.[55] Three additional circuit courts have since disagreed with the *Kiobel* majority, holding that the ATS applies to corporate defendants.[56] In late 2011, the Supreme Court agreed to review the *Kiobel* decision and heard arguments on the issue in early 2012.[57] However, the court then asked for reargument on a separate question the extraterritorial application of the ATS:[58] (an issue that will be discussed in the next section). The *Kiobel* decision, released in April 2013, does not directly address whether corporations can be sued at all under the ATS.[59] Instead, the court held that the particular corporate-defendant claim at issue in that case cannot be litigated under the ATS, and it appeared to bar most, if not all, *Kiobel*-type claims: those filed by foreign plaintiffs to address claims that arose in a foreign state against a foreign corporation with a minimal presence in the United States.[60]

The *Kiobel* court did not discuss the threshold question of whether the federal courts have jurisdiction over any ATS claims against corporate defendants, including claims against U.S. corporations, against foreign corporations with a substantial presence in the United States, or where some of the conduct at issue took place in the United States. Because jurisdiction is always at issue in federal courts, and should always be resolved before addressing the merits of a dispute, the failure to discuss jurisdiction may indicate that a majority of the court concluded that the ATS does provide jurisdiction over corporate-defendant cases. In the absence of a more definitive ruling from the Supreme Court, however, the lower courts will have to decide which, if any, corporate-defendant

---

54.   621 F.3d 111.

55.   Romero v. Drummond Co., 552 F.3d 1303, 1315 (11th Cir. 2008).

56.   Sarei v. Rio Tinto, PLC, 671 F.3d 736 (9th Cir. 2011) (en banc) *judgment vacated*, 133 S. Ct. 1995 (2013); Doe v. Exxon Mobil Corp., 654 F.3d 11 (D.C. Cir. 2011); Flomo v. Firestone Natural Rubber Co., 643 F.3d 1013, 1017 (7th Cir. 2011).

57.   Kiobel v. Royal Dutch Petroleum Co., 621 F.3d 111 (2d Cir. 2010), *cert. granted*, 132 S. Ct. 472 (mem.) (Oct. 17, 2011) (No. 10-1491).

58.   Reargument Order, Kiobel v. Royal Dutch Petroleum Co., 132 S. Ct. 1738 (mem.) (2012).

59.   Kiobel v. Royal Dutch Petroleum Co., 133 S. Ct. 1659, 1669 (2013).

60.   *Id.* at 1662, 1669.

cases can be litigated under the ATS, and final resolution of the question may require yet another appeal to the Supreme Court.

Does the ATS Apply to Conduct That Occurs in the Territory of Another Sovereign State?

In March 2012, after the *Kiobel* oral argument on the question of corporate ATS liability, the Supreme Court ordered the *Kiobel* litigants to brief and argue the following issue: "Whether and under what circumstances the [ATS] allows courts to recognize a cause of action for violations of the law of nations occurring within the territory of a sovereign other than the United States."[61] Almost all cases decided up to this point had assumed that the statute applies outside of the United States. *Sosa*, for example, involved conduct that occurred in Mexico. Although the U.S. government raised concerns about the issue in its *Sosa* brief,[62] the *Sosa* decision applied the statute to extraterritorial acts without discussion. The issue of extraterritorial application of the statute was raised in a handful of dissenting opinions in subsequent cases,[63] and several justices raised questions about it during the first *Kiobel* oral argument.

In the *Kiobel* opinion, issued in April 2013, the court unanimously rejected application of the ATS to the claims at issue in that case: foreign plaintiffs suing a foreign corporation for events that took place in a foreign country.[64] The majority opinion, joined by five judges, emphasized that application of the ATS to events arising in the territory of foreign states could lead to friction with other nations[65] and posed "the danger of unwarranted judicial interference in the conduct of foreign policy."[66] The opinion concluded:

> On these facts, all the relevant conduct took place outside the United States. And even where the claims touch and concern the territory of the United States, they must do so with sufficient force to displace the presumption against extraterritorial application. Corporations are often present in many countries, and it would reach too far to say that mere corporate presence suffices. If Congress were to determine otherwise, a statute more specific than the ATS would be required.[67]

Kiobel leaves unresolved the status of claims that have a greater connection to U.S. territory than those at issue in *Kiobel*,[68] such as claims filed against U.S. citizens, including

---

61. Reargument Order, Kiobel v. Royal Dutch Petroleum Co., 132 S. Ct. 1738 (mem.) (2012).

62. Brief for the United States as Respondent Supporting Petitioner, at 46–50, Sosa v. Alvarez-Machain, 542 U.S. 692 (2004) (No. 03-339), 2004 WL 182581.

63. *See, e.g.*, Doe v. Exxon Mobil Corp., 654 F.3d 11, 74–81 (D.C. Cir. 2011) (Cavanaugh, J., dissenting).

64. Kiobel v. Royal Dutch Petroleum Co., 133 S. Ct. 1659, 1669 (2013).

65. *Id.* at 1664.

66. *Id.*

67. *Id.* at 1669.

68. Justice Kennedy, a member of the five-judge majority, noted in a short concurring opinion that

U.S. corporations; claims against individuals living in the United States; and claims that involve events occurring in the United States. A concurring opinion signed by four justices looked to "international jurisdictional norms" to determine the scope of the statute and identified three situations in which ATS claims could proceed:

> (1) the alleged tort occurs on American soil, (2) the defendant is an American national, or (3) the defendant's conduct substantially and adversely affects an important American national interest, and that includes a distinct interest in preventing the United States from becoming a safe harbor (free of civil as well as criminal liability) for a torturer or other common enemy of mankind.[69]

In the immediate aftermath of the decision, commentators staked out competing views about how much connection to the United States is necessary to support a post-*Kiobel* ATS claim. Litigators predicted that the issues would be fought in every pending ATS case. If the lower courts do not reach a consensus, resolution of the scope of the ATS will probably await a future Supreme Court decision. The most that can be said with confidence is that *Kiobel*-like claims against foreign corporations are not permitted.

What Standard Governs Whether a Defendant Can Be Held Liable for Aiding and Abetting Violations of International Law?

Corporate-defendant human rights cases often allege that a corporation assisted the government or paramilitary security forces that committed human rights abuses. Although defendants have argued that ATS liability only extends to the direct perpetrator of the abuses, the courts have reached a general consensus in favor of aiding and abetting liability.[70] A central unresolved question, however, is exactly how much involvement in the violation must be shown to find a corporation legally responsible for aiding and abetting abuses committed by others. Addressing the question in 2002 in *Doe v. Unocal*, the Ninth Circuit held that a defendant can be held liable for a human rights violation if it provides "knowing practical assistance or encouragement that has a substantial effect on the perpetration of the crime."[71]

Since *Unocal*, courts have split on whether aiding and abetting liability requires that the actor have *knowledge* of the consequences of the assistance offered to the tortfeasor

---

the majority opinion ". . . leave[s] open a number of significant questions regarding the reach and interpretation of the Alien Tort Statute." *Id.* at 1669 (Kenedy, J., concurring). Justices Alito and Thomas, also members of the majority, stated in a separate concurring opinion that the majority opinion "leaves much unanswered." *Id.* (Alito, J., concurring).

69.   *Id.* at 1671 (Breyer, J. concurring).

70.   *See* Doe v. Exxon Mobil Corp., 654 F.3d 11, 19 (D.C. Cir. 2011) (noting that [v]irtually every court to address the issue [of aiding and abetting liability], before and after *Sosa,* has . . . held" that it applies to ATS claims).

71.   Doe v. Unocal Corp., 395 F.3d 932, 951 (9th Cir. 2002).

or the defendant must also *intend* that the abuses take place—that is, must the defendant *purposefully* assist the violations?

The D.C. Circuit and Eleventh Circuit have held that the standard requires only knowledge, not intent or purpose.[72] The Eleventh Circuit reached this result in a noncorporate case, *Cabello v. Fernández-Larios*.[73] There, the court affirmed a jury instruction that stated that the defendant, a Chilean military officer, could be held liable for aiding and abetting torture and extrajudicial killing if he "substantially assisted some person or persons who personally committed or caused . . . the wrongful acts" and "knew that his actions would assist in the illegal or wrongful activity at the time he provided the assistance."[74] The Second and Fourth Circuits, however, have held that international law requires "purpose rather than knowledge alone."[75] The Ninth Circuit declined to address the issue in a full-bench decision.[76] The opinion noted, however, that the international law requirement of "purpose" might be comparable to general intent under U.S. criminal law, not specific intent.[77] That is, a perpetrator might be found to act with "purpose" when aware of the likely outcome of intentional acts.[78] This circuit split may remain unresolved until the Supreme Court reviews the issue.

Determining the Proper Forum for ATS Cases

Several corporate-defendant ATS lawsuits have triggered monumental battles over whether a U.S. court is the appropriate forum or courts in the place where the events occurred. Defendants can raise the issue either with a *forum non conveniens* challenge or as an asserted failure to exhaust domestic remedies. Both doctrines require defendants to show that the plaintiffs have an adequate remedy in the place where the abuses took place. A *forum non conveniens* motion also requires demonstrating that a list of private- and public-interest factors weighs in favor of the alternative forum, including, for example, the location of witnesses and evidence and the forum state's interest in the subject of the lawsuit.

Given that the plaintiffs often allege abuses in which the foreign government was complicit, defendants are frequently unable to show that the alternative forum is "adequate."

---

72. Doe v. Exxon Mobil Corp., 654 F.3d 11, 33–39 (D.C. Cir. 2011); Cabello v. Fernández-Larios, 402 F.3d 1148 (11th Cir. 2005).

73. 402 F.3d 1148 (11th Cir. 2005).

74. *Id.* at 1158.

75. Presbyterian Church of Sudan v. Talisman Energy, Inc., 582 F.3d 244, 259 (2d Cir. 2009); Aziz v. Alcolac, Inc., 658 F.3d 388, 398–401 (4th Cir. 2011).

76. Sarei v. Rio Tinto, PLC 671 F.3d 736 (9th Cir. 2011). The Supreme Court has vacated this decision and remanded for reconsideration in light of *Kiobel*, 133 S. Ct. (2013). The Ninth Circuit later affirmed the district court's dismissal. 722 F. 3d 1109 (9th Cir. 2013).

77. *Sarei*, 671 F.3d at 766–67.

78. *Id.* at 767 (citing Doug Cassel, *Corporate Aiding and Abetting of Human Rights Violations: Confusion in the Courts*, 6 Nw. J. Int'l Hum. Rts. 304, 312–13 (2008) ("'[P]urpose' in the ICC Statute need not mean the exclusive or even primary purpose. A secondary purpose, including one inferred from knowledge of the likely consequences, should suffice.").

In a case involving workers trafficked to Curacao, for example, a district court denied a *forum non conveniens* motion after finding that plaintiffs would be in danger if they returned to that country to file suit.[79] Other corporate-defendant cases have been dismissed after a showing both that another forum was available and that the private- and public-interest factors weighed in favor of litigating there. For instance, in *Türedi v. Coca-Cola Co.*, a case alleging violent attacks on workers during a labor dispute, the court dismissed the case after finding that Turkey provided an adequate, alternative forum.[80]

Courts have split on whether plaintiffs should be required to exhaust domestic remedies before bringing suit in the United States if the place where the event occurred would provide an adequate forum. The Eleventh Circuit, for instance, concluded that the ATS does not require exhaustion of domestic remedies.[81] The Ninth Circuit, in a full-bench decision that produced three splintered opinions, held that exhaustion may be required for some claims, but only if the nexus to the United States is weak and the claims do not involve issues of universal concern.[82] Applying this standard on remand, the district court held that exhaustion was not required for claims of war crimes, crimes against humanity, and racial discrimination, although it was required for the specific claims of environmental destruction and cruel, inhuman, or degrading treatment alleged by the plaintiffs.[83]

When cases are dismissed based on either of these doctrines, the plaintiffs often are unable to refile in the foreign country, so the dismissal of the U.S. claims leaves those injured without a remedy.[84] That is, even though the U.S. courts have determined, as part of the required analysis for *forum non conveniens* or exhaustion of domestic remedies, that an adequate, alternative forum exists, the practical realities facing the litigants may make litigation in that forum impossible. Common problems include the inability to find legal counsel in the foreign country because of the absence of public-interest law offices or contingency-fee arrangements; the lack of discovery procedures in the foreign country; or narrower definitions of the causes of action.[85]

In some human rights cases in which plaintiffs have obtained a judgment in a foreign legal system, defendants have argued that the judgments cannot be enforced in the United

---

79. Licea v. Curacao Drydock Co., 537 F. Supp. 2d 1270, 1274–75 (S.D. Fla. 2008).

80. 343 F. App'x. 623 (2d Cir. 2009).

81. Jean v. Dorelien, 431 F.3d 776, 781 (11th Cir. 2005).

82. Sarei v. Rio Tinto, PLC, 550 F.3d 822, 830–31 (9th Cir. 2008), *judgment vacated*, 133 S. Ct. 1995 (2013) (explaining factors that influence application of "prudential exhaustion" rule).

83. Sarei v. Rio Tinto, PLC, 650 F. Supp. 2d 1004, 1030-31 (C.D. Cal. 2009) *aff'd* 722 F. 3d 1109 (9th Cir. 2013).

84. For a discussion of the difficulties faced by plaintiffs after dismissals in the United States, *see* Jacqueline Duval-Major, Note, *One-Way Ticket Home: The Federal Doctrine of Forum Non Conveniens and the International Plaintiff*, 77 CORNELL L. REV. 650 (1992).

85. For a discussion of these issues, *see* Beth Stephens, *Translating Filártiga: A Comparative and International Law Analysis of Domestic Remedies for International Human Rights Violations*, 27 YALE J. INT'L L. 1 (2002).

States because of alleged irregularities in the foreign legal proceedings. Litigation against ChevronTexaco Corporation for environmental harms caused in Ecuador provides a salient example. At the defendant's request, the ATS claims were dismissed on a motion for *forum non conveniens* after the defendants agreed to submit to jurisdiction in Ecuador.[86] Years later, when plaintiffs successfully obtained a multibillion-dollar judgment in the courts of Ecuador, the defendant launched a multipronged attack on the plaintiffs, their lawyers, and the Ecuadorean legal system, designed to prevent courts in the United States or elsewhere from enforcing the judgment.[87]

This legal maneuvering illustrates an unfortunate reality: the international legal system today has yet to develop effective means to hold corporations accountable when they violate human rights. U.S. courts may eventually resolve the particular questions raised by challenges based on *forum non conveniens* and failure to exhaust domestic remedies. Resolution of the larger question—the appropriate forum in which to seek redress for harms committed by multinational corporations—will require international action.

U.S. Human Rights Litigation and the Global Accountability Movement

International law requires states to provide redress for international human rights violations. Each state, however, responds to this mandate through substantive norms and procedural rules appropriate to its legal system. Most states permit some means by which the victims can seek redress through criminal, civil, or administrative proceedings appropriate to the structure of their legal systems.[88] Civil human rights litigation in U.S. courts is a product of particular U.S. laws and procedures.

Why Are Civil Human Rights Lawsuits Feasible in U.S. Courts?

U.S. human rights litigation is a product of a combination of substantive law and procedural rules that is unique to the United States.

As explained by the Supreme Court in *Sosa v. Alvarez-Machain*, the ATS grants federal courts jurisdiction over claims of international law violations; federal courts have the

---

86. Aguinda v. Texaco, Inc., 303 F.3d 470 (2d Cir. 2002).

87. For an overview of almost two decades of legal proceedings before multiple U.S. and Ecuadorean courts and before an international arbitration panel, *see* Business & Human Rights Resource Centre, *Case Profile: Texaco/Chevron Lawsuits (re Ecuador)*, http://www.business-humanrights.org/Categories /Lawlawsuits/Lawsuits regulatoryaction/LawsuitsSelectedcases/TexacoChevronlawsuitsreEcuador (last visited Dec. 2, 2013).

88. For a comparison of U.S. human rights proceedings and those used in other legal systems, *see* Stephens, *supra* note 85.

authority to recognize common law causes of action for those claims.[89] As a result, aliens can sue in U.S. courts for widely accepted, clearly defined international law norms if they can obtain personal jurisdiction over the defendant. Two additional statutes permit suits for human rights violations committed in other countries:

1. The Anti-terrorism Act permits claims by U.S. citizens for injuries caused by "an act of international terrorism," defined as a violent crime intended to intimidate or coerce a civilian population or a government.[90] The statute applies to organizational defendants, including corporations, as well as individual defendants.[91]

2. The Torture Victim Protection Act permits suits against an individual for torture or extrajudicial execution committed "under . . . color of law, of any foreign nation."[92] The Supreme Court ruled in 2012, however, that the statute does not permit suit against corporations.[93]

Procedural rules also smooth the path for civil human rights litigation in U.S. courts. First, personal jurisdiction rules permit suit against a corporation that has continuous and systematic business ties with the United States such that it is essentially "at home" in the United States, even if the corporation is not incorporated or headquartered in this country and the cause of action arose in a foreign state.[94] Similarly expansive rules permit U.S. courts to assert personal jurisdiction over an individual who is served process while physically present in the state where the lawsuit is filed, even if the presence is transitory.[95]

Second, the U.S. legal system includes several plaintiff-friendly procedures and customs that are of particular importance when a plaintiff with limited or no resources seeks redress under a novel legal theory.[96] Perhaps most important, the United States does not follow the *loser pays* system, under which the losing party is required to pay the legal fees of the victorious opponent. As a result, litigants can bring difficult claims without fear of a huge penalty if they lose. Similarly, contingency fees and the possibility of punitive damages may make some longshot human rights claims financially attractive to private law firms. At the

---

89. Sosa v. Alvarez-Machain, 542 U.S. 692 (2004).

90. 18 U.S.C. §§ 2331-2339C.

91. *See, e.g.*, Rothstein v. UBS AG, 708 F.3d 82 (2d Cir. 2013) (applying the ATA to claims against a bank, although dismissing those claims for failure to state a claim). *Rothstein* also held that the ATA does not permit aiding and abetting claims. *Id.* at 97–98.

92. Torture Victim Protection Act of 1991, 28 U.S.C. § 1350 (note), § 2(a).

93. Mohamad v. Palestinian Authority, 132 S. Ct. 1702 (2012) (holding that TVPA does not permit suit against corporations).

94. Goodyear Dunlop Tires Operations, S.A. v. Brown, 131 S. Ct. 2846, 2857 (2011).

95. *See* Kadic v. Karadzic, 70 F.3d 232 (2d Cir. 1995) (citing Burnham v. Superior Court of California, 495 U.S. 604) (holding that personal jurisdiction over the leader of the Bosnian Serbs could be based on service of summons and complaint while he was physically present in the United States).

96. For a discussion of the procedural and substantive features that facilitate U.S. human rights litigation and comparisons to other legal systems, *see* Stephens, *supra* note 85.

same time, a tradition of public-interest litigation and nonprofit law offices has created a pool of lawyers willing to litigate cases even if the possibility of collection is remote. Finally, broad U.S. discovery rules enable plaintiffs to prove their cases through documents and other information obtained from defendants. This enables plaintiffs to consider filing cases even when all or most of the necessary evidence is in the defendant's control.

Analogous Human Rights Claims in Other Systems

Not surprisingly, human rights claims outside of the United States have not followed the U.S. civil lawsuit model. Some of these systems will be discussed later in this book.

In many foreign legal systems, substantive requirements bar civil human rights litigation in the form common in the United States. For example, many systems require that conduct that constitutes a crime must first be prosecuted through the criminal justice system; under such rules, claims for torture or execution cannot be litigated as independent civil lawsuits, or at least not until the criminal proceeding is final. In other systems, a claim cannot be based on an international law violation in the absence of a statute creating a civil cause of action for the underlying conduct.

However, despite the absence of civil human rights lawsuits, similar claims may be pursued through various analogous mechanisms. In civil law systems, victims can often join a criminal prosecution as a *partie civile*, with the right to seek compensation for their injuries.[97] This process is similar to a U.S. civil lawsuit for the same conduct. Administrative actions, including efforts to seize or freeze bank accounts of those accused of international law violations, also serve similar goals. Finally, in some legal systems, private parties regularly file domestic tort claims against corporations for human rights abuses committed in their operations abroad.[98]

These varied procedures have much in common: each seeks legal redress for human rights abuses in a domestic forum, asking for remedies that include both compensation to those injured and punishment of the perpetrators.

Conclusion

Even in the absence of a large number of cases resulting in enforceable judgments, corporate-defendant ATS cases have had a remarkable impact, both on the individuals involved in particular cases and on the global movement to find means to hold corporations accountable for human rights violations.

---

97.   *See* Muchlinski and Rouas's chapter 12 for further detail on business and human rights litigation in civil systems.

98.   *See* Srinivasan's chapter 11 for details on this type of litigation in the UK.

First, even if the cases do not result in enforceable damage awards and, at times, even if the cases are not successful, victims and survivors may take some satisfaction from the process of pursuing their claims. A lawsuit may produce a public accounting of the facts and assign responsibility for the injuries they and their family members have suffered. Given how few victims of human rights abuses have access to justice, civil human rights litigation offers some survivors a rare opportunity to take action against those responsible.

Second, even a small number of corporate-defendant cases may help deter future human rights abuses. Consultants working with corporations report that fear of litigation has led at least some corporate leaders to pay more attention to their possible liability for human rights abuses committed in the course of their operations.

Third, lawsuits focus attention on corporate human rights violations, energize public campaigns against abusive corporations, and place additional pressure on governments and international bodies to take action. This pressure contributes to the eventual development of binding, enforceable norms governing corporations and international human rights. By highlighting the problem of corporate accountability, the U.S. human rights cases help push governments to recognize the issues and begin to address them.

The Supreme Court narrowed the permissible scope of U.S. human rights litigation against corporations in the 2013 *Kiobel* decision. Future litigation will need to resolve several remaining contentious issues, including which corporations can still be sued and for which acts outside of the United States; the definition of aiding and abetting liability; and the test for determining a proper forum. Even if corporate-defendant litigation under the ATS is further limited, human rights litigation against corporate defendants will likely continue through other legal avenues, including, for example, lawsuits based on state common law claims or another federal statute. As long as the international community fails to provide a comprehensive means to provide redress to victims of human rights violations, plaintiffs and their advocates will continue to search for legal means to hold accountable the individuals and corporations responsible for those abuses.

Chapter 7

The Implications of *Kiobel* for Corporate Accountability Litigation under the Alien Tort Statute

Paul Hoffman

Introduction

The Supreme Court's decision in *Kiobel v. Royal Dutch Petroleum*[1] was expected to bring clarity to the litigation of corporate complicity claims under the Alien Tort Statute (ATS). The first question presented when the court granted *certiorari* in October 2011 was whether corporations could be sued at all under the statute.[2] After the February 2012 *Kiobel* argument, the court expanded the issues before it to whether, and under what circumstances, the ATS applies to acts occurring on the territory of foreign sovereigns.[3]

After two arguments, accompanied by full briefing and nearly one hundred amicus briefs, including two from the United States, the Supreme Court's April 17, 2013, decision appears to raise more questions than it answers. Moreover, the alignment of justices in

---

1. 133 S. Ct. 1659 (2013).
2. "Whether corporations are immune from tort liability for violations of the law of nations such as torture, extrajudicial executions or genocide, as the court of appeals decision provides, or if corporations may be sued in the same manner as any other private party defendant under the ATS for such egregious violations, as the Eleventh Circuit has explicitly held." Kiobel v. Royal Dutch Petroleum Co., 132 S. Ct. 472 (2011) (mem.). The Second Circuit dismissed the plaintiffs' claims on the grounds that there was no corporate liability under the ATS. Kiobel v. Royal Dutch Petroleum Inc., 621 F. 3d 111, 145 (2d Cir. 2010).
3. "Whether and under what circumstances the Alien Tort Statute, 28 U.S.C. § 1350, allows courts to recognize a cause of action for violations of the law of nations occurring within the territory of a foreign sovereign other than the United States." Kiobel v. Royal Dutch Petroleum Co., 132 S. Ct. 1738 (2012) (mem.).

Kiobel suggests that the future meaning of the ATS is largely in the hands of Justice Kennedy, whose concurrence offers little guidance regarding what that future might look like.

This chapter first examines the *Kiobel* opinions in search of *Kiobel*'s meaning, albeit inescapably from the perspective of the plaintiffs' lawyer.[4] The following section addresses some of the issues most likely to arise in post-*Kiobel* ATS corporate cases and suggests some possible alternative avenues for redress for human rights victims if the scope of the ATS is further narrowed.[5] Ultimately, the chapter concludes that *Kiobel* will not stop corporate complicity litigation; it may shift such litigation to other fora, in particular, state courts.

The *Kiobel* Framework

Background

Prior to the Supreme Court's decision in *Kiobel*, no court had ever accepted the argument that the presumption against extraterritorial application of U.S. statutes limited the scope of the ATS.[6] The Justice Department advanced this argument in *Sosa v. Alvarez-Machain*.[7] No justice considered the argument, even though *Sosa* was a case involving a foreign plaintiff, a foreign defendant, and acts occurring only on Mexican territory. Indeed, virtually every ATS case since *Filártiga v. Peña-Irala*[8] has involved acts occurring on the territory

---

4. Predictably, the defense bar started to spin the decision as erecting an insurmountable barrier to extraterritorial ATS claims before the ink was dry on the *Kiobel* opinions. *See, e.g.*, John Bellinger, *Reflections on Kiobel*, Lawfare (Apr. 22, 2013, 8:52 PM), http://www.lawfareblog.com/2013/04/reflections-on-kiobel. As the court noted in Sosa v. Alvarez-Machain, 542 U.S. 692, 731 (2004), the ideological debate over the scope of the ATS has been ongoing at least since the debate between Judge Bork and Judge Edwards in Tel-Oren v. Libyan Arab Republic, 726 F. 2d 774, 775, 798 (D.C. Cir. 1984). Perhaps the defense spin will turn out to be true, and the *Kiobel* majority opinion, in retrospect, will have signaled an ideologically driven intent to reject *Sosa* and ATS jurisprudence as it has developed since Filártiga v. Peña-Irala, 630 F. 2d 876 (2d Cir. 1980). However, nothing in the court's *Kiobel* opinions announces that this day has come. This chapter assumes that *Kiobel* should be read as written, not as a disguised exercise in raw judicial power to reject *sub rosa* all future ATS litigation.

5. Paul Hoffman & Beth Stephens, *International Human Rights Cases under State Law and in State Courts*, 3 UCI L. Rev. 9 (2013). This article is part of a February 2013 Symposium issue devoted to the questions raised by human rights litigation in state courts under state law.

6. The argument was advanced in a handful of dissenting opinions. *See, e.g.*, Doe v. Exxon Mobil Corp., 654 F.3d 11, 72–73 (D.C. Cir. 2011) (Kavanaugh, J., dissenting in part), vacated, No. 09–7125 (D.C. Cir. July 26, 2013); Sarei v. Rio Tinto, PLC, 671 F.3d 736, 797, 809 (9th Cir. 2011) (en banc) (Kleinfeld, J., dissenting), vacated, 133 S. Ct. 1995 (2013) (mem.). Notably, Judge Kleinfeld did believe that the ATS applies extraterritorially to the conduct of U.S. citizens. *Id.* at 803–04 ("What little authority there is for one world state to impose a law having effect in another has generally been limited to circumstances where the conduct affects its own citizens or interests."). In describing the origin of the ATS, Kleinfeld explains that the "concern was that U.S. citizens might engage in incidents that could embroil the young nation in war," and in analyzing the Bradford opinion, he notes that "it spoke to Americans' actions abroad, not foreign-cubed cases such as this." *Id.* at 802, 811.

7. 542 U.S. 692 (2004). Brief for the United States as Respondent Supporting Petitioner, at 8, 46–48, Sosa v. Alvarez-Machain, 542 U.S. 692 (2004) (No. 03-339), 2004 WL 182581.

8. 630 F.2d 876 (2d Cir. 1980).

of foreign sovereigns. Moreover, the ATS cases that the court endorsed in *Sosa* were all extraterritorial cases.[9] The *Sosa* majority recognized that the modern international law of human rights often arose in the context of acts taking place within the territory of foreign sovereigns.[10] Thus, six members of the Supreme Court found that modern federal courts could recognize federal common law causes of action based on modern international human rights norms, as long as the norms were of the same character as the norms recognized by Blackstone at the time that the ATS was enacted.[11]

From the outset of the first *Kiobel* oral argument, it was clear that some justices, including Justice Kennedy, were troubled by the application of the ATS to the facts of the case.[12] The *Kiobel* plaintiffs were Nigerian citizens who had been subjected to human rights violations in Ogoni in Nigeria by Nigerian security forces in the 1990s.[13] The primary theory of liability was that Shell's Nigerian subsidiary aided and abetted the Nigerian security

---

9.   *Sosa*, 542 U.S. at 732 (citing *Filártiga*, 630 F.2d 876; *In re* Estate of Marcos Human Rights Litig., 25 F.3d 1467 (9th Cir. 1994); and Kadic v. Karadzic, 70 F.3d 232 (2d Cir. 1995)).

10.   *See Sosa*, 542 U.S. at 727–28. During the *Kiobel* litigation, the U.S. government recognized this pattern as well. *See* Supplemental Brief for the United States as Amicus Curiae in Partial Support of Affirmance, at 10; Kiobel v. Royal Dutch Petroleum Co., 133 S. Ct. 1659 (2013) (No. 10-1491), 2012 WL 2161290 [hereinafter Supp. U.S. Br.] ("Modern litigation under the ATS has focused primarily on alleged law-of-nations violations committed within foreign countries. . . . [I]n the ensuing decades since *Filártiga*, federal courts have either assumed or, in at least one case, expressly held that violations of the law of nations arising in a foreign country could be brought based on the ATS.").

11.   *Sosa*, 542 U.S. at 725 ("Accordingly, we think courts should require any claim based on the present-day law of nations to rest on a norm of international character accepted by the civilized world and defined with a specificity comparable to the features of the 18th-century paradigms we have recognized.").

12.   Several comments from Justices Kennedy and Alito at the outset of the argument suggested that the Justices were of the view that the *Kiobel* claims should not be resolved in a U.S. court:

> JUSTICE KENNEDY: But, counsel, for me, the case turns in large part on this: . . . "International law does not recognize corporate responsibility for the alleged offenses here"; and . . . the amicus brief for Chevron saying "No other nation in the world permits its court to exercise universal civil jurisdiction over alleged extraterritorial human rights abuses to which the nation has no connection." And in reading through the briefs, I was trying to find the best authority you have to refute that proposition, or are you going to say that that proposition is irrelevant? Transcript of First Oral Argument, at 3:19-4:6, Kiobel v. Royal Dutch Petroleum Co., 133 S. Ct. 1659 (2012) (No. 10-1491).

> JUSTICE ALITO: There's no connection to the United States whatsoever. The Alien Tort Statute was enacted, it seems to be—there seems to be a consensus, to prevent the United States—to prevent international tension, to—and—does this—this kind of a lawsuit only creates international tension. *Id.* at 12:1-7.

> JUSTICE KENNEDY: But I agree that we can assume that Filártiga is a binding and important precedent, it's the Second Circuit. But in that case, the only place they could sue was in the United States. He was an individual. He was walking down the streets of New York, and the victim saw him walking down the streets of New York and brought the suit. In this case, the corporations have residences and presence in many other countries where they have much more—many more contacts than here. *Id.* at 13:21-14:5.

13.   The plaintiffs had received political asylum in the United States because of these violations and were all U.S. residents. *Kiobel*, 133 S. Ct. at 1662–63.

forces, which actually committed these violations. The defendants in *Kiobel* were Royal Dutch Petroleum Company and Shell Transport and Trading Company plc—the parent corporations based in the Netherlands and the United Kingdom, respectively. The only connection to the United States, apart from the plaintiffs' residence, was the presence of these parent corporations in New York; in particular, the parent corporations used an investor assistance office in New York and were listed on the New York Stock Exchange.[14]

Thus, though the court framed the new question presented broadly, the specific question in *Kiobel* was whether the federal courts should recognize a cause of action under the ATS for acts of torture, extrajudicial execution, or arbitrary detention committed by Nigerian security forces in Nigeria in the 1990s—acts that a subsidiary of the defendants before the court, foreign holding companies, had allegedly aided and abetted—where the only U.S. connection was the court's general jurisdiction over these corporate defendants.

Significantly, both the Dutch and UK governments submitted briefs arguing that the assertion of ATS jurisdiction over their corporations for acts taking place in Nigeria would itself violate international law.[15] Thus, unlike most ATS cases, the court was faced with a conflict over the appropriate reach of U.S. action, consistent with international law, and an argument that the court should avoid this conflict by restricting the reach of the ATS itself. The Dutch and UK governments did not dispute the legitimacy of extraterritorial ATS jurisdiction in other contexts, such as over the extraterritorial conduct of U.S. citizen defendants in particular.[16] Thus, the briefing and argument in *Kiobel* were influenced by the fact that the actual case before the court was a so-called "foreign-cubed" case and not a case with a more significant geographic or substantive connection to the United States.

The Roberts Majority Opinion

The *Kiobel* majority opinion by Chief Justice Roberts recognizes that the presumption against extraterritorial application of federal statutes does not strictly apply to the ATS because it is a jurisdictional statute that applies federal common law causes of action based on the law of nations and treaties of the United States.[17] Nonetheless, the opinion finds

---

14. In a prior case involving similar claims, the Second Circuit upheld a finding of personal jurisdiction over the same defendants and overturned a *forum non conveniens* dismissal. Wiwa v. Royal Dutch Petroleum Co., 226 F.3d 88 (2d Cir. 2000), cert. denied, 532 U.S. 941 (2001) (mem.). In *Kiobel* the defendants waived any challenge to personal jurisdiction by failing to object on this basis in their first motion to dismiss; they did not make a *forum non conveniens* motion.

15. *See* Brief of the Governments of the Kingdom of the Netherlands and the United Kingdom of Great Britain and Northern Ireland as Amici Curiae in Support of Neither Party, at 27–28, Kiobel v. Royal Dutch Petroleum Co., 133 S. Ct. 1659 (2013) (No. 10-1491), 2012 WL 2312825 [hereinafter UK/Dutch Br.]. Other amici advance this argument as well. *See, e.g.*, Supplemental Brief of Chevron Corp., et al., as Amici Curiae in Support of Respondents at 24–29, Kiobel v. Royal Dutch Petroleum Co., 133 S. Ct. 1659 (2013) (No. 10-1491), 2012 WL 3245485 [hereinafter Chevron Supp. Br.].

16. Dutch/UK Br., *supra* note 15, at 35–36.

17. *Kiobel*, 133 S. Ct. at 1664.

it appropriate to apply the *principles* underlying the established presumption to analyze whether the ATS ought to recognize such federal common law claims.[18]

According to these principles, courts should be wary of "the danger of unwarranted interference in the conduct of foreign policy"[19] and ought to protect against "unintended clashes between our laws and those of other nations."[20] The majority rejected the argument that *Sosa*'s limitation—recognizing only ATS claims founded upon "specific, universal, and obligatory" international norms supported by the same quality of evidence as the norms recognized by Blackstone in the eighteenth century—was sufficient to address these concerns.[21]

Although the majority found that the presumption's principles applied in *Kiobel*, the opinion does not indicate what weight the courts should give to these concerns in the post-*Kiobel* calculus. Some ATS cases will involve extraterritorial conduct where these concerns are not present or where the failure to afford a remedy will create the conflict or tension the court wishes to avoid.[22] The ATS was enacted to remedy the absence of a federal judicial forum, not because of a concern that federal courts would exacerbate tensions by deciding cases based on the law of nations.[23]

In section III of the majority opinion, the court rejects petitioners' arguments that the presumption is overcome by the text, purpose, and history of the statute.[24] Undoubtedly ATS defendants will encourage courts to read this language as a categorical rejection of

---

18.   *Id.* at 1665.

19.   *Id.* at 1664.

20.   *Id.* (quoting EEOC v. Arabian American Oil Co., 499 U.S. 244, 248 (1991)).

21.   *Id.* at 1665 (quoting *Sosa*, 542 U.S. at 732).

22.   In *Filártiga*, the State Department informed the Second Circuit that it furthered U.S. foreign policy interests to provide a federal forum for foreign human rights victims under the ATS. Memorandum for the United States as Amicus Curiae at 23, Filártiga v. Peña-Irala, 630 F.2d 876 (2d Cir. 1980) (No. 79-6090), 1980 WL 340146 ("[T]here is little danger that judicial enforcement will impair our foreign policy efforts. To the contrary, a refusal to recognize a private cause of action in these circumstances might seriously damage the credibility of our nation's commitment to the protection of human rights."). *See also* Supp. U.S. Br., *supra* note 10, at 4–5 ("This Office is informed by the Department of State that, in its view, after weighing the various considerations, allowing suits based on conduct occurring in a foreign country in the circumstances presented in Filártiga is consistent with the foreign relations interests of the United States, including the promotion of respect for human rights.").

23.   *Sosa*, 542 U.S. at 715–16 ("Before there was any ATS, a distinctly American preoccupation with these hybrid international norms had taken shape owing to the distribution of political power from independence through the period of confederation. The Continental Congress was hamstrung by its inability to 'cause infractions of treaties, or of the law of nations to be punished'" (citing J. MADISON, JOURNAL OF THE CONSTITUTIONAL CONVENTION 60 (E. Scott ed. 1893).).

24.   *Kiobel*, 133 S. Ct. at 1669 (Roberts, C.J.) ("We therefore conclude that the presumption against extraterritoriality applies to claims under the ATS, and that nothing in the statute rebuts that presumption."). In the author's opinion, the Court's analysis is flawed in many respects and will be the subject of much scholarly debate. My purpose here is not to provide a comprehensive critique of the decision but rather to sketch what the post-*Kiobel* battleground will look like. Of course, identifying the majority's misunderstanding of the relevant history may be part of that battle.

extraterritorial ATS claims and hope that the courts will stop reading the opinion at the end of section III.[25]

Section IV of the majority opinion, however, makes it clear that the language at the end of section III only concludes that a presumption applies, leaving open the question of whether that presumption applies to any particular set of facts. Section IV contains the majority's holding, and it clearly applies only to the limited context of this "foreign-cubed" case. Section IV reads in full as follows:

> On these facts, all the relevant conduct took place outside the United States. And even where the claims touch and concern the territory of the United States, they must do so with sufficient force to displace the presumption against extraterritorial application. *See Morrison*, 130 S. Ct. 2883–2888. Corporations are often present in many countries, and it would reach too far to say that mere corporate presence suffices. If Congress were to determine otherwise, a statute more specific than the ATS would be required.[26]

This paragraph provides the holding of the case: "mere corporate presence," such as that involved in *Kiobel*, is insufficient to overcome the new presumption, but ATS claims that "touch and concern the territory of the United States" with "sufficient force" will overcome the presumption. Claims based on conduct occurring in part on U.S. territory,[27] or with some other substantial connection to the United States, may not be barred. The majority opinion, though, provides little guidance about the meaning of the new term, *touch and concern*.[28] The Kennedy Concurrence

Justice Kennedy supplied the crucial fifth vote for the majority opinion. His concurrence reads in full as follows:

> The opinion for the Court is careful to leave open a number of significant questions regarding the reach and interpretation of the Alien Tort Statute. In my view that is a proper disposition. Many serious concerns with respect to human rights abuses

---

25. *See, e.g.*, Al Shimari v. CACI Int'l, Inc., 2013 WL 3229720 (E.D. Va., June 25, 2013).

26. *Kiobel*, 133 S. Ct. at 1669 (Kennedy, J., concurring).

27. Cases arising on U.S. bases abroad where the United States is in control of the base may also be considered "U.S. territory" for this purpose. *See* Rasul v. Bush, 542 U.S. 466, 484–85 (2004) (finding that the ATS applies to the U.S. bases at Guantanamo). Certainly the reasoning in the majority opinion concerning potential conflict with other nations does not apply where the United States exercises such control. The court in Mwani v. Bin Laden recently found that "events that occurred in and around the grounds of the United States Embassy in Nairobi, Kenya, on August 7, 1998, 'touched and concerned' the United States with 'sufficient force' to displace the presumption." 2013 WL 2325166 (D.D.C. May 29, 2013).

28. This formulation has never appeared previously in an ATS case. There is no apparent body of existing law to which the Court is referring in using this formulation.

committed abroad have been addressed by Congress in statutes such as the Torture Victim Protection Act of 1991 (TVPA), 106 Stat. 73, note following 28 U.S.C. § 1350, and that class of cases will be determined in the future according to the detailed statutory scheme Congress has enacted. Other cases may arise with allegations of serious violations of international law principles protecting persons, cases covered neither by the TVPA nor by the reasoning and holding of today's case; and in those disputes the proper implementation of the presumption against extraterritorial application may require some further elaboration and explanation.[29]

Justice Kennedy's concurrence also suggests that the majority holding is found in section IV of the opinion, not in the two categorical sentences rejecting extraterritorial application of the ATS. Thus, for Justice Kennedy, "a number of significant questions regarding the reach and interpretation of the Alien Tort Statute" remain open.[30] Because a categorical ban on the extraterritorial application of the ATS would have wiped out virtually all pending and potential future ATS cases, the existence of this caveat demonstrates that there are circumstances in which the ATS applies to extraterritorial conduct. Justice Kennedy reinforces this reading of the court's holding by emphasizing that there will be cases under the ATS falling outside both the scope of the TVPA and the "reasoning and holding" of *Kiobel*, which "may require some further elaboration and explanation" of the new *Kiobel* presumption.[31]

The reasoning of *Kiobel* is based heavily on the policy concerns underlying the presumption against extraterritoriality, including interference with foreign policy and clashes between the laws of the United States and those of other countries.[32] However, foreign states often do not object to litigation of ATS claims arising in their territory. They have even expressly endorsed such claims, particularly when the defendants have fled their home country and sought protection in the United States.[33] At a minimum, Justice Kennedy's

---

29. *Kiobel*, 133 S. Ct. at 1669 (Kennedy, J., concurring).

30. *Id.*

31. *Id.*

32. *Id.* at 1664–67 (noting, *inter alia*, that the presumption "serves to protect against unintended clashes between our laws and those of other nations which could result in international discord" (quoting EEOC v. Arabian American Oil Co., 499 U.S. 244, 248 (1991)); highlighting that "the danger of unwarranted judicial interference in the conduct of foreign policy is magnified in the context of the ATS"; finding that *Sosa* does not sufficiently "diminish[]" these concerns; and underscoring that piracy cases "carr[y] less direct foreign policy consequences").

33. *See, e.g.*, Trajano v. Marcos, 878 F. 2d 1439, *2 (9th Cir. 1989) ("Marcos is a private citizen residing in the United States. Neither the present government of the Republic of the Philippines nor the United States government objects to judicial resolution of these claims."); *In re* Estate of Marcos Human Rights Litig., 978 F.2d 493, 498 n.11 (9th Cir. 1992) (discussing the Philippine government's "statement of non-objection to the litigation against former President Marcos"); Paul v. Avril, 812 F. Supp. 207, 210 (S.D. Fla. 1993) (highlighting that the government of Haiti "waived any and all immunity enjoyed by Prosper Avril.").

opinion indicates that *Kiobel* does not bar claims when neither the U.S. executive branch nor the relevant foreign state objects to the litigation.[34]

The Alito Concurrence

The concurring opinion by Justice Alito (joined by Justice Thomas) expresses agreement with the majority's "narrow approach."[35] Therefore, the concurring opinion underscores the unanimous understanding of the justices that the *Kiobel* holding is a limited one, leaving many important questions for future decisions. Justices Alito and Thomas write separately to emphasize that they would approve an ATS cause of action only if "the domestic conduct is sufficient to violate an international law norm that satisfied *Sosa*'s requirements of definiteness and acceptance among civilized nations."[36] Significantly, only justices Alito and Thomas take this view. Thus, seven justices allow for the possible recognition of ATS claims where some, or perhaps all, of the conduct giving rise to the claims arose outside U.S. territory. At a minimum, seven justices failed to express support for Justice Alito's "broader standard" for what cases fall within the scope of the presumption against extraterritoriality.[37]

The Breyer Concurrence

Since Justice Breyer, joined by justices Ginsburg, Sotomayor, and Kagan, concurred in the rejection of the ATS claims in *Kiobel*, no member of the court supported the application of the ATS to the claims in *Kiobel*.[38] However, although the Breyer opinion rejects the claims in *Kiobel* itself, it also rejects the presumption against extraterritoriality as the proper analytical framework to govern when extraterritorial ATS claims should be recognized.[39] Instead, Justice Breyer, relying heavily on established U.S. foreign relations law, finds jurisdiction[40] under the ATS when:

---

34. Even where a foreign state or the United States objects to the litigation, courts turn to established jurisprudence under the political question doctrine to guide them. *See, e.g.*, Japan Whaling Ass'n v. Am. Cetacean Soc., 478 U.S. 221, 229–30 (1986); Kadic v. Karadzic, 70 F.3d 232, 248–50 (2d Cir. 1995); *In re* S. Afr. Apartheid Litig., 617 F. Supp. 2d 228, 284 n.349 (S.D.N.Y. 2009) ("A speculative conflict with the goal of maintaining good relations with a foreign nation—as opposed to a conflict with the authority of the political branches—is not the type of conflict that normally triggers dismissal under the political question doctrine.").

35. *Kiobel*, 133 S. Ct. at 1670 (Alito, J., concurring).

36. *Id.*

37. *Id.*

38. The Roberts and Breyer opinions have the appearance of the respective ideological blocks on the Court vying for Justice Kennedy's crucial fifth vote, with Justice Kennedy not fully in either camp at this point.

39. *Kiobel*, 133 S. Ct. at 1671 (Breyer, J., concurring in the judgment) ("Unlike the Court, I would not invoke the presumption against extraterritoriality.").

40. It is not clear whether Justice Breyer views the application of the presumption as an issue of subject matter jurisdiction or a merits question. The Roberts majority opinion treats the issue as a merits decision and finds that "the principles underlying the presumption against extraterritoriality thus constrain

1. the alleged tort occurs on American soil,
2. the defendant is an American national, or
3. the defendant's conduct substantially and adversely affects an important American national interest, and that includes a distinct interest in preventing the United States from becoming a safe harbor (free of civil as well as criminal liability) for a torturer or other common enemy of mankind.[41]

As the facts stood in *Kiobel*, however, the Breyer opinion finds that "the parties and relevant conduct lack sufficient ties to the United States for the ATS to provide jurisdiction."[42] As such, "it would be farfetched to believe, based solely upon defendants' minimal and indirect American presence, that this legal action helps to vindicate a distinct American interest, such as in not providing a safe harbor for an 'enemy of mankind.'"[43]

Some General Observations

It is impossible to predict how the Supreme Court will interpret the ATS in the future. Justice Kennedy possesses the decisive vote, and his opinion lacks any indication of how he would resolve the significant issues that *Kiobel* leaves open. Yet, some initial observations seem appropriate.

First, the court did not overrule *Sosa*. Indeed, the court treated *Sosa* as a binding authority. The *Kiobel* opinion, therefore, should be read in a way that reconciles its holding with *Sosa*. For example, *Sosa* endorsed the majority of ATS cases that had been decided before 2004 and specifically cited the *Filártiga* and *Marcos* cases,[44] all of which involved extraterritorial conduct. *Kiobel* only rejects ATS claims in the specific fact situation of that case, a factual setting, of course, very different from the factual setting in *Sosa*.

Fundamentally, *Sosa* determined that the federal courts could recognize modern law-of-nations violations based on international human rights law.[45] International human rights law is concerned with the way states treat their own citizens and others on their own territory. Indeed, the universal application of customary international human rights norms is at the heart of post–World War II developments and the entire line of ATS cases since

---

courts exercising their power under the ATS." 133 S. Ct. at 1665 (Roberts, C.J.). The Court has treated the application of the presumption against extraterritoriality as a merits issue. *See, e.g.*, Morrison v. Nat'l Austl. Bank Ltd., 130 S. Ct. 2869, 2876–77 (2010).

41. *Kiobel*, 133 S. Ct. at 1671 (Breyer, J., concurring).

42. *Id.*

43. *Id.*

44. Sosa v. Alvarez-Machain, 542 U.S. 692, 732 (2004) (citing Filártiga v. Peña-Irala, 630 F.2d 876, 890 (2d Cir. 1980)); and *In re* Estate of Marcos Human Rights Litig., 25 F.3d 1467, 1475 (9th Cir. 1994). *See also* Brief of Amicus Curiae The Rutgers Law School Constitutional Litigation Clinic in Support of Petitioners, on Re-Argument of the Case, at 9, 24, 33; Kiobel v. Royal Dutch Petroleum Co., 133 S. Ct. 1659 (2013) (No. 10-1491), 2012 WL 2165328.

45. *Sosa*, 542 U.S. at 712.

Filártiga. At a minimum, a categorical bar on ATS cases based on human rights violations arising on foreign soil would be in tension with a core holding in *Sosa* and with the way the ATS has been interpreted since *Filártiga.*

Sosa found that Congress authorized federal courts to recognize claims based on modern violations of fundamental human rights.[46] The *Kiobel* majority ignored this aspect of *Sosa* but did not overrule it. Justice Kennedy was part of the *Sosa* majority that brought the ATS into the twenty-first century, and he rejected arguments that would have relegated the ATS to history. The Kennedy concurrence in *Kiobel* leaves room for the Kennedy of *Sosa* to reconcile with the Kennedy of *Kiobel.*

Second, the court appears unanimous in its understanding that the *Kiobel* holding is a narrow one, leaving the resolution of many significant issues about the scope of the ATS open for future decisions. Even the justices who would bar all extraterritorial claims acknowledge that this is not what the court held.[47]

Third, the Roberts opinion concedes that the usual presumption against the extraterritorial application of U.S. substantive statutes does not apply to the ATS; in fact, the presumption had never before been applied to any jurisdictional statutes.[48] Moreover, the usual presumption is overcome when Congress intends to apply its norms outside U.S. territory and even on the high seas[49]—one of the primary areas to which the law of nations applied when the ATS was enacted.[50]

Traditionally, the court attempts to ascertain whether Congress intends to apply its own substantive law outside U.S. territory. When Congress imposes substantive requirements not universally shared by other countries, the potential for conflicting substantive requirements over extraterritorial conduct exists. Because the ATS is limited to the enforcement of a modest number of universally accepted international norms, concern about the substantive conflict of laws is greatly reduced. At a minimum, these concerns arise in a

---

46. *Id.* at 724–25 ("We assume . . . that no development in the two centuries from the enactment of § 1350 to the birth of the modern line of cases beginning with Filártiga . . . has categorically precluded federal courts from recognizing a claim under the law of nations as an element of the common law. . . . We think courts should require any claim based on the present-day law of nations to rest on a norm of international character accepted by the civilized world and defined with a specificity comparable to the features of the 18th-century paradigms we have recognized.").

47. *Kiobel,* 133 S. Ct. at 1669–70 (Alito, J., concurring).

48. Morrison v. Nat'l Austl. Bank Ltd., 130 S. Ct. 2869, 2877–78 (2010) (applying the presumption to the Exchange Act, regulating securities trading); Doe v. Exxon Mobil Corp., 654 F.3d 11, 23 (D.C. Cir. 2011) ("As a jurisdictional statute, [the ATS] would apply extraterritorially only if Congress were to establish U.S. district courts in foreign countries. To say that a court is applying the ATS extraterritorially when it hears an action such as appellants have brought makes no more sense than saying that a court is applying 28 U.S.C. § 1331, the federal question statute, extraterritorially when it hears a TVPA claim brought by a U.S. citizen based on torture in a foreign country."), vacated, No. 09-7125 (D.C. Cir. July 26, 2013).

49. Indeed, the Court recognized that the fact that the ATS applies to piracy would usually overcome the presumption. *See, e.g.,* Sale v. Haitian Ctrs. Council, Inc., 509 U.S. 155, 173–74 (1993).

50. *Sosa,* 542 U.S. at 719, 724.

wholly different context than in the application of the presumption to a substantive U.S. statute, requiring a different analysis even within a *Morrison* framework.

As a jurisdictional statute, the founders assumed that the courts would recognize common law claims based on universally accepted law-of-nations norms under the ATS. As the court recognized in *Kiobel*, such claims might be extraterritorial.[51] The possibility of conflict over the substance of norms applying to extraterritorial conduct does not exist in ATS cases—at least not in the same way that it does with respect to U.S. substantive statutes. Because international norms already apply in other countries, the only potential conflict in ATS cases concerns whether damage awards in the common law method applicable at the time the ATS was enacted will enforce the shared international norms. The majority opinion suggests that the recognition of a claim for damages amounts to an extension of U.S. substantive law extraterritorially.[52] Given all the ways states enforce international norms through their legal systems, it seems likely that the court will revisit this aspect of its rationale in a case with a closer nexus to U.S. territory or U.S. citizens.[53]

In *Kiobel*, the court dealt not with ascertaining congressional intent concerning the scope of the ATS but rather with its own self-imposed limitations on its willingness to recognize federal common law causes of action under the ATS based on the law of nations.[54] Thus, the jurisprudence governing the usual application of the statutory presumption against extraterritoriality may not provide an adequate guide to the application of the principles underlying the presumption to ATS cases.

If Justice Kennedy agrees to it, the courts may morph *Kiobel*'s nuanced approach to the presumption against extraterritoriality into the more traditional application of the presumption. However, it is more likely that the courts will have to develop a matrix of factors more relevant to the international norms enforced by the ATS to govern the application of the new presumption in the myriad factual settings in which ATS cases arise.

What is less clear is how Justice Kennedy thinks the presumption or the principles underlying the presumption should be applied. Does the application of the new presumption consider principally the geography of relevant contacts? To what extent does international law matter?

---

51. *Kiobel*, 133 S. Ct. at 1666–67. For example, a U.S. citizen could have attacked a French Ambassador on foreign territory and created exactly the same diplomatic issue as was created by the Marbois incident—one of the events that led to the inclusion of the ATS in the First Judiciary Act. *Sosa*, 542 U.S. at 716–17.

52. *Kiobel*, 133 S. Ct at 1671 ("We added that the statute gives today's courts the power to apply certain 'judge-made' damages law to victims of certain foreign affairs-related misconduct.").

53. *See, e.g., In re* Chiquita Brand Int'l., Inc., Alien Tort Statute and Shareholder Derivative Litig., 792 F. Supp. 2d 1301, 1313–14 (S.D. Fla. 2011), appeal pending; Adhikari v. Daoud, 697 F. Supp. 2d 674 (S.D. Tex. 2009).

54. *Kiobel*, 133 S. Ct. at 1665–66 (Roberts, C. J.). For example, the Court indicates that the *Kiobel* plaintiffs had properly pled causes of action under the ATS. *Id.* at 1664. The issue, though, was whether the Court was prepared to recognize these causes of action given the fact that the conduct occurred on Nigerian territory and was committed by the Nigerian military, aided and abetted by foreign corporations. *Id.* at 1662.

Is the most important issue the connection with U.S. territory or is it the overall connection with the United States? Do citizenship ties or U.S. interests, policies, or obligations matter as much as connections to territory? Justice Kennedy joins the majority in rejecting "mere corporate presence" as an adequate basis for the recognition of ATS claims. His failure to join the Breyer opinion suggests that Justice Kennedy is not prepared to agree to every aspect of Justice Breyer's comprehensive framework, or perhaps to any such framework at this point. However, this does not mean that Justice Kennedy has rejected all of the analysis in the Breyer concurrence or accepted the more categorical language in the first three sections of the majority opinion. A case with a different factual context may well lead to a new alignment.

Fourth, whether the presumption is nearly insurmountable or limited, *Kiobel* has introduced a new screening mechanism for ATS cases. The courts will have to find a methodology to interpret the new presumption in pending cases across the country. Had this presumption been in effect from the beginning, at least some claims in ATS corporate complicity cases would have been dismissed.[55] It is not clear how the *Kiobel* majority views the relationship between the new presumption and existing limiting doctrines (for example, *forum non conveniens*, political question, international comity) that have been the usual issues litigated in ATS cases. Will the new *Kiobel* presumption become the last line of defense against ATS claims, raised whenever the courts are dissatisfied with the results of the more traditional screening doctrines?

Despite the fact that *Kiobel* restricts the scope of the ATS in as yet undefined ways, the most important observation may be that predicting the future application of the new presumption is impossible.

The Issue of Corporate Liability

The *Kiobel* court did not decide or discuss the issue upon which it initially granted *certiorari*. Between the grant of *certiorari* in October 2011 and the time of the first *Kiobel* argument in February 2012, three additional circuits had rejected the Second Circuit's position on corporate liability.[56] Even in the Second Circuit in early 2011, the active

---

55. The most obvious of these is Wiwa v. Royal Dutch Petroleum, a case settled in June 2009 for $15.5 million. Jad Mouawad, *Shell to Pay $15.5 Million to Settle Nigerian Case*, N.Y. TIMES June 8, 2009) at B1. The ATS claims in *Wiwa* would have been barred by *Kiobel*. In the immediate aftermath of *Kiobel*, the plaintiffs in Sarei v. Rio Tinto, PLC, a case pending for nearly fifteen years, conceded that they could not meet the *Kiobel* standard. Plaintiffs-Appellants/Cross-Appellees' Supplemental Brief, at 1, Sarei v. Rio Tinto, PLC, 722 F. 3d 1109 (9th Cir. 2013) (Nos. 02-52666, 02-56390, 09-56381), 2013 WL 3357740 (9th Cir. June 28, 2013). Without explanation, an en banc panel of the Ninth Circuit dismissed the case with prejudice. Sarei v. Rio Tinto PLC, Nos. 02-56256, 02-56390, 09-56381, 2013 WL 3357740 (9th Cir. June 28, 2013).

56. Doe v. Exxon Mobil Corp., 654 F.3d 11, 57 (D.C. Cir. 2011), vacated, No. 09-7125 (D.C. Cir. July 26, 2013); Flomo v. Firestone Nat'l Rubber Co., 643 F.3d 1013, 1019 (7th Cir. 2011); Sarei v. Rio Tinto, PLC., 671 F. 3d 736, 765 (9th Cir. 2011) (en banc), vacated, 133 S. Ct. 1995 (2013) (mem.). These circuits joined the Eleventh Circuit in explicitly holding that corporations could be sued under the ATS. Romero v. Drummond Co., 552 F.3d. 1303, 1315 (11th Cir. 2008).

judges were evenly divided over the panel's decision to exclude corporations from the scope of the ATS.[57] The United States supported corporate liability under the ATS in the first round of *Kiobel* briefing.[58]

There is no way to know why the court decided not to address this issue in its *Kiobel* decision, but there is little basis for a categorical exclusion of corporations from the scope of the ATS. The only hint of the court's thinking on corporate liability under the ATS is indirect and does not appear to question it. If corporations were not covered by the ATS, there would be no reason to consider whether *mere corporate presence* was sufficient to overcome the *Kiobel* presumption.[59] Indeed, all of the *Kiobel* opinions assume that, in principle, corporations are proper ATS defendants.

The Second Circuit's exclusion of corporations seems unlikely to stand in that circuit or in any other circuit for the reasons set forth in the decisions affirming corporate liability since the circuit's decision.[60] Of course, the defense bar will no doubt continue to press this argument in the post-*Kiobel* era.

The Application of the *Kiobel* Presumption

Categorical or Case-by-Case Analysis

The most crucial threshold issue in the post-*Kiobel* world is whether the court's opinion will be interpreted to require a case-by-case application of the principles underlying the presumption to ATS claims or whether it will be interpreted as a categorical ban on extraterritorial ATS cases.

The language of section IV of the majority opinion, stating that there could be extraterritorial cases that "touch and concern" U.S. territory with "sufficient force" to displace the presumption, can only mean that courts must examine whether the facts of particular cases "touch and concern" U.S. territory sufficiently to displace the presumption. This language defies a categorical ban, instead calling for the examination of the facts and circumstances of each case to see if the connection with the United States is sufficient.

Defendants will argue that the *Kiobel* majority decided that the presumption applies categorically, banning all extraterritorial ATS cases, using the analysis set forth in

---

57. A petition for rehearing en banc failed by a five-to-five vote. Kiobel v. Royal Dutch Petroleum Co., 642 F.3d 268 (2d Cir. 2011). Three new judges have joined the Second Circuit since that decision, making it likely that a future case will be taken en banc.

58. Brief for the United States as Amicus Curiae Supporting Petitioners at 12–13, Kiobel v. Royal Dutch Petroleum Co., 133 S. Ct. 1659 (2013) (No. 10-1491), 2011 WL 6425363.

59. *Kiobel*, 133 S. Ct. at 1669 (2013).

60. The Second Circuit may address this issue in several pending cases, including the Apartheid cases. *See, e.g.*, Balintulo v. Daimler A.G., No 09-2778-cv (2d Cir. 2009). *See also* Judge Leval's scathing opinion in Kiobel v. Royal Dutch Petroleum Co., 621 F.3d 111, 149 (2d Cir. 2010) (Leval, J., concurring).

Morrison.[61] Though this is one possible reading of the majority opinion, it is not the most plausible reading. At a minimum, it begs the question of how the court will define *extraterritorial* in the context of causes of action based on international-law norms, as opposed to U.S. securities law.

During the completion of this chapter, a district judge in *Al Shimari v. CACI International, Inc.*[62] dismissed ATS claims arising in Iraq based on a categorical view of the *Kiobel* presumption, without a deep analysis of the differences between the ATS and a substantive U.S. statute. It is useful to examine this initial foray into the meaning of the new presumption, although the *Al Shimari* decision will not be the last word on the meaning of *Kiobel.* A split in the circuits is likely to arise quickly.[63]

The judge in *Al Shimari* focused on the need for legislative action to overcome the presumption, found in the first three sections of the Roberts opinion, and on the court's many references to the *Morrison* case. *Morrison* employed a categorical approach typical of statutory presumption analyses to determine whether Congress intended its substantive laws to reach extraterritorial conduct. As a result, the *Al Shimari* judge apparently concluded that *Kiobel* also calls for a typical, ordinarily categorical statutory presumption analysis.[64]

Unsurprisingly, the *Al Shimari* judge had difficulty reconciling this categorical view—that the statute either reaches or does not reach extraterritorial claims—with the *touch and concern* language contained in section IV of the majority opinion. The district court conveniently describes that language as "textually curious" and treats it as irrelevant to the application of the *Kiobel* presumption.[65]

The *Al Shimari* court's analysis cannot be reconciled with the opinions in *Kiobel*. *Al Shimari* essentially ignores, or treats as surplusage, section IV of the majority opinion, which contains the majority's holding in *Kiobel*. *Al Shimari* ignores the recognition in the

61.   *Kiobel*, 133 S. Ct. at 1664–67, 1669 (citing Morrison v. Nat'l Austrl. Bank Ltd., 130 S. Ct. 2869, 2878 (2010)).

62.   2013 WL 3229720, at *7 (E.D. Va. June 25, 2013) ("[The *Kiobel* Court] held that the text of the ATS failed to rebut the presumption that the statute would not be extraterritorially applied."). Recently, some courts have dismissed pro se complaints based on *Kiobel* without much reasoning, sometimes taking a categorical approach to the extraterritoriality presumption. *See, e.g.*, Ahmed-Al-Khalifa v. Trayers, No. 3:13-CV-00869, 2013 WL 3326212, at *2 (D. Conn. July 1, 2013).

63.   In *Al Shimari*, the judge recognized this possibility, noting that the "touch and concern" language "may be interpreted by some as leaving the proverbial door ajar for courts to eventually measure its width." 2013 WL 3229720, at *9. The U.S. magistrate judge in Mwani v. Bin Laden also recognized the impending split, immediately certifying to the Court of Appeals his decision on subject matter jurisdiction. No. 99-125, 2013 WL 2325166, at *4 (D.C. Cir. May 29, 2013). The judge found the presumption against extraterritoriality sufficiently rebutted in an ATS case where the claims arose from the bombing of a U.S. embassy in Kenya. *Id.*

64.   *Al Shimari*, 2013 WL 3229729, at *9 ("[T]he presumption's best practice . . . is the universal application of the presumption, providing the stable backdrop against which Congress is free to indicate otherwise.").

65.   *Id.*

Kennedy and Alito concurrences that the majority opinion was a narrow one, leaving the scope of the presumption open for future decisions.

The *Al Shimari* decision will not withstand careful analysis on appeal for the reasons set forth in pages 202–212. Specifically, only two members of the court share the view of the presumption advanced in *Al Shimari* and apply the presumption to exclude all extraterritorial ATS cases. Although Justice Kennedy's position is ambiguous, no reading of his concurrence can be squared with the categorical exclusion of all extraterritorial ATS cases. Justice Kennedy explicitly conditions his vote on the idea that some extraterritorial ATS cases will fall outside *Kiobel*'s reasoning and narrow holding, potentially requiring further elaboration of the presumption. There would be no need for future elaboration if *Kiobel* had, in fact, eliminated all such cases.

Unlike a substantive statute, the ATS allows for the enforcement of treaties and customary norms. It is open ended in the sense that it applies to future treaty and customary norms that may arise.[66] There is no mechanism for Congress to specify which international norms should or should not have extraterritorial effect under the ATS. Unless the majority has overruled *Sosa sub silentio*,[67] it cannot be the case that Congress must pass implementing legislation before a particular international norm can be enforced with respect to extraterritorial conduct under the ATS. As such, the post-*Kiobel* analysis somehow must take into account the nature of the norm being enforced.

However, to do so, courts cannot rely slavishly on the usual application of the presumption, which *Kiobel* does not require, or on the analysis in *Morrison* concerning the application of the presumption to a securities regulation, which is inapposite to jurisdictional statutes. Rather, the majority finds that the *principles* underlying the presumption apply to the federal common law process of recognizing an ATS cause of action.[68] Thus, jurisprudence developed in the context of the ordinary statutory presumption does not

---

66. *Sosa*, 542 U.S. 692, 730 ("The First Congress, which reflected the understanding of the framing generation and included some of the Framers, assumed that federal courts could properly identify some international norms as enforceable in the exercise of §1350 jurisdiction.").

67. *Id.* at 724 ("[A]lthough the ATS is a jurisdictional statute creating no new causes of action, the reasonable inference from the historical materials is that the statute was intended to have practical effect the moment it became law.").

68. The *Al Shimari* court found that the presumption was a matter of subject matter jurisdiction under the ATS. *Al Shimari*, 2013 WL 3229720, at *1 ("As the Court held in *Kiobel*, the presumption against extraterritorial application applies to the ATS. . . . Therefore, Plaintiffs' claims under the ATS [arising from acts occurring exclusively in Iraq] are dismissed for want of jurisdiction."). However, the *Kiobel* majority opinion seems clearly to find that the allegations in plaintiffs' complaint in *Kiobel* were adequate to establish subject matter jurisdiction under the statute. *Kiobel*, 133 S. Ct. at 1664 ("The question here is not whether petitioners have stated a proper claim under the ATS, but whether a claim may reach conduct occurring in the territory of a foreign sovereign."). The merits question the Court considered was whether the courts should recognize the cause of action under the ATS because of the principles underlying the presumption. The majority found that those principles prevented the courts from recognizing these causes of action where the only U.S. connection was the "mere corporate presence" of two foreign corporate defendants. *Id.* at 1669.

easily translate to the issue of whether the principles underlying the presumption should lead a court to limit the territorial scope of an ATS cause of action.

Finally, if the *Kiobel* presumption were categorical, one would expect that the court would have noted that its new rule was inconsistent with virtually every judicial ATS decision since *Filartiga*, including *Sosa* and the cases endorsed by the *Sosa* court. Admittedly, there is no requirement that a majority of the court provide a decent burial to more than three decades of jurisprudence, including its own cases. Regardless, courts are more likely to adopt the noncategorical understanding of *Kiobel* given that a contrary view would require concluding that *Kiobel* overturned an entire body of law *sub silentio*.

Cases against U.S. Defendants

One of the most important issues left open by *Kiobel* is whether or to what extent the new presumption immunizes the extraterritorial actions of U.S. corporations.[69] In many ways this goes to the heart of the court's rationale. Is *Kiobel* about geography, thus potentially barring cases where a court has personal jurisdiction over a corporation but where the corporation's relevant acts occurred abroad, or is *Kiobel* about a broader concept of connection to the United States and its interests, potentially allowing corporations present in the United States to be sued for their actions elsewhere?

The majority opinion does not discuss the significance of U.S. citizenship to its presumption analysis because it was confronted with a *foreign-cubed* case. However, the majority's discussion of the Bradford opinion indicates a potential distinction between U.S. and foreign defendants.[70] Historical research presented by *amici* in *Kiobel* makes it clear that the Bradford opinion found that the ATS is available not only for violations on the high seas but also for violations committed on foreign soil.[71] The majority deflected the

---

69. As this chapter was being completed, a district court found that the U.S. citizenship of a corporate defendant did not overcome the *Kiobel* presumption. Giraldo v. Drummond Co., No.2:09-cv-01041-RDP (N.D. Ala. filed July 25, 2013) (mem.). This decision is unlikely to be the last word on this issue. As the district court acknowledged, "Kiobel has not given courts a road map for answering [the] question of what, more than corporate presence, is *enough* for foreign conduct to displace the presumption, *id*. at 8.

70.   *Id*. at 1667–68.

71.   Supp. U.S. Br. *supra* note 10, at 6-8 (recognizing that the Bradford opinion is one of the few historical records addressing what causes of action are cognizable under the ATS and that the opinion concerns a historical incident that "occurred in part on land" and "within the territory of a foreign sovereign"; and recognizing that Bradford himself "plainly knew that some of the conduct at issue occurred within the territory of Sierra Leone, and his reference to 'acts of hostility' for which the ATS afforded a remedy could have been meant to encompass that conduct"). *See also* Supplemental Brief of Amici Curiae Professors of Legal History William R. Casto et al. in Support of Petitioners, at 18–22; Kiobel v. Royal Dutch Petroleum Co., 133 S. Ct. 1649 (2013) (No. 10-1491), 2012 WL 2165337 ("Bradford then opined that the ATS offered a civil remedy for acts that had been committed in British sovereign territory. . . . The Bradford Opinion unequivocally demonstrates that he understood the ATS to provide civil jurisdiction over the tortious acts that were transitory and had occurred in British Sierra Leone."). *See also* Curtis A. Bradley, *Attorney General Bradford's Opinion and the Alien Tort Statute*, 106 Am. J. Int'l L. 509, 520–21 (2012) ("Some judges have suggested that in referring to the ATS, Bradford had in mind only conduct that occurred either in the United States or on the high seas. That seems unlikely,

significance of the Bradford opinion by noting that the Sierra Leone incident involved U.S. citizens and a possible treaty violation. Attorney General Bradford's conclusion, only six years after the ATS was enacted, that the statute applied to international law violations committed by U.S. citizens on foreign soil will be more difficult to ignore or distinguish.

It is one thing to exclude foreign-cubed cases from the reach of the ATS but another to find that the ATS was not meant to apply to extraterritorial international-law violations committed by U.S. citizens, including U.S. corporations.

First, less controversy arises when a U.S. court applies international law to U.S. citizens, including corporations, when they act abroad than when U.S. courts attempt to hold foreign citizens accountable for conduct on foreign territory.

Second, the United States has an indisputable right to police the conduct of its own citizens. In *Kiobel*, the Netherlands and United Kingdom,[72] supported by several prominent *amici*,[73] claimed that it was a violation of international law for the United States to apply the ATS to the actions of foreign corporations on foreign territory. Respondents in *Kiobel* suggested that the ATS ought to be interpreted as not reaching this foreign-cubed situation, based on the canon of statutory interpretation that directs courts to interpret federal statutes to avoid conflict with international law unless no other interpretation is possible.[74]

Though that argument might have some plausibility in the context of a foreign-cubed case, it has no force if the defendant is a U.S. citizen.[75] Such a case, with a U.S. citizen defendant, may well be one of the cases that Justice Kennedy had in mind when he anticipated that some ATS cases would fall outside the reasoning of the *Kiobel* decision.

---

however, given the nature of the complaints that he was addressing. Many of the allegations specifically concerned pillaging and destruction of property in Freetown. . . . Moreover, the letter from Hammond and the Macaulay/Tilley memorial were focused on breaches of neutrality by the U.S. citizens, offenses that can occur just as easily on land as at sea."); William R. Casto, *The Federal Courts' Protective Jurisdiction over Torts Committed in Violation of the Law of Nations*, 18 Conn. L. Rev. 467, 503 (1986) ("The plunder of Sierra Leone is of particular importance because the Attorney General's opinion—like much of the modern litigation under [the ATS]—dealt with a transitory tort action arising out of events in a foreign country."). These materials convinced the United States to reverse its past views on the Bradford opinion and extraterritoriality. Supp. U.S. Br. *supra* note 10, at 8 n.1 ("The United States advanced a different reading of the 1795 opinion in a previous submission to this Court. . . . On further reflection, and after examining the primary documents, the United States acknowledges that the opinion is amenable to different interpretations.").

72.   Dutch/UK Br., *supra* note 15, at 17–18.

73.   *See, e.g.*, Chevron Supp. Br., *supra* note 15, at 13–24; Brief of *Amici Curiae* BP America et al. in Support of Respondents, at 26–27, Kiobel v. Royal Dutch Petroleum Co., 133 S. Ct. 1659 (2013) (No. 10-1491), 2012 WL 392536.

74.   Supplemental Brief for Respondents, at 37, Kiobel v. Royal Dutch Petroleum Co., 133 S. Ct. 1659 (2013) (No. 10-1491), 2012 WL 3127285 ("[A]n act of Congress ought never to be construed to violate the law of nations if any other possible construction remains." (quoting Murray v. Schooner Charming Betsy, 2 Cranch 64, 118 (1804))).

75.   One issue that will arise in this context is whether the acts of non-citizen individuals or corporations who are agents of U.S. corporations acting abroad would be treated the same way.

The Netherlands and United Kingdom conceded that the United States had authority under international law to apply its laws to the extraterritorial actions of its own citizens abroad.[76] After all, this is an established principle of international law,[77] long recognized by the Supreme Court.[78] Moreover, eliminating claims against U.S. citizens for international law violations conflicts more clearly with the history and purpose of the ATS in ways the exclusion of foreign-cubed cases does not.

Cases Involving Both Domestic and Extraterritorial Conduct

If the primary focus of the *Kiobel* presumption is the relationship between the conduct at issue and U.S. territory, then the courts will be faced with a wide array of factual circumstances when applying the presumption. In the *Sosa* case, for example, all of the acts Dr. Alvarez complained of took place on Mexican territory, not within the territory of the United States. However, U.S. officials within U.S. territory directed all these acts.[79] The *Kiobel* Court did not give any indication that it overruled or limited *Sosa* in any respect.

It seems likely that extraterritorial human rights violations committed at the direction of actors, natural or corporate, acting within U.S. territory would overcome the *Kiobel* presumption. For example, if ATS defendants acting within U.S. territory conspire to assassinate an Israeli ambassador in Canada, it would be absurd to exclude such actions from the scope of the ATS, given the statute's historical origins and purpose.

In many cases, though, the U.S.-based acts will amount to less than specific directions to engage in human rights violations abroad. In such cases the courts will have to develop principles to govern the significance of the domestic acts, given the purposes of the presumption.

The Lessons of *Morrison*

Chief Justice Roberts's majority opinion cites *Morrison* several times. Even if the new *Kiobel* presumption operates in a similar manner as the statutory presumption cases do, the courts will be confronted with many cases where it is not self-evident whether the

---

76. *See* Dutch/UK Br., *supra* note 15, at 12–13.
77. RESTATEMENT (THIRD) OF THE FOREIGN RELATIONS LAW OF THE UNITED STATES § 402 (1987) (explaining that, subject to § 403, the links of territoriality and nationality are "universally recognized" to be sufficient to support jurisdiction, where the links of nationality are described as "the activities, interests, status, or relations of its nationals outside as well as within its territory").
78. *See, e.g.*, Blackmer v. United States, 284 U.S. 421, 436 (1932) ("By virtue of the obligations of citizenship, the United States retained its authority over [the defendant], and he was bound by its laws made applicable to him in a foreign country.").
79. The United States argued that the ATS did not reach extraterritorial acts in *Sosa*; however, no Justice commented on this argument in any of the opinions. Reply Brief for the United States as Respondent Supporting Petitioner, at 19, Sosa v. Alvarez-Machain, 542 U.S. 692 (2004) (No. 03-339), 2004 WL 577654.

presumption applies. The difficulties that the lower courts have had in implementing the *Morrison* decision are instructive.

Since *Morrison*, lower courts have faced uncertainty about what constitutes domestic transactions. The *Morrison* court rejected the Second Circuit's "conduct and effects" test and found that the Securities Exchange Act applied only to "transactions in securities listed on domestic exchanges" and "domestic transactions in other securities."[80] However, *Morrison* did not define what constitutes a "domestic transaction," just as the court in *Kiobel* did not explain what it means to "touch and concern" the territory of the United States.

In *Absolute Activist Value Master Fund Ltd. v. Ficeto*, the Second Circuit found that a transaction was "domestic" if "irrevocable liability was incurred or title was transferred within the United States."[81] This test has led to case-by-case evaluations to determine whether the transaction is "domestic" or "extraterritorial" and the presumption applies.[82]

The courts have faced similar challenges in the context of other substantive statutes, including the Racketeering Influenced and Corrupt Organizations Act (RICO). Courts have adopted two approaches in RICO cases: the *enterprise* approach, focusing on where the enterprise is located geographically,[83] or an alternate approach focusing on where the racketeering activity has taken place.[84]

The point is that the lower courts have had significant difficulty applying *Morrison*, even in the context of considering its application to particular substantive statutes. This task will be far more difficult in the ATS context because the ATS is a congressional directive to enforce international law arising in widely varying contexts.

Cases Advancing U.S. Foreign Policy Interests

What about ATS cases that advance U.S. foreign policy positions or clear legislative policy?[85] For example, what if the United States embargos certain goods, preventing them from being exported to a given country,[86] and U.S. corporations violate the embargo, aid-

---

80.   Morrison v. Nat'l Austrl. Bank Ltd., 130 S. Ct. 2869, 2884 (2010).

81.   677 F.3d 60, 67–68 (2d Cir. 2012).

82.   *Cf.* Elliott Associates v. Porsche Automobil Holding SE, 759 F. Supp. 2d 469, 476 (S.D.N.Y. 2010) (interpreting *Morrison* to turn on whether "purchases and sales of securities [were] explicitly solicited by the issuer in the U.S."), *with* Wu v. Stomber, 883 F. Supp. 2d 233, 253 (D.C. Cir. 2012) (interpreting *Morrison* to turn on "where the plaintiff's purchase occurred"). This approach has been criticized. *See* recent case, Absolute Activist Value Master Fund Ltd. v. Ficeto, 677 F.3d 60 (2d Cir. 2012), 126 HARV. L. REV. 1430, 1436 (2013).

83.   *See, e.g.,* Mitsui O.S.K. Lines, Ltd. v. Seamaster Logistics, Inc., 871 F. Supp. 2d 933, 941 (N.D. Cal. 2012).

84.   *See, e.g.,* United States v. Chan Fan Xu, 706 F.3d 965, 977–79 (9th Cir. 2013).

85.   In Mwani v. Bin Laden, 2013 WL 2325166, at *4 (D.D.C. May 29, 2013), a district court allowed ATS claims arising out of the attack on the U.S. Embassy in Nairobi, Kenya, involving foreign plaintiffs and defendants, to proceed notwithstanding *Kiobel*. As the Court stated, "[i]t is obvious that a case involving an attack on the United States Embassy in Nairobi is tied much more closely to our national interests than a case whose only tie to our country is a corporate presence here." *Id.*

86.   A variation of this argument is being advanced by the plaintiffs in Balintulo v. Daimler A.G., No

ing and abetting serious international human rights violations as a result? Would *Kiobel* bar ATS cases based on such extraterritorial conduct in violation of official U.S. policy? There is no reason to apply the new presumption if the underlying conduct also violates other substantive U.S. laws.

What if an alleged perpetrator of serious human rights violations is found within the United States, and neither the U.S. nor the foreign government raises any concerns about litigation of a civil lawsuit against him or her? What if both governments actively support such a lawsuit?

The *Kiobel* case did not present a situation in which the United States had acted with respect to the underlying violations.[87] The Roberts opinion suggests that one of the primary principles underlying the presumption against extraterritoriality is to avoid conflicts with other countries and unanticipated conflicts between U.S. foreign policy and the litigation. Where the political branches have condemned the violations, the potential for these sorts of conflicts is reduced.

Some ATS cases involving extraterritorial conduct will arise to which neither foreign governments nor the U.S. government will object. Some ATS cases will plainly advance U.S. foreign policy and interests. Indeed, given the limitation in *Sosa* to very serious human rights violations, such situations seem likely. Where the concerns reflected in the presumption against extraterritoriality do not exist, there would be no reason to bar ATS claims on the sole ground that the challenged conduct took place on foreign soil.

No Safe Haven

In *Kiobel* the plaintiffs had other fora in which they could have pursued their claims. It was conceded that the courts in the United Kingdom and the Netherlands were open to the plaintiffs.[88] The initial questions by Justices Kennedy and Alito at the February 2012

09-2778-cv (2d Cir. 2009), based on U.S. adherence to embargos on Apartheid South Africa.

87.   One example of a case where the United States did act with respect to the underlying violations in a subsequent ATS suit is *In re* Chiquita Brand Int'l., Inc., Alien Tort Statute and S'holder Derivative Litig., 792 F. Supp. 2d 1301 (S.D. Fla. 2011), appeal pending. The U.S. government had filed criminal charges against Chiquita for its payments to a right-wing terrorist group in Colombia whose acts were at the heart of plaintiffs' allegations. *Id.* at 1310. These charges resulted in a guilty plea. *Id.*

88.   Transcript of Oral Argument, at 6:4-13, Kiobel v. Royal Dutch Petroleum Co., 133 S. Ct. 1659 (2013) (No. 10-1491). In fact, during the pendency of *Kiobel*, the Dutch courts were becoming more open to asserting jurisdiction over extraterritorial torts including so-called foreign-cubed cases. For example, in a March 2012 foreign-cubed case, a Dutch District Court awarded a Palestinian-Bulgarian physician, Dr. Ashraf El-Hojouj, one million Euros in damages in a civil suit against Libyan officials who tortured him. Ashraf Ahmed El-Hojouj v. Harb Amer Derbal, Rechtbank's-Gravenhage 21 maart 2012, No. 400882 (Neth.), http://jure.nl/bv9748 (in Dutch). *See also* Mike Corder, *Dutch Court Compensates Palestinian for Libya Jail*, Associated Press (Mar. 27, 2012) 3/27/12 AP Worldstream 14:45:36. Dutch and UK courts also asserted jurisdiction over Shell's Nigerian subsidiary for environmental degradation in the Niger Delta. *See* Oguru v. Royal Dutch Shell, Rechtbank's-Gravenhage 30 December 2009, No. 330891 (Neth.) http://jure.nl/bk8616; Bodo Community v. Shell Petroleum Co. of Nigeria, Claim No. HQ 11X01280, High Court (QB) (Eng.) (filed Apr. 6, 2011). *See also* Joeie A. Kirshner, *Why Is the U.S.*

Kiobel argument suggested that they did not think it was appropriate for U.S. courts to sit in judgment over foreign corporations when their home fora were available to the plaintiffs.[89]

Justice Kennedy expressed a view in the first *Kiobel* argument that his discomfort did not extend to cases against individuals where there was no other available forum.[90] This is certainly the view expressed in the Breyer concurrence, which stresses the need not to allow the United States to become a safe haven for human rights violators.[91] Thus, the *Filartiga* line of cases against individual defendants found in the United States should survive the new *Kiobel* presumption. In many of these cases, foreign governments have not objected to ATS suits.[92]

Whether this rationale can be applied to foreign corporate defendants is less clear. What if ATS plaintiffs cannot pursue their claims against a corporate defendant because it is not possible for them to bring a case in the defendant's home forum? What if American Jewish plaintiffs seek to pursue their claims against an Iranian corporation doing substantial business in the United States? Would the presumption apply to foreign corporations with more extensive operations in the United States than the defendants in *Kiobel*? *Kiobel* does not answer these questions.

The *Kiobel* majority did not accept the argument that existing doctrines such as *forum non conveniens* were sufficient to screen ATS cases with insufficient links to the United States. The new *Kiobel* presumption can be seen as a broader, more discretionary tool to screen out additional ATS cases—beyond those that the existing screening mechanisms catch—that the court believes lack an adequate connection to the United States or threaten U.S. foreign policy.[93]

Abdicating the Policing of Multinational Corporations to Europe?: Extraterritoriality, Sovereignty, and the Alien Tort Statute, 30 BERKELEY J. INT'L L. 259, 285 (2012) (highlighting the trend in Europe to apply domestic law to the extraterritorial conduct of European corporations and of their foreign subsidiaries).

89. One oddity in *Kiobel* was that the defendants never made a motion to dismiss for lack of personal jurisdiction or based on *forum non conveniens*. This was probably because the Second Circuit had rejected both defenses in Wiwa v. Royal Dutch Petroleum, 226 F. 3d 88 (2d Cir. 2000). After *Kiobel*, the Court granted certiorari to determine the standards for personal jurisdiction over corporate subsidiaries in the context of another ATS case arising out of the Dirty War in Argentina. Bauman v. DaimlerChrysler Corp., 644 F.3d 909 (2011), cert. granted, 133 S. Ct. 1995 (2013).

90. *See supra* note 12.

91. *Kiobel*, 133 S. Ct. at 1671 (Breyer, J., concurring).

92. *See, e.g.*, Trajano v. Marcos, 878 F.2d 1439, *2 (1989) ("Neither the present government of the Republic of the Philippines nor the United States government objects to judicial resolution of these claims, or sees any resulting potential embarrassment to any government.").

93. In *Sosa*, the Court discussed a number of limiting principles that apply to ATS cases, including a sufficiently definite international norm, exhaustion of remedies outside the United States, and the "policy of case-specific deference to the political branches." 542 U.S. 692, 733 n.21. It is possible that the new *Kiobel* presumption will operate in a similar, case-specific manner, although the *Kiobel* Court did not explicitly tie its new presumption to this doctrine.

The Transitory Tort Doctrine

The ATS, after *Sosa*, enforces certain widely accepted universal, international norms accepted by all states. One of the questions that *Kiobel* raised without resolving explicitly is whether the ATS was an exercise in adjudicative jurisdiction—that is, U.S. courts adjudicating transitory tort claims between parties over which the courts had personal jurisdiction[94]—or in prescriptive jurisdiction—that is, applying U.S. substantive law to the parties before the court.[95]

The Roberts opinion sides with Royal Dutch Petroleum's view that the decision to recognize a cause of action seeking damages for violations of the law of nations is not a traditional application of the transitory tort doctrine.[96]

Now that other states are exercising jurisdiction over extraterritorial torts,[97] will the court again address the transitory tort doctrine and its relevance to the ATS? The assumption in 1789 was that the law of nations was part of the common law; therefore, the drafters of the ATS would not have considered the cause-of-action question discussed by Chief Justice Roberts. The distinction Chief Justice Roberts made was that in transitory tort cases, courts apply foreign law in the ATS context; courts have to decide whether to recognize a cause of action based on international law as a matter of federal common law.[98]

If more states were to accept tort claims based on the law of nations, would the ATS be available to provide relief in U.S. federal courts for human rights victims who find perpetrators, natural or corporate, in the United States if the other relevant states provide for the same or similar relief? Given the history of the ATS, it would make no sense to relegate such claims to U.S. state courts, because it was a primary purpose of the ATS to ensure that law-of-nations claims be heard in a federal forum.[99] Indeed, one of the

---

94. *See* William S. Dodge, *Alien Tort Litigation and the Prescriptive Jurisdiction Fallacy*, 51 HARV. INT'L L. ONLINE 35, 42 (2010), http://www.harvardilj.org/2010/05/online_51_dodge/ ("In sum, there is no evidence that the ATS was originally understood as an exercise of prescriptive jurisdiction, and plenty of evidence that torts in violation of the law of nation[s] were considered a subset of transitory torts.").

95. Respondents argued that the decision to apply a cause of action for damages based on international law was an application of U.S. substantive law. Supplemental Brief for Respondents, at 14–15; Kiobel v. Royal Dutch Petroleum Co., 133 S. Ct. 1659 (2013) (No. 10-1491), 2012 WL 3127285.

96. *Kiobel*, 133 S. Ct. at 1665–66 (Roberts, C.J.) (relying on the perspective advanced in Cuba R. Co. v. Crosby, 222 U.S. 473, 479 (1912), that the transitory tort doctrine only "allow[s] a party to recover when the cause of action arose in another civilized jurisdiction" if there is a "well founded belief that it was a cause of action in that place").

97. *See* El-Hojouj v. Harb Amer Derbal et al., Oguru v. Royal Dutch Shell, and Bodo Cmty. v. Shell Petroleum Co. of Nigeria, *supra* note 88. In recent years, plaintiffs have brought claims in the United Kingdom concerning indefinite detention and mistreatment in Iraq under the UK Human Rights Act of 1998, which provides for claims arising from breaches of international human rights norms as well. *See, e.g.*, R. (Ali Zaki Mousa) v. Sec'y of State for Defence, [2011] EWCA (Civ) 1334 (Eng.); R. (Al-Sweady and Others) v. Sec'y of State for Defence, [2009] EWHC (Admin) 1687 (Eng.).

98. *Kiobel*, 133 S. Ct. at 1660.

99. *See, e.g.*, William R. Casto, *The Federal Courts' Protective Jurisdiction on Torts Committed in Violation of the Law of Nations*, 18 CONN. L. REV. 467, 480–81 (1985–86).

historical purposes of the transitory tort doctrine was to ensure that there was a forum in which the wrongdoer could be brought to civil justice.[100]

The majority opinion's treatment of the transitory tort doctrine is cursory. As such, it is impossible to know whether the court will recognize future ATS cases based on recognition of tort claims that foreign countries recognize as valid claims rooted in international law. The recognition of such claims is the mechanism for the enforcement of the law of nations adopted by the founders in the ATS. The court in *Sosa* found that this mechanism was still viable.[101] It would be ironic if *Kiobel* prevented a human rights victim from asserting an international law claim recognized in foreign law despite the transitory tort doctrine and the conflict this situation would present with the basic design of the ATS.

The Future Direction of Corporate Complicity Litigation

Though it is too early to determine the impact of *Kiobel* on corporate complicity litigation under the ATS, two effects are likely: (1) ATS litigation will move into state courts,[102] and (2) plaintiffs will name individual corporate executives and managers as defendants under the Torture Victim Protection Act (TVPA).[103]

In many ATS cases, plaintiffs have asserted state-law tort claims along with ATS and other federal claims. In *Doe v. Unocal Corp.*,[104] for example, after the district court granted Unocal's motion for summary judgment on the plaintiffs' ATS claims,[105] the plaintiffs filed a complaint

---

100. *See* Mostyn v. Fabrigas (1774) 98 Eng. Rep. 1021, 1024–26 (K.B.) (Lord Mansfield) (holding that "an action of trespass can be brought in England for an injury done abroad" because "[i]t is a transitory action, and may be brought any where"; noting that "[t]he true distinction . . . between transitory and location actions [is] the former . . . may be tried any where"; and concluding that "the action which is a transitory one is clearly maintainable in this country, though the cause of action arose abroad"). One of the rationales of the transitory tort doctrine is to ensure that tortfeasors do not escape justice. *Id.* at 1025–26 (noting that in the case of 1 Salk. 404, the court rejected defendants' argument that the court lacked jurisdiction where the claims arose in another government's territory because "otherwise there might be a failure of justice if the Chancery could not hold plea in such case, the party being here" and concluding that if Mr. Fabrigas "should be deprived of that satisfaction in damages which the jury gave him" then Governor Mostyn is merely "*hic est damnatus inani judicio*" [condemned by an empty judgment] and the "*at tu victrix provincia ploras*" [you, whining Province, win]).

101. Sosa v. Alvarez-Machain, 542 U.S. 692, 724 (2004) ("The jurisdictional grant is best read as having been enacted on the understanding that the common law would provide a cause of action for the modest number of international law violations with a potential for personal liability at the time.").

102. As more foreign courts assume jurisdiction over extraterritorial torts, some cases may be brought in foreign courts. *See supra* notes 88, 97.

103. Torture Victim Protection Act of 1991, Pub. L. No. 102-256, 106 Stat. 73 (1992), codified at 28 U.S.C. § 1350 (1994).

104. Doe v. Unocal, 963 F. Supp. 880, 897–98 (C.D. Cal. 1997) (denying in part a motion to dismiss plaintiffs' ATS claims arising in Burma against a U.S. corporation, finding that "[s]ubject-matter jurisdiction over plaintiffs' claims against the remaining defendants is available under the Alien Tort Claims Act").

105. Subsequently, the summary judgment was reversed in part. Doe v. Unocal Corp., 395 F.3d 932,

asserting state-law tort claims in Los Angeles Superior Court.[106] These claims had been scheduled for trial in April 2005, but the parties reached a settlement in the fall of 2004.[107]

Corporate complicity cases filed in state courts will raise a host of new issues. State tort law, rather than international law, will define the human rights violations at issue. In many cases, the elements of state-law tort claims may be easier to satisfy than the elements of international human rights violations. Indeed, common law complicity theories are broader than international theories largely derived from international criminal law.[108]

State courts will have to wrestle with threshold issues potentially involving both state and federal dimensions such as personal jurisdiction, *forum non conveniens*, international comity, and the act-of-state doctrine. The state tort statutes of limitations will vary but usually will be shorter than the ten-year ATS statute of limitations. Similarly, tolling doctrines will vary from state to state.

Defendants are likely to argue that federal law and policy preempt state tort claims. At least one district court has accepted this argument,[109] but this theory goes far beyond existing doctrine.[110] Of course, any argument that the ATS was intended to preempt state courts from resolving international law disputes flies in the face of the history set forth in detail in *Sosa*.[111]

Future corporate complicity cases may also focus on individual corporate executives or managers under the TVPA. In *Mohamad v. Palestinian Auth.*,[112] the Supreme Court

---

962 (9th Cir. 2002) (reversing the district court's grant of summary judgment in favor of Unocal on plaintiffs' ATS claims for forced labor, murder, and rape but not for torture). The Circuit took the case en banc on February 14, 2003.

106. Doe v. Unocal, Nos. BC 237 980, BC 237 679 (Cal. Super. Ct. Oct. 4, 2000). The state case was scheduled for trial in the spring of 2005, based, *inter alia*, on plaintiffs' agency theory that Unocal could be held liable for the actions of its foreign subsidiaries in Burma.

107. *See Settlement Reached in Doe v. Unocal*, EARTHRIGHTS INT'L (Mar. 21, 2005), http://www .earthrights.org/legal/final-settlement-reached-doe-v-unocal.

108. *Cf.* RESTATEMENT (SECOND) OF TORTS §§ 876 (a) (civil conspiracy), (b) (aiding and abetting), *with* Presbyterian Church of Sudan v. Talisman Energy, Inc., 582 F.3d 244, 258–59 (2d Cir. 2009).

109. Mujica v. Occidental Petroleum, Corp., 381 F. Supp. 2d 1164, 1188 (C.D. Cal. 2005) ("Since these strong federal foreign policy interests outweigh the weak state interests involved, the Court dismisses Plaintiffs' state law claims pursuant to the foreign affairs doctrine."), appeals pending, Nos. 10-55515, 10-55516, 10-55587.

110. *See* Crosby v. Nat'l Foreign Trade Council, 530 U.S. 363, 388 (2000) (finding the state legislative act preempted by a federal act through which Congress had specifically prescribed that the president should have "flexible discretion" and should "develop a comprehensive, multilateral strategy under the federal Act"); Am. Ins. Ass'n v. Garamendi, 539 U.S. 396, 420–25 (2003) (finding that a provision of California's state Holocaust Victim Insurance Relief Act impermissibly conflicted with "a matter well within the Executive's responsibility for foreign affairs" thereby preempting the California statute).

111. Sosa v. Alvarez-Machain, 542 U.S. 692, 715–22 (2004) (noting that "there is every reason to suppose that the First Congress did not pass the ATS as a jurisdictional convenience to be placed on the shelf for use by a future Congress *or state legislature*" and explaining the historical relationship between common and positive law that makes it logical for the Continental Congress to have "encouraged *state legislatures* to pass criminal statutes to the same effect" as the ATS, providing remedies for violations of the law of nations. (emphasis added)).

112. 130 S. Ct. 1702, 1710 (2012) ("The text of the TVPA convinces us that Congress did not extend liability to organizations, sovereign or not.").

found that the TVPA did not apply to corporate defendants. However, the TVPA is explicitly extraterritorial and applies to torture and extrajudicial killings. One might expect TVPA claims brought in federal court against individuals to be joined with state claims against U.S. corporations, based on diversity jurisdiction or supplemental jurisdiction.[113] Moreover, corporate executives and managers will likely be the subject of TVPA claims.

Without analyzing all of these issues comprehensively, it is clear that any further narrowing of the extraterritorial scope of the ATS after *Kiobel* will shift litigation to state or federal courts based on diversity or other bases of federal subject matter jurisdiction.

Conclusion

The struggle over the modern meaning of the ATS is in equipoise. Four members of the court, now led by Chief Justice Roberts, will undoubtedly seek to limit the scope of the ATS so that its application would be occasional and exceptional. It appears that four members of the court, now led by Justice Breyer, will seek to give a modern meaning to the ATS based on its history and purpose, in the same cautious manner initiated by Justice Souter's opinion in *Sosa*.

No member of the court is a champion of a more robust application of the ATS to vindicate a broader range of human rights violations. Indeed, no justice voted to sustain the human rights claims in either *Sosa* or *Kiobel*.

Where does Justice Kennedy stand? He joined the Souter majority opinion in *Sosa*, which affirmed the modern vitality of the ATS and its application to serious human rights violations, including extraterritorial claims. Justice Kennedy joined a narrow *Kiobel* majority rejecting "mere corporate presence" as a sufficient basis for ATS jurisdiction. He agreed to a framework in which ATS claims must be examined through the prism of the principles underlying the presumption against extraterritoriality.

Thus, Justice Kennedy's conception of the scope of the ATS, at least the geographic scope, lies somewhere between the territorial views advanced by Justice Alito and the international-law–oriented framework advanced by Justice Breyer.

It could be that Justice Kennedy, and perhaps other members of the court, simply have not come to a comprehensive approach to the scope of the ATS and are prepared to allow ATS jurisprudence to develop using common law methods familiar to the founding generation. Thus, those looking for bright-line rules for ATS cases may have a long wait.

---

113. Diversity jurisdiction would be available in almost any corporate complicity case with foreign plaintiffs and U.S. corporate defendants. *See, e.g.*, Doe v. Exxon Mobil Corp., 654 F.3d 11, 71 (2011) (finding that if a party were nondiverse, the court could dismiss that party because "Federal Rule of Civil Procedure 21 permits dismissal of 'jurisdictional spoilers'" (quoting *In re* Lorazepam & Clorazepate Antitrust Litigation, 631 F.3d 537, 542 (D.C. Cir. 2011))).

Chapter 8

Environmental Litigation against Corporations: Where Now?

Neil A.F. Popović

Framing the Issue(s)

As a matter of well-documented fact, corporate conduct that harms the environment sometimes leads to human suffering that implicates—even where it might not violate—human rights.[1] These include civil and political rights, such as the right to freedom from discrimination and the right to participate in decision-making, as well as economic, social, and cultural rights, including the right to health and the right to an adequate standard of living. As a matter of law, the situation sometimes gets more complicated. Issues may arise, including the following:

- choice of law—for example, between international law and the domestic law of multiple countries;
- the substantive content and scope of international environmental law and international human rights—that is, whether it covers the conduct and injuries at issue;
- the role of domestic courts (in the United States and elsewhere) in adjudicating essentially international (or in some cases, foreign) disputes;

---

1. *See, e.g.*, Human Rights Council, *Report of the Independent Expert on the Issue of Human Rights Obligations Relating to the Enjoyment of a Safe, Clean, Healthy and Sustainable Environment*, ¶ 49-50, UN Doc. A/HRC/22/43 (Dec. 24, 2012) (by John H. Knox); Special Representative of the Secretary-General on the Issue of Human Rights and Transnational Corporations and Other Business Enterprises, *Report of the Special Representative of the Secretary-General on the Issue of Human Rights and Transnational Corporations and Other Business Enterprises, Addendum, Corporations and Human Rights: A Survey of the Scope of Alleged Corporate-Related Human Rights Abuse*, ¶¶ 73-84, UN Doc. A/HRC/8/5/Add.2 (May 23, 2008) (by John Ruggie).

- the standing of one country's nationals to invoke another country's legal system, including domestic courts; or
- the parameters of corporate liability.

In some situations, the analysis depends heavily on the environmental aspects of a case; in others, environmental considerations have little bearing on the legal issues, even though they might provide the source of the problem and serve as an important catalyst for seeking relief.

Defining the Problem (Factually)

In some cases, the environmental harm itself affects human rights, and in other cases, environmental harm may be accompanied by violations of human rights. Examples of the former include oil and gas development and mining, which may cause air and water pollution or harm flora and fauna in ways that implicate the right to life, health, and food and water, as well as the right to safe working conditions. These kinds of cases present the most direct connection between human rights and the environment. One step removed are cases where environmentally harmful activities may be facilitated, exacerbated, or carried out with impunity because of human rights violations, including procedural rights violations, such as infringement of free speech and assembly, access to information, public participation or access to justice, or substantive rights violations such as forced labor, murder, torture, and rape.

In the latter cases, government officials sometimes commit violations while providing security or military protection in connection with environmentally risky projects. The environmental harm in cases of this sort might not deprive a person of the right to speak freely or seek redress, but the deprivation of rights may enable or intensify the environmental harm. Similarly, violations such as forced labor, murder, torture, and rape might not directly harm the environment, but the terror such violations invoke may make it possible to pursue projects that would otherwise face insurmountable opposition from local peoples.

The types of cases described above involve differing factual connections between corporate conduct and environmental harm. They involve different kinds of human rights, and they raise different legal issues as well; but they have in common a link between corporate conduct that harms the environment and human suffering that implicates human rights.

Defining the Challenge (Legally)

In litigation involving corporation-caused environmental harm that directly affects the enjoyment of human rights, the legal status of environmental human rights may pose a threshold issue, as in *Beanal v. Freeport-McMoran*,[2] where the court held that the plain-

---

2.   197 F.3d 161, 167 (5th Cir. 1999).

tiff "failed to articulate environmental torts that were cognizable under international law." In doctrinal terms, this means a claimant must establish the substantive content of environmental human rights violation to show that the alleged conduct and injury implicate legally recognized human rights principles. In other words, the plaintiff must demonstrate that the facts alleged establish a violation of human rights law. Thus, a court must determine the environmental content or coverage of the human rights norms at issue, as well as whether the norm qualifies as binding international law.

In cases where a corporation is sued in connection with human rights violations perpetrated by government actors, the character of the relationship between the corporation and the allegedly offending government may hold the key to corporate liability. This so-called "nexus" requirement considers the extent to which the corporation knew of or had reason to expect and participated in human rights violations committed by government officials.

The Range of (Litigation) Approaches and Their Varying Effectiveness

The Alien Tort Statute

The primary, although not exclusive, vehicle for raising environmental human rights claims in U.S. courts has been the Alien Tort Claims Act (referred to by the Supreme Court as the Alien Tort Statute, or ATS),[3] which provides the following:

> The district courts shall have original jurisdiction of any civil action by an alien for a tort only, committed in violation of the law of nations or a treaty of the United States.

As with other types of human rights claims under the ATS, environmental claims must satisfy the substantive legal standard for violations of "the law of nations or a treaty of the United States."

For human rights norms included in treaties to which the United States is a party, the substantive standard is straightforward: if the treaty norm covers the wrong alleged, then a violation of that norm qualifies as a violation of a treaty of the United States, and it provides a basis for *jurisdiction* under the ATS. For a treaty provision to provide a *claim for relief* under the ATS, however, it must also be self-executing, or Congress must have implemented it by enacting the treaty obligations into federal law. Thus, for a treaty-based claim, the court must determine whether the United States is a party to the treaty, whether the treaty norm encompasses the alleged wrongful conduct, and whether the treaty is either self-executing or has been implemented. This rule applies to all treaty-based

---

3.   28 U.S.C. § 1350 (2006).

claims, whether rooted in environmental treaties or human rights treaties.[4] Given the U.S. practice of including a declaration of non–self-execution with its ratification of human rights treaties,[5] the analysis for claims based on such treaties skips directly to whether the United States has implemented the treaty—that is, executed its treaty obligations—in a way that establishes a cause of action.

For claims not based on provisions of a U.S. treaty, courts interpret "the law of nations" to mean customary international law—that is, international custom—as evidence of a general practice accepted as law.[6] To identify norms of customary international law, courts consider the usage and practice of states and attempt to discern whether states adhere to a particular custom out of a sense of legal obligation rather than for social, moral, or political reasons.[7]

This determination may be particularly challenging in the context of environmental claims because other than "the general obligation of States to ensure that activities within their jurisdiction and control respect the environment of other States or of areas beyond national control,"[8] international environmental law includes relatively few principles uncontroversially accepted as customary international law.[9] The substantive requirement that the alleged wrong must violate an established rule of international law applies whether the norm is found in a U.S. treaty or in customary international law; and it applies whether the situation involves environmental harm that directly implicates human rights or environmental harm associated with other violations of human rights.

Direct Attack—Environmental Harm as Human Rights Violation
In cases where the environmental harm and the alleged human rights violation involve the same conduct, claimants may face an uphill battle to convince a court that the environmental harm at issue fits within the substantive scope of the human rights norm upon

---

4.   The United States is a party to more than 100 environmental treaties and four human rights treaties. *See* U.S. Dep't of State, Treaties in Force: A List of Treaties and Other International Agreements of the United States in Force on January 1, 2011 (2011), http://www.state.gov/documents/organization/169274.pdf. The figure is not precise for environmental treaties because there is no universally agreed upon definition of what qualifies as an "environmental" treaty.

5.   *See, e.g.,* U.S. Reservations, Declarations, and Understandings to Human Rights Treaties, Univ. of Minn. Human Rights Library, http://www1.umn.edu/humanrts/usdocs/usres.html (last visited Mar. 14, 2012).

6.   ICJ Stat., Art. 38(1)(b).

7.   Courts may also look to "general principles of law" accepted by the civilized nations of the world as a source of international law (i.e., the "law of nations"). *See* Doe v. Exxon Mobil, 654 F.3d 11, 53–54 (D.C. Cir. 2011).

8.   *See* Legality of the Threat or Use of Nuclear Weapons, Advisory Opinion, 1996 I.C.J. 226, 241–42 (July 8).

9.   *See, e.g.,* Philippe Sands, Principles of International Environmental Law 143–50 (2d ed. 2003); Daniel Bodansky, *Customary (and Not So Customary) International Environmental Law*, 3 Ind. J. Global Legal Stud. 105 (1995); Geoffrey Palmer, *New Ways to Make International Environmental Law*, 86 Am. J. Int'l L. 259 (1992).

which they base their claims. For example, in *Beanal v. Freeport-McMoran*,[10] Tom Beanal, the leader of the Amungme people in Irian Jaya, Indonesia, sued U.S. mining company Freeport-McMoran, Inc., in connection with Freeport's operation of the Grasberg Mine, an open-pit copper, gold, and silver mine in Jayawijaya Mountain in Irian Jaya. Beanal alleged that Freeport engaged in environmental abuses, human rights violations, and cultural genocide. He specifically alleged that Freeport's mining activities caused harm to the Amungme's environment and habitat, and that Freeport engaged in cultural genocide by destroying his people's habitat and religious symbols. Beanal further alleged that Freeport acted in concert with the Indonesian government to violate international human rights.

Freeport successfully moved to dismiss Beanal's claims in the district court for failure to state a claim. The Fifth Circuit Court of Appeals upheld the dismissal, concluding that Beanal failed to show that Freeport's mining activities "violate any universally accepted environmental standards."[11]

In *Flores v. Southern Peru Copper Corp.*,[12] plaintiff residents of Ilo, Peru sued Southern Peru Copper Corporation, a U.S. company, alleging that pollution from the company's mining, refining, and smelting operations caused them to suffer severe lung disease, violating their right to life, health, and sustainable development. The district court dismissed the case, holding that the plaintiffs had not "demonstrated that high levels of environmental pollution within a nation's borders, causing harm to human life, health, and development, violated well-established, universally recognized norms of international law."[13]

On appeal, the Second Circuit Court of Appeals undertook a lengthy, albeit somewhat confused, analysis of the sources and content of customary international law, concluding that the right to life and right to health "are insufficiently definite to constitute rules of customary international law."[14] The court reached a similar conclusion with respect to intranational pollution, holding that no treaties, nonbinding General Assembly declarations, other "multinational declarations of principles," decisions of multinational tribunals, or expert statements by international law scholars establish that intranational pollution violates customary international law. The court also stated that even if the right to health set forth in the International Covenant on Economic, Social, and Cultural Rights created

---

10. Beanal v. Freeport-McMoran, 197 F.3d 161 (5th Cir. 1999).

11. *Id.* at 166.

12. 414 F.3d 233 (2d Cir. 2003).

13. Flores v. Southern Peru Copper Corp., 253 F. Supp. 2d 510, 525 (S.D.N.Y. 2002).

14. 414 F.3d at 254. The court apparently conflated the test for whether a norm qualifies as customary international law with the test for whether a norm is sufficiently precise to support a claim for relief under ATS. The former is a question of international law; the latter is a question of U.S. law. The court also misconstrued the sources of law listed in Article 38 of the Statute of the International Court of Justice as embodying "the understanding of States as to what sources offer competent proof of the content of customary international law." *Id.* at 251. To the contrary, Article 38 lists multiple primary sources of international law recognized by the World Court, *including* customary international law, along with conventions and general principles of law. *See* Statute of the International Court of Justice, art. 38, ¶ 1.

a rule of customary international law, and even if the rule covered intranational pollution, "the rule would apply only to state actors because the provision addresses only 'the steps to be taken *by the States Parties* [to the ICESCR],' . . . and does not profess to govern the conduct of private actors such as defendant SPCC."[15]

The legal analysis in cases where the environmental harm itself implicates human rights involves drawing out and evaluating the environmental aspects of existing, recognized human rights. For example, pollution that endangers human life may implicate the right to life; if it adversely affects human health, it may implicate the right to health, and so on for other human rights.[16] These kinds of rights are sometimes referred to as environmental human rights, signifying that they involve application of recognized human rights to environmental issues. Environmental application of human rights has been recognized—at least as creating legal obligations for governments—in nonlitigation contexts, including in the UN human rights system and regional human rights bodies.[17] But these traditional human rights mechanisms do not provide direct recourse against private companies.

---

15.   414 F.3d at 259 (emphasis in original).

16.   For additional examples, including the environmental content of the right to life, health, work, privacy and personal security, food and water, housing, and nondiscrimination; the rights of indigenous peoples, the right to information, freedom of expression, education, and participation; freedom of association; and access to justice, *see* Neil A. F. Popović, *In Pursuit of Environmental Human Rights: Commentary on the Draft Declaration of Principles on Human Rights and the Environment*, 27 COLUM. HUM. RTS. L. REV. 487 (1996), reprinted in HUMAN RIGHTS AND THE ENVIRONMENT (Dinah L. Shelton, ed., 2011).

17.   *See, e.g.*, UN Human Rights Committee, *General Comment No. 34, Article 19: Freedoms of Opinion and Expression*, ¶ 30, UN Doc. CCPR/C/GC/34 (2011) (disapproving use of treason laws to prosecute environmental activists for disseminating information of public interest); UN Human Rights Committee, Lubicon Lake Band v. Canada, Comm. No. 167/1984, ¶ 2.3, UN Doc. Supp. No. 40 (A/45/40) (Mar. 26, 1990) (exploitation of oil, gas and land resources in areas traditionally inhabited by Lubicon Lake Band of Indians found to violate ICCPR, art. 27, right to culture); Kawas Fernandez v. Honduras, Merits, Reparations, and Costs, Judgment, Inter-Am. Ct. H. R. (ser. C) No. 196 (Apr. 3, 2009) (finding multiple violations of Inter-American Convention on Human Rights in connection with persecution and murder of environmental activist); Inter-American Commission on Human Rights, *Report on the Situation of Human Rights in Ecuador*, OEA/Ser.L/V/II.96, Doc. 10 rev. 1 (Apr. 24, 1997) (finding, inter alia, that severe environmental pollution may be inconsistent with "the right to be respected as a human being," and "the quest to guard against environmental conditions which threaten human health requires that individuals have access to: information, participation in relevant decision-making processes, and judicial recourse.").

This is to be contrasted with the *right to environment*, which signifies an independent human right to protection of the environment, regardless of whether the harm at issue otherwise implicates human rights. The right to environment, often qualified with an adjective such as *healthy* or *sustainable* (as in the right to a healthy or sustainable environment), appears in several regional human rights instruments but has yet to find expression in a globally applicable human rights treaty. *See* African Charter on Human and Peoples' Rights art. 24, June 26, 1981, 21 I.L.M. 59, 63 ("All peoples have the right to a general satisfactory environment favorable to their development."); Additional Protocol to the American Convention on Human Rights in the Area of Economic, Social and Cultural Rights art. 11(1), Nov. 7, 1988, O.A.S.T.S. No. 69, 28 I.L.M. 161 ("Everyone shall have the right to live in a healthy environment and to have access to basic public services.").

Indirect Attack—Environmental Harms Associated with Human Rights Violations
Environmentally destructive projects may sometimes be associated with violations of human rights where the human rights violations are not the same as the environmental harm. Cases that focus on well-recognized, non-environmental human rights principles, such as the prohibitions against torture, genocide, or forced labor, may make it easier for courts to recognize a claim under the ATS because the non-environmental coverage of human rights has a firmer historical foundation. In cases based on non-environmental human rights violations, plaintiffs may obtain compensation for their non-environmental injuries, but addressing the human rights violations does not necessarily alleviate the environmental problems. Nevertheless, obtaining redress for human rights violations may furnish sufficient incentives for plaintiffs to pursue litigation and for corporations to avoid it. Such litigation may indirectly ameliorate environmental problems, especially in situations where honoring human rights might result in public denouncement of an environmentally harmful project or where complying with human rights principles might render a project economically unattractive.

In cases involving non-environmental human rights violations associated with environmentally harmful corporate activities, the direct perpetrator of human rights violations may be a representative of the host government, such as a member of the military rather than a representative of the corporation. The foreign governments involved in such abuses may be immune to suit in the domestic courts of the United States under such laws as the Foreign Sovereign Immunities Act. Private corporations, however, generally do not enjoy sovereign immunity. A plaintiff pursuing a claim against a private company based on governmental conduct must overcome a different hurdle—namely, the claimant must establish a basis to hold the corporation vicariously liable for the conduct of government actors. The requisite nexus between government and private company remains unsettled in environmental cases.

In *Doe v. Unocal*, a group of villagers from the Tenasserim region in Burma alleged in a federal lawsuit in California that Unocal Corporation and French oil and gas company Total SA directly or indirectly subjected the villagers to forced labor, murder, rape, and torture when the companies constructed a gas pipeline through the region to supply natural gas to Thailand. The Burmese military provided security and other services for the project. Plaintiffs alleged that the military forced them, under threat of violence, to work on and serve as porters for the project, and that in furtherance of the forced labor, the military subjected them to murder, rape, and torture.[18]

The district court dismissed Total from the case for lack of jurisdiction[19] and subsequently granted summary judgment in favor of Unocal on the claims based on murder,

---

18. *See* Doe v. Unocal, 395 F.3d 932 (9th Cir. 2002), reh'g en banc granted, 395 F.3d 978 (9th Cir. 2003).

19. Plaintiffs then sued Total in Belgium (case dismissed because plaintiffs were not Belgian nationals), and then in France, leading eventually to an out-of-court settlement.

rape, and torture on the grounds that the plaintiffs could not show that Unocal engaged in "state action" or controlled the Burmese military. The court granted summary judgment on the forced-labor claims because the plaintiffs could not show that Unocal "actively participated" in the forced labor. On appeal, the Ninth Circuit Court of Appeals recognized that torture, murder, and slavery are *jus cogens* violations, and thus violations of the law of nations. The court also noted that rape can be a form of torture. Environmental problems associated with the pipeline project provided context, but the plaintiffs did not present them as a basis for liability.

The appellate court further explained that although some crimes require state action, "there are a 'handful of crimes,' including slave trading, 'to which the law of nations attributes *individual liability*,' such that state action is not required."[20] The court found that forced labor is a modern variant of slavery for which state action is not required for individual liability, and that Unocal could be liable under the ATS for aiding and abetting the Burmese military in subjecting the plaintiffs to forced labor. The environmental elements of the case did not enter into this aspect of the court's analysis.[21]

Unocal successfully petitioned for rehearing *en banc*, and after oral argument on the rehearing, the parties reached a settlement.[22] Although the settlement terms were confidential, Unocal reportedly agreed to pay upwards of $60 million.[23] The pipeline project raised environmental concerns—including clear-cutting of the pipeline path, construction-related pollution, and environmental risks associated with operation of the pipeline—but the legal claims, and the human rights claims in particular, focused on forced labor, murder, rape, and torture. The settlement did not affect the operation of the pipeline project and thus did not directly ameliorate the environmental risks, but it provided compensation to individuals, families, and communities affected by the project, thus putting them in a better position to deal with threats to their environment.

In *Doe v. Exxon Mobil Corp.*, the plaintiffs, who were citizens and residents of Indonesia, alleged that government-affiliated security forces hired by Exxon Mobil Corporation, in connection with the operation of a natural gas extraction and processing facility in Aceh Province, committed murder, torture, sexual assault, battery, and false imprisonment.[24] The plaintiffs alleged that Exxon hired the security forces knowing that the troops had previously committed human rights violations, that they were tortured by the troops in

---

20. Doe v. Unocal, 395 F.3d at 945–46 (quoting Tel-Oren v. Libyan Arab Republic, 726 F.2d 774, at 794–95 (D.C. Cir. 1984) (Edwards, J., concurring) (emphasis added by court in *Doe*).

21. The court affirmed summary judgment as to plaintiffs' claims under RICO based on lack of subject matter jurisdiction.

22. *See* Doe v. Unocal Corp., 403 F.3d 708 (9th Cir. 2005) (postsettlement order granting the parties' stipulated motion to dismiss).

23. The amount of the settlement was reportedly revealed in insurance coverage litigation between Unocal and its insurers. *See* Daphne Eviatar, *A Big Win for Human Rights*, THE NATION (Apr. 21, 2005), http://www.thenation.com/article/big-win-human-rights.

24. 654 F.3d 11 (D.C. Cir. 2011).

facilities inside the Exxon Mobil compound, and that the company did nothing to prevent or curtail the violations. As in *Doe v. Unocal*, the alleged human rights violations occurred in connection with an environmentally dangerous project, but the environmental harms were legally distinct from the alleged human rights violations. Although the case arose because of an environmentally risky project, the legal sufficiency of the claims did not depend on environmental harm.

In one of relatively few ATS cases to go to trial (with both sides participating), the plaintiffs in *Bowoto v. Chevron* alleged that Chevron, acting in concert with Nigeria's military and police, committed systematic violations of human rights—including summary execution, torture, and cruel and inhuman treatment—to suppress protests about Chevron's environmental practices.[25] The case went to trial after ten years of pretrial litigation. At trial, the claims included common law torts under California and Nigerian law as well as international law claims under the ATS. On appeal, the court considered whether the Death on the High Seas Act (DOHSA)[26] preempts ATS claims for wrongful deaths that occur more than three miles from shore. The court held that DOHSA does not necessarily preempt all wrongful-death claims, but because the jury rejected twenty common law wrongful-death claims brought under Nigerian law, it was highly unlikely the jury would have found a summary-execution claim meritorious under the ATS in any event. The court held that survivor claims were preempted by DOHSA. As in other ATS cases, neither the plaintiffs' claims nor the legal analysis rested on the existence of environmental harm, although the underlying protests that gave rise to the case arose directly from Chevron's allegedly destructive environmental practices.

"Mixed" Claims

Based on the foregoing examples (and there are many others), U.S. courts appear more receptive to recognizing the substantive legal sufficiency of environmental claims based on human rights violations when the human rights norms at issue are not dependent on, or specific to, environmental harm. Thus, courts have left more room for plaintiffs to pursue human rights claims against corporations where the alleged human rights violations do not themselves depend on the existence of environmental harm. Human rights claims based on violations such as murder, rape, and forced labor more easily satisfy the standard for torts in violation of the law of nations, no more or less so when the underlying corporate activities involve threats to the environment.

---

25.   *See* Bowoto v. Chevron, 312 F. Supp. 2d 1229 (N.D. Cal. 2004). The trial focused on a protest at a Chevron offshore drilling facility in Parabe, allegedly broken up in a violent confrontation when Chevron called in the Nigerian military to provide security. The soldiers shot a number of the protestors, killing two. *See* Bowoto v. Chevron, 621 F.3d 1116 (9th Cir. 2010).

26.   46 U.S.C. §§ 30301-30308 (2006).

Although the legal theories may be distinct, the real-world circumstances involving environmentally harmful corporate activities in a particular case may give rise to claims based directly on harm to the environment *and* claims based on other harms associated with the environmentally harmful activities. For example, in *Sarei v. Rio Tinto plc*, plaintiff residents of Bougainville, Papua New Guinea alleged that Rio Tinto's mining operations on Bougainville "destroyed the island's environment, harmed the health of its people, and incited a ten-year civil war, during which thousands of civilians died or were injured."[27] The plaintiffs asserted claims for crimes against humanity, war crimes, and murder; violations of the rights to life, health, and security of the person; racial discrimination; cruel, inhuman, and degrading treatment; violation of international environmental rights; and a consistent pattern of gross violations of human rights.[28]

The district court evaluated each of the plaintiffs' claims under the ATS, considering the following: "(1) whether they identify a specific, universal, and obligatory norm of international law; (2) whether that norm is recognized by the United States; and (3) whether they adequately allege its violation."[29] Remarking that "it is well-settled that racial discrimination is a violation of the law of nations," the court deemed the plaintiffs' allegations that Rio Tinto's decision to build the mine, take land, destroy the environment, and encourage military action was motivated "at least in part" by racial discrimination, sufficient to state a claim for racial discrimination under the ATS.[30]

The court separately analyzed the claims based on environmental harm *per se*, comprising claims based on the rights to life and health, sustainable development, and the United Nations Convention on the Law of the Sea (UNCLOS). The court found that plaintiffs failed to meet their burden of proving that environmental harm that endangers human health violates a specific, universal, and obligatory norm of international law and granted Rio Tinto's motion to dismiss the claim based on violation of the rights to life and health.[31] Because the court could not "identify the parameters of the right created by the principle of sustainable development," it concluded that sustainable development could not form the basis for a claim under the ATS.[32]

The plaintiffs asserted that Rio Tinto's operation of the mine violated two provisions of UNCLOS: (1) the provision requiring states to take "all measures . . . that are necessary to prevent, reduce and control pollution of the marine environment that involves 'hazards to human health, living resources and marine life through the introduction of substances into the marine environment'"; and (2) the provision mandating that states

---

27.   221 F. Supp. 2d 1116 (C.D. Cal. 2002).
28.   *Id.* at 1127–28.
29.   *Id.* at 1132.
30.   *Id.* at 1154–55.
31.   *Id.* at 1160.
32.   *Id.* at 1160–61.

"adopt laws and regulations to prevent, reduce, and control pollution of the marine environment caused by land-based sources."[33] Recognizing that UNCLOS reflects customary international law—and is therefore part of the law of nations regardless of whether the United States has ratified it—the court denied Rio Tinto's motion to dismiss plaintiffs' UNCLOS-based claims.[34]

As a matter of legal theory, there is nothing inherently different about claims based directly on environmental harm when compared to claims based on other types of harm. The same analysis applies to both, including whether the harm implicates a recognized norm of international law and whether that norm is sufficiently universal, specific, and obligatory to support a claim under the ATS. Courts have tended to be more receptive to claims not based directly on environmental harm, but there is no rule of international law, nor any reason under the ATS, that environmental claims are inherently less valid.

Aiding and Abetting

Cases involving human rights claims based directly on harm to the environment typically focus on a company's own conduct, such as oil extraction or mining; the environmental harm caused by that activity, such as pollution or damage to flora and fauna; and ways that the environmental harm infringes on the human rights of affected people and communities. In those kinds of cases, corporate liability, if established, rests on a corporation's own environmentally harmful conduct. In contrast, in cases involving claims based on non-environmental human rights violations—such as forced labor, torture, or wrongful killing—corporations more typically are not alleged to be primary violators of human rights, and harm to the environment is less likely to provide the factual predicate for a human rights violation. Such cases more likely involve primary wrongdoing by government-affiliated security or military personnel that the company relies on to provide security or other logistical support in connection with its (environmentally harmful) activities on the ground. A private company may have primary responsibility for the project, including any adverse environmental impacts, but the host government may be the primary, or even the sole, direct perpetrator of human rights violations. To hold a private company legally responsible for a host government's conduct, plaintiffs must establish a basis for vicarious liability.[35]

---

33. *Id.* at 1161.

34. As discussed below at pages 240–41, the Ninth Circuit Court of Appeals subsequently concluded that most of plaintiffs' claims could be tried in the United States, holding that the district court erred in dismissing the claims as presenting nonjusticiable political questions. Sarei v. Rio Tinto, PLC, 487 F.3d 1193, 1197 (9th Cir. 2007). With respect to the UNCLOS claim, the appellate court also rejected dismissal based on international comity. *Id.* Rio Tinto filed a petition for certiorari in the Supreme Court on December 21, 2011. On April 22, 2013, the court granted Rio Tinto's petition, vacated the judgment, and remanded the case for further consideration in light of Kiobel v. Royal Dutch Petroleum Co., 133 S. Ct. 1659 (2013).

35. In most (but not all) such cases, the government does not directly damage the environment, and the private corporation does not directly violate human rights.

As the D.C. Circuit Court of Appeals framed the issue in *Doe v. Exxon Mobil*, "[w]hat intent must be proved for aiding and abetting liability under the ATS?"[36] The standard for intent focuses on the extent to which a corporation knew or should have known that government actors would (or were likely to) commit human rights violations. The knowledge standard does not depend on the existence or severity of environmental harm. That said, at least in certain politically volatile areas (for example, oil fields in Nigeria or mining areas in Indonesia), corporations engaged in environmentally sensitive activities may have good reason to expect that their activities will generate protests, and that if they call on government security forces for assistance, human rights violations will likely occur.

The aiding and abetting issue in environmental cases has tended to center on a corporation's knowledge that government personnel called on to assist with activities (such as providing security) ancillary to environmentally harmful projects may commit non-environmental human rights violations. Thus, environmentally harmful and locally unpopular corporate conduct may provide the context for the need (or perceived need) to call on government forces for assistance, but the ensuing human rights violations are at least one step removed from the environmental harm. In this paradigm, a corporation is the direct perpetrator of environmental harm and an aider and abettor of human rights violations.

The Special Problem of Corporate Liability

Although not unique to cases involving environmental harm, courts in ATS cases have recently focused attention on the legal question of whether corporations can be liable at all for violations of international human rights. The issue of corporate liability played a key role in the outcome of two recent cases in which plaintiffs sought relief for alleged violations of human rights associated with, although not resulting directly from, corporate oil-development activities that harmed the environment. Both cases arose from environmentally harmful corporate projects, but neither involved claims that environmental harm itself violated human rights.

In *Kiobel v. Royal Dutch Petroleum*, plaintiff residents of the Ogoni region of Nigeria sued holding companies Royal Dutch Petroleum Company (incorporated in the Netherlands) and Shell Transport and Trading Company *plc* (incorporated in the United Kingdom) for aiding and abetting the Nigerian government, through a Nigerian Shell subsidiary, in committing human rights abuses. The Nigerian subsidiary had been engaged in oil development in the Ogoni region, in response to which the Ogoni people organized a group to protest the environmental effects of oil exploration in the region.

The district court dismissed claims based on property destruction, forced exile, extrajudicial killing, and violations of the rights to life, liberty, security, and association, on the grounds that customary international law did not define the violations with sufficient

---

36.   654 F.3d 11, 32 (D.C. Cir. 2011).

particularity. Neither side raised the issue of whether a corporation could be liable under the ATS for violations of human rights. The Second Circuit raised the issue *sua sponte*, holding that (1) international law determines whether corporations can be liable for violations of "its norms," and (2) "corporate liability has not attained a discernible, much less universal, acceptance among nations of the world in their relations *inter se*, and it cannot, as a result, form the basis of a suit under the ATS."[37] However, the court's ruling did not depend on the environmental aspects of the case, even though environmental concerns led to the protest that provoked the government conduct that allegedly violated human rights.

In *Doe v. Exxon Mobil*, another case arising out of environmentally sensitive corporate conduct (discussed above), the D.C. Circuit held that

> under the ATS, domestic law, i.e., federal common law, supplies the source of law on the question of corporate liability. The law of the United States has been uniform since its founding that corporations can be held liable for the torts committed by their agents.[38]

Like the Second Circuit, the D.C. Circuit did not rely on the environmental origins of the controversy in reaching its conclusions regarding corporate liability.

The U.S. Supreme Court granted *certiorari* in the *Kiobel* case on October 17, 2011, and heard oral argument in February 2012. In March 2012, the Supreme Court issued an order restoring the case to the argument calendar and directing the parties to brief the following question: "Whether and under what circumstances the Alien Tort Statute, 28 U.S.C.§ 1350, allows courts to recognize a cause of action for violations of the law of nations occurring within the territory of a sovereign other than the United States." The court issued its decision April 17, 2013.

According to the (five to four) majority opinion by Chief Justice Roberts, the question was "not whether petitioners have stated a proper claim under the ATS, but whether a claim may reach conduct occurring in the territory of a foreign sovereign."[39] The court did not directly address the issue of corporate liability, deciding instead that nothing in the ATS overcomes the presumption against extraterritorial application of U.S. law, and because "all the relevant conduct took place outside the United States," the plaintiff's claim "seeking relief for violations of the law of nations occurring outside the United States is barred."[40]

Though not specific to environmental cases, the majority opinion suggests that the ATS might not provide jurisdiction where both the environmental harm and the conduct that

---

37. Kiobel v. Royal Dutch Petroleum Co., 621 F.3d 111, 148–49 (2d Cir. 2010).
38. 654 F.3d at 57.
39. Kiobel v. Royal Dutch Petroleum Co., 133 S. Ct. 1659, 1664 (2013).
40. *Id.* at 1669.

caused the harm occurred outside the United States.[41] In contrast, it would not necessarily preclude jurisdiction in a case where important decisions that affect the environment overseas might have been made in the United States, as alleged in *Doe v. Unocal*, or where an individual defendant resides in the United States, as in *Filártiga v. Peña-Irala*.[42] The *Kiobel* decision unquestionably restricts the scope of liability under the ATS, including for environmental harm and human rights violations that occur within the territory of another sovereign, but it does not provide immunity for corporations.

Justiciability Issues

Environmental cases that involve conduct attributable to a foreign sovereign—like non-environmental cases that involve conduct attributable to a foreign sovereign—may also trigger concerns about justiciability. For example, in *Sarei v. Rio Tinto*, discussed above, plaintiffs alleged that the government of Papua New Guinea acted at the direction of mining company Rio Tinto and that the government and Rio Tinto "conspired to commit . . . violations of customary international law," including human rights violations and violations of international environmental law. Plaintiffs thus put acts of the government at issue, even though the government was not named as a defendant.[43] Justiciability issues include the political-question doctrine, the act-of-state doctrine, and international comity. Justiciability issues are not inherently linked to environmental considerations, but situations involving a host government's treatment of its own natural resources often include sensitive foreign policy considerations that may trigger concerns about justiciability.

In *Doe v. Exxon Mobil*, the plaintiffs based their claims on alleged human rights abuses committed in Indonesia by the Indonesian military, with the knowledge and assistance of Exxon Mobil. Exxon Mobil argued that the case was nonjusticiable because (1) the court should defer to the foreign policy views of the executive branch; (2) adjudication of the case would interfere with an international agreement supported by the United States; and (3) comity is owed to the judicial, legislative, and executive acts of the government of Indonesia.[44]

Indeed, "matters relating to the conduct of foreign relations . . . are so exclusively entrusted to the political branches of government as to be largely immune from judicial

---

41. Justice Breyer, in a concurring opinion joined by three other members of the Court, takes the position that the ATS should apply: where (1) the alleged tort occurs on American soil, (2) the defendant is an American national, or (3) the defendant's conduct substantially and adversely affects an important American national interest, and that includes a distinct interest in preventing the United States from becoming a safe harbor (free of civil as well as criminal liability) for a torturer or other common enemy of mankind. *Kiobel*, 133 S. Ct. at 1671 (Breyer, J., concurring in judgment).

42. 630 F.2d 876 (2d Cir. 1980).

43. Sarei v. Rio Tinto, PLC, 487 F.3d 1193, 1209 (9th Cir. 2007) (en banc) (quoting plaintiffs' complaint).

44. 654 F.3d 11, 58 (D.C. Cir. 2011).

inquiry or interference."[45] However, just because a case arises in a "politically charged context" does not mean adjudicating the case would interfere with U.S. foreign relations. A court may not shirk its constitutionally committed responsibility to adjudicate tort claims out of concern that the case is politically controversial, although it may receive input from other branches of government, either at the court's invitation or on the initiative of the other governmental entity.

In *Sarei v. Rio Tinto*, the State Department submitted a statement of interest (SOI) stating, "[i]n our judgment, continued adjudication of the claim . . . would risk a potentially serious adverse impact on the peace process [in Papua New Guinea], and hence on the conduct of our foreign relations."[46] The SOI described the allegations in the complaint, including that Papua New Guinea government officials were responsible for despoliation of the environment and that the defendants' mining operations "destroyed the island's river system and fish supply, and polluted the atmosphere."[47] The SOI did not, however, invoke the adverse environmental impacts to support its conclusion regarding potential adverse impact on the peace process. The court concluded that adjudication of the claims presented would not infringe on the prerogatives of the executive branch but, echoing the SOI, it did not overtly rely on environmental considerations in reaching its conclusion.[48]

In *Kiobel*, the U.S. government expressed its views by submitting an amicus brief on the merits, implicitly supporting justiciability and arguing that the Second Circuit erred in ruling that a corporation cannot be held liable in a federal action under the ATS. The government's brief, submitted jointly by the Department of State, Department of Commerce, solicitor general, attorney general, and Department of Justice, included a statement setting forth the interest of the United States:

> The United States has an interest in the proper application of the ATS because such actions can have implications for the Nation's foreign and commercial relations and for the enforcement of international law.

Thus, the government recognized that the case was political, but it did not consider that fact a reason for the court to stand down in favor of another branch of government. Yet again, the government did not invoke the environmental aspects of the case in support of justiciability or with respect to the merits.[49]

---

45. *Id.* at 59 (quoting Regan v. Wald, 468 U.S. 222, 242 (1984)).
46. 487 F.3d at 1205–06.
47. Letter from William H. Taft IV, Legal Adviser to Hon. Robert D. McCallum Jr., Asst. U.S. Atty. Gen (Oct. 31, 2001), on file with the author.
48. 487 F.3d at 1206.
49. On rehearing, the government submitted another amicus brief, this time signed only by the Solicitor General, the Attorney General, and the Department of Justice—i.e., not the Department of State or the Department of Commerce. The government argued that the court should fashion a rule that allows

Procedural Hurdles—Jurisdiction, Venue, and Extraterritoriality

Cases involving environmental harm outside the United States may invite challenges to jurisdiction and venue because they necessarily involve parties, events, and physical locations outside the forum, which may also raise questions about extraterritorial application of U.S. law. Non-U.S. defendants may challenge personal jurisdiction based on the insufficiency of their contacts with the U.S. judicial forum. Thus, in *Doe v. Unocal*, the French company Total SA, which was Unocal's co-venturer in the Tenasserim pipeline project in Burma, successfully challenged personal jurisdiction in the Central District of California based on its lack of contacts with California, only to be sued in Belgium (resulting in dismissal) and France (leading to settlement). Foreign subsidiaries of U.S. companies have also challenged the jurisdiction of U.S. courts on the grounds that, unlike their American parents, they lack sufficient forum contacts.

In cases involving environmental harm, the physical activities and adverse environmental impacts typically occur in the host country (even if the corporate parent makes decisions at its U.S. headquarters), which may mean the foreign subsidiary lacks sufficient U.S. contacts to be required to defend litigation in U.S. courts. U.S. companies may also challenge jurisdiction on the premise that U.S. law, whether the ATS or the common law of torts, does not apply to events occurring outside the United States.[50]

In cases where the jurisdictional foundation is solid, a corporate defendant may still try to avoid litigation in the United States by seeking dismissal based on *forum non conveniens*. Cases involving environmental harm that occurs outside the United States often invite such challenges, because they inevitably involve at least one alternative forum: the jurisdiction where the environmental harm occurred. Application of *forum non conveniens* in ATS litigation has not generated significant controversy regarding the applicable law, although application of the law in particular cases has been controversial.

To obtain dismissal on *forum non conveniens* grounds, a defendant "must demonstrate that an adequate alternative forum exists, and that private and public interests favor trial in the alternative forum."[51] Private-interest factors regarding access to proof and

---

a cause of action under the ATS for extraterritorial violations of the law of nations in limited circumstances, and only after considering doctrines such as exhaustion and *forum non conveniens,* as well as international comity, act of state, and political question. Support Brief for the United States as Amicus Curiae in Partial Support of Affirmance, Kiobel v. Royal Dutch Petroleum Co., 133 S. Ct. 1659 (2013) (No. 10-1491).

50.   To the extent a case involves damage to property outside the U.S., it could also trigger local law that favors or mandates adjudication of property disputes in local courts. *See* Nadia de Araujo & Frederico de Valle Magalhães Marques, *Recognition of Foreign Judgments in Brazil: The Experience of the Supreme Court and the Shift to the Superior Federal Court*, 1 World Arb. & Mediation Rev. 211 (2007) (courts of Brazil have exclusive jurisdiction over actions regarding real property located in Brazil); Mo Zhang, *International Civil Litigation in China: A Practical Analysis of the Chinese Judicial System*, 25 B.C. Int'l & Comp. L. Rev. 59 (2002) (Chinese courts have exclusive jurisdiction over disputes involving Chinese-foreign cooperative exploration and development of natural resources).

51.   Sarei v. Rio Tinto, 221 F. Supp. 2d 1116, 1164 (C.D. Cal. 2002). Public interest factors include:

the possibility of viewing the premises could be particularly important in cases involving environmental harm in foreign territory, because the environmental harm and the affected premises are, by definition, outside the United States.

Perhaps the most notorious example of *forum non conveniens* in a case involving overseas environmental harm is the Chevron/Texaco–Ecuador litigation, in which Texaco convinced a federal court in New York in 2001 (after nearly a decade of pretrial litigation) to decline jurisdiction over claims of environmental and human rights violations arising from Texaco's oil development activities in Ecuador in favor of allowing the claims to be litigated in Ecuadorean courts, finding "these cases have everything to do with Ecuador and nothing to do with the United States."[52] Unlike some cases, in which plaintiffs may lack the inclination or ability to pursue litigation overseas, the Ecuadorean plaintiffs, aided by an international team of lawyers and a receptive local court system, proceeded with litigation in Ecuador, leading to a judgment of $18.6 billion against Chevron, as corporate successor to Texaco.

Chevron sought to prevent enforcement of the Ecuadorean judgment on the grounds that the proceedings in Ecuador had been subject to corruption. The U.S. District Court for the Southern District of New York granted Chevron's request for a worldwide anti-enforcement injunction, which the Second Circuit reversed on the grounds that New York's recognition of foreign-judgments law did not imbue the court with authority to issue a preemptive injunction in advance of efforts to enforce an actual foreign judgment.[53]

Another set of multiple-jurisdiction issues arose in connection with litigation against Union Carbide, arising out of the tragic 1984 Bhopal, India gas leak that killed more than 5,000 people and injured several hundred thousand.[54] The accident spawned 145 lawsuits in federal courts in the United States, all of which were consolidated in multidistrict litigation (MDL). The court presiding over the MDL proceedings granted Union Carbide's motion to dismiss on grounds of *forum non conveniens* on the condition that the company submit to jurisdiction in India and waive defenses based on the statute of limitations.

The Indian legislature adopted the Bhopal Act, pursuant to which the government decided to represent exclusively all victims of the disaster in a suit against Union Carbide

---

(1) court congestion; (2) burdening citizens in an unrelated forum with jury duty; (3) interest in having localized controversies decided locally; (4) interest in trying a case in a forum familiar with the applicable law; and (5) interest in avoiding unnecessary conflict of laws. Private interest factors include: (1) relative ease of access to sources of proof; (2) availability of compulsory process for unwilling witnesses; (3) comparative cost of securing willing witnesses; (4) possibility of viewing the affected premises; (5) ability to enforce an eventual judgment; and (6) "other practical problems that make trial of a case easy, expeditious and inexpensive." *Id.* (quoting Gulf Oil Corp. v. Gilbert, 330 U.S. 501, 508 (1947)).

   52.   Aguinda v. Texaco, Inc., 142 F. Supp. 2d 534, 537 (S.D.N.Y. 2001).

   53.   Chevron v. Naranjo, 667 F.3d 232 (2d Cir. 2012). The Court of Appeals also noted that international comity would weigh against issuing an order purporting to restrict enforcement in third countries where Chevron might have assets. *Id.*

   54.   *See* Bano v. Union Carbide, 2000 U.S. Dist. LEXIS 12326 (S.D.N.Y., Order of Aug. 28, 2000).

and to use the money it obtained in such a suit to process the claims of all victims. The litigation proceeded in India for several years, leading eventually to a judicially prescribed settlement, which included payment of $470 million by Union Carbide to the government of India and termination of the Indian litigation.

In *Sarei v. Rio Tinto*, the case arising out of Rio Tinto's mining operations in Papua New Guinea, the company sought dismissal on *forum non conveniens* grounds in favor of litigation in Papua New Guinea, Australia, or Britain. The court found that Papua New Guinea was an adequate alternative forum, notwithstanding the unavailability of class actions and possible unavailability of contingency-fee counsel, as well as constraints on discovery. It found that private-interest factors weighed in favor of denying dismissal, and public-interest factors were neutral, leading the court to deny Rio Tinto's motion. The court noted that dismissal on *forum non conveniens* grounds "is particularly inappropriate given that the case is brought under the ATCA and alleges violations of international law."[55]

In *Wiwa v. Royal Dutch Petroleum*,[56] plaintiffs sued Royal Dutch Petroleum and Shell Transport and Trading Co. plc—incorporated in the Netherlands and the United Kingdom, respectively—for human rights abuses suffered at the hands of Nigerian authorities, including allegations of substantial air and water pollution.[57] Defendants moved to dismiss for lack of personal jurisdiction and *forum non conveniens*. The district court denied the motion challenging jurisdiction and granted the *forum non conveniens* motion in favor of proceeding in the United Kingdom. On appeal, the Second Circuit held that the defendants' maintenance of an investor-relations office in New York established sufficient contacts with New York to justify general jurisdiction, and that the inconvenience to the defendants of litigating in New York would not be so great as to render it unfair under the Due Process Clause.

Addressing *forum non conveniens*, the Court of Appeals assumed that Britain would provide an adequate alternative forum but held that the district court failed to give sufficient weight to three significant considerations: (1) the choice of forum by lawful U.S. residents (three of the plaintiffs had emigrated from Nigeria); (2) the interest of the United States in providing a forum to litigate claims based on violation of international human rights; and (3) the weakness of the factors that led the district court to dismiss in favor of a British forum.[58] The defendants did not argue that the case should be litigated in Nigeria, where both the environmental harm and the alleged human rights violations occurred.[59]

---

55.   221 F. Supp. 2d at 1175 (citing Wiwa v. Royal Dutch Petroleum Co., 226 F.3d 88, 108 (2d Cir. 2000)).

56.   226 F.3d 88.

57.   The *Wiwa* case involved the same defendants as *Kiobel*, and it arose out of the same oil development activities, but the plaintiffs and the particular claims were different.

58.   226 F.3d at 101.

59.   The *Wiwa* case preceded Gbemre v. Shell Petroleum Development Company Nigeria Ltd., in which a Nigerian domestic court ruled that a Nigerian subsidiary of Shell Oil and its Nigerian state-owned

Plaintiffs in *Cariajano v. Occidental Petroleum Corp.*[60]—twenty-five members of the Achuar indigenous group dependent on rain-forest lands and waterways along the Rio Corriente in Peru, along with U.S. nongovernmental organization Amazon Watch—sued Occidental Petroleum Corporation and its Peruvian subsidiary OxyPeru for environmental contamination and release of hazardous waste in connection with the companies' petroleum and oil exploration activities. Plaintiffs sued in California state court, asserting claims for common law torts and violation of California Business and Professions Code section 17200. The defendants removed the case to federal court and moved to dismiss based on *forum non conveniens*.

The district court granted the defendants' motion without imposing any conditions on dismissal. On appeal, the Ninth Circuit Court of Appeals held that the district court abused its discretion by failing to consider whether a lawsuit in Peru would be time barred, failing to give adequate weight to whether Peruvian law would provide a remedy for co-plaintiff Amazon Watch, and failing to consider evidence of corruption in the Peruvian judicial system. With respect to environmental factors, the Court of Appeals noted that Occidental's withdrawal from the site in 2000 undermined its argument that evidence found at the physical site was more important than evidence found at Occidental's corporate headquarters in California.[61] Similarly, the court held that California's "significant interest in providing a forum for those harmed by the actions of its corporate citizens" outweighed Peru's interest in adjudicating a case that involved "environmental regulation of Peruvian territory, and the allegedly tortious conduct carried out against Peruvian citizens."[62]

The legal standard for *forum non conveniens* does not depend on whether a case involves environmental harm, but on whether the circumstances of such a case may affect application of the relevant factors, including access to evidence, the possibility of a site visit, the applicable law, and the availability of adequate remedies. In cases where such motions succeed, litigation in non-U.S. forums might not in fact proceed (due to practical and/or legal limitations), and when it does proceed, it may be influenced by the home government and subject to challenge at the enforcement stage in U.S. courts.[63]

The Supreme Court's decision in *Kiobel* makes clear that even where a court has personal jurisdiction over the defendant and declines to dismiss based on *forum non conveniens*,

---

co-venturer must stop flaring gas in the Niger Delta. The court held that gas flaring violated the fundamental rights to life and dignity of the human person, including the right to a "clean, poison-free, pollution-free healthy environment." The court found these rights in the Nigerian Constitution and the African Charter on Human and Peoples' Rights. Gbemre v. Shell Petroleum Dev. Co. Nigeria Ltd..

60. 626 F.3d 1137 (9th Cir. 2010).

61. *Id.* at 1153.

62. *Id.* at 1154.

63. Such cases may raise difficult issues, as the same parties who argued in favor of a foreign forum at the *forum non conveniens* stage, later attack the integrity of the foreign forum at the enforcement stage. *See generally*, Christopher A. Whytock & Cassandra Burke Robertson, *Forum Non Conveniens and the Enforcement of Foreign Judgments*, 111 Colum. L. Rev. 1444 (2011).

the presumption against extraterritorial application of the ATS may still divest the court of jurisdiction. If, as the court found in *Kiobel*, "all the relevant conduct took place outside the United States," then the case is barred. "And even where the claims touch and concern the territory of the United States, they must do so with sufficient force to displace the presumption against extraterritorial application." In the case of an individual defendant, as in *Filártiga*, presence in the United States might suffice to overcome the presumption, but because corporations "are often present in many countries . . . it would reach too far to say that mere corporate presence suffices."[64] What more than mere corporate presence will suffice to overcome the presumption remains to be litigated.[65]

Common Law Tort Theories

Some of the legal issues claimants face in pursuing environmental human rights claims against corporations under the ATS are specific to the ATS, such as whether the substantive claim is based on a norm of international law that is *universal, specific, and obligatory*, and whether the claims *touch and concern* the United States with sufficient force to overcome the presumption against extraterritorial application. These issues may arise with respect to claims based directly on harm to the environment, and in cases based on human rights violations, indirectly related to environmentally harmful conduct. Either way, they may prevent a court from reaching the merits, and at the very least, they may result in substantial delays while the parties litigate preliminary issues.

In some cases, plaintiffs have attempted to avoid ATS-specific issues by pursuing claims based on legal theories that do not rest on substantive international law or the ATS. Indeed, notwithstanding the limitations imposed on ATS suits by the decision in *Kiobel*, plaintiffs' lawyers surely will not stop filing lawsuits; they will develop alternative legal theories. Non-ATS claims may be pursued in conjunction with ATS claims or in separate litigation. The same factual scenario that plaintiffs allege implicates international human rights may also implicate common law torts, either under the law of the forum or the law of the place where the conduct or harm occurred. Issues such as personal jurisdiction and *forum non conveniens* remain, but under a non-ATS theory of relief, there is no need for state action, and the presumption against extraterritorial application of U.S. statutory law does not apply.

In *Doe v. Unocal*, plaintiff Burmese villagers filed a state court complaint based on the same alleged abuses pled in the federal complaint in connection with the construction of

---

64.   Kiobel v. Royal Dutch Petroleum Co., 133 S. Ct. 1659, 1669 (2013).

65.   Although not directly addressing the *touch and concern* standard, the court will likely address a related issue in DaimlerChrysler AG v. Bauman, 644 F.3d 909 (9th Cir. 2011), *cert. granted*, 81 U.S.L.W. 3028 (U.S. Apr. 22, 2013) (No. 11–965), where the question presented is: "whether it violates due process for a court to exercise general personal jurisdiction over a foreign corporation based solely on the fact that an indirect corporate subsidiary performs services on behalf of the defendant in the forum State."

a natural gas pipeline in the Tenasserim region of Burma. The plaintiffs' claims included wrongful death, battery, false imprisonment, assault, intentional infliction of emotional distress, negligent infliction of emotional distress, negligence and recklessness, negligence *per se*, conversion, negligent hiring, negligent supervision, violation of California Business and Professions Code section 17200 (unfair business practices), violation of the California Constitution (slavery and involuntary servitude), and unjust enrichment. As in the federal case, environmental issues figured prominently in the community's concerns about the project, but the legal claims focused on forced labor and physical abuse.[66]

Unocal sought summary adjudication of the intentional tort and negligence claims on multiple grounds. The superior court rejected Unocal's choice of law challenge because the "snippets and portions" of Myanmar law cited by the company's foreign-law expert were inadequate to identify a conflict with California law.[67] The court further held that although there was a possibility that Unocal's investment in the pipeline project perpetuated the risk that plaintiffs would be subjected to forced labor, Unocal did not owe a duty to the plaintiffs under California law.[68]

The court rejected Unocal's argument that the plaintiffs' Business and Professions Code section 17200 claim and their forced labor and slavery claims under the California Constitution could not be brought in California for injuries occurring outside the state as long as some of the allegedly wrongful conduct (in this case, corporate decision-making) occurred in California. The court further ruled—again referencing prior rulings in the federal court litigation—that the plaintiffs' claims were not preempted by federal law, including the Burma Sanctions Act, and that consideration of the claims did not conflict with U.S. foreign policy. None of the legal rulings turned on environmental considerations.

By framing the very same factual allegations that supported human-rights–based ATS claims in federal court as common law torts in state court, the plaintiffs eliminated two key issues that have proven difficult in ATS litigation: (1) determination of the legal status of particular international norms under the ATS, and (2) establishing the potential for corporate liability. The plaintiffs still must satisfy the factual and legal requirements for substantive liability, including establishing that U.S. corporations owe a duty of care to overseas communities with respect to corporations' own conduct and the conduct of third parties, such as government security forces, acting in concert with the corporations.

---

66. In contrast, the original complaint in the Texaco-Ecuador litigation included common law tort claims for negligence, public and private nuisance, medical monitoring, and trespass, all arising directly out of environmental degradation linked to Texaco's oil exploration and drilling activities in the Ecuadorean Amazon. *See* Complaint, Aguinda v. Texaco Inc., 945 F. Supp. 625 (S.D.N.Y. 1996) (No. 93 Civ. 07527).

67. Doe v. Unocal, Nos: BC 237 980, BC 237 679, 2002 WL 33944506 (Cal. Super. Ct. June 11, 2002).

68. *Id.*

Proceeding on a tort theory also adds at least one potential issue not present in ATS claims: conflict of laws. In contrast to ATS cases, in which the statute specifies the substantive law (the law of nations), asserting a common law tort claim invites the court to undertake a choice of law analysis. In *Doe v. Unocal*, Unocal failed to convince the Los Angeles Superior Court to apply Burmese law. In theory, core environmental claims that focus on damage to the physical environment and residents of another country should weigh more heavily toward application of the law of the jurisdiction where the harm occurred, to reflect that jurisdiction's interest in the proceedings.

The case of *Calcaño Pallano v. AES Corporation*[69] arose out of alleged unlawful dumping of toxic waste in the Dominican Republic from a coal-fired power plant located in Puerto Rico. Several residents of the Dominican Republic sued the plant's operator, the AES Corporation, in Delaware state court, asserting claims for negligence, nuisance, fraud, abnormally dangerous and/or ultrahazardous activities, battery, intentional infliction of emotional distress, violation of international environmental law and international human rights, willful and wanton misconduct, and wrongful death. According to plaintiffs, Puerto Rican officials required AES to transport and dispose of highly toxic coal ash and fly ash (composed of arsenic, cadmium, nickel, beryllium, chromium, lead, mercury, and vanadium) outside Puerto Rico. The court concluded that Dominican Republic law should apply because the Dominican Republic had the most significant relationship to the parties and events at issue. Relying extensively on the plaintiffs' expert on Dominican law, the court held that the plaintiffs sufficiently pled four causes of action in tort.

The plaintiffs also alleged violations of (a) the Basel Convention on the Control of Transboundary Movements of Hazardous Wastes and Their Disposal, (b) the Cairo Guidelines for the Environmentally Sound Management of Hazardous Wastes, (c) the United Nations Norms on the Responsibilities of Transnational Corporations and Other Business Enterprises with Regard to Human Rights, (d) international human rights law,[70] (e) UNCLOS, (f) the Convention on the Prevention of Marine Pollution by Dumping of Wastes and Other Matter, and (g) the international law against bribery. Borrowing from jurisprudence under the ATS, the court set the legal standard as whether each claim rested "on a norm of international character accepted by the civilized world and defined with a specificity comparable to the features of the 18th-century paradigms" prohibiting piracy and assaults against ambassadors. The court held that none of the international instruments or legal principles invoked by the plaintiffs satisfied the quoted standard and, therefore, dismissed the plaintiffs' claims for violation of international law and human rights.

---

69.   Nos. N09C–11–021 JRJ, N10C–04–054 JRJ, 2011 WL 2803365 (Del. Super. Ct. July 15, 2011).
70.   Plaintiffs alleged that international human rights law recognizes that "the illegal disposal of toxic and dangerous substances can result in violation of traditional human rights such as the right to life, personal security, health, and well-being, physical security and integrity, property, freedom from discrimination, and inviolability of the home and privacy." *Id.*

Pursuing claims in state court does not eliminate the substantive limitations of international law, but including claims based on common law tort theory may provide a more robust legal theory of relief. Depending on where the offending conduct and injuries occurred, the relevant law may be that of the forum, the place where the challenged conduct occurred or the place where the environmental injuries occurred.

Where Now?

The environmental impact of corporate activities provides the backdrop for a wide range of transnational litigation, in the United States and elsewhere, with diverse factual circumstances and multiple legal theories. In cases where the environmental impact directly impairs human rights, claimants who rely on the ATS must establish that (a) the human rights principles they rely on encompass environmental harm; (b) the principles qualify as international law (either customary international law, general principles, or a treaty of the United States); (c) the norms at issue are sufficiently specific, universal, and obligatory to support a cause of action under the statute; and (d) the claims "touch and concern the territory of the United States . . . with sufficient force to displace the presumption against extraterritorial application."[71]

In cases where environmental impacts and human rights violations are factually distinct, although causally connected, claimants may have an easier time establishing the substantive basis for a cause of action, but to the extent the primary wrongdoing is committed by third parties, such as military personnel, claimants must establish a basis for vicarious liability on the part of a private corporation. Moreover, because the legal violation in such cases does not relate directly to environmental harm, the legal remedies available may be less likely to improve environmental conditions.

The Supreme Court's decision in *Kiobel* may lead injured plaintiffs to shift their focus to legal claims based on common law tort theories, as they have already done in some cases. However, proceeding on a common law tort theory may highlight other obstacles for plaintiffs, such as *forum non conveniens* and choice of law. Some plaintiffs may choose or be forced to litigate their claims outside the United States, although that is not always a realistic option, especially when the plaintiffs are represented by U.S.-based nongovernmental organizations.

Regardless of whether the Supreme Court further limits human rights litigation against corporations under the ATS, victims (and their lawyers) undoubtedly will continue to develop and pursue alternative legal theories to hold corporations legally responsible for

---

71.   *Kiobel*, 133 S. Ct. at 1669.

environmental harm that adversely affects human rights. At the same time, corporations (and their lawyers) will surely continue their efforts to avoid and defend against such claims.

Examples of alternative (non-ATS) legal strategies include the following, some of which have been tried and some of which are still in formative stages:

- enforcement of SEC environmental reporting obligations, such as required disclosures related to climate change;[72]
- imposition of supply-chain reporting requirements, such as the Dodd-Frank Act's disclosure requirements regarding conflict minerals and payments made by natural-resource companies to governments in connection with development of oil, gas, or minerals, and the California Transparency in Supply Chains Act of 2010's requirement to report on human trafficking;
- challenging credit applications by U.S. corporations to the U.S. Export-Import Bank on the grounds that the requested financing would contravene U.S. interests in environmental protection and human rights, pursuant to 12 U.S.C. § 635(b)(1)(B)(ii);[73]
- enforcement of the Overseas Private Investment Corporation's (OPIC) environmental and social obligations pursuant to the OPIC Social and Environmental Policy Statement;[74] and
- use of the International Finance Corporation's (IFC) Office of the Compliance Advisor/Ombudsman complaint mechanism to address adverse social and environmental impacts of projects financed by the IFC.[75]

---

72. *See* Commission Guidance Regarding Disclosure Related to Climate Change, 17 C.F.R. §§ 211, 231, 241 (2010). To date, climate change litigation against corporations in the United States has not fared well. *See, e.g.*, Native Village of Kivalina v. Exxonmobil Corp., 663 F. Supp. 2d 863 (N.D. Cal. 2009) (dismissing climate change claims against corporations based on political question doctrine and lack of standing).

73. This strategy was employed to oppose Ex-Im Bank support for participation by U.S. companies in the Three Gorges Dam project, based on the dam's environmental and social impacts, only to have the Chinese government contract instead with non-U.S. companies that were not subject to similar constraints. *See* Peter H. Gleick, *Water Brief 3: Three Gorges Dam, Yangtze River, China*, in The World's Water, 2008–2009: The Biennial Report on Freshwater Resources (Peter H. Gleick et al. eds., 2009) (charting timeline of Ex-Im Bank disapproval followed by approval from analogous German agency); Press Conference Transcript, Export-Import Bank, Three Gorges Project in China (May 30, 1996) (reporting that information received "fails to establish the project's consistency with the Bank's environmental guidelines"), on file with the author.

74. The U.S. NGO Accountability Counsel filed complaints with the OPIC Office of Accountability in connection with the proposed Cerro do Oro Hydroelectric Power Project in Mexico. *See* Overseas Private Investment Corporation, Environmental and Social Policy Statement, ¶ 1.3 (Oct. 15, 2010), http://www.opic.gov/sites/default/files/consolidated_esps.pdf. As a result, OPIC initiated a compliance review process to address claims that the project is negatively affecting the surrounding communities' health, environment, and livelihoods. *See Cases and Reports*, Overseas Private Investment Corporation (July 23, 2013), http://www.opic.gov/cerrodeorocomplaint.

75. *See generally* Office of the Compliance Advisor/Ombudsman (CAO), Terms of Reference (1999), http://www.cao-ombudsman.org/about/whoweare/documents/TOR_CAO.pdf.

Developments in international law, such as the United Nations' appointment of an independent expert on human rights and the environment, and its efforts to address corporate responsibility for human rights, may lead to further law reform that facilitates resolution of environmental human rights claims against corporations.[76] Developments in domestic law, in the United States and elsewhere, may provide additional reference points and legal tools to address environmental harm that implicates human rights. Corporations themselves may address the issue by implementing voluntary measures to improve the protection of human rights and the environment, whether out of the corporations' desire to enhance their contribution to society, ward off externally imposed regulations, or avoid potentially devastating legal proceedings.

Increasing media attention, including mainstream media and social media, on the links between environmental harm and human rights may hasten improved corporate behavior toward the environment and human rights. Ultimately, corporations and the communities they affect have a shared interest in protecting the environment—to minimize human suffering, protect natural resources, and maximize the positive impact corporations can have on society.

---

76. *See* Human Rights Council, Human Rights and the Environment, UN Doc. A/HRC/19/L.8/Rev.1 (Mar. 20, 2012) (Human Rights Council resolution deciding to appoint independent expert on human rights and environment); Human Rights Council, Human Rights and Transnational Corporations and Other Business Enterprises, UN Doc. A/HRC/RES/17/4 (July 6, 2011) (Human Rights Council resolution endorsing Guiding Principles on Business and Human Rights).

Chapter 9

Influencing the Impact of Business on Human Rights

Corporate Social Responsibility through Transparency and Reporting

Erika R. George

Introduction

International human rights instruments emphasize the central role of states in ensuring that fundamental rights are protected. The conventional focus of human rights advocacy, therefore, has aimed at exposing rights abuses by states and governments. However, more recently, several multinational corporations have come under scrutiny as potentially complicit in human rights abuses based on their conduct abroad.

Interest in the role of business in human rights violations and the relationship of business to human rights has increased in recent years as more information on the impacts of various industry practices becomes available to the public. Human rights and environmental campaigners have exposed the ways in which the business practices of certain multinational corporations are inconsistent with international environmental and human rights law. Using traditional and nontraditional forms of media, campaigners in cooperation with conscious consumers and activist investors are seeking more transparency from the business community regarding ways in which business practices impact society. Members of affected communities, in cooperation with human rights and environmental campaigners, are demanding that corporate actors be held accountable for the adverse impacts associated with particular business practices. Corporations increasingly confront the challenge of reputational risks that are bad for business when the ways that they conduct business are perceived by a conscious segment of the public to be bad for people or the planet.

Concurrently, efforts to bring corporate conduct into alignment with respect for human rights by expanding the social responsibility of business have increased. Campaigners fighting to ensure corporate accountability for abuses have opted for adjudication in courts of law, advocacy in the court of public opinion, or, increasingly, both. For example, in recent years, several lawsuits have been brought against corporations in federal courts across the United States under the Alien Tort Statute (ATS), a statutory provision that allows aliens access to federal courts when the law of nations has been violated.[1] Many of these lawsuits have concerned the conduct of multinational corporations with operations in developing countries. Claimants in these suits often alleged that business enterprises have engaged in or been complicit in violations of international human rights guarantees. Comparable actions to hold corporations accountable for involvement in human rights violations have been filed in foreign domestic courts and before international tribunals.[2]

Rights campaigners seeking to challenge corporate conduct outside the United States in U.S. federal courts can no longer count on the ATS as an avenue to access remedies for individuals and communities injured abroad. In *Kiobel v. Royal Dutch Petroleum*, the U.S. Supreme Court held that the extension of jurisdiction over tort claims by aliens for incidents that occurred overseas would run counter to the strong presumption against extraterritorial application of the laws of the United States.[3] The presumption precludes remedy for violations of the law of nations that occur outside the United States.[4] Though the court held that the ATS does not apply to conduct that occurs entirely within a foreign nation, it did leave open a number of significant questions "regarding the reach and interpretation" of the statute, leading Justice Kennedy to suggest in his concurrence that "proper implementation of the presumption against extraterritorial application may require some further elaboration and explanation" in future cases involving allegations of grave abuses of the "international law principles protecting persons."[5] Justice Breyer, in his concurrence, argued that federal courts could conceivably assert jurisdiction over cases consistent with foreign relations law where "(1) the alleged tort occurs on American soil,

---

1.   28 U.S.C. § 1350.

2.   *See, e.g.*, Ian Cobain, *British Mining Company Faces Damages Claim after Allegations of Torture in Peru*, Guardian (UK, Oct. 18) 2009, http://www.guardian.co.uk/world/2009/oct/18/peru-mon terrico-metals-mining-protest (reporting on suit brought in UK); Sarah Arnott, *Farmers Sue Shell Over Oil Spills in Niger Delta*, Independent (UK, Dec. 3, 2009) http://www.independent.co.uk/news/business /news/farmers-sue-shell-over-oil-spills-in-niger-delta-1833087.html (reporting on suit brought in Dutch court); John Lichfield, *French Oil Firm Accused of Complicity with Military Regime*, Independent (UK, Oct. 4, 2007) http://www.independent.co.uk/news/world/asia/french-oil-firm-accused-of-complic ity-with-military-regime-395921.html (reporting on suit brought in Belgian court); Ian Traynor, *Gypsies Win Right to Sue IBM Over Role in Holocaust*, The Guardian (UK, June 22, 2004) http://www.guardian .co.uk/technology/2004/jun/23/secondworldwar.internationalnews (reporting on suit brought in Swiss court).

3.   Kiobel v. Royal Dutch Petroleum, 133 S. Ct.. 1659, 1669 (2013).

4.   *Id.*

5.   *Id.* at 1669 (Kennedy, J., concurring).

(2) the defendant is an American national, or (3) the defendant's conduct substantially and adversely affects an important American national interest, and that includes a distinct interest in preventing the United States from becoming a safe harbor (free of civil as well as criminal liability) for a torturer or other common enemy of mankind."[6] Absent a statute with greater specificity, even where tort claims do "touch and concern the territory of the United States," the court has held that "the claims must do so with sufficient force to displace the presumption against extraterritorial application."[7] The court did not determine whether the law of nations recognizes corporate liability for human rights violations.[8]

Recent legislation in the United States may offer alternative options to the accountability arsenal of those who are working to better understand the connection between corporate conduct and human rights abuses. The contested new social reporting requirements contained in financial-reform legislation will provide the public with more information on the relationship between commerce and human rights conditions. The new reporting requirements may also offer an opportunity for some corporations to promote their better business practices and capture a competitive advantage among conscious consumers and socially responsible investors.

This chapter reviews recent initiatives in the United States and abroad, aside from litigation, that attempt to address the human rights consequences of how business is conducted at home and abroad.

The following section on Federal Legislation will discuss recently enacted and proposed legislation at the federal and state levels that addresses the relationship between human rights and corporate conduct through various reporting requirements. Specifically, this part will examine the trend toward leveraging securities law to promote corporate accountability through information and disclosure. It also briefly outlines examples of efforts to hold corporations accountable for alleged abuses and to regulate the relationship of corporations to human rights in other jurisdictions.

The section on Leveraging Securities Law will discuss recent international frameworks and industry-specific, multi-stakeholder initiatives combining the efforts of the business community, investors, activists, and consumers to address corporate complicity in rights abuses and define best practices for businesses. Specifically, this part will consider initiatives in the extractive industry and retail manufacturing sectors. It will also examine the potential for greater self-regulation and expanded corporate social-responsibility commitments consistent with international human rights standards pursuant to international and industry-specific initiatives. This part will also review, in particular, the UN "Protect,

---

6.   *Id.* at 1671 (Breyer, J. concurring); Justices Ginsberg, Sotomayor, and Kagan joined the concurrence.
7.   *Id.* at 1669.
8.   *Id.* at 1663.

Respect and Remedy" Framework and Guiding Principles on Business and Human Rights and the UN Global Compact. Private initiatives led by industry will also be outlined.

The chapter concludes with an assessment of the practical implications for business of the growing trend toward greater transparency in a context of escalating expectations on the part of conscious consumers and activist investors. In sum, recent developments will require corporations that have not considered the ways their conduct could impact the enjoyment of human rights to move beyond business as usual.

Federal Legislation: Corporate Accountability through Information and Disclosure

In the aftermath of the 1929 market crash that led the world into the Great Depression, Congress enacted the Securities Act of 1933 (Securities Act).[9] Because misstatements, omissions, and other fraud on the part of securities issuers were central factors contributing to the crash, the Securities Act required companies to disclose certain specified information about themselves upon the issuance of new securities to protect investors and prevent fraud.[10] The Securities Exchange Act of 1934 (Exchange Act) further expanded the circumstances under which mandatory information disclosures must be made and the nature of the information that must be disclosed to address similar perceived information asymmetries relating to securities purchased and sold in capital markets.[11] The integrated disclosure requirements of the Securities Act and the Exchange Act govern mandatory disclosure for statements, reports, and schedules filed with the Securities and Exchange Commission (SEC).[12]

Disclosures made to the SEC and the public are subject to a *materiality* test that sets a basic benchmark for the information firms are required to report.[13] The materiality

---

9.   Securities Act of 1933, 15 U.S.C § 77 *et seq.*

10.   For a comprehensive discussion of the history of securities regulation and origins of the Securities and Exchange Commission, *see generally,* JOEL SELIGMAN, THE TRANSFORMATION OF WALL STREET: A HISTORY OF THE SECURITIES AND EXCHANGE COMMISSION AND MODERN CORPORATE FINANCE (2003); *see also* Daniel M. Firger, Note, *Transparency and the Natural Resource Curse: Examining the New Extraterritorial Information Forcing Rules in the Dodd-Frank Wall Street Reform Act of 2010,* 41 GEO. J. INT'L L. 1043 (2010) (emphasizing the importance of Congressional intent "to insist that every issue of new securities to be sold in interstate commerce shall be accompanied by full publicity and information, and that no essentially important element attending the issue shall be concealed from the buying public" (citing 77 Cong. Rec. 937 (1933))).

11.   Securities Exchange Act of 1934, 15 U.S.C. § 78 *et seq.*; *see also* Joan MacLeod Heminway, *Materiality Guidance in the Context of Insider Trading: A Call for Action,* 52 AM. U.L. REV. 1131, 1170–71 (2003) (discussing the key legislative, regulatory, and judicial rationales supporting disclosure under the 1934 Act).

12.   *See* SEC, Adoption of Integrated Disclosure System, Securities Act Release No. 33-6383 (1982), http://www.sec.gov/rules/final/33-8591.pdf.

13.   *See* Cynthia A. Williams, *The Securities and Exchange Commission and Corporate Social Transparency,* 112 HARV. L. REV. 1197, 1208–09 (1999).

requirement arises from gap-filling and antifraud rules contained in the Securities and Exchange Acts to ensure that disclosures made by issuers are not misleading. Information that is not required by the mandatory disclosure provisions contained in the Securities Act and the Exchange Act, or other information that does not meet the materiality benchmark, is deemed immaterial and need not be disclosed. The Supreme Court has held that "there must be a substantial likelihood that the disclosure of [an] omitted fact would have been viewed by the reasonable investor as having significantly altered the 'total mix' of information made available" by the issuer for information to be deemed material and meet the benchmark.[14] When there is a substantial likelihood that a reasonable investor would consider information important in making a voting or investment decision, the information is material. Under the theory of efficient capital markets, absent the disclosure of mandated information and any additional *material* information, investors would be unable to value securities properly or take measures to protect against fraud, waste, or corporate mismanagement.[15]

Federal Statutes and Regulations: Obligations and Objectives

Specific provisions of the recently adopted Dodd-Frank Wall Street Reform and Consumer Protection Act amend the Exchange Act to require firms to produce information on the extent, if any, to which their commercial activities can be associated with either conflict or corruption. The new disclosure regime contained in Dodd-Frank, in effect, makes matters that pertain to human rights material. A summary of significant provisions and proposals follows.

Section 1502

In July 2010, President Obama signed the Dodd-Frank Wall Street Reform and Consumer Protection Act (Dodd-Frank) into law.[16] Section 1502 of Dodd-Frank amends section 13 of the Securities Exchange Act of 1934 (15 U.S.C § 78m) and requires disclosures, largely on corporate due diligence procedures, relating to conflict minerals that originate in the Democratic Republic of the Congo (DRC).[17]

---

14. T.S.C. Indus., Inc. v. Northway, Inc., 426 U.S. 438, 449 (1976); *see also* Basic Inc. et al. v. Levinson, 485 U.S. 224, 232 (applying materiality standard set forth in *T.S.C. Indus.* in the merger context).

15. The Efficient Capital Markets hypothesis holds that stock prices reflect available information relevant to their values. *See* Lynn A. Stout, *The Unimportance of Being Efficient: An Economic Analysis of Stock Market Pricing and Securities Regulation*, 87 MICH. L. REV. 613, 619 (1988); Ronald J. Gilson & Reinier H. Kraakman, *The Mechanisms of Market Efficiency*, 70 VA. L. REV. 549, 564–65 (1984).

16. The Dodd-Frank Wall Street Reform and Consumer Protection Act, Pub. L. No. 111-203, 124 Stat. 1376 (2010) [hereinafter the Dodd-Frank Act]. *See also* Helene Cooper, *Obama Signs Overhaul of Financial System*, NEW YORK TIMES (Jul. 21, 2010) http://www.nytimes.com/2010/07/22/business /22regulate.html.

17. Dodd-Frank Act, § 1502, 124 Stat. 2213–18 (2010)(to be codified at 15 U.S.C. § 78m(p)).

Conflict Commerce in the Context of the Democratic Republic of the Congo

Although a significant portion of the world's mineral wealth lies beneath the soil of the DRC, the country suffers from a particularly acute case of the *resource curse*. A term coined by economists, the resource curse refers to the counterintuitive *inverse relationship* between a country's economic growth and its abundance in mineral or natural resources.[18] The condition is common in countries that have economies with a high ratio of natural resource exports to gross domestic product (GDP).[19] Countries afflicted with the resource curse are more likely to experience slower and lower economic growth than comparable economies,[20] and frequently they are less democratic, more corrupt, and have a higher risk of violent conflict.[21] Mineral exports from the DRC were estimated to exceed $6 billion in 2008.[22] Tin, tantalum, tungsten, and gold are the primary minerals mined in the DRC for international trade.[23]

According to the United Nations, the eastern region of the DRC—where large deposits of the ores of tin, tantalum, tungsten, and gold are located—remains "the site of one of the world's worst humanitarian crises."[24] Replicating past patterns of exploitation, enslavement, and abuse established under the colonial rule of King Leopold II and Belgium, current competition for control over mineral wealth by armed factions continues to claim the lives of many civilian Congolese.[25] An estimated 5.4 million people have died as a result of civil war and conflict in the DRC.[26]

---

18. *See* Jeffrey D. Sachs & Andrew M. Warner, *Natural Resource Abundance and Economic Growth,* 21 Nat'l Bureau of Econ. Research, Working Paper No. 5398 (1995) (documenting correlation between natural resource abundance and negative growth), http://www.nber.org/papers/w5398.

19. *Id.* at 22.

20. *See also* Paul Collier, *Laws and Codes for the Resource Curse,* 11 Yale Hum. Rts. & Dev. L. J. 9 (2008).

21. *See, e.g.,* Paivi Lujala, *Deadly Combat Over Natural Resources: Gems, Petroleum, Drugs and the Severity of Armed Civil Conflict,* 53 J. Conflict Resol. 50 (2009); James D. Fearon, *Primary Commodities Exports and Civil War,* 49 J. Conflict Resol. 483 (2005); Macartan Humphreys, *Natural Resources, Conflict, and Conflict Resolution: Uncovering the Mechanisms,* 49 J. Conflict Resol. 508, 510–13 (2005); Michael L. Ross, *How Does Natural Resource Wealth Influence Civil War? Evidence from Thirteen Cases,* 58 Int'l Org. 35 (2004).

22. *See* John Burchill, *Out of the Heart of Darkness: A New Regime for Controlling Resource Extraction in the Congo,* 10 Asper Rev. of Int'l Bus. and Trade L. 99, 100 (2010) (citing United States Geological Survey, 2008 Minerals Yearbook: Africa (Washington, D.C.: United States Department of the Interior, Feb. 2010)).

23. U.S. Gov't Accountability Office, GAO-10-1030, The Democratic Republic of the Congo: U.S. Agencies Should Take Further Actions to Contribute to the Effective Regulation and Control of the Minerals Trade in the Eastern Democratic Republic of the Congo 6 (2010) [Hereinafter GAO Report: DRC].

24. *UN: DRC One of World's "Worst Humanitarian Crises,"* Mail & Guardian Online (South Africa, June 11, 2010), http://mg.co.za/article/2010-06-11-un-drc-one-of-worlds-worst-humanitarian-crises; *see also* GAO Report: DRC *supra* note 23 at 1.

25. Global Witness, Same Old Story: A Background Study on Natural Resources in the Democratic Republic of Congo 3 (2004) [hereinafter Same Old Story].

26. International Medical Corps, http://internationalmedicalcorps.org/sslpage.aspx?pid=359 #.UsBoJrK9KSM (last updated Dec. 4, 2013); Benjamin Coghlan et al., International Rescue

Despite peace accords that formally ended the civil war, conflict still persists in the DRC, fueled by an illegal and illicit trade in minerals that relies on forced and slave labor. Proceeds from the sale of minerals enable belligerent groups in the eastern DRC to sustain conflict and instability.[27] According to UN estimates, the minerals trade accounts for 20 to 40 percent of the revenue of armed groups operating in the region.[28] Profits are primarily derived from exploitation and extortion of the Congolese civilian population. Illegal armed groups in control of mines force civilians to work extracting minerals under conditions that are unsafe and exploitative.[29]

Corrupt elements of the Congolese national military are also involved in the illicit minerals trade and abuses against the civilian population.[30] The worst instances of extreme violence against the civilian population—massacres, mutilations, and rapes—often occur when illegal armed groups and some elements of the Congolese national military compete to consolidate control over resource-rich areas and economic activities along trading routes through abuse and intimidation.[31]

The United States is the largest donor to the UN Organization Stabilization Mission in the Democratic Republic of the Congo (MONU.S.CO),[32] currently the UN's largest and most expensive peacekeeping operation.[33] The Democratic Republic of Congo Relief, Security and Democracy Promotion Act of 2006 announced the policy of the United States

---

COMMITTEE, MORTALITY IN THE DEMOCRATIC REPUBLIC OF CONGO: AN ONGOING CRISIS ii (2007) (estimating that between 1998 and 2007, approximately 5.4 million, or 8 percent of the DRC population, died as a result of the conflict).

27. John R. Crook, *New U.S. Legislation Requires Transparency in Conflict Minerals Trade*, 104 AM. J. INT'L L. 668 (2010) (citing U.S. Dep't of State Press Release No. 2010/627, Industry Representatives Discuss Conflict Minerals at the U.S. Department of State (May 14, 2010), http://www.state.gov/r/pa/prs/ps/2010/05/121880.htm).

28. GAO Report: DRC, *supra* note 23 at 16.

29. HUMAN RIGHTS CENTER ET AL., LIVING WITH FEAR: A POPULATION-BASED SURVEY ON ATTITUDES ABOUT PEACE, JUSTICE, AND SOCIAL RECONSTRUCTION IN EASTERN DEMOCRATIC REPUBLIC OF CONGO 2 (2008), http://www.law.berkeley.edu/HRCweb/pdfs/LivingWithFear-DRC.pdf.

30. GAO Report: DRC, *supra* note 23 at 16; *see also* Thomas Fessy, *Congo General "Profits from Blood Gold"*, BBC (Nov. 10, 2010), http://www.bbc.co.uk/news/world-africa-11722142 (discussing the involvement of a top DRC military personnel in gold mining in conflict regions).

31. GAO Report: DRC, *supra* note 23 at 15. Sexual violence has been a prevalent feature of the conflict. For a discussion of rates of rape among Congolese women, *see* Amber Peterman et al., *Estimates and Determinants of Sexual Violence against Women in the Democratic Republic of Congo*, 101 AM. J. PUB. HEALTH 1060, 1063, 1064 tbl. 2 (2011). For a discussion of the injuries inflicted on the civilian population, *see* HUMAN RIGHTS CENTER, ET AL, LIVING WITH FEAR: A POPULATION-BASED SURVEY ON ATTITUDES ABOUT PEACE, JUSTICE, AND SOCIAL RECONSTRUCTION IN EASTERN DEMOCRATIC REPUBLIC OF CONGO 2 (2008), http://www.law.berkeley.edu/HRCweb/pdfs/LivingWithFear-DRC.pdf.

32. GAO Report: DRC *supra* note 23 at 1; *see also Improving Governance in the Democratic Republic of the Congo: Testimony Before the Senate Foreign Relations Comm. and the African Affairs Subcomm.*, 112th Cong. (2011) (statement of Johnnie Carson, Asst. Sec'y, Bureau African Affairs).

33. Shannon Raj, *Blood Electronics: Congo's Conflict Minerals and the Legislation That Could Cleanse the Trade*, 84 S. CAL. L. REV. 981, 988 (2011) (citing UN S.C. Rep. of the Security Council Mission to Central Africa (Nov. 21–25, 2004) at 5, 26, UN Doc. S/2004/934 (Nov. 20, 2004)).

to promote peace and security in the DRC by disarming illegal armed groups, protecting civilians, and ensuring that those responsible for abuses and destabilizing the DRC would be held accountable.[34] Section 1502 can be seen as an effort on the part of Congress to promote these aims and ensure that American businesses are not unwittingly complicit in providing further fuel to the conflict in the DRC.

The Content of Section 1502: Objectives and Obligations

Appreciating the urgent need to address the human rights abuses associated with the ongoing violence in the DRC, fueled in significant part by the proceeds from the illicit trade in conflict minerals by armed groups in the eastern region, Congress crafted provisions pertaining to the trade of DRC conflict minerals that were included into Dodd-Frank.[35] The broad aim of the provision is to disrupt the connection between violent conflict and commercial activity.[36] Section 1502 of Dodd-Frank is a federal, legally binding regulatory initiative in the United States that is intended to curtail commercial complicity in international human rights violations.[37]

Section 1502 requires publicly traded companies that utilize certain conflict minerals to report the due diligence steps they have taken to determine the source of their minerals. The goal of this provision is to ensure that companies demonstrate that links along their product supply chains are not, in effect, providing further financial support for the violent conflict in the DRC or otherwise contributing to the country's emergency humanitarian situation.[38] To serve these ends, issuers must annually disclose whether "conflict minerals" that are "necessary to the functionality or production" of a manufactured product

---

34.   GAO Report: DRC *supra* note 23 at 1.

35.   The conflict minerals provision in the Dodd-Frank Act was approved by a voice vote on an amendment proposed by Senator Sam Brownback (R-KS). In a statement issued after the vote, Senator Russ Feingold (D-WI), who cosponsored the amendment, explained that their aim was to address reports issued by the UN Group of Experts in support of UN S.C. Res. 1857 (2008), which called on Member States to take measures "to ensure that importers, processing industries and consumers of Congolese mineral products under their jurisdiction exercise due diligence on their suppliers and on the origin of the minerals they purchase." *See* Lucinda A. Low et al., *FCPA Self-Reporting and the Effects of the Dodd-Frank Whistleblower Provisions: A New Calculus*, PRACTICING LAW INSTITUTE (May 5, 2011).

36.   *See* 145 CONG. REC. S3816–17 (daily ed., May 17, 2010) (statement of Sen. Durbin) (Section 1502 "encourages companies using [conflict] minerals to source them responsibly" and also seeks to "address where the armed groups are receiving their funding").

37.   For legislative history of section 1502, *see* Conflict Minerals, 75 Fed. Reg. 80948, 80950–75 (proposed Dec. 23, 2010), http://www.gpo.gov/fdsys/pkg/FR-2010-12-23/pdf/2010-31940.pdf; 156 Cong. Rec. S3976 (daily ed., May 19, 2010) (statement of Sen. Feingold). In his statement before Congress, Senator Feingold described section 1502 as a unique contribution to securities regulation in that it is intended to ensure "greater transparency around how international companies are addressing issues of foreign corruption and violent conflict that relate to their business." 156 Cong. Rec. S3976.

38.   *See* Dodd-Frank Act, *supra* note 16, at §1502(a). Due diligence standards are also contained in the UN Guiding Principles on human rights endorsed in 2011 by the UN Human Rights Council. However, the two due diligence frameworks are quite different, as will be discussed below.

originated in the DRC or an adjoining country.[39] For the purposes of section 1502, "conflict minerals" are defined to include columbite-tantalite (coltan), cassiterite (tin), wolramite (tungsten), and gold, or their derivatives, as well as any others determined by the secretary of state to fund conflict in the DRC or an adjoining country that shares an internationally recognized border with the DRC. The DRC is bordered by Angola, Burundi, the Central African Republic, the Republic of Congo, Rwanda, Sudan, Tanzania, Uganda, and Zambia.

Section 1502 imposes a duty on corporations using conflict minerals from the DRC, or nations neighboring the DRC, to submit a report to the SEC detailing measures taken to exercise due diligence with respect to determining the source and chain of custody of its minerals. According to section 1502, the report must disclose the facilities used to process the conflict minerals, the country of origin of the conflict minerals, the issuer's efforts to determine the specific originating mine, and whether products manufactured or contracted for manufacture by the corporation are "DRC conflict free."[40]

Under section 1502, due diligence must include at a minimum an independent private-sector audit of the corporation's report, conducted in a manner consistent with standards that are to be established by the comptroller general of the United States in consultation with the secretary of state.[41] Congress intends for certified audits to constitute a "critical component" of due diligence in establishing the source and chain of custody for minerals used in manufacturing.[42] In addition to SEC reporting and certified audits, section 1502 requires issuers to provide the same information to the public on their Internet Web site.

Under the language of the statutory provision, products are "DRC conflict free" when they "do not contain minerals that directly or indirectly finance or benefit armed groups in the DRC or an adjoining country."[43] Products originating from areas "under the control of armed groups" are not DRC conflict free. In particular, products are not conflict free if they contain materials from those areas within the DRC or its neighboring nations where armed groups physically control mines or force civilians to mine, transport, or sell conflict minerals; tax, extort, or control any part of trade routes; or tax, extort, or control trading facilities in whole or in part.[44]

The secretary of state in consultation with the administrator of the United States Agency for International Development (U.S.AID) is tasked with developing a strategy to address the connections between commercial products, conflict minerals, armed groups, and human rights abuses.[45] Among other things, the strategy will seek to develop a plan to provide guidance to commercial actors in conducting due diligence on the origin of

---

39. *Id.* § 1502(b).
40. *Id.*
41. *Id.*
42. *Id.*
43. *Id.*
44. *Id.* § 1502(e)(5).
45. *Id.* § 1502 (c)(1)(A).

minerals that may make it into the formal sector from the informal and illicit activities of armed groups.[46] The strategy will also set forth a description of punitive measures that can be taken against individuals or entities whose commercial activities are supporting armed groups and perpetuating rights abuses.[47] In accordance with the recommendation of the UN Group of Experts on the Democratic Republic of Congo, the secretary of state is also to produce and make available to the public a map of mineral-rich regions and trade routes under the control of armed groups.

The comptroller general must assess the efficacy of the legislation in promoting peace and security in the DRC and adjoining countries and evaluate the issues encountered by the SEC in enforcing the provisions of the amended reporting requirements.[48] The secretary of commerce must assess the accuracy of the independent private-sector audits and due diligence processes and make recommendations for improving the accuracy of audits and establishing standards of best practice.[49]

The SEC has promulgated rules changing the annual reporting requirements of issuers that file reports pursuant to sections 13(a) or 15(d) of the Securities Exchange Act of 1934 to implement section 1502.[50] Under the rules, all issuers that manufacture, or contract to manufacture, products for which conflict minerals are necessary to functionality or production must make conflict-minerals disclosures.[51] The rules do not exempt foreign private issuers or smaller reporting companies.[52] In addition to announcing new rules, the SEC has also adopted a new form, Form SD, to faciliate the disclosures consistent with section 1502.[53]

The rules apply equally to those issuers who manufacture and those who contract to manufacture products. Therefore, issuers selling products, irrespective of the level of their influence over the manufacturing process, must still report if they have contracted with another party to have products manufactured specifically for the issuer.[54] However, pure retailers that have no influence over the manufacture of products and no contractual or other involvement in manufacturing would not be required to provide information

---

46. *Id.* § 1502 (c)(1)(B)(ii).

47. *Id.* § 1502 (c)(1)(B)(iii).

48. *Id.* § 1502 (d)(2)(A) and (B).

49. *Id.* § 1502 (d)(3)(B).

50. *See* Conflict Minerals, 77 Fed. Reg. 56,274 *et seq.* (Sept. 12, 2012) (to be codified at 17 C.F.R. pts. 240 and 249b).

51. *See* Conflict Minerals, 77 Fed. Reg. 56,290–92 (Sept. 12, 2012) (to be codified at 17 C.F.R. pts. 240 and 249b).

52. *See* Conflict Minerals, 77 Fed. Reg. 56,290–92 (Sept. 12, 2012) (to be codified at 17 C.F.R. pts. 240 and 249b). *See* Proposed Rules, 77 Fed. Reg. at 56,277, http://www.gpo.gov/fdsys/pkg/FR-2012-09-12/pdf/2012-21153.pdf.

53. 77 Fed. Reg. 56,274 (Sept. 12, 2012).

54. *See* Conflict Minerals, 77 Fed. Reg. 56,290–92 (Sept. 12, 2012) (to be codified at 17 C.F.R. pts. 240 and 249b).

regarding any conflict minerals in products sold in retail stores.[55] Also, mining issuers are not considered manufacturers under the rules.[56]

The SEC has divided the disclosure process into three stages. First, the issuer must determine whether it is subject to the Conflict Minerals Provision. The term *conflict mineral* is defined in the rules to include cassiterite, columbite-tantalite, gold, wolframite, and their derivatives, limited to tantalum, tin, and tungsten.[57] If the issuer is not one for whom these "conflict minerals" are necessary to the function or production of products manufactured or contracted for manufacture, the issuer would not be required to take any action, make any disclosures, or submit any reports.[58]

Although the SEC did not define "necessary to the functionality or production," the rules do provide guidance in the form of a factor analysis to inform the determination.[59] Whether conflict minerals are "necessary" will depend on the particular context and circumstances of an issuer's product or production.[60] Accordingly, the factors set forth by the SEC either individually or in the aggregate may be determinative regarding whether conflict minerals are "necessary" to a given product.[61] However, where a conflict mineral is contained in a product, the rules state that it should be considered "necessary to the functionality or production" of that product.[62] The rules do not provide for *de minimis* content exceptions.[63]

If the issuer is one for whom any of the aforementioned conflict minerals are necessary to the production of products manufactured or contracted for manufacture, the issuer must move to the second stage of the disclosure process. Stage two requires the issuer to determine whether its conflict minerals originated in the DRC or neighboring nations after conducting a "reasonable country of origin inquiry."[64] If the issuer determines that its minerals did not originate in the DRC or neighboring nations, it must disclose this determination as well as the process it used to conduct its reasonable country-of-origin inquiry, demonstrating the basis for its conclusions in the body of its specialized disclosure report on Form SD. The issuer must also provide a link on its Internet Web site.[65]

The rules do not state what a reasonable country-of-origin inquiry should entail; rather, the SEC has indicated that the amount of inquiry depends on the issuer's "particular facts

55. *Id.*
56. *Id.* at 56,292.
57. *Id.* at 52,685.
58. *Id.* at 56,279.
59. *Id.* at 56,295–98.
60. 77 Fed. Reg. at 56,295.
61. *Id.*
62. *Id.* at 56,296.
63. *Id.* at 56,298.
64. *Id.* at 56,310–14.
65. *Id.* at 56,315.

and circumstances" as well as "the available infrastructure at a given point in time."[66] However, the rules do contemplate that as systems for discovering the origin of minerals improve, the facts and circumstances informing reasonable inquiry may also change.[67] In sum, as access to information concerning the flow of conflict minerals in the stream of commerce improves, a mode of inquiry that might be adequate under present circumstances could become inadequate in the future.[68]

If after conducting a reasonable country-of-origin inquiry, "the issuer knows that it has necessary conflict minerals that originated in the Covered Countries and did not come from recycled or scrap sources, or if the issuer has reason to believe that its necessary conflict minerals may have originated in the Covered Countries and may not have come from recycled or scrap sources," the issuer must proceed to the final stage of the disclosure process.[69] The third stage requires the issuer to prepare a Conflict Minerals Report (CMR).[70] Issuers are to use an internationally or nationally recognized due diligence framework, if available, for the specific conflict mineral at issue.[71] The rules reference the OECD Due Diligence Guidance for Responsible Supply Chains of Minerals from Conflict Affected and High Risk Areas as satisfying the criteria for due diligence.[72] The CMR must contain "a description of the measures the issuer has taken to exercise due diligence on the source and chain of custody" of conflict minerals where it has reason to believe that its minerals may have originated in the countries covered under section 1502 and may not have come from scrap or recycled sources.[73]

For a temporary period, the rules allow issuers that are unable to determine the mineral origins through due diligence to label their products "DRC conflict undeterminable."[74] After the temporary period, issuers that cannot determine minerals origins through due diligence can label their products not been found to be "DRC Conflict Free."[75] Unless an issuer's products are "DRC Conflict Free," the CMR must include a description of the facilities used to process the issuer's minerals, the country of origin, and the issuer's efforts to determine the specific location of the mine.[76]

The CMR must also include, among other things, a description of measures taken by the issuer to exercise due diligence in sourcing minerals and securing the chain of custody

---

66. *Id.* at 56,311.
67. *Id.* at 56,311–12.
68. *Id.*
69. *Id.* at 56,280, 56,313.
70. *Id.* at 56,320.
71. *Id.* at 56,281.
72. *Id.* at 56,326. *See also* OECD, OECD Due Diligence Guidance for Responsible Supply Chains of Minerals from Conflict-Affected and High-Risk Areas (2011), http://www.oecd.org/daf/internationalinvestment/guidelinesformultinationalenterprises/46740847.pdf.
73. *Id.* at 56,320.
74. *Id.* at 56,321–22.
75. *Id* at 56,322.
76. *Id.* at 56,320.

of its minerals.[77] The SEC is requiring that the description of measures taken by issuers to exercise due diligence include a certified independent private-sector audit, and that this audit report also be provided with the CMR.[78]

Under the rules, the CMR will be filed as an exhibit to Form SD.[79] The language of section 1502 requires these reports to be "submitted."[80] The SEC distinguishes between materials "furnished" to it and materials "filed" with it; issuers are subject to less liability for false or misleading statements in materials "furnished."[81] The rules now require that issuers file Form SD, which must include the issuer's reasonable country-of-inquiry process and, where required, the CMR.[82] The rules require each issuer "to provide its annual conflict minerals information in its specialized disclosure report on Form SD for every calendar year from January 1 to December 31 and the specialized disclosure report will be due to the Commission on May 31 of the following year. The first reporting period for all issuers will be from January 1, 2013, to December 31, 2013 and the first specialized disclosure report must be filed on or before May 31, 2014."[83]

The National Association of Manufacturers, the Chamber of Commerce of the United States of America, and the Business Roundtable sued to challenge the SEC's final rule,[84] seeking review on a number of points, including the following:

1. Whether the commission violated its duty and did not conduct adequate economic analysis;
2. Whether the commission erroneously concluded it lacked authority to adopt a *de minimis* exception;
3. Whether the commission's interpretation of "did originate" in 15 U.S.C § 78m(p) (1)(A) is erroneous or arbitrary and capricious;
4. Whether the rule's "reasonable country of origin inquiry" is too costly an approach to monitoring supply chains;
5. Whether the commission's interpretation of 15 U.S.C § 78m(p)(2)(B) is erroneous;

---

77. *Id.* at 56,320.
78. *See id.* at 46.
79. *See id.* at 49–50.
80. *See* Dodd Frank Act, *supra* note 16, at § 1502 (b).
81. *See* Conflict Minerals, 75 Fed. Reg. at 80,960.
82. *Id.* In a letter to the SEC, Senator Durbin and Representative McDermott objected to the SEC's treatment of the term *submit* in Section 1502, arguing that Congress intended for the term to be synonymous with *file*, not *furnish*. Letter from Sen. Richard J. Durbin & Rep. Jim McDermott to Mary L. Schapiro, Chairman SEC 2 (Feb. 28, 2011), http://www.sec.gov/comments/s7-40-10/s74010-88.pdf.
83. Conflict Minerals, 77 Fed. Reg. at 56,305.
84. Conflict Minerals, 77 Fed. Reg. 56,274 (Sept. 12, 2012) (codified in 17 C.F.R. Parts 240 and 249b) and Section 1502 of the Dodd-Frank Wall Street Reform and Consumer Protection Act of 2010, Pub. L. No. 111-203, § 1502, 124 Stat. 1376, 2213–18 (2010) (codified in relevant part at 15 U.S.C. § 78m(p)). As stated under rule 15 U.S.C. § 78c(f) and 15 U.S.C. § 78w(a)(2).

6. Whether the shorter transition period for big companies is arbitrary and capricious when the adherence to the rule depends on smaller companies to comply; and

7. Whether the rule violates the First Amendment to the U.S. Constitution by compelling speech.

Amnesty International intervened in the litigation, arguing that the SEC's final rules should be upheld.[85] On July 23, 2013, the U.S. District Court for the District of Columbia concluded that the challenge to the SEC's final rules lacked merit.[86] The SEC's final rules currently stand as promulgated.

Even though the proposed rules to implement section 1502 were considerably delayed before being released in final form and remained in litigation for several months, according to an early report by the UN Group of Experts on the DRC, section 1502 had already generated "a massive and welcome impact," requiring "the world to take due diligence and conflict financing seriously."[87] The group reported a reduction in the level of conflict financing as commercial actors seeking conflict-free status have stopped purchasing from suspect sources and have demonstrated interest in taking ownership over greater lengths of the supply chain to create a closed system of custody over minerals from production to export.[88] However, the group has also called for "correct calibration" of the SEC regulations on disclosure to allow trade from areas that would improve the situation in the DRC.[89] Some commentators have cautioned that an unintended consequence of section 1502 could be the creation of a de facto embargo on minerals from the DRC, costing civilians their livelihood.[90] The interim report of the Group of Experts, though supportive of

---

85. *See* Petitioners' Preliminary Statement of Issues at 1–2, Nat'l Ass'n of Mfr. v. S.E.C. (Nov. 12, 2012) (No. 12-1422) *and* Motion for Leave to Intervene as Respondents at 9-13, Nat'l Ass'n of Mfr. v. S.E.C. (Nov. 19, 2012) (No. 12-1422).

86. Nat'l Ass'n of Mfrs. v. S.E.C., No. 13-CV-635, 2013 WL 3803918 at *1 (D.D.C., Jul. 23, 2013)

87. Letter from Fred Robarts, Coordinator Group of Experts on the DRC reestablished pursuant to resolution 1952 (2010), to Mary Schapiro, Chairman Securities and Exchange Commission (Oct. 21, 2011), http://www.sec.gov/comments/s7-40-10/s74010-346.pdf.

88. UN Group of Experts on the Democratic Republic of the Congo, Rep., transmitted by letter dated Nov. 18, 2011, from the Chair of the Security Council Comm. established pursuant to resolution 1533 (2004) concerning the Democratic Republic of the Congo addressed to the President of the Security Council, ¶¶ 368–70, UN Doc. S/2011/738 (Dec. 2, 2011), *www*.un.org/ga/search/view_doc.asp?symbol=S /2011/738.

89. *Id.* at 3.

90. *See, e.g.*, Laura Seay, *What's Wrong with Dodd-Frank 1502: Conflict Minerals, Civilian Livelihoods, and the Unintended Consequences of Western Advocacy* 11–16 (Center for Global Development, Working Paper No. 284, 2012), http://www.cgdev.org/content/publications/detail/1425843; Jonny Hogg, *Congo Miners Suffer as Traceability Rule Bite*, REUTERS (May 5, 2011), http://www.reuters.com/article /2011/05/05/congo-democratic-minerals-idU.S.LDE7431UG20110505; Christiana Ochoa & Patrick J. Keenan, *Regulating Information Flows, Regulating Conflict: An Analysis of United States Conflict Minerals Legislation*, GOETTINGEN J. OF INT'L L. 3, 1, 129–54 (2011); Celia R. Taylor, *Conflict Minerals and*

section 1502, also contained similar concerns.[91] Other commentators have called attention to the need for policymakers to remain mindful of the potential risk of imposing adverse impacts on the very communities affected by conflict when considering various strategies to curb commercial contribution to conflict in the region.[92]

The final report of the Group of Experts credits the SEC for recognizing OECD standards, and by extension the group's due diligence framework, in the final rules.[93] However, the group has criticized the failure to recognize the importance of risk mitigation in the final rules.[94] The group favored the adoption of a risk-mitigation process that would have allowed businesses to continue purchasing minerals in areas where state security forces are present, provided the businesses implement a strategy to assess the situation and substantiate improvement.[95] Under the risk-mitigation approach, a company would cease to conduct business in the region only when the security situation did not improve.[96]

Section 1504: Resource-Extraction Payment Reporting Legislation

Section 1504 of Dodd-Frank amends section 13 of the Securities Exchange Act of 1934 to require disclosures by issuers engaged in resource extraction.[97] A resource-extraction issuer has a duty to disclose under the section if it is ordinarily required to file an annual report with the SEC and if it engages in the "commercial development of oil, natural gas, or minerals."[98] Commercial development includes exploration, extraction, processing, exporting, acquiring a license, and other activities related to oil, natural gas, or minerals.[99]

Resource-extraction issuers, within the meaning of section 1504, must report to the SEC any payments made directly, through a subsidiary, or through an entity under its control to a foreign government or the federal government.[100] Covered corporations—those required to file an annual report with the SEC and engaged in commercial development of

---

SEC Disclosure Regulation, HARV. BUS. L. REV. ONLINE, www.hblr.org/2012/01/conflict-minerals-and-sec-disclosure-regulation/ (January 10, 2012).

91.   Group of Experts on the Democratic Republic of the Congo, Interim Report of the Group of Experts on the Democratic Republic of the Congo in Accordance with Paragraph 4 of Security Council Resolution 2021 (2012) UN Doc. S/2012/348 at ¶¶ 140, 151 (June 21, 2012).

92.   Louise Arimatsu & Hemi Mistry, International Law Programme Paper IL PP 2012/01, *Conflict Minerals: The Search for a Normative Framework* (Sept. 2012), http://www.chathamhouse.org/sites/default/files/public/Research/International%20Law/0912pparimatsu_mistry.pdf.

93.   Group of Experts on the Democratic Republic of the Congo, Final Report of the Group of Experts on the Democratic Republic of the Congo in Accordance with Paragraph 4 of Security Council Resolution 2021 (2012), annex 72 at 193–94, UN Doc. S/2012/843 (Nov. 15, 2012).

94.   *Id.*

95.   *Id.*

96.   *Id.*

97.   Dodd-Frank Act, *supra* note 16 §1504 (amending Section 13 of the Securities Exchange Act of 1934 (15 U.S.C. 78m)).

98.   *Id.*

99.   *Id.* § 1504 (q)(1)(A).

100. *Id.* § 1504 (q)(2)(A).

oil, natural gas, or minerals—must report how much they pay governments for activities related to commercial development on a country-by-country and project-by-project basis.[101] All payments that are "not *de minimis*" must be reported.[102] According to observers, this may potentially be consistent with an understanding of *de minimis* implying "payment so insignificant as to be irrelevant to an analysis (e.g., an investor's risk assessment)."[103] The final rules promulgated by the SEC define "not *de minimis*" to mean "any payment, whether a single payment or a series of related payments that equals or exceeds $100,000 during the most recent fiscal year."[104]

Section 1504 shares much in common with the Foreign Corrupt Practices Act (FCPA). The express aim of section 1504 is to decrease corruption by increasing transparency in the resource extraction sector.[105] The FCPA regulates the overseas conduct of U.S. businesses and companies traded in U.S. capital markets, and it prohibits payments to "foreign officials" in exchange for favorable treatment.[106]

The FCPA prohibits bribery, and section 1504 mandates transparency. Under the FCPA, businesses monitor certain interactions with governments and government officials where the opportunity for or appearance of bribery or corruption may be more likely.[107] Section 1504 is more expansive on one level and perhaps more restrictive on another. For example, the rules implementing section 1504 require a broader range of reporting, in that *all* payments to governments must be disclosed without respect to whether there is elevated risk of illegality.[108] In this respect, section 1504 will require greater specificity in monitoring than many corporations may currently assume, thus expanding obligations.[109] On another level, the definition of "foreign government" in the rules differs from the definition in the FCPA pertaining to "foreign officials," and it appears to be at variance with prior enforcement actions.[110] Under the rules, a foreign government must have a majority

---

101. *Id.* § 1504 (q)(2)(A)(i)–(ii).

102. *Id.* § 1504 (q)(1)(C)(i)(II).

103. *See, e.g.,* Revenue Watch Institute, Disclosure Rules: U.S. and EU Standards (June 16, 2011), www.revenuewatch.org/sites/default/files/EU-U.S.-rules.pdf.

104. 77 Fed. Reg. 56,365 *et seq.* at 56,368 (Sept. 12, 2012) (to be codified at 17 C.F.R. pts. 240 and 249b).

105. *Id.* at 56,365 (Congressional intent informing increased transparency was "to help empower citizens of resource-rich countries to hold their governments accountable for the wealth generated by those resources.").

106. 15 U.S.C. § 78dd-1(f)(1)(A), 78dd-2(h)(2)(A), 78 dd-3(f)(2)(A) (defining "foreign official" as "any officer or employee of a foreign government or any department, agency, or instrumentality thereof, or of a public international organization, or any person acting in an official capacity or on behalf of any such government or department, agency, or instrumentality, or for or on behalf of any such public international organization").

107. *See* Ernst & Young, Understanding the Effects and Challenges of Section 1504 at 3 (April 2013), http://www.ey.com/Publication/vwLUAssets/Dodd_Frank_section_1504/$FILE/Understanding_the_effects_and_challenges_of_Section_1504.pdf.

108. *Id.*

109. *Id.*

110. Debevoise & Plimpton LLP, FCPA Update at 3–4 (Oct. 2012), http://www.debevoise.com/files/

ownership share of a company for a company to be considered controlled by a foreign government.[111] Prior FCPA enforcement actions have found entities with less than 50 percent foreign government ownership or control to be instrumentalities of foreign governments and the employees of such entities to be foreign officials.[112]

The rules do not contain a specific definition of the term *project*, appreciating that "depending on the particular industry or business in which an issuer operates, and other factors such as size," the definition could vary.[113] However, the SEC has determined that the scope of the definition of a *foreign government* is not limited to foreign national governments but extends to subnational entities, "including a state, province, county, district, municipality, or other level of subnational government."[114] The American Petroleum Institute (API), concerned that the costs of compliance will have negative effects on the profits of its members, has opposed such disaggregated reporting.[115] The campaign group Publish What You Pay (PWYP) is a proponent of the measure and counters that disclosure of detailed information is essential for civil society efforts to monitor corporate and government interactions.[116] Oxfam America, a member of the PWYP coalition, filed suit against the SEC, seeking to compel the agency to issue a final rule pursuant to section 1504 and alleging, among other things, that the SEC's failure to comply with section 1504's statutory deadline to promulgate a final rule constitutes unreasonable and unlawful delay.[117]

However, when at last the SEC issued the final rules, the API, the Chamber of Commerce of the United States of America, the Independent Petroleum Association of America (IPAA), and the National Foreign Trade Council (NFTC) brought suit to challenge the rules. They argued, among other things, that the rules violate the First Amendment by compelling speech on a controversial matter to influence political affairs.[118] They also contended that the rules were arbitrary and capricious, in violation of the commission's statutory duty to consider the effect of a rule on efficiency, competition, and capital formation.[119] Oxfam America intervened in the litigation. On July 2, 2013, the U.S. District

Publication/8cc917ab-1009-43b3-b10a-78f694d59dc7/Presentation/PublicationAttachment/017a004d-a359-492d-8e94-7cfd2aac79e4/FCPA_Update_October_2012.pdf.

111. 77 Fed. Reg. at 56,389.

112. Debevoise & Plimpton LLP, FCPA UPDATE at 3–4 (Oct. 2012), http://www.debevoise.com/files/Publication/8cc917ab-1009-43b3-b10a-78f694d59dc7/Presentation/PublicationAttachment/017a004d-a359-492d-8e94-7cfd2aac79e4/FCPA_Update_October_2012.pdf.

113. 77 Fed. Reg. at 56385.

114. Id. at 56,388–89.

115. *Costs & Criticisms: The Facts about Disclosure Rules*, REVENUE WATCH (Sept. 7, 2011), http://www.revenuewatch.org/publications/fact_sheets/costs-criticisms-facts-about-disclosure-rules.

116. Daniel Kaufmann & Veronika Penciakova, *Transparency, Conflict Minerals and Natural Resources: Debating Sections 1502 and 1504 of the Dodd-Frank Act*, THE BROOKINGS INSTITUTION (Dec. 20, 2011), http://www.brookings.edu/opinions/2011/1220_debating_dodd_frank_kaufmann.aspx.

117. *See* Compl. at ¶¶ 21–31, 39–45, Oxfam America, Inc. v. S.E.C. (D. Mass. 2012) (No. 12-10878).

118. Brief for Petitioners at 2, Am. Petroleum Inst. v. S.E.C. (D.C. Cir. 2012) (No. 12-1398).

119. *Id.* at 3; *see also* Brief of Intervenor Oxfam Am., Inc., Am. Petroleum Inst. v. S.E.C. (D.C. Cir. 2012) (No. 12-1398).

Court for the District of Columbia vacated the final rules and remanded the matter back to the SEC for further proceedings to remedy deficiencies.[120] The SEC's failure to allow exemptions to reporting for countries that prohibit payment disclosure, such as Angola, Cameroon, China, and Qatar, was ruled an arbitrary and capricious error.[121] The court also found fault with the scope of public disclosures mandated by the SEC, observing that "the Commission fundamentally miscalculated the scope of its discretion at critical junctures, viewing itself as shackled by the words 'report' and 'compilation.'"[122] The SEC must now remedy the rule's "deficiencies" as identified by the court on remand.

Leveraging Securities Law to Promote Corporate Social Responsibility and Protect Human Rights

As noted above, these new duties to disclose are not without detractors. Indeed, these legally binding transparency initiatives have been challenged in court and confront a common set of criticisms concerning costs and institutional capacity. Moreover, commentators and corporations troubled by the transparency trend argue that the significant compliance costs associated with new disclosure requirements would be disproportionate to any benefits to investors.[123] The SEC estimates that approximately 1,200 corporations may be required to file disclosures pursuant to section 1502, but other observers anticipate that the number of companies required to report could be up to five times larger.[124] Indeed, because the conflict minerals found in the DRC are also found in a wide variety of consumer and industrial products, including laptop computers, cell phones, jewelry, cars, and planes, Dodd-Frank stands to impact an array of different industries.

These legislative changes are also likely to have extraterritorial effects, whether or not similar measures are taken in other countries.[125] All U.S. and foreign corporations registered with the SEC must report.[126] Companies outside the United States that want to develop business relationships with SEC-listed companies will also need to meet the standards to remain attractive potential partners.[127] Consistent with the demands of conscious consumers, corporations down the supply chain that are not demonstrably conducting business in

---

120. Am. Petroleum Inst. v. S.E.C., No. 12-1668, 2013 WL 3307114, at *1, U.S. District Court (D.D.C.) for the District of Columbia (2013).

121. *Id.* at *12.

122. *Id.* at *4.

123. David M. Lynn, *The Dodd-Frank Act's Specialized Corporate Disclosure: Using the Securities Laws to Address Public Policy Issues*, 6 J. Bus. & Tech. L. 327, 330–31 (2011).

124. Jason Zweig, *Can Annual Reports Save Lives?* THE WALL STREET JOURNAL (Dec. 17, 2011), http://online.wsj.com/article/SB10001424052970203733304577102412994084008.html.

125. *See Conflict Minerals—Detailed Guidance*, FOREIGN & COMMONWEALTH OFFICE (UK), http://www.fco.gov.uk/en/global-issues/conflict-minerals/legally-binding-process/ (last visited Dec. 29, 2013).

126. *See Dodd-Frank Section 1504: Transparency Legislation*, FOREIGN & COMMONWEALTH OFFICE (UK), http://www.fco.gov.uk/en/global-issues/conflict-minerals/legally-binding-process/dodd-frank-act-section-1504 (last visited Dec. 29, 2013).

127. *See Legally Binding Process*, FOREIGN & COMMONWEALTH OFFICE (UK), *supra* note .

a manner that supports respect for human rights could become disfavored. Retailers may increase efforts to source from suppliers with better business practices to avoid reputational risks associated with disclosures that could link a brand with conflict or slavery.[128]

Beyond the potential cost and scope of mandatory reporting regimes, institutional capacity has been raised as an objection. Some commentators have argued that sections 1502 and 1504 of Dodd-Frank are improper interventions, motivated by public policy concerns rather than concerns for shareholders or potential investors being misled, which is the primary problem reporting to the SEC is intended to prevent.[129] Critics also question the institutional competence of the SEC for managing social, as distinct from financial, reporting.[130] It is argued that the information requirements of Dodd-Frank regarding conflict minerals appear to mark an unwarranted departure from the SEC's mission to "protect investors, maintain fair, orderly, and efficient markets and facilitate capital formation."[131]

Alternatively, it would be conceivable to see the recent proliferation of social reporting duties as an appropriate interpretation of evolving market trends that have made social criteria more important to investors. As some commentators have observed, this view is consistent with that espoused by the Guiding Principles (to be discussed below) as outlined by the UN secretary-general's special representative on the issue of human rights and transnational corporations and other business enterprises.[132] For instance, Guiding Principle 3(d) offers that states should "encourage, and where appropriate require, business enterprises to communicate how they address their human rights impacts," and it supports the development of reporting requirements for human rights: "[f]inancial reporting requirements should clarify that human rights impacts in some instances may be 'material' or 'significant' to the economic performance of the business enterprise."[133]

---

128. For discussions of how a corporation's approach to social and environmental issues can affect its reputation and long-term financial performance, *see, e.g.,* DELOITTE RESEARCH, DISCLOSURE OF LONG-TERM BUSINESS VALUE: WHAT MATTERS? 2–3 (2012), http://www.deloitte.com/assets/Dcom-UnitedStates /Local%20Assets/Documents/us_scc_materialitypov_032812.pdf; UNEP FINANCE INITIATIVE, ENVIRONMENTAL AND CORPORATE GOVERNANCE ISSUES TO EQUITY PRICING: 11 SECTOR STUDIES BY BROKERAGE HOUSE ANALYSTS AT THE REQUEST OF THE UNEP FINANCE INITIATIVE ASSET MANAGEMENT WORKING GROUP 7 (2004), http://www.unepfi.org/fileadmin/documents/amwg_materiality_equity_pricing_report _2004.pdf.

129. *See* Lynn, *supra* note 123 at 330–31.

130. *See* Lynn, *supra* note 123 at 330–31.

131. *See* Lynn, *supra* note 123 at 330.

132. *See generally* J.C. Drimmer & N.J. Phillips, *Sunlight for the Heart of Darkness: Conflict Minerals and the First Wave of SEC Regulation of Social Issues,* 1 HUM. RTS. & INT'L LEGAL DISCOURSE 131 (2012).

133. *Id.* (citing Ruggie Report § 3(d) & (cmt)). "The commentary to the draft Guiding Principles released in November 2010 was even more explicit on this point: 'Financial reporting requirements should clarify that human rights impacts in some instances may be "material" or "significant" from the investors' point of view and indicate when they should be disclosed.'" *See Draft Guiding Principles for the Implementation of the United Nations 'Protect, Respect and Remedy' Framework* (Nov. 22, 2010), http://www.reports-and-materials.org/Ruggie-UN-draft-Guiding-Principles-22-Nov-2010.pdf § 5 (cmt) ("2010 Draft Ruggie Report")).

Regarding the institutional challenge the provisions may present for the SEC, sections 1502 and 1504 are not entirely without precedent. There are other examples of the SEC reaching into the realm of social concerns with respect to security threats and climate change. The SEC established the Office of Global Security Risk within its Division of Corporation Finance to develop procedures to identify all listed companies operating in "terrorist-sponsoring states" as identified by the Department of State.[134] The commission has also issued interpretive guidance to companies on reporting the impact of climate change on their businesses.[135] Because section 1502 requires the involvement of the secretary of state and the comptroller general, any institutional limitations on the part of the SEC could be addressed with support from other agencies with relevant experience. This approach is supported in Guiding Principle 8, which calls for horizontal policy coherence between governmental departments and agencies.

Finally, through cooperation, corporations may be able to reduce the costs of compliance. For example, the Electronic Industry Citizenship Coalition (EICC) has partnered with the Global e-Sustainability Initiative (GeSI) to form the voluntary Conflict-Free Smelter (CFS) assessment program, which will aid companies in identifying sources that are conflict free.[136] The Public Private Alliance for Responsible Minerals Trade (PPA), led by a governance committee consisting of the State Department, the U.S.AID, industry, and other civil society organizations such as the Enough Project, intends to pilot supply-chain systems to enable corporations to source from mines audited and certified as conflict free.[137] Over time, cooperative efforts such as these could reduce the costs any one corporation will incur.

Proposed Legislation: Business Transparency on Trafficking and Slavery

Further human rights–related amendments to the Securities and Exchange Act could be on the horizon. A federal proposal to require supply-chain transparency would have reached a wide range of business enterprises. The U.S. State Department has observed in its report on human trafficking, "with the majority of modern slaves in agriculture and mining around the world . . . it is impossible to get dressed, drive to work, talk on the

---

134. Amy Deen Westbrook, *What's in Your Portfolio? U.S. Investors Are Unknowingly Financing State Sponsors of Terrorism*, 59 DePaul L. Rev. 1151, 1195–1221 (2010) (describing and analyzing the effectiveness of the Office of Global Security Risk), http://www.washburnlaw.edu/faculty/westbrook-amy-fulltext/2010-59depaullawreview1151.pdf.

135. *See* John M. Broder, *S.E.C. Adds Climate Risk to Disclosure List*, N.Y. Times (Jan. 28, 2010) at B1.

136. *See* Electronic Industry Citizenship Coalition & Global E-Sustainability Initiative, EICC-GeSI Conflict Free Smelter (CFS) Assessment Program: Frequently Asked Questions (2012) http://www.gesi.org/DesktopModules/Bring2mind/DMX/Download.aspx?TabId=129&Command=Core_Download&EntryId=515&PortalId=0&TabId=129.

137. *See* U.S. State Dep't, Public-Private Alliance for Responsible Minerals Trade (Nov. 15, 2011), http://www.state.gov/r/pa/prs/ps/2011/11/177214.htm.

phone, or eat a meal without touching products tainted by forced labor."[138] House Bill 2759, titled the Business Transparency on Trafficking and Slavery Act, proposed to amend section 13 of the Securities Exchange Act of 1934 by adding another new subsection that would mandate disclosures relating to slavery conditions within product supply chains.[139]

Under the proposal, issuers would have been required to include in their annual reports to the SEC a disclosure describing measures, if any, the company had taken to identify and address conditions of forced labor, slavery, human trafficking, and the worst forms of child labor within its supply chains.[140] The text of the bill explained that the worst form of child labor is work performed by children that would violate international standards, including those set forth in the International Labour Organization Convention No. 182.[141] The bill was referred to the House Financial Services Committee and later failed in the Subcommittee on Capital Markets and Government Sponsored Enterprises.[142] The mea-

---

138. U.S. STATE DEP'T, TRAFFICKING IN PERSONS REPORT 30 (10th ed. 2010), http://www.state.gov/documents/organization/142980.pdf.

139. Business Transparency on Trafficking and Slavery Act of 2011, H.R. 2759, 112th Cong. (1st Sess. 2011). *See also* Tawnee Vevacqua, *Investors Support the Business Transparency on Trafficking and Slavery Act*, FTS BLOG (Jan. 27, 2012), http://ftsblog.net/2012/01/27/investors-support-the-business-transparency -on-trafficking-and-slavery-act/ (reporting that the bill was supported by the Interfaith Center on Corporate Responsibility and the Forum for Sustainable and Responsible Investment); *ATEST National Call on Business Transparency Legislation*, ATEST (June 27, 2012), http://www.endslaveryandtrafficking.org /legislative_updates/atest-national-call-business-transparency-legislation; Bill Summary & Status Search Results, THE LIBRARY OF CONGRESS THOMAS, http://thomas.loc.gov/cgi-bin/bdquery/?&Db=d112 &querybd=@FIELD%28FLD001+@4%28Human+trafficking%29%29 (last visited June 6, 2013); *see also* Trafficking Victims Protection Reauthorization Act of 2013, H.R. 898, 113th Congress (1st Sess. 2013) (proposing increased government oversight of industries using forced and child labor, encouraging publicly traded and private entities to "disclose annually on their Web sites and to the Secretary any measures taken to address conditions of forced labor, slavery, human trafficking, and child labor within their supply-chains." The bill was referred to committee on February 28, 2013); *See also* California Transparency in Supply Chains Act, CAL. CIV. CODE § 1714.43 (West 2012); Michael F. Taveira, *United States: California Transparency in Supply Chains Act*, MONDAQ (April 22, 2013), http://www.mondaq .com/unitedstates/x/235020/California+Transparency+In+Supply+Chains+Act; Anna Williams Shavers, *Human Trafficking, the Rule of Law, and Corporate Social Responsibility*, S.C. J. INT'L L. & BUS. (Fall, 2012) n.243.

140. *Id.*

141. The ILO Convention No. 182, Article 3, provides in pertinent part that the term "the worst forms of child labour" comprises:

> (a) all forms of slavery or practices similar to slavery, such as the sale and trafficking of children, debt bondage and serfdom, and forced or compulsory labor, including forced or compulsory recruitment of children for use in armed conflict;
> (b) the use, procuring, or offering of a child for prostitution, for the production of pornography or for pornographic performances;
> (c) the use, procuring, or offering of a child for illicit activities, in particular for the production and trafficking of drugs as defined in the relevant international treaties;
> (d) work which, by its nature or the circumstances in which it is carried out, is likely to harm the health, safety or morals of children.

http://www.ilo.org/public/english/standards/relm/ilc/ilc87/com-chic.htm.

142. *Business Transparency on Trafficking and Slavery Act*, GOVTRACK, http://www.govtrack.us/

sure was unsuccessfully reintroduced, and though there has not been further action on it to date, the effort does illustrate an increasing interest in business transparency.

Modern Slavery in the Stream of Commerce

The United States is the world's largest importer.[143] In 2010, the Department of Labor identified 134 goods from 74 countries around the world made by forced labor and child labor.[144] According to a U.S. Department of State Human Smuggling and Trafficking Center report, an estimated 800,000 men, women, and children are trafficked across international borders each year.[145] Of these, approximately 80 percent are women and girls, and up to 50 percent are children under the age of eighteen.[146]

Though the Smoot-Hawley Tariff Act of 1930 (Smoot-Hawley) already prohibits importation of goods made with forced labor or convict labor, it has broad exceptions.[147] Moreover, because the original legislative intent of Smoot-Hawley was to protect American manufacturers from unfairly priced goods and not to protect consumers from tainted goods, courts have held that consumers do not have standing to bring a civil action in U.S. courts for enforcement of the labor provision of Smoot-Hawley.[148]

Objectives and Obligations

The proposed legislation reflected an understanding that forced labor, slavery, human trafficking, and the worst forms of child labor are serious human rights abuses committed for commercial profit, and that the current legislative and regulatory framework to prevent goods produced under abusive conditions from entering the stream of commerce flowing into the United States remains gravely inadequate.[149] Consequently, the proposed Business Transparency on Trafficking and Slavery Act was intended to offer information

---

congress/bills/112/hr2759#overview. *See* http://thomas.loc.gov/cgi-bin/bdquery/z?d112:hr2759 (last visited Dec. 29, 2013).

143. *Statistics Database: United States*, WORLD TRADE ORG. (Apr. 2013), http://stat.wto.org/CountryProfile/WSDBCountryPFView.aspx?Language=E&Country=U.S. (reporting U.S. rank in world trade number one in imports, number two in exports).

144. U.S. DEP'T LABOR, LIST OF GOODS PRODUCED BY CHILD LABOR OR FORCED LABOR 1 (2012), http://www.dol.gov/ilab/programs/ocft/2012TVPRA.pdf.

145. *See* U.S. STATE DEP'T, TRAFFICKING IN PERSONS REPORT 7 (2008), http://www.state.gov/documents/organization/105655.pdf.

146. *Id.*

147. *See* Business Transparency on Trafficking and Slavery Act of 2011, *supra* note 142 at § 1(b)(4).

148. *Id.* §1 (b)(5). 21 J. OF POL'Y HIST. No. 2 (2009). For a discussion of historical and political factors that contributed to the creation of Smoot-Hawley, *see generally* Kumiko Koyama, *The Passage of the Smoot-Hawley Tariff Act: Why Did the President Sign the Bill?*

149. The Fair Labor Standards Act of 1938 (FLSA), 29 U.S.C. §§ 206, 207, 212, 215 (2011) (establishes a minimum wage, sets a forty-hour week, guarantees overtime compensation, and prohibits child labor; also includes a "Hot Goods" provision, prohibiting the sale or transport of goods from factories with conditions violating its provisions).

to the public and to encourage businesses to identify and address abusive conditions that may exist along links in their supply chains.[150]

The proposed legislation would have imposed a duty on issuers having annual global receipts in excess of $100 million to disclose information in a report titled *Policies to Address Forced Labor, Slavery, Human Trafficking and the Worst Forms of Child Labor*.[151] The required disclosure under the proposal would have described the extent to which, if any, the issuer:

1. "[m]aintains a policy to identify and eliminate risks of forced labor, slavery, human trafficking, and the worst forms of child labor within its supply chain";

2. prohibits the use of its "products, facilities, or services to obtain or maintain someone under conditions of forced labor, slavery, human trafficking, and the worst forms of child labor";

3. "[e]ngages in verification of product supply chains to evaluate and address risks of forced labor, slavery, human trafficking and the worst forms of child labor;"

4. "[a]ssesses supply chain management and procurement systems" to verify that suppliers have systems in place "to identify risks of forced labor, slavery, human trafficking and the worst forms of child labor;"

5. "[r]equires its suppliers . . . to certify that materials incorporated into . . . product[s] comply with the laws regarding forced labor . . . in the country or countries in which they [conduct] business;"

6. "[m]aintains internal accountability standards . . . and [sets] procedures" for failure to implement systems to uphold such standards;

7. educates employees with "direct responsibility for supply chain management" about issues associated with "forced labor, slavery, human trafficking and the worst forms of child labor" to "mitigat[e] risks within the supply chain;" and

8. "audits labor recruiters and ensures that recruitment practices are compliant with company standards."[152]

If the issuer maintains a policy to identify and eliminate risks of labor abuses, the disclosure shall include the text of the policy or a substantive description of the elements of the policy.[153] In its disclosure, the issuer should describe the greatest risks that it has identified within the supply chain and the steps it has taken toward ameliorating potential

---

150. Business Transparency on Trafficking and Slavery Act of 2011, § 1(b)(4), §1(c)(3), H.R. 2759, 112th Cong. (1st Sess. 2011).

151. *Id.* § 2(r)(4), §2(r)(5)(B).

152. *See id.* § 2(r)(1)(A)-(J).

153. *Id.* § 2(r)(1)(A).

abuses.[154] The issuer should also state whether its supply-chain assessments to address potential abuses and identify risks were conducted by an independent third party.[155] In addition, the issuer should specify whether its verification process includes consultations with independent unions, workers' associations, or workers within workplaces.[156]

An issuer filing disclosures under the proposed legislation would be required to make the information contained in its disclosure to the SEC available to the public with a "conspicuous and easily understood link to the relevant information" that is located on the issuer's home page and clearly labeled "Policies to Address Forced Labor, Slavery, Human Trafficking, and the Worst Forms of Child Labor."[157] Issuers without a Web site would be required to respond within thirty days after receiving a written request for the disclosure from an investor or consumer. Such issuers would achieve compliance with the disclosure provision by providing that party with the information it reported to the SEC pursuant to the legislation.[158] In instances where the issuer has identified issues within its supply chain, it should ensure that remediation is provided to those who have been identified as victims of forced labor, slavery, human trafficking, and the worst forms of child labor, and it must report on remedial measures taken.[159]

Though this particular proposal did not succeed, the growing public concern about product origins suggests that similar measures may be introduced in the future.

State Legislation: Objectives and Obligations

In addition to federal legislative action to promote greater transparency to protect human rights, there is similar activity at the state level. A variety of state and local governments have undertaken initiatives aimed at improving transparency and alleviating poverty that could have positive impacts on the promotion of human rights. A few illustrations of these efforts are described below.

California Transparency in Supply Chains Act (CTSCA)

In 2010, California enacted the first state law requiring manufacturers and retail companies to publicly disclose their policies to eradicate slavery, forced labor, and human trafficking within their supply chains.[160] The CTSCA was the inspiration for the proposed federal bill,[161] and therefore the two acts are very similar. The CTSCA differs from the federal proposal in that the federal proposal limits disclosure requirements to publicly traded companies and therefore requires disclosure to be made in companies' annual reports to

---

154. *Id.* § 2(r)(1)(C)(i).
155. *Id.* § 2(r)(1)(C)(ii).
156. *Id.* § 2(r)(1)(C)(iii).
157. *Id.* § 2(r)(4).
158. *Id.*
159. *Id.* § 2(r)(1)(J).
160. CAL. CIV. CODE § 1714.43 (West 2012) [hereinafter Cal. Supply Chain Act].
161. Business Transparency on Trafficking and Slavery Act of 2011, §2 (b)(3).

the SEC.[162] The CTSCA, on the other hand, requires all retailers and manufactures that do business in California and have over $100 million in annual gross receipts to disclose on their company Web site any efforts being made to eradicate slavery and human trafficking from their supply chains.[163]

The law takes up a "critical clarion call for action" made by the California Department of Justice in a 2007 report entitled *Human Trafficking in California*, which contained a comprehensive list of recommendations to combat human trafficking.[164] The report concluded that "California bears a moral responsibility to exert leadership, through government and business purchasing practices, to implement and monitor codes of conduct assuring fair and humane labor practices throughout their supply chain."[165] As the world's ninth-largest economy—after the United States, China, Japan, Germany, France, the United Kingdom, Italy, and Brazil[166]—California passed the CTSCA to leverage the substantial economic power of California consumers to promote social responsibility in the business community and prevent the use of forced labor in its supply chains.

The CTSCA became effective January 1, 2012. Retailers and manufacturers subject to its provisions are required to disclose their efforts, if any, to ensure that their supply chains are free from slavery and human trafficking by evaluating and addressing risks along links of the supply chain. Initial estimates indicate that California's supply-chain transparency reporting requirements will reach approximately 3,200 companies.[167]

As with the requirement under the failed federal provision, the disclosure must be prominently displayed on the retail seller's or manufacturer's Web site and include a link to the required information placed on the business's home page.[168] Those retailers or manufacturers without an Internet presence are required to provide a written disclosure of efforts to eradicate trafficking within thirty days of receiving a written request for the disclosure from a consumer.[169]

The disclosure must, at a minimum, explain the extent to which the business entity is engaged in activities to eradicate slavery and trafficking, including (1) verifying product

---

162. *Id.* preamble.
163. Cal. Supply Chain Act § 1714.43(a)(1), (b).
164. *The California Transparency in Supply Chains Act of 2010: New Information to Aid Consumer Purchasing Decisions: Hearing on S.B. 657 before the Assemb. Comm. on Judiciary,* at 1–2 (June 23, 2010) http://www.leginfo.ca.gov/pub/09-10/bill/sen/sb_0651-0700/sb_657_cfa_20100628_112914_asm _comm.html (last visited July 10, 2012).
165. *Id.* at 1.
166. CTR. FOR CONTINUING STUDY OF THE CAL. ECONOMY, 2010 CALIFORNIA ECONOMY RANKINGS (2012), http://www.ccsce.com/PDF/Numbers-Jan-2012-CA-Economy-Rankings-2010.pdf; *California Economy Ranking in the World,* ECONOMIC POST (Feb. 3, 2011), http://econpost.com/californiaeconomy /california-economy-ranking-among-world-economies.
167. Jonathan Todres, *The Private Sector's Pivotal Role in Combating Human Trafficking,* 3 CALIF. L. REV. 80, 81 (2012).
168. *See* Cal. Supply Chain Act, *supra* note 163 at § 1714.43(b).
169. *Id.*

supply chains to evaluate and address risks of human trafficking and slavery; (2) auditing suppliers to evaluate supplier compliance with company standards for trafficking and slavery in supply chains; and (3) requiring direct suppliers to certify that materials incorporated into the product comply with the laws regarding slavery and human trafficking of the country or countries in which they are doing business.[170] These disclosures must note whether audits for information were conducted by an independent third party and were unannounced.[171] Failure to comply with California's reporting requirements may result in an action brought by the attorney general of California for injunctive relief.[172]

Although the only relief available under the CTSCA for failure to report is injunctive, the enforcement strength of the statute may be in consumer choice and consciousness. California's Business and Professions Code permits consumer claims for unfair business practices (section 17200) and for false advertising (section 17500) which complement the CTSCA.[173] A California resident sued Nike under this code for making false and misleading statements about labor conditions in its factories in Asia.[174] After the U.S. Supreme Court declined to review the lower court's decision,[175] Nike settled the suit.[176]

The recent disclosure duties placed on industry by new federal and state legislation have faced both praise and criticism from various stakeholders. For example, in California the new law was celebrated by a broad coalition of human rights, law enforcement, and employee rights organizations as an important advance in protecting human rights. However, it was condemned as costly and burdensome by a coalition of business trade organizations including the California Chamber of Commerce, California Grocers Association, California Manufacturers and Technology Association, California Retailers Association, and TechAmerica.[177] Similarly, at the federal level, reporting requirements and due diligence obligations were welcomed by rights campaigners but met with resistance from some segments of the business community.[178] Nonetheless, voluntary CSR reporting continues

---

170. *Id.* at (c)(1)–(3).

171. *Id.* at (c)(2).

172. *Id.* at (d).

173. CAL. BUS. & PROF. CODE § 17,200 *et seq.* (2003).

174. Kasky v. Nike, Inc., 45 P.3d, 243, 119 Cal. Rptr.2d 296 (Cal. 2002).

175. Nike, Inc. v. Kasky, 539 U.S. 654, 657–58 (2003) (dismissing grant of certiorari as improvidently granted).

176. Press Release, Fair Labor Association, Fair Labor Association Receives $1.5 Million in Settlement of Kasky v. Nike First Amendment Case: Funds to Be Used to Benefit Factory Workers and Consumers (Sept. 12, 2003). *See also* Jan Wouters & Leen Chanet, *Corporate Human Rights Responsibility: A European Perspective*, 6 Nw. J. INT'L. HUM. RTS. 262, 286 n.168 (2008) (citing William Baue, *The Implications of the Nike and Kasky Settlement on CSR Reporting*, ETHICAL CORPORATION (September 23, 2003)).

177. *Bill Analysis: Hearing on S.B. 657 before the Assembly Comm. on Judiciary* 12–13 (CA Jun. 29, 2010), http://www.leginfo.ca.gov/pub/09-10/bill/sen/sb_0651-0700/sb_657_cfa_20100628_112914_asm_comm.html.

178. *See, e.g.*, David M. Lynn, *The Dodd-Frank Act's Specialized Corporate Disclosure: Using the Securities Laws to Address Public Policy Issues*, 6 J. BUS. & TECH. L. 327, 336–39 (2011); Cecelia R. Taylor, *Conflict Minerals and SEC Disclosure Regulation*, 2 HARV. BUS. L. REV. ONLINE 105, 120 (2012);

unabated in response to political and market pressures. There is no reason to discount the increasing relevance of transparency initiatives. However, questions remain about how these efforts will ultimately impact industry.

Living-Wage Ordinances

Several U.S. jurisdictions have adopted policies intended to improve socioeconomic conditions in their communities by elevating the wages of employees through the contractual choices made for provision of public services.[179] Because governments award contracts to private businesses to provide services to the public, and taxpayers fund these contracts, living-wage ordinances reflect a growing sentiment that it is appropriate to direct taxpayer funds toward advancing the interests of municipalities and taxpayers.[180] Government contracts are intended to promote economic development, job creation, and retention. Also chief among the interests articulated by local governments are creating jobs that keep workers (who are also taxpayers) and their families out of poverty.[181] Yet evidence suggests that people who provide municipal services often work for low wages and live at or below the poverty line.[182] Evidence further suggests that paying living wages tends to improve the quality of government services by reducing the instability of absenteeism and high turnover.[183]

Living-wage ordinances require that government service contracts be awarded only to those employers that pay employees at a specified minimum compensation level.[184] Though the wage levels vary among regions, this level is usually above that set under a legally mandated minimum wage and is meant to allow individuals employed full-time to provide food, housing, health care, child care, and basic transportation for themselves and their families.[185] Currently, thirty-two California cities and counties have living-wage ordinances.[186]

Although the base wage in living-wage ordinances varies, certain basic features are shared among different jurisdictions. For example, the basic type of employer covered

---

Letter from the U.S. Chamber of Commerce to the SEC (Feb. 28, 2011), http://www.sec.gov/comments/s7-40-10/s74010-87.pdf.

179. Clayton P. Gillette, *Local Redistribution, Living Wage Ordinances, and Judicial Intervention*, 101 Nw. U. L. Rev. 1057, 1057 (2007).

180. T. WILLIAM LESTER & KEN JACOBS, CTR. FOR AM. PROGRESS ACTION FUND, CREATING GOOD JOBS IN OUR COMMUNITIES: HOW HIGHER WAGE STANDARDS AFFECT ECONOMIC DEVELOPMENT AND EMPLOYMENT (Nov. 2010), http://www.americanprogressaction.org/issues/2010/11/pdf/living_wage.pdf.

181. *Id.*

182. Los Angeles Admin. Code Ordinance No. 172336, Art. 11 Living Wage, Sec. 10.37 Legislative Findings at 1 (1996), http://bca.lacity.org/index.cfm?nxt=lco&nxt_body=content_lwo.cfm.

183. *Id.*

184. Jon Gertner, *What Is a Living Wage?* eq N.Y. TIMES (Jan. 15, 2006), http://www.nytimes.com/2006/01/15/magazine/15wage.html?pagewanted=all.

185. *See Living Wage Overview*, UC BERKELEY LABOR CTR., http://laborcenter.berkeley.edu/livingwage/overview.shtml (last visited Mar. 14, 2012).

186. *Id.*

depends on the size of the contract and the number of employees.[187] Generally, wages are adjusted upward annually from a set level linked to an accepted index.[188] For instance, San Diego's ordinance requires annual upward adjustments to reflect changes in the consumer price index for all urban consumers within its metropolitan statistical area.[189] In addition to meeting the fair-wage floor, covered employers are required to provide covered employees with a minimum number of compensated days of leave for illness, vacation, or personal necessity upon the employee's request.[190] Covered employers must also grant a set number of uncompensated days of leave to covered employees who have exhausted compensated days off.[191] Employees are to be notified of their rights pursuant to living-wage provisions, and employers must post such notifications and others at the work site in a prominent place in an area frequently and easily accessed by employees.[192]

In the instance of an employer's violation of a living-wage ordinance, the municipality with which the employer has contracted may declare a material breach of contract and exercise remedies including contract termination and a monetary refund for payments on services not yet rendered.[193] Furthermore, an employer in violation of a living-wage ordinance may be prohibited from future contracts for a term of years or until restitution has been fully paid.[194] Governments may also sue a covered employer for failure to comply with living-wage ordinances and seek remedies including, among others, payments to covered employees for unpaid wages and health care premiums.[195] Additionally, employers that fail to comply with these ordinances risk incurring fines for each violation; a greater fine is accrued for each day the violations remain uncured.[196]

Public Procurement Ordinances

Like living-wage ordinances, public procurement programs also use contractual choices to promote economic development and social justice.[197] Public procurement ordinances frequently give preference to local businesses for awarding bids on public projects.[198]

---

187. *See, e.g., Living Wage and Self-Sufficiency Resources*, UC BERKELEY LABOR CTR., http://laborcenter.berkeley.edu/livingwage/resources.shtml (last visited Dec. 29, 2013).

188. *Id.*

189. *See* San Diego Municipal Code, Art. 2 Admin. Code, Div. 42: City of San Diego Living Wage Ordinance § 22.4220 (b) [hereinafter San Diego Living Wage Ordinance].

190. *See, e.g., Living Wage and Self-Sufficiency Resources*, UC BERKELEY LABOR CTR., http://laborcenter.berkeley.edu/livingwage/resources.shtml (last visited Dec. 29, 2013).

191. *Id.*

192. *Id.*

193. *See, e.g.,* San Diego Living Wage Ordinance § 22.4230 (d)(1)(enforcement provisions).

194. *See, e.g.,* San Diego Living Wage Ordinance § 22.4230 (d)(2).

195. *See, e.g.,* San Diego Living Wage Ordinance § 22.4230 (d)(4)(i).

196. *See, e.g.,* San Diego Living Wage Ordinance § 22.4230 (d)(4)(ii).

197. For an examination of how governments use contracting to promote social justice, *see generally* CHRISTOPHER MCCRUDDEN, BUYING SOCIAL JUSTICE: EQUALITY, GOVERNMENT PROCUREMENT AND LEGAL CHANGE (2007).

198. *See* California Small Business Procurement and Contract Act, CAL. GOV'T CODE § 14835–47

On occasion, however, local government contracting choices have been used to impact global issues by structuring incentives to create changes in social policies.[199] For example, public authorities in the United States and Europe used procurement practices to protest apartheid by threatening corporations operating in South Africa with the loss of government contracts.[200]

Public procurement promises to be an important avenue for influencing corporate conduct, as sustainable and social procurement concepts gain ground and government authorities exercise such preferences. In the European Union, purchases by public authorities already account for an estimated 20 percent of GDP.[201] The European Commission has long acknowledged the potential social dividends public procurement policies in the EU member states could pay in promoting corporate respect for human rights and environmental protection.[202] In fact, the European Parliament has asked the European Commission to explore how social and environmental considerations could be integrated into public procurement and to educate public purchasers about the opportunities for greater integration of these considerations in their purchasing decisions.[203] The commission has also issued an interpretive communication on European community law relevant to public procurement.[204] Therefore, it is clear that governments are leveraging their dual

---

(West 2012). Public procurement ordinances allow governments to prefer domestic producers when procuring goods over producers from other countries. A simple example of public procurement is the government's purchase of domestically manufactured automobiles for police vehicles and other government uses. Such ordinances are often viewed as barriers to trade because they allow governments to procure goods from domestic producers that may be less efficient than those of foreign producers. Developing countries often use public procurement as a way to strengthen infant industries, and public procurement policies have been shown to have a meaningful impact on development. Victor Mosoti, *The WTO Agreement on Government Procurement: A Necessary Evil in the Legal Strategy for Development in the Poor World?* 25 U. PA. J. INT'L ECON. L. 593, 599 (2004). At the state level, procurement ordinances like California's allow the state government to give preference to companies that are either registered in or have their principle place of business in California when purchasing goods for government use. *See* Cal. Gov't Code §§ 14835–47. "Nothing in the purposes animating the commerce clause prohibits a State, in the absence of congressional action, from participating in the market and exercising the right to favor its own citizens over others." Hughes v. Alexandria Scrap Corp., 426 U.S. 794 (1976).

199. Christopher McCrudden, *Using Public Procurement to Achieve Social Outcomes*, 28 NATURAL RESOURCES FORUM, 257, 263 (2004).

200. *See* McCrudden, BUYING SOCIAL JUSTICE, *supra* note 197 at 9–10.

201. Christopher Bovis, *Where Does the Regulation of Public Procurement and Public Private Partnerships Take the Member States of the EU*, 2 EUR. PUB. PRIVATE PARTNERSHIP L. REV. 53, 53 (2011).

202. *See* Jan Wouters & Leen Chanet, *Corporate Human Rights Responsibility: A European Perspective*, 6 NW J. INT'L HUM. RTS. 262, 290 (2008); Peter Kunzlik, *Making the Market Work for the Environment: Acceptance of (Some) "Green" Contract Award Criteria in Public Procurement*, 15 J. ENVTL. L. 175,189 (2003).

203. *See* Wouters, *Corporate Human Rights Responsibility, supra* note 201 at 290 n.198 (citing Parliament Resolution 2002/278 on the Commission Green Paper on Promoting a European Framework for Corporate Social Responsibility (COM (2001) 366-C5-0161/2002/2069 (COS) of 30 May 2002, 2003 O.J. (C 187 E), Preamble, Recital J.)).

204. *Commission Interpretative Communication on the Community Law Applicable to Public Procurement and the Possibilities for Integrating Social Considerations into Public Procurement*, COM (2001).

role in the market as regulators and purchasers through procurement programs that take account of social criteria.

Comparative Approaches to Corporate Social Responsibility

As illustrated by socially conscious public procurement policies in the European Union, the United States is not alone in experimenting with creating incentives to promote greater corporate social responsibility. Legislative organs in other jurisdictions have also undertaken efforts to further define the responsibilities of corporations in global society. Additionally, courts outside the United States have exercised jurisdiction over corporations accused of engaging in conduct contrary to respect for human rights.[205] A few examples are discussed below.

Litigation

Though the future of civil litigation in the United States against corporations for their role in human rights abuses has been sharply curtailed by the Supreme Court's recent decision in *Kiobel* (discussed earlier), similar suits against corporations have been and continue to be filed in other jurisdictions. Several resolutions of the European Parliament speak to the question of civil liability for corporate conduct abroad alleged to involve human rights abuses.[206] European conflict-of-laws regulations allow the courts of EU member states to assert jurisdiction over cases against corporations registered or domiciled in the European Union for damages sustained in third countries.[207] Therefore, "courts of EU Member States are competent to adjudicate civil proceedings against corporations based in the EU for acts which have taken place outside the EU even if the damage occurred outside the EU and the victim is not domiciled in the EU."[208]

Such cases have been filed in the English High Court against companies such as BP Exploration Co. for their environmental impact in Colombia. A Belgian court entertained the claims of refugees from Myanmar who brought suit against TotalFinaElf, alleging the company was complicit in crimes associated with the construction and operation of a pipeline committed against civilians by the Myanmar military.[209] One episode has spawned litigation across multiple jurisdictions against the Dutch multinational Trafigura after a ship chartered by its London office unloaded a waste shipment in the Côte d'Ivoire and residents near

---

205. For additional information on such developments outside the U.S., see the chapters by Chambers and Tyler, Srinivasan, and Muchlinski and Rouas in this book.

206. *See, e.g.,* Wouter, *supra* note 201, at 295 n.234.

207. *See, e.g.,* Wouter, *supra* note 201, at 295 n.235.

208. *See, e.g.,* Wouter, *supra* note 201, at 295.

209. *Case Profile: Total Lawsuit in Belgium (re Myanmar)*, Bus. & Human Rights Res. Ctr., http://www .business-humanrights.org/Categories/Lawlawsuits/Lawsuitsregulatoryaction/LawsuitsSelectedcases/ TotallawsuitinBelgiumreBurma (last visited Dec. 29, 2013).

the disposal sites became ill.[210] Proceedings were instituted against the corporation in the Netherlands, the United Kingdom, and France.[211] A case commenced by Nigerian farmers and the Friends of the Earth against Shell in the Netherlands seeking reparation for environmental contamination concluded with the court finding the firm's Nigerian subsidiary liable for damage and ordering the subsidiary to pay compensation.[212]

Reporting Regulation

Though some European commentators lament that European approaches to corporate social responsibility are "both broad and underdeveloped,"[213] to the extent that certain member states of the European Union already do mandate reporting on matters that are not financial, the European policy agenda on corporate social responsibility appears more established than current U.S. efforts. On the other hand, it was after the U.S. Congress passed section 1504 of the Dodd-Frank Act that the European Commission issued draft directives requiring companies listed on EU stock exchanges to disclose their payments to governments for oil, gas, minerals, and timber.[214] Individual European nations appear to be working toward transparency on social issues relevant to corporate respect for human rights, even though EU law currently does not formally require companies to adopt policies or report on CSR efforts.[215] Nevertheless, a conceptual shift in the status of CSR is emerging in the European Union as the commission has explicitly departed from an earlier definition of CSR as "a concept whereby companies integrate social and environmental concerns in their business operations and in their interaction with their stakeholders on a

---

210. Case *Profile: Trafigura Lawsuits (re Cote d' Ivoire)*, BUS. & HUMAN RIGHTS RES. CTR., http://www.business-humanrights.org/Categories/Lawlawsuits/Lawsuitsregulatoryaction/LawsuitsSelectedcases/TrafiguralawsuitsreCtedIvoire (last visited Apr. 27, 2012).

211. *See* Rob Evans, *Trafigura Fined €1M for Exporting Toxic Waste to Africa*, THE GUARDIAN (UK, July 23, 2010).

212. *Shell Nigeria Case: Court Acquits Firm on Most Charges*, BBC NEWS AFRICA (Jan. 30, 2013) http://www.bbc.co.uk/news/world-africa-21258653. *See also* Friday Alfred Akpan v. Royal Dutch Shell, PLC, Judgment District Court of the Hauge, Docket No. C/09/337070/HA ZA 09-1580 (Jan. 30, 2013) (declaratory judgment: subsidiary committed specific tort of negligence insufficiently securing against sabotage and oil spills and ordering compensation for damages suffered).

213. *See, e.g.*, Ruben Zandvliet, *Corporate Social Responsibility Reporting in the European Union: Towards a More Univocal Framework*, 18 COLUM. J. EUR. L. F. 38 (2011).

214. *See* Revenue Watch, U.S. and EU Standards, *supra* note 103, at 1. *See also*, Barbara Lewis, *EU Politicians Vote for Tough Oil, Gas Anti-corruption Law*, REUTERS CANADA (Sept. 18, 2012), http://ca.reuters.com/article/topNews/idCABRE88H0LE20120918.

215. The current EU CSR Strategy makes clear that while it is planning to legislate in the area of reporting and public procurement pertaining to human rights, CSR remains a voluntary initiative within the EU sphere. *Communication from the Commission to the European Parliament, the Council, the European Economic and Social Committee and the Committee of the Regions: A Renewed EU Strategy 2011-14 for Corporate Social Responsibility*, EUROPEAN COMMISSION, http://ec.europa.eu/enterprise/policies/sustainable-business/files/csr/new-csr/act_en.pdf. For a review of measures taken by different jurisdictions, *see* STEVE LYDENBERG & KATIE GRACE, INNOVATIONS IN SOCIAL AND ENVIRONMENTAL DISCLOSURE OUTSIDE THE UNITED STATES (2008), http://www.domini.com/common/pdf/Innovations_in_Disclosure.pdf.

voluntary basis."[216] More recently, in its renewed CSR strategy communication, the commission defines CSR as "the responsibility of enterprises for their impacts on society,"[217] wording conceptually more in line with that presented in the Guiding Principles on business and human rights, discussed below. It also emphasizes the importance of having processes in place for corporations to "integrate social, environmental, ethical, human rights, and consumer concerns into their business operations and core strategy in close collaboration with their stakeholders" to minimize adverse impacts and maximize "the creation of shared value" for shareholders and society at large.[218]

Two directives of the European Parliament are worthy of note with respect to recent developments in CSR and human rights in the region: the Accounts Modernization Directive and the Unfair Commercial Practices Directive. The Accounts Modernization Directive amends earlier directives that had informed provisions of company law in Europe with respect to reporting and accounting. It provides that annual reports should, where "necessary" to understand a company's position or performance, include "non-financial key performance indicators relevant to the particular business, including information relating to environmental and employee matters."[219] Reporting requirements under the Modernization Directive have been deemed by some as "ambiguous" due to the lack of clarity on what actually encompasses an environmental or employment issue to be reported.[220] The Modernization Directive has been seen as "undemanding" due to the wide discretion vested in corporations regarding whether and what to report.[221]

Several member states of the European Union have implemented, and many have even enhanced, the non-financial reporting measures of the directive. For instance, French law mandates disclosure of non-financial performance measures.[222] This requirement means that corporations listed on the French stock exchange are required to comment on the social and environmental consequences of their activities in their annual reports.[223] Belgium, Germany, and the United Kingdom all mandate disclosures by pension-fund managers.[224] Under these disclosure requirements, managers of pension funds must

---

216. *See* Beate Sjafjell & Linn Anker-Sorensen, *Directors' Duties and CSR* (forthcoming 2013) (citing COM (2001) 366 final).

217. *Id.* (citing COM (2011) 681 final, Section 3.1).

218. *Id* (citing COM (2011) 681 final, section 3.2).

219. *Id.* (citing Parliament and Council Directive L 178/16, Amending Directives 78/660/EEC, 83/349/EEC, 86/635/EEC and 91/674/EEC on the annual and consolidated accounts of certain types of companies, banks, and other financial institutions and insurance undertakings, 2003 O.J. (L 178) 16 (EC) (Articles 1.4 and 2.10 of the Directive pertains to annual reporting and consolidated annual reporting)).

220. *Id.*

221. Zandvliet, *supra* note 213 at 39.

222. Anna Triponel, *Business & Human Rights Law: Diverging Trends in the United States and France*, 23 Am. U. Int'l L. Rev., 855, 878 (2007) (citing Law No. 2001-420 of May 15, 2001, Journal Officiel de la Republique Francaise [J.O.] [Official Gazette of France], May 16, 2001 at 7776).

223. *Id.*

224. *See* Occupational Pension Schemes (Investment, and Assignment, Forfeiture, Bankruptcy, etc.)

reveal whether and how social, environmental, and ethical issues inform investment decisions.[225] Denmark has integrated international CSR instruments (discussed below) into its reporting requirements.[226]

The Unfair Commercial Practices Directive prohibits false and misleading advertisements and renders the use of unfair commercial practices that improperly distort transactional decision-making actionable under EU law.[227] This directive does not exclude representations made by corporations with respect to social or environmental impacts. Therefore, it is feasible that "inaccurate or incomplete representations by corporations about CSR or their adherence to and compliance with voluntary codes of conduct [could] be attacked."[228] Litigation brought against Nike in California under state laws prohibiting unfair business practices and false advertising raised similar claims.

The directive prohibits commercial practices that (1) conflict with professional diligence obligations and (2) alter materially or are likely to alter materially the typical consumer's choices, distorting his or her decision-making with respect to a product.[229] Put another way, it is unfair under EU law for commercial advertisements to "appreciably impair the consumer's ability to make an informed decision, thereby causing the consumer to take a transactional decision that he [or she] would not have taken otherwise."[230] The efforts of EU member states to enforce the directive range widely from self-regulation to regulations enforced by government agencies, which suggests that application of the directive in relation to social and environmental considerations might be inconsistent. Nevertheless,

---

Amendment Regulations, 1999 S.I. 1999/1849, reg. 11A(a) (UK) (amending Occupational Pension Schemes (Investment) Regulations, 1996, SI 1996/3127 (UK)); Local Government Pension Scheme (Management and Investment of Funds) (Amendment) Regulations, 1999, S.I. 1999/3259 (UK) (amending Local Government Pension Scheme (Management and Investment of Funds) Regulations, 1998, S.I. 1198/1831 (UK)); Law Concerning Supplementary Pensions and the Fiscal Regime of Such Pensions and of Certain Supplementary Benefits Concerning Social Security (April, 28, 2003) art. 42, §1 (F.R.G.); *see also* Wouters, *supra* note 176, at 285 n.158 (listing citations to the laws of member states that have exceeded EU reporting requirements).

225. *See* Wouters, *supra* note 176, at 285 n. 158.

226. Karin Buhmann, *Migration of CSR-Related International Norms into Companies Self-Regulation Through Company Law: The Danish CSR Reporting Requirement*, 2 EUR. BUS. L. REV. 187, 187–216 (2013) (Danish reporting provisions allow companies participating in the United Nations Global Compact that have submitted a Communication of Progress (CoP) to "double" as the company's CSR report for statutory purposes).

227. *Id.* at 287.

228. *Id.* at 287.

229. *Id.* at 287 n.174 (citing Parliament Directive (EC) 2005/29, Concerning Unfair Business-to-Consumer Commercial Practices in the Internal Market and Amending Council Directive 84/450 (EEC), Directives 97/7 (EC), 98/27 (EC) and 2002/65 (EC) of the Council of the European Parliament and the Council and Regulation (EC) No 2006/2004 of the European Parliament and of the Council, (November 6,2005) sec. 1, 2006 O.J. (L 149) 22. Arts. 5, 6).

230. Parliament Directive (EC) NO 2006/2004 of the European Parliament and of the Council, (November 6, 2005) Sec. 1, 2006 O.J. (449) 22. Art. 2(e).

the directive does demonstrate a trend toward demanding greater transparency on the part of businesses where business practices may place human rights at risk.

Multi-stakeholder Processes Taking Stock of Stakeholder Interests

Complementing the binding regulatory moves toward greater transparency are several nonbinding policies, principles, and cooperative platforms now in place to promote greater corporate social responsibility. In some instances voluntary initiatives have informed the content of binding regulations. A few examples are outlined briefly below, starting with the most recent global project to articulate more clearly the responsibilities of corporations with respect to human rights.

The UN Framework and Guiding Principles

The UN secretary-general special representatives for business and human rights issued Guiding Principles for the Implementation of the UN "Protect, Respect and Remedy" Framework after consultation with a broad range of stakeholders. The Guiding Principles offer operative guidance to states and businesses and clarify the roles and responsibilities of each as to three core principles: (1) the duty of states to protect against human rights abuses by third parties, including business enterprises; (2) the responsibility of corporations to respect human rights by avoiding human rights infringements and by addressing adverse human rights impacts in which they are involved; and (3) access to judicial and nonjudicial remedies for victims of rights abuses. The Guiding Principles offer both foundational and operational guidance to corporations concerning their human rights responsibilities.[231]

Some human rights campaign groups have expressed disappointment that the Framework and Guiding Principles did not go further in creating binding obligations for corporations and regret that the international community has failed to produce a legally binding framework for ensuring accountability.[232] Proponents of the process that generated the Framework and Guiding Principles point out that industry's involvement indicates that it is a pragmatic way of addressing the problems that concern campaigners. Though it is early to assess the likelihood of their success, the Framework and Guiding Principles

---

231. UN Spec. Rep. of the Sec'y-Gen., *Protect, Respect and Remedy: A Framework for Business and Human Rights*, UN Doc. A/HRC/8/5 (April 7, 2008), http://www.reports-and-materials.org/Ruggie-report-7 -Apr-2008.pdf. For further detail on the Guiding Principles, *see* Part I of this book.

232. *Joint Civil Society Statement on the draft Guiding Principles on Business and Human Rights*, FIDH-WORLDWIDE HUMAN RIGHTS MOVEMENT (Jan. 2011), http://www.fidh.org/Joint-Civil-Society-Statement-on ,9066. For a discussion of the shortcomings of soft law and voluntary instruments to address the role of business in rights abuses, *see generally* Christopher Albin-Lackey, *Without Rules: A Failed Approach to Corporate Accountability*, in WORLD REPORT 2013 (Human Rights Watch ed. 2013) http://www.hrw.org /world-report/2013/essays/without-rules.

provide a salient starting point from which to advance human rights and to put the issue of business practices that impair the enjoyment of human rights on the public agenda.

The U.S. government, among others, has embraced the Guiding Principles and made them the basis of the U.S. Government Approach on Business and Human Rights. It cites the Guiding Principles as a "minimum" standard of conduct for states and businesses and points to both reputational and legal benefits of adherence. The approach also appears to frame human rights standards as a basis of business innovation and economic growth.[233]

At the conclusion of the special representative's mandate, the UN Human Rights Council established a "working group on the issue of human rights and transnational corporations and other business enterprises."[234] The working group consists of five independent experts who are appointed by the council with an appreciation for achieving a balanced geographical representation of stakeholders to serve for a three-year term. Among other things, the group has been charged with the responsibility to "promote the effective and comprehensive dissemination and implementation" of the Guiding Principles; to "seek and receive information from all relevant sources, including governments, transnational corporations and other business enterprises, national human rights institutions, civil society and rights-holders" to promote good practices for implementing the Guiding Principles; to "provide support for efforts to promote capacity-building" and "provide advice and recommendations regarding the development of domestic legislation and policies relating to business and human rights"; to "integrate a gender perspective throughout the mandate"; and to "explore options and make recommendations at the national, regional, and international levels for enhancing access to effective remedies available to those whose human rights are affected by corporate activities."[235]

The working group also conducts country visits to support the work of its mandate.[236] The working group made its first country visit to Mongolia in 2012 and conducted a country visit to the United States in 2013. It will report its findings annually to the Human Rights Council and the General Assembly.[237]

The UN Global Compact

A strategic policy initiative of the United Nations, the UN Global Compact provides a forum for businesses that have expressed a commitment to aligning their business practices with ten principles in the areas of human rights, labor, the environment, and anticorruption.

---

233. *U.S. Government Approach on Business and Human Rights*, U.S. STATE DEP'T, BUREAU OF DEMOCRACY, HUMAN RIGHTS AND LABOR (May 1, 2013), http://www.humanrights.gov/2013/05/01/u-s-government-approach-on-business-and-human-rights/.

234. Human Rights and Transnational Corporations and Other Business Enterprises, Human Rights Council, 17th Sess. Agenda item 3 A/HRC/17/L.17/Rev. 1.

235. *Id* at ¶ 5.

236. *Id* at ¶ 5(d).

237. A/HRC/17/L.17/Rev.1.

The human rights principles contained in the compact provide the following: "(1) [b]usi-nesses should support and respect the protection of internationally proclaimed human rights; and (2) make sure that they are not complicit in human rights abuses."[238]

Understanding business as a driver of globalization and appreciating the challenges and opportunities businesses confront in a global economy, the Global Compact serves as a platform for business to collaborate and partner with governments, civil society, labor, and the United Nations. Hopefully these partnerships will ensure that more ben-efits than burdens accrue to society as a result of cooperation and collaboration to confront common challenges.

To achieve better human rights outcomes, the Global Compact "seeks to combine the best properties of the UN, such as moral authority and convening power, with the pri-vate sector's solution-finding strengths, and the expertise and capacities of a range of key stakeholders."[239] Its stated approach is to do so as a complement, rather than as a sub-stitute, for regulatory regimes. Still, it commands a measure of accountability associated with participation in the compact, and it has periodically expelled participants for failure to comply with compact commitments.[240]

After the Guiding Principles were adopted, the compact and the United Nations Office of the High Commissioner for Human Rights (OHCHR) issued a statement on the rela-tionship between the Guiding Principles and compact commitments.[241] According to the OHCHR, the Guiding Principles "provide further conceptual and operational clarity" to the human rights commitments contained in the compact.[242] Because the Guiding Principles are a global standard and apply to all business enterprises, they "provide an authoritative framework" for compact participants to implement their commitments.[243] Because the compact has a global network of participants, it is well positioned to provide the support necessary to put the Guiding Principles into practice.[244]

---

238. *The Ten Principles*, UN GLOBAL COMPACT, http://www.unglobalcompact.org/aboutthegc/thetenprinciples/index.html (last visited Dec. 29, 2013).

239. *Id.*

240. Jo Confino, *Cleaning up the Global Compact Dealing with Corporate Free Riders*, THE GUARD-IAN (Mar. 26, 2012), http://www.guardian.co.uk/sustainable-business/cleaning-up-un-global-compact-green-wash (analyzing the reasons 3,100 businesses have been delisted by the UN Global Compact in recent years); Cristina Garza, *U.S. Companies Drag their Feet on UN Global Compact*, TRIPLE PUNDIT: PEOPLE, PLANET, PROFIT (May 24, 2013), http://www.triplepundit.com/2013/05/companies-dragging-f eet-sign-global-compact/ (reporting that as of May 2013 6 percent of the large U.S. participants and 23 percent of small and medium size U.S. participants have been delisted from the UN Global Compact).

241. *The UN Guiding Principles on Business and Human Rights: Relationship to UN Global Compact Commitments* (July 2011), http://www.unglobalcompact.org/docs/issues_doc/human_rights/Resources/GPs_GC%20note.pdf (describing the Guiding Principles as providing "further conceptual and operational clarity" for Principle 1 and Principle 2 of the Global Compact), http://www.unglobalcompact.org/docs/issues_doc/human_rights/Resources/GPs_GC%20note.pdf.

242. *Id.*

243. *Id.* at 2.

244. E-mail from Michael Addo, Member of the United Nations Working Group on Business and

The UN Human Rights Council recently commended the compact for its work on human rights tools.[245] The compact reports that the working group considers the Global Compact network to be "one of the most important channels" through which to achieve uptake and implementation of the Guiding Principles.[246] The compact also hosted the working group's roundtable dialogue with representatives of the business community during the group's recent country visit to the United States.[247]

The executive director of the Global Compact contributed to the development of the Framework and Guiding Principles issued by the UN secretary-general's special representative on business and human rights development. The compact continues to maintain a close relationship with the UN working group that was created to continue the work of the special representative and put the principles into practice.[248] In fact, a member of the UN working group is based in the Global Compact office.[249]

Where the Guiding Principles set forth a minimum standard, participants in the Global Compact have committed to strive for more than the minimum. For example, though the Guiding Principles speak of undertaking efforts to avoid adverse impacts, the compact speaks of undertaking efforts to advance the realization of human rights.[250] Perhaps for this reason, Global Compact publications continue to refer to companies possessing "spheres of influence,"[251] a term expressly rejected by the Guiding Principles in favor of the term *leverage*. However, because the compact predated the Guiding Principles, compact materials are being updated to better reflect the Guiding Principles.[252] The processes and priorities of each are different but complementary; both the Guiding Principles and

---

Human Rights, Special Procedures of the United Nations Human Rights Council to Erika George, Professor of Law, University of Utah, S.J. Quinney College of Law (June 6, 2013) (on file with author).

245. Human Rights Council Res. 21/5, Rep. of the Human Rights Council, 21st Sess., UN Doc. A/HRC/RES/21/5 (Oct. 16, 2012); Robert C. Blitt, *Beyond Ruggie's Guiding Principles on Business and Human Rights: Charting an Embracive Approach to Corporate Human Rights Compliance*, 48 Tex. Int'l L.J. 33, 51–61 (Fall 2012); Jena Martin Amerson, *"The End of the Beginning?" A Comprehensive Look at the UN's Business and Human Rights Agenda from a Bystander Perspective*, 17 Fordham J. Corp. & Fin. L. 871, 890–96 (treating the UN Global Compact as a piece of the history building toward the Guiding Principles).

246. E-mail from Ursula A. Wynhoven, General Counsel UN Global Compact Office, to Erika George, Professor of Law, University of Utah, S.J. Quinney College of Law (Jun. 3, 2013)(on file with author).

247. Press Release, UN Global Compact, U.S. Companies Discuss Guiding Principles on Business and Human Rights (Apr. 29, 2013) (on file with author).

248. *Id.*

249. *Id.*

250. *The UN Guiding Principles on Business and Human Rights: Relationship to UN Global Compact Commitments* (July 2011), http://www.unglobalcompact.org/docs/issues_doc/human_rights/Resources/GPs_GC%20note.pdf (describing the Guiding Principles as providing "further conceptual and operational clarity" for Principle 1 and Principle 2 of the Global Compact).

251. UN Global Compact brochure, http://www.unglobalcompact.org/docs/news_events/8.1/GC_brochure_FINAL.pdf.

252. E-mail from Michael Addo, Member of the United Nations Working Group on Business and Human Rights, Special Procedures of the United Nations Human Rights Council, to Erika George, Professor of Law, University of Utah, S.J. Quinney College of Law (Jun. 6, 2013) (on file with author).

the compact are "part of a wider process within the UN to secure business engagement with human rights."

Voluntary Initiatives, Nongovernmental Advocacy, Shareholder Activism

Though campaigners tend to speak the language of human rights, some corporations have engaged with human rights issues using the language of corporate social responsibility. For instance, some corporations have created codes of conduct in cooperation with multiple stakeholders.[253] Discussed below are a few examples of voluntary initiatives, selected for their contribution to the creation of recent binding reporting legislation (as reviewed above) or for their potential to inform future efforts to further define corporate obligations to respect human rights.

Extractive Industries Transparency Initiative

The Extractive Industries Transparency Initiative[254] (EITI) is of particular relevance given the Dodd-Frank conflict-mineral provisions. It is a multi-stakeholder organization of governments, corporations engaged in resource extraction, and concerned civil society groups. EITI is considered "a focal point for the movement to promote greater transparency" between extractive companies and governments in resource-rich, but often economically poor, countries.[255] This initiative aims to "increase transparency over payments and revenues in the extractives sector in countries heavily dependent on these resources."[256] In other words, EITI is an effort to reverse the *resource curse* by disclosing financial transactions to counter the kinds of corruption often at the root of rights violations.[257]

The EITI framework contains twelve principles related to transparency, government accountability, sustainable economic growth, and national sovereignty, among other topics.[258] Countries can commit to being EITI compliant by requiring extractive companies that operate within their borders "to report their oil, gas and mining payments, which are then reconciled against reported receipts from the government and made public."[259] Currently,

---

253. *See, e.g.*, THE VOLUNTARY PRINCIPLES ON SECURITY AND HUMAN RIGHTS, http://www.voluntaryprinciples.org; EXTRACTIVE INDUSTRIES TRANSPARENCY INITIATIVE, http://eitransparency.org/eiti/principles; GLOBAL REPORTING INITIATIVE, https://www.globalreporting.org/Pages/default.aspx (last visited Dec. 29, 2013)

254. EXTRACTIVE INDUSTRY TRANSPARENCY INITIATIVE, http://eiti.org/ (last visited May 11, 2012).

255. Matthew Genasci & Sarah Pray, *Extracting Accountability: The Implications of the Resource Curse for CSR Theory and Practice*, 11 YALE HUM. RTS. & DEV. L.J. 37, 51 (2008).

256. *Statement of Principles and Agreed Objectives*, EXTRACTIVE INDUSTRIES TRANSPARENCY INITIATIVE, http://info.worldbank.org/etools/docs/library/57454/eiti_stat_of_principles.pdf (last visited Dec. 29, 2013).

257. *Id.*

258. *Id.*

259. Genasci & Pray, *supra* note 255, at 51.

there are twenty-one EITI-compliant countries and sixteen EITI candidate countries.[260] Additionally, extractive companies operating in EITI-implementing countries can choose to become EITI-supporting companies by declaring support and endorsement of the EITI principals, and supporting EITI through annual financial contributions.[261] Over eighty oil, gas, and mining companies have chosen to support the EITI in this way.[262]

Before EITI, governments of resource-rich countries kept confidential the revenues obtained from commercial actors engaged in natural resource extraction. The shroud of secrecy cloaked corruption. Multinational firms seeking to secure valuable concessions to exploit resource-rich areas often ignored misappropriation. Now, many EITI countries are demonstrating significant improvements in their interactions with extractive companies. For example, Nigeria, which was one of the first countries to begin implementing the EITI process, is now not only an EITI-compliant country, but it has initiated transparency measures that go beyond the EITI requirements.[263]

The EITI's efficacy has been questioned because it is a purely voluntary organization.[264] Nevertheless, the EITI's impact has been far-reaching.[265] The Dodd-Frank provisions and other reporting legislation build on the efforts of the EITI in promoting corporate transparency and accountability regarding the human rights impacts of extractive companies. In fact, it was referenced in the floor debates over section 1504 of the Dodd-Frank Act, and an explicit reference is made to the EITI in the legislation.[266]

The Kimberley Process

Another voluntary global initiative developed by government, industry, and civil society representatives is the Kimberley Process Certification Scheme (KPCS).[267] KPCS seeks to stem the flow of conflict diamonds into the stream of commerce to reduce the ability of armed groups to use rough diamonds to finance violent opposition against legitimate

---

260. *EITI Countries*, EXTRACTIVE INDUSTRY TRANSPARENCY INITIATIVE, http://eiti.org/countries (last visited May 11, 2013).

261. *Supporting Companies*, EXTRACTIVE INDUSTRY TRANSPARENCY INITIATIVE, http://eiti.org/supporters /companies (last visited May 29, 2013).

262. *Company Support of the EITI*, EXTRACTIVE INDUSTRY TRANSPARENCY INITIATIVE, http://eiti.org /supporters/companies/howto (last visited May 29, 2013).

263. Dr. Peter Eigen, *Fighting Corruption in a Global Economy: Transparency Initiatives in the Oil and Gas Industry*, 29 HOUS. J. INT'L L. 327, 339–40 (2007).

264. Martin Sandbu, *Regulation: Voluntary Transparency Scheme Faces Scrutiny*, FIN. TIMES (June 17, 2010), http://www.ft.com/intl/cms/s/0/dd252206-78da-11df-a312-00144feabdc0.html#axzz2gQEsFebV.

265. *See, e.g.*, Paul D. Ocheje, *The Extractive Industries Transparency Initiative (EITI): Voluntary Codes of Conduct, Poverty and Accountability in Africa*, 8 J. SUSTAINABLE DEV. IN AFR. 222, 232–33 (2006) (assessing implementation of the EITI audit program in Nigeria as a significant shift from *business as usual* with broader consequences for transparency in other areas).

266. Dodd-Frank § 1504 (codified at 15 U.S.C. § 78m(q)(1)(C)(ii) (2012)).

267. Governments from Angola to Zimbabwe are members. For a full list of the fifty participating governments in the KPCS as of January 2012, *see* http://www.kimberleyprocess.com/web/kimberley-process /kp-participants-and-observers.

governments. Proponents of the KPCS have credited it with reducing conflict in several countries. Opponents critical of KPCS contend that incentives to comply have not been sufficiently resolved, such that the benefits of noncompliance significantly outweigh the costs of compliance, resulting in even more diamonds on the black market.[268]

Recently, the KCPS has come under serious challenge from Global Witness, a nongovernmental organization instrumental in its creation.[269] In 2011, Global Witness left the KCPS in protest over a series of "shoddy compromise[s]" that have "turned an international conflict prevention mechanism into a cynical corporate accreditation scheme" and served to undermine the integrity and earlier achievements of the KCPS.[270]

The two predecessor bills to Dodd-Frank § 1502 (U.S., Bill S. 891, Congo Conflict Minerals Act of 2009, 111th Cong., 2009, and U.S., Bill H.R. 4128, Conflict Minerals Trade Act of 2009, 111th Cong., 2009) did incorporate the critiques of KPCS into their deliberations and intended to overcome some of its shortcomings.[271]

The Electronic Industry Citizenship Coalition

The Electronic Industry Citizenship Coalition (EICC) administers a code of conduct throughout the information and communications technology (ICT) supply chain.[272] Currently, nearly eighty member companies located across Asia, the Americas, and Europe make up the EICC.[273] The overall objectives of the EICC are to (1) create a code of conduct common across the industry; (2) establish a process for the assessment and administration of supply chains to address sourcing, employment, and environmental concerns; (3) provide training and education to improve social and environmental performance in the supply chain; and (4) raise external awareness through stakeholder engagement.[274]

Before the EICC was formed, the global electronics industry had no systems in place that would permit a corporation to determine easily the origins of materials used in products or the production process. Participation in the program is entirely voluntary

---

268. Competitive Enterprise Institute, In the Matter of Public Comments Proposed Rule: Conflict Minerals, Before the U.S. Securities and Exchange Commission Release No. 34-63547, File No. S7-40-10, 75 Fed. Reg. 80,948 (Dec. 23, 2010).

269. *Our History*, GLOBAL WITNESS, http://www.globalwitness.org/about-us/our-history (last visited Dec. 29, 2013) ("Our campaigning led to the creation of the precedent-setting Kimberley Process Certification Scheme and to our joint nomination for the Nobel Peace Prize.").

270. *Why We Are Leaving the Kimberley Process*, GLOBAL WITNESS (Dec. 5, 2011), http://www.globalwitness.org/library/why-we-are-leaving-kimberley-process-message-global-witness-founding-director-charmian-gooch.

271. Statement from Sen. Feingold about the Conflict Minerals Provision, S4697 (Apr. 23, 2009).

272. *See* Bob Leet, Presentation, *Introduction to the Electronic Industry Citizenship Coalition* (Apr. 12, 2011) [hereinafter EICC Introduction].

273. *Membership List*, ELECTRONIC INDUS. CITIZENSHIP COALITION, http://www.eicc.info/about_us05.shtml (last viewed May 11, 2013).

274. *Id.*

and limited to corporations.[275] Although corporate only, another EICC aim is to "solicit feedback from stakeholders" outside industry to better "focus efforts on positive social and environmental change and improvement."[276] The outcomes the EICC would like to achieve are increased efficiency and productivity for customers and suppliers, greater economic development, better working conditions, and cleaner environmental conditions.[277]

Because suppliers may have several different customers with different codes of conduct and different demands for implementation, multiple audits and assessments of the same supplier by different corporations can lead to an inefficient use of resources and inconsistent assessment findings.[278] Particularly given the rapid growth of initiatives to create better social and environmental outcomes in the supply chain, members of the coalition agreed to come together to create a common approach to aid suppliers. Though the trend in responsible supply-chain management is to form industry initiatives to tackle human rights problems in the supply chain,[279] it is important to note that these initiatives continue to have limited success. For instance, Apple (an EICC member) recently faced significant negative publicity surrounding its Foxconn supplier in China, where several workers committed suicide, allegedly due to poor working conditions at the factory.[280]

Conscious Consumers and Activist Investors

Recent transparency initiatives appear to share two related underlying rationales: (1) the influence of industry (such as those initiatives described above) can make a difference, and (2) the consuming public actually cares about people worlds away and will make different purchasing choices as they become conscious of the high costs imposed on others. For example, the author of the CTSCA deemed the bill a "consumer empowerment measure," explaining,

> Consumer spending and corporate investment in business are leverage points that can turn around a system that has for too long allowed traffickers and economies

---

275. *Id.*

276. *Id.*

277. *Id.*; *see generally* GHGM, SOCIAL AND ENVIRONMENTAL RESPONSIBILITY IN METAL SUPPLY TO THE ELECTRONIC INDUSTRY (2008), http://www.eicc.info/documents/SERMetalsSupplyreport.pdf.

278. *See, e.g,* The Global Enabling Trade Report 2012: Reducing Supply Chain Barriers, World Economic Forum 2012 (Robert Z. Lawrence, Margareta Drzeniek Hanous & Sean Doherty eds., 2012), http://www3.weforum.org/docs/GETR/2012/GlobalEnablingTrade_Report.pdf.

279. Sune Skadegaard Thorsen & Signe Andreasen, *Remodelling Responsible Supply Chain Management: The Corporate Responsibility to Respect Human Rights in Supply Chain Relationships*, in THE UN GUIDING PRINCIPLES ON BUSINESS AND HUMAN RIGHTS: FOUNDATIONS AND IMPLEMENTATION (Radu Mares ed., 2012).

280. Terrence O'Brien, *Apple and Foxconn Agree to Drastically Improve Working Conditions Following Fair Labor Association Report*, ENGADGET (Mar. 29, 2012), http://www.engadget.com/2012/03/29/apple-and-foxconn-agree-to-drastically-improve-working-condition/.

to operate with impunity. There is an increasing push for consumer transparency, certification, and more rigorous regulation.[281]

Similarly, the federal proposal to require supply-chain reporting is informed by an appreciation for the possibility that

> legislation is necessary to provide the information the public demands, recognizing that businesses can be part of the solution to these problems when they transparently provide information to consumers and investors, and subsequently respond to consumer and investor demands for business reasons, rather than solely reacting to governmental prescriptions on how to conduct their business.[282]

These fundamental assumptions about the market for altruism, if correct, could place a value on respect for human rights that has been largely absent in corporate social responsibility programs. Because these transparency initiatives solely and simply require information disclosure to the relevant regulatory authorities and the public without expressly prohibiting any particular business practice, enforcement appears to rest on whether consumers decide to make different choices. By preferring, perhaps, a conflict-free consumer electronic product assembled without using forced laborers, slaves, trafficking victims, or children over products associated with abuses, transparency may create a taste for respecting human rights.[283] For instance, consumer collaborations that share information about a variety of products provide support for the position that the recently enacted disclosure requirements could make a difference to a significant number of consumers.[284]

The Impact of Responsible Consumerism

Consumers who care about the environment and social issues are using social media to raise awareness about the origins of a wide range of consumer products and educate the public about human rights abuses. Consider the following examples:

---

281. The California Transparency in Supply Chains Act of 2010: New Information to Aid Consumer Purchasing Decisions, Before the Assembly Committee on the Judiciary (June 29, 2010), http://www.leginfo.ca.gov/pub/09-10/bill/sen/sb_0651-0700/sb_657_cfa_20100628_112914_asm_comm.html.

282. *Supra* note 177 §1(c)(3).

283. For profiles and analysis of social-conscious consumers and cause-marketing, *see generally* NIELSEN, THE GLOBAL, SOCIALLY-CONSCIOUS CONSUMER (2012); Jens Hainmueller, Michael J. Hiscox & Sandra Sequeira, *Consumer Demand for the Fair Trade Label: Evidence from a Field Experiment* (2011), http://papers.ssrn.com/sol3/papers.cfm?abstract_id=1801942; Maria Loureiro & Justus Lotade, *Do Fair Trade and Eco-Labels in Coffee Wake Up the Consumer Conscience?* 53 ECOLOGICAL ECON. 129 (2005); DANISH FASHION INST., THE NICE CONSUMER: RESEARCH SUMMARY AND DISCUSSION PAPER (2012).

284. *See, e.g.*, Richard E. White & Philip D. Kare, *The Impact of Consumer Boycotts on the Stock Prices of Target Firms*, 6 J. APPLIED BUS. RES. 63, 69 (2011) ("[C]onsumer Boycott announcements appear to have a statistically significant negative effect on stock prices."); *cf.* Martinne Geller, *Wal-Mart Shares Drop 4.7 Percent after Bribery Allegations*, REUTERS (Apr. 23, 2012).

- The Web site www.slaveryfootprint.org helps consumers detect whether slave labor may have been used to produce an item.[285] Visitors to this Web site are invited to take a scored survey to understand the way their product choices contribute to modern-day slavery. The Web site encourages visitors to share their total "slave score" with their friends and ask their favorite brands for information about modern slavery in their supply chains. Slaveryfootprint's mobile application Free World allows consumers to find out about products at point of purchase.

- The Web site www.chainstorereaction.com, in collaboration with the Alliance to Stop Slavery and End Trafficking (ASSET), facilitates forwarding e-letters to industry from concerned consumers. To date, more than 150,000 communications have been forwarded to more than 1,700 companies.

- The Web site www.sourcemap.com offers an interactive platform for exchanging information about sourcing and supply-chain links. An open, "crowdsourced" directory of product supply chains and carbon footprints, the Web site allows members to learn where products come from, what they are made of, and how the product may impact people or the planet.

- The mobile application Buycott, available for free on iOS and Android, allows consumers to create "campaign" lists of issues they do not want their purchasing to support. Users simply scan the barcode of a product using Buycott, and the application checks its crowdsourced databases for parent companies and their connections to the user's campaigns. Users also create campaigns and provide information on unknown products and company contact information.[286]

- The Web site www.goodguide.com provides a rating system that allows users to evaluate the negative impact of products they use on issues they care about. It also allows users to create and share products lists that receive positive ratings for their issues.

Additionally, a certain segment of consumers make purchasing decisions based on their social commitments to respect for human rights and environmental protection.[287] For instance, with respect to the conflict in the DRC, university students participating in the Conflict Free Campus Initiative have urged their universities to adopt investment and technology-procurement policies that avoid contributing to humanitarian crises.[288] These

---

285. Beth Duff-Brown, *Slave Labor Targeted in Calif. Law, Social Media*, ASSOCIATED PRESS (Dec. 30, 2011) (reporting project was developed with grant from Google).

286. *About Buycott*, BUYCOTT, http://www.buycott.com/about (last visited June 6, 2013). *See also* Andrew Leonhard, *App of the Week: Buycott*, SALON (June 2, 2013), http://www.salon.com/2013/06/02 /app_of_the_week_buycott/ (reviewing the application).

287. *See, e.g.*, CONE LLC, 2010 CONE CAUSE EVOLUTION STUDY 14 (2010) (reporting survey results on consumer attitudes and behaviors toward corporate support of social and environmental issues).

288. *See, e.g.*, Kate Dailey, *How to Offset Your Conflict Mineral Guilt*, BBC NEWS MAGAZINE (Jan. 19, 2012), http://www.bbc.co.uk/news/magazine-16535620. University student groups using Facebook as a platform are working to raise awareness of issues associated with conflict minerals and advocated

types of consumer campaigns are not new; they follow initiatives such as the state and university divestment campaign to protest apartheid. [289] However, as these conscious consumers share their concerns about business practices with others, there are bound to be implications for industry.

The Impact of Activist Investing

Similarly, the increasing popularity of sustainable and responsible investing (SRI) offers evidence that expectations are escalating with respect to the social responsibility of business.[290] Although SRI remains a niche area, it is expanding rapidly.[291] By April 2013, the UN Principles for Responsible Investment reported that its signatory institutions accounted for socially responsible investments approximating $34 trillion in assets under management.[292] Although only about 11 percent of investments target companies that meet criteria based on social, environmental, or good corporate-governance criteria,[293] the SRI market has grown at a faster pace than the market for conventional investments.[294] Furthermore, the

---

for universities to adopt procurement policies that do not contribute to worsening crisis. *See* Conflict-Free Campus Initiative Facebook page, FACEBOOK, http://www.facebook.com/conflictfreecampus; *see also Conflict Free Campus Initiative*, RAISE HOPE FOR CONGO, http://www.raisehopeforcongo.org/content/conflict-free-campus-initiative.

289. Margaret Jungk, *Shareholders Pressure McDonald's to Report Human Rights Impacts*, HUFF POST BUSINESS: THE BLOG (May 22, 2013), http://www.huffingtonpost.com/margaret-jungk/mcdonalds-shareholders-no_b_3317423.html (citing the pressure investors put on religious institutions during apartheid as the parent of more recent shareholder resolutions demanding companies such as Halliburton, Yahoo, and Google assess their human rights impacts).

290. According to a 2011 report, nearly one out of every eight dollars invested in the U.S. using professional management is invested according to SRI strategies. Meg Voorhes & Joshua Humphreys, *Recent Trends in Sustainable and Responsible Investing in the United States*, 20 J. OF INVESTING 90, 90 (2011).

291. Forbes reports regularly on stocks that receive positive rankings from ETF Channel's rankings of socially responsible dividends. Recent U.S. companies to receive such praise include Texas Instruments (3.3% yield) and AvalonBay Communities, Inc. (3.2% yield). *See Why Texas Instruments Is a Top 25 Socially Responsible Dividend Stock*, FORBES DIVIDEND CHANNEL (Mar. 22, 2013), http://www.forbes.com/sites/dividendchannel/2013/03/22/why-texas-instruments-is-a-top-25-socially-responsible-dividend-stock/; *AVB Named Top 25 Socially Responsible Dividend Stock*, FORBES DIVIDEND CHANNEL (May 31, 2013), http://www.forbes.com/sites/dividendchannel/2013/05/31/avb-named-top-25-socially-responsible-dividend-stock/; ETF Channel Staff, *25 Top Ranked Socially Responsible Dividend Stocks*, ETF CHANNEL (updated June 6, 2013), http://www.etfchannel.com/slideshows/socially-responsible-dividends/.

292. *About the PRI Initiative*, PRINCIPLES FOR RESPONSIBLE INVESTMENT, http://www.unpri.org/about-pri/about-pri/ (last visited May 16, 2013).

293. Katherina Glac, *The Influence of Shareholders on Corporate Social Responsibility* 21 (Center for Ethical Business Culture, Working Paper No. 2 (2010)), http://www.cebcglobal.org/uploaded_files/Glac_paper_on_Social_Investment_FINAL.pdf; BUSINESS FOR SOCIAL RESPONSIBILITY, ENVIRONMENTAL, SOCIAL, AND GOVERNANCE: MOVING TO MAINSTREAM INVESTING? 6 (2008), http://bsr.org/reports/BSR_ESG_Mainstream_Investing.pdf.

294. *See* PRICEWATERHOUSECOOPERS, DO INVESTORS CARE ABOUT SUSTAINABILITY?: SEVEN TRENDS PROVIDE CLUES 3 (2012), http://www.pwc.com/us/en/corporate-sustainability-climate-change/publications/investors-and-sustainability.jhtml. *See also* Michael Chamberlain, *Socially Responsible Investing: What You Need to Know*, FORBES (Apr. 24, 2013), http://www.forbes.com/sites/feeonlyplanner/2013/04/24/socially-responsible-investing-what-you-need-to-know/ (Reporting that SRI investing has increased 22

legislative history of section 1502 of Dodd-Frank indicates an appreciation on the part of Congress that social issues do inform investment decisions.[295] Moreover, certain socially responsible investors have opposed the legal challenges brought against transparency regulations by certain business interests.[296] Investors are also working in cooperation with rights organizations. For example, Calvert Investments, the Interfaith Center on Corporate Responsibility, and the Institute for Business and Human Rights have published a guide for "mainstream investors across all asset classes, including hedge funds."[297] The guide, *Investing the Rights Way*, outlines recent developments and key provisions of the UN Guiding Principles relevant to investors, among other things.

Conclusion

Taken together with recent legislation, these trends toward an increasingly conscious consumer and activist investor segment with a greater interest in transparency should inspire industry to revisit the adage that "the only social responsibility of business is to make profits for its shareholders within the constraints of the law."[298] A number of popular brands such as GAP and Nike adopted clean-labor policies after instances of bonded, child, or forced labor in their supply chains were exposed to the purchasing public.[299]

---

percent since 2011 and now represents $3.74 trillion in managed assets. Furthermore, Chamberlain suggests that one in every nine dollars of U.S. investments is used for SRI investments.).

295. *See* 156 CONG. REC. S3965-03, S3976 (daily ed. May 19, 2010) statement of Sen. Feingold, "Transparency . . . will help the United States and our allies more effectively deal with . . . complex problems . . . they will also help American consumers and investors make more informed decisions.".

296. Investor Statement in Support of SEC Rule 1502 on Conflict Minerals, Responsible Sourcing Network (June 3, 2013), http://www.sourcingnetwork.org/storage/minerals-investors-group/CM%20Investor%20Statement%202013-05-28%20FIN.pdf (Notifying public that on June 3, 2013, a group of 275 faith-based investment organizations signed a statement opposing a lawsuit against the SEC seeking to overturn Section 1502 of Dodd-Frank filed by the U.S. Chamber of Commerce, the National Association of Manufacturers, and the Business Roundtable. These organizations represent $458,670,218,008 of assets under management).

297. INSTITUTE FOR HUMAN RIGHTS ET AL., INVESTING THE RIGHTS WAY: A GUIDE FOR INVESTORS ON BUSINESS AND HUMAN RIGHTS (2013).

298. *See* Milton Friedman, *Social Responsibility of Business Is to Increase Its Profits*, N.Y. TIMES MAG, (Sept. 13, 1970).

299. *See* Amelia Gentleman, *Gap Moves to Recover from Child Labor Scandal*, N.Y. TIMES (Nov. 15, 2007), http://www.nytimes.com/2007/11/15/business/worldbusiness/15iht-gap.1.8349422.html; *Online Extra: Nike's New Game Plan for Sweatshops*, BLOOMBERG BUSINESSWEEK MAGAZINE (Sept. 19, 2004), http://www.businessweek.com/stories/2004-09-19/online-extra-nikes-new-game-plan-for-sweatshops (Reporting Nike's solutions to late-1990s labor violations, including inspections staff and a monitoring collective that allows protestors to deal directly with Nike if violations are found in their factories); Steven Greenhouse, *Groups Press Big Retailers on Safety Overseas*, N.Y. TIMES (May 16, 2013), http://www.nytimes.com/2013/05/17/business/global/investors-and-religious-groups-press-retailers-on-safety.html?ref=business&_r=0 (reporting that 123 religious groups and investment organizations representing $1.1 trillion in investment assets signed a letter asking retailers to comply with a new factory safety plan. An additional letter signed by investment and pension funds representing $1.35 trillion in assets was sent

Apple eventually had to respond with action after it became apparent that a segment of its consumers were concerned about reports of the human costs involved in manufacturing its products in China.[300] Apple is now reporting its efforts to address these conditions. Such a large and influential business actor could well change how the business of manufacturing is done, for the better.

The recent tragic deaths of thousands of laborers buried under collapsed buildings or consumed by fires while working in unsafe conditions in Bangladesh's garment factories, manufacturing *fast fashion* apparel for export, reflected poorly on popular brands.[301] Again, in the face of pressure from investors and consumers, the apparel sector has been forced to engage in greater due diligence and devise ways to do business in a manner that respects worker rights.[302] Several companies have agreed to accords that would provide (1) "independent, rigorous factory safety inspections with public reports and mandatory repairs and renovations underwritten by Western retailers" and (2) "for workers and their unions to have a substantial voice in factory safety," among other things.[303] The tragedies have resulted in multi-stakeholder dialogues and debates over how best to protect workers and what level of responsibility brands should assume for ensuring their products are not the result of a factory system that routinely places lives at risk.[304] For instance, the UN working group has announced that it will host a special session on managing human

---

to retailers urging changes in safety standards in Bangladesh. The organizations are responding to the deadly collapse of a textile factory building in Bangladesh in April). *See also Diverse Coalition of Global Investors Managing More Than $1.5 Trillion Calls for Systemic Reform to End Human Rights Abuses in Apparel Supply Chains*, Boston Common Asset (May 22, 2013), http://www.bostoncommonasset .com/news/BangladeshHumanRights.php.

300. *Apple Press Info: Fair Labor Association Begins Inspection of Foxconn*, Apple (Feb. 13, 2012), http://www.apple.com/pr/library/2012/02/13Fair-Labor-Association-Begins-Inspections-of-Foxconn .html; Kevin Drew, *Apple's Chief Visits iPhone Factory in China*, N.Y. Times (Mar. 29, 2012), http://www .nytimes.com/2012/03/30/technology/apples-chief-timothy-cook-visits-foxconn-factory.html; Charles Duhigg & Steven Greenhouse, *Electronic Giant Vowing Reforms in China Plants*, N.Y. Times (Mar. 29, 2012) at A1, http://www.nytimes.com/2012/03/30/business/apple-supplier-in-china-pledges-chan ges-in-working-conditions.html?; Poornima Gupta & Edwin Chan, *Apple, Foxconn Set New Standard for Chinese Workers*, Reuters (Mar. 30, 2012), http://www.reuters.com/article/2012/03/30/ us-apple-foxconn-idU.S.BRE82S19720120330.

301. *See* Steven Greenhouse, *Major Retailers Join Bangladesh Safety Plan*, N.Y. Times (May 13, 2013), http://www.nytimes.com/2013/05/14/business/global/hm-agrees-to-bangladesh-safety-plan.html?_r=0; *see also* Charlie Campbell, *Retailers Sign Bangladesh Garment Factory Safety Deal*, Time: World (May 14, 2013), http://world.time.com/2013/05/14/retailers-sign-bangladesh-garment-factory-safety-deal-as-c ollapse-rescue-efforts-wind-up/.

302. *See Clothing Brands Must Work with Bangladesh to Prevent Another Disaster—UN Experts*, UN News Centre (May 8, 2013), http://www.un.org/apps/news/story.asp?NewsID=44859&Cr=bangladesh &Cr1=#.UcNCZJytxrk.

303. Steven Greenhouse, *supra* note 299; *see also Unions Commend Deal after Bangladesh Collapse*, Deutshe Welle (May 17, 2013), http://www.dw.de/unions-commend-deal-after-bangladesh-collapse /a-16820215.

304. *Avoiding the Fire Next Time*, Economist (May 4, 2013), http://www.economist.com/news/business /21577078-after-dhaka-factory-collapse-foreign-clothing-firms-are-under-pressure-improve-working.

rights risks in the garment-sector supply chain.[305] Exposure of abuses through transparency regulations could force innovations in better ways of doing business, ultimately improving corporate governance and avoiding tragic outcomes.

These new national and state laws, as well as new global standards, signal a shift toward the creation of monitoring mechanisms to ensure that corporations meet their responsibility to respect human rights. To the extent that efforts such as deploying the power of public purchasing and leveraging securities laws prove successful in changing corporate conduct and curtailing rights violations, an expansion of similar efforts to incorporate social criteria in the market can be expected. The proliferation of voluntary codes of conduct crafted by individual corporations, industry associations, and multi-stakeholder organizations provided the normative foundation for mandatory disclosures measures. The added element of the SEC's power to enforce can only promote greater transparency and increase the possibility that human rights will be better respected by corporations.

---

305. *Working Group on the Issue of Human Rights and Transnational Corporations and other Business Enterprises*, UNITED NATIONS HUMAN RIGHTS: OFFICE OF THE HIGH COMMISSIONER FOR HUMAN RIGHTS, http://www.ohchr.org/EN/Issues/Business/Pages/WGHRandtransnationalcorporationsandother business.aspx (last visited June 20, 2013); *see also Managing Human Rights Risk in the Garment Sector Supply Chain—What Lessons Learned from the Perspective of the UN Guiding Principles on Business and Human Rights?*, BUSINESS & HUMAN RIGHTS RESOURCE CENTRE, http://www.business-humanrights .org/Links/Repository/1019610 (last visited June 20, 2013).

Chapter 10

The UK Context for Business and Human Rights

Rachel Chambers and Katherine Tyler

Introduction

The questions of if and how to regulate the human rights impacts of businesses operating abroad have long been contentious ones. Companies have been accused of a wide range of human rights violations, yet all too often the victims and survivors are left without access to an effective remedy.

In June 2011, the United Nations Human Rights Council (UNHRC) unanimously endorsed[1] the United Nations Guiding Principles on Business and Human Rights (UNGPs).[2] The principles seek to provide an authoritative global standard for preventing and addressing the risk of adverse human rights impacts linked to business activity. As a member of the UNHRC, the United Kingdom endorsed the UNGPs with the following statement:

> The UK has always been a strong supporter of John Ruggie's work, and fully endorses the conceptual framework set out in his Guiding Principles which gives excellent, comprehensive guidance on how to ensure that human rights are respected in this corporate context. . . . [T]he UK is co-sponsoring this resolution subject to our understanding that the Principles do not all necessarily reflect the current state of international law. . . . In particular whilst the UK agrees that certain treaty provisions

---

1. Human Rights Council, *Human Rights and Transnational Corporations and Other Business Enterprises*, UN Doc. A/HRC/RES/17/4 (July 6, 2011).

2. Special Representative of the Secretary-General on the Issue of Human Rights and Transnational Corporations and Other Business Enterprises, *Guiding Principles on Business and Human Rights: Implementing the United Nations "Protect, Respect and Remedy" Framework*, UN Doc. A/HRC/17/31 (Mar. 21, 2011) [hereinafter UNGP], http://www.ohchr.org/Documents/Issues/Business/A-HRC-17-31_AEV.pdf (by John Ruggie) (last accessed Dec. 10, 2013).

may impose an express or implied duty on States to protect against nonstate human rights abuses, it does not consider that there is a general State duty to protect under the core United Nations human rights treaties, nor that such a duty is generally agreed to exist as a matter of customary international law.[3]

Since then, the UK government has made its commitment to the UNGPs clear through the Foreign and Commonwealth Office's publication of a National Action Plan[4] and through public commitments in the House of Commons and most recently through the UK's National Action Plan on Business and Human Rights.[5]

In this chapter, we examine current trends in UK legislation and litigation that are relevant to the liability of corporations domiciled in the United Kingdom for human rights abuses committed outside the territory. The first part of this chapter explores the limitations of the United Kingdom's existing legislation in providing a remedy for victims of corporate-related harm committed abroad. We identify relevant developments in English criminal law, and in light of the difficulty of prosecuting companies for human rights violations committed abroad under existing criminal law provisions, we move on to look at another means of bringing about corporate accountability: company law, specifically

---

3.   The full text of the statement is http://www.business-humanrights.org/media/documents/ruggie /statements-norway-uk-business-human-rights-16-jun-2011.pdf (last accessed Dec. 10, 2013).

4.   *See* UK FIRST TO LAUNCH ACTION PLAN ON BUSINESS AND HUMAN RIGHTS, Sept. 2013, https://www .gov.uk/government/news/uk-first-to-launch-action-plan-on-business-and-human-rights (last accessed Dec. 10, 2013); *see also* The Secretary of State for Foreign and Commonwealth Affairs' Response to the Third Report from the Foreign Affairs Committee Session 2012-13 (Dec. 2012), http://www.official-documents .gov.uk/document/cm85/8506/8506.pdf (last accessed Dec. 10, 2013)..

5.   The House of Commons is the lower house of Parliament of the United Kingdom. It is composed of 650 elected Members of Parliament (MPs). MPs consider and propose new laws, and can scrutinize government policies by asking ministers questions about current issues either in the Commons Chamber or in committee. The debates in the House of Commons are recorded in Hansard. The Hansard record of July 14, 2011, records the following interchange of relevance: "*Grahame M. Morris (Easington) (Lab): What steps he is taking to increase international legal protection for those affected by corporate abuses in conflict zones.*"

The Parliamentary Under-Secretary of State for Foreign and Commonwealth Affairs (Mr. Henry Bellingham): "The Government totally deplore any company anywhere in the world that ignores human rights. It is especially important that companies set the highest possible standards when operating in failed states or conflict zones. That is why we support the excellent work being carried out by Professor John Ruggie, the United Nations expert on business and human rights. We particularly welcome the final version of his guiding principles, which deals with this subject."

Grahame M. Morris: "I am grateful to the Minister for that reply, but will he go just a little further? Given the effect that legal protections could have on the lives of ordinary people in countries such as Peru, Indonesia, Mexico and even the Israeli-occupied Palestinian territories, where there have been cases of abuse, torture and even killings when citizens have protested against large-scale private sector projects, will the Government confirm that they are supporting Professor Ruggie's recommendation that the UK Government explore additional legal protections for victims of corporate abuse in conflict zones?"

Mr Bellingham: "I had the chance to meet Professor John Ruggie the other day, and I am working hard to ensure that the guiding principles are incorporated and endorsed by the UN Human Rights Council in Geneva, as that would provide extra clout and credibility."

the laws regulating non-financial disclosures. Recent developments in company reporting requirements both at the UK and at the EU level have led to the proposed, and in some cases realized, tightening up of corporate disclosure requirements on human rights issues. The impetus for this law reform certainly at the EU level is not, however, a sense of responsibility to victims of human rights violations—a fact we explore further in this section.

The second part of the chapter briefly explores recent litigation trends, the changes to the procedural laws governing this litigation, and the effect of these changes. Having identified various difficulties for victims in accessing the courts of the United Kingdom, we canvas possible solutions for those who have suffered human rights violations at the hands of corporations. We conclude the chapter by looking at the government's approach to corporate responsibility since its endorsement of the UNGPs. Has the United Kingdom's endorsement of the UNGPs resulted in any developments that illustrate a shift in the government's understanding of corporate responsibility?

Limitations of the United Kingdom's Existing Legislation

At present there is no statutory provision under which a company can be held to account in civil law for human rights abuses committed abroad. The Human Rights Act 1998 (Eng.) (HRA) does not provide such a cause of action,[6] and the United Kingdom has no legislation allowing the pursuit of tort claims for violations of international law of the kind that have been brought under the Alien Tort Statute (ATS) in the United States.[7]

---

6.   The HRA only applies to the acts of public authorities (§6(1)). It will not apply to a company unless that company is exercising functions of a public nature (§6(3)(b)). *See YL v Birmingham City Council* [2007] 3 W.L.R. 112 (Eng.) in which the House of Lords found that a privately owned care home was not exercising functions of a public nature and did not therefore attract liability under the HRA. The circumstances in which HRA protection will extend to acts committed abroad is highly contentious, and an analysis of the arguments on this question is beyond the scope of this chapter. There have been a number of controversial decisions by the European Court of Human Rights, in particular *see* Bankovic v. Belgium (2007) 44 E.H.R.R. SE5; Al-Skeini v. UK [2011] 53 E.H.R.R. 18. For an analysis of this issue, *see* Max Shaefer, *Al-Skeini and the Elusive Parameters of Extraterritorial Jurisdiction*, E.H.R.L.R (2011) No.5, 566–81. More recently, in Smith (and others) v. MOD (2013) UKSC 41 the United Kingdom's Supreme Court concluded that the UK government exercised extraterritorial jurisdiction over the claimant soldiers at the time of their death, based on the authority and control, which the UK, through the chain of military command, had over the individual.

7.   28 U.S.C. § 1350. This statute is also called the Alien Tort Claims Act (ATCA). Up until recently those who had suffered human rights violations had attempted to use the ATCA to seek redress from those responsible for their abuse—be they individuals or corporations. However, in the 2013 decision of Kiobel v. Royal Dutch Petroleum Co., 133 S. Ct. 1659, 1669 (2013), the Supreme Court significantly limited ATCA's application holding that the Act does not apply to human rights violations committed in other countries unless there is an adequate connection to the United States. The Justices unanimously agreed that the mere presence of a multinational corporation was not a clear enough connection for the purposes of the ATCA. For more detail on the ATCA and Kiobel, *see* Stephens', Hoffman's, and Popović's chapters in this book.

Because there is no cause of action provided for by statute in the United Kingdom, most cases in which corporations have been taken to court in the United Kingdom for human rights abuses and corporate-related harm committed abroad have been brought as tort claims alleging a breach of the company's duty of care. These claims seek to impose direct liability for actions or omissions by the parent company in respect of harm committed abroad.[8] The advantage of bringing claims in this way is that they avoid the difficulty that traditionally the laws of England and Wales are limited to the jurisdiction and territories of those two countries unless there is express provision to the contrary.[9] Such claims also allow the victims to pursue the head office of a company rather than the local subsidiary, which may be impecunious.[10]

The lack of any statute creating civil liability does not, however, necessarily discount other forms of statute-based remedies for this kind of harm. Over the past seven years there has been a marked shift in criminal law toward increased standards of corporate accountability, including for harm committed abroad. Recent developments in English criminal law illustrate this trend.

English Criminal Law

As a general rule, English criminal law is limited to acts performed within the territory of England and Wales,[11] and only a statutory provision asserting extraterritorial jurisdiction will criminalize acts committed abroad.[12] Under English criminal law, a corporation may

---

8. *For example*, in Connelly v. RTZ Corp. Plc [1998] A.C. 854 (H.L.) a claim for compensation was brought in England by Richard Connelly, a Scottish laryngeal cancer victim who had been employed at Rio Tinto's Rossing uranium mine in Namibia. He alleged that key strategic technical and policy decisions relating to Rossing were taken by the England-based RTZ companies. It was alleged that Rio Tinto had devised the mine's policy on health, safety, and the environment and/or had advised the mine at to the contents of the policy.

9. Since England and Wales is treated as a single jurisdiction to the other parts of the United Kingdom (namely, Scotland and Northern Ireland), for the purposes of this chapter, only the jurisdiction of the courts of England and Wales will be considered. References to the English courts, English law, and England shall be deemed to include Wales.

10. In *Lubbe and Ors v Cape Plc* [2000] UKHL 41, [2000] W.L.R. 1545, [2000] 4 All E.R. 268, the claimants proceeded against the parent company Cape, which was the only realistic target for legal action due to the insolvency of Cape's South African subsidiaries.

11. As to when a crime is committed within the territory of England and Wales, see BLACKSTONE'S CRIMINAL PRACTICE (Lord Justice Hooper & D. Ormerod eds., 2012), 156 "An offence may be committed within England and Wales even where some elements or consequences occur abroad, at least in cases where the last essential constituent element of the offence takes place within England and Wales." Treacy v. DPP [1971] A.C. 537 at 552–53 (H.L.); *but see also* R. v. Smith (Wallace Duncan) (No. 4) [2004] Q.B. 1418 (Eng.) in which the Court of Appeal held that courts may assume jurisdiction to try an offence if a substantial part of it took place within their jurisdiction, provided that there was no reason of international comity why the court should not do so.

12. See BLACKSTONE'S CRIMINAL PRACTICE at 162 (Lord Justice Hooper & D. Ormerod eds., 2012); *see also* OXFORD PRO BONO PUBLICO, OBSTACLES TO JUSTICE AND REDRESS FOR VICTIMS OF CORPORATE HUMAN RIGHTS ABUSE 285 (2008), http://www.reports-and-materials.org/Oxford-Pro-Bono-Publico-su bmission-to-Ruggie-3-Nov-08.pdf (last accessed Dec. 10, 2013).

be held liable just as a natural person may be held liable and may be convicted of common law and statutory offences. For those offences requiring a criminal intent, corporate liability is generally attributed through the identification principle,[13] which requires that the natural person who committed the offence must fall within the category of individuals who are the directors of the company or are entrusted with the exercise of the powers of the company.[14] The creation of legislation such as the Corporate Manslaughter and Corporate Homicide Act 2007, the Serious Crime Act 2007, and the Bribery Act 2010 all demonstrate a shift away from these general rules toward increased levels of corporate accountability and an expanded assertion of extraterritorial jurisdiction.[15]

Corporate Manslaughter and Corporate Homicide Act 2007

The Corporate Manslaughter and Corporate Homicide Act 2007 (CMCHA) came into force on April 6, 2008. It allows for a corporation to be convicted of corporate manslaughter when someone is killed as a result of the way the organization is managed or organized and when the organization's actions constitute a gross breach of the "relevant duty of care" owed to the deceased person.[16] This legislation is a departure from the common law rules requiring a "directing mind" and makes it easier for a corporation to be found guilty of this specific offence.[17] The CMCHA significantly changed the standards of corporate accountability, and had the act been extraterritorial in its application, it would have provided an important method of regulating the actions of companies abroad.

---

13. The identification principle is the primary rule of attribution and it is specifically relevant here in so far as it was identified in the UNGPs as being one of the barriers to corporate accountability, see FN 14. However, there are other ways in which a prosecution can be brought against a corporation, for example for offences of strict liability or for certain statutory offences which impose duties on corporations as distinct from its employees or managers. Also, a company can be personally or vicariously liable for the acts of its employees or agents where a natural person would similarly be liable for such acts, for example where a statute imposes a strict duty. For more information see Blackstone's Criminal Practice at 111-4 (Lord Justice Hooper and D. Ormerod eds. 2012).

14. The circumstances in which an identified individual's conduct can be attributed to the company have been considered by the courts with inconsistent results, see Tesco Supermarkets Ltd v. Nattrass [1972] A.C. 153 (H.L.); John Henshall (Quarries) Ltd v. Harvey [1965] 2 Q.B. 233 (Eng.); AG's Ref (No. 2 of 1999) [2000] Q.B. 796.

15. Both of these concepts were identified in the UNGPs as obstacles to the criminal liability of companies for human rights abuses committed abroad. UNGP supra note 2 at 7, 23.

16. So far only three companies have been prosecuted under the CMCHA; they are Cotswold Geotechnical Holdings Ltd, JMW Farms, and most recently, in July 2012, Lion Steel Equipment Limited. The companies were fined £385,000.00 (U.S. $600,000.00) (see R. v Cotswold Geotechnical (Holdings) Ltd [2011] All E.R. (D) 100 (May)), £187,500.00 (U.S. $290,000), and £480,000.00 (U.S. $750,000) respectively.

17. The extent to which the CMCHA departs from the common law identification principle is apparent from the Ministry of Justice Guidance Notes to the Act, which state that: "the Act does not require the prosecution to prove specific failings on the part of individual or senior managers. It will be sufficient for a jury to consider that the senior management of the organization collectively were not taking adequate care, and this was a substantial part of the organization's failure." See BLACKSTONE'S CRIMINAL PRACTICE, supra note 11, at 112.

However, albeit that on its passage through Parliament the Home Affairs and Work and Pensions Committee[18] was petitioned to expand the CMCHA's jurisdictional reach[19] by a number of high-profile organizations,[20] the government refused to extend the CMCHA to encompass extraterritorial actions in its application, relying in part on the fact that such a step would be impractical and difficult to police.[21] As a result, this piece of legislation is limited to the jurisdiction of the United Kingdom and, as such, is entirely ineffective for regulating companies' actions abroad.[22] By way of contrast, the Bribery Act 2010 is not limited by traditional rules of jurisdiction.

Bribery Act 2010

Bribery and corruption have long been considered inimical to the attainment of human rights.[23] They have been considered to impact on a range of human rights[24] and, in particular, have been found to exert a negative effect on certain economic and social rights as they remove from the public domain all-important revenues and make the attainment of due process almost impossible.[25] Following serious criticism from both the Organization

---

18. Members of the Home Affairs and Work and Pensions Committee are appointed by the House of Commons to examine the expenditure, administration, and policy of the Home Office and the Department for Work and Pensions. The Committee heard oral evidence and received live evidence that was relevant to the drafting of the CMCHA.

19. The Home Affairs and Work and Pensions Committees, Draft Corporate Manslaughter Bill: Written Evidence, 2005-6, H.C. 540-II.

20. *Id.* at 17, 25, 30 (In particular see the written representations of the Trade Union Congress at 17, the Transport and General Workers Union at 25, and the Public and Commercial Services Union at 30).

21. *See* Secretary of State for the Home Department, The Government Reply to the First Joint Report from the Home Affairs and Work and Pensions Committees Session 2005-06 HC 540 at 24–25 (2006) http://www.official-documents.gov.uk/document/cm67/6755/6755.pdf.

22. *See* Corporate Manslaughter and Corporate Homicide Act, 2007, c. 19, § 28 (UK); Health and Safety at Work Act, 1974, c. 37, § 15 (UK); but *see id.* § 84(3), under which there is a broad power to extend, by order, the application of the provisions of the Act outside Great Britain. Realistically, this power is very rarely used, and when it is, it is in relation to specific projects such as the offshore installation and pipelines. *See* Health and Safety at Work Order 1989 (Application outside Great Britain).

23. *See* Int'l Council on Human Rights Policy & Transparency Int'l, Corruption and Human Rights: Making the Connection (2009), http://www.ichrp.org/files/reports/40/131_web.pdf; Human Rights Watch, Everyone's in on the Game: Corruption and Human Rights Abuses by the Nigerian Police Force (2010), http://www.hrw.org/sites/default/files/reports/nigeria0810webwcover .pdf (last accessed Dec. 10, 2013).

24. Everyone's in on the Game, *id.*, at 47–54 (examples of bribery in breach of Article 2 of the European Convention on Human Rights ("ECHR") (the right to life); *id.* at 41–44 (examples in breach of Article 3 ECHR, the right to be free from torture, inhuman, and degrading treatment); *id.* at 31–40 (examples in breach of Article 5 ECHR, the right not to be arbitrarily detained). *See* Corruption and Human Rights: Making the Connection, *supra* note 22, at 31–58.

25. Such rights include the right to an adequate standard of living, the right to public participation, and the right to an effective remedy. *See* Corruption and Human Rights: Making the Connection, *supra* note 22.

for Economic Cooperation and Development[26] and the European Commission,[27] in July 2011 the UK government enacted the Bribery Act 2010 (BA).[28] The BA is relevant to both the consideration of increased standards of corporate accountability and the assertion of extraterritorial jurisdiction because it creates an offence that is specifically aimed at companies operating abroad.

The offences created by the BA include the bribery of another person,[29] being bribed,[30] and bribing a foreign official.[31] Though not necessarily aimed at companies, each of these three offences can apply to a corporation just as they can apply to a natural person.[32] The scope of the BA is wide with respect to both the actions and the persons that will fall within its jurisdiction. For example, a body incorporated under the law of the United Kingdom, among others, may be prosecuted for one of these offences, irrespective of where the criminal act occurs, on the basis that by virtue of its incorporation the company in question has a "close connection with the UK."[33] Non-UK companies and partnerships can also commit these offences if an act or omission, which forms part of the offence, takes place within the United Kingdom.[34]

The corporate offence of failing to prevent bribery,[35] which, unlike the others, is specifically aimed at companies, can be committed by any "relevant commercial organization,"[36] irrespective of where the act occurred and irrespective of the identity of the person who committed the act.[37] It is a defense for the corporation to prove that it had in place ade-

---

26. ORG. FOR ECON. COOPERATION AND DEV. ("OECD") WORKING GROUP ON BRIBERY, ANNUAL REPORT 2008, at 43 (2009), http://www.oecd.org/daf/anti-bribery/anti-briberyconvention/44033641.pdf (last accessed Dec. 10, 2013) (in which the UK is criticized for failing to comply with the requirements of the OECD Anti-Bribery Convention).

27. *Report from the Commission to the Council based on Article 9 of the Council Framework Decision 2003/568/JHA of 22nd July 2003 on Combating Corruption in the Private Sector*, COM (2007) 328 final (June 18, 2007).

28. The Bribery Act, 2010, c. 23 (UK) (came into force in the UK on July 1, 2011).

29. *Id.* § 1.

30. *Id.* § 2.

31. *Id.* § 6.

32. *See id.* § 14 (which defines the circumstances in which a body corporate will be held liable.).

33. *Id.* §§ 12(2), 12(4).

34. *Id.*, § 12(1).

35. *Id.* § 7.

36. *Id.* § 7(5) (defines a relevant commercial organization as: (a) a body that is incorporated under the law of any part of the United Kingdom and that carries on a business (whether there or elsewhere), (b) any other body corporate (wherever incorporated) that carries on a business, or part of a business, in any part of the United Kingdom, (c) a partnership that is formed under the law of any part of the United Kingdom and that carries on a business (whether there or elsewhere), or (d) any other partnership (wherever formed) that carries on a business, or part of a business, in any part of the United Kingdom, and (for the purposes of this section) a trade or profession is a business.).

37. *Id.* § 8 (Meaning of associated person for the purposes of section 7, a person ("A") is associated with C if (disregarding any bribe under consideration) A is a person who performs services for or on behalf of C (§ 8(1)). The capacity in which A performs services for or on behalf of C does not matter (§ 8(2)). Accordingly, A may (for example) be C's employee, agent, or subsidiary (§ 8(3)). Whether or not A is a person who performs services for or on behalf of C is to be determined by reference to all the

quate procedures to prevent bribery. The UK government has published guidance to assist companies to put in place these procedures however, the weight to be attributed to this guidance has not yet been considered by the UK courts.[38]

The BA attracted a lot of attention when it came into force, specifically because of the reach of the new corporate offence.[39] This new offence was deemed important because, like the CMCHA, it circumvents the common law principles of corporate liability, which require the participation of a "directing mind," such that in this context a company may be guilty even if no one in the company knew that bribery was taking place. It places the burden firmly on corporations to ensure that their anticorruption procedures are sufficiently robust to prevent bribery, even by third parties, and most unusually, as mentioned, it allows companies to be held accountable for their actions abroad.

Serious Crime Act 2007

The Serious Crime Act 2007 (SCA), to which the common law principles of corporate liability apply, expands the traditional limitations on criminal jurisdiction.[40] The SCA criminalizes conduct that takes place in England and Wales if that conduct is capable of encouraging or assisting the commission of an offence abroad.[41] This legislation is another example of an exception to the traditional rules of jurisdiction, and though the provisions of the SCA are not aimed at companies in quite the same way as the provisions of the BA, the SCA theoretically provides a mechanism whereby companies could be prosecuted for actions abroad, including those that might constitute human rights harm. In reality, such a prosecution is unlikely ever to take place, even if the necessary offence could be made out. This is for two reasons. First, it would be difficult to prove a *mens rea*. Second, any

---

relevant circumstances and not merely by reference to the nature of the relationship between A and C (§ 8(4)). But if A is an employee of C, it is to be presumed unless the contrary is shown that A is a person who performs services for or on behalf of C (§ 8(5)).

38.   Ministry of Justice, The Bribery Act 2010: Guidance on Procedures Which Relevant Commercial Organisations Can Put into Place to Prevent Persons Associated with Them from Bribing (Section 9 of the Bribery Act 2010) (2011), www.justice.gov.uk/guidance/docs/bribery-act-2010-guidance.pdf (last accessed Dec. 16, 2013) (It identifies six principles that should assist all companies, irrespective of size, to put in place adequate procedures to prevent bribery. It requires that all companies take action proportionate to the risks that the company faces and to the size of its business; that there is a top level commitment to conducting business without bribery; that the corporation assesses its risk of being subjected to bribery; that it conducts due diligence; that it communicates these policies to its staff, and that it monitors and reviews its antibribery measures to keep pace with any possible changes in practice and business development.).

39.   *See* Alex Bailin, *Revamped Bribery Act Is Giving Firms the Jitters*, Guardian Online (Apr. 1, 2011), http://www.guardian.co.uk/law/2011/apr/01/revamped-bribery-act-firms-jitters.

40.   Serious Crime Act 2007, c. 27, §§ 52-53, sch. 4 (UK).

41.   *See id.* §§ 44–46, 52 (§§ 44–46 requires a different *mens rea* for each offence to be made out. Importantly, per §52 and ¶ 2 of Schedule 4 of the SCA, a person who through his actions in the UK encourages or assists the commission of conduct that constitutes an offence in the territory in which that conduct occurs will be guilty of an offence under the SCA. In such a case there is no requirement for the conduct that was encouraged or assisted to constitute an offence in the UK.).

such prosecution requires the consent of the attorney general—a fact that might be seen to politicize the application of these extraterritorial provisions.[42]

Offenses Attracting Universal Jurisdiction

In addition to the BA and the SCA, the United Kingdom asserts extraterritorial jurisdiction for certain specific criminal offences to which universal jurisdiction applies, including genocide, torture, crimes against humanity, and war crimes.[43] The statutory provisions through which the UK asserts extraterritorial jurisdiction with respect to these crimes have never been used to proceed against companies, and for some of the reasons identified earlier a prosecution may struggle to establish corporate liability along common law principles. In addition, because all of these offences carry a maximum sentence of thirty years of imprisonment,[44] and because a corporation cannot be convicted of a crime for which imprisonment is the only punishment,[45] it is highly unlikely that these provisions will ever offer any form of remedy to the victims of human rights abuses committed abroad.

Though the criminal law has developed significantly in the past seven years—creating two new offences aimed specifically at companies and two statutes that criminalize actions abroad—there is no specific statute aimed at regulating the criminal liability of companies for human rights violations committed abroad. The legislative provisions considered here were not designed to serve such a purpose and could not properly be said to be effective in addressing that harm.[46]

The lack of any criminal statute under which companies may be held accountable for human rights harm committed abroad demonstrates the limitations of the existing UK legislation in this field. With these limitations in both criminal and civil law in mind, it is perhaps preferable to look to other legislative provisions that may be of relevance. Arguably, the most important development in legislation relating to the accountability of companies for human rights violations committed abroad has been the recent European-led changes to the non-financial disclosure obligations of companies. In the next part of

---

42. Any prosecution under Schedule 4 (which makes provision for the prosecution of offences committed abroad), unless it is a prosecution under the Bribery Act 2010, requires the consent of the attorney general (§ 53 SCA).

43. *See* International Criminal Court Act, 2001, c. 17, § 51(1) (Eng.); Criminal Justice Act, 1988, c. 33, § 134 (Eng.) (which implements the UN Convention against Torture and Other Cruel, Inhuman or Degrading Treatment or Punishment.).

44. Geneva Conventions Act, 1957, Eliz. 2, c. 52, §1(2) (UK) (as amended) ("liable for a term not exceeding 30 years"); International Criminal Court Act, 2001, c. 17, § 53(6)("term not exceeding 30 years").

45. *See* R v. ICR Haulage Ltd., [1944] K.B. 551 at 554 (Eng.); Law Society v. United Service Bureau Ltd., [1934] 1 K.B. 343 at 350 (Eng.).

46. *See* UNGP *supra* note 2 at 10 (and the associated commentary at 11 that states, "Where they identify gaps, States should take appropriate steps to address them. This may include exploring civil, administrative or criminal liability for enterprises domiciled or operating in their territory and/or jurisdiction that commit or contribute to gross human rights abuses.").

this chapter, we consider these developments, which were underway before the UNHRC's endorsement of the UN Guiding Principles in June 2011, but which have quite clearly been reinforced by the adoption of the Guiding Principles.

Company Reporting Law

Since the global economic crisis in 2007 and 2008, a number of countries have strengthened their non-financial disclosure obligations for companies.[47] There is a strong argument that this has been in an attempt to boost shareholder confidence and company sustainability rather than from any benevolent motivation.[48] However, irrespective of the impetus, the effect has been to encourage certain companies to think more actively about their human rights impacts.[49]

---

47.   For an overview of recent CSR disclosure requirements by governments and stock exchanges, *see Global CSR Disclosure Requirements*, INITIATIVE FOR RESPONSIBLE INVESTMENT, http://hausercenter.org /iri/about/global-csr-disclosure-requirements (last accessed July 24, 2013); *see also* Special Representative of the United Nations Secretary-General on the Issue of Human Rights and Transnational Corporations and other Business Enterprise, *Survey of State Corporate Social Responsibility Policies Summary of Key Trends* (June 2010).

48.   As David Massey, North American Securities Administrators Association President, explained in his presidential address, the Dodd-Frank Wall Street and Consumer Protection Act 2010, which, among other things, requires disclosure of payments to foreign governments and the use of conflict minerals, was ushered in to "better protect investors." www.nasaa.org/389/2010-presidential-speech-North-Car-olina-deputy-securities-administrator-david-massey/ (last accessed Nov. 26, 2013) Also of note is the increase in responsible investing, which has seen a marked growth in the past four years as pension funds in particular recognise the link between human rights and sustainable investment. *See* SHARE ACTION: THE MOVEMENT FOR RESPONSIBLE INVESTMENT, http://www.fairpensions.org.uk/investors (last visited July 24, 2013); *see also* Richard Wachman, *Vedanta Under Fire from Amnesty International Over Human Rights*, GUARDIAN (July 23, 2011), http://www.guardian.co.uk/business/2011/jul/24/amnesty-internatio nal-slams-vedanta (reports of Aviva's involvement with Vedanta following allegations of human rights abuses). And *see also* p.11, COM (2011) 681 final (October 25, 2011) at n.49 where the the European Commission stated that "In response to the financial crisis, the Commission is making a number of regulatory proposals to ensure a more responsible and transparent financial system. By taking adequate account of relevant non-financial information, investors can contribute to a more efficient allocation of capital and better achieve longer-term investment goals."

49.   In March 2011, the Hong Kong Stock Exchange delisted China's leading gold-copper mining company, Zijin, for a short period after contending that two of its subsidiaries, rather than the parent company, should be held responsible for causing the deaths of 22 people and the destruction of 523 homes in the south-eastern province of Guangdong after the tailing dam at a tin mine collapsed under the onslaught of a typhoon. Hong Kong requires that mineral companies comply with specific listing requirements that, as yet, have no counterpart in the UK. These include disclosure of: environmental, social, health, and safety issues; impacts on sustainability of exploration projects; claims that may exist over the land on which mining activity is being carried out, and the company's historical experience of dealing with concerns of local governments and communities on the sites of its mines and exploration properties. *See* LONDON MINING NETWORK, UK LISTED MINING COMPANIES AND THE CASE FOR GREATER OVERSIGHT 7–8 (2012), http://www.stakeholderforum.org/fileadmin/files/Mining%20report.pdf; *see also* Hong Kong Stock Exchange Listing Rules (in particular 18.05 in Chapter 18), http://www.hkex.com.hk /eng/rulesreg/listrules/mbrules/documents/chapter_18.pdf.

Of all developments in this area, those at the European level have been particularly noticeable. In October 2011, the European Commission announced its intention to encourage responsible business[50] and to build on the existing reporting requirements for companies. through which the UK asserts extraterritorial jurisdiction with respect to these crimes[51] obligations of companies involved in the extractive or logging industries, which was incorporated into the new Directive,[52] adopted in June 2013, which imposes an obligation on Member States to require large undertakings and all public interest entities active in the extractive industry or the logging of primary forests to prepare and make public a report on payments made to government on an annual basis.[53]

The European Commission also published a new definition of and agenda for the responsibility of enterprises for their impacts on society. This new definition seeks to align European and global approaches to corporate social responsibility (CSR) in line with five of the key international agreements.[54] This initiative gained greater force last year when, in February 2013, the European Parliament adopted two resolutions[55] reiterating the importance of company transparency on environmental and social matters calling for specific measures to combat misleading and false information regarding commitments to corporate social responsibility and relating to the environmental and social impact of

---

50. *See Communication from the Commission to the European Parliament, the Council, The European Economic and Social Committee and the Committee of the Regions, A Renewed Strategy 2011–2014 for Corporate Social Responsibility*, COM (2011) 681 final (October 25, 2011).

51. *See* European Union's Press Release, "Commission moves to enhance business transparency on social and environmental matters" (16 April 2013) available at http://europa.eu/rapid/press-release _IP-13-330_en.htm?locale=en.

52. Directive 2013/34/EU of the European Parliament and of the Council of 26 Jun 2013 on the annual financial statements, consolidated financial statements and related reports of certain types of undertakings amending Directive 2006/43/EC of the European Parliament and of the Council and repealing Council Directives 78/660/EEC and 83/349/EEC.

53. *See* Chapter 10, Articles 41–47 of Directive 2013/34/EU, ibid. Further, Article 19 of the new directive requires companies, where appropriate and to the extent necessary for an understanding of the company's development, performance, or position, to include in the annual report non-financial information including information relating to environment and employee matters.

54. Those five international agreements are: OECD Guidelines for Multinational Enterprises; Principles of the UN Global Compact; UN Guiding Principles on Business and Human Rights; ILO Tri-partite Declaration of Principles on Multinational Enterprises and Social Policy; and ISO 26000 Guidance Standard on Social Responsibility.

55. European Parliament, *Report on Corporate Social Responsibility: Accountable, Transparent and Responsible Business Behavior and Sustainable Growth* (2012/2098(INI)), A7-0017/2013 (Jan. 28, 2013), http://www.europarl.europa.eu/sides/getDoc.do?pubRef=-//EP//NONSGML+REPORT+A7-2013-0017+0+DOC+PDF+V0/EN (last accessed Nov. 26, 2013); European Parliament, *Report on Corporate Social Responsibility: Promoting Society's Interests and a Route to a Sustainable and Inclusive Recovery* (2012/2097(INI)), A7-0023/2013 (Jan. 29, 2013), http://www.europarl.europa.eu/sides/getDoc.do ?pubRef=-//EP//NONSGML+REPORT+A7-2013-0023+0+DOC+PDF+V0//EN (last accessed Nov. 26, 2013).

products and services,[56] and expressly acknowledging the UNGPs in improving standards of corporate practice.[57]

In its proposal of 16 April 2013, the European Commission went one step further than it had on previous occasions and proposed an amendment to existing accounting legislation to improve the transparency of certain large companies on social and environmental issues, in particular with regard to human rights impacts. Should the proposals be adopted, companies concerned will need to disclose information on, among other things, policies, risks, and risk management with respect to human rights and anticorruption and bribery issues.[58] These developments are encouraging, albeit that they have not yet been formalized in the way that those relating to the extractive industries were. If they are adopted in full, which seems unlikely in the short term at least,[59] they will have an impact on the development of UK non-financial reporting law, which we explore below.

As far back as September 2011, in tandem with the European Commission's initiative[60] and shortly after the public adoption of the UNGPs, the UK government's Department for

---

56. *See* p.5 of the European Parliament's 'Report on Corporate Social Responsibility: Accountable, Transparent and Responsible Business Behaviour and Sustainable Growth (2012/2098(INI)), A7-0017/2013 (Jan.28 2013)

57. This followed an announcement in February 2012 that the European Commission would be developing sector-specific guidance on the implementation of the UNGPs. The first three sectors to be the focus of the forthcoming guidance would be employment and recruitment agencies, information and communication technology, and the oil and gas sectors.

58. The companies concerned are those whose average number of employees exceed 500 and exceed either a balance sheet total of €20 million (U.S. $26 million) or a net turnover of €40 million (U.S. $52 million). It is estimated that the new requirement will cover around 18,000 companies in the EU. *See The Proposal for a Directive of the European Parliament and of the Council Amending Council Directives 78/660/EEC and 83/349EEC as Regards Disclosure of Non-Financial and Diversity Information by Certain Large Companies and Groups*, art. 1(a), COM (2013) 207 final (April 16, 2013), http://eur-lex .europa.eu/LexUriServ/LexUriServ.do?uri=COM:2013:0207:FIN:EN:PDF (last accessed Dec. 19, 2013) *See also* Press Release, European Commission, Commission Moves to Enhance Business Transparency on Social and Environmental Matters (Apr. 16, 2013), http://europa.eu/rapid/press-release_IP-13-330_en .htm (last accessed Nov. 23, 2013)

59. European apathy spells end for corporate social responsibility rules, as reported in the Guardian, 19 November 2013, http://www.theguardian.com/global-development/2013/now/19/european-corp orate-social-responsibility-eu (last accessed Nov. 23, 2013).

60. In November 2010, the European Commission launched an online public consultation to gather views on the disclosure of nonfinancial information by enterprises. At present, European law makes the following requirement on companies, not necessarily including small- and medium-sized companies: "To the extent necessary for an understanding of the company's development, performance or position, the analysis [in the annual review] shall include both financial and, where appropriate, nonfinancial key performance indicators relevant to the particular business, including information relating to environmental and employee matters." Eur. Parl. & Council, *Directive 2003/51/EC of the European Parliament and of the Council, June 18, 2003, Amending Directives 78/660/EEC, 83/349/EEC, 86/635/EEC and 91/674/EEC on the Annual and Consolidated Accounts of Certain Types of Companies, Banks and Other Financial Institutions and Insurance Undertakings*, L 178/17 (July 17, 2003), http://eur-lex.europa.eu/LexUriServ/ LexUriServ.do?uri=OJ:L:2003:178:0016:0022:en:PDF (last visited Dec. 10, 2013) (The consultation seeks both to expand these and to make the requirements more effective.). The results of this consultation and the expert group discussions are http://ec.europa.eu/internal_market/accounting/non-financial_reporting /index_en.htm (last accessed on July 24, 2013).

Business, Innovation and Skills[61] published a consultation paper on The Future of Narrative Reporting.[62] This was followed in October 2012 by the publication of The Future of Narrative Reporting: A New Structure for Narrative Reporting in the UK, which sets out draft regulations that make up the Companies Act 2006 (Strategic Report and Directors Report) Regulations 2013.[63] These regulations, which came into force as recently as 1st October 2013, require quoted companies to disclose information about "social, community and human rights issues" to the extent necessary for an understanding of the development, performance, or position of the company's business. This should include information about any policies in relation to these matters and the effectiveness of these policies. If any of these are not covered the company should explain that they are not covered.[64] Prior to these regulations coming into force there was no requirement under UK law for companies to include information on human rights impacts in their company reports.[65]

The previous scheme (that existing prior to the implementation of the 2013 regulations) had been criticized as being vague and weakly enforced,[66] and these criticisms had some force. Companies whose actions have serious human rights impacts do not always disclose such impacts in their company reports and are rarely, if ever, held to account for failing to do so. No doubt, some will be watching carefully to see what material impact the inclusion of a specific human rights requirement has on companies' disclosures and whether or not it makes any difference to the enforcement of the reporting provisions themselves. The organization responsible for enforcing these provisions is now the Conduct Committee, previously the Financial Reporting Review Panel (FRRP)[67] of the Financial

---

61. The Department for Business, Innovation and Skills is a government department responsible for regulating and fostering business. For more information, *see* https://www.gov.uk/government/organisations /department-for-business-innovation-skills (last accessed July 24, 2013).

62. THE DEPARTMENT FOR BUSINESS, INNOVATION AND SKILLS, THE FUTURE OF NARRATIVE REPORTING: CONSULTING ON A NEW REPORTING FRAMEWORK (Sept. 2011), https://www.gov.uk/government /uploads/system/uploads/attachment_data/file/31402/11-945-future-of-narrative-reporting-consulting-new-framework.pdf.

63. THE DEPARTMENT FOR BUSINESS, INNOVATION AND SKILLS, THE FUTURE OF NARRATIVE REPORTING: A NEW STRUCTURE FOR NARRATIVE REPORTING IN THE UK (Oct. 2012), https://www.gov.uk/ government/uploads/system/uploads/attachment_data/file/34745/12-979-future-of-narrative-reporting-new-structure.pdf (last accessed Dec. 10, 2013)

64. *See* Companies Act, 2006, c. 1, § 414C(7).

65. The scheme under the Companies Act 2006 prior to the implentation of th e2013 regulation requires only that quoted companies disclose environmental, employee, social, and community issues "to the extent necessary for an understanding of the company's development, performance or position." S-417 (5)

66. JENNIFER A. ZERK, CORE, SIMPLY PUT: TOWARDS AN EFFECTIVE UK REGIME FOR ENVIRONMENTAL AND SOCIAL REPORTING BY COMPANIES (2011), http://corporate-responsibility.org/simply-put-towards-an-effective-uk-regime-for-environmental-and-social-reporting-by-companies/.

67. The Financial Reporting Review Panel was established in 1990 as part of the Financial Reporting Council. The panel now forms part of the Conduct Committee, the division of the FRC responsible, amongst other things, for ensuring that the provision of financial information by public and large private companies complies with relevant requirement. For more information see www.frc.org.uk/our-work /conduct/corporate-reporting-review.aspx.

Reporting Council.[68] As the law currently stands, the mechanism to refer a company to the FRRP for failing to meet the necessary reporting standards is rarely used. However, it was taken up in July 2010 by the nongovernmental organization ClientEarth, which referred mining company Rio Tinto. The FRRP found that Rio Tinto had failed to make material disclosures regarding its environmental, employee, social, and community issues, in particular at the group's nonmanaged Grasberg mine in Indonesia.[69] Following this finding, the FRRP closed its enquiry after Rio Tinto's directors included some more information about environmental matters, social and community issues, and related reputational risk in their report and accounts for the year ending in December 2010. No other sanction was applied.[70] This case demonstrates the limits to the FRRP's powers. It can seek the correction of defective accounts, or it may refer a company against whom a complaint has been made to other relevant bodies such as the Financial Services Authority, the Accountancy and Actuarial Disciplinary Board,[71] or another professional institute, now the Financial Conduct Authority, but it cannot directly punish a company for failing to comply with reporting law. ClientEarth criticized both the manner of the FRRP's investigation and its outcome as providing no clarity about how the law is to be interpreted by companies.[72]

Comment on Legislation

The conclusion to be drawn from the above analysis is that despite the proposed developments in EC and UK company law, which certainly demonstrate an increased awareness of the responsibility of businesses for their human rights impacts, the statute-based options in

---

68. The Financial Reporting Council is the UK's independent regulator. Its role is to promote good corporate reporting and governance to foster investment. The FRRP is one of the organs of the FRC. At the time of this writing, the FRC is the subject of a proposal for reform. For more information, *see* www .frc.org.uk (last visited July 25, 2013).

69. CLIENTEARTH, REFERRAL TO THE FINANCIAL REPORTING REVIEW PANEL: RE: THE RIO TINTO GROUP ANNUAL REPORT 2008, http://www.clientearth.org/reports/clientearth-submission-to-frrp-re-r io-tinto-annual-report-2008.pdf (last accessed Dec. 10, 2013) (Rio Tinto had been accused of large-scale environmental destruction and human rights abuses, in relation to some of which the company was facing litigation in the U.S.. The FRRP concluded that in respect of the company's report and accounts for the years ended December 31, 2008, and December 31, 2009, additional information comprising details of the potential health risks posed to workers and local communities from exposure to harmful substances at the company's uranium mines ought to have been included. Likewise, details of the sensitivities the group faces in dealing with local communities, such as the La Granja copper development in Peru and the Eagle project in Michigan in the United States, were omitted.).

70. *See Statement by the Financial Reporting Review Panel in Respect of the Report and Accounts of Rio Tinto Plc*, FINANCIAL REPORTING COUNCIL (Mar. 15, 2011), http://www.frc.org.uk/News-and-Events /FRC-Press/Press/2011/March/Statement-by-the-Financial-Reporting-Review-Panel.aspx.

71. The Financial Services Authority is the UK regulator of the financial services industry; the Accountancy and Actuarial Disciplinary Board is the independent, investigative, and disciplinary body for accountants and actuaries in the UK.

72. *See First Test of UK's New Corporate Environmental and Social Law Falls Short*, CLIENTEARTH (Mar. 24, 2011), http://www.clientearth.org/news/press-releases/uk-corporate-law-falls-short-1255 (last accessed Dec. 10, 2013).

the United Kingdom for victims of human rights abuses committed abroad are extremely limited. As identified at the outset, the most viable option for such claimants to secure a remedy remains a civil action in tort. In the next part of this chapter, we consider the merit of such actions and provide details of recent cases brought in England and Wales against multinational corporations (MNCs) for their harmful activities overseas. The details of these cases make it clear just how important it is for victims of these abuses to have a remedy, and just how vital the described litigation is to ensuring access to that remedy.

Litigation: For Human Rights Abuses and Corporate-Related Harm Committed Outside the United Kingdom

The past eight years have seen an increase in the number of corporate-related human rights cases. Beginning with a claim against BP, which was commenced in 2005, a total of six such cases have been filed, of which four have resulted in settlement.[73] Though this may not seem a great number, it represents twice as many such claims as had been brought prior to 2005.[74] We set out the details of the cases to provide a backdrop to our general comment on the litigation and to our discussion later in the chapter about legislative changes that will affect the ability of claimants to bring such claims.

BP Claims (2005 and 2008)

There are two cases against BP concerning human rights violations, both of which arise out of the actions of its subsidiary company, BP Exploration Company (Colombia) Ltd., in constructing the Oleoducto Central S.A. (OCENSA) oil pipeline in Colombia in the late 1990s. The claimants in the first case were fifty-three Colombian farmers. They asserted that their land had been seriously damaged because the pipeline construction contaminated soil and water resources, rendering their land no longer suitable for farming. Specifically, the claimants alleged that the pipeline dissected important water sources, leading to soil erosion, ruined crops, and water deficits in the rivers where they fish.

The claimants sent a letter of claim to BP alleging breach of contract; breach of agreements to compensate them properly for harm to their land; and in the tort of negligence, failure to take adequate steps to prevent the harm from occurring. The farmers asked for £15 million (U.S. $23 million) in damages. Following negotiations, which took place in June 2006, this first batch of claims was settled without an admission of liability from

---

73. These cases are: two claims against BP (2005 and 2008); Trafigura claim (2006); Monterrico claim (2008); Shell claim (2011); and Anglo-American claim (2011).

74. Previously there had only been three such claims: Sithole and Others v. Thor Chemicals Holdings Ltd. [1995] T.L.R. 110; Connelly v. RTZ Corporation Plc [1998] A.C. 854 (H.L.); Lubbe and Ors v Cape Plc [2000] UKHL 41, [2000] W.L.R. 1545 [2000] 4 All E.R. 268.

the company. The terms of the settlement were not disclosed, but BP did announce that it would establish a trust fund to pay compensation to the farmers, and that it would also pay for workshops to help the farmers cope with environmental management, business development, and other topics they requested.[75] The settlement figure was reported to be a "substantial multimillion pound payout."[76] However, less than two years later, seventy farmers from a group not part of the original action filed suit in the English High Court.[77] A group litigation order was granted in September 2008, and the case remains pending.[78]

Trafigura Claim (2006)

This claim arose out of the disposal of 500 tons of toxic waste materials from a ship, the *Probo Koala*, at various landfill sites around Abidjan, Côte d'Ivoire, on the night of August 19, 2006. Trafigura is the Dutch petroleum trading company whose UK subsidiary, Trafigura Ltd., had chartered the ship. Puma Energy, an Ivorian subsidiary of Trafigura, had contracted with a local company registered only one month previously to handle the waste materials. Local people living in Abidjan suffered ill health allegedly as a result of exposure to the toxic chemicals contained in the waste. In February 2007, Trafigura reached a negotiated settlement with the Ivorian government, which exempted it from legal proceedings in the West African country. The company agreed, without admission of liability, to pay approximately £122 million (U.S. $200 million) for a waste-treatment plant, health provision for local people, and a compensation fund for the victims.[79] The government subsequently drew up a list of over 95,000 victims to compensate; however, the government compensation process was never completed, and questions remain about how much compensation the victims actually received. As many as 30,000 of the victims had already brought legal proceedings against the company in the High Court in London in November 2006, seeking £100 million (U.S. $156 million) in damages.[80] A preliminary hearing took place in March 2009, when the claimants sought an injunction to prevent Trafigura from making contact with them. Evidence was adduced to show that the company or its representatives had put pressure on individual claimants to change their statements in the case. A temporary injunction was granted and shortly afterward, in September 2009,

---

75.   Robert Verkaik, *BP Pays Out Millions to Colombian Farmers*, INDEPENDENT (July 22, 2006).

76.   *Id.*

77.   Pedro Emiro Florez Arroyo v. BP Petroleum (Colombia) Ltd., Particulars of Claim, Claim No. HQO8X00328 (High Court of Justice Dec. 1, 2008).

78.   A group litigation order is akin to a class action. *See* Diane Taylor, *BP Faces Damages Claim over Pipeline through Colombian Farmland*, THE GUARDIAN (Nov. 11, 2009).

79.   AMNESTY INT'L AND GREENPEACE NETHERLANDS, THE TOXIC TRUTH ABOUT A COMPANY CALLED TRAFIGURA, A SHIP CALLED THE PROBO KOALA, AND THE DUMPING OF TOXIC WASTE IN CÔTE D'IVOIRE 133 (2012), http://issuu.com/greenpeaceinternational/docs/the-toxic-truth?mode=a_p (last accessed Dec. 10, 2013)

80.   Yao Essaie Motto & Ors v. Trafigura Ltd & Trafigura Beheer BV, Claim No. HQ06X03370 (Nov. 2006).

the case was settled with payment of approximately £1,000 (U.S. $1,500) in damages to each claimant but no admission of liability from the company.

Further litigation has followed over the sum of money in costs sought by lawyers for the claimants, which was £105 million (U.S. $164 million). The Court of Appeal decided in October 2011 that a lower court had been right to reduce this figure to reflect the case's higher-percentage chance of success than the lawyers had rated it as having.[81] Costs for other preparatory work were also disallowed.[82] Additionally, there has been libel litigation brought by Trafigura and threats of the same against various media outlets concerning their coverage of the matter, as well as against Leigh Day, solicitors for the claimants. One such case against BBC London was successful, resulting in the payment of £28,000 (U.S. $44,000) in damages, a retraction, and an on-air apology. A successful criminal prosecution was brought against Trafigura in the Netherlands, but this case was the subject of an appeal after a lower court ordered the company to pay a €1 million (U.S. $1.33 million) fine. The matter was finally settled between the Dutch prosecution service and the company in November 2012, with the company agreeing to pay €1.3 million (U.S. $1.7 million) in fines.[83] A complaint was also filed with the Paris prosecutor on behalf of Ivorian victims; however, a decision was taken in April 2008 not to investigate this matter further.[84]

Monterrico Claim (2008)

Monterrico is a mining company that was incorporated in the United Kingdom. The claim in the English High Court against the company concerned protests that took place in Peru in 2005 regarding its proposal to develop a copper mine there. The claimants were thirty-one protesters and their family members, who sought compensation for false imprisonment and trespass to the person (torture), which they suffered at the hands of the Peruvian police, allegedly incited to do so by the mine management. The protesters were hooded, bound, and detained over a period of days. Two women alleged that they were sexually assaulted. One protester died. Monterrico vehemently denied that its officers had any involvement in the mistreatment of the protesters but nonetheless settled the claim out of court in 2011, just months before the case was due to be heard at trial. The company did so without admission of liability.

The claimants won a preliminary legal point in 2009 when they successfully applied for a freezing injunction that ensured that £5 million (U.S. $7.8 million) of the company's assets remained in the United Kingdom—sufficient funds to cover the level of damages

---

81. The percentage chance of success affected the amount that could be recovered from Trafigura as a success fee because the case was taken by lawyers on a *no win no fee* basis.

82. Motto v. Trafigura [2011] EWCA Civ 1150.

83. *See* Statement from the Management Board of Trafigura Beheer BV (Nov. 16, 2012), http://www .trafigura.com/media-centre/probe-kcala/statements/amsterdam-settlement/?lang=grr (last accessed Dec. 10, 2013).

84. The Toxic Truth, *supra* note 76, at 168.

sought by the claimants and their costs.[85] Monterrico had been bought by a Chinese company, Zijin, in 2007, and in 2009 announced its decision to de-list from the AIM UK stock exchange. Thus, the claimants' concern was that the company would remove its assets from the jurisdiction, which might make their legal action futile. Lawyers for the company, as part of their defense to the application, sought to argue that there was no justification for freezing its assets, because the claimants did not have an arguable case against Monterrico. This argument was rejected by the court, which held that "the alleged facts as to Monterrico's responsibility and participation in the alleged brutality against the protesters would appear to be sufficient to found a cause of action."[86]

Shell Claim (2011)

The history of oil companies operating in the Niger Delta, Nigeria, is long and complex. Allegations against these companies range from pollution of the Delta to mistreatment of those who protest about their activities. The claims in the English High Court concern the environmental damage caused to land and waterways in the Delta following massive oil spills that took place in 2008 and 2009. A class-action lawsuit was brought by the affected fishing community, the Bodo community, against Shell and its subsidiary, Shell Petroleum Development Company (SPDC), in April 2011 on behalf of 69,000 claimants.[87] The case was settled just four months later, with an admission of liability on SPDC's part that equipment failures were responsible for the two oil spills but not for the amount of oil spilled or the extent of the damage caused.[88] The company began negotiating a compensation package with the claimants' law firm, but in March 2012, these talks broke down and further papers were filed with the High Court.[89]

The original admission of liability came just days before a UN report detailing the extent of environmental degradation in the Niger Delta brought about by oil pollution was released. Shell was heavily implicated in the report. Further litigation against Shell for environmental damage in the Niger Delta has been conducted in the Netherlands. On January 30, 2013, the District Court of The Hague issued a decision ordering Shell to pay compensation to one of the claimants, Friday Alfred Akpan, but it dismissed the balance of the claims.[90] Litigation is also underway in the United States, where a case was

---

85. Guerrero v. Monterrico Metals Plc [2009] EWHC 2475.
86. Guerrero, *Id.* at ¶ 27.
87. Bodo Cmty. v. Shell Petroleum Dev. Co. of Nigeria, Claim No. HQ11X01280.
88. John Vidal, *Shell Accepts Liability for Two Oil Spills in Nigeria*, Guardian (Aug. 3, 2011); Sylvia Pfeifer & Jane Croft, *Shell's Nigeria Pay-out Could Top £250m*, Fin. Times (Aug. 3, 2011).
89. Jane Croft, *Shell Faces Claims Over Niger Delta Spills*, Fin. Times (Mar. 22, 2012). A recent news item from Leigh Day cites 11,000 claimants, not 69,000 as was originally reported, *see Martyn Day Condemns Oil Pollution Clean Up Operation in Niger Delta as 'Totally Amateurish'*, Leigh Day (Sept. 23, 2012), http://www.leighday.co.uk/News/2012/September-2012/Martyn-Day-condemns-oil-pollution-clean-up-operati (last accessed Dec. 10, 2013)
90. Akpan v. Shell, 337050 / HAZA 09-1580. (District Court of the Hague, Jan 30, 2013)

filed in the district court in Detroit in October 2011 on behalf of the village of Ogale in Rivers State. In this case, U.S. $1 billion is being sought in compensation for long-time environmental damage brought by oil production. The lawsuit accuses Shell of "willful" negligence in its fifty years of oil production through a local subsidiary and relies heavily on the UN report mentioned above to substantiate this allegation.[91]

Anglo-American Claim (2011)

This claim was issued in September 2011 on behalf of 450 named laborers from South Africa and neighboring countries, such as Lesotho, who worked in the company's gold mines until 1998.[92] It alleged that these workers are suffering from diseases such as silicosis brought on by exposure to dust at the mines. Disparity of treatment between black and white workers resulting in greater exposure by black workers is also alleged.[93] According to Leigh Day, solicitors for the claimants, the case was filed in the United Kingdom because of the better-developed case management procedures, which make this jurisdiction friendlier to claimants, and because of the UK measure of damages that would have been awarded if the case is successful.[94]

The claim was against Anglo-American South Africa and was brought on the basis of the present control and management of this company by its UK-headquartered parent, Anglo-American plc. The company challenged jurisdiction and in July 2013 the High Court accepted this argument and dismissed the claim.[95] This litigation follows a series of three test cases brought against Anglo-American South Africa in the Johannesburg High Court.[96] These cases were brought by local lawyers in collaboration with overseas specialist lawyers and had the financial support of the South African Legal Aid Board. The decision to pursue the latest claim in England and Wales rather than South Africa is likely to have been premised on the fact that a type of class action can be brought in this jurisdiction. The Leigh Day press release announcing the litigation specifically references the fact that the proceedings include a representative claim on behalf of unnamed claimants in similar circumstances to the named claimants.

---

91.   The fate of this case, Okpabi v. Royal Dutch Shell, must now be in doubt in light of the Supreme Court's decision in *Kiobel, supra* note 7, due to the limited connection between the U.S. and the alleged violation in this case.

92.   Vava & Ors v. Anglo-American South Africa Ltd. [2012] EWHC 1969.

93.   For example, it is alleged that black workers did not have access to showers unlike their white counterparts.

94.   *See Gold Miners with Lung Disease Start UK Legal Action*, LEIGH DAY (Sept. 11, 2011), http://www.leighday.co.uk/News/2011/September-2011/Gold-miners-with-lung-disease-start-UK-legal-actio (last accessed Dec. 10, 2013) (given that damages awarded under the Rome II Regulations are done so according to the law of the country where the harm occurred, see above, it is unclear why Leigh Day has asserted that UK damages would be awarded in this case. It may be that the claims predate Rome II.).

95.   Vava v. Anglo American South Africa Ltd. (2013) EWHC 2131 (QB).

96.   Hempe & Ors v. Anglo-American South Africa Ltd., South Guateng High Court, Johannesburg Case No 18273/04. It is referred to in Richard Meeran's article *supra note* 112.

In March 2011, the Constitutional Court of South Africa heard a similar case against AngloGold Ashanti Ltd., a successor company to Anglo-American South Africa.[97] The claimant, Thembekile Mankanyi, was a disabled South African miner who sought compensation for silicosis. Mr. Mankanyi worked high-risk jobs as a miner for sixteen years and suffered exposure to harmful dusts and gases that caused his lung disease. The court held that the ex-mineworker could claim damages of more than 2.6 million rand (U.S. $366,440) from his former employer because he had acquired a lung disease while working at one of its mines. This award came despite the fact that he had previously received a small sum under the South African industrial-disease compensation scheme.[98] The success of this litigation has opened the door to further claims, which may be brought by the hundreds of thousands of mine workers affected by the same type of disease.

The importance of these six cases cannot be underestimated. Although they represent only a tiny minority of all allegations leveled at corporations for human rights violations perpetrated abroad, they demonstrate to both companies and victims that justice may be sought and achieved in this way. This is really the only effective method in the United Kingdom of holding companies accountable for harm committed abroad. However, the effects of changes to procedural law and funding of civil litigation have the potential to severely impact this kind of litigation. (See chapter 11 by Srinivasan for further detail.)

Procedural Law Affecting the Ability to Bring Claims against Corporations in the UK Courts

With no statutory footing on which to take a company to court for human rights abuses committed abroad, claimants are reliant on actions in tort and are heavily affected by changes to the procedural law affecting such claims.

Until recently these cases have been beset by expensive preliminary arguments on grounds of *forum non conveniens* (FNC), in which defendants sought to argue that the UK courts were not the appropriate forum for the case to be heard. These FNC arguments were severely limited by two major legal developments relating to the conflict of laws: the enactment of Brussels Regulations (EC) No. 44/2001 on jurisdiction and the recognition and enforcement of judgments in civil and commercial matters (the Brussels Regulation),[99]

---

97.   Mankayi v. AngloGold (CCT 40/10) [2011] ZACC 3; 2011 (5) BCLR 453 (CC); 2011 (3) SA 237 (CC) (Mar. 3, 2011).

98.   IRIN, *Glimmer of Justice for Sick Gold Miners in South Africa*, Guardian (Mar. 29, 2011), http://www.theguardian.com/global-development/2011/mar/29/south-africa-gold-miners-compensation (last accessed Dec. 10, 2013)

99.   *See* The European Commission's Application of European Union Law Web site on Regulations, http://ec.europa.eu/eu_law/introduction/what_regulation_en.htm (last visited July 26, 2013) (The Brussels Regulation of December 22, 2000, came into force on March 1, 2002. It was devised to add certainty to

and the decision of the European Court of Justice (ECJ) in *Owusu v. Jackson*.[100] In *Owusu*, the ECJ decided that the terms of the Brussels Convention[101] prohibit the courts of England and Wales from declining jurisdiction on the grounds of *forum non conveniens* in respect of defendants domiciled therein.[102] As a result of this judgment, it is now widely accepted that the common law rules on *forum non conveniens* will not apply in cases where the corporate defendant is domiciled in the regulation state[103] in which the claim is brought, and that the court will have to accept jurisdiction.[104] It is only when the corporate defendant has no domicile in the regulation state[105] and does not otherwise fall within the terms of the regulation[106] that the question of jurisdiction is a matter to be determined within the national law of the court seized,[107] which in the United Kingdom is in accordance with *Spiliada Maritime Corp v. Cansulex Ltd.*[108]

Regulation (EC) 864/2007 on the Law Applicable to Non-Contractual Obligations (known as the Rome II Regulation) has also made a number of changes to the preexisting legislative scheme in the United Kingdom governing the procedural aspects of claims brought against companies for harm committed abroad.[109] The Rome II Regulation came into force in the United Kingdom on January 11, 2009, and has as one of its aims the introduction of uniform choice-of-law rules in respect of noncontractual obligations arising

---

the resolution of civil disputes and to harmonise the differences between the laws of the different member states of the European Union in relation to conflict of laws. Regulations are the most direct form of EU law—as soon as they are passed, they have binding legal force throughout every Member State, of which the UK is one, on a par with national laws. National governments do not have to take action themselves to implement EU regulations.).

100. [2005] EUECJ C-281/02 (Mar. 1, 2005). The leading authority on the subject of the conflict of laws states that although the European Court made its findings in terms of the Brussels Convention, that is "no basis for supposing that the answer would have been any different if the English Court had been given jurisdiction under another provision of the 1968 convention of the judgments regulation." DICEY, MORRIS & COLLINS, THE CONFLICT OF LAWS 472 (14th ed. 2006).

101. The Brussels Convention was an earlier incarnation of what is now the Brussels Regulation. The Brussels Regulation supersedes the Brussels Convention of 1968, which was applicable between the EU countries before the Regulation entered into force. The Convention continues to apply with respect to those territories of EU countries that fall within its territorial scope and that are excluded from the regulation pursuant to Article 299 of the Treaty establishing the European Community (now Article 355 of the Treaty on the Functioning of the European Union). *See Jurisdiction, Recognition and Enforcement of Judgments in Civil and Commercial Matters ("Brussels I")*, EUROPA, http://europa.eu/legislation _summaries/justice_freedom_security/judicial_cooperation_in_civil_matters/l33054_en.htm (last visited July 26, 2013).

102. *Id.*

103. Or Convention State.

104. Brussels Regulation at art. 2(1); *see* DICEY, MORRIS AND COLLINS, *supra* note 97, at 472; *see supra* note 82, *Guerrero & Ors v Monterrico Metals plc*, ¶ 23.

105. Or Convention State.

106. Or Convention.

107. *See* Brussels Regulation at art. 4; Ionnou v Frangos [1999] 2 Lloyds rep. 337 (CA).

108. [1987] A.C. 460.

109. Private International Law (Miscellaneous Provisions) Act 1995.

out of a tort or delict.[110] The regulation made three important changes that will affect the victims of human rights abuses committed by companies who are seeking remedy in the UK courts. It clarified the law regarding the choice of applicable law, the law governing the assessment of damages, and the law governing the period of limitation.

Under the Rome II Regulation, the general rule is that the applicable law will "be the law of the country in which the damage occurs irrespective of the country . . . in which the indirect consequences of that event occur."[111] In some senses, this scheme is similar to the one that existed previously. Under the Private International Law (Miscellaneous Provisions) Act 1995, the general rule was that the applicable law was that of the country in which the injury occurred, which is not significantly different from the test of "where the damage occurs." Where the pre- and post-Rome schemes differ is in the test to be applied when a party seeks to argue that a law of a country other than that country in which the harm occurred should be the applicable law. In the pre-Rome scheme, the test was as follows: Having considered the significance of factors that connect the tort to each of the respective countries, was it substantially more appropriate for the law of the other country to apply?[112] The Rome II Regulation requires the existence of a manifestly closer connection with that other country.[113]

Though it is clear that two different tests apply, in reality the practical difference is often negligible. The areas where the choice of applicable law does have an impact, and where Rome II has made significant changes to the existing legislative scheme in the United Kingdom, are in the assessment of damages and the calculation of limitation periods,[114] which will have a serious impact on the financial viability of any particular claim and whether the court will have jurisdiction to hear it. Another area where the choice of applicable law will have an impact is in claims arising from employment where local workmen's compensation law bars claims against employers.[115]

Previously, damages were calculated in accordance with the law of the state,[116] even

---

110. The Rome II Regulation was directly applicable in the United Kingdom and no UK legislation was required to bring it into effect. However, in this instance domestic legislation has been created specifically to clarify the position. 864/2007, on the Law Applicable to Non-Contractual Obligations (Rome II), 2007 O.J. (L 199) 40 (EC) [hereinafter Rome II Regulation].

111. Rome II Regulation at art. 4(1) (EC) No. 864/2007.

112. Private International Law (Miscellaneous Provisions) Act 1995, §12(1)(2).

113. Rome II Regulation at art. 4(3).

114. A limitation period is the time within which a party to a claim must bring that claim. A failure to do so will, in all but the most exceptional circumstances, mean that the court has no jurisdiction to hear the claim. There are different limitation periods for different causes of action.

115. In his article, *Tort Litigation Against Multinationals for Violation of Human Rights: An Overview of the Position Outside the U.S.*, Richard Meeran identifies this as a class of of case in which the choice of applicable law may make a fundamental difference to the determination of the substantive issues. 3 CITY U. HONG KONG L. REV. 16-17 (Fall 2012). According to Meeran, a highly regarded solicitor and partner at Leigh Day who acted for the claimants in these cases, such bars were raised in: *Connelly, Lubbe* and *Sithole, supra* note 71, as well as in the 2011 Anglo-American litigation, *supra* note 89.

116. *See* Harding and Wealands [2006] UKHL 32, [2007] 2 A.C. 1 [24].

when the applicable law of the substantive claim was that of another country. This meant that damages would be determined in accordance with English law, which is often more generous than the equivalent provisions of the law of the MNC host state. The Rome II Regulation provides that damages will be assessed in accordance with the law and procedure of the country in which the harm occurred.[117]

The Rome II Regulation has also standardized the approach to limitation periods. Article 15(h) provides that the law chosen as the applicable law will govern the rules of prescription and limitation. This, again, is similar to the situation prior to Rome II, which was governed by the Foreign Limitations Periods Act 1984 (FLPA 1984).[118]

Whether this is a positive or a negative thing for claimants will depend very much on the limitation periods under the applicable law. The real difference is that the undue hardship exception—expressly provided for in the FLPA 1984, and which allowed a court to disregard foreign limitation law if its application would constitute undue hardship—is conspicuously missing from the Rome II Regulation.[119]

Under Rome II, a court can only disregard foreign limitation law if applying it would be contrary to public policy, that is, the first strand of the FLPA 1984 test. Such an exception is clearly only to be invoked in exceptional cases.[120] But as the leading authority on the subject observes, though, "there may be foreign causes of action or categories of damage based on laws which when scrutinized as to content and effect of application are found

---

117. Rome II Regulation, art. 4, 15.
118. § 1 states: "(1) Application of foreign limitation law

(1) Subject to the following provisions of this Act, where in any action or proceedings in a court in England and Wales the law of any other country falls (in accordance with rules of private international law applicable by any such court) to be taken into account in the determination of any matter—
(a) the law of that other country relating to limitation shall apply in respect of that matter for the purposes of the action or proceedings; and
(b) except where that matter falls within subsection (2) below, the law of England and Wales relating to limitation shall not so apply.
(2) A matter falls within this subsection if it is a matter in the determination of which both the law of England and Wales and the law of some other country fall to be taken into account."
119.   See also § 4; Durham v. T & N Plc, [1993] 4 S.C.R. 289 (Can.), in which a claim brought in England against T & N by an asbestos victim who worked at T & N's subsidiary factory in Quebec was struck out when the Court of Appeal held that the law of Quebec (which had a one-year limitation period) should apply (Meeran, *supra* note 112, at 9). S.2 FLPA 1984 states, in so far as it is relevant, the followingIn any case in which the application of section 1 above would to any extent conflict (whether under subsection (2) below or otherwise) with public policy, that section shall not apply to the extent that its application would so conflict.
The application of section 1 above in relation to any action or proceedings shall conflict with public policy *to the extent that its application would cause undue hardship* to a person who is, or might be made, a party to the action or proceedings. (emphasis added)
120. *See* DICEY, MORRIS & COLLINS, SUPPLEMENT 2011 TO THE CONFLICT OF LAWS 513 (14th ed. 2006).

to be contrary to fundamental principles of public policy, for example, where a law or its consequences represent a gross infringement of fundamental human rights."[121]

Funding of Cases

In addition to the changes made by the Brussels II Regulation, another legislative development that will affect victims' ability to bring litigation against companies for human rights abuses and corporate-related harm committed abroad are the reforms to the civil costs scheme suggested by Lord Justice Jackson and incorporated into the Legal Aid, Sentencing and Punishment of Offenders Act 2012 (Legal Aid Act). Part 2 of the Legal Aid Act, which reforms payment for legal services in civil cases, came into force in April 2013 and is anticipated to have a severe impact on firms conducting this kind of litigation. These are dealt with in detail by Srinivasan in chapter 11.

As elaborated in that chapter, claimant lawyers previously were able to take on cases against MNCs on a no win no fee basis, under which they agreed to fund all legal costs and expenses on the understanding that they would recoup those costs from the MNC if the case was successful.[122] The Legal Aid Act abolished the success fee and introduced a new, tougher proportionality test to the assessment of costs, which requires MNCs to pay back only those legal costs that are proportionate to the compensation received. Success fees, if they are to be paid, would need to be deducted from claimants' damages, thus decreasing their much-needed compensation for injury and loss. This scheme has attracted significant criticism from a number of organizations,[123] including a personal letter from John Ruggie, the former UN special representative on business and human rights, to Jonathan Djanogly, MP, the Parliamentary Under-Secretary of State at the Ministry of Justice.[124] In this letter the UK government was roundly criticized for a measure that was seen to be entirely contrary to the promotion of the UNGPs.

The European-led reforms to procedural law identified above are important, but they do not demonstrate any trend toward increased or decreased corporate accountability. The changes that these measures have made to the process of litigating against companies for human rights violations committed abroad were brought about as part of wide-ranging reform to almost all conflict-of-laws cases, irrespective of subject matter or grounds of claim. Other than a wholehearted effort to standardize these kinds of cases, there does not

---

121. *See* DICEY, MORRIS & COLLINS, THE CONFLICT OF LAWS 228I (15th ed. 2012).

122. This was authorised by §58 and §58A of the Court and Legal Services Act 1990.

123. *See, e.g., Report of the Committee on the Elimination of Racial Discrimination, 79th Sess., 8 August–2 September 2011* ¶29, CERD/C/GBR/CO/18-20.

124. Letter from the Special Representative of the Secretary-General for Business and Human Rights dated May 16, 2011, http://www.guardian.co.uk/law/2011/jun/16/united-nations-legal-aid-cuts-trafigura (last accessed Dec. 10, 2013).

appear to be a political agenda. The extent to which these reforms will impact this kind of litigation over and above the impact of the *Owusu* decision will depend very much on the way the courts apply the principles enunciated in the Rome II Regulation. For example, it remains to be seen whether the courts will apply the public policy exception to prevent denials of justice based on short limitation periods. In contrast to the generic European regulations, the United Kingdom's position on civil costs is more instructive and seems to undermine the UK government's statements endorsing the UNGPs—a matter clearly drawn to its attention by John Ruggie himself. Irrespective of this, the UK government has refused to make an exception in the legislation for cases brought against MNCs for corporate-related harm committed abroad.[125]

Comment on the Litigation

The cases we have set out in detail above have been brought predominantly in the tort of negligence,[126] with some exceptions, such as the BP breach of contract claim and the Monterrico tort of wrongful imprisonment claim. The negligence claims allege that the parent company has breached its duty of care to the claimants in each matter with the result that they have suffered harm.[127] By targeting the parent company, claimants have avoided having to argue that the corporate veil should be pierced to trace liability for the actions of the local subsidiary back to the parent company or other branch of the business in the United Kingdom. As yet there has been no judicial determination of a case argued in this way, although the recent decision of the UK Court of Appeal in the case of *Chandler v. Cape* advanced and clarified the law in this area.[128] Prior to *Chandler*, the closest the courts had come was a decision in response to a strike-out application in the case of *Thor Chemicals*.[129] In this matter the cause of action was negligence, and the claim was against the UK parent company of a South African manufacturer of mercury-based chemicals. Liability was asserted on the basis of negligent design, transfer, setup, operation, supervision, and monitoring of the intrinsically hazardous processes at the South African plant.

---

125. On September 13, 2011, the Government's Public Bill Committee debated an amendment to the Legal Aid, Sentencing and Punishment of Offenders Bill, tabled by a Labour MP, that would have exempted claims brought by foreigners against UK multinationals from the civil litigation reforms. A majority rejected the amendment; Conservative and Liberal Democrat MPs voted with the government and against the amendment.

126. The tort of negligence was established in the case of *Donoghue v Stevenson* [1932] A.C. 562 (Eng.).

127. In the Anglo-American case, *supra* note 89, for example, it is argued that the company was negligent in its management and control of the local subsidiary's health and safety procedures including dust control measures.

128. [2012] E.W.C.A. Civ 525 (Eng.).

129. Ngcobo & Others v. Thor Chemical Holdings & Desmond Cowley (Maurice Kay J, Nov. 7, 1996, unreported).

The strike-out application was unsuccessful. The judge accepted that the claimants "went well beyond establishing a clear evidential basis" for liability against the parent company.

The case of *Chandler* is an important development, even though it is a domestic case concerning events at a factory in Uxbridge (near London) that produced asbestos. The claimant worked at the factory during the late 1950s and early 1960s loading bricks. He recently contracted asbestosis as a result of inhaling dust in this workplace. His employer was Cape Products, a company that had gone out of business some years ago but that had been a subsidiary of Cape plc. Mr. Chandler brought proceedings against the parent company, arguing that it had assumed responsibility for the employees of Cape Products and was therefore liable for Cape Products' admitted negligence, despite the separate legal identities of Cape *plc* and Cape Products. Giving the leading judgment in Mr. Chandler's favor, Lady Justice Arden set out the principles that apply in such cases. She held that the law may impose responsibility on a parent company for the health and safety of its subsidiary's employees in "appropriate circumstances," such as where the businesses of parent and subsidiary are similar and the parent's superior knowledge of relevant health and safety matters is relied on by the subsidiary. She was prepared to find that Cape *plc* had assumed responsibility toward the Cape Products' employees in circumstances where the latter had installed its asbestos production business at the Cape Products' site and maintained a certain level of control over the business. Cape *plc* involved itself in the health and safety of the Cape Products' employees through its chief medical adviser, who personally visited the factory when an employee was found to be suffering from asbestosis.[130]

The question remains as to why the international cases concerning human rights violations committed abroad have not gone before the courts and thus been the subject of judicial determination on the question of parent-company liability. It has been argued that the reasons are "the financial realities and risks to the MNC, the claimants and the claimants' lawyers of not settling."[131] Risks to the company include damage to reputation and consequential impact on share price, as well as creating unwanted legal precedent, whereas risks to the claimants include the fact that they are using an untested legal argument in circumstances where the imperative for them to win is great because of lost livelihood, health, and so on. There is also risk to the claimants' lawyers, who are generally working on a *no win no fee* basis and who will have already expended significant financial outlay investigating and pursuing the claim. In these circumstances there is impetus from all sides to seek to settle the case rather than argue this point in court.

---

130. Arden LJ was aware of the significance of the judgment. At ¶ 2 she said: "We understand that this is one of the first cases in which an employee has established at trial liability to him on the part of his employer's parent company, and thus this appeal is of some importance not only to the parties but to other cases."

131. Meeran, *supra* note 112, at 10.

The question of the choice of law is also pertinent in this type of case. As we stated above, often the practical difference that the choice of the applicable law makes to determination of the substantive issues in a case is negligible. By way of example, in the case against Monterrico Metals, the claims were formulated using both the English law of negligence and equivalent provisions under the Peruvian civil code. The claimants' lawyers felt confident that the same issues would need to be determined under both.[132] The choice of applicable law may, however, have worrying consequences for the claimants in this type of claim if, for example, tort law is not well developed in the host state or, in the extreme case, where amnesty laws have been passed exempting violators from liability.[133]

The tactic employed by companies fighting these cases has been the vigorous pursuit of preliminary or ancillary issues, followed by negotiation to reach a settlement before the case reaches trial. We have already discussed the reasons on both sides for reaching negotiated settlements in these cases. Examples of issues that have been the subject of preliminary or ancillary litigation in these cases include an unsuccessful application for the claimants to disclose the "after the event" insurance premium in the BP case[134] and the libel action against Leigh Day in the Trafigura case, regarding statements on the firm's Web site alleging that people had died and suffered miscarriages following exposure to the toxic waste.[135] Claimants in these cases have also successfully used preliminary issues to progress their claims. In the Monterrico case, the claimants applied for a freezing injunction to ensure that enough of the company's assets remained in the United Kingdom, and in the Trafigura case, the claimants applied for a temporary injunction to prevent the company from making contact with them personally.

Conclusion

Recent years have seen major developments in the understanding of the responsibility of corporations for human rights violations. The UK government has been at the forefront of some of these, as illustrated by the fact that the UK was one of the countries that endorsed

---

132. Meeran, *supra* note 112, at 16.

133. This did happen in the context of the long-running Ok Tedi litigation in Australia. The Ok Tedi Mine Continuation (Ninth Supplemental) Act 2001 was passed into law in Papua New Guinea and purported to exempt Australian mining company BHP from environmental claims regarding pollution of the Ok Tedi River. Dagi v. Broken Hill Proprietory Co., Supreme Court of Victoria, Sept 22, 1995, unreported.

134. Pedro Emiro Florez Arroyo and Others v. BP Exploration Company (Colombia) Limited: Ocensa Pipeline Group Litigation [2010] EWHC 1643 (Eng.) (Heard before the Senior Master on May 6, 2010. After the event insurance is used to protect claimants against the cost of losing their case).

135. *See* Agreed Final Joint Statement which Records the Settlement of the Libel Action Against Leigh Day, BBC NEWS, http://news.bbc.co.uk/1/shared/bsp/hi/pdfs/20_09_09_trafigura_statement.pdf (last visited July 27, 2013).

the UNGPs when they were adopted by the UNHRC in 2011.[136] It was also one of the first states to launch a national action plan on businesses and human rights. However, with the exception of the amendments to the Companies Act 2006, the focus of the government is on soft-law standards and voluntary initiatives, rather than legally enforceable norms. This position is fortified by the fact that the government does not accept itself as duty bound to protect against human rights violations by nonstate actors; thus, it does not feel legally obligated to protect against the excesses of corporate behavior.[137] In these circumstances, the government's rejection of the proposed amendment to the Legal Aid Act, which would have carved out a funding exception for claims against multinationals, is unsurprising, even in the face of protest from the architect of the UNGPs. The government's plan for implementing the UNGPs, while containing some small indications of a more robust approach, provides no sanctions for the non-compliance with the UNGPs and thus continues the same vein as earlier government initiatives in this area.[138]

Regarding legislation, the main discernible legislative trend is that of consultation on increased company reporting requirements both at the national level and at the EU level. It appears that the trigger for these enhanced reporting standards has not been exclusively concern about human rights violations by corporations, but rather the global economic crisis of 2007 to 2008 and the need to ensure greater corporate accountability for shareholders. However, there is no doubt that the proposals have gained speed since the adoption of the UNGPs. Whether the legislative amendments go far enough is open to question, but they certainly represent a step in the right direction.[139] Developments in criminal legislation demonstrate a gradual willingness, which began pre-UNGPs, to hold companies accountable for specific offences, namely bribery and corporate manslaughter. It is also

---

136. The UK government has also pioneered improvements to the complaints mechanism for breaches of the OECD Guidelines on Multinational Enterprises.

137. *See* the Secretary of State for Foreign and Commonwealth Affairs's response to the *Third Report from the Foreign Affairs Committee Session 2012–13*, where in response to the suggestion that guidance and voluntary initiatives do not meet the spirit of the UNGPs the governments replied as follows: "The Government is grateful for the Committee's endorsement of its intention to develop a strategy based on the UN Guiding Principles. The Guiding Principles include an important focus on the State and its duty to protect human rights. The UK already has a mix of policies, legislation and regulations that help protect human rights and have been developed over many years. But gaps may still exist and the strategy under preparation makes clear that we are committed to having in place all the necessary measures and instruments to require and enable businesses to respect human rights. We also recognize the good work done, over many years, through the use of "soft law" initiatives. For example the UK was a founding member of the Voluntary Principles on Security and Human Rights, set up in 2000, and which has been an important mechanism for spreading best practice among companies and states involved in the extractive industries sector." *Supra* note 4, at 19–20.

138. *See* launch and report, *supra* note 4, the more robust in relation to public procurement and export credit.

139. UNGP *supra* note 2, at 6 states that "States must protect against human rights abuse within their territory and/or jurisdiction by third parties, including business enterprises. This requires taking appropriate steps to prevent, investigate, punish and redress such abuse through effective policies, legislation, regulations and adjudication."

clear that the traditional limitations on extraterritorial jurisdiction are being chipped away and that in some cases this will have relevance for companies operating abroad. However, despite these developments, existing UK criminal legislation is insufficient to hold such companies legally to account . There is no suggestion that sufficient legislation is on the horizon; rather, the UK government is taking steps to prevent such a possibility. By way of example, the UK government, pre-UNGPs, did have the opportunity to legislate to make companies liable for some of the serious harm they can cause abroad, yet the government consciously limited the scope of the legislation.[140] More recently, and noticeably after its public endorsement of the UNGPs, the UK government filed a joint amicus brief with the government of the Netherlands in support of Shell in the U.S. Supreme Court case *Kiobel et al. v. Royal Dutch Petroleum*, agreeing with the Second Circuit's holding that international law does not impose liability on corporations, and arguing that application of the ATS to foreign nationals for actions in foreign countries with no nexus to the United States violates international law.[141] Further still, in its recent response to the Foreign Affairs Committee, the UK government conspicuously avoided the question of whether, in taking steps to meet the requirements of the UNGPs, it would go beyond mere guidance and voluntary initiatives.[142]

With regard to litigation, although recent years have seen an increase in the number of claims against MNCs for their harmful activities overseas, these cases represent just a few examples of such harm. The reality is that only a tiny percentage of victims will be able to seek justice in the English courts, for reasons including their lack of knowledge of the option of bringing a case in this forum and their lack of connection to suitable lawyers. The courts of England and Wales have shown themselves to be receptive to the arguments raised in the cases that have so far been filed. Moreover, substantive decisions are few in number, but the application for a freezing injunction in the Monterrico litigation is one useful precedent. As part of her decision in that matter, Mrs. Justice Gloster accepted that the claimant protesters had a "good arguable case."[143] The settlement of cases, though not resulting in helpful legal precedent, does mean that individual victims have been compensated for corporate harm, and a message has been sent to other companies that they could be next.

Recent legislative developments to reform the funding of civil litigation and the enactment of Rome II demonstrate how precarious the monetary element of such claims has become. The reforms brought about by the Legal Aid Act in particular are likely to have a chilling effect on the ability of lawyers to take on this type of litigation. It is therefore of

---

140. *See* CMCHA.

141. *See* Kiobel, et al. v. Royal Dutch Petroleum, NAT'L CHAMBER LITIGATION CTR., http://www.chamberlitigation.com/kiobel-et-al-v-royal-dutch-petroleum (last visited July 27, 2013).

142. *See supra* note 134. The Third Report from the Foreign Affairs Select Committee.

143. Monterrico 2009, *supra* note 82, ¶ 26.

paramount importance that other sources of funding are identified to ensure that victims do have access to the courts of England and Wales in appropriate cases. One option might be to follow the model used in the United States by organizations such as EarthRights International, which is a charitable body that raises funds from the public to pay for litigation against corporate defendants and works in conjunction with lawyers and other NGOs to pursue such claims. This model was also used in the Netherlands for the case against Shell: the NGO Friends of the Earth raised funds to supports its legal case on behalf of affected individuals from the Niger Delta.[144]

The difficulty of funding this type of litigation also leads to questions about what other routes to seeking justice are available to victims of human rights violations by MNCs. One option is the use of the grievance mechanism provided through the Organization for Economic Cooperation and Development (OECD) Guidelines on Multinational Enterprises. The UK National Contact Point (NCP), set up under the auspices of the guidelines, does provide a route to complain about an MNC's conduct and to seek redress. However, the fact that no compensation may be awarded, and that no findings of the NCP are legally enforceable, means that this is not always an attractive or viable reparations option for victims. Also, due to the nature of the process that seeks mediation or conciliation in the first instance, this kind of grievance mechanism is quite likely to be limited to specific kinds of harm. Complaints arising from gross human rights violations such as torture or inhuman or degrading treatment might well be inappropriate for such a forum. The NCP, as the history of its cases shows, is far better suited to mediating disputes arising from breaches of economic and social rights, such as the right to participation.[145] Victims of the more egregious violations, such as the protesters and their families in the Monterrico case, must therefore be able to pursue their claims in the English courts despite the government's stance that it is not legally obliged to protect them. Their lawyers must work creatively to find ways to fund their cases and overcome the procedural obstacles they face. There is much work to be done.

---

144. Akpan, *supra* note 87.

145. *See, e.g.*, the NCP report of *Complaint Against Unilever plc on India's Doom Dooma Factory* (Oct. 2010), https://www.gov.uk/uk-national-contact-point-for-the-organisation-for-economic-co-operation-and-development-oecd-guidelines-for-multinational-enterprises (last accessed Dec. 10, 2013). In this case the IUF (International Union of Food, Agricultural, Hotel, Restaurant, Catering, Tobacco and Allied Workers' Associations) made a number of allegations of breaches of the guidelines by Unilever plc in its factory in Doom Dooma in Assam, India. The main allegation was that Hindustan Unilever's management at the Doom Dooma factory had failed to respect the right of their employees to be represented by a legitimate trade union by requiring employees to renounce their membership of the Hindustan Lever Workers Union and instead join the Hindustan Unilever Democratic Workers Union, which the IUF alleged had been established by the management following a lockout announced by management on July 15, 2007. Unilever denied all of the allegations made by the IUF. The parties entered conciliation and agreed to the application of a secret ballot at the Doom Dooma factory. In light of the conciliation, the UK NCP did not carry out an examination of the allegations contained in IUF's complaint or make a statement as to whether there was a breach of the guidelines.

Chapter 11

Current Trends and Future Effects in Transnational Litigation against Corporations in the United Kingdom

Shubhaa Srinivasan

Introduction

Economic globalization has made the "governance gap"[1] that existed between the operational capacities of corporations and the regulatory capacities of states even more stark. Human rights abuses in the extractive, security, finance, natural resource, and other sectors in developing and developed countries—with the direct and indirect participation of transnational corporations (TNCs)—reveal that corporate impunities are an international legal problem because of the enormous global reach of corporations.[2] The scale of devastation that can be caused by corporate practice, such as BP's conduct in the Gulf of Mexico and the alleged indiscriminate dumping of potentially hazardous waste by Trafigura in the Côte d'Ivoire, affects the lives of tens of thousands of individuals, clearly signaling a need for serious analysis of how to plug the increasing governance gap. Though it is necessary for states, particularly developing states, to strengthen their regulatory capacity, it

---

1. Special Representative of the Secretary-General on the Issue of Hum. Rts. and Transnat'l Corp. and Other Bus. Enters., *"Protect, Respect and Remedy": A Framework for Business and Human Rights*, 3, 7, UN Doc. A/HRC/8/5 (Apr. 7, 2008) (by John Ruggie). Professor Ruggie postulates at the outset of his report that "the root cause of the business and human rights predicament today lies in the governance gaps created by globalization—between the scope and impact of economic forces and actors, and the capacities of societies to manage their adverse consequences."

2. For example, Anglo-American plc, one of the largest mining companies in the world, has business operations in over thirteen countries. *See Where We Operate*, ANGLOAMERICAN, http://www.angloamerican .com/about/operate (last visited July 23, 2013).

has also been argued that the home state of the TNC, typically (but not always) a Western state, should fill the regulatory vacuum.[3]

The emergence and development of transnational litigation under private law in the context of business and human rights in the United Kingdom reveals the inherent complexities of such litigation. Such complexities include the challenges faced by the foreign litigants and their lawyers and the UK courts' approach to addressing the access to justice barriers typically faced by such litigants.

Development of Transnational Litigation in the United Kingdom

Transnational litigation is the term used in this paper to describe business-related human rights civil claims brought in the United Kingdom by overseas victims who have suffered harm alleged to have been caused by an act or omission of a multinational corporate defendant either based in the United Kingdom or over which the UK court is able to exercise jurisdiction. Such cases are therefore not litigated in the country where the harm occurs (sometimes referred to as the "host state") but in the "home state" where the TNC is domiciled.[4] The UK courts may also accept jurisdiction over a defendant outside the United Kingdom in relation to a tort where damage has been sustained within UK jurisdiction or damage resulted from an act committed within the jurisdiction.[5]

In such cases, victims whose human rights have been infringed by corporate acts and/or omissions have been using existing domestic civil law principles, mainly English tort law, to provide themselves a remedy.[6] The foundation of a claim is grounded in principles of domestic tort law (mainly the law of negligence), not upon a breach of international law. Like many other jurisdictions, the United Kingdom has not adopted specific legislation that governs and regulates the overseas activities of TNCs domiciled in the United Kingdom, and that provides victims specific causes of action or remedies against the TNCs for their violation of such human rights or in causing harm. This fundamental inadequacy poses

---

3.   Jan Wouters & Cedric Ryngaert, *Litigation for Overseas Corporate Human Rights Abuses in the European Union: The Challenge of Jurisdiction*, 40 GEO. WASH. INT'L L. REV. 939.

4.   The Civil Jurisdictions and Judgment Act 1982 as amended, later largely superseded by EC Regulation (EC) 44/2001 (December 22, 2000), which has direct effect in the UK. The specific provisions are set out later in this chapter.

5.   Civil Procedure Rules ("CPR"), 6.20(8).

6.   Transnational litigation claims have also been brought under the law of contract. For example, a legal claim brought by seventy-three Colombian rural farmers for alleged breach of contract and negligence against a former BP subsidiary is currently progressing through the UK courts. Pedro Emiro Florez Arroyo & 72 Ors v. Equion Energia Limitada, Claim No: HQ08X00328. Victims of business-related human rights violations also use public law to establish corporate accountability through indirect means. Such claims, brought by way of an application for judicial review, are challenges to the legality of the acts and omissions of public bodies. It is principally a method used to hold to account the UK government for conduct engaged by corporations domiciled in the UK who may be complicit in violations of international humanitarian law and international human rights law (therefore, corporations are not directly held accountable).

serious challenges to a victim's ability to sue a TNC to obtain appropriate redress, not least because remedies under the law of negligence[7] are limited or may not be sufficient or adequate for certain types of harm occasioned. The nature of *harm* is wide-ranging and particularly problematic in business and human rights cases. Some of these abuses fall into traditional concepts of harm under criminal and civil law, yet others may be articulated as a breach of a human right. While others (such as environmental harm) fall into a category where the offending company has liability under national law to provide redress, but there is no appropriate means of redress to compensate sufficiently for the harm. Often a case raises a range of *harm*. Some cases speak the human rights language, but others do not, and often a particular cause of action, such as pursuing a case under tort law, restricts the type of redress available.

In the vast majority of UK transnational cases, such as *Lubbe v. Cape plc*, *Connelly v. RTZ*, and the *Trafigura* case, the relief sought by the claimants was monetary compensation for personal injury. In *Alphaeus Zonsile Blom v. Anglo-American South Africa Ltd.*, Case No. 18267/04 (an ongoing South African litigation), the litigants, a group of ex-goldminers, are claiming for monetary damages to be used to set up a fund for periodic medical monitoring and treatment of silicosis and other lung disease. The claimants argue that they contracted these diseases due to alleged negligent exposure to unacceptable levels of silica dust when they worked in Anglo's gold mines in the Free State. The silicosis case is an example of how the traditional remedy of monetary compensation is being used creatively to address the wider problem of the lack of sustained access to proper medical treatment for the overwhelmingly black miners in South Africa.

Bringing litigation outside the country where harm occurs can also result in a limitation on types of redress available. For example, in relation to torts to immovable property (such as land), section 30 of the Civil Jurisdiction and Judgments Act 1982 extends the jurisdiction of the courts of England, Wales, and Northern Ireland to cover proceedings for trespass to, or any other tort affecting, immovable property in which the property in question is situated outside that part of the United Kingdom, unless the proceedings are principally concerned with a question of the title to, or the right to possession of, that property.[8]

---

7.   The basic elements of the law of negligence are that there exists a legal duty of care owed by one person to another, which is breached by an individual (the tortfeasor) thereby directly causing harm or injury to the victim of a tortious act resulting in damage suffered by the victim that is not too remote. Donoghue v. Stevenson, [1932] UKHL 100. The main remedy against tortious loss is compensation in monetary terms. In the case of a continuing tort, the courts may grant an injunction restraining the continuation or threat of harm.

8.   *See also* DICEY, MORRIS & COLLINS, THE CONFLICTS OF LAWS ¶ 23-034 (14th ed. 2006).

Essential Requirements for Transnational Litigation
to Be Brought in the United Kingdom

There are two principal requirements for a business-related human rights claim to proceed on its merits in the United Kingdom. First, the claimants must establish jurisdiction over the TNC's conduct abroad. Second, the availability of a possible cause of action must exist in the United Kingdom and in the host state where the damage or tort occurred.

EU Regulation (EC) No. 44/2001 of December 22, 2000 (sometimes referred to as "Rome II"),[9] stipulates that jurisdiction is to be exercised by the EU country in which the defendant is domiciled.[10] Chapter V, article 60 (1)–(3) provides that a company or other legal person is domiciled at the place where it has its

(a) statutory seat,
(b) central administration,[11] or
(c) principal place of business.

For the purposes of the United Kingdom and Ireland, "statutory seat" means the registered office, the place of incorporation, and/or the place under the law of which the formation took place.

Even if jurisdiction is established in the United Kingdom, it is quite likely that the law of the host state will be found to be the applicable law.[12] When foreign law (of the host state) applies to the dispute, it is that system of law that will provide the available causes of action to victims.[13]

---

9.   This EU Regulation on jurisdiction and the recognition of enforcement of judgments in civil and commercial matters has direct effect in the UK. In other words, it need not be transposed into domestic law to have effect.

10.   EU Regulation (EC) No. 44/2001 (Dec. 22, 2000), art. 2.1, § 1.

11.   A related action to the South African gold mining claim has been brought by additional hundreds of claimants against Anglo-American South Africa Ltd ("AASA") in England in 2012 on the grounds that AASA has its "central administration" in Anglo-American plc in London [Flatela Vava & Ors v Anglo-American South Africa Ltd: Jessica Margaret Young (by her Father and Litigation friend Kenneth Niall Young) v Anglo-American South Africa Ltd & 5 ors [2013] EWHC 2131 (QB)]. In May 2013, Mr Justice Andrew Smith ruled that the fact that AASA's entrepreneurial functions may be heavily influenced by the decisions taken, and policies and strategies adopted by Anglo-American plc in England does not mean that AASA's central administration can be said to be in England within the meaning of article 60(a)(b) (paragraph 71 and 72 of the judgment). The Vava action comprised two sets of Claimants, the South African victims and Jessica Margaret Young, who also brought an action against AASA for disabilities suffered resulting from a late diagnosis of phenylketonuria after her birth in Botswana in 1990, was negligently treated by five doctors, four of whom AASA is said to be vicariously liable. Miss Young is appealing against the first instance decision.

12.   Council Regulation 864/2007, art. 4, 2007 O.J. (L 199) (EU) [hereinafter Rome II]. Civil law claims brought in the UK in relation to torts occurring overseas are subject to the provisions of the EC Rome II Regulation, the provisions of Part III of the Private International Law (Miscellaneous Provisions) Act 1995 and common law rules in order to determine the applicable law to the dispute.

13.   Private International Law (Miscellaneous Provisions) Act, 1995, c. 42, Part II (UK). Equally under

Developments in Overcoming the Jurisdiction Hurdle

Overcoming the jurisdiction hurdle is one of the principle challenges faced by foreign litigants in their attempts to seek legal accountability of TNCs in the United Kingdom and other home states, such as the United States and Canada.[14]

Since the 1990s, the United Kingdom has experienced an increase in litigation for social and environmental damage caused by TNCs' overseas business operations.[15] Arguably, this trend has been possible because of a combination of important factors; the availability of British legal aid for non-British claimants and a developed judicial procedure for handling group actions[16] are two such factors. Perhaps most importantly, however, British judges have been willing to allow foreign claimants to use a British forum for adjudicating disputes on the basis that denying them a British forum would be a "denial of justice." The House of Lords,[17] in *Connelly (A.P.) v. RTZ Corporation plc & Ors,*[18] articulated such jurisprudence rooted in the concept of access to justice. This was a case where Mr. Connelly, who allegedly contracted laryngeal cancer as a result of exposure to uranium when he worked in a uranium mine in Namibia for RUL, a subsidiary of RTZ, sued RTZ in the British courts. Mr. Connelly successfully secured British legal aid to fund his case. The defendant, RTZ, argued that the appropriate venue for the claim would be Namibia. The House of Lords held that although Namibia was a more appropriate venue for the claim, it would not be in the interests of justice to make Mr. Connelly litigate his claim

---

common law tort principles, the *forum non conveniens* rule would require an analysis of the country to which the dispute has the closest connection.

14. TNC litigation is replete with examples where corporations have repeatedly applied to the home state courts in the UK, U.S., and Canada to stay legal proceedings brought against them by victim litigants on the basis that the more appropriate venue for the case is the host state where the harm occurred. In fact, corporate defendants in the majority of the UK cases referred to in this chapter have challenged the appropriateness of a British forum to hear the claims against them. In respect to Canadian cases, the Anvil case is a typical illustration of how jurisdictional arguments can potentially deprive victims a right to redress. In November 2010, the Canadian Association Against Impunity (CAAI) filed a class action on behalf of families of Congolese victims against Anvil Mining accusing it of having provided logistical support to the Congolese army who raped, murdered, and brutalised the people of the town of Kilwa in the DRC. In January 2012, the Quebec Court of Appeal overturned an earlier Quebec Superior Court decision that found Quebec had jurisdiction to hear the case on the basis that the claimants will not have any other avenue to obtain justice (either in the DRC or in Australia, where Anvil previously had its head office). The Court of Appeal reversed the earlier court decision despite acknowledging and expressing sympathy for the obstacles faced by the victims in seeking justice. CAAI filed an application with the Supreme Court of Canada on March 26, 2012, appealing the decision of the Appellate Court. In November 2012, the Supreme Court dismissed the application for leave to appeal, thus ending any possibility for the victims to obtain justice through the Canadian courts.

15. Jedrzej George Frynas, *Social and Environmental Litigation Against Transnational Firms in Africa,* 42 J. MOD. AFRICAN STUD. 363 (2004).

16. Almost all transnational litigation in the UK is brought by a large number of claimants, often as a group action under Part 19 of the UK's civil procedure rules.

17. The House of Lords was then the court of last resort and the highest appellate court in the United Kingdom. Its judicial function has since been superseded by the Supreme Court, which was established by Part 3 of the Constitutional Reform Act 2005 and started work on October 1, 2009.

18. [1998] A.C. 854, 874 (H.L.).

in Namibia because he would not have the legal, financial, and technical resources to be able to do so.

Lord Goff of Chieveley, in delivering the lead judgment, held,

[i]t is clear that the nature and complexity of the case is such that it cannot be tried at all without the benefit of financial assistance. There are two reasons for this. The first is that, as Sir Thomas Bingham M.R. recognized, there is no practical possibility of the issues which arise in the case being tried without the plaintiff having the benefit of professional legal assistance; and the second is that his case cannot be developed before a court without evidence from expert scientific witnesses. It is not in dispute that in these circumstances the case cannot be tried in Namibia; whereas, on the evidence before the Court of Appeal and before your Lordships, it appears that if the case is fought in this country the plaintiff will either obtain assistance in the form of legal aid, or failing that, receive the benefit of conditional fee agreement with his solicitor. . . . In these circumstances I am satisfied that this is a case in which, having regard to the nature of the litigation, substantial justice cannot be done in the appropriate forum, but can alone be done in this jurisdiction where the resources are available.[19]

Similar judicial reasoning surfaced in another landmark House of Lords decision that paved the way for foreign litigants to sue British TNCs in the British courts for harmful events that occurred abroad: *Lubbe v. Cape plc.*[20] This case concerned thousands of former Cape plc[21] workers in South Africa who suffered from asbestos-related illnesses as a result of alleged exposure to asbestos fiber while working in Cape's mines. Because Cape *plc* has had no presence in South Africa after 1989, a claim was brought by nearly 7,500 South African former mine workers against Cape *plc* in the English court in February 1997. As in *Connelly v. RTZ*, the claimants were successful in obtaining British legal aid, but the defendant argued that the British court had no jurisdiction to hear the claims. When the case went to the House of Lords on the matter of jurisdiction, the Law Lords ruled that the suit should be tried in England for a number of important reasons. Lord Bingham, in delivering the leading judgment, recognized that

if these proceedings were stayed in favor of the more appropriate forum in South Africa the probability is that the plaintiffs would have no means of obtaining the professional representation and the expert evidence which would be essential if these

19.   [1998] A.C. 854, 874 (H.L.).
20.   [2000] 1 WLR 1545.
21.   Cape plc is a leading British TNC manufacturer of insulation materials.

claims were to be justly decided. This would amount to a denial of justice. In the special and unusual circumstances of these proceedings, lack of means, in South Africa, to prosecute these claims to a conclusion provides a compelling ground . . . for the refusal to stay the proceedings here.[22]

In arriving at this decision, the Law Lords also took into account the content of a letter written by the South African Legal Aid Board to the plaintiffs' lawyers.[23] In this letter the board confirmed that it had decided to withdraw legal aid in personal injury cases due to an acute shortage of financial resources. This withdrawal of funding, according to the lordships, strongly suggested that legal aid was unlikely to be made available in South Africa to fund the potentially protracted and expensive litigation were the claims pursued there.

Lord Bingham recognized that the absence of developed procedures for handling group actions in South Africa reinforced the plaintiff's argument on the issue of funding. He saw the pragmatic problems that may arise in litigating a case of such complexity by a South African High Court and South African judges and practitioners inexperienced in the conduct of such proceedings. In his view, this must lead to an

increased likelihood of interlocutory decisions which are contentious, with the likelihood of appeals and delay. It cannot be assumed that all judges will respond to this new procedural challenge in the same innovative spirit. The exercise of jurisdiction by the South African High Court through separate territorial divisions, while not a potent obstacle in itself, could contribute to delay, uncertainty, and cost. The procedural novelty of these proceedings, if pursued in South Africa, must in my view act as a further disincentive to any person or body considering whether or not to finance the proceedings.[24]

These decisions from the highest court in the land signaled a watershed moment for foreign litigants. For the first time they had legal clarity that, through bringing their case in the English courts, they could overcome the difficult jurisdictional hurdle if they were able to demonstrate that substantive justice could not be obtained in their home country.

The decline in the availability of legal aid for transnational litigation in the early 2000s did not appear to deter foreign claimants from initiating claims in the United Kingdom, because the conditional fee regime that had already been introduced by then[25] encouraged

---

22.   *Id.* at 1559. See the leading judgment of Lord Bingham of Cornhill.
23.   *Id.* at 1558. The letter was dated September 20, 1999.
24.   *Id.* at 1560.
25.   The background to the abolition of legal aid in personal injury cases and the introduction of conditional fee agreements in the UK by primary legislation is discussed later in this chapter.

claimant lawyers to take on the risk of bringing legitimate claims on behalf of such claimants, thereby continuing to allow claimants access to justice.

The provisions of Rome II have made it easier for foreign litigants to bring legal claims against Britain-domiciled corporations in the British courts even if the claims involve a tort that occurred abroad. However, this does not mean foreign litigants are unlikely to face a jurisdictional challenge. The effect of Rome II in certain circumstances is less clear. For example, it becomes altogether unclear whether a UK court will exercise jurisdiction where an action between identical parties on similar or related grounds is already proceeding in another jurisdiction, or where there are several defendants, each with different domicile status.[26] In relation to such questions, it is possible that many complex legal arguments will need to be resolved at an early stage in the proceedings, adding to the cost and duration of litigation.

Further, the lack of certainty at the outset on matters relating to jurisdiction adds to the risk profile of a case. For example, in *Yao Essaie Motto and Others v. Trafigura Ltd. & Anor*,[27] a British subsidiary of a Dutch company was sued in Britain, where the company's operations center was located. The case was brought by 30,000 Ivorian claimants and concerned the alleged illegal disposal of hazardous waste in Côte d'Ivoire by one of the parent company's ships. In analyzing the risk profile of the case, the claimants identified potential arguments on forum as a reason for justifying a higher success-fee level as the claims progressed under conditional fee agreements (CFAs). This analysis came about because it was not possible to determine at the early stages of the litigation whether Tommy, the operator allegedly authorized to dispose the waste, played a significant role in the management of the alleged hazardous waste. It was also considered significant that Trafigura had not filed an acknowledgment of service, which is required under UK rules. The consequence of not filing one suggested that Trafigura was considering making a challenge on forum grounds.

Corporate Veil, Parent Company Responsibility, and the Acts of Subsidiaries

One of the most challenging issues in transnational litigation is establishing direct liability against a parent company domiciled in the United Kingdom in circumstances where its subsidiary based overseas may have contributed to certain acts or omissions said to have caused harm. This difficulty arises because companies rely on the notion of the *corporate veil*. This characterization means that each company is recognized as a separate

---

26. Thus far, the author is not aware of any cases involving transnational litigation where such matters have been the subject of judicial deliberation, but the scenarios identified above are quite common in business related human rights complaints and are mentioned here to demonstrate that jurisdictional challenges may still pose a significant access to justice barrier and potentially bar a victim from seeking an effective remedy.

27. SCCO Ref: PTH 1002160 & 1002161.

legal person, and this legal personality cannot be bypassed in order to attribute its rights and responsibilities to its shareholders or parent company.[28] The corporate veil will only be *pierced* in very limited circumstances, which are onerous to prove.[29]

A number of UK tort cases against corporations have sought to circumvent the corporate veil theory by seeking to argue for the existence of *parent company responsibility*. This approach argues that the defendant company's intimate knowledge and role in the conduct that led to harm or damage gave rise to a direct duty of care between the parent company and the claimant, and that this duty of care was breached. Until recently, this principle had not been directly tested by the British courts, but in transnational litigation, this principle has been accepted at interlocutory hearings[30] in many cases, and defendants have settled significant claims premised upon this concept.

However, in 2012 a Court of Appeal judgment endorsed the principle of parent company responsibility as part of the principle of assumption of responsibility under common law. In the recent case of *Chandler v. Cape*,[31] the Court of Appeal ruled that

> in appropriate circumstances the law may impose on a parent company responsibility for the health and safety of its subsidiary's employees. The circumstances include a situation where, as in the present case, (1) the business of the parent and subsidiary are in a relevant respect the same; (2) the parent has, or ought to have, superior knowledge on some relevant aspect of health and safety in the particular industry; (3) the subsidiary's system of work is unsafe as the parent company knew, or ought to have known; and (4) the parent knew or ought to have foreseen that the subsidiary or its employees would rely on its using that superior knowledge for the employees' protection. For the purposes of (4) it is not necessary to show that the parent is in the practice of intervening in the health and safety policies of the subsidiary. The court will look at the relationship between the companies more widely.

---

28. Salomon v. A. Salomon & Co., [1897] A.C. 22.

29. In practice, courts may only consider lifting the corporate veil when (a) construing a statute, contract, or other document, (b) a company is a "mere façade" concealing the true facts, or (c) a subsidiary company was acting as an authorised agent of its parent: *see* the leading judgment of Adams v. Cape Indus. Plc. [1990] Ch. 433 (C.A.) (Eng.).

30. This was in part the basis of the claim before the House of Lords in Lubbe and more recently in Guerrero v. Monterrico Metals Plc. [2009] EWHC 2475.

31. [2012] EWCA Civ 525. The appeal to the Court of Appeal was brought by Cape plc, the parent company of Mr. Chandler's (the claimant) former employer. The principle issue was whether Cape owed a direct duty of care to the employees of its subsidiary to advise on or ensure a safe system of work for them. Mr. Chandler had recently contracted asbestosis as a result of a short period of employment over fifty years ago with Cape Building Products Ltd, which is no longer in existence. However, its parent company, Cape, formerly the well-known asbestos producer Cape Asbestos plc, is still in existence. On April 14, 2011, Wyn Williams J (at the High Court) held that Cape was liable to Mr. Chandler on the basis not of any form of vicarious liability or agency or enterprise liability, but on the basis of the common law concept of assumption of responsibility. Cape appealed against that decision but lost at the Court of Appeal.

The court may find that element (4) is established where the evidence shows that the parent has a practice of intervening in the trading operations of the subsidiary, for example production and funding issues.[32]

In transnational litigation, the ability to hold TNCs to account legally in the home states where their head offices are usually located is important for the following reasons:

1. The head office orchestrates and is a focal point of the organization. Often group corporate policies emanate from the head office, and notwithstanding the application of local law, holding the parent accountable at home will make compliance with uniform standards across the global operations with the TNCs more likely.
2. The parent is usually more able to meet any financial sanctions than its overseas subsidiaries are.
3. Obstacles to access to justice locally due to fear of persecution, corruption, or lack of resources to fight a case against MNCs frequently preclude any practical possibility of legal action in MNC host states. In some instances the host state's laws may not be fully developed, or its legal system may not be able to cope with large and complex multiparty or class action cases (which transnational litigation invariably is).
4. Sometimes suing the parent company is the only possible avenue of redress available to the wronged victim. This was the position for the thousands of ex–South African miners in *Lubbe v. Cape*.

The apparent willingness of the English courts to work around the old doctrine of "corporate veil" has enormous implications for transnational litigation and is another reason the United Kingdom seems to be creating an environment conducive to such claims.[33] However, suing the parent company in the home country significantly increases the stakes at all levels, making such cases procedurally, legally, and financially riskier and more challenging.

In *Lubbe v. Cape*, by alleging direct parent-company responsibility, the claimants were careful not to rely on a liability doctrine that located the defendant's violations in South Africa (for example, liability as occupier of the South African factory or as the source of contamination in South Africa). Instead, they relied on the defendant's violations of a duty of care that could be traced back to corporate headquarters in the United Kingdom. In the House of Lords decision, Lord Bingham of Cornhill observed,

---

32. *Id.* ¶ 80.
33. Alex Twanda Magaisa, *Suing Multinational Corporate Groups for Torts in Wake of the Lubbe Case*, Law, Soc. Just. & Global Dev. J. 5 (2001) (where the author refers to the House of Lord's decisions in *Lubbe* and Connelly v. RTZ as undoubtedly "victim-friendly").

[t]he central thrust of the claims made by each of the plaintiffs is not against the defendant as the employer of that plaintiff or as the occupier of the factory where that plaintiff worked, or as the immediate source of the contamination in the area where that plaintiff lived. Rather, the claim is made against the defendant as a parent company which, knowing (so it is said) that exposure to asbestos was gravely injurious to health, failed to take proper steps to ensure that proper working practices were followed and proper safety precautions observed throughout the group. In this way, it is alleged, the defendant breached a duty of care which it owed to those working for its subsidiaries or living in the area of their operations (with the result that the plaintiffs thereby suffered personal injury and loss).[34]

The judgment also noted the following:

Resolution of this issue will be likely to involve an inquiry into what part the defendant played in controlling the operations of the group, what its directors and employees knew or ought to have known, what action was taken and not taken, whether the defendant owed a duty of care to employees of group companies overseas and whether, if so, that duty was broken. Much of the evidence material to this inquiry would, in the ordinary way, be documentary and much of it would be found in the offices of the parent company, including minutes of meetings, reports by directors and employees on visits overseas and correspondence.[35]

Lord Bingham's observations highlight the complex legal issues a claimant would have to address in determining the existence of direct parent-company responsibility for which it, as opposed to its subsidiary or other third party, can be held legally liable. It will involve an inquiry into the factual role played by the parent company in controlling its subsidiaries and its knowledge of material facts. Often these matters are wholly within the knowledge of one party: the corporate defendant. This is a reason why the process of disclosure of relevant documents in the company's control can be a very important step for claimants in establishing company knowledge and control.

Although transnational litigation in the United Kingdom has proved viable, Lord Bingham's observations in *Cape v. Lubbe* demonstrate these cases are by no means straightforward. In fact, litigants must be prepared for the fact that such cases are inherently complex and raise difficult legal, jurisdictional, and procedural issues. They reveal a striking power imbalance between the parties,[36] and due to the inherent legal and practical

---

34. *Lubbe*, 1 W.L.R. at 1545, ¶ 6.
35. *Id.* at 1546.
36. Peter Muchlinski, *Corporations in International Litigation: Problems of Jurisdiction and the United Kingdom Asbestos Cases*, 50 INT'L & COMP. L.Q. 1, 7 (2001). In Motto v. Trafigura, the claims were

difficulties in commencing them, the outcome of such litigation is often difficult to predict, adding to the risk of commencing such cases in the first place.

Inherent Challenges in Transnational Litigation in the United Kingdom

There is usually very little commonality among transnational litigation cases, which thwarts a meaningful analysis to determine how effective the current mechanisms are for litigants who commence transnational litigation.[37] It also makes a determination of the main inherent challenges difficult. Because of these problems, providing a generalized account of the obstacles facing victims of corporate human rights abuses in the United Kingdom is almost impossible. Each particular cause of action will have its own obstacles: different tests to be satisfied, different rules affecting jurisdiction, and different burdens of proof.[38]

Therefore, a meaningful and effective enquiry must consider the factual circumstances of the particular case, which will inform and determine both the causes of action available to a claimant and tease out the potential obstacles the claimant might face (which can be different and vary by degrees). That said, some common, congenital obstacles can be identified that will typically be faced by claimants. These obstacles can be substantial, procedural, or practical.

Civil Wrongs Do Not Speak the Language of Rights

As previously mentioned, the United Kingdom does not have specialized legislation that governs business-related human rights cases and has had to rely primarily on traditional tort law principles to attract legal accountability and provide meaningful redress to claimants. This type of approach has also been adopted in a number of other countries, such as Argentina, Australia, India, and Japan.[39]

---

brought on behalf of 30,000 largely illiterate and economically impoverished Ivorian claimants against Trafigura, an oil company with a turnover of $122 billion in 2011. Trafigura, http://www.trafigura.com /about-us/performance (last visited July 23, 2013).

37.   *Obstacles to Justice and Redress for Victims of Corporate Human Rights Abuse*, Oxford Pro Bono Publico (2008), http://www2.law.ox.ac.uk/opbp/Oxford-Pro-Bono-Publico-submission-to-Ruggie-3 -Nov-2008.pdf.

38.   In *Guererro*, the applicable law to the dispute was Peruvian law. In *Florez*, *supra* note 6, the claims are advanced under Colombian contract law and extracontractual civil responsibility which although broadly comparable to English law of negligence requires different tests to be applied in order to establish liability.

39.   Anita Ramasastry & Robert C. Thompson, Fafo, Commerce, Crime and Conflict: Legal Remedies for Private Sector Liability for Grave Breaches of International Law (2006), http://www.fafo.no/pub/rapp/536/536.pdf. In their study of national legal systems, Ramanastry and Thompson found that fifteen out of sixteen countries they surveyed responded that it would be possible to bring a civil claim against a corporation for a violation of international human rights law if the wrong were characterised as a civil wrong, a tort, or a delict. The report explains that it is a question of legal culture as to whether a particular country allows for civil litigation to be used in dealing with violations of international human rights law.

There is a fundamental inadequacy with a tort-based approach, which arguably does not give much-needed incentive for a corporation to ensure that respect for human rights underpins its core business philosophy. Existing tort law, or indeed other UK civil laws, does not directly refer to human rights even if in some instances domestic law may cover the same or similar area of conduct—for example, "torture" as "trespass" under the law of tort. This omission affects all human rights litigation undertaken against TNCs. Under the civil wrong approach, in each particular case, the availability and effectiveness of any remedy will turn on the substance and facts of the actions or omissions of the TNC and its agents, rather than on whether there has been a violation of a human right. In certain circumstances, this distinction may result in an inadequate outcome.

In instances where a litigant is complaining of a harm that may be a gross human rights violation (such as torture, extrajudicial killing, war crimes, or crimes against humanity), it is often important to the litigant that he or she be able to articulate his or her complaint in the language of human rights. This presentation reflects the gravity of the alleged harm and is more likely to attract an appropriate and commensurate remedy. This outcome is especially so where there is no real likelihood that criminal law may offer an effective remedy. There are no known cases of UK authorities initiating investigations against corporate employees for alleged violations of international humanitarian law. In part, this is attributable to the lack of specific legislation in the United Kingdom that clearly allows for the application of extraterritorial jurisdiction to cases of corporate abuse abroad by corporate *nationals* based in the foreign state (for example, a subsidiary to a UK parent company).[40]

In *Guerrero and Others v. Monterrico Metals plc*,[41] a total of thirty Peruvian litigants alleged they suffered torture at the hands of the state police, who it was said acted at the behest of the company, which allegedly facilitated the torture. The litigants had to frame their case under the law of tort and characterize the harmful corporate conduct as "trespass to persons" rather than "torture" to find legal liability under UK law. Though using traditional tort law principles helped to advance the claimants' case, it can be argued that being able to hold the company accountable for "torture," a universally recognized heinous crime, would have properly reflected the gravity of the offence from the victims' perspective and would have had significant reputational implications for the company. These reputational consequences are precisely the kind of deterrent needed to bring about a fundamental change in corporate culture.

---

40. However, under certain legislative provisions, such as the Criminal Justice (Terrorism and Conspiracy) Act of 1998, the UK does occasionally extend jurisdiction over offences committed abroad, but only on the basis that: (a) the offender, either individual or corporation, was a UK national offender, and (b) part of the offence took place in the UK. Nevertheless, the exercise of extraterritorial jurisdiction is still subject to the proviso that it is not an unreasonable interference with the domestic affairs of the foreign state where the alleged criminal offence was committed.

41. *Supra* note 30.

The law on which the general (as opposed to specific) causes of action are based is not intended to address infringements of human rights. Therefore, the many specific and unusual issues that arise with respect to transnational human rights litigation—such as what type of *harm* is capable of redress, the difficulties in pursuing parent company responsibility, and the limitations on the types of relief a court may grant under traditional tort law or contractual principles—result in a civil-wrong approach that sometimes appears ill-suited to addressing infringements of human rights.

No Extraterritorial Operation

Generally, criminal or civil causes of action are not intended to operate outside of the state in which they are established;[42] this is the case in the United Kingdom. This fact poses a serious obstacle to commencing human rights litigation for overseas violations and is one of the main reasons the use of traditional civil law doctrines is inherently unsuitable for transnational human rights litigation. A classic illustration of this problem is regulatory standards (such as health and safety standards) with which a company is required to comply in the home state but not in a foreign state where there is no corresponding regulation. One of the unintended consequences of this jurisdictional dichotomy is that it encourages so-called "double standards" to be adopted. This outcome is unsatisfactory because it creates an environment in which corporations are not legally required to develop and implement key common policies such as health, safety, employment, and environmental standards across their global business operations.[43] As a result, foreign employees of a parent company's subsidiary harmed by that parent company's business operations are unlikely to be able to invoke statutory liability against the parent company or subsidiary for breach of the provisions of the United Kingdom's health and safety legislation. This lacuna has the potential to undermine

---

42. The UK's extensive Health & Safety legislation, which imposes certain obligations and duties on employers to provide a safe system of work for employees, expressly limits its application to UK jurisdiction. *See* Health and Safety at Work etc. Act 1974. According to the Health and Safety Executive, "British health and safety legislation only applies within the baseline of Great Britain (GB), to certain offshore facilities, and to certain other activities within territorial waters, subject to the Health and Safety at Work etc. Act 1974 (Application Outside Great Britain) Order 2001." *The Health and Safety at Work etc. Act 1974 (Application outside Great Britain) Order 2001*, LEGISLATION.GOV.UK, http://www.legislation.gov.uk/uksi/2001/2127/contents/made.

43. The potential *double standard* created by the UK's lack of an effective extraterritorial regulation of its TNCs overseas business operations is illustrated in the *Cape* case. *See* Richard Meeran, *Liability of Multinational Corporations: A Critical Stage* (1999), http://www.labournet.net/images/cape/campanal.htm. The commentary was written by Richard Meeran, the claimants' lawyer in the *Cape* litigation. According to the commentary, "Cape closed its principal UK factory in 1968 due to the prevalence of asbestos-related disease. However, it continued to engage in bad working practices in South Africa until 1979. In South Africa, Cape's operations took full advantage of the apartheid regime, including the use of young children in its mines and mills. In 1973, Cape gave evidence to a UK Government Committee which was concerned about the company's treatment of South African workers. The profits from the South African operations owned by Cape flowed back to the UK."

the primary reason for holding corporations accountable: to ensure that corporations implement common human rights standards across their global operations no matter where their business operations are located.

Legal and Procedural Obstacles

The significant hurdle of establishing jurisdiction to bring a claim in transnational litigation has been addressed elsewhere in this chapter and in the preceding chapter by Chambers and Tyler. Although limiting the application of the doctrine of *forum non conveniens* and the introduction of Rome II have, on balance, created a more conducive environment for foreign litigants to bring claims against multinational corporations in British courts, there are still circumstances that can easily arise in transnational cases and make the application of Rome II unclear. For example, this situation arises when there is the possibility of suing multiple defendants or there has been a legal action instituted in the host state on similar or related grounds to the action to be pursued in the United Kingdom. No known cases have grappled with these issues as yet, and in the face of this uncertainty, it is likely that a litigant bringing a transnational claim may still have to face a long, drawn-out battle to establish jurisdiction in the United Kingdom.

The ability to bring transnational litigation will also turn on the applicable law and differing tests to be satisfied in a given case, as well as the different burdens of proof.

Host-State Compensation Levels

In Europe, the introduction of Rome II, which came into effect in 2009, has an added complication. Since Rome II, for claims that deal with events giving rise to damage occurring on or after August 19, 2007, compensation levels in transnational litigation will be determined in accordance with the applicable law to the dispute and not with UK damages levels, as was the case before.[44] This change poses a quandary for victims and their lawyers. One of the reasons a legal case is brought against the parent company in the home state is that the relevant host-state laws, which provide an actionable cause, are underdeveloped and have rudimentary judicial guidelines to evaluate damages levels for personal injury or other types of harm.[45]

---

44. The position pre-Rome II was that matters relating to assessing the compensation resulting from damages should be treated as matters of procedure to be determined by the law of the forum, which is English law. Therefore, while the heads of loss are matters of substance (determined by the applicable law), damages assessments are calculated by applying English law and according to English levels. In the *Trafigura* case, for example, the levels of damages for various alleged personal injuries were based on English levels.

45. A brief internal survey of potential damages levels in four different developing countries (Philippines, Argentina, Chile, and Libya) by Leigh Day revealed judicial guidelines to evaluate damages levels for personal injury or other types of harm are potentially underdeveloped and are often left to judicial discretion on a case-by-case basis. Limited resources means a large number of cases go unreported, making it very difficult for practitioners in transnational litigation to assess the potential value of business-related

For example, large-scale environmental damage is complex to evaluate even in a highly advanced and sophisticated legal system, and in most instances it is unlikely that the host state has a legal system sufficiently robust to deal with such complexity.[46] A victim whose way of life has been changed due to a company's conduct may have to face the harsh reality of fighting a major multinational corporation that has seemingly unlimited resources. This victim must also overcome significant substantive, procedural, and practical obstacles, only to be faced with obtaining limited compensation assessed at very low levels while incurring significant legal costs (at home-state levels). Therefore, there is a real danger that host-state mechanisms used to assess damages may not be suitable for business-related human rights cases. The significant disparity that may arise between legal costs and the level of compensation awarded may have the unintended consequence that claimant lawyers become increasingly cautious and cherry-pick cases, even within a pool of potentially legitimate cases. What is clear is that the quantum value of a case may well be a more significant factor in determining whether claimant lawyers would be willing to litigate a claim that otherwise has merit.

Identifying the Parties

Identification of the defendant and potential claimant cohort can be a complex process, particularly in large environmental disasters. Tort law principles are premised on the idea that any duty of care owed by a potential defendant ought to be owed to a defined class of individuals, therefore creating a need to identify a defined class of claimants. This requirement can pose difficulties in transnational litigation because the consequences of corporate wrongdoing may affect a very large victim class, all of whom may have a legitimate right to bring a legal claim but who may not be easily identified.

In the Bangladesh arsenic-poisoning litigation,[47] the British Geological Survey (BGS), a world-renowned research unit of the National Environmental Research Council, was sued in the United Kingdom by a group of four hundred Bangladeshi farmers who alleged negligent omission in testing arsenic levels in groundwater as part of a water report prepared by the BGS. The result was that the natural presence of high levels of arsenic was

---

human rights cases at the outset without the involvement of legal experts who have specialist knowledge of the applicable law to the dispute.

46. The Bodo Community v. SPDC, Claim No: HQ11X01280, HQ12X04933, currently proceeding in the British Courts, represents the first time Shell or any oil company has faced claims in the UK for environmental damage caused by its oil extraction operations from a community in the developing world. The claims are brought in respect of two massive oil spills in the Niger Delta in 2008 that the claimants allege had a devastating impact on the environment surrounding the community of Bodo and devastated over nintey square kilometres of the local land, mangroves, and waterways, estimated to be equivalent to the amount of coastline affected by the BP Deepwater Horizon disaster. The costs of cleanup are estimated by the claimants to be in the millions. See *11,000 Nigerians Sue Shell in London Courts*, LEIGH DAY (Mar. 22, 2012), http://www.leighday.co.uk/News/2012/March-2012/11,000-Nigerians-sue-Shell-in-London-Courts.

47. Binod Sutradhar FC v. Natural Envtl. Research Council, [2006] UKHL 33.

not detected in the groundwater, leading to potential arsenic poisoning of a very large and potentially undefined victim class. In that case, the House of Lords heard evidence of criteria that had been drawn up by the claimant litigants' lawyers in an attempt to identify the pool of litigants that could legitimately bring a legal claim. Nevertheless, the House of Lords considered that the claim put forth could still lead to a victim class that was too large and undefined, and could potentially include "the entire population of Bangladesh, or at the very least that of the areas tested during the 1992 survey [carried out by the defendant]."[48] On this basis, it ruled that the BGS could not be said to owe a duty of care toward an undefined and unidentifiable class of victims.

On the other hand, business-related human rights cases usually involve several actors who are all linked in some way, and to sue the correct defendant, a forensic analysis needs to be conducted to determine which entity may be the most liable for the harm, and in which forum an appropriate suit can be brought to maximize the availability of an effective redress. For instance, one set of facts might give rise to several private claims in several different jurisdictions against separate subsidiaries or joint ventures of a TNC. This plurality of claims, jurisdictions, and parties was an issue in a complaint brought by a group of Colombian farmers against BPXC. In this case, a wholly owned subsidiary of BP *plc* was alleged to be responsible for the alleged environmental damage caused by the construction of an oil pipeline on their private land.[49] In that complaint, it appeared that some of the farmers had instituted separate legal actions for certain environmental damages in Colombia against the Colombian joint-venture company that operated the pipeline. However, it also appeared there was a real possibility the claims would not progress through the Colombian courts, not least because there seemed to be a real risk that the farmers in the Colombian action would not be able to obtain legal representation.[50] In the event that a British judge is required to consider a jurisdictional challenge by the potential defendant, it is arguable that due to the special circumstances of the case, the court may well be persuaded that in the interests of justice the claims ought to proceed in the United Kingdom. However, these are fact-sensitive issues.

Another difficulty in identifying defendants is the confusing corporate structures of TNCs. At times, these structures are designed to avoid liability. It therefore becomes very difficult to assess whether a viable claim can be brought against the parent company where one or more of the subsidiaries (or another TNC) are also implicated. For

---

48. *Id.* ¶ 48 (judgment of Lord Walker of Gestingthorpe).

49. This claim raised substantially similar complaints to those in *Florez, supra* note 6. Proceedings were not issued in respect of this group of claimants as their claims were settled by way of mediation on the basis that BPXC did not accept liability. The settlement terms are subject to a confidentiality agreement between the company and the Colombian farmers. *See* Robert Verkaik, *BP Pays Out Millions to Colombian Farmers*, THE INDEPENDENT (July 2006), http://www.independent.co.uk/news/world/americas /bp-pays-out-millions-to-colombian-farmers-408816.html.

50. *Id.*

example, in *Guererrero and Others v. Monterrico*, the Peruvian mine operator was initially named as the second defendant in the action. However, because there was no reciprocity treaty between Peru and the United Kingdom, any judgment reached would not have been enforced and potentially would have left the claimants without any compensation. This was one of the reasons the Peruvian operator was later removed as a defendant in the UK action.

Limitation/Prescription

As discussed earlier, the applicable law to a dispute in transnational litigation generally is the law of the host country. This choice of law means the host state's limitation-of-prescription rules apply to the dispute, creating another layer of uncertainty and complexity in these cases. UK courts generally have discretion in allowing a case to be brought outside the limitation period, and the discretion is based on a number of considerations, such as: (a) lack of a demonstrable prejudice caused to the defendant; (b) public policy concerns about preventing the claimants from bringing the claim (an argument deployed in the Mau Mau litigation involving British colonial atrocities against the Mau Mau rebels in Kenya);[51] or (c) certain special circumstances pertinent to individual cases.[52]

Evidential Difficulties

It is difficult to investigate and identify the parent company's own role because its level of involvement in the subsidiary's activity and its level of knowledge and control for the purposes of mounting a claim can be hard to demonstrate. Moreover, transnational litigation is unlike other litigation in that there is an inherent power imbalance between the corporate defendant and the victim who has suffered harm. There is not only a big gulf in the respective parties' financial capacity but also a knowledge gap between the parties relevant to the dispute. The issues central to establishing the corporate acts or omissions causing the alleged harm are often the exclusive knowledge of the corporate defendant. This imbalance makes it difficult for parties to litigate on equal footing in practical terms.

---

51. Ndiku Mutua & Ors v. Foreign & Common Wealth Office, [2011] EWHC 1913 (QB). *See Kenyan Victims of Colonial Torture to Give Evidence at the High Court in London*, LEIGH DAY (Mar. 29, 2011), www.leighday.co.uk/news/2011/March-2011/Kenyan-Victims-of-colonial-torture-to-give-evidenc; MoD v. AB & Ors, [2012] UKSC 9 (also known as the *Atomic Veteran's Litigation*). This claim involves a group of approximately 1,000 former UK servicemen who claimed damages for personal injury as a result of alleged exposure to radioactive fallout during or after British nuclear tests in Australia and the South Pacific in the 1950s. In a majority decision of 4 to 3, the House of Lords ruled that the claimants' claims could not proceed as they had been brought out of time.

52. In *Monterrico*, *supra* note 30, Peruvian law advice was necessary to determine whether the action brought by the claimants was time barred under Peruvian law (which was two years for a noncontractual claim), the applicable law to the dispute.

Potential Costs Involved in Conducting Transnational Litigation

The costs involved in bringing transnational litigation cannot be underestimated. Transnational litigation results in complex cases that are time and resource intensive. Often litigants are domiciled in remote areas, areas of poor security, or postconflict areas. This reality poses significant logistical challenges in contacting clients to obtain client evidence and instructions, and may well add to the risk profile of a case. In addition, the litigant class may be a vulnerable group marginalized within its own society; these groups often require careful handling. Many litigants are not familiar with judicial processes, the concept of burden of proof, and how to discharge this obligation. These are all significant issues for claimant lawyers to negotiate in mounting such claims.

The UK cost rules generally require the losing party to meet the legal costs of the successful party. In the United Kingdom, up until April 1, 2013, claimant lawyers primarily funded legal costs during the case under a conditional-fee agreement;[53] lawyers were reimbursed only if successful. Given the sizeable costs, lengthy litigation, and uncertain outcomes, embarking on transnational litigation entailed acceptance of substantial risk on the part of claimant lawyers.[54] As mentioned by Chambers and Tyler in the previous chapter, the *no win, no fee* system allowed claimant lawyers to contract with their clients for payment of a "success fee"—an uplift of base costs payable if the claim is successful. Under the pre–April 1 costs rules, the success fee was paid by an unsuccessful defendant. This was intended to promote access to justice by encouraging claimants' lawyers to accept greater risk. The litigants were also able to purchase insurance (referred to as "after the event insurance") to cover themselves from the risk of losing and becoming liable for the defendant's legal costs. The associated premium payable was also recoverable from the losing party, and in transnational litigation, the premium can be substantial.

The Future of Transnational Litigation in the United Kingdom

A recent change in law that transforms the civil-litigation costs regime in the United Kingdom has raised significant concerns that many working in the field of business and human

---

53. Conditional Fee Agreements were introduced by the Courts and Legal Services Act (1990) (as amended by the Access to Justice Act 1999). A conditional fee agreement (CFA) is an agreement pursuant to which a lawyer agrees with his client to be paid a success fee in the event of the client's claim succeeding, where the success fee is not calculated as a proportion of the amount recovered by the client. A typical example of a CFA is one retained on a *no win no fee* basis. CFAs were introduced in the UK at the same time that legal aid was abolished for personal injury and other cases with the intention that such claims not be funded by the public purse but by the private sector.

54. The House of Common debates on the implications of the Government's Legal Aid Sentencing and Punishment of Offenders Bill (LASPO) included consideration of the impact of the Bill on transnational litigation. MP Kate Green referred to how costs were driven by several factors in such cases, including the fact that such cases are generally costly to bring, that the lawyers have to bear the risks and associated costs while the cases proceed, and that there is a huge imbalance in the ability of the parties to meet the costs. *See* Public Bill Committee Legal Aid Sentencing and Punishment of Offenders Bill (September 13, 2011), on Clause 41, Column No 480 by Kate Green MP.

rights consider will have a dramatic impact on the ability and willingness of claimant law-yers to bring transnational litigation in the United Kingdom.[55] The Legal Aid, Sentencing and Punishment of Offenders Act 2012 (LASPO) contains a series of very wide-ranging civil-costs reforms that threaten to become an effective barrier to legitimate business-related human rights claims.[56] As Chambers and Tyler have mentioned, the furor over the legal changes under LASPO prompted Professor John Ruggie, the UN secretary-general's special representative for business and human rights, to write to UK Justice Minister Jona-than Djanogly, raising his concerns about the "disincentives" being introduced[57] that may have a potential impact "on the position of legitimate claimants in civil actions . . . par-ticularly in cases involving large multinational enterprises." He argued that the reforms proposed, when taken together, have the effect of constituting an "effective barrier to legitimate business-related human rights claims being brought before UK courts in situ-ations where alternative sources of remedy are unavailable."

The main elements of LASPO and associated changes to the UK Civil Procedure Rules that may have major implications for the conduct of transnational litigation are as follows:

(a) The recoverability of success fees from the defendant has been abolished. Instead, success fees may only be deducted from the claimants' compensation (capped at 25 percent of damages).[58]

(b) The recoverability of the insurance premium for claimants who take out a costs insur-ance policy in all personal injury cases, except in certain clinical negligence cases,[59] has been abolished.[60] One-way qualified cost shifting has been introduced in personal injury cases by rule 44 of the Civil Procedure Rules, which now largely removes the risk previously faced by claimants of potentially having to pay the defendant's legal costs should the claim be unsuccessful. Though this is a positive outcome for claimants generally, because it seems they are now protected from the risk of having to pay the substantial costs of a corporate defendant should they lose their claim, the fact that this protection is not guaranteed[61] means that if a particular case war-

---

55. Owen Bowcott, *Legal Aid Cuts Will Stop Cases Like Trafigura, UN Official Warns*, THE GUARD-IAN (June 2011), http://www.guardian.co.uk/law/2011/jun/16/united-nations-legal-aid-cuts-trafigura.

56. Richard Meeran, *Multinationals Will Profit from the Government's Civil Litigation Shakeup*, THE GUARDIAN (May 2011), http://www.guardian.co.uk/commentisfree/libertycentral/2011/may/24/civil-litigation-multinationals. Richard Meeran is a leading practitioner in transnational litigation and has represented claimants in several of the cases brought by Leigh Day referred to in this chapter. The article was written during the early stages of LASPO Bill consultation process.

57. *Id*. The article attaches the letter from John Ruggie to Jonathan Djanogly dated May 16, 2011.

58. Legal Aid, Sentencing and Punishment of Offenders Act, 2012, § 44(4) (UK).

59. *Id*. § 46(1).

60. *Id*. § 46(1).

61. The exceptions to qualified one-way costs shifting are set out under Rule 44.15 and 44.16 of the UK Civil Procedures Rules. These are: where the claimant has disclosed no reasonable grounds for bring-ing the proceedings (Rule 44.15(a)); the proceedings are an abuse of the court's process (Rule 44.15(b));

rants it, a claimant may still need to take out insurance to protect against the risk of an adverse-costs order but would be unable to recover the insurance premium against the defendant if the claimant is successful in bringing his or her claim. The substantial premium amount would have to come out of the claimant's damages.

(c) New rules on assessment of costs have come into force. The new rule 44.3 of the Civil Procedure Rules means that for claims whereby proceedings were issued after April 1, 2013, courts will not allow recoverability of costs that have been unreasonably incurred or are an unreasonable amount, even though it can be shown that such costs were necessarily incurred to progress the litigation; this argument is more readily available under the old cost-assessment rules.

Two aspects of LASPO have implications regarding access to justice for victims and a claimant's rights to a remedy. First, the abolition of the ability to recover a success fee, instead deducting the fee from the claimants' damages (capped at 25 percent), poses difficulties in business-related human rights cases. Contingency-fee agreements (CFAs) are the principle method of funding these sorts of cases.[62] The potential effect is that in complex transnational litigation, it is quite possible that the success fee could equal or even exceed the compensation awarded. This effect may lead to a perverse situation in which successful claimants could still walk out of court no better off than at the start of the litigation, thus left without access to an effective remedy.[63]

Second, in circumstances where a defendant may be liable to meet the claimant's costs, the new cost assessment rules make it clear that a defendant should only pay the claimant's legal costs if such costs are "proportionate," meaning that the costs must bear a reasonable relationship to the compensation at issue in the proceedings, the value of any nonmonetary relief at issue in the proceedings, the complexity of the litigation, any additional work generated by the conduct of the paying party, and significant wider factors such as reputation or public importance (rule 44.3 (5 a–e)). Though in theory the new *proportionality* rules may allow a party to recover its costs despite them being *disproportionate*, it is clear this will very much be the exception rather than the norm. This rule

the conduct of the claimant or a person acting on the claimant's behalf (with the claimant's knowledge of such conduct) is likely to obstruct the just disposal of the proceedings (Rule 44.15(c i and ii)); and the claimant is found to have been fundamentally dishonest (Rule 44.16).

62. There has been a serious decline for some considerable time in the availability of legal aid for multi-party litigation involving multinational enterprises, as referred to by Professor Ruggie in his letter to Justice Minister Jonathan Djanogly, *supra* note 57. *See also* the High Court decision in the Trafigura case, *supra* note 27.

63. *See* Public Bill Committee Legal Aid Sentencing and Punishment of Offenders Bill, 2010-12, H.C. cl. 41, col. 480 by Kate Green MP, where the Bill Committee debated a proposal to amend the bill in its current form, which would allow success fees to be recovered by claimant litigants in transnational litigant cases, among other things, in recognition of the significant imbalance in the parties' ability to meet costs in such litigation. The amendments were defeated.

could constitute a real disincentive to what is already a small pool of lawyers willing to take on transnational litigation.

Transnational litigation in the United Kingdom has generally been against multinational parent companies rather than local operating subsidiaries; it is intrinsically challenging for the reasons already examined above. With much at stake, both from a monetary and reputational perspective, UK multinationals, which are some of the wealthiest corporations in the country and the world, usually have a *no holds barred* approach to litigation and defend cases against them vigorously.[64] Consequently, legal costs invariably substantially exceed compensation (at UK levels). As already stated elsewhere, costs in the *Trafigura* case were more than three times higher than the damages agreed.[65]

Unsurprisingly, Trafigura defended the case against it vigorously at all stages, always arguing that it was not responsible for the waste dumping. In part, it was able to do so because it had very large resources at its disposal, given that it is one of the largest private companies in the world. The costs in the litigation were astronomical, with fifty lawyers working on the case at one stage on behalf of the claimants. The expenses that the claimant law firm had to bear throughout the life of the case ran into millions of pounds. The claim ultimately settled three years after it was brought by an out-of-court negotiated settlement, the terms of which are strictly confidential.

The principle claimant lawyer who represented the largely impoverished Ivorian victims has publicly acknowledged that the claim would not have been brought if there was not the prospect of recovering the success fees from the defendant as under the current *no win no fee* system.[66]

The new proportionality test, when taken together with the existing Rome II regulations, would have the unintended effect of further increasing the disparity between *proportionate* and actual costs. Though it is open to claimant lawyers to argue for higher than *proportionate* costs at the conclusion of the case, it is certain that this will be a hotly disputed issue between the parties, with the potential for protracted, detailed costs hearings.[67] The challenge to costs recovery has the potential to deter claimants' lawyers from accepting the risk of litigating business-related human rights cases in the first place.

---

64. *See* Public Bill Committee Legal Aid Sentencing and Punishment of Offenders Bill, 2010-12, H.C. cl. 41, col. 480 by Andrew Slaughter MP.

65. Meeran, *supra* note 56.

66. O. Bowcott, *Legal aid cuts will stop cases like Trafigura, UN official warns*, THE GUARDIAN 16 June 2011. In the article, Mr. Martyn Day, senior partner at Leigh Day gives his view on the government's proposal and its impact on cases like the one against Trafigura.

67. Under the UK civil procedure rules, when legal costs are not agreed at the conclusion of a case, parties have to go through a detailed costs hearing according to the procedures set out under Part 44 of the Civil Procedure Rules.

Conclusion

The *Cape*, *Connelly*, and *Thor Chemicals* cases show that British judges are acutely aware of the peculiar complexities of transnational litigation. They were not prepared to allow a *denial of justice* for victims of corporate harm in the stark circumstances of those cases, which are typical scenarios faced by victims in such cases. NGOs, lawyers, the government, and the media should keep a close and watchful eye on the effects of the LASPO to ensure that it does not undermine the effects of these cases and to make sure victims have the opportunity to access British justice and a means to pursue a meaningful and effective remedy against British or British-based corporations. Legal suits of this nature may well have the positive effect of shaping British corporate behavior, which is beneficial to British society and Britain's image on the world stage. If such cases are under threat because of the unintended consequences of the LASPO, it may well call into question Britain's commitment at an international level to support and enhance corporate regulation to ensure corporate accountability for human rights violations committed abroad.

Part III

Looking to the Future

Chapter 12

Foreign Direct-Liability Litigation

Toward the Transnationalization of

Corporate Legal Responsibility

Peter Muchlinski and Virginie Rouas

School of Law, SOAS, University of London

The rise of multinational enterprises (MNEs) as major players in the global economy has led to calls for greater corporate accountability. This rise has resulted in calls for greater accountability for legal wrongs, including alleged human rights abuses. Various legal systems have responded to this call in different ways, ranging from the development of a detailed human rights-based case law in the United States arising under the Alien Tort Claims Act (ATCA) to mass tort actions in the United States, Canadian, English, and Australian courts and, more recently, civil law actions in the French, Belgian, Dutch, German, and Swiss courts.[1] In addition, European human rights law may provide new avenues of argumentation and redress in this context.

---

1.   For the purpose of this chapter, we will focus on the study of foreign direct-liability litigation in France, Belgium, and the Netherlands as regards civil law countries. However, it is worth mentioning litigation efforts in Germany and Switzerland. On April 25, 2013, the European Center for Constitutional and Human Rights (ECCHR) together with Global Witness filed a criminal complaint against a senior manager of the Danzer Group, a Swiss and German timber manufacturer, for his alleged participation in grave human rights violations against members of a forest community in the Democratic Republic of Congo. The State Prosecutor's office in Tubingen, Germany, was asked to investigate the case. *See Criminal Complaint Filed Accuses Senior Manager of Danzer Group of Responsibility Over Human Rights Abuses Against Congolese Community*, ECCHR (Apr. 25, 2013), http://www.ecchr.de/index.php/danzer-en.html. Furthermore, on March 5, 2012, the ECCHR together with the Colombian trade union SINALTRAINAL submitted a criminal complaint to the public prosecution of Zug in Switzerland directed against Nestlé and five former members of the firm's top management. The complaint related to the role of the company and its managers in the murder of a Colombian trade unionist in 2005. The case was passed on to the public prosecution of Waadt, which on May 1, 2013, issued a "no-proceedings order" announcing the

In non-Western jurisdictions, such claims are also beginning to surface.[2] The most established system in the developing world is the public-interest litigation jurisdiction of the Indian appellate and supreme courts. Litigation strategies are increasingly used as part of a wider political strategy to mobilize opposition to the social and political effects of globalization on local communities. This mobilization has resulted in what de Sousa Santos has termed "subaltern cosmopolitan legality," the process by which excluded and marginalized groups can use existing laws in a counter-hegemonic way to undermine the dominance of institutions and practices that seek to further the interests of the minority of social actors who benefit from globalization.[3] One part of such a strategy is to further litigation against MNEs either in the host country, where the alleged wrongs have taken place, or in the home country of the parent, emphasizing the responsibility that comes from the operation of an integrated transnational enterprise regardless of the formal corporate separation between parent and subsidiaries. It should be noted that, as in the case of India, most litigation in developing countries involving MNEs has hitherto concerned the liability of foreign parent companies for acts of subsidiaries within the jurisdiction, rather than direct liability of home-country firms. However, as developing countries increasingly become homes to new MNEs, this position may change, and foreign direct-liability claims may also begin to arise in traditionally host states.

A further significant development has arisen recently on the international plane with the endorsement of the Guiding Principles on Business and Human Rights (UN Guiding Principles) in June 2011 by the UN Human Rights Council. These Guiding Principles were designed to implement the UN "Protect, Respect and Remedy" Framework on which they are premised.[4] These Guiding Principles can be said to constitute "the first global standard for preventing and addressing the risk of adverse impacts on human rights related

---

decision not to open an investigation because the case was statute-barred. The widow of the trade unionist lodged an appeal against that decision on May 16, 2013. *See Nestlé Precedent Case: Charges Filed in Murder of Colombian Trade Unionist*, ECCHR (Mar. 6, 2012), http://www.ecchr.de/index.php/nestle-518 .html; *Nestlé Has Nothing to Fear from Swiss Legal System*, ECCHR (May 10, 2013), http://www.ecchr .de/index.php/nestle-518.html; *UPDATE in the Nestlé Case: Prosecutor under Court Review*, ECCHR (May 17, 2013), http://www.ecchr.de/index.php/nestle-518.html.

2.   *See generally* Law and Globalization from Below: Towards a Cosmopolitan Legality (Boaventura de Sousa Santos & Cesar A. Rodriguez-Garavito eds., 2005).

3.   *See* Boaventura de Sousa Santos & Cesar A. Rodriguez-Garavito, *Law, Politics and the Subaltern in Counter-Hegemonic Globalization*, *in id.* at 12–18; Boaventura de Sousa Santos, Toward a New Legal Common Sense ch. 9 (2d ed. 2002).

4.   UN Human Rights Council, *Guiding Principles on Business and Human Rights Implementing the United Nations "Protect, Respect and Remedy" Framework*, UN Doc A/HRC/17/31 (2011), http://www .ohchr.org/documents/issues/business/A.HRC.17.31.pdf. The Guiding Principles were adopted by Resolution 17/4 of the Human Rights Council on June 16, 2011. *See* UN Human Rights Council, *Human Rights and Transnational Corporations and Other Business Enterprises*, UN Doc A/HRC/RES/17/4 (2011), http://www.business-humanrights.org/media/documents/un-human-rights-council-resolution-re-human -rights-transnational-corps-eng-6-jul-2011.pdf.

to business activity."[5] A key element in the UN Framework is the corporate responsibility to respect human rights, which is to be operationalized by way of a *human rights due diligence* concept. The concept of due diligence has more recently acquired a wider role in relation to the recently revised OECD Guidelines for Multinational Enterprises (OECD Guidelines), where it is endorsed as a general principle of corporate action across a wide range of issues covered by the guidelines, including but also going beyond human rights observance.[6] In addition, the International Finance Corporation's (IFC) Human Rights Impact Assessment Guide (IFC Guide) for corporations was launched in 2010, providing guidance on all elements of human rights due diligence as advanced in the UN Framework.[7] The use of due diligence as a standard of corporate action has significant implications for the further development of foreign direct-liability litigation, as will be examined further in the section on the contribution of European and international human rights developments.

The main aim of this chapter is to use a comparative approach to detail the broad nature of different national and international legal responses to the issue of corporate human rights liability that have arisen in what has become known as "foreign direct liability."[8] Given the predominantly Anglo-American, common law–based focus of much of this litigation, this analysis prompts the question of whether anything distinctive in such legal orders suggests that they may be the *natural* home for the development of this kind of litigation. It connotes an analysis based on the notion of *legal families* and their characteristics. Such an approach has already arisen in the context of company law more generally. Thus, La Porta *et al.* argue that the common law countries are more suited to the development of financial markets because they offer on average better minority-shareholder protection than countries following a civil law tradition.[9] Is it possible that

---

5.   *See* Navi Pillay, UN High Comm'r for Human Rights, Statement to the Employer's Group at the International Labour Conference (June 7, 2011), *quoted in* OFFICE OF THE UN HIGH COMM'R FOR HUM. RTS., THE CORPORATE RESPONSIBILITY TO RESPECT HUMAN RIGHTS: AN INTERPRETATIVE GUIDE 2 (2012), http://www.ohchr.org/Documents/Publications/HR.PUB.12.2_En.pdf.

6.   OECD, OECD GUIDELINES FOR MULTINATIONAL ENTERPRISES: 2011 EDITION (2011), http://www.oecd.org/daf/inv/mne/48004323.pdf.

7.   Desiree Abrahams & Yann Wyss, *Guide to Human Rights Impact Assessment and Management*, INT'L BUS. LEADERS FORUM AND INT'L FIN. CORP. (2010), http://www.ifc.org/hriam.

8.   "Foreign Direct Liability" may be defined as, "A new wave of legal actions in the UK, U.S., Canada and Australia [that] aims to hold parent companies legally accountable in developed country courts for negative environmental, health and safety, labour or human rights impacts associated with the operations of members of their corporate family in developing countries. These 'foreign direct liability' claims represent the flip side of foreign direct investment. They complement campaigners' calls for minimum standards for multinational corporations by testing the boundaries of existing legal principles, rather than by calling for new regulation." Halina Ward, *Governing Multinationals: The Role of Foreign Direct Liability* 1 (Chatham House Briefing Paper No. 18, 2001), http://www.chathamhouse.org/publications/papers/view/107528.

9.   *See* Rafael La Porta, Florencio Lopez de Silanes, Adrei Shleifer & Robert W. Vishny, *Legal Determinants of External Finance*, 52 J. FIN. 1131 (1997); Rafael La Porta, Florencio Lopez de Silanes, Adrei Shleifer & Robert W. Vishny, *Law and Finance*, 106 J. POL. ECON. 1113 (1998). This view does not in fact stand up to closer empirical examination, on which *see* Katerina Pistor, Yoram Keinan, Jan

these countries also are more suited to foreign direct-liability litigation and, if so, why? Equally, are civil law countries ill suited to such litigation?

The chapter will begin with an overview of the origins of foreign direct-liability litigation in common law jurisdictions. It will then consider the rise of similar litigation in civil law countries. Then the development of litigation against corporate defendants in developing countries will be considered. The final section of the chapter will assess the impact of European human rights standards and the recent international developments in the UN Framework on the further development of foreign direct liability.

Origins in Common Law Jurisdictions

Foreign direct-liability claims emerged around two sets of cases starting in the 1990s.[10] First, there are the U.S. cases brought under ATCA that center on alleged violations of human rights by corporate actors through their foreign operations. Second, a series of cases brought before U.S., UK, Canadian, and Australian courts have sought to hold the parent company accountable before the courts of the home state for wrongs committed by its subsidiaries abroad. Here the emphasis is not so much on human rights abuses, though they may be an aspect of the case, but on civil law, especially tort liability under the laws of the home state. The main characteristics of each set of cases will be considered briefly because an understanding of these is essential before any comparative analysis of their impact on other jurisdictions can be made.

The ATCA cases represent, to date, the most advanced attempt to establish human rights responsibilities in law for legal persons. In the case of *Doe v. Unocal*,[11] it was held for the first time that in principle, MNEs could be directly liable for gross violations of human rights under ATCA.[12] Initially, the district court in that case held that Unocal could not be held liable for alleged violations of fundamental labor rights on the grounds that it was necessary to show that a corporate actor had taken direct steps to violate those

---

Kleinheisterkramp & Mark D. West, *The Evolution of Corporate Law: A Cross-Country Comparison*, 23 U. Pa. J. Int'l Econ. L. 791 (2002).

10.   *See* Ward, *supra* note 8.

11.   Doe v. Unocal Corp., 963 F. Supp. 880 (C.D. Cal. 1997), *aff'd*, 395 F.3d 932 (9th Cir. 2002), *reh'g* ordered by, 395 F.3d 978 (9th Cir. 2003) (en banc). *See also* in this regard Kadic v. Karadzic, 70 F.3d 232 (2d Cir. 1995), where it was held that the Alien Tort Claims Act reaches the conduct of private parties provided that their conduct is undertaken under the colour of state authority or violates a norm of international law that is recognised as extending to the conduct of private parties.

12.   *See* 28 U.S.C. § 1350 (2006). ATCA states: "The district courts shall have original jurisdiction of any civil action by an alien for a tort only, committed in violation of the law of nations or a treaty of the United States." *See also* Sarah Joseph, Corporations and Transnational Human Rights Litigation, chs. 2–4 (2004).

rights.[13] The United States Court of Appeal (U.S.CA) for the Ninth Circuit overturned this decision.[14] The U.S.CA held that the essential element in such liability was to show that the corporation had either directly violated fundamental norms of human rights or had aided and abetted the host-state government authorities in their alleged violations. Thus the U.S.CA accepted that a corporate actor could be complicit in a human rights violation even when there was no direct involvement. Accordingly, different levels of complicity, both direct and indirect, could be invoked as the basis of a corporate liability claim.[15] This approach was affirmed in 2007 by the U.S.CA for the Second Circuit, which overturned the dismissal of claims arising out of claims of corporate complicity with the apartheid regime in South Africa, on the grounds that aiding and abetting liability was a part of customary international law and so could be invoked under ATCA.[16]

Whether this case law will survive is now at issue. In 2010, the U.S.CA for the Second Circuit dismissed a series of claims under ATCA against the Shell Petroleum Development Company of Nigeria on the grounds that, following the precedent of *Sosa v. Alvarez-Machain*,[17] in ATCA suits alleging violations of customary international law, the scope of liability was determined by customary international law itself.[18] Because customary international law consisted of only those norms that were specific, universal, and obligatory in the relations of states among themselves, and because no corporation had ever been subject to any form of liability (whether civil or criminal) under the customary international law of human rights, the U.S.CA held that corporate liability was not a discernible, much less universally recognized, norm of customary international law that could be

13. Doe v. Unocal Corp., 110 F. Supp. 2d 1294 (C.D. Cal. 2000). *See also* William Branigin, *Claim Against Unocal Rejected: Judge Cites Evidence of Abuses in Burma but No Jurisdiction*, WASH. POST, Sep. 8, 2000, at E10.

14. Doe v. Unocal Corp., 395 F.3d 932 (9th Cir. 2002) This decision was in turn vacated on February 14, 2003, to be reheard by the *en banc* Court of Appeal for the Ninth Circuit. *See* Doe v. Unocal Corp., 395 F.3d 978 (9th Cir. 2003). The case settled in December 2004. *See Unocal Settles Burma Abuse Case*, FIN. TIMES (Dec. 14, 2004), at 12. Since then, the District Court opinion of 2000 has also been vacated by the U.S. Court of Appeal for the Ninth Circuit. *See* Doe v. Unocal Corp., 403 F.3d 708 (9th Cir. 2005) (filed April 13, 2005).

15. On the issue of corporate complicity in human rights violations, *see also* Anita Ramasastry, *Secrets and Lies? Swiss Banks and International Human Rights*, 31 VAND. J. TRANSNAT'L L. 325 (1998); Anita Ramasastry, *Corporate Complicity from Nuremberg to Rangoon: An Examination of Forced Labor Cases and Their Impact on the Liability of Multinational Corporations*, 20 BERKELEY J. INT'L L. 91 (2002); Andrew Clapham & Scott Jebri, *Categories of Corporate Complicity in Human Rights Abuses*, 24 HASTINGS INT'L & COMP. L. REV. 339 (2001).

16. Khulumani et al. v. Barclays Bank, 504 F.3d 254 (2007). Affirmed without opinion by an equally divided Court at Am. Isuzu Motors Inc. v. Ntsebeza, 553 U.S. 1028, 128 S. Ct. 2424, 171 L. Ed. 2d 225 (2008). On the issue of aiding and abetting liability, *see also* Doug Cassel, *Corporate Aiding and Abetting of Human Rights Violations: Confusion in the Courts*, 6 NW. UNIV. J. INT'L HUM. RTS. 304 (2007–2008); Richard Hertz, *The Liberalizing Effects of Tort: How Corporate Complicity Liability Under the Alien Tort Statute Advances Constructive Engagement*, 21 HARV. HUM. RTS. J. 208 (2008).

17. Sosa v. Alvarez-Machain, 542 U.S. 692 (2004). *See* SARAH JOSEPH, CORPORATIONS AND TRANSNATIONAL HUMAN RIGHTS LITIGATION (2004), http://www.hartpub.co.uk/updates/pdfs/sj.pdf (for comment)

18. Kiobel v. Royal Dutch Petroleum Co., 621 F.3d 111 (2010).

applied pursuant to ATCA. Accordingly, the plaintiffs' claims were dismissed for lack of subject-matter jurisdiction.[19]

The case was appealed to the U.S. Supreme Court.[20] The petitioners argued, among other things, that the lower court erred in holding that corporate liability was not recognized under international law or that only international law determined the nature of the claim because it was open to the federal courts to allow a claim against a corporation based on tort for an alleged violation of international law.[21] Respondents argued that the lower court was correct to assert that corporate liability under ATCA was improper because corporate liability had never been recognized under customary international law, aiding and abetting liability was not available, and ATCA did not have extraterritorial reach.[22] The U.S. Supreme Court issued a writ of *certiorari* on April 17, 2013.[23]

One striking aspect of this decision is that the U.S. Supreme Court avoided answering the original question, whether the law of nations does recognize corporate liability. Instead, it focused on the extraterritorial application of the ATCA, holding that the presumption against extraterritoriality applies to claims under the ATCA and that nothing in the statute rebuts that presumption. Although some commentators have interpreted this decision as the end of human rights litigation against global corporations in the United States,[24] it appears that the U.S. Supreme Court's avoidance of the question relating to corporate liability under the ATCA actually leaves the door ajar for further claims against MNEs.[25] However, future plaintiffs will have to demonstrate a strong nexus of their claim with the U.S. jurisdiction. This requirement will certainly narrow the number of claims brought against foreign MNEs but may have the benefit of legitimizing litigation against corporations before the U.S. district courts.

---

19. *Id.* at 48–50.

20. Transcript of Oral Argument, Kiobel v. Royal Dutch Petroleum Co., 133 S. Ct. 1659 (2013) (No. 10-1491) http://www.supremecourt.gov/oral_arguments/argument_transcripts/10-1491.pdf (argued Feb. 28, 2012).

21. Brief for the Petitioners, Kiobel v. Royal Dutch Petroleum Co., 133 S. Ct. 1659 (2013) (No. 10-1491), http://www.americanbar.org/content/dam/aba/publications/supreme_court_preview/briefs /10-1491_petitioner.authcheckdam.pdf.

22. Brief for the Respondents, Kiobel v. Royal Dutch Petroleum Co., 133 S. Ct. 1659 (2013) (No. 10-1491), http://www.americanbar.org/content/dam/aba/publications/supreme_court_preview/briefs /10-1491_petitioner.authcheckdam.pdf.

23. Kiobel v. Royal Dutch Petroleum Co., 133 S. Ct. 1659 (2013).

24. Jen Alic, *Shell vs. Kiobel: Green Light for Multinational Human Rights Abuses*, OILPRICE.COM (Apr. 22, 2013), http://oilprice.com/Energy/Energy-General/Shell-vs.-Kiobel-Green-Light-for-Multinatio nal-Human-Rights-Abuses.html; Amol Mehra, *Supreme Court Undermines Human Rights*, PROVIDENCE J. (Apr. 25, 2013), http://blogs.providencejournal.com/ri-talks/this-new-england/2013/04/amol-mehra-su preme-court-undermines-human-rights.html.

25. Justice Kennedy, who joined the majority opinion in full, also concurred separately. He held that "the opinion for the Court is careful to leave open a number of significant questions regarding the reach and interpretation of the Alien Tort Statute." *See also* Katie Redford, *Commentary: Door Still Open for Human Rights Claims after Kiobel*, SCOTU.S.BLOG (Apr. 17, 2013), http://www.scotusblog.com/2013 /04/commentary-door-still-open-for-human-rights-claims-after-kiobel/.

The second set of original *foreign direct liability* cases arose in the United States, Canada, Australia, and England. Such liability was sought in the United States in the Bhopal case against Union Carbide, which was said to be liable on the ground that it designed, built, and operated the Bhopal pesticides plant from which a gas leak killed and injured thousands in December 1984.[26] In Canada, Quebec mining company Cambior faced litigation over pollution from its gold mine in Guyana.[27] In Australia, the company BHP faced claims arising out of pollution in Papua New Guinea.[28] In England, actions were brought against Rio Tinto arising out of alleged industrial health injuries at its Rossing Uranium Mine in Namibia, former asbestos mining company Cape because of its operations in South Africa, and Thor Chemicals over mercury poisoning suffered by workers at its South African mercury-recycling plant.[29]

In all these cases, the issue was whether the parent company could be liable in tort for the acts of its overseas subsidiaries. A preliminary question was whether the home country had jurisdiction over the claims made by nationals of the host country. Thus, the U.S. Bhopal case was unsuccessful on grounds of *forum non conveniens* because India was seen as the appropriate forum for the claims against Union Carbide. The Canadian litigation against Cambior failed on the same grounds, because Guyana would be a preferable alternative forum given the location of the evidence and witnesses and the interests of justice. The BHP claim was admissible on jurisdictional grounds because of Australia's generally pro-plaintiff approach to the forum-selection issue, but it was ultimately settled.[30] The English cases established that *forum non conveniens* was no bar to bringing the relevant claims because the requirements of justice in each case could not be met by sending the case to the host-country forum. The case against Rio Tinto ultimately failed on the grounds that the statute of limitations had run out, whereas the Cape *plc* and Thor Chemicals cases ended in settlements.[31] The *forum non conveniens* issue should no longer

---

26. *In re* Union Carbide Corp. Gas Plant Disaster at Bhopal, India, 634 F. Supp. 842 (S.D.N.Y. 1986), aff'd and modified, 809 F.2d 195 (2d Cir. 1987), cert denied, 108 S. Ct. 199 (1987). For analysis, *see also* Peter T. Muchlinski, *The Bhopal Case: Controlling Ultrahazardous Industrial Activities Undertaken by Foreign Investors*, 50 MO. L. REV. 545 (1987); Upendra Baxi, *Mass Torts, Multinational Enterprise Liability and Private International Law*, 276 HAGUE RECUEIL 301 (1999).

27. Recherches internationales du Québec v. Cambior Inc., [1998] Q.J. No. 2554.

28. Dagi v Broken Hill Proprietary Co. Props. *(No 2)* (1995) 1 V.R. 428.

29. Connelly v Rio Tinto Zinc [1997] 4 All E.R. 335 (H.L.); Lubbe v Cape Plc [1998] C.A.C. 1559 (CA July 30, 1998), [2000] 2 Lloyds Rep 383 (H.L.), [2000] 4 All E.R. 268 (H.L.); *See* Ngcobo v. Thor Chemical Holdings Ltd (9th Cir. Oct. 1995) (unreported).

30. *See also* PETER T. MUCHLINSKI, MULTINATIONAL ENTERPRISES AND THE LAW 159 (2d ed. 2007).

31. Thor Chemicals settled the initial claims against them in 1997 for £1.3 million. In July 1998 Thor's attempt to stay these proceedings was rejected by Garland J. and leave to appeal was refused by the Court of Appeal. *See* Sithole v. Thor Chemicals Holding Ltd. (July 31, 1998) (unreported). For background, *see* Richard Meeran, *The Unveiling of Transnational Corporations: A Direct Approach*, in HUMAN RIGHTS AND THE RESPONSIBILITY OF TRANSNATIONAL CORPORATIONS, 161–70 (Michael Addo ed., 1999). The *Cape* cases settled for £7.5 million compensation to the 7,500 members of the Group action brought in England. *See* Coombs, Pickering and Partners, *Press Release: End of Struggle for Cape*

provide a major procedural obstacle to foreign direct-liability litigation in the English courts. The European Court of Justice held that the doctrine of *forum non conveniens* is incompatible with European regulations on jurisdiction.[32] The dominant European principle is that mandatory jurisdiction based on the domicile of the defendant is available as of right to the claimant, subject to certain specific exceptions. In relation to tort claims, the only exception to this rule is that the claimant can choose between the jurisdiction where he or she has suffered harm and the jurisdiction of domicile of the defendant. Thus, English law appears to be moving away from the discretionary approach of common law doctrine and coming closer to European doctrine, under which no discretion over the exercise of jurisdiction by a national court is recognized.[33] By contrast, U.S. law retains a strong discretion under the *forum non conveniens* doctrine.

As to substantive law principles, very few cases have ever reached a final determination on the merits. Most such cases settle out of court. Accordingly, there is very little guidance on the extent of a parent company's duty of care for the acts of its subsidiaries. This dearth of guidance is compounded by the continued adherence to a strict separation in law between the parent and subsidiary. Only in the most extreme cases of control by the parent over the subsidiary has liability been accepted.[34] This situation has involved the direct liability of the parent for acts that, in combination with the acts of its closely controlled subsidiaries, could be seen as the acts of joint tortfeasors. Thus, these are not cases in which the *corporate veil* has been lifted between parent and subsidiary. Indeed, the questions of corporate separation and limited liability severely limit the chances of success where the alleged liability of the parent is indirect, such as when it has not taken an active part in the chain of events leading to the harm or has negligently omitted to act to stop the harmful conduct undertaken by the subsidiary. However, in the recent case of *Chandler v. Cape plc*, the High Court held that the parent company, Cape plc, was

---

Asbestos Victims, MAC: Mines and Communities (Mar. 13, 2003), http://www.minesandcommunities .org/article.php?a=739.

32. Case C-281/02, Owusu v. Jackson [2005] 2 W.L.R. 942. 363. The ECJ has also ruled that the Brussels Convention applies to give jurisdiction against a defendant, domiciled in an EC Member State, to claimants domiciled in a country that is not a party to the Convention. *See* Case C-412/98, Société Group Josi Reinsurance Company SA v. Compagnie d'Assurances Universal General Insurance Company, E.C.R. [2000] I-5925.

33. *See* S & W Berisford plc v. New Hampshire Insurance Co. [1990] 2 All E.R. 321 at 332 (Com. Ct.), a-e citing the Schlosser Report on the 1968 Convention, OJ [1979] C 59, ¶ 76, 78 at 97–99. For a critical appraisal of this tendency, including a scathing critique of Owusu v. Jackson, *see also* Trevor C. Hartley, *The European Union and the Systematic Dismantling of the Common Law of Conflict of Laws*, 54 Int'l & Comp. L. Q. 813 (2005).

34. *See* The Amoco Cadiz [1984] 2 Lloyds Rep. 304; CSR v. Wren (1997) 44 N.S.W.L.R. 463 (CA NSW). For a detailed discussion of English law, *see* Myfanwy Badge, *Transboundary Accountability for Transnational Corporations: Using Private Civil Claims* (working paper, Mar. 2006), http://www .chathamhouse.org/sites/default/files/public/Research/International%20Law/ilp_tnc.pdf. On U.S. law, *see* Philip I. Blumberg, Kurt A. Strasser, Nicholas L. Georgakopoulos & Eric J. Gouvin, Blumberg on Corporate Groups 2, chs. 57–65 (2d ed. 2005).

liable through negligence for asbestos-related illness suffered by the claimant as a result of his employment in a subsidiary of Cape, Cape Building Products Limited, where he had worked with asbestos products.[35] On April 25, 2012, the Court of Appeal upheld this decision and provided some guidance on the circumstances in which to hold a parent company liable for its subsidiary's activities.

> In summary, this case demonstrates that in appropriate circumstances the law may impose on a parent company responsibility for the health and safety of its subsidiary's employees. Those circumstances include a situation where, as in the present case, (1) the businesses of the parent and subsidiary are in a relevant respect the same; (2) the parent has, or ought to have, superior knowledge on some relevant aspect of health and safety in the particular industry; (3) the subsidiary's system of work is unsafe as the parent company knew, or ought to have known; and (4) the parent knew or ought to have foreseen that the subsidiary or its employees would rely on its using that superior knowledge for the employees' protection.[36]

Despite the fact that this case is concerned with the liability of a parent company for the activities of its subsidiary in the United Kingdom, it will be interesting to see in the future how the decision of the Court of Appeal may influence litigation brought against

---

35.   Chandler v. Cape PLC [2011] EWHC 951 (QB). The parent company admitted that the risk of injury to the claimant was foreseeable but that it owed no duty of care to employees of subsidiaries. Williams J held that, on the facts, a direct duty of care was owed to the claimant as it was Cape PLC that dictated health policy and that it, "retained responsibility for ensuring that its own employees and those of its subsidiaries were not exposed to the risk of harm through exposure to asbestos. In reaching that conclusion I do not intend to imply that the subsidiaries, themselves, had no part to play—certainly in the implementation of relevant policy. However, the evidence persuades me that the Defendant retained overall responsibility. At any stage it could have intervened and Cape Products would have bowed to its intervention. On that basis, in my judgment, the claimant has established a sufficient degree of proximity between the Defendant and himself. . . . No argument was advanced to me . . . that if foreseeability and proximity were established nonetheless it was not fair, just and reasonable for a duty to exist. Had such an argument been advanced I would have rejected it. By the late 1950s it was clear to the Defendant that exposure to asbestos brought with it very significant risk of very damaging and life threatening illness. I can think of no basis upon which it would be proper to conclude in those circumstances that it would not be just or reasonable to impose a duty of care upon an organisation like the Defendant." *Id.* ¶ 75–76.

36.   Chandler v. Cape PLC [2012] E.W.C.A. Civ 525, ¶ 80. Lady Justice Arden held, "Given Cape's state of knowledge about the Cowley Works, and its superior knowledge about the nature and management of asbestos risks, I have no doubt that in this case it is appropriate to find that Cape assumed a duty of care either to advise Cape Products on what steps it had to take in the light of knowledge then available to provide those employees with a safe system of work or to ensure that those steps were taken. The scope of the duty can be defined in either way. Whichever way it is formulated, the injury to Mr. Chandler was the result. As the judge held, working on past performance and viewing the matter realistically, Cape could, and did on other matters, give Cape Products instructions as to how it was to operate with which, so far as we know, it duly complied. In these circumstances, there was, in my judgment, a direct duty of care owed by Cape to the employees of Cape Products. There was an omission to advise on precautionary measures even though it was doing research and that research had not established (nor could it establish) that the asbestosis and related diseases were not caused by asbestos dust." *Id.* ¶ 78–79.

multinational enterprises headquartered in the United Kingdom with subsidiaries in developing countries.[37] We will see further in this chapter that the application of *Chandler v. Cape plc* to multinational enterprises was interpreted narrowly by the District Court of the Hague in the case it heard against Shell.

Why have these cases arisen in the common law world in particular? There are no simple answers because the motives for such litigation and the procedural opportunities for it are varied even among these jurisdictions.[38] As already noted, there is no uniform approach to the question of jurisdiction among these countries. Equally, the substantive law may approach matters differently in each case. The lack of decided cases simply covers up this possibility. One possible answer is that common law jurisdictions often offer more claimant-friendly procedures, such as the availability of contingency or conditional fees, easier discovery, and, in the case of the United States, a jury trial. However, such advantages must be weighed against the chances of success, and they are not present in every jurisdiction that has entertained foreign direct-liability actions. Moreover, in the United Kingdom, the implementation of the Legal Aid Sentencing and Punishment of Offenders Act 2012 (LASPO) is expected to have a substantial impact on litigation costs, including cuts in the legal aid budget and changes in the regime of success fees and after-the-event (ATE) insurance premiums.[39] NGOs have held that LASPO will have a direct impact on the number of transnational cases brought against multinational enterprises in the United Kingdom.[40]

Perhaps the real answers lie in the legal-professional culture and the extent to which common law countries tend to hand the direction of litigation to party discretion. As to the former, it appears that American lawyers, and to a lesser extent their English, Australian, and Canadian counterparts, see legal practice in more entrepreneurial terms than lawyers who may be steeped in the civilian tradition, who see themselves more as political actors dedicated to the defense of the public interest.[41] Equally, the adversary system

---

37. *See Historic Judgement as Asbestos Victim Wins Damages from Employer's Parent Company*, LEIGH DAY (April 25, 2012), http://www.leighday.co.uk/News/2012/April-2012/Historic-Judgment-as-Asbestos-Victim-Wins-Damages-.

38. *See also* Badge, *supra* note 34.

39. The Legal Aid, Sentencing and Punishment of Offenders Act 2012 came into force on April 1, 2013.

40. *See* CORE, Amnesty International, CAFOD & OXFAM, *Government Reforms Undermine UN Guiding Principles on Business and Human Rights and Encourage Impunity for Abuses*, CORE COALITION (Mar. 23, 2012), http://corporate-responsibility.org/wp-content/uploads/2012/03/Legal-Aid-Bill-Briefing-Lords-3rd-reading-March-20121.pdf.

41. *See* LAWYERS AND THE RISE OF WESTERN LIBERALISM: EUROPE AND NORTH AMERICA FROM THE EIGHTEENTH TO THE TWENTIETH CENTURIES (Terence Halliday & Lucien Karpik eds., 1998). The authors identify a new American model of legal practice after the Second World War, "which has become strongly favoured throughout the world in the train of United States' economic and political influence and the energetic entrepreneurialism of American lawyers" *Id.* at 13. This influence is seen in particular in the building of market-based legal solutions to economic globalization but is more resistant in relation

of justice encourages placing the interests of the client first and hands control over the presentation of evidence to the lawyers rather than to the court, which has such control in civilian systems.[42] Both practices would tend toward giving lawyers in these countries a sense that they can use their initiative to develop cases.

A further important factor arises out of the fact that many of the leading NGOs concerned about corporate social responsibility were founded in the Anglo-American world, though as will be noted below, similar organizations are now active in some civil law jurisdictions as well. They have been at the forefront of activism in relation to foreign direct liability.[43] Perhaps the best example is the UK-based Corporate Responsibility (CORE) Coalition, formed in 2000. It aims to make changes in UK law to "minimize companies [*sic*] negative impacts on people and the environment and to maximize [their] contribution to sustainable societies."[44] The main themes of the coalition's work include "the need for greater corporate *accountability* of key decision makers in companies, the importance of openness and *transparency* and better *access to justice* for victims of corporate abuse." In this connection, CORE has advocated the further reform of English law to accommodate foreign direct liability through changes in statutory obligations of corporations and through litigation.[45]

Equally, public-interest law firms in these countries have developed a unique expertise in such litigation. For example, the English firm of Leigh Day, which was responsible for bringing the Cape and Thor Chemicals cases, and which settled the claims against Trafigura concerning oil pollution in the Côte d'Ivoire,[46] states that its ethos is

> to ensure that the ordinary person has just as good quality legal advice as our state
> bodies, insurers and multi-nationals which has led us to take on many "David and

---

to political and constitutional issues. A good example of this entrepreneurial domination is the prevalence of U.S.- and UK-based law firms in international investor-state arbitration.

42. *See also* Stephen Gillers, *The American Legal Profession*, in Fundamentals of American Law 151, 166–68 (Alan B. Morrison ed., 1996).

43. *See also* Michael Yaziji & Jonathan Doh, NGOs and Corporations: Conflict and Collaboration (2009).

44. *About Us,* CORE Coalition, http://corporate-responsibility.org/about/ (last visited July 23, 2013). Members of CORE include Amnesty International, Action Aid, Friends of the Earth, Traidcraft, and War on Want and WWF (UK).

45. *See also* London School of Economics and Political Science & CORE Coalition, *The Reality of Rights: Barriers to Accessing Remedies When Business Operates Beyond Borders*, Amnesty Int'l (Mar. 2009), http://www.amnesty.org.uk/uploads/documents/doc_19465.pdf.

46. *See* David Leigh, *Trafigura Reaches a Global Settlement,* The Guardian (Sept. 16, 2009), http://www.guardian.co.uk/world/2009/sep/16/trafigura-toxic-dump-global-settlement.; *see Cheques Will Be Paid to Côte d'Ivoire Waste Claimants from 1st March 2010,* Leigh Day (Feb. 26, 2010), http://www.leighday.co.uk/News/2010/February-2010/Cheques-will-be-paid-to-Ivory-Coast-waste-claimant, on the problems relating to the paying out of the settlement monies in the Côte d'Ivoire. *Agreement Gives Hope to Ivorian Toxic Waste Claimants,* Leigh Day (Feb. 14, 2010), http://www.leighday.co.uk/News/2010/February-2010/Agreement-gives-hope-to-Ivorian-toxic-waste-claima; *Victims of Toxic Waste in Despair at Court Ruling,* Leigh Day (Jan. 22, 2010), http://www.leighday.co.uk/News/2010/January-2010/Victims-of-toxic-waste-in-despair-at-Court-ruling.

Goliath" legal struggles for justice. Our aim is to remain a niche firm specializing in the more complex aspects of personal injury and human rights law. We are committed to achieving access to justice for all including full, fair compensation by providing first-rate legal advice.[47]

Thus, in the English legal system there is a strong civil society presence that seeks to further what it sees as an imbalance of rights and responsibilities in the law where the liability of MNEs is concerned. Indeed, the examples of NGOs and public-interest law firms taken from the English context can be multiplied by similar institutional phenomena in the United States, Canada, and Australia, though space prohibits any more-detailed description.[48]

Foreign Direct-Liability Litigation in Civil Law Jurisdictions

Turning to civil law jurisdictions, the *legal family* argument that common law jurisdictions are better fora for foreign direct-liability cases can now be tested by reference to the recent experience of litigation in civil law jurisdictions aimed at securing compensation from corporate non-state actors for harm, including for violations of human rights. Examples from France, Belgium, and the Netherlands are examined here.

In France, under the leadership of the human rights NGO Sherpa, a number of cases have been instituted over the past fifteen years against French MNEs for alleged violations of human rights by their overseas subsidiaries.[49] In particular, Sherpa filed a lawsuit

---

47. *See About Us*, LEIGH DAY, http://www.leighday.co.uk/about-us (last visited July 23, 2013). In 2012, Leigh Day commenced proceedings in the English High Court against Royal Dutch Shell arising out of two oil spills in the Niger Delta in 2008, after settlement negotiations broke down. *See Shell Sued in UK over Nigeria Spills*, FIN. TIMES (Mar. 23, 2012), at 22; *11,000 Nigerians Sue Shell in London Courts*, LEIGH DAY (Mar. 22, 2012), http://www.leighday.co.uk/News/2012/March-2012/11 ,000-Nigerians-sue-Shell-in-London-Courts.

48. On the U.S., *see e.g.,* the national network of Public Interest Research Groups (PIRGs). The national network U.S. PIRG states that its mission is to act as "an advocate for the public interest. When consumers are cheated, or the voices of ordinary citizens are drowned out by special interest lobbyists, U.S. PIRG speaks up and takes action. We uncover threats to public health and well-being and fight to end them, using the time-tested tools of investigative research, media exposés, grassroots organizing, advocacy and litigation. U.S. PIRG's mission is to deliver persistent, result-oriented public interest activism that protects our health, encourages a fair, sustainable economy, and fosters responsive, democratic government." *See About Us*, U.S. PIRG, http://www.uspirg.org/about-us/mission (last visited July 23, 2013). Similar bodies have been established in Canada. In Australia, the NGO community is also active in the field and lawyers specialising in public interest actions are well organised. *See, e.g.,* the Public Interest Law Clearing House (VIC) Inc. (PILCH). *See About PILCH*, PILCH, http://www.pilch.org.au/about / (last visited July 23, 2013).

49. Among the cases instituted by Sherpa, three of them are worth mentioning. In 2002, a claim was lodged against Rougier in respect of alleged corrupt practices in Cameroon, but it was dismissed by the Paris Court of Appeal on February 13, 2004, on the ground of lack of jurisdiction over the parent company for the acts of its subsidiary. Plaintiffs appealed the decision, which was upheld by the French

in France on August 26, 2002, on behalf of eight Myanmar nationals against the French oil company Total, citing "complicity in unlawful confinement."[50] The plaintiffs alleged that they had been forced by the Myanmar army to provide what they deemed to be compulsory labor for the construction of the Yadana gas pipeline, in which Total had been a participant. Total has always maintained that the accusations made against the company were without substance as a matter of fact and as a matter of law. Total and Sherpa entered into a settlement agreement on November 29, 2005. Under the terms of the agreement, Total created a €5.2 million solidarity fund to compensate the eight plaintiffs as well as any other persons who could demonstrate that they suffered a similar experience in the area near the pipeline construction corridor.[51] The fund would also be used to finance humanitarian actions benefiting Myanmar refugees in the region.

A similar case was filed against Total in Belgium on April 25, 2002 by four Myanmar refugees, who cited "complicity in crimes against humanity" under Belgium's Universal Jurisdiction Law of June 16, 1993, relative to serious violations of international human rights.[52] The 1993 law was repealed by the law of August 5, 2003, which included a procedure for terminating certain proceedings that were underway. The Belgian Cour de Cassation subsequently dismissed the proceedings against Total on jurisdictional grounds in a ruling dated June 29, 2005. On June 21, 2006, the Belgian Cour d'Arbitrage annulled the procedure provided for by the law of August 5, 2003. However, the consequences of this decision do not affect the Cour de Cassation's ruling under the principle of *res judicata*. In two rulings dated March 28, 2007 and October 29, 2008, this court confirmed that the proceedings had been dismissed definitely.

In neither case against Total could it be said that the national laws of France and Belgium had fully accepted foreign direct liability as a basis for claims. The French litigation ended in an out-of-court settlement. The Belgian case was found to have been based on an inappropriate assumption of universal jurisdiction under the Belgian statute of 1993 and was correctly dismissed on the basis of the repealing statute of 2003. Is this indicative of a civilian bias against foreign direct-liability actions?

Court of Cassation in 2005. *See* Marie-Caroline Caillet, *Note didactique: Comprendre les obstacles à la mise en œuvre de la responsabilité des entreprises multinationales*, Sherpa & CCFD Terre Solidaire (Oct. 2009), at 5. Furthermore, during the same year a claim was brought against Total arising out of its involvement in the construction of the Yadana pipeline in Burma/Myanmar. The third complaint was lodged by Sherpa, Global Witness, and partner NGOs in 2009 against DLH for its involvement in the Liberian civil war (1989–2003). *See International Timber Company DLH Accused of Funding Liberian War*, Global Witness (Nov. 18, 2009), http://www.globalwitness.org/library/international-timber-company-dlh-accused-funding-liberian-war. For the latest campaigns, *see Action Plan 2010–2012*, Sherpa, http://asso-sherpa.org/sherpa-content/docs/english/SHERPA_Action_plan.pdf (last visited July 23, 2013).

50. This account is taken from the Total Web site. *See Total au Myanmar*, Total, http://burma.total.com/en/controverse/p_4_2.html (last updated 2013).

51. *See also* Sherpa, Annual Report 2006, at 2 (May 2, 2007), http://asso-sherpa.org/sherpa-content/docs/association/histoire/Rapport_activites_2006.pdf.

52. This summary is also taken from Total's Web site. *See Total au Myanmar*, *supra* note 50.

The validity of foreign direct-liability claims remains uncertain in France. Civilian legal systems generally view a criminal trial and conviction as the requisite basis for compensation in grave human rights abuse cases.[53] Equally, in the *Lipietz* litigation, a case concerning the extent to which the French national railway company SNCF and the French government could be held responsible for complicity in the deportation of French Jews during the Second World War. The liability of both was accepted at first instance, but SNCF's liability was overturned on appeal.[54] The Conseil d'État upheld the ruling of the Administrative Court of Appeals on the ground that the tribunal of first instance lacked jurisdiction to hear a compensation claim against SNCF, which was at the relevant time a mixed-economy entity exercising both public and commercial functions, and on the ground that it was acting under orders, as the Court of Appeal had correctly concluded.[55] The overruling of the decision against SNCF can be seen as a brake on development in relation to corporate liability for human rights violations.

The interesting issue in the *Lipietz* case is why the plaintiffs made a claim of this kind at all. This case stands out as an example of a legal strategy being employed in a way that connotes a creative transplantation, or *sampling*, of foreign legal solutions to common problems of liability for major breaches of human rights by corporate and governmental actors.[56] Some have suggested that it represents the first time a French court has accepted an Anglo-American type of solution to a major public interest claim and has entertained a private, tort-based analysis of a struggle for justice that would normally be played out through criminal law, and through the resulting direction of the legal process, by the court as the representative of the protecting power of the state.[57] This approach developed through activism on the part of lawyers who represented the victims and who used the threat of a U.S.-based ATCA action to get the case heard in France.[58]

---

53. *See* Vivian Grosswald Curran, *Globalization, Legal Transplantation and Crimes against Humanity: The Lipietz Case,* 56 Am. J. Comp. L. 363, 379 (2008).

54. Tribunal administratif de Toulouse, *M. A. et consorts Lipietz ci Préfet de la Haute-Garonne et Société nationale des chemins de fer français,* No. 0104248 (June 6, 2006), http://www.acaccia.fr/IMG/pdf/JudgmentLipietzenglish.pdf. *See generally* Curran, *supra* note 53.

55. *See* Conseil d'État, *M. A. et Consorts Lipietz ci Préfet de la Haute-Garonne et Société nationale des chemins de fer français,* No. 305966 (Dec. 21, 2007) ("Whereas the Administrative Court is competent to hear claims seeking to establish the liability of a legal person governed by private law only if the damage is related to the exercise by such legal person of its prerogative of public power conferred for the execution of the mission of public service it was invested; Regarding the plea alleging an error of law on the date to take into account in determining the legal nature of the SNCF; Whereas the Administrative Court of Appeal of Bordeaux used, to retain jurisdiction of the ordinary court, the legal nature of the SNCF at the time of the facts, which was then a semi-public company operating the industrial and commercial public service rail transport under the agreement approved by the Decree-Law of 31 August 1937, and not the SNCF's current status of public industrial and commercial establishment, the Administrative Court has not vitiated its judgment by an error of law."). (Unofficial translation by the authors.)

56. Legal "sampling" is used here on analogy with the process of sampling in music whereby a part of an existing piece of music is incorporated into a new piece of music to produce an original sound.

57. *See* Curran, *supra* note 53, at 366.

58. Curran, *supra* note 53, at 391.

Also, in other cases, the existence of Sherpa has supplied the kind of institutionalized support that seems necessary for foreign direct-liability actions to develop. The civilian character of French law appears not to be the main reason for the comparative lack of public-interest tort litigation; it seems to be the relatively recent development of awareness among French lawyers that makes such cases possible at all. Indeed, in the field of environmental liability, civil claims for compensation have only recently been accepted in principle and remain subject to significant limitations, although the standing of environmental NGOs as claimants has been accepted.[59]

In addition, the *Lipietz* case can be seen as a *transnationalization* of law by way of legal changes occurring under unchanged forms of law in response to the threat of forum shopping, and in response to the need for an approach to cross-border issues of justice. Indeed, the main line of criticism of the *Lipietz* case in French legal circles, that the plaintiff's aim was not justice but profit and that the case trivialized the important historical and moral issues involved because it was a civil claim, can be explained as a reaction to the role of globalization in blurring the otherwise clear distinction between public and private interests in French law.[60] It is suggested that the common law–style tort action is being imported into France, and that even in France a *cosmopolitan legality* is developing, which is strongly influenced by the development of, among other types of claims, the foreign direct-liability action in common law jurisdictions.[61] That said, the case was brought as a *recours administrative* and/or a claim for *responsabilité administrative*, where the key question was the public- or private-law character of SNCF and whether the administrative courts had consequential subject-matter jurisdiction. Thus, it may be argued that the case retains an essentially French legal character while being motivated by social and legal initiatives that are common to a number of jurisdictions containing activist lawyers and NGOs.

Similarly, in the Netherlands the civilian character of the legal system has not been a barrier to the acceptance, for the first time in Dutch legal history, of jurisdiction over a foreign direct-liability claim based on references to an emergent *cosmopolitan legality*. In 2009, victims of oil pollution from Shell's installations in Nigeria, in conjunction with Milieudefensie (Friends of the Earth Netherlands), started legal proceedings against Shell Nigeria and Royal Dutch Shell plc, its parent company.[62] The claimants alleged that Shell Nigeria was liable for the pollution as the operator of the relevant plants in the Niger

---

59. *See also* Danai Papadopoulou, *The Role of French Environmental Associations in Civil Liability for Environmental Harm: Courtesy of Erika*, 21 J. ENVTL. L. 87 (2009) (discussing the implications of the judgment of the Paris Tribunal Correctionnel in the Erika oil spillage case, T. Corr. Paris (Jan. 16, 2008), No. 99-34-895010).

60. Curran, *supra* note 53, at 375.

61. *Id.*

62. *See* Milieudefensie, *Factsheet: The People of Nigeria Versus Shell: The First Session in the Legal Proceedings*, FRIENDS OF THE EARTH NETHERLANDS (Dec. 2009), http://milieudefensie.nl/publicaties/factsheets/factsheet-the-first-session.

Delta, while Royal Dutch Shell was liable on the basis of its duty of care as the parent company to prevent environmental damage on the part of its subsidiary. This principle of liability is supported, according to the claimants, in other legal systems, especially in U.S. and English law, as well as under Dutch law and international standards contained in international soft-law instruments, such as the OECD Guidelines on Multinational Enterprises and the UN Global Compact, and Global Reporting Initiative.[63]

On December 30, 2009, the District Court of the Hague ruled that the claimants had the right to bring the case before a Dutch court.[64] Jurisdiction over the parent company was established under Articles 2(1) and 60(1) of Council Regulation (EC) No. 44/2001 on jurisdiction and the recognition and enforcement of judgments in civil and commercial matters (Brussels I Regulation) on the basis that the parent company's domicile was in the Netherlands.[65] Regarding Shell Nigeria, because there was no connection to the Netherlands to justify competence through the EU regulation, the court relied on Article 7(1) of the Dutch Code of Civil Procedure, which allows the court, once it has established competence to hear the case concerning one defendant, to exercise jurisdiction over all concerned defendants if the complaint against parties is *connected* to such an extent that judicial economy (efficiency) justifies joining them. The court held that this was the situation in the present case because the constellation of facts was identical and the complaint held the parent and subsidiary jointly responsible.[66] Since the hearing on jurisdiction, a number of ancillary hearings have taken place in relation to disclosure of documents. In the course of these hearings, the District Court of the Hague made clear that Nigerian substantive law governed the claims and that, at the merits stage, the claimants had to substantiate their claims in accordance with the requirements of that law.[67]

---

63.   Oguru et al. Subpoena, ¶ 203-28 (2008), http://milieudefensie.nl/publicaties/bezwaren-uitspraken/subpoena-oruma/.

64.   Plaintiff 1 & Milieudefensie v. Royal Dutch Shell Plc & Shell Petroleum Development Company of Nigeria Ltd, LJN: BK8616, Rechtbank's-Gravenhage, HA ZA 330891 09-579 (2009) (judgement in motion contesting jurisdiction), http://milieudefensie.nl/publicaties/bezwaren-uitspraken/judgment-courtcase-shell-in-jurisdiction-motion-oruma.

65.   Council Regulation (EC) 44/2001 of 22 December 2000 on Jurisdiction and the Recognition and Enforcement of Judgments in Civil and Commercial Matters (2001) O.J. L 12/1.

66.   Plaintiff 1 & Milieudefensie v. Royal Dutch Shell Plc & Shell Petroleum Development Company of Nigeria Ltd, LJN: BK8616, Rechtbank's-Gravenhage, HA ZA 330891 09-579, ¶ 3.6: ("In the main action, [the plaintiffs] hold RDS and SPDC liable for the same damage, which also follows from the claim for a joint and several order for RDS and SPDC. This means that the same complex of facts in Nigeria must be assessed in respect of the claims against both RDS and SPDC. The court finds that this fact alone demonstrates a connection to such an extent that reasons of efficiency justify a joint hearing of the claims against RDS and SPDC. That all or part of these facts and circumstances did not occur in the Netherlands is not exceptional in Dutch case law and does not lead to a difference opinion on sufficient connection and efficiency in the sense of Section 7 DCCP.").

67.   Akpan v. Royal Dutch Shell Plc & Shell Petroleum Development Company of Nigeria Ltd, 337050 / HA ZA 09-1580; Oguru Efanga & Milieudefensie v. Royal Dutch Shell Plc & Shell Petroleum Development Company of Nigeria Ltd, 330891 / HA ZA 09-0579; Dooh & Milieudefensie v. Royal Dutch Shell Plc & Shell Petroleum Development Company of Nigeria Ltd, 337058 / HA ZA 09-1581

On January 30, 2013, the District Court of the Hague reached a decision. The court established that four of the contested oil spills were caused by sabotage from third parties. In its view, the oil spills were not caused by defective maintenance by Shell Nigeria, which had taken sufficient precautions to prevent sabotage from its underground oil pipelines. Applying Nigerian law, the District Court of the Hague found that an oil company is not liable for oil spills caused by sabotage and dismissed the lawsuits based on these oil spills.[68] However, in the proceedings concerning two further oil spills near the village of Ikot Ada Udo, the district court held that the Nigerian subsidiary of Shell, pursuant to applicable Nigerian law, had violated its duty-of-care obligation and found the oil company liable for tort of negligence.[69] The district court held,

> [a]s an operator acting reasonably, SPDC [Shell Petroleum Development Company of Nigeria] should have properly secured the IBIBIO-I well because it could and should have considerably limited or excluded such a large and obvious risk of sabotage—which was easy to commit— at relatively low cost. This leads to the conclusion that in this specific case, SPDC violated its duty of care in respect of Akpan. The parties do not disagree regarding the fact that the oil spills would not have occurred if the IBIBIO-I well simply had already been closed before 2006 or 2007 using a concrete plug. . . . Thus, there is a causal link between the violation of this specific duty of care by SPDC and the stated damage of Akpan. The above brings the District Court to the conclusion that SPDC committed a specific tort of negligence against Akpan by insufficiently securing the IBIBIO-I well to prevent the sabotage that was committed in a simple manner prior to the subject two oil spills, and that SPDC is liable for the damage that Akpan suffered as a result.[70]

With regard the liability of the British parent company, Royal Dutch Shell, the District Court of the Hague dismissed all claims. The district court was of the opinion that under

---

(2011). Judgments in the ancillary action concerning the production of exhibits and in the main action, http://milieudefensie.nl/english/shellinnigeria/oil-leaks/documents-on-the-shell-legal-case#legal..

68.   Oguru & Milieudefensie v. Royal Dutch Shell Plc & Shell Petroleum Development Company of Nigeria Ltd, LJN: BY9850, Rechtbank's-Gravenhage, C/09/330891 / HA ZA 09-0579 (2013); Dooh & Milieudefensie v. Royal Dutch Shell Plc & Shell Petroleum Development Company of Nigeria Ltd, LJN: BY9845, Rechtbank's-Gravenhage, C/09/337058 / HA ZA 09-1581 (2013). *See Dutch Judgements on Liability Shell*, DE RECHTSPRAAK (Jan. 30, 2013), http://www.rechtspraak.nl/Organisatie/Rechtbanken/Den-Haag/Nieuws/Pages/DutchjudgementsonliabilityShell.aspx.

69.   Akpan & Milieudefensie v. Royal Dutch Shell Plc & Shell Petroleum Development Company of Nigeria Ltd, LJN: BY9854, Rechtbank's-Gravenhage, C/09/337050 / HA ZA 09-1580 (2013), http://www.milieudefensie.nl/publicaties/bezwaren-uitspraken/final-judgment-akpan-vs-shell-oil-spill-ikot-ada-udo/view. Milieudefensie and the plaintiffs from two villages have submitted an appeal to the rulings dated January 30, 2013. *See Nigerians and Milieudefensie Appeal in Shell Case*, MILIEUDEFENSIE (May 1, 2013), http://www.milieudefensie.nl/english/shell/news/nigerians-and-milieudefensie-appeal-in-shell-case.

70.   *Akpan* case, *supra* note 69, ¶ 4.45.

applicable Nigerian law, a parent company is not obliged to prevent its subsidiaries from harming third parties abroad. Interestingly, the district court gave a narrow interpretation of the application of the abovementioned *Chandler v. Cape plc* case. The district court found that the special relation or proximity between a parent company and the employees of its subsidiary that operates in the same country cannot be unreservedly equated with the proximity between the parent company of an international group of oil companies and the people living in the vicinity of oil pipelines and oil facilities of its (sub-)subsidiaries in other countries. Subsequently, the district court held,

> The duty of care of a parent company in respect of the employers of a subsidiary that operates in the same country further only comprises a relatively limited group of people, whereas a possible duty of care of a parent company of an international group of oil companies in respect of the people living in the vicinity of oil pipelines and oil facilities of (sub-) subsidiaries would create a duty of care in respect of a virtually unlimited group of people in many countries. The District Court believes that in the case at issue, it is far less quickly fair, just and reasonable than it was in *Chandler v Cape [PLC]* to assume that such a duty of care on the part of [the parent company] exists.[71]

A second notable recent case that has arisen in the Netherlands concerns claims against Trafigura arising out of its transfer of toxic oil waste in the tanker the *Probo Koala* on charter to Trafigura.[72] On board the *Probo Koala*, washes of contaminated naphtha were carried out for Trafigura. Trafigura offered the waste materials generated in this process to Amsterdam Port Services (APS) for processing. The actual cost of dealing with this waste turned out to be substantially higher than had been agreed. Trafigura was unwilling to pay these higher costs. APS wanted to pump the waste back into the *Probo Koala*. The act was forbidden by the police, the public prosecution service, and the municipal environmental health department because the *Probo Koala* was not a recognized waste processor. After APS had consultations with the municipal environmental health department, it was agreed that the waste could be pumped back into the *Probo Koala*. The tanker subsequently headed to Côte d'Ivoire with the waste. There, it was alleged that deaths and injuries were caused by the processing of that waste in the Côte d'Ivoire. Without

---

71. Akpan case, *supra* note 69, § 4.29.
72. *See Trafigura Beheer B.V.*, LJN: BU9237, Gerechtshof Amsterdam, 23-003334-10; LJN: BU9239, Gerechtshof Amsterdam, 23-003335-10; LJN: BU9240, Gerechtshof Amsterdam, 23-004035-10 (2011), http://www.rechtspraak.nl/Organisatie/Gerechtshoven/Amsterdam/Nieuws/Pages/FineimposedonTrafigura.aspx. The facts are taken from the English summary. For more background material, *see Case Profile: Trafigura Lawsuits (re Côte D'Ivoire)*, Bus. Hum. Rts. Resource Centre, http://www.business-humanrights.org/Categories/Lawlawsuits/Lawsuitsregulatoryaction/LawsuitsSelectedcases/TrafiguralawsuitsreCtedIvoire (last visited July 23, 2013).

admitting liability, Trafigura reached a settlement with the Côte d'Ivoire government in 2007 that exempted the company from suit there.[73] In parallel, Leigh Day brought a group claim on behalf of 31,000 Côte d'Ivoire residents against Trafigura before the London High Court. In 2009, the litigation was settled out of court, with Trafigura agreeing to pay damages of £30 million.[74]

In December 2011, the Amsterdam Court of Appeal upheld a €1 million fine imposed on Trafigura by the court of first instance.[75] Trafigura had failed to disclose the hazardous character of the waste to APS. Moreover, Trafigura illegally exported the waste to Côte d'Ivoire after it had been returned by APS. The Court of Appeal asserted that the requirements on waste-producing companies were very strict in relation to the handing over and disposal of such hazardous waste in an environmentally sound manner. This standard was an important aspect of socially responsible entrepreneurship exercised on a worldwide basis. The fact that, as a group of companies operating globally, Trafigura could not have been unaware of this weighed heavily in the Court of Appeal's judgment.[76] The Amsterdam Court of Appeal also took into consideration the wave of negative publicity and the damage to Trafigura's image caused by this case, as well as the positive contribution to global welfare in the form of the Trafigura Foundation.[77] Trafigura has filed an appeal in *cassation* at the Supreme Court.

In addition to the action against Trafigura, separate actions were also taken against APS and the Municipality of Amsterdam. The Court of Appeal held that APS violated the Environmental Management Act (*Wet milieubeheer*) by handing over waste to the *Probo Koala*, a nonrecognized processor unauthorized by law to handle such waste. However, APS was not subject to punishment because it had relied on the notification of the municipal environmental health department, which had indicated that this handing over was permitted. APS was therefore discharged from further prosecution.[78] As to the Municipality of Amsterdam, the Court of Appeal, like the court of first instance, established that it

---

73. AFP, *Trafigura Toxic Waste Trial Begins in Amsterdam*, FRANCE 24 NEWS (June 1, 2010), http://www.france24.com/en/20100601-swiss-trafigura-toxic-waste-trial-begins-amsterdam-ivory-coast-koala.

74. David Leigh, *Trafigura Reaches a Global Settlement*, THE GUARDIAN (Sept. 16, 2009).

75. This summary is based on the English summary of the judgments. *See Trafigura Beheer B.V*, *supra* note 72. The Dutch court of first instance also convicted a Trafigura employee and the Ukrainian captain of the Probo Koala for their roles in the matter. These convictions were upheld by the Court of Appeal.

76. *Trafigura Beheer B.V.*, LJN: BU9237, Gerechtshof Amsterdam, 23-003334-10, §6 (2011). "The suspect is well aware of this in its capacity as a globally operating group. This sits all the more uneasily with an enterprise such as the suspect applying a special, in the sense of aberrant, production process." (Unofficial translation by the authors.)

77. "The court acknowledges the wave of negative publicity and the damage it has inflicted on the reputation of Trafigura, as well as the positive contribution through the Trafigura Foundation (established in November 2007) to the global well-being." (Unofficial translation by the authors.) *See Fine Imposed on Trafigura*, DE RECHTSPRAAK (Dec. 23, 2011), http://www.rechtspraak.nl/Organisatie/Gerechtshoven/Amsterdam/Nieuws/Pages/FineimposedonTrafigura.aspx.

78. *See Trafigura Beheer B.V.*, case LJN: BU9239, Gerechtshof Amsterdam, 23-003335-10.

had immunity from prosecution because the granting of permission to pump back waste or failure to take enforcement action was an action performed within the scope of an exclusive administrative responsibility assigned to the municipality. Prosecution of the municipality of Amsterdam was therefore barred.[79]

While these cases were going on, Greenpeace filed a complaint with the Hague Court of Appeal to compel the public prosecutor to prosecute Trafigura for more than just the export of hazardous waste. However, in April 2011, the appeal court ruled that the public prosecution department was not required to prosecute Trafigura for the dumping of the waste in Côte d'Ivoire. In addition, the issue of whether to prosecute Trafigura's co-founder and director, Claude Dauphin, has been raised before the Dutch courts. When the regional court in Amsterdam decided in 2008 not to prosecute, the prosecutors appealed the court's decision. The prosecutors were turned down and later lodged another appeal before the Supreme Court, which sent the case back to the Amsterdam Court of Appeal to review the original decision. In January 2012, the appeal court decided that Claude Dauphin could be prosecuted for the alleged illegal export of waste by Trafigura.[80] Trafigura's director filed an appeal with the Supreme Court against this decision.

However, on November 16, 2012, the Dutch Prosecution Service and Trafigura reached a settlement whereby the appeals to the Dutch Supreme Court regarding the handling of the *Probo Koala* waste within the port of Amsterdam in 2006 would all be withdrawn. Furthermore, all the remaining cases regarding the company and its executives in relation to this incident were settled. None of the executives of Trafigura faced any conviction, nor were they required to make any admission of liability or guilt as part of this settlement.[81] The public prosecution service stated that "continuing the proceedings might take many more years." Nevertheless, "the cases will be concluded in a way that makes clear that violation of international regulations for hazardous waste will not be tolerated."[82] This settlement was, nonetheless, strongly criticized by NGOs that denounced the plea bargain as "a very weak slap on the wrist for a large corporation like Trafigura."[83]

In light of the foregoing examples, it appears that much remains to be done in some civilian jurisdictions to match the development of foreign direct liability in common law jurisdictions. The traditional French approach would put a brake on the development of foreign direct liability by reason of insistence on the presence of a criminal element in the

---

79. *See Trafigura Beheer B.V.*, case LJN: BU9240, Gerechtshof Amsterdam, 23-004035-10.

80. *See Case Profile: Trafigura Lawsuits (re Côte d'Ivoire)*, *supra* note 72.

81. *See* Press Release, Openbaar Ministerie Functioneel Parket, Trafigura's Punishment Final, Top Executive Settles (Nov. 16, 2012), http://www.trafigura.com/1524/dutch_authorities_statement_english .pdf; Trafigura Beheer BV, *Statement from the Management Board of Trafigura Beheer BV* (Nov. 16, 2012), http://www.trafigura.com/1524/amsterdam_settlement_statement_from_trafigura_english.pdf.

82. *See* Openbaar Ministerie Functioneel Parket, *supra* note 81.

83. *Trafigura Fine a Set-back for Africa's Environmental Justice*, GREENPEACE AFRICA (Nov. 21, 2012), http://www.greenpeace.org/africa/en/News/news/Greenpeace-Trafigura-fine-a-set-back-for-Afric as-environmental-justice/.

acts of the corporate defendant, taking the vast majority of cases outside the purview of the action. Thus, it is not surprising that activist lawyers in France are attempting to adapt common law tort actions to the French context. By contrast, their Dutch colleagues seem to have had an easier time persuading the District Court of the Hague that Dutch law is consistent with U.S. and English law regarding the possibility of a foreign direct-liability claim, and that this is also supported by international standards on corporate responsibility. Accordingly, jurisdiction over such a claim should be granted, and it was. Equally, the willingness of the Dutch prosecution authorities to bring a case against Trafigura and other parties involved in that incident shows a growing awareness of the legitimacy of holding MNEs to account through the courts where this is warranted on the facts. Thus, it would appear that the civil law nature of the legal system is not in itself decisive with regard to whether foreign direct-liability claims can be brought. Instead, it appears that specific public policy–based considerations about how best to deal with such claims, the presence of a sufficiently motivated and organized community of activist lawyers and NGOs, and prosecutors responding to the need for justice will support such claims.

Litigation against MNEs and Other Economic Actors in Developing Countries

An activist approach to litigation against MNEs and other economic actors has also evolved in non-European jurisdictions. Of greatest significance is perhaps the public interest litigation (PIL) jurisdiction of the appellate and supreme courts of India. Again, this is a common law jurisdiction but with some unique features that make it, at times, a distant cousin of its English heritage. Perhaps the most significant difference is that the Indian Constitution contains, in part IV, the Directive Principles of State Policy, which in effect enshrine certain political and social values into the legal order. These Principles assert a vision of an improving society requiring, among other things, the distribution and control of the material resources of the community to serve the common good, the control of the economic system to prevent the concentration of the means of production to the common detriment, the provision of equal justice and legal aid, the right to work in just and humane conditions, and the improvement of public health, all of which may be motives for PIL.[84]

In 1976, Article 48A was added to the list and introduced a duty on the state to "endeavor to protect and improve the environment and to safeguard the forests and wildlife of the country." This provision was supplemented by a new chapter on "Fundamental Duties," which under Article 51A(g) includes a duty on every citizen to protect

---

84. INDIA CONST. art. 39–47.

the natural environment.[85] The Directive Principles are not legally binding but are often cited by judges as complementary to the fundamental rights of the Constitution.[86] PIL has helped to bridge the gap between the Fundamental Rights of the Indian Constitution in part III and the Directive Principles in part IV, and it has allowed the latter to become binding rights through judicial development.[87] Against this background, PIL evolved as a response to the lack of inclusion of the poor and dispossessed from legal remedies. It is a system that allows for their representation through the extension of standing to representative plaintiffs who could bring a claim on behalf of those who, by reason of their poverty, ignorance, or fear, would not bring an action in their own name.[88] This extension of standing has been attributed to the initiatives of judges of the Indian Supreme Court, most notably judges Krishna Iyer and P. N. Bhagwati.

PIL has played a role in the control of MNE activity in India, though there appears to have been no case that is specifically a foreign direct-liability action against an Indian-based parent company. Rather, PIL has been used to test the legality of the operations of foreign investors in India; with variable levels of success. For example, in the course of the litigation arising out of the Bhopal disaster, a piece of PIL was brought in *Mehta v. Union of India*,[89] which concerned a leak of oleum gas from a caustic chlorine plant resulting in some 340 injuries and, possibly, one fatality. In the course of its judgment, the Supreme Court laid down a new principle of absolute liability for enterprises engaged in hazardous or inherently dangerous industry.[90] This decision was taken to ensure that the Bhopal case would be determined on the basis of this new principle, rather than on traditional common law notions of fault-based liability. It was in this sense that the Indian courts applied the *Mehta* doctrine in the *Bhopal* case, during the course of hearings on interim measures.[91] Of particular importance is the judgment of Seth J., given in the High Court

---

85. SHYAM DIVAN & ARMIN ROSENCRANZ, ENVIRONMENTAL LAW AND POLICY IN INDIA: CASES, MATERIALS AND STATUTES 45 (2d ed. 2001).

86. *Id.*

87. *See also* Upendra Baxi, *The State and Human Rights Movements in India*, in PEOPLE'S RIGHTS SOCIAL MOVEMENTS AND THE STATE IN THE THIRD WORLD 335, 341–44 (Manoranjan Mohanty, Partha Nath Mukherji & Olle Tornquist eds., 1998).

88. *Id.* at 134–35.

89. Mehta v. Union of India, A.I.R. 1987 S.C. 965, 1086. This summary is taken from PETER MUCHLINSKI, *supra* note 30 at 314–15.

90. Mehta v. Union of India, A.I.R. 1987 S.C. ¶ 31 33, at 1098 1100. The Supreme Court formulated the applicable principle as follows: "An enterprise which is engaged in a hazardous or inherently dangerous industry which poses a potential threat to the health and safety of the persons working in the factory and residing in the surrounding areas owes an absolute and non-delegable duty to the community to ensure that no harm results to anyone on account of hazardous or inherently dangerous nature of the activity which it has undertaken. The enterprise must be held to be under an obligation to provide that the hazardous or inherently dangerous activity in which it is engaged must be conducted with the highest standards of safety and if any harm results on account of such activity, the enterprise must be absolutely liable to compensate for such harm and it should be no answer to the enterprise to say that it had taken all reasonable care and that the harm occurred without any negligence on its part." *Id.* ¶ 31 at 1099.

91. Union of India v. Union Carbide Corporation (Gas Claim Case No. 113 of 1986) (Order Dec.

of Jabalpur, on appeal from the order of the Bhopal District Court.[92] Having held that the doctrine elaborated in *Mehta* provided the substantive law by which the final decision on the merits would be made, Seth J. lifted the corporate veil between the Union Carbide Corporation (UCC) and its Indian subsidiary, holding the former liable for the tort and, in addition, holding that a *prima facie* case could be made showing that UCC had real control over the Bhopal plant for purposes of liability. The Bhopal case eventually settled without a decision on the liability of the parent for the acts of its Indian subsidiary. More recently, litigation has continued in the United States over the environmental responsibility for the site after Dow Chemicals acquired Union Carbide.[93]

A second example concerns the litigation arising out of the Narmada Valley Dam dispute.[94] Though not involving MNEs as such, this case did have a significant transnational dimension in that the World Bank was heavily involved in the funding of the dam building project until it withdrew in 1993 in response to the campaign that had grown around the project. The principal legal issues in the case concerned the rights of the local population, who were displaced by the project, to compensation and rehabilitation. However, in due course, the dispute took on a wider environmental perspective. A transnational coalition of activist groups emerged in the late 1980s to challenge the social and environmental implications of the project, which had been planned since the 1940s and which was given the go-ahead in 1979. The Narmada Bacho Andolan (NBA, Save the Narmada) led the activist coalition and the legal challenge to the dam. In 1995, the Supreme Court issued a stay order against further construction of the dam. However, in 1999, the stay order was cancelled, and in 2000, the Indian Supreme Court ruled against the claim on the grounds that the vital role played by the dam project in the development of the Narmada River region outweighed the issues of human displacement.[95]

Though only two examples have been offered, from these it can be seen that PIL is not a sure route to social change or justice.[96] The turnaround of the Supreme Court in the

---

17, 1987) (Deo J. upheld in part: Union of India v. Union Carbide Corporation Civil Revision No. 26 of 1988 (Apr. 4, 1988) Seth J.).

92. The District Court had ordered Union Carbide to pay 3,500 million Rupees (U.S. $270 million) by way of interim relief. That order was upheld by the High Court though the sum awarded was reduced to 2,500 million Rupees (U.S. $190 million).

93. *See* the Sahu v. Union Carbide Corp. and Bano v. Union Carbide litigation before U.S. courts. For more information, *see International Campaign for Justice in Bhopal*, BHOPAL.NET, http://www.bhopal .net (last visited July 23, 2013).

94. *See* Balakrishnan Rajagopal, *Limits of Law in Counter-Hegemonic Globalization: The Indian Supreme Court and the Narmada Dam Struggle*, in Boaventura de Sousa Santos & Cesar A. Rodriguez, *supra* note 2, at 183; Divan and Rosencranz, *supra* note 85, at 441–58.

95. Narmada Bachao Andolan v. Union of India (2005) 10 S.C.C. 664.

96. For a fuller analysis, *see* Upendra Baxi, *Taking Suffering Seriously: Social Action Litigation in the Supreme Court of India*, 29 REV. INT'L COMMISSION JURISTS 37 (1982); G. L. Peiris, *Public Interest Litigation in the Indian Subcontinent: Current Dimensions*, 40 INT'L & COMP. L. Q. 66 (1991); SANGEETA AHUJA, PEOPLE, LAW AND JUSTICE: A CASEBOOK ON PUBLIC-INTEREST LITIGATION (1997).

Narmada dam case shows that, among other things, the composition of the bench and its underlying beliefs will have a significant impact on outcomes.[97] The PIL approach is one that has its roots in U.S. practice.[98] However, it would be wrong to see it as a mere transplant. It is a unique development of Indian legal practice emerging out of local judicial activism and social awareness. What is significant, however, is the fact that civil society activism is highly developed in India and has a long history. Again, it is the social and political context that appears to explain the legal phenomenon. The emphasis of PIL on foreign firms and intergovernmental organizations, and the Indian state's responsibility for their actions, no doubt reflects India's more recent economic history as a predominantly host country to foreign investment.

As India's own MNEs continue to invest worldwide, it remains to be seen whether Indian civil society groups will initiate foreign direct-liability actions in Indian courts and whether PIL could be used for this purpose. Though mainly directed at the state, PIL is sufficiently flexible to allow for actions against nonstate actors, given that the scope of this jurisdiction is dependent to a considerable degree on judicial discretion. That said, as the Indian legal system contains basically the same tort remedies as the English system, there is no obstacle in principle to developing specialized foreign direct-liability actions against India-based firms for their overseas activities.

Do developing countries that follow a civilian legal tradition bear the same burdens regarding the growth of foreign direct liability as their developed-country counterparts? Again the crucial variable appears to be not so much the *family of law* to which the legal system in question belongs as the presence or absence of organized legal groups and legal professionals willing to articulate a public interest strategy and apply it to claims against corporate as well as state actors, as has occurred in France. This analysis is also the case in Brazil, where public interest litigation over land rights has increased in recent years due to such contextual developments in legal activism.[99] In addition, in South Korea public interest law groups have used shareholder derivative actions to further the ends of economic justice in the aftermath of the Asian financial crisis by challenging unlawful corporate governance practices.[100] This litigation was led by the People's Solidarity for Participatory Democracy, and major claims were lodged in 1997 and 1998 against the management

---

97. *See* Rajagopal, *supra* note 94, at 203, who accepts that bench composition is one factor, but that ingrained scripts reflected in the text of the judgment indicate that law creates certain assumptions that militate toward a statist and developmentalist approach that downgrades the human suffering involved in such a project.

98. *See also* C. D. Cunnigham, *Public Interest Litigation in Indian Supreme Court: A Study in the Light of American Experience*, 29 J. INDIA L. INST. 494 (1987).

99. *See also* Peter P. Houtzager, *The Movement of the Landless (MST), Juridical Field and Legal Change in Brazil*, in LAW AND GLOBALIZATION FROM BELOW: TOWARDS A COSMOPOLITAN LEGALITY 218 (De Sousa Santos & Rodriguez-Garavito eds., 2005), *supra* note 3.

100. *See* Tae-Ung Baek, *Public Interest Litigation in South Korea*, in PUBLIC INTEREST LITIGATION IN ASIA 115, 124–25 (Po Jen Yap & Holning Lau eds., 2011).

of major conglomerates, including Korea First Bank, Samsung Electronics, and Daewoo Corporation. These claims resulted in large compensation awards.[101]

The possibility of developing foreign direct-liability litigation in civil law jurisdictions is reinforced by the fact that many developing countries from within the civilian legal tradition have in place laws and practices conducive to public interest litigation. For example, China has a system of rules for class actions, and lawyers practice an informal system of contingency fees, leading to an increase in such actions, particularly in the consumer field.[102] Equally, Brazil has developed its own system of class action suits, though many problems remain.[103] Moreover, South Korea amended its securities laws in 2005 to facilitate securities class actions by shareholders.[104] This set of legal developments may be contrasted with a lack of such rules in France, where the belief that justice should be individualized has led to a rejection of class actions.[105] However, in such jurisdictions actual foreign direct-liability cases have not yet made a mark. All that can be said for now is that such cases might be more probable in developing countries, regardless of which legal *family* they belong to, where procedural rules exist to facilitate public interest litigation, and where there are organized political groups and activist lawyers willing to develop such cases.

The Contribution of European and International Human Rights Developments

The final section of this chapter looks forward and considers how developments in European human rights law, and the recent adoption of a general responsibility to respect human rights by corporations in the UN Guiding Principles, which might help to shape the future of foreign direct liability. Both tools offer avenues for innovative argumentation on the part of human rights claimants and further suggest that the possibility of convergence in this field exists. This assessment is based on the use of comparative law approaches focused on other national jurisdictions and also on the adaptation of concepts found in these supranational sources.

The European contribution to the development of foreign direct liability centers on the development of arguments based on the European Convention on Human Rights (ECHR)

---

101. *Id.* at 119.

102. *See* Benjamin Liebman, *Class Action Litigation in China*, 111 HARV. L. REV. 1523 (1998); Michael Palmer & Chao Xi, *China*, 622 ANNALS AM. ACAD. POL. SOC. SCI. 270–79 (2009); Michael Palmer, *Towards a Greener China? Accessing Environmental Justice in the People's Republic of China*, in ACCESS TO ENVIRONMENTAL JUSTICE: A COMPARATIVE STUDY 205 (Andrew Harding ed., 2007).

103. *See* Antonio Gidi, *Class Actions in Brazil: A Model for Civil Law Countries*, 51 AM. J. COMP. L. 311 (2003).

104. *See* Tae-Ung Baek, *supra* note 100, at 128.

105. *See* Curran, *supra* note 53, at 398–99.

and European Union law.[106] In particular, Article 6 of the ECHR can potentially contribute to the development of foreign direct-liability litigation. This article protects the right to a fair trial; "[i]n the determination of his civil rights and obligations or of any criminal charge against him, everyone is entitled to a fair and public hearing within a reasonable time by an independent and impartial tribunal established by law." In the English case of *Lubbe v. Cape Industries plc*,[107] the plaintiffs relied on Article 6 of the ECHR to fend off a motion to stay the proceedings on grounds of *forum non conveniens*. They claimed that a stay of the proceedings in favor of South African courts would violate their rights guaranteed by Article 6 of the ECHR. The lack of funding and legal representation in South Africa would deny them a fair trial on terms equal with those of the defendant in the litigation. Although the House of Lords did base its opinion on the *Spiliada Maritime Corp. v. Cansulex Ltd.* case and not on Article 6 of the ECHR, it nevertheless refused to decline jurisdiction in favor of South Africa due to the absence of adequate funding and legal representation in South Africa. Lord Bingham of Cornhill acknowledged that

> since, as the *Spiliada* case [1987] AC 460 makes clear, a stay will not be granted where it is established by cogent evidence that the plaintiff will not obtain justice in the foreign forum, I cannot conceive that the court would grant a stay in any case where adequate funding and legal representation of the plaintiff were judged to be necessary to the doing of justice and these were clearly shown to be unavailable in the foreign forum although available here. I do not think Article 6 supports any conclusion which is not already reached on application of *Spiliada* principles. I cannot, however, accept the view of the Second Court of Appeal that it would be right to decline jurisdiction in favor of South Africa even if legal representation were not available there.

Equally, the claimants in the Dutch cases against Royal Dutch Shell argued, in ancillary proceedings, that Article 6 required the disclosure of certain documents by the defendant company. The District Court of the Hague held that the Dutch Civil Code upheld the principle of equality of arms under Article 6 and that the restrictions on disclosure that it contained were compatible with Article 6 unless there were exceptional circumstances. On

---

106. *See* Karl Hofstetter, *Parent Responsibility for Subsidiary Corporations: Evaluating European Trends*, 39 Int'l Comp. L. Q. 576 (1990); Olivier De Schutter, *The Accountability of Multinationals for Human Rights Violations in European Law*, Ctr. for Human Rights and Global Justice, Working Paper No. 1 (2004); Jan Wouters & Cedric Ryngaert, *Litigation for Overseas Corporate Human Rights Abuses in the European Union: The Challenge of Jurisdiction*, 40 Geo. Wash. Int'l L. Rev. 939 (2009); Liesbeth Enneking, *Crossing the Atlantic? The Political and Legal Feasibility of European Foreign Direct Liability Cases*, 40 Geo. Wash. Int'l L. Rev. 903 (2009); Stéphanie Khoury, *Transnational Corporations and the European Court of Human Rights: Reflections on the Indirect and Direct Approaches to Accountability*, 4 Sortuz Oñati J. Emergent Socio-legal Stud. 68 (2010).

107. *See* Lubbe v. Cape Industries Plc [2000] 1 W.L.R. 1545; [2000] 4 All E.R. 268 (H.L.) 277.

the present facts, no such exceptional circumstances were shown to exist by the claimants to justify the requested disclosure.[108] Thus, the court accepted the relevance of Article 6 even though, in the circumstances of the case, it could not help the claimants obtain the disclosure for which they had asked.

EU law is also of relevance in relation to issues of jurisdiction and extraterritoriality. The Brussels I Regulation[109] is a key legal instrument in the context of foreign direct-liability litigation because it governs the choice of jurisdiction in cross-border disputes in civil and commercial matters. The Brussels I Regulation establishes the rules of jurisdiction when persons are domiciled in EU member states. A defendant company domiciled in an EU member state must be sued before the courts of that state. When a defendant company is domiciled outside the European Union, questions of jurisdiction are mainly governed by the domestic rules of the member state. Consequently, there is no uniform system of rules regarding the choice of jurisdiction when the defendant company is domiciled outside the European Union because member states have differing approaches. Some member states have adopted domestic rules that support access to their courts by victims of corporate activities in the context of foreign direct-liability litigation. For instance, the United Kingdom and the Netherlands enable victims to sue a parent company together with its subsidiary domiciled outside the European Union.[110] Another example is the application of the *forum necessitatis* rule in the Netherlands, which allows Dutch courts to exercise jurisdiction over cases that have no nexus with the Dutch legal order in certain circumstances defined by the law.[111]

In December 2010, the European Commision (EC) presented a proposal for a recast Brussels I Regulation (Proposal) that aimed to remedy a number of deficiencies in the operation of the regulation and to further enhance access to justice.[112] The proposal sought to increase legal certainty by harmonizing member states' laws and providing for additional grounds of jurisdiction applicable to non–EU-domiciled defendants. Various organizations expressed their concerns that the proposal would limit existing opportunities of foreign direct-liability litigation in some EU member states.[113] Although the extension

---

108. *See Akpan & Milieudefensie*, LJN: BY9845, Rechtbank's-Gravenhage, 337050 / HA ZA 09-1580; *Oguru Efanga & Milieudefensie*, LJN: BY9850, Rechtbank's-Gravenhage, 330891 / HA ZA 09-0579; *Dooh & Milieudefensie*, LJN: BY9845, Rechtbank's-Gravenhage, 337058/HA ZA 09-1581.

109. *See* Brussels I Regulation, *supra* note 65.

110. *See* UK CPR RULES & PRACTICE DIRECTIONS § 6B ¶ 3.1(3); WETBOEK VAN BURGERLIJKE RECHTVORDERING [Rv] [CODE OF CIVIL PROCEDURE] art. 7 (Neth.). In Plaintiff 1 & Milieudefensie v. Royal Dutch Shell Plc & Shell Petroleum Development Company of Nigeria Ltd, the District Court of the Hague found that the claims against both the subsidiary and the parent company were connected to such an extent that they could be heard together. LJN: BK8616, Rechtbank's-Gravenhage, HA ZA 330891 09-579, ¶ 3.4–3.7.

111. *See* Rv art. 9 (Neth.).

112. *See Commission Proposal for a Regulation of the European Parliament and of the Council on Jurisdiction and the Recognition and Reinforcement of Judgements in Civil and Commercial Matters*, COM (2010) 748 final (Dec. 14, 2010).

113. *See* Amnesty International, *Amnesty International Submission on Brussels I Regulation Legislative*

of the Brussels I Regulation to non–EU-domiciled defendants would have enhanced legal certainty, favorable national rules governing jurisdiction over non–EU-domiciled companies no longer would have applied. For example, the proposal would have allowed the *forum necessitatis* rule only on an *exceptional basis*, thus reducing opportunities for victims to bring claims against subsidiaries in the Netherlands.

Finally, a recast of Brussels I Regulation was adopted in December 2012.[114] The basic jurisdictional rules of the original Brussels I Regulation are left unchanged in the recast version. The general distinction between defendants domiciled in the European Union and outside the European Union is maintained. The recast Brussels I Regulation, however, introduces new rules on *lis pendens*, which can have a direct impact on foreign direct-liability claims. EU courts have discretion to stay proceedings in favor of non-EU courts, even when the EU courts have jurisdiction. Yet several conditions must be met: there must be prior proceedings pending before the non-EU court; the judgment given by the non-EU court can be enforced in the EU member state concerned; and a stay is necessary for the proper administration of justice. The extent of the application of the new rules of *lis pendens* is still unclear though, especially when it comes to the interpretation of the necessity of proper administration of justice. In this context, one wonders whether the application of the new rules of *lis pendens* will jeopardize the existence of foreign direct-liability claims before the courts of EU member states.

As to extraterritoriality, according to the EU *Study of the Legal Framework on Human Rights and the Environment Applicable to European Enterprises Operating Outside the European Union*, the case law of the European Court of Human Rights (ECtHR) on the extraterritorial application of the ECHR is informed by an "essentially territorial notion of jurisdiction" that the court derives from Article 1 of the ECHR.[115] Although an extraterritorial application of the ECHR rights constitutes the exception rather than the norm, the EU study suggests that the ECHR has given a broad interpretation of the duty of states to protect human rights "within their jurisdiction," encompassing both instances of direct extraterritorial jurisdiction and domestic measures with extraterritorial implications.[116]

Proposal, IOR 61/012/2011 (2011), http://www.amnesty.org/ar/library/asset/IOR61/012/2011/en/ba67b e74-3127-48af-a1f0-ead6d92717c5/ior610122011en.pdf .

114. Regulation No. 1215/2012, of the European Parliament and of the Council of 12 December 2012 on Jurisdiction and the Recognition and Enforcement of Judgements in Civil and Commercial Matters (2012) O.J. (L 351) 1 (EU). The recast Brussels I Regulation came into force on January 10, 2013, but will apply only to legal proceedings instituted and to court settlements approved or concluded on or after January 10, 2015. This means that initial Brussels I Regulation will continue to apply until January 9, 2015.

115. Daniel Augenstein, Univ. of Edinburgh, Study of the Legal Framework on Human Rights and the Environment Applicable to European Enterprises Operating Outside the European Union 23 (2010), http://ec.europa.eu/enterprise/policies/sustainable-business/files/business-human-rights /101025_ec_study_final_report_en.pdf.

116. *Id.* ¶ 67 at 25 ("It should be noted that under the Court's current jurisprudence, the State duty to protect human rights against corporate violations that take place or produce effects outside the State's

Thus, the possibility of invoking the rights protected under the ECHR in cases where the alleged violations have arisen outside the jurisdiction of the state party to the ECHR remains live. That said, it is still uncertain how far ECHR rights can be invoked in such cases, given the need to show a jurisdictional link between the claim and the ECHR member state and its actions.[117] Arguably, it should be enough to show that the defendant parent company, domiciled in the home state, has a sufficient link to the activities of its overseas subsidiaries for their actions to be deemed within the jurisdiction of the home-state forum. Such was the logic used by the District Court of the Hague to establish jurisdiction in the abovementioned case against Royal Dutch Shell. However, in that case the company was not acting as an agent of the Netherlands, and so it remains uncertain to what extent the ECHR could supply the basis of a claim, which needs to show that the ECHR member state committed a violation of convention rights.

In the cases brought against Royal Dutch Shell, the District Court of the Hague considered whether the Rome II Regulation applied to the facts of the cases before it.[118] Adopted in 2007, the Rome II Regulation applies, in situations involving a conflict of laws, to noncontractual obligations in civil and commercial matters in the European Union.[119] According to its Article 4(1), "the law applicable to a non-contractual obligation arising out of a tort/delict shall be the law of the country in which the damage occurs irrespective of the country in which the event giving rise to the damage occurred and irrespective of the country or countries in which the indirect consequences of that event occur." Pursuant to its primary aim of predictability, the Rome II Regulation limits the domestic courts in determining the law that is applicable to a transboundary tort case.[120] The Rome II Regulation shall apply to events giving rise to damage that occurs after its entry into force, which was January 11, 2009.[121] The Court of Justice of the European Union (ECJ) also interpreted the Rome II Regulation as applying only to events giving rise to damage occurring after January 11, 2009.[122]

---

territory is more limited than the corresponding duty to protect human rights within its own territory. State responsibility for corporate human rights violations committed outside the State's territory (direct extraterritorial jurisdiction) presupposes the State exercises at least 'decisive influence' over (a person in) the area outside its territory. On the logic of *Issa*, the Court may also be prepared to accept State responsibility for extraterritorial corporate human rights violations where the corporate conduct can be directly attributed to the State (corporations acting as State agents). As far as domestic measures with extraterritorial implications are concerned, the Court's jurisprudence may be taken as an indication that, in cases such as transboundary environmental pollution, Convention States can be liable for failures to regulate corporate activities within their territory that result in human rights violations outside their territory.").

117. *See Id.*; Enneking, *supra* note 106, at 920–21.

118. *Akpan & Milieudefensie*, LJN: *BY9845*, Rechtbank's-Gravenhage, C/09/337050 / HA ZA 09-1580.

119. Regulation (EC) 864/2007 on the Law Applicable to Non-Contractual Obligations (2007) O.J. 199/40, art. 1.

120. *See* Enneking, *supra* note 106, at 927.

121. Rome II Regulation, *supra* note 119, art. 32.

122. Case C-412/10, Deo Antoine Homawoo v. GMF Assurances (2010) E.C.R. EUR-Lex CELEX

The cases before the District Court of the Hague presented several oil spills that had occurred in Nigeria between 2004 and 2007. Referring to Articles 31 and 32 of the Rome II Regulation and an ECJ's ruling dated November 17, 2011,[123] the district court stated, "[t]he alleged harmful events occurred before 11 January 2009; this means that the case falls outside the temporal scope of Regulation (EC) No 864/2007 on the law applicable to non-contractual obligations (Rome II Regulation)." Subsequently, the district court applied the Dutch legislation governing conflicts of law (*Wet Conflictenrecht Onrechtmatige Daad*) to the question regarding the law under which the district court must substantively assess the initiated claims.[124]

In the context of foreign direct-liability litigation, the applicable law is the law of the host country. In such litigation, the choice of the governing law may be a crucial issue. As noted by Enneking,

> There may be major differences in the outcome when they are governed by the developed home country's tort law as opposed to the developing host country's tort law. Important factors like the standards of care, regulatory standards, and damage awards usually will be much higher in the home country than in the host country.[125]

However, there are a few exceptions to this rule, the most important being the situation of environmental damage. According to Article 7 of the Rome II Regulation, "the law applicable to a non-contractual obligation arising out of environmental damage or damage sustained by persons or property as a result of such damage shall be the law determined pursuant to Article 4(1), unless the person seeking compensation for damage chooses to base his or her claim on the law of the country in which the event giving rise to the damage occurred."

The state duty to protect human rights, as defined in the UN Framework, may add weight to the argument that the presence of the parent company in the home state is enough to require access to effective remedies by claimants from the host states where its subsidiaries are located. According to the UN Guiding Principles, the state duty to protect implies a duty to regulate nonstate actors so that they do not infringe on human rights. The Guiding Principles assert, "[s]tates must protect against human rights abuse within their territory and/or jurisdiction by third parties, including business enterprises. This

---

LEXIS (Nov. 17, 2011).

123. *Akpan & Milieudefensie*, LJN: BY9845, Rechtbank's-Gravenhage, C/09/337050 / HA ZA 09-1580; *Oguru & Milieudefensie*, LJN: BY9850, Rechtbank's-Gravenhage, C/09/330891 / HA ZA 09-0579; *Dooh & Milieudefensie*, LJN: BY9845, Rechtbank's-Gravenhage, C/09/337058 / HA ZA 09-1581.

124. *Id.*

125. *Id.* at 928.

requires taking appropriate steps to prevent, investigate, punish and redress such abuse through effective policies, legislation, regulations and adjudication."[126]

The final reference to adjudication may be taken as requiring the provision of adequate remedies for corporate human rights violations taking place within their jurisdiction or territory. In a case of foreign direct liability, the territorial link is present where the parent company is present and by virtue of the fact that its responsibility is in issue. Thus, this distinction should not form a bar to jurisdiction. Also, as noted above, although some jurisdictions do apply rules on the appropriate forum, others accept as a matter of principle that corporate domicile can found jurisdiction as of right.

In any case, the Guiding Principles suggest that procedural barriers to redress should be avoided as part of the state's duty to provide effective redress. This point is emphasized by Principle 26 of the Guiding Principles, which demands that "states should take appropriate steps to ensure the effectiveness of domestic judicial mechanisms when addressing business-related human rights abuses, including considering ways to reduce legal, practical and other relevant barriers that could lead to a denial of access to remedy."[127]

The commentary to Principle 26 lists a number of legal barriers that can prevent legitimate cases involving business-related human rights abuse from being addressed. These include the following:

- The way in which legal responsibility is attributed among members of a corporate group under domestic criminal and civil laws facilitates the avoidance of appropriate accountability.
- Claimants face a denial of justice in a host state and cannot access home-state courts regardless of the merits of the claim.
- Certain groups, such as indigenous peoples and migrants, are excluded from the same level of legal protection of their human rights that applies to the wider population.[128]

This list connotes some of the key procedural and substantive legal barriers to foreign direct-liability claims and suggests that the home state ought to provide redress where the claimants risk a denial of justice in the host state.

Regarding the issue of extraterritoriality, the Guiding Principles note the following in the commentary to Principle 2:

At present States are not generally required under international human rights law to regulate the extraterritorial activities of businesses domiciled in their territory and/

---

126. UN Guiding Principles, *supra* note 4 at Principle 1.
127. UN Guiding Principles, *supra* note 4, at Principle 26.
128. *Id.*

or jurisdiction. Nor are they generally prohibited from doing so, provided there is a recognized jurisdictional basis. Within these parameters some human rights treaty bodies recommend that home States take steps to prevent abuse abroad by business enterprises within their jurisdiction.

There are strong policy reasons for home States to set out clearly the expectation that businesses respect human rights abroad, especially where the State itself is involved in or supports those businesses. The reasons include ensuring predictability for business enterprises by providing coherent and consistent messages, and preserving the State's own reputation.[129]

Thus, though the Guiding Principles stop short of recommending the adoption of extraterritorial measures concerning the control of human rights abuses by corporate actors domiciled within the home state, they do not rule such developments out. Rather, the general message is that when the home state feels it is right to offer the possibility of foreign direct-liability claims, it should ensure that these are effective and that barriers to such effectiveness are avoided.

Finally, in relation to the substantive basis of foreign direct-liability claims, the corporate responsibility to respect human rights, as formulated under the Guiding Principles, suggests the possibility of further bases of claims against the parent company. In particular, the due diligence element of this responsibility appears capable of generating legal liabilities under domestic law, even though the corporate responsibility to respect is formulated as a nonlegally binding obligation in the Guiding Principles. Principle 17 states that due diligence

(a) should cover adverse human rights impacts that the business enterprise may cause or contribute to through its own activities, or which may be directly linked to its operations, products or services by its business relationships;
(b) will vary in complexity with the size of the business enterprise, the risk of severe human rights impacts, and the nature and context of its operations;
(c) should be ongoing, recognizing that the human rights risks may change over time as the business enterprise's operations and operating context evolve.[130]

Adherence to a corporate responsibility to respect human rights and avoid adverse impacts through due diligence may lead to the creation of a duty of care in this regard. Normally, due diligence mechanisms create direct duties of care for the person or entity carrying out such an assessment. Once a due diligence obligation is accepted, failure to use due diligence

---

129. UN Guiding Principles, *supra* note 4, at Principle 2.
130. UN Guiding Principles, *supra* note 4, at Principle 17.

is evidence of a breach of such a duty, as is the careless operation of such a process. In this respect, the due diligence element of the Guiding Principles appears no different, and any failure to carry out this process in a way that avoids, or at least mitigates, adverse human rights impacts on the part of companies could form the basis of a legal action against the company.[131] That said, it remains a tenuous form of potential liability, and much depends on what may be seen to constitute adequate human rights due diligence and whether it will be more than a mere *tick-box* exercise designed to cover a minimal duty of care. In this determination, the approach of national laws and courts will be crucial.

Concluding Remarks

This chapter has examined the rise of foreign direct-liability litigation in a comparative context. Foreign direct-liability litigation arises out of the need for greater accountability for MNEs and their overseas operations, especially when those operations occur in less-developed host countries that have fewer avenues for legal redress. In this regard, foreign direct-liability litigation is an interim measure that fills a remedial void in the host state. The main conclusion is that such litigation is capable of becoming more generalized and that its success or failure, though influenced by the characteristics of the legal family to which the forum's jurisdiction belongs, does not depend on those characteristics. Rather, the main variables are whether the jurisdiction contains entrepreneurial lawyers and activists who are motivated to explore the development of such litigation and the extent of the awareness among policymakers of the need to provide redress in such cases.

Furthermore, as noted earlier, it is already possible to bring human rights and social-responsibility–oriented lawsuits in certain developing countries against MNEs and other corporate entities, given the right mix of legal developments and activist lawyers and campaigners. Foreign direct-liability litigation may also develop in such countries as they become home states of MNEs in their own right. Again, whether the country espouses a common law or civil law tradition appears to be of limited relevance.

Finally, the role of foreign direct-liability litigation is reinforced by the UN Framework through the establishment of a positive responsibility to respect human rights on the part of corporate actors, accepting a due-diligence–based approach to that responsibility, coupled with the need for access to an effective remedy as part of the state duty to protect human rights. Foreign direct-liability litigation may be one such remedy that the state may wish to promote. Equally, European law may be able to assist in the further development of

---

131. For a full discussion, *see* Peter T. Muchlinski, *Implementing the New UN Corporate Human Rights Framework: Implications for Corporate Law, Governance and Regulation*, 22 Bus. Ethics Q. 145 (2012).

foreign direct-liability litigation, although its precise impact is not settled at present, save in the use of Article 6 of the ECHR to protect due process and in the eradication of the *forum non conveniens* doctrine from EU jurisdictions.

Of particular note in this regard is that in October 2011, the EC presented the new EU CSR strategy for the period 2011 to 2014.[132] This strategy follows the 2001 EU Green Paper *Promoting a European Framework for Corporate Social Responsibility* and seeks to promote a modern vision of CSR through an updated definition and a new agenda for action. In its new CSR strategy, the EC has taken into consideration the latest developments on the issue of business and human rights, including the UN Framework and its Guiding Principles. First, a new definition of CSR is put forward: CSR is "the responsibility of enterprises for their impacts on society."[133] Contrary to the definition found in the 2001 Green Paper, this broad definition does not put emphasis on the voluntary nature of CSR but on the responsibility of enterprises—a concept directly inspired by the UN Framework.[134] Furthermore, it is stressed that respect for applicable legislation is a prerequisite for meeting that responsibility. More specifically, European policy should be made fully consistent with internationally recognized principles and guidelines, including the UN Framework and its Guiding Principles. Thus, a section is dedicated to the implementation of the UN Guiding Principles within EU policies.[135]

The EC indicates that a "better implementation of the UN Guiding Principles will contribute to EU objectives regarding specific human rights issues and core labor standards." The EC intends to improve the coherence of EU policies with the UN Guiding Principles through a set of measures. The EC is currently developing human rights guidance for three business sectors—employment and recruitment agencies, information and communications technology/telecommunications, and oil and gas—that will be consistent with the UN Guiding Principles. Completion is expected in the course of 2013.[136] Furthermore, EU member states have been invited to develop national plans for the implementation of the UN Guiding Principles.

In conclusion, it can be said that the UN Framework and its Guiding Principles have

---

132. Communication from the Commission for a Renewed EU Strategy 2011–2014 for Corporate Social Responsibility, COM (2011) 681 final (Oct. 25, 2011), http://ec.europa.eu/enterprise/newsroom/cf/_getdocument.cfm?doc_id=7010.

133. *Id.* at 6.

134. The UN Framework rests on differentiated but complementary responsibilities. It comprises three core principles, including "the corporate responsibility to respect human rights." *See* John Ruggie, "Protect, Respect and Remedy": A Framework for Business and Human Rights, 4 UN Doc. A/HRC/8/5 (Apr. 7, 2008); UN Guiding Principles, *supra* note 4.

135. *See* Communication from the Commission for a Renewed EU Strategy 2011–2014 for Corporate Social Responsibility, *supra* note 132, § 4.8.2.

136. *See European Commission Human Rights Sector Guidance Project: Developing Guidance on the Corporate Responsibility to Respect Human Rights in the Employment & Recruitment Agencies, Information & Communication Technology, and Oil & Gas Sectors,* INST. FOR HUM. RTS. BUS., http://www.ihrb.org/project/eu-sector-guidance/index.html (last visited July 24, 2013).

renewed the debate about corporate responsibility not only at the global level but also at the regional level. These instruments have allowed the EU to reconceptualize its CSR strategy, which, until now, had been criticized for its inadequacy to impose strong obligations on corporations.[137] Undoubtedly, the UN Framework and its Guiding Principles will impact in the near future the development of new EU policies regarding corporate responsibilities for human rights abuses and environmental degradation, as well as the evolution of foreign direct-liability litigation in Europe.

---

137. Olivier De Schutter, *Corporate Social Responsibility European Style*, 14 EUR. L. J. 203 (2008).

Chapter 13

Labour Rights in the World Economy

Sheldon Leader

This is a study of the fragmentation of labor rights. It is a fragmentation that arises from the insertion of undertakings made to labor into different domains of law: laws regulating commercial companies, investment, and trade. Each incorporates a place for labor rights, but does so in a different way than happens within labor law. The result is one of fundamental conflict among the principles shaping labor rights within the world economy. The reason for this conflict does not simply arise from the encroachment of economic logic into a domain designed to protect basic rights. It also resides within a tacit theory of law at work within the world economy, which we shall call one of functional pluralism, and which we will contrast with another form of pluralism that could offer a form of protection for labor rights that is more faithful to their origin and sense.

Imagine that the world has reached the stage at which it has successfully built into the standards governing socially responsible enterprises the protection of labor rights according to ILO requirements. That is, imagine that alongside a multinational system of labor law there is in place within the corporate laws of states, as well as international investment law, a demand that these same labor rights be respected. This is slowly happening. Multinational companies regularly place into the center of their public commitment to corporate social responsibility a declaration of their support for these rights. Many do so as part of their wider commitment to supporting human rights. ExxonMobil has, for example, recently said, "[We are] steadfast in promoting respect for human rights throughout the world. We believe corporations play an important role in supporting human rights and that our presence in developing countries positively influences issues relating to the treatment of people."[1] Although these undertakings are not yet interpreted as forming part of the company's constitutional norms, on which lawsuits could be grounded, this evolution is imaginable. Alongside

---

1. [2] ExxonMobil, 2003 Corporate Citizenship Report Summary, http://www.exxonmobil.com /corporate/files/corporate/CCR_2003.pdf.

this, the International Finance Corporation (IFC), an affiliate of the World Bank that lends to the private sector, demands as part of its project standards that borrowers respect ILO standards.[2] These requirements are paralleled by the same demand made by private lending banks grouped together in what are called the Equator Principles.[3]

With these connections in place, we then face the next issue: what will actually count as *violation* of any given right? Here arise issues of balance. Labour rights have to enter into the set of competing rights and interests that might on some occasions override those entitlements, even as the enterprise pays due respect to them. That is a standard feature of all schemes of regulation. Very few of the basic guarantees provided will be impervious to any compromise. However strong the commitments to fairness in the workplace might be, they will face the threat of legitimate adjustment as company directors grapple with their requirements to perform their fiduciary duties within company law, their obligations to lenders under investment law, and so on. There is, however, a distinction to notice. This is between the vulnerability of any given labor right to compromise and adjustment *per se* and its vulnerability to *varying degrees* of compromise and adjustment depending on the domain of law in which it appears. One and the same right can take on a different profile within each such domain. Corporate decisions sit in the middle of these crosscutting bodies of rules and principles. A great deal is a stake here in trying to work out the strength of labor rights in the world economy.

Consider an example. Imagine that in the course of building the petroleum pipeline for the export of oil from Chad through Cameroon, ExxonMobil has tried to fit, if practical to do so, with the movement of world markets for the petroleum. The volatility of world prices can, and has, placed a premium on speed of completion of pipelines to begin oil flowing as soon as possible. It is not difficult to imagine the following scenario arising in this situation. The imaginary CEO of the company—we can call him Mr. Jones—has been told that if he can begin use of the pipeline within a year, he will be able to take advantage of a high price of oil, which may decline after that. The prediction is also that even after a decline in prices, it will still be profitable to produce the oil, but the company's marketing manager tells him that if the company can move ahead quickly, it will earn revenues of such magnitude that this will have a significant impact on its long-term plans for developing new fields, and therefore on long-term shareholder returns.

Mr. Jones would like to accelerate the pace of construction but realizes that most of his workforce currently lacks the skills necessary to do this while still maintaining the requisite level of workplace health and safety on the project. His technical advisors tell him that the risk of fatal accidents will increase. He has a choice. He can provide some marginal extra training for employees in health and safety procedures and immediately

---

2.   *Id.*
3.   The Equator Principles 2013, http://www.equator-principles.com/index.php/about-ep.

order an increased speed of construction—knowing that the number of fatal accidents will go up—or he can take more time to increase the pace of construction in order to give more thorough training, and thereby aim to keep the risk of accidents at their present level. The latter option risks missing the chance to take advantage of the high oil price on world markets.

What should Mr. Jones do? Several different specialists offer him advice.

The *financial planning* officer advises Mr. Jones to take the first approach. He knows that it will raise the level of risk of accidents but indicates that the company has a contingency fund, ready to compensate individuals if the company is found at fault in its health and safety provision.

The company's *company law* advisor tells Mr. Jones that if he chooses to delay the increase in speed of construction, and thereby causes a significant and long-term loss of an opportunity for increased profits, then he could be found to be in breach of his fiduciary duty to the company. That profit would not, the advisor insists that, be earned at the expense of violating the rights of employees, because they will be fully compensated if and when such a breach occurs. The advisor insists this approach is fully compliant even with that company law, which carves out an explicit place for the protection of employees as part of the personal duties of the director. An example of this can be found in the UK Companies Act 2006:

> A director of a company must act in the way he considers, in good faith, would be most likely to promote the success of the company for the benefit of its members [such as shareholders] as a whole, and in doing so have regard . . . to: (a) the interests of the company's employees, (b) the impact of the company's operations on the community and (c) the environment.[4]

Applying that formula to our case, if Mr. Jones were to choose the first option, it is a solution that would, we can assume based on the facts as given, better serve the long-term interest of the shareholders than would the second. He would, in the process, "have regard to the interests of the company's employees," but being careful to compensate the workers for accidents caused by inadequate safety measures could discharge this portion of his duties. He might think that he captures the best of both worlds: benefiting the shareholders and respecting, via the compensation, the rights of his employees. He would produce, in the eyes of company law, an optimal solution.

Mr. Jones next contacts the IFC, which has made a loan for the pipeline. This body has rather different advice. It points to a fundamental requirement that it makes of its

---

4. Companies Act (2006), § 172 (Eng.), http://www.legislation.gov.uk/ukpga/2006/46/pdfs/ukpga_20060046_en.pdf.

borrowers, which can be called the *avoidance over compensation* principle. It reads as follows:

> The mitigation hierarchy to address identified risks and impacts will favor the avoidance of impacts over minimization, and, where residual impacts remain, compensation/offset, wherever technically and financially feasible. [5]

The IFC's view tempts Mr. Jones to follow the second solution, but he runs up against the advice of his financial officer and company law counsel, who say that although the slower pace for construction may help to avoid risk, in fact this course is not *financially feasible* within the terms of the IFC principle. It is a solution that will cause the company to lose the chance to increase its profits significantly, and hence lies beyond the boundaries of what a company director can reasonably have as his priorities.

Mr. Jones, still not certain, turns to his labor law advisor. This specialist informs him of a basic principle of labor law, which is seen most clearly in the law of dismissal, but he says it can be applied by analogy to this situation. The principle says that an employer may legitimately introduce changes that override employee rights for a *good business reason*. The leading book for practitioners in the United Kingdom says of this principle that

> in practice if this is merely to make a profitable business more profitable, tribunals are likely to view the change with disapproval. Where the employees are adversely affected financially, tribunals are in practice more likely to need persuading that it is *necessary* for the employer to impose the burden on them. The fact that the *well-being of the business will be improved* is unlikely to be enough.[6]

In the area of health and safety, the law requires that the employer attend to "the gravity of the harm, the costs and practicability of preventing it, and the justification for running the risk."[7] In deciding what counts as a "justification for running the risk of accidents," the same principle, says the advisor, should apply.

In other words, even if the first choice for the director might be recommended by company law, as part of his fiduciary duty to work for the benefit of the corporation, that solution stands condemned by labor law. Whatever company law says about the director's internal, personal duty to the corporation on this matter, labor law takes an external view and can condemn the company itself as an entity for wrongly overriding employees' rights

---

5.   INTERNATIONAL FINANCE CORPORATION, PERFORMANCE STANDARD 1: SOCIAL AND ENVIRONMENTAL ASSESSMENT AND MANAGEMENT SYSTEMS, IFC Performance Standard 1, ¶ 14, January 2012.

6.   HARVEY ON INDUSTRIAL RELATIONS AND EMPLOYMENT LAW ¶ 1875 (Peter Wallington ed., 2007). Emphasis added.

7.   N. M. SELWYN, SELWYN'S LAW OF EMPLOYMENT 129, ¶ 11 (2004).

to adequate levels of health and safety. It can condemn the company on the ground that benefit to it cannot justify the higher level of risk, whereas company law can exonerate the director precisely on the ground that benefit can justify the higher level of risk. Both solutions are simultaneously possible.

Finally, Mr. Jones consults a human rights specialist. She tells him that if he chooses the first option, the company may well put the state in violation of its obligation under the International Covenant on Economic, Social, and Cultural Rights (ICESCR) to provide the *highest attainable* level of health protection within its available resources, as per Article 12 of the covenant.[8] The state is able to raise the level of regulation on the project by forbidding, via injunctions, the increased pace of construction. If the state chooses not to do so knowing the increased risk to health and safety that this will provoke, then it has failed to provide the highest attainable level of protection. If the state has backed away from issuing these injunctions because of pressure from the company, then the latter might be a party to the violation of rights that occurred.

Mr. Jones tells the human rights specialist about the other advice he received—to the effect that the company had to stand ready to compensate employees for damage done to them—but also tells her he would be wrong from the perspective of company law to go further. She says, politely, that Mr. Jones seems to have lost the plot—failing to understand the nature of a basic right. Readiness in advance to pay compensation for violating such a right is not a justification for going ahead and violating it. Priority always has to be given to avoidance of damage to human rights rather than simply standing ready to compensate for it. She agrees with the IFC on this point but insists that it is *financially feasible* to take the steps necessary to avoid the higher risk. The company, she says, need simply follow the approach taken by labor law rather than by company law on this matter.

Standing away from these possibilities there is, as was said, a good deal at stake. Human rights are given a clear role in all of these domains of law, but the *level* at which those rights are protected is strongly affected by the *direction of adjustment* that is chosen between commercial imperatives and human rights imperatives. Company law proposes that, from among the various ways open to giving respect to a human right, the method needs to be chosen that will do least damage to the company's commercial imperatives. Human rights law proposes the opposite: that from among the various ways open to giving respect to commercial imperatives, the method chosen must be the one that will do the least damage to the full implementation of human rights. Investment law, as we have seen, contains elements of the latter approach, but when brought into contact with the logic of company law, it shifts to the first perspective.

How might the legal system reconcile these different perspectives?

---

8. International Covenant on Economic, Social, and Cultural Rights Art.12, Dec. 16, 1966, http://www.c-fam.org/docLib/20080625_ICESCR.pdf.

An Attempted Resolution

The attractions of the compensation strategy are two: first, it seems to allow the company the policy space to pursue its best strategy and to integrate the cost of violating worker rights into its balance sheet. Second, the compensation paid by the company for violating labor law will not turn into a personal liability of the director, requiring him to indemnify the company for its extra expense in paying damage to the injured employee. As long as he has acted in good faith and with adequate skill and care for the good of the enterprise, the company cannot turn around and demand that the director compensate it out of his own pocket for having knowingly led the company to increase the risk of accidents.

These two attractions are precisely what makes it difficult to effectively link company law and adequate respect for labor rights—many of which are also internationally recognized human rights. It is important to close this gap between directors' duties to their company and the company's duties to employees if labor rights are to receive the coherent and constant level of protection that they were designed to have. It is necessary to build into the content of the fiduciary duty of the director to the company the principle that one of his duties of care is not to allow the company to commit certain illegal acts, such as serious violations of labor law that are anticipated in the first option in front of Mr. Jones. Those employee interests would then be built into the *interests of the company*, though not in the way they are in the Companies Act 2006. Not only must a director *have regard* for employee interests, as the legislation provides, he or she must also, as part of his or her personal obligation to the company, avoid placing it in violation of the fundamental legal rights of those employees. The *interests* of the employee to which the act refers, as seen above, would then be divided into two: (1) interests that correspond to basic legal rights, such as the right to health and safety as articulated by both labor law and international human rights law and (2) interests that do not amount to rights of such importance. If the director fails in the former domain, he or she would owe an obligation to reimburse the company for the compensation it had to pay from its treasury for the violation of the law. This would be the case even if he or she led the company to violate those basic rights out of a sincere desire to further the best interests of the enterprise. In other words, this principle would reverse the direction of adjustment between a company's commercial interests and its employees' basic rights. The insulation of the director from personal responsibility that is designed to free him or her to pursue the commercial benefit of the enterprise would be reduced, compelling the director to find a mode of pursuing the company's financial gain that does the least damage to the employees' basic rights. It is the opposite of the direction in which, as has been seen, adjustment runs at the moment. For other employee entitlements that do not correspond to rights of such importance, the classical direction of adjustment, as stipulated by company law, would remain in place.

This is a perspective on company law, and allied areas of investment law, designed to induce both to support rather than subvert the fundamental objectives of labor law. A director's personal responsibility to his or her company would become partly symmetrical with the company's responsibility to its employees. Any violation of the basic rights of those employees becomes a violation of the director's duty to the company. This is a position on corporate governance that seems to accord with the American Law Institute's *Principles of Corporate Governance*. The Institute writes,

> [i]t is sometimes maintained that whether a corporation should adhere to a given legal rule may properly depend on a kind of cost-benefit analysis, in which probable corporate gains are weighed against either probable social costs, measured by the dollar liability imposed for engaging in such conduct, or probable corporate losses, measured by potential dollar liability discounted for likelihood of detection. [Our principles of corporate governance do] not adopt this position. With few exceptions, dollar liability is not a "price" that can properly be paid for the privilege of engaging in legally wrongful conduct. Cost-benefit analysis may have a place in the state's determination whether a given type of conduct should be deemed legally wrongful. Once that determination has been made, however, the resulting legal rule normally represents a community decision that the conduct is wrongful as such, so that cost-benefit analysis whether to obey the rule is out of place.[9]

Although the Institute does not say this, it should follow from what it does say that the company director would be responsible to the company itself for knowingly placing the latter in violation of the fundamental elements of labor law. He or she should not have the inducement to lead the company to *purchase* a violation of rights to health and safety with a decision in advance to pay compensation.

Two Types of Pluralism and Globalization

The issue that arises is one of coherence. Can we tolerate a polity in which a basic right receives these different weightings? The answer is that this depends on how we understand the distinct domains of law being considered. In one view, it is legitimate that each domain be treated as autonomous. That is, the distinct objectives of labor, company, and investment law should be allowed to drive the order of values and rights within it. Even if some of these values and rights are imported from *outside* these domains, as is true of labor and human rights brought inside the branches of commercial law we have been considering, it is thought to be correct that they receive different weightings in each context.

It is this tacit theory of law, which can be labeled *functional pluralism*, that contributes to the threat that globalization poses to basic labor rights in the world economy. This is not a threat stemming from a failure to take such labor rights seriously. People of good

---

9.   AM. LAW INST., PRINCIPLES OF CORPORATE GOVERNANCE § 2.01(b)(1) cmt. g (1992).

faith in claiming they take those rights seriously implement each of the different solutions to the problem described in our example. They feel, nevertheless, bound to adjust those rights to the specific priorities that set off one domain of law from the other. There is a different theory of law underpinning the proposals advanced here. It aims to bring the distinct branches of norms into a coherent relationship while also preserving many, though not all, of their unique sets of priorities. It understands basic labor rights, like other internationally recognized fundamental rights, as designed to have the same weight as part of an emerging constitution of civil society—both national and international. It can be called *civic pluralism*.[10] This spread of a basic right with the same force across different domains of law is part of what can be understood by the claim that human rights are indivisible. Indivisibility means that different human rights are meant to complement one another, but it also means that one and the same human right is meant to avoid fragmentation. The vice of globalization is that it threatens to produce this type of fragmentation. A varying hierarchy of commitments, which specialized bodies of law in civil society see themselves as bound to further, overtakes the spread of commitments that human rights impose. A *constitution* of international civil society threatens to disappear, replaced by separate sets of norms, each competing with the other and hence open to capture by the force of private power within the economy.

---

10.   For further treatment of these varieties of pluralism *See* Sheldon Leader, *The Collateral Protection of Rights in a Global Economy*, 53 N.Y.L. Sch. L. Rev. 805, 805 (2009); *see also Collateralism* in ROGER BROWNSWORD, GLOBAL GOVERNANCE AND THE QUEST FOR JUSTICE 53–67 (2005).

Chapter 14

Financial Institutions and Human Rights

Dr. Mary Dowell-Jones

The succession of political dramas in Europe . . . again shows the financial markets
acting like a global supra-government. They oust entrenched regimes where normal
political processes could not do so. They force austerity, banking bail-outs and other
major policy changes. Their influence dwarfs multilateral institutions such as the
International Monetary Fund. Indeed, leaving aside unusable nuclear weapons, they
have become the most powerful force on earth. . . . Whether this power is healthy
or not is beside the point. It is permanent.[1]

The globalization of financial services has far outstripped the capacity of international
human rights law to oversee its effects, as the latest financial crisis has so amply demonstrated. The integration of human rights principles into the day-to-day operations and
management of the international financial sector has so far been geared toward a few key
target issues where the negative impact of financial activity is highly visible, and where the
causative financial act can be most directly traced to a given financial institution, largely
by human rights and corporate social responsibility (CSR) advocates without expertise
in the more technical corners of the financial system. Under this approach, major strides
have been made in applying human rights to certain areas of finance; there have been
high-profile campaigns and international initiatives around issues such as project finance,
ethical investing, microfinance, and corruption, to cite the most visible. Most, if not all,
of these have been the subject of significant nongovernmental organization (NGO) campaigns targeting banks and asset managers,[2] international stakeholder initiatives such as

---

1. Roger Altman, *We Need Not Fret Over Omnipotent Markets*, Fin. Times (Dec. 1, 2011),
http://www.ft.com/cms/s/0/890161ac-1b69-11e1-85f8-00144feabdc0.html (Altman is a former U.S.
deputy treasury secretary under President Bill Clinton).
2. Banking and asset managers have been the main focus of efforts on the financial sector. More
specialist operators like hedge funds, insurers, and private equity are notable for their absence from the

the Equator Principles,[3] and thousands of pages of academic analysis. The industry buy-in has been widespread, with the United Nations Principles for Responsible Investment, for example, now boasting more than a thousand signatory institutions with combined assets under management (AUM) of roughly U.S. $30 trillion.[4] Most, if not all, of the major banking organizations now have corporate social responsibility teams in place that often report directly to the chief executive and are responsible for implementing publicly available human rights policies. The Web sites of major banking and financial services companies have extensive sections devoted to CSR, including a commitment to internationally recognized human rights standards, and these tend to be reproduced in glossy segments of the companies' annual reports.[5]

Viewed solely from the vantage point of the business and human rights debate, and without any grounding in finance, these efforts may give the impression that the financial sector has wholeheartedly embraced human rights principles and made strenuous efforts to implement them across their many activities. In practice, aside from the problems on the ground of making sure high-sounding statements of principle translate into actual practice, the events that have shaken the world since the beginning of the credit crisis in 2007 leave any observer with profound questions about the ethics and human rights impacts of the global financial services industry. Even regulators have questioned the social utility of finance. Mark Carney, chairman of the G20's Financial Stability Board and successor to Mervyn King as governor of the Bank of England has said, "[t]he old normal was deformed. . . . For all the perceived difficulties the industry has with regulatory overload . . . it pales in comparison to the difficulties, the lost output, the lost jobs . . . quite frankly, the suffering that's happening in a variety of economies."[6] On reading accounts of the crisis, it is manifestly clear that statements of human rights principle made by major financial institutions did not reach very far into actual operations, and they certainly were not deemed relevant to the creating and selling of complex financial instruments based on esoteric mathematical formulas, despite the fact that these instruments rested upon the right to housing of the lowest-rated borrowers in America.[7] Similarly, banks have

---

debate. The suite of financial products that have come under review are similarly limited and are mainly confined to lending, long-only equity investing, and providing corporate/customer accounts.

3.   Equator Principles (2011), www.equator-principles.com. See below p. 417.

4.   *About the PRI Initiative*, Principles for Responsible Investment, http://www.unpri.org/about-pri/ (last visited Dec. 6, 2013). See below p. 421.

5.   See below p. 431.

6.   Brooke Masters, *FSB Chief in Call to Rein in "Shadow Banking,"* Fin. Times (Jan. 15, 2012) (quoting Mark Carney, chair of the Financial Stability Board).

7.   For a comprehensive account of the crisis and the attitudes and actions of major banks that led to it, *see*: Financial Crisis Inquiry Commission, The Financial Crisis Inquiry Report: Final Report of the National Commission on the Causes of the Financial and Economic Crisis in the United States (2011); UK Financial Services Authority, The Turner Review: A Regulatory Response to the Global Banking Crisis (2009). For an analysis of the subprime crisis and human rights law, *see*: Mary Dowell-Jones & David Kinley, *The Monster Under the Bed: Financial Services and*

not linked the events currently unfolding across Europe as a result of bank bailouts and years of reckless lending to their human rights or sustainability commitments.[8] In practice, human rights as an issue have been viewed from quite a limited perspective in the financial sector—as much by human rights activists themselves as by financiers.

Certainly, the complexity of modern finance makes much of it difficult to reconcile with international human rights law. Despite the fact that specialized financial transactions in centers like New York and London can now have global socioeconomic impacts that are often the most devastating for the *bottom billion* who are already on the margins of daily survival, international human rights law is generally not part of the debate. For example, although there is growing disquiet among regulators and financiers over exchange traded funds and their potential to trigger a major financial crisis, reference to human rights law *per se* offers no way of arguing to a solution—even were it to be invoked—despite the fact that any financial crisis will inevitably have severe consequences for human rights enjoyment.[9] The simple fact is that modern finance is so technically specialized and complex that human rights law has barely left the starting gate in responding to the growing threat it poses to the enjoyment of human rights, not only by the poorest of the poor but by everyone whose livelihoods and socioeconomic rights are impacted by the whirlwinds of unstable financial markets. This is as much a challenge for the future development of human rights law as it is for the reform of financial institutions, and it raises many questions about what the proper role of human rights law should be in the financial sector.

The Human Rights Response to the Crisis

It is notable how small a role human rights law has played in the aftermath of the subprime financial crisis and in the unfolding Eurozone crisis. Despite a flurry of statements at the outset of the global meltdown of 2008 to 2009 on the need to embed human rights into the foundations of the financial system,[10] the human rights community has largely failed

---

the Ruggie Framework, in THE UN GUIDING PRINCIPLES ON BUSINESS AND HUMAN RIGHTS: FOUNDATIONS AND IMPLEMENTATION 193–216 (R. Mares ed., 2012).

8.   Roger McCormick, *What Makes a Bank a "Sustainable Bank"?* 1 LAW & ECON. YEARLY REV. 77 (2012).

9.   *See, e.g.*, Srichander Ramaswamy, *Market Structures and Systemic Risks of Exchange-Traded Funds,* (Bank for International Settlements, BIS Working Paper No. 343 (2011), http://www.bis.org/publ/work343.pdf. As concerns centre on the systemic risks generated by the lengthening of the chain of intermediation and its complexity, particularly where derivatives are used, it is immediately apparent that international human rights law would have little direct relevance to the substantive problem, no matter how dire the human rights consequences of such systemic risk manifesting.

10.   UN Human Rights Council, 10th Sess., *The Impact of the Global Economic and Financial Crises on the Universal Realization and Effective Enjoyment of Human Rights*, Statement of Navanethem Pillay, UN High Commissioner for Human Rights, UN Doc. A/HRC/S-10/2 (Feb. 20–23, 2009); INT'L NETWORK FOR ECON., SOC. & CUL. RTS., ESCR-NET STATEMENT ON THE FINANCIAL CRISIS AND

to follow up on this. There has been little active engagement of regulators, policymakers, and financial institutions in meaningful dialogue on the changes needed to insulate human rights from the daily activities of financial institutions. In fact, it is notable how few human rights bodies have risen to this challenge. Certainly, there has been little active participation from formal human rights bodies at the national or international level in financial sector discussions, and although a few NGOs have started to address regulatory reform, their output remains distant from formal negotiations.[11] Even for the Committee on Economic, Social, and Cultural Rights, the backdrop of crisis has not intruded much into their work. In 2008, the committee issued a statement on the world food crisis, and in 2012, the chairperson of the committee addressed a letter to states parties on the financial and economic crisis and its impact on socioeconomic rights. This two-page document does not address the issue of problems and failures within financial institutions themselves.[12]

To a large extent, this rather remarkable omission is understandable; the source of the problems that result in broad-based negative human rights harm from the activities of financial institutions lies in the technical architecture of the system itself, and in the complex products and processes that are generally remote from immediate human rights abuses. They are therefore largely beyond the area of focus of traditional human rights lawyers and activists. Moreover, structural failings within finance require targeted structural solutions—they cannot be addressed by a simple overlay of human rights and sustainability criteria—because much more is at stake than simply whether financial behavior is ethical or not.[13] This issue immediately creates a problem for human rights lawyers, who tend to be highly specialized in their own discipline but lacking in the necessary background to wade into regulatory debates on derivatives, capital adequacy, ringfencing, liquidity coverage ratios, proprietary trading, and other issues that are at the forefront of the current regulatory-reform agenda. Moreover, the economics of regulation is just as important as

---

GLOBAL ECONOMIC RECESSION: TOWARDS A HUMAN RIGHTS RESPONSE (2008), www.escr-net.org/usr _doc/EconomicCrisisHRStatement_ESCR-Net_final_eng_withendorsements.pdf.; BANKTRACK, BANK TO THE FUTURE: EL ESCORIAL STATEMENT ON BANKS AND THE FINANCIAL CRISIS (2008), www.banktrack .org/download/bank_to_the_future_el_escorial_statement/escorial_declaration_final.pdf; CTR. FOR ECON. & SOC. RTS., HUMAN RIGHTS AND THE ECONOMIC CRISIS: A TRANSFORMATIVE MOMENT? (2009), www .cesr.org/atricle.php?id=368; R. BALAKRISHNAN, H. HEINTZ, & S. SEGUINO, RUTGERS CTR. FOR WOMEN'S GLOBAL LEADERSHIP, A HUMAN RIGHTS RESPONSE TO THE ECONOMIC CRISIS IN THE U.S. (2009), www .cwgl.rutgers.edu/globalcenter/whatsnew/RBhumanrightsresponse2009.pdf.

11. *See, e.g.,* Description of the work of SOMA's financial sector, SOMA, http://somo.nl/dossiers-en /sectors/financial (last visited July 27, 2013).

12. UN Comm. on Econ., Soc. & Cultural Rights, Rep. on its 40th Sess., Apr. 28-May 16, 2008, *Statement of the Committee on the World Food Crisis,* UN Doc. E/C.12/2008/1 (May 20, 2008); UN Comm. on Econ., Soc. & Cultural Rights, Letter from the CESCR Chairperson to States Parties in the Context of the Economic and Financial Crisis, Ref. CESCR/48th/SP/MAB/SW (May 16, 2012).

13. The breadth and technicality of much of the content of the updated international regulatory framework for banks, so-called Basel III, illustrates this perfectly. *See International Regulatory Framework for Banks (Basel III),* BANK FOR INT'L SETTLEMENTS, http://www.bis.org/bcbs/basel3.htm?ql=1 for documents (last visited Dec. 6, 2013).

the legal aspects of regulation; that is, responding to the crisis is not simply an issue of enacting more laws but of enacting the right law given the structure and dynamics of international finance. This distinction can be lost on human rights lawyers, but it is extremely important to the successful stabilization of financial markets.

Developments within human rights law have also overshadowed the immediate challenge of tackling the crisis and the role of financial institutions in negatively impacting human rights. The 2011 endorsement of the UN Guiding Principles on Business and Human Rights[14] came as the culmination of a very long process of discussion and intensive consultation at the UN on the nature of the responsibilities of businesses for their human rights impacts. This research had been ongoing since the early work of the Sub-Commission on the Promotion and Protection of Human Rights on the ill-fated draft *Norms on the Responsibilities of Transnational Corporations and Other Business Enterprises with Regard to Human Rights*,[15] and through the six-year mandate of the UN Special Representative of the Secretary-General on the issue of human rights and transnational corporations and other business enterprises, Professor John Ruggie.[16] The latter's work was not sector specific but focused on identifying a common framework that would apply right across the business landscape. As such, although sectoral consultations were held under the auspices of the high commissioner on human rights,[17] the Guiding Principles do not refer to any particular sector, nor do they provide guidelines on how they can be implemented within a sectoral context, beyond the specification that businesses must have human rights policies in place and due diligence procedures to underpin them.[18]

The enormous challenge and success of Professor Ruggie's work drew the focus of most business and human rights participants during these years because it was, of course, expected that the Guiding Principles would provide the framework for the financial sector's human rights responsibilities. The work needed to develop a comprehensive understanding of how human rights responsibilities apply to an industry as complex as finance was pushed onto the back burner because there was a drive for theoretical coherence in defining the responsibilities of corporations, and perhaps a failure to understand the unique nature and power of the international financial markets relative to other sectors. Operationalization of the principles was also left to phase two of the mandate, which has now

---

14. UN Special Representative of the Secretary-General, *Guiding Principles on Business and Human Rights: Implementing the United Nations "Protect, Respect and Remedy" Framework*, UN Doc. A/HRC/17/31 (Mar. 21, 2011).

15. Comm'n on Human Rights, 55th Sess., UN Doc. E/CN.4/Sub.2/2003/12/Rev.2 (Aug. 26, 2003).

16. For an introduction and overview of the two stages of the UN's work in this area, *see* R. Mares, *Business and Human Rights After Ruggie: Foundations, the Art of Simplification and the Imperative of Cumulative Progress*, in THE UN GUIDING PRINCIPLES ON BUSINESS AND HUMAN RIGHTS (R. Mares ed., 2012) *supra* note 7, at 1–49.

17. *See, e.g.*, Report of the United Nations High Commissioner on Human Rights on the sectoral consultation entitled "Human Rights and the Financial Sector", UN Doc. A/HRC/4/99 (Mar. 6, 2007).

18. *Guiding Principles on Business & Human Rights, supra* note 14, principles 16–21.

been taken up by the UN working group on the issue of human rights and transnational corporations and other business enterprises. In choosing its initial themes to guide its work, it has also chosen a non-sectoral perspective because its mandate does not specifically give it the authority to look in detail at the challenges of applying the Guiding Principles to any specific business sector.[19] The entire approach of the UN to the issue of corporate accountability for human rights impacts is understandable as a matter of law, but its practical effect has been to sideline and obfuscate the enormous challenge of dealing with the accountability of financial institutions of all types for the global human rights impacts of their dealings.

This is the core of the challenge for the business and human rights agenda in the financial sector in light of the crisis—to focus on defining principles and methodologies that are practically applicable to the complex array of products, processes, and services that make up modern finance, using the UN Guiding Principles as the normative framework. This reconciliation is something that will require a cognitive leap by human rights defenders, who have not yet proven very good at understanding the problem. For example, a paper by a coalition of four NGOs submitted to the European Union's 2011 consultation on updating the Capital Requirements Directive included the following recommendations "[b]anks that engage in, or finance . . . commodity derivatives, foreign exchange derivatives, and credit derivatives should assess the sustainability risks of these derivatives," and, "[l]iquidity stress should be avoided by ensuring that all risk management assesses if specific loans, investments or financial products are contrary to principles of sustainable and socially equitable development."[20] Honorable as these sentiments are, there is currently no way of assessing what the sustainability risks of derivatives are or how they could be measured or applied in trading these instruments—indeed, the financial sector's usual argument for derivatives trading is that they play a crucial role in hedging risk and thereby in ensuring (hopefully) the sustainability of the financial system. The NGO submission fails to address the crucial operational point of whether these arguments are in fact justified, and if not, how the colossal world of derivatives could be made more sustainable, for example by exchange-based trading and/or increased collateralization. Similarly, liquidity stress could not be preempted by using unspecified sustainability criteria upon which, again, the submission does not elaborate. In fact, to suggest that it could be is arguably to display a lack of understanding of the mechanics of liquidity stress and

---

19.   Human Rights Council Res. 17/4, 17th Sess., Human Rights and Transnational Corporations and Other Business Enterprises, UN Doc. A/HRC/RES/17/4 (July 6, 2011). For the mandate of the Working Group, *see* paragraph 6. The Working Group has chosen the three following thematic priorities: Dissemination of the Guiding Principles, Promoting Their Effective Implementation, and Embedding Them in Global Governance Structures. *See Methods of Work*, OHCHR.org, http://www.ohchr.org/EN/Issues /Business/Pages/WorkingMethods.aspx (last visited July 29, 2013).

20.   BankTrack, Berne Declaration, CRBM & Friends of the Earth Europe, How to Integrate Sustainability Criteria in Capital Requirements ¶¶ 2, 4 (Mar. 2011).

maturity transformation inside major financial institutions and how it precipitates crisis.[21] It also shows a failure to understand how risk management methodologies embedded in financial regulation contribute to liquidity stress and unsustainable financial markets. At this current juncture, however, the theoretical body of work that would enable the bridging of this manifest gap between financial reality and the ethos of human rights is simply lacking. In fact, it has barely begun to be tackled. Ultimately, human rights defenders face the challenge of making themselves relevant to the major issues in managing the global financial system and containing the human fallout of periodic malfunctions by looking in depth at the technical challenges posed by the governance and operation of the international financial system. The simple statement of high ethical ideals will not do much to transform practice within the sector.

This chapter will explore some of these issues and the challenges they raise for the Guiding Principles and for embedding human rights holistically across the operations of the financial sector. It will start by providing an overview of the financial sector and why it is crucially relevant to global human rights enjoyment. It will then review the current debate around financial institutions and human rights by examining three major areas in which human rights have so far been linked to financial institutions: project finance, ethical investing, and corporate social responsibility (CSR). The limitations of these initiatives will be outlined, including their very limited scope when viewed against the backdrop of the financial system as a whole. This topic will be followed by a case study of the controversy surrounding Vedanta Resources *plc*, which neatly illustrates the shortcomings of project finance, ethical investing, and CSR as a framework for protecting human rights in financial institutions. This chapter will then provide a brief comment on the challenges that current gaps in a human rights approach to the financial sector raise for the implementation of the UN Guiding Principles on Business and Human Rights in the sector. Finally, it will conclude with some recommendations for future research and action.

Financial Institutions and Human Rights: Understanding the Context

Some figures on the scale of today's financial markets will put the debate on the proper role of human rights law into context. World GDP is roughly U.S. $70 trillion.[22] The value

---

21. *See* the account of the events between September and December 2008 when severe liquidity stress cascaded through the U.S. financial system causing the failure of Lehman's and other major financial institutions like AIG, Citigroup, Morgan Stanley, Washington Mutual, and Wachovia, which were either bailed out or sold with extensive government guarantees for any potential losses. FINANCIAL CRISIS INQUIRY REPORT, *supra* note 7, at 324–86. The FCIC comments (at 324) that: "Solvency should be a simple financial concept"—as the crisis demonstrated, it is anything but. *Id.*

22. INTERNATIONAL MONETARY FUND, WORLD ECONOMIC OUTLOOK DATABASE, 2012 FIGURES, http://www.imf.org/external/pubs/ft/weo/2012/02/weodata/index.aspx. (latest full year figures available).

of shares trading on world exchanges is not much lower than this, at U.S. $63 trillion, before taking into account any other type of financial market.[23] Amounts outstanding on the global bond markets hit a record of U.S. $100 trillion in 2012, up from U.S. $40 trillion ten years earlier.[24] The combined face value of derivatives contracts in existence is a staggering U.S. $700 trillion—ten times world GDP.[25] According to data from the International Swaps and Derivatives Association, most of these contracts are concentrated among a small handful of financial institutions. In 2010 (latest figures available), the four-teen largest global derivatives dealers, the G14 Group, accounted for U.S. $354.6 trillion of derivatives exposures—roughly five times current world GDP; and the five largest U.S. dealers had U.S. $172.3 trillion of contracts—a value equivalent to two and one-half times world GDP concentrated in just five financial institutions.[26]

As these figures indicate, financial institutions themselves have grown enormously in size over the last two decades, and many of the large global banks (the large, complex financial institutions, or LCFIs, at the heart of the system) now have balance sheets that are bigger than the GDP of their home country. The predicament is, in essence, the too big to fail problem that came to the fore during the bailouts of major financial institu-tions in 2008 and 2009—they are too large and too interconnected to be allowed to fail because the disruption to the world financial system and economy would simply be too great. However, they are also increasingly too big to save because their home govern-ments simply do not have the resources to rescue them, particularly given the debt loads that most advanced economies now carry.

Enjoyment of human rights is inextricably bound up with this problem, even though the link between systemic risk and human rights has not so far received much attention: the failure of such an institution would undoubtedly be catastrophic for both human rights and the financial system, as it was when Lehman Brothers collapsed in 2008. This level of impact raises the question whether the LCFIs bear more onerous responsibilities under the UN Guiding Principles than other financial institutions that are less systemi-cally vital. The legal form of human rights does not, however, provide any type of ready

---

23. WORLD FEDERATION OF EXCHANGES, WFE MARKET HIGHLIGHTS (Jan. 26, 2012), http://www .world-exchanges.org/files/file/stats%20and%20charts/2011%20WFE%20Market%20Highlights.pdf.

24. THECITYUK, BOND MARKETS 2012 1, c.1 (Oct. 2012). A proportion of this total is made up of securitized assets of the sort that triggered the financial meltdown. One financial commentator has noted: "We are today securitizing ever-larger chunks of the global economy with everything from credit-card debt to home mortgages." Keith Fitzgerald, *Bond Market Outlook: 4 Ways to Hedge the Looming Fixed-Income Fiasco*, SEEKING ALPHA (Mar 9, 2011), www.seekingalpha.com/article/257363-bond-mar-ket-outlook-4-ways-to-hedge-the-looming-fixed-income-fiasco.

25. *See Derivative Statistics*, BANK FOR INT'L SETTLEMENTS, http://www.bis.org/statistics/derstats.htm (last visited June 2012) (*see* Table 23A: Derivative financial instruments traded on organized exchanges, and Table 19: Amounts Outstanding of Over-the-Counter (OTC) Derivatives).

26. INT'L SWAPS & DERIVATIVES ASS'N, 2010 MID-YEAR MARKET SURVEY, *www*.isda.org/statistics/ recent.html. The survey was discontinued in 2010.

solution to what is an enormously challenging theoretical and practical problem in the governance of the global financial system, one that has been made worse by the crisis. As the U.S. Financial Crisis Inquiry Commission (FCIC) comments, "[a]s a result of the rescues and consolidation of financial institutions through failures and mergers during the crisis, the U.S. financial sector is now more concentrated than ever in the hands of a few very large, systemically significant institutions."[27] The shadow banking system—which is made up of financial institutions outside the traditional banking regulatory structure but which engage in banking functions like granting credit—is also now worth around U.S. $67 trillion, itself nearly equivalent in size to world GDP.[28]

Once the colossal scale of today's financial markets and financial institutions relative to the world economy is grasped, it is easier to see why they are so relevant to human rights. In the post-war era, as financial services have been liberalized, we have moved into an increasingly financialized world where, rather than providing a support service to the real economy, banking and the architecture of finance now drive and dominate the world's economy.[29] The socioeconomic rights laid out in the International Bill of Human Rights—such as the rights to work, to an adequate standard of living, and to food, water, housing, social security, health care, and education—are intimately dependent upon the economic environment in which they are enjoyed.[30] Thanks to financialization, these rights are now extremely vulnerable to volatility in the financial markets, from small changes in sentiment to the storms of crisis that can wipe away years of antipoverty gains and economic growth. Socioeconomic rights are inevitably dragged along in the slipstream of malfunctioning financial markets and are difficult, if not impossible, to isolate from them. The impact on American households of the subprime mortgage abuses, the global human costs of the economic downturn, and the shock to European welfare systems coming from problems in sovereign bond markets all testify to this inextricable interconnection. According to World Bank analysis, the global economic crisis sparked by the financial meltdown

---

27. FINANCIAL CRISIS INQUIRY REPORT, *supra* note 7, at 386.

28. FINANCIAL STABILITY BOARD, STRENGTHENING OVERSIGHT AND REGULATION OF SHADOW BANKING: A POLICY FRAMEWORK FOR STRENGTHENING OVERSIGHT AND REGULATION OF SHADOW BANKING ENTITIES 1 (2012), http://www.financialstabilityboard.org/publications/r_121118a.pdf. Shadow banking is described as "credit intermediation involving entities and activities (fully or partially) outside the regular banking system." *Id. at* ii.

29. *See, e.g.,* FINANCIALIZATION AND THE WORLD ECONOMY (Gerald Epstein ed., 2005); T. Palley, *Financialization: What It Is and Why It Matters,* Levy Economics Institute, Working Paper No. 525 (2007).

30. Universal Declaration of Human Rights, G.A. Res. 217 (III) A, UN Doc. A/Res/217(III) at Articles 22–27 (Dec. 10, 1948); International Covenant on Economic, Social and Cultural Rights, G.A. Res. 2200A(XXI), UN Doc. A/Res/21/2200 (Dec. 16, 1966). Systemic financial risk imperils these rights directly via its economic consequences like unemployment and sharp falls in the standard of living, and also indirectly through the costs it imposes on the State. These costs are now so substantial because of the size of the financial sector that they entail broad consequences for social spending and public services. This is not to downplay the importance of civil and political rights that can also be impacted: social unrest stemming from economic problems can also lead to negative impacts on civil and political rights.

of 2007 to 2009 pushed the number of people living in extreme poverty to 53 million more than would have otherwise been the case by 2015. It has had long-term negative impacts on prospects for attaining the Millennium Development Goals, notably in the areas of hunger, child and maternal health, access to clean water, and disease control.[31] The World Bank has also warned developing countries to start contingency planning for a potential economic downturn worse than that of 2008 to 2009, in the face of another potential financial crisis stemming from the Eurozone—something that will once again hit human rights very heavily.[32]

Consequently, there are persuasive arguments that the way financial institutions are managed—both internally and externally via supervision and regulation—should take into account a broad human rights framework to financial stability as well as the more traditional perspective of solvency, financial stability, and returns. Similarly, there are persuasive arguments that complex products, such as credit derivatives, that are capable of such global human consequences should be brought within the ambit of human rights law, despite the current perception that financial institutions are only responsible for human rights impacts in a very narrow range of areas. Because the same states who oversee global financial markets are also party to the International Covenant on Economic, Social, and Cultural Rights (except of course the United States and surprisingly South Africa, which have both signed but not ratified this instrument),[33] and because the UN Human Rights Council has unanimously endorsed the UN Framework on Business and Human Rights, which establishes a business responsibility to respect human rights across their operations,[34] there is an increasingly clear basis in law for arguing this position. Under the state duty to protect, the Guiding Principles also clearly set out the expectation that states should "enforce laws that are aimed at, or have the effect of, requiring business enterprises to respect human rights."[35] Clearly, the architecture of international financial services, both its regulation and the broad impact of financial activity on socioeconomic conditions, is just as relevant to human rights as the few core areas of operations that have currently benefitted from so much focus.

The Debate So Far: A Subsidiarity Approach to Human Rights Accountability

Despite this context, the debate so far on human rights and financial institutions has been driven largely by the narrow perception that it is only where financial services companies

---

31. WORLD BANK & INTERNATIONAL MONETARY FUND, GLOBAL MONITORING REPORT 2010: THE MDGs AFTER THE CRISIS (2010).

32. WORLD BANK, GLOBAL ECONOMIC PROSPECTS—JANUARY 2012 (2012).

33. For the status of ratifications, see Ratification Status of International Covenant on Economic, Social and Cultural Rights, UN TREATY COLLECTION, http://treaties.un.org/Pages/ViewDetails.aspx ?src=TREATY&mtdsg_no=IV-3&chapter=4&lang=en (last visited April 24, 2013).

34. Guiding Principles on Business and Human Rights, supra note 14.

35. Guiding Principles on Business and Human Rights, supra note 14, Principle 3(a).

come very visibly and immediately into contact with individuals' rights that human rights issues arise at all. A CEO briefing on human rights prepared by the UN Environment Programme Finance Initiative in 2008, during the height of the financial crisis, listed the following three core areas of interaction between financial services and human rights: (1) when a customer's business causes or contributes to human rights violations or its products/services are used for such purposes (for example, military equipment); (2) when project finance lending for large projects causes or contributes to human rights violations; (3) and when financial services facilitate capital flight and money laundering. Beyond these, the briefing notes that the financial sector can help promote human rights through statements supporting human rights or deploring situations of violation, or by contributing to development activities.[36]

This rather limited list is an example of the *micro level* impacts[37] of financial institutions on human rights; the instances where definable human rights harm upon identifiable individuals can be attributed to the activities of an identifiable financial institution through direct funding and/or customer relationships. It is based on a legalistic model of causality that requires reasonably direct attribution of individual harm to a corporate actor. This is the cognitive model that has driven thinking about human rights and financial institutions so far, and as a consequence, the debate has largely been limited to a few key areas where this model most readily applies—instances where impacts are easiest to trace and attribute directly to the activities of a particular financial institution. Based on this model, human rights themselves have also been seen in quite narrow legalistic terms—for example, as instances of egregious violations, such as the funding of large infrastructure or mining projects where local communities' rights are blatantly ignored. Although this model could potentially have been extended to encompass other product and/or process areas within financial institutions (such as subprime), the expertise to do this within the human rights community has largely been lacking and financial institutions themselves are unlikely to volunteer to more onerous accountability. The broader concept of human rights, which encompasses their macro dimensions such as the rights of everyone to work, social security, healthcare, housing, and so on, has also been largely absent from debate. This broader concept of human rights, which is facilitated by the economic and financial architecture of the state, would more readily link them to the more systemic dimensions of international finance.

As deeply necessary as the legalistic angle is, it can only ever capture within its purview a small fragment of daily activity in financial institutions, and the financial sector is rather let off the hook for responsibility for the socioeconomic impacts of the rest of

---

36. RORY SULLIVAN & PHILLIPA BIRTWELL, UNITED NATIONS ENVIRONMENT PROGRAMME FINANCE INITIATIVE, CEO BRIEFING ON HUMAN RIGHTS 4 (2008).

37. Mary Dowell-Jones & David Kinley, *Minding the Gap: Global Finance and Human Rights*, 25 ETHICS & INT'L AFFAIRS 183, 188 (2011).

its colossal operations. This approach cannot be readily scaled up to encompass more intractable *macro* dimensions of the interaction between rights and finance, particularly where there are complex financial products or activities such as those that span several financial entities in chains of intermediation. *Macro level* impacts refer to the way the activities of different market participants, intermediated through different market and regulatory structures, interact with international human rights standards through their impact on socioeconomic conditions around the world. This covers, for example, their impact on the livelihoods of individuals and on the capacity of states to implement policies required to fulfill their international obligations. This relates to constraints on fiscal policies that affect social policies[38]—both directly, through the costs of bailing out ailing financial institutions in the United States and Europe, and indirectly, through the socioeconomic costs of economic recession triggered by activities within the financial sector. It also includes the way the lobbying power of financial institutions can overshadow human rights and social welfare concerns. A report by the Consumer Education Foundation found that in the decade leading up to the crisis (1998 to 2008), the financial sector spent U.S. $1.7 billion on campaign contributions and another U.S. $3.4 billion on lobbyists in the United States. During this period, crucial reforms central to the crisis were enacted, such as the Financial Services Modernization Act 1999 and the SEC Rule on Consolidated Supervised Entities 2004, which enabled banks like Lehman Brothers and Bear Sterns to reduce their net capital by up to 30 percent.[39]

Another important ingredient of the approach taken so far to integrating human rights into financial institutions is that the financial sector is just one subsector of the world economy, alongside other industry segments such as pharmaceuticals, retail, and extractive industries. Efforts have then focused on mapping human rights onto banking or asset management,[40] where those companies can be seen to come most visibly into direct contact with well-understood areas of human rights concern, along the same lines as other industries. For example, the Business Leaders Initiative on Human Rights was a multisector, voluntary initiative that ran from 2003 to 2009, with the aim of finding "practical ways of implementing the Universal Declaration on Human Rights in a business context."[41] It brought together major companies from across the corporate spectrum, including Barclays, to develop a human rights matrix that all companies could use to embed respect for

---

38.   The cost of unemployment payouts in the U.S. rose from $31.1 billion in the twelve months leading up to June 30th, 2006, to $159.4 billion in the year leading up to June 30th, 2010, as unemployment soared from 4.6% to 9.1%. The cost of this has exacerbated fiscal deficits and led to cuts in the number of weeks for which claimants are eligible for payments, leaving many without work or unemployment insurance. *See* Matt Kenard, *U.S. Jobless Face Benefits Squeeze*, Fin. Times (Sept. 2, 2011), http://www.ft.com/intl/cms/s/0/e3afed80-c99d-11e0-9eb8-00144feabdc0.html.

39.   Consumer Education Foundation & Essential Information, Sold Out: How Wall Street and Washington Betrayed America 6 (2009), www.wallstreetwatch.org/reports/sold_out.pdf.

40.   *See supra* note 2.

41.   *See* www.integrating-humanrights.org/home for the toolkit and matrix that was developed.

human rights into their operations. Human rights issues specific to financial institutions were not separated out for targeted analysis because it was assumed that they could be addressed in the same way as other businesses.

A corollary of this approach is that financial-services companies have been widely characterized in business and human rights circles as coming into contact with human rights only "in the zone of complicity," through their business relationships with companies that directly infringe human rights: "the human rights and financial worlds meet, to a great extent, in the zone of complicity, where the financial services supplier potentially enables other business activities that abuse human rights."[42] The then UN Special Representative of the Secretary-General on the issue of human rights and transnational corporations, Professor John Ruggie, said the following at a consultation on "human rights and the financial sector" hosted by the UN High Commissioner for Human Rights in 2007,

> While attention in the business and human rights arena has thus far been on so-called front-line businesses, i.e. those that interact with communities directly such as the extractive industries and infrastructure, there is now a growing interest in finance because the financial sector provides the means for front-line industries to operate.[43]

Taken together, the combined effect of this approach to the relationship between human rights and the financial sector is to interpret human rights risk in the sector as a subsidiary of the human rights risks generated by front-line businesses in other sectors with which they have commercial relationships. So, for example, in the project-finance arena, the human rights risks stem from the front-line project that the bank is funding. The bank becomes implicated in any negative human rights impacts through its commercial and/or funding relationship with the company operating the project on the ground. The impetus behind current initiatives has been in essence to use the financial sector as another way to address human rights issues in underlying companies, as another route to human rights accountability. The bigger picture, which is to scrutinize the human rights risks generated by financial activity proper and more complex financial products, has largely proved to be a step too far. As we shall see below, for example, ethical investing initiatives have provided human rights principles and checklists for screening potential investments, but they have ignored potential human rights issues raised directly by the asset management business, such as fees and costs and the way they affect retirement income, market instability generated by fund managers selling in droves, and the human rights impacts of investments that are not long-only equity.

---

42. RITA ROCA & FRANCESCA MANTA, DANISH INSTITUTE FOR HUMAN RIGHTS, VALUES ADDED: THE CHALLENGE OF INTEGRATING HUMAN RIGHTS INTO THE FINANCIAL SECTOR 17 (2010).

43. UN Doc. A/HRC/4/99, *supra* note 17, at ¶ 6.

Although financial institutions do indeed fund the commercial activities that make up the global economy—and so can influence companies that are undermining human rights, or indeed be held vicariously liable for those risks—human rights issues in financial institutions should not be viewed as merely a subsidiary of abuses or violations that occur in front-line businesses in other sectors. This approach cannot address the fact that the global financial system and financial institutions are in practice a separate system that is much bigger than the underlying world economy, and that this system has profound and far-reaching human rights impacts of its own. Indeed, although many of the linkages are not yet well understood, it is plainly inconceivable that a system of the size and influence of modern finance—a system that is deeply integrated into the socioeconomic fabric of the world and can cause enormous damage—raises no direct human rights issues of its own. The evidence for this comprises the debris of not only the most recent financial crisis but a whole litany of crises that have occurred since markets globalized: the Latin American crisis of 2001 to 2003, the dot-com crisis in 2000, the Brazilian crisis in 1999, the Russian crisis in 1998, the Asian financial crisis of 1997 to 1998, the Mexican crisis of 1994 to 1995, the bond market crisis of 1994, the European exchange-rate mechanism crisis of 1992 to 1993, and the stock market crisis of 1987. All of these have had a significant impact on standards of living, social welfare, and government policies of varying duration, which can be tied to state obligations and company responsibilities under international human rights law. On reading the comprehensive wording of the UN Guiding Principles and comparing it to the human debris of the crisis in the financial markets that has been ongoing since 2007, it is difficult to conceive of only a very restrictive subsidiary responsibility of financial institutions for human rights impacts perpetrated by other companies. The responsibility to respect requires that financial institutions "avoid causing or contributing to adverse human rights impacts through their own activities, and address such impacts when they occur" (principle 13(a)). It is also difficult to accept that the broad-based impacts of crises or complex products that are difficult to shoehorn into the subsidiary model are somehow excluded from this framework, and hopefully the Guiding Principles will serve as the catalyst for a major reconsideration of the way human rights responsibilities are approached in financial institutions going forward.

Current Initiatives: An Overview

To highlight the limitations of current thinking about human rights accountability in the financial sector, three key areas at the forefront of the integration of respect for human rights into the activities of financial institutions will be reviewed: project finance, ethical investing, and corporate social responsibility.

Project Finance

Project finance has been at the forefront of the interpolation of human rights into the financial sector for the simple reason that major infrastructure and mining projects have caused untold and highly visible damage to the human rights and environment of the peoples and communities they affect. It is also an issue that straddles the operations of international financial institutions (the World Bank and IMF) and private financial institutions, and the huge amount of NGO attention on the former during the 1980s and 1990s helped force the issue.

The Equator Principles are a voluntary initiative developed under the auspices of the International Finance Corporation in coordination with four private-sector banks—ABN Amro, Barclays, Citi, and West LB—in 2002. They are a set of ten principles that provide a credit-risk management framework for controlling the environmental and social risks of project finance transactions, including human rights.[44] There are currently seventy-nine signatory institutions, known as the Equator Principles Financial Institutions (EPFIs) (seventy-seven are EPFIs, two are associate members).[45] They commit to ensuring, among other things, that borrowers have conducted an environmental and social impact assessment of the proposed project, which includes human rights risks;[46] that the assessment has been properly conducted in compliance with the IFC Performance Standards or equivalent and addresses any issues of compliance with host-country laws, regulations, and permits;[47] that affected communities have been consulted "in a structured and culturally appropriate manner" that ensures their free and informed participation;[48] that the borrower has established a grievance mechanism as part of the project's management;[49]

---

44. For a history of the principles and the principles themselves, *see About the Equator Principles*, EQUATOR PRINCIPLES, http://www.equator-principles.com/index.php/about (last visited April 24, 2013). The Principles were updated in 2006 and are currently in the process of another formal review. The updated Principles, designated Equator Principles III, are due to be adopted in 2013. For details, *see The Equator Principles III*, EQUATOR PRINCIPLES, http://www.equator-principles.com/index.php/ep3/about-ep3 (last visited April 24, 2013).

45. For a list of members, *see Members & Reporting*, EQUATOR PRINCIPLES, http://www.equator-principles.com/index.php/members-reporting (last visited April 24, 2013).

46. Principle 2 requires EPFIs to ensure: "For each project . . . the client [will] conduct a [Social and Environmental] Assessment . . . process to address, to the EPFI's satisfaction, the relevant environmental and social risks and impacts of the proposed Project."

47. Principle 3 requires: "For projects located in Non-Designated Countries . . . the Assessment process evaluates compliance with the then applicable IFC Performance Standards . . . and the (then applicable industry specific) World Bank Group Environmental, Health and Safety Guidelines. . . . The Assessment process will establish to the EPFI's satisfaction the Project's overall compliance with, or justified deviation from" these standards. Moreover, "the Assessment process . . . evaluates compliance with relevant host country laws, regulations and permits that pertain to environmental and social issues."

48. Principle 5 states: "For projects with potentially significant adverse impacts on Affected Communities, the process will ensure their free, prior and informed consultation and facilitate their informed participation as a means to establish, to the satisfaction of the EPFI, whether a project has adequately incorporate affected communities' concerns."

49. Principle 6 states: "This will allow [the borrower] to receive and facilitate resolution of concerns

and that an independent environmental and/or social expert is retained for the life of the project to monitor it.[50]

The Equator Principles encapsulate the concept of the subsidiarity of human rights risk in financial institutions in relation to front-line companies. In effect, EPFIs take on a watchdog function over borrower companies; their role is to monitor whether the company operating the project (to whom they have lent money specifically to fund the project) has appropriate safeguards in place to identify and address any environmental or human rights risks that the project raises—and project financing is tied to this criteria.[51] Although the Equator Principles have a high profile in development and human rights circles, and undoubtedly broke new ground in establishing the principle that financial institutions do bear some responsibility for the social, environmental, and human rights impacts of their financing decisions, they also highlight some of the limitations of the current piecemeal, soft-law approach to managing the human rights impacts of financial institutions in the context of complex and far-reaching global markets and financial institutions.

Aside from the fact that the principles make up a voluntary, unenforceable initiative that depends on the willingness and diligence of the lender in scrutinizing the performance of the borrower, a key limitation is the very narrow scope of their application in terms of the panoply of financial products. The framework for international banking regulation (the Basel Accords) defines project finance as

> a method of funding in which the lender looks primarily to the revenues generated by a single project both as a source of repayment and as security for the exposure. . . . In such transactions, the lender is usually paid solely or almost exclusively out of the money generated by contracts for the facility's output, such as the electricity sold by a power plant. The borrower is usually an SPE [special purpose entity] that is not permitted to perform any function other than developing, owning and operating the installation.[52]

---

and grievances about the project's environmental and social performance . . . raised by individuals or groups from among project-affected communities."

50. Principle 9 requires the "appointment of an Independent Environmental and Social Consultant, or [that the EPFI] require that the client retain qualified and experienced external experts to verify its monitoring information which would be shared with EPFI."

51. Principle 8 requires the inclusion of covenants in the loan agreements that provide scope to the lender to seek legal means of redress should the borrower breach the stipulations of the Principles.

52. Bank for International Settlements, Basel II: International Convergence of Capital Measurement and Capital Standards: A Revised Framework, at ¶¶ 221, 222 (June 2006). This revised version forms part of the documents that make up Basel III, see supra note 13. It is interesting to note that during 2002 when the Equator Principles were being drafted, three of the four banks involved (ABN Amro, Citigoup, and West LB) were simultaneously engaged in negotiating a discounted capital treatment for project finance loans under the new international capital adequacy framework with the Basel Committee on Banking Supervision. This was followed up by a study by BIS staff on the "peculiar nature of credit risk in project finance," which led to it being given lower capital treatment than had originally

This highly specific definition of project finance is also used by the Equator Principles.[53] When viewed from the vantage point of vast financial institutions, the limited scope of their operational application becomes immediately apparent.[54] The principles only apply to one very specific type of project funding and are therefore easily circumvented by the use of other types of financing. UBS, one of the world's systemically important, too big to fail banks, with assets of over U.S. $1.3 trillion,[55] is not a signatory of the Equator Principles because it does not have a project finance division. Though it may not directly fund projects using this precise format, it is inconceivable that a global financial institution with a balance sheet of that size does not maintain a whole range of commercial relationships with and exposures to companies that may be engaged in mining or infrastructure projects that raise human rights concerns. For example, a bank may have a traceable commercial relationship to a problem project through foreign exchange or derivatives transactions, by providing global commercial banking services to the company or its subsidiaries, or even through brokerage services to a hedge fund or private equity fund that may be a major investor in a controversial project. Currently, many of these types of funding relationships effectively fall between the cracks of disparate human rights initiatives, principles, and commitments that major banks have signed up for, and the market incentive for them to join the dots does not currently exist.

The Guiding Principles do create a normative framework within which this problem should be addressed; they stipulate that there needs to be a coherent approach to addressing human rights risk across business operations (principle 16, commentary) and that the responsibility to respect requires that businesses "seek to prevent or mitigate adverse human rights impacts that are linked to their operations, products or services by their business relationships, even if they have not contributed to those impacts" (principle 13 (b)). However, for this to happen it is likely to take a concerted push from human rights lawyers and stakeholders—including financial institution investors and bondholders; it is unlikely that the initiative will come from within financial institutions themselves in the absence of external pressure. This author was told by the head of CSR at one of the global, systemically important financial institutions that the Guiding Principles would

---

been envisaged. Benjamin Esty & Aldo Sesia Jr., *Basel II: Assessing the Default and Loss Characteristics of Project Finance Loans,* Harvard Business School, Publishing Case No. 203-035 (2003), http://papers .ssrn.com/sol3/papers.cfm?abstract_id=374800; Blaise Gadanecz & Marco Sorge, *The Term Structure of Credit Spreads in Project Finance,* Bank for International Settlements, Working Papers No. 159 (Aug. 2004), http://www.bis.org/publ/work159.pdf.

53.   *See* Equator Principles, The Equator Principles (June 2006), http://www.equator-principles .com/resources/equator_principles.pdf.

54.   There is nothing to stop EPFIs applying the Principles to other methods of funding projects as an aid to risk management, but in order for the loan to benefit from the reduced regulatory capital requirements under the Basel framework, the loan would have to comply with the stated definition.

55.   UBS, Annual Report 2012, at 6 (2012). Balance sheet size at December 31st, 2012, converted from CHF 1,259 billion.

merely cement the status quo because banks are under too much regulatory pressure on other fronts for them to have the appetite for much else.[56]

The Equator Principles are also easily circumvented by the sheer size of global financial markets. When a sector such as mining or infrastructure, or indeed the emerging markets as an asset class, are a flavor of the month for global investors, as they have been for most of the last decade, a very large number of global investors from asset managers to hedge funds, sovereign wealth funds, and private equity investors (of which only seventy-nine banks are party to the principles) will be looking for investment opportunities. This means a vast pool of global liquidity chasing opportunities in mining and infrastructure that they can access in a whole variety of ways. Where one Equator bank refuses to fund a problematic project, a long line of investors will be looking to take its place, or alternative financing structures could be used to secure funding for the project.

Vallares provides a case in point. In 2011, this shell company set up by Nathaniel Rothschild and Tony Hayward, former CEO of BP, raised £1.3 billion from investors in the space of a month to invest in oil and gas projects in emerging markets despite being "a newly formed entity with no operating history, no revenues and no basis on which to evaluate its ability to achieve its objectives."[57] This cash shell was designed to be used to reverse-engineer London listings of emerging market resource stocks with the aim of giving London investors better access to these stocks at a time of growing demand and to increase the stocks' value by overlaying London standards of corporate governance onto these companies. In reality, these ambitions descended into a long drawn-out feud among directors involving an Indonesian coal miner (Bumi Resources *plc*), where there were substantial allegations of irregularities and manifest governance failings, as has been documented in the financial press. Similarly, according to figures from the London Stock Exchange (LSE), mining companies listed on the LSE raised over U.S. $12 billion in initial public offerings and secondary offerings in 2011, and nearly U.S. $70 billion between 2000 and 2011.[58] This provides an example of one way of providing an ample source of project funding that does not fall within the ambit of the Equator Principles.

Moreover, the rise of the emerging markets over the last decade means that there are now emerging-market banks providing project finance that are beyond the reach of the principles, for example in China. Recent commentators have noted

---

56. Private discussion, April 2011.

57. Richard Lambert, *Lessons in Capitalism for the FTSE 100 Founders*, FIN. TIMES (June 28, 2011). The company became Genel Energy in November 2011 after it acquired an oil company operating in Kurdistan and Africa. *See* GENEL ENERGY (2012), www.genelenergy.com.

58. LONDON STOCK EXCHANGE, RAISING CAPITAL IN THE HEART OF THE WORLD'S FINANCIAL MARKETS FOR GLOBAL MINING COMPANIES 11 (June 2012), http://www.global-mining-finance.com/preciousmetals/presentations2012/LSE.pdf.

Though they are just as welcome to join the Equator Principles as their Australian, European and U.S. counterparts, China's commercial banks are different creatures from the privately-owned, profit-driven banks for which the Principles were designed. This is a serious matter, and one that is certain to figure large in the next 10 years of the life of the Equator Principles.[59]

In these circumstances, the practical limits of the Equator Principles must be recognized. What they do, they do well, but "they are unenforceable, do not themselves prevent corporate malpractice, and do not cover other sources from which project finance is raised (not least form a corporation's own cash reserves)."[60] Addressing human rights risks embedded in project finance transactions is just one step toward addressing and mitigating the whole range of human rights risks that can be raised by the operations of financial institutions, particularly LCFIs with balance sheets and exposures in the trillions of dollars.

Ethical Investing

The embedding of human rights principles into asset management has similarly been driven by voluntary stakeholder initiatives like the UN Principles for Responsible Investment[61] (UNPRI) and the UN Environment Programme Finance Initiative[62] (UNEPFI) and by demand from investors for ethical products. Regulatory and/or legal measures have not, on the whole, driven this process. Such voluntary codes of principle provide another example of subsidiarity—that is, approaching human rights risk in the financial sector as a derivative of the risks in other corporate sectors. The starting point is again the assumption that asset managers may come into contact with human rights risk through their investments in companies with poor human rights records. Through their ownership of assets (equity), they become complicit in the harmful practices of those companies, and they can provide an important lever of influence in fostering ethical behavior in corporations. This is an idea encapsulated by a statement from the Norwegian Ministry of Finance in relation to the government pension fund:

> The Fund is managed according to a set of Ethical Guidelines. Through the guidelines and the mechanisms under the guidelines, we signal expectations towards companies in the portfolio to respect and uphold widely shared fundamental ethical norms, such as human rights, in the conduct of their operations.[63]

---

59. Fiona Cunningham & David Kinley: *The Trinity and the Dragon: Reconciling Finance, Human Rights and the Environment in China*, 3 J. HUM. RTS. & ENV'T 116, 118 (2012).

60. DAVID KINLEY, CIVILISING GLOBALIZATION 172–73 (2009).

61. PRINCIPLES FOR RESPONSIBLE INVESTMENT, www.unpri.org (last visited April 24, 2013).

62. UNEP FINANCE INITIATIVE, www.unepfi.org (last visited April 24, 2013).

63. UNEP FINANCE INITIATIVE, FIDUCIARY RESPONSIBILITY: LEGAL AND PRACTICAL ASPECTS OF

So far this approach has not been followed up by looking at the whole suite of financial products that asset managers invest in from a human rights perspective or by efforts to look at whether there are any direct human rights issues raised by the fund management industry itself (for example, the way that fund managers can exacerbate financial instability and economic crisis by selling into falling markets, or the way they may affect human rights enjoyment by piling into favored asset classes). Similarly, ethical investing initiatives tend to target only a particular sector of the fund management business: mainstream asset managers and pension funds. Other vehicles, such as hedge funds, private equity, insurance, and exchange traded funds are largely, if not entirely, off the radar.

Human rights commitments are generally combined with other ethical criteria in socially responsible investing (SRI) or environmental, social, and governance (ESG)[64] codes and initiatives that encourage institutional investors to overlay human rights criteria and due diligence onto the research and stock selection process. This integration of human rights into standard business processes, it is hoped, will both foster better attention to human rights issues in underlying companies—by showing that any human rights risks affecting the company will be taken into account by institutional investors in deciding to buy or sell their stock—and prevent fund managers from benefiting from a company that is violating human rights. A report from the Danish Institute for Human Rights noted that socially responsible investment and/or the use of ESG criteria in investment decision-making

> distinguishes itself from mainstream investment by the importance it places on linking capital provision and finance to long-term sustainable social and environmental goals. . . . An important assumption sustaining SRI is that financial instruments are intrinsically—albeit indirectly—connected to society and the environment, and that they have the potential to positively or negatively impact sustainable development outcomes.[65]

The sensitivity of companies to their share price and reputation in the investment community are thus key incentives for them to manage their exposures to any human rights

---

Integrating Environmental, Social and Governance Issues into Institutional Investment 7 (July 2009), http://www.unepfi.org/fileadmin/documents/fiduciaryII.pdf.

    64. It is difficult to find a precise definition of these terms and a list of the factors that they include, although the "social" factors generally encompass human rights. According to one commentator, ESG "focuses on the economic implications of long-term risks and opportunities that are associated with strategies of the companies in which investments are made," while SRI is more generic, covering "any type of investment process that combines investors' financial objectives with their concerns about ESG." Lars Hassel, *How is ESG Integration Effective?*, PRI Digest (Feb. 2011), www.academic.unpri.org/index.php?option=com_content&view=article&id=276:editorial-by-lars-hassel-february-2011&catid=49&Itemid=10033.

    65. R. Roca & F. Manta, Values Added, *supra* note 42, at 11.

issues and SRI/ESG issues. Ethical investing is again a way of using the financial system to foster better behavior in frontline companies.

A core foundation of ethical investing initiatives has been efforts to challenge narrow interpretations of the fiduciary duty of fund managers, which had been interpreted as preventing them from actively taking note of human rights concerns. A leading report on the issue by the UNEPFI noted that "those seeking a greater regard for ESG issues in investment decision-making often encounter resistance on the basis of a belief that institutional principals and their agents are legally prevented from taking account of such issues."[66]

A cross-country study of corporate law undertaken by Professor John Ruggie while UN Special Representative of the Secretary-General for transnational corporations and human rights found that in certain jurisdictions, corporate law prohibited institutional investors from considering human rights issues in their investment decisions because they were bound to act in the economic interests of the fund; that is, they were limited to maximizing return on assets under management, rather than venturing out into consideration of what were then deemed social issues ancillary to their mandate.[67] Stakeholder initiatives such as those listed above have been instrumental in challenging this viewpoint by promoting acceptance of human rights as a material issue. Two landmark reports prepared for the UNEPFI set out a multijurisdictional analysis that established the materiality of human rights and ESG considerations in the management of assets, "[i]n our view, decision-makers are required to have regard (at some level) to ESG considerations in every decision they make. This is because there is a body of credible evidence demonstrating that such considerations often have a role to play in the proper analysis of investment *value*."[68]

Arguments that human rights are material to the issue of value have been central to the drive for their inclusion in ethical investing, both to avoid limiting interpretations of fiduciary duty and to establish them as credible issues for fund managers to engage with in the stock selection process.[69] The limitations of this approach from the vantage point of financial services (rather than from the legal perspective) are immediately apparent. First, many such arguments are of necessity premised on the longer-term time horizons required to capture the benefits of sustainability and managing human

---

66. UNEP FINANCE INITIATIVE, ASSET MANAGEMENT WORKING GROUP, A LEGAL FRAMEWORK FOR THE INTEGRATION OF ENVIRONMENTAL, SOCIAL AND GOVERNANCE ISSUES INTO INSTITUTIONAL INVESTMENT 6 (October 2005).

67. UN Special Representative of the Secretary-General, *Human Rights and Corporate Law: Trends and Observations from a Cross-National Study Conducted by the Special Representative*, add. 2, UN Doc. A/HRC/17/31/Add.2 (May 23, 2011).

68. A LEGAL FRAMEWORK, *supra* note 66, at 10–11. This was followed up by the UNEPFI's FIDUCIARY RESPONSIBILITY, *supra* note 63.

69. The report from the Danish Institute, for example, sets out to challenge the perception that "social issues are little understood, and are hard to quantify, and thus suffer the fate of being labelled as not only intangible, but also as not-material, and thus marginally relevant or irrelevant to the valuation process." R. ROCA & F. MANTA, VALUES ADDED, *supra* note 42, at 12.

rights risks (up to ten years).[70] For example, the UN Global Compact's *Who Cares Wins* report of 2004 was one of the first to use the concept of ESG in relation to financial markets, and it set out to "better integrate environmental, social and corporate governance issues in asset management, securities brokerage services and associated research functions."[71] It argued that "the use of longer time horizons in investment is an important condition to better capture value creation mechanisms linked to ESG factors." It encouraged investors to "include longer time horizons in investment mandates."[72] In light of the recent financial crisis, the Global Compact has reiterated this position by stressing that "recent events in global financial markets underscore the importance of transparency, accountability, and a focus on long-term investment horizons over 'short termism.'"[73]

Similarly, the report of the Danish Institute for Human Rights focused specifically on "long-term investors" because

> a great deal of asset management is a long-term affair, and therefore asset managers have an interest in thorough research and analysis about the value of assets before they invest or provide credit to them. Mainstreaming extra-financial issues into all institutions has become a strategic aspect of data and investment research management, together with branding and reputation issues.[74]

This long-term investment focus has been described as the "holy grail"[75] of arguments for including human rights in investment analysis; that it will enable investors to achieve better returns because the human rights performance of a company can in the long run affect its share price. The Global Compact's *Who Cares Wins* report argued that "companies that perform better with regard to [ESG] issues can increase shareholder value by, for example, properly managing risks, anticipating regulatory action, or accessing new markets, while at the same time contributing to the sustainable development of the societies in which they operate."[76]

---

70.   The UNEPFI, in Fiduciary Responsibility, goes into detail on the legal and practical issues involved in long-term investment strategy in order to include ESG criteria effectively into investment processes. UNEP Finance Initiative, *supra* note 63.

71.   The Global Compact, Who Cares Wins: Connecting Financial Markets to a Changing World, at i (2004).

72.   Who Cares Wins, *id.* at 5.

73.   *The UN Global Compact and Financial Markets*, UN Global Compact, http://www.unglobalcompact.org/issues/financial_markets/index.html (last visited Jan. 16, 2013).

74.   R. Roca & F. Manta, Values Added, *supra* note 42, at 18.

75.   Insight Investment, Effective Integration of ESG Issues Into Investment Decision-Making 2 (2009), www.insightinvestment.com/global/documents/riliterature/821056/Effective_integration.pdf.

76.   Who Cares Wins, *supra* note 71, at i.

Though such arguments are understandable from a legal perspective, from a broader financial perspective they appear to put the proverbial cart before the horse. The trend in equity trading and investment management has, in fact, been in the opposite direction over the last forty years, with shorter and shorter holding periods for stocks. The average holding period is now measured in months, not years. It is estimated to be just seven months in the United Kingdom and United States (that is, on average any given stock will only be owned continually for a seven-month period, though the fund may well buy and sell it many times), and for international equity markets, it is also typically less than one year.[77] Though much of the decline has been driven by the advancement of computer-driven trading,[78] the asset management business has also seen its holding periods decline. This phenomenon is called "portfolio turnover," and it is a hidden cost to investors that benefits fund managers through generating extra commissions. Some funds can have an annual turnover rate of equity holdings as high as 500 percent, meaning that they buy and sell their entire portfolio five times during the year.[79] Moreover, under the European Union's Undertakings for Collective Investment in Transferable Securities (UCITS) IV directive, which came into force in July 2011, institutional investors no longer have to disclose their turnover rate to investors, so it can actually be invisible.[80]

Second, there are many factors that drive asset valuations in financial markets, and it is difficult in reality to sustain the argument that human rights practices are a substantial source of an equity's value. A significant and growing proportion of equity market activity is now computer driven and intensely short term, with holding periods of just a few seconds or even a few milliseconds. This type of market activity comes under various headings, including algorithmic trading, high-frequency trading, and high-velocity trading, and it is estimated to account for up to 70 percent of trading volume in U.S. equities, 30 to 40 percent

---

77.   Andrew Haldane, Executive Director for Financial Stability, Bank of England, Patience and Finance 16–17 (Sep. 2, 2010), http://www.bankofengland.co.uk/publications/speeches/2010/speech445 .pdf. The impact of "short-termism" on equity market performance and governance was the central focus of the Kay Review of the UK Markets, commission by the UK Department for Business, Innovation and Skills. *See* JOHN KAY, THE KAY REVIEW OF UK EQUITY MARKETS AND LONG-TERM DECISION MAKING (Final Report, July 2012), *www*.bis.gov.uk/kayreivew.

78.   The market uncertainty and volatility this can generate is an increasing source of concern for regulators. *See* Andrew Haldane, Executive Director for Financial Stability, Bank of England, *The Race to Zero* (July 8, 2011), http://www.bankofengland.co.uk/publications/Documents/speeches/2011/speech509 .pdf.

79.   Alice Ross, *The Hidden Costs of Portfolio Turnover*, FIN. TIMES (Apr. 1, 2011). *See also* IRRC INSTITUTE, INVESTMENT HORIZONS: DO MANAGERS DO WHAT THEY SAY? (Feb. 2010), http://www .irrcinstitute.org/pdf/IRRCMercerInvestmentHorizonsReport_Feb2010.pdf; Ed Moisson, *Are Marathon Runners Trying to Sprint?* in LIPPER EMEA RESEARCH INSIGHTS 25–26 (2012), http://funds.uk.reuters .com/UK/pdf.asp?language=UNK&dockey=1523-4337-0UF62R7S60HJ2T3GH4V9AI4JVA.

80.   Council Directive 2009/65/EC, 2009 O.J. (L302) 32 (EU); Commission Regulation 583/2010, of July 1, 2010, Implementing Directive 2009/65/EC of the European Parliament and of the Council as Regards Key Investor Information and Conditions to Be Met When Providing Key Investor Information or the Prospectus in a Durable Medium Other Than Paper or by Means of a Web site, 2010 O.J. (L176) 1 (EU).

of volume in Europe, and 5 to 10 percent of equity trading volume in Asia.[81] The hedging of various derivatives products through purchasing and holding shares (for example, a covered warrant on a particular stock will be hedged by the issuer through purchasing some of the stock to cover the exposure) also accounts for another sizeable chunk of market activity, as does so-called technical trading, whereby traders use a system of complex charts that identify patterns in markets. Exchange traded funds (ETFs) and index tracking products also account for another chunk of market activity. Taken together, price dynamics in the equity markets are driven by many different forces and do not heavily reflect the long-term sustainability performance of a company. In practice, this factor is of little relevance to many trading decisions in today's computer-driven, high-speed markets.

It is also worth noting that the UK's FTSE100 index—which contains some of the largest and highest-profile companies in the world, many of which have led the way in adopting detailed human rights policies—is, at the time of writing, barely back to the level it stood at twelve years ago and has been through two substantial bear markets in that period that wiped billions of pounds off its value. In the United States, the Dow Jones Industrial Average has also been through two major bear markets in this period, although it is currently higher than it was twelve years ago. In contrast, the Mexican stock market has posted a return of over 500 percent in the same period, and the Russian stock market is up over 600 percent.[82] One may surmise that the human rights policies and records of London- or U.S.-listed companies are (or should be) on the whole more robust than those of Mexico or Russia, showing that the value arguments for human rights–based investing decisions are not as weighty as proponents would hope. They are relevant, but broader market reality is that they are far less relevant than market dynamics—a reality that would limit their appeal to fund managers as a tool for stock selection. They seem to be drawn from an ardent desire to see human rights issues more visibly respected in corporate practice rather than from an understanding of equity market dynamics.

For those fund managers already deeply committed to sustainability, the logic of long-term value linked to human rights sells itself, but for the broader fund-management or investing community, the arguments around long-term valuation must surely play a subsidiary role alongside much more pressing considerations. It is thus to be wondered just how important the long-term considerations are for asset managers, whether in the initial selection of a stock or in reviewing that company's performance. Are they really an

---

81. Andrew Haldane, *Patience and Finance, supra* note 77, at 17. The U.S. Securities and Exchange Commission has undertaken an enquiry into the impact of electronic trading on equity market structure. *See* Mary Shapiro, SEC Chairman, *Strengthening Our Equity Market Structure* (Sept. 7, 2010), *available at* http://www.sec.gov/news/speech/2010/spch090710mls.htm; U.S. Securities and Exchange Commission, *Roundtable on Technology and Trading: Promoting Stability in Today's Markets* (Oct. 2, 2012), http://www.sec.gov/news/otherwebcasts/2012/ttr100212-transcript.pdf.

82. Data from TRADING ECONOMICS (2013), www.tradingeconomics.com (last visited April 24, 2013).

important factor in stock selection, or are they a compliance issue? And do they feature in decision-making for active trading?

Once investors have bought a stock, it also appears that in practice, most investors are reluctant to engage forcefully with companies on human rights issues when problems do arise. As the head of responsible investment at one asset manager has argued,

> there are, at present, few incentives anywhere in the investment system for investors to engage proactively with companies in which they are invested. This is a well-recognized problem. . . . The transaction costs of taking action and the reality that the benefits are difficult to measure and accrue to the investment industry as a whole (rather than to the individual investor) limit the level of willingness and interest . . . to commit significant resources to this.[83]

Key reasons for this, he argues, are skepticism about the investment benefits of focusing on human rights; the perception that being an activist on human rights issues may hurt the fund's performance relative to that of its peers; lack of pressure from clients, stakeholders, or industry peers; an unwillingness to take a leadership position on something that is perceived as ancillary to their main mandate; and a perception that focusing on these issues may result in additional costs.[84]

The interpretation of what is and is not a human rights risk can, in any case, be subject to divergent viewpoints and is a matter of ongoing controversy, particularly in relation to socioeconomic rights, which are deeply entwined with issues of economic policy and national economic sovereignty. The long-running arguments over whether cheap labor and a lack of labor rights constitute a competitive advantage are very familiar.[85] Similarly, a mining project that concerns human rights advocates due to its disruption of traditional livelihoods and potential environmental impact can be presented by a company as a creator of employment and generator of tax revenue for government, which can in turn be used to provide social services essential to human rights realization. Generally phrased commitments to human rights can in reality mean different things to different stakeholders, and undertaking such commitments can often signal the beginning, not the end, of the arguments for fund managers. Fund managers are, in general, not well placed and lack

---

83.   Rory Sullivan & Nicolas Hachez, *Human Rights Norms for Business: The Missing Piece of the Ruggie Jigsaw—The Case of Institutional Investors*, in THE UN GUIDING PRINCIPLES ON BUSINESS AND HUMAN RIGHTS 217, 239 (R. Mares ed., 2012) *supra* note 7. Rory Sullivan was Co-Chair of the UNEPFI human rights workstream and is head of Investor Responsibility at Insight Investments.

84.   R. Sullivan & N. Hachez, *supra* note 83, at 239–40.

85.   Gary Chartier, *Sweatshops, Labor Rights, and Competitive Advantage*, 10 OREGON REV. OF INT'L LAW 149 (2008); Jehangir Pocha, *The Last "Competitive Advantage": Letter from China*, YALE GLOBAL ONLINE (2007), http://yaleglobal.yale.edu/content/last-competitive-advantage-letter-china.

the training necessary to navigate human rights arguments.[86] Indeed, there is no overall clarity on what SRI means.

> No consensus on a unified definition of SRI exists within Europe, regardless of whether that definition focuses on the processes used, societal outcomes sought or the depth and quality of ESG analysis applied. For investors, in particular retail investors, this represents a challenge to understanding the various product offerings. For providers (asset managers), this also represents a challenge as different national markets may require various product strategies to be deployed depending on local investor preferences.[87]

In the absence of such clarity, it is arguably easy for many institutional investors to adhere to rather vague principles of high purpose without significant will to push a strong vision of human rights onto their investment agenda.[88] It is difficult to see how the UNPRI, for example, would significantly affect the strategic allocation of funds in any fundamental way because they are more likely to affect investment relations with a particular company (Would they change the decisions a fund manager would make in their absence?). This may not even be the objective of the principles. Even when there are very visible human rights issues affecting a company, the principles merely encourage engagement but not divestment; "[t]he Principles are designed for large investors that are highly diversified and have large stakes in companies, often making divestment or avoidance impractical."[89] In any case, this position assumes that fund managers can be an effective force for human rights realization and fails to reflect the well-documented problems with agency capitalism.

> With money managers needing to preserve their jobs through providing satisfactory investment performance quarter by quarter, they certainly [aren't] likely to endanger their positions through sticking their neck out in opposition to a powerful corporate management. Separating themselves from the herd and confronting corporate big

---

86. Sullivan and Hachez write: "The creation of an agreed normative framework would also help bypass some of the problems presented by the general lack of knowledge about human rights issues in the investment world. It is likely that investors would articulate their expectations of companies by reference to 'compliance with' the framework." R. Sullivan & N. Hachez, *supra* note 83, at 239.

87. Eurosif, European SRI Study 2012, at 7 (2012), http://www.eurosif.org/research/eurosif-sri-study/sri-study-2012.

88. The UNPRI, for example, is in reality just six short principles that commit signatories to, *inter alia*, "incorporate ESG issues into investment analysis" and "seek appropriate disclosure on ESG issues by the entities in which we invest." *The Six Principles*, Principles for Responsible Investment, www.unpri.org/principles/ (Principles 1 & 3) (last visited April 24, 2013).

89. *FAQs*, Principles for Responsible Investment, www.unpri.org/faqs (last visited April 24, 2013).

shots, when in any case they [speak] for only perhaps 5% of the company's stock, [goes] entirely against [their] instincts.[90]

Whether most investors would compromise on returns for the sake of a strong stand on human rights principles is a moot point.

Third, this approach continues the notion of an indirect relationship between financial products and processes and human rights—that is, asset managers are relevant to human rights via the interface of the companies they invest in, rather than directly through their own actions. This approach lets them somewhat off the hook because it fails to look at how the market dynamics fueled by the activities of the global fund management industry may themselves impact human rights. As the wreckage of the subprime crisis so clearly attests, human rights outcomes are profoundly and directly influenced by financial processes and complex financial activity, as the U.S. housing market was by Wall Street demand for mortgages to securitize, and as human rights globally were by the collapse in financial markets. Although the Danish Institute report sets out to "integrate human rights into the financial sector," it really only focuses on identifying "how social risk, particularly human rights risk, can be translated into a format that is digestible to financial analysts,"[91] which is in practice a much more limited objective. As the report openly acknowledges, most of the vast universe of financial products was deliberately left off the table.

> Actors and assets such as *hedge funds, brokerage houses, insurance, derivatives, private equity and variable income investments* have proved difficult to include in the present analysis. Hedge funds involve a great deal of short-term products, and the actors and the assets are not compatible with long-term only thinking. Structured finance, built on a series of complex intermediate operations linking one asset to multiple others, to future dividends, or to funds of funds, makes it difficult to create a feasible methodology that includes social concerns, considered not to be significant to valuation. The high frequency of transactions and the volatility of these assets also make long-term thinking irrelevant. Moreover, it is a considerable challenge to track financial operations and movements of capital which may span several territorial sites and pass through various financial entities, especially considering operations with private equity.[92]

Effectively, then, this approach typifies conventional thinking about the relationship between finance and human rights, and it leaves out of the analysis most activity that

---

90. KEVIN DOWD & MARTIN HUTCHINSON, ALCHEMISTS OF LOSS: HOW MODERN FINANCE AND GOVERNMENT INTERVENTION CRASHED THE FINANCIAL SYSTEM 400 (2010).

91. R. ROCA & F. MANTA, VALUES ADDED, *supra* note 42, at 5 & report title.

92. R. ROCA & F. MANTA, VALUES ADDED, *supra* note 42, at 19. This typifies the approach that has been taken so far by the human rights community to financial institutions.

takes place on a daily basis inside financial institutions, particularly large financial institutions. The methodology is designed such that these activities cannot be factored in. Even mainstream asset managers will have holdings of derivatives and structured products, for example, and it seems anachronistic to limit their human rights responsibilities solely to their long-only equity holdings. Although this position is perhaps understandable, given that long-only equities are much easier to understand for nonspecialists in finance like human rights lawyers, this approach very narrowly circumscribes the application of human rights to finance. Arguably, the methodology is backward insofar as it posits that those areas amenable to existing human rights methodology will be covered but the rest will not be. It is human rights led, rather than starting from the reality of financial markets themselves and then working to tie them broadly to human rights.

In fact, institutional investors control an enormous amount of funds that can exacerbate the destabilization of markets once they start selling in droves into falling markets. According to recent figures, conventional asset managers control some U.S. $84.1 trillion of assets—more than world GDP. Pension assets accounted for U.S. $33 trillion of the total. When the assets held in alternative vehicles are included—such as sovereign wealth funds, hedge funds, private equity funds, exchange-traded funds, and funds of wealthy individuals—assets of the global fund management industry total around U.S. $120 trillion.[93] The Financial Crisis Inquiry Commission noted some of the effects these asset managers can have on markets and living standards.

> The performance of the stock market in the wake of the crisis . . . reduced wealth. The Standard and Poor's 500 Index fell by a third in 2008—the largest single year decline since 1974—as big institutional investors moved to Treasury securities and other investments that they perceived as safe. Individuals felt these effects not only in their current budgets but also in their prospects for retirement. By one calculation, assets in retirement accounts such as 401(k)s lost $2.8 trillion, or about a third of their value, between September 2007 and December 2008.[94]

Public pension plans were also severely impacted.

> In Colorado, state budget officials warned that losses of $11 billion, unaddressed, could cause the Public Employees Retirement Association plan—which covers 450,000 public workers and teachers—to go bust in two decades. The state cut retiree benefits to adjust for the losses. Montana's public pension fund lost $2 billion,

---

93.   TheCityUK, Fund Management Report 2012, at 1 (Nov. 2012); Press Release, TheCityUK, Global Funds Under Management Reach $84 Trillion (Nov. 13, 2012).
94.   Financial Crisis Inquiry Report, *supra* note 7, at 393.

or a fourth of their value, in the six months following the 2008 downturn, in part because of investments in complex Wall Street securities."[95]

Another potential human rights issue for the global fund management industry that is rarely mentioned in analysis is the effect of fees and charges on personal savings. Research by the Financial Times found that charges by pension fund managers can reduce the value of pensions by up to a third of their value because fees and commissions can take tens of thousands of pounds off the value of pension savings.[96] Undoubtedly, this has a significant impact on the right to an adequate standard of living in old age, but so far it has not attracted much attention from human rights lawyers.[97]

Viewed from this broader perspective, efforts to apply human rights to asset management via ethical investing initiatives are in practice quite narrowly focused, and they do not go far enough to embed human rights principles into the heart of the fund management industry. Under this approach, human rights are more of a high-level overlay than foundational principles of equity markets, and the weight given to them in the stock selection process probably has more to do with the discretion of the manager than any clear industry standard. Adding human rights to the responsibilities of the fund management industry is a persuasive proposition, and it has certainly raised the profile of human rights as issues relevant to finance, but it does not go very far in embedding human rights in the workings of gigantic world financial markets that periodically sweep away the world economy.

Corporate Social Responsibility

Most, if not all, major financial-services companies now have corporate social responsibility (CSR) teams and policies in place, which include publicly available human rights policies or statements setting out the organization's commitment to respecting international human rights. This is one of the key requirements of the Guiding Principles, which set out the expectation that business enterprises will have human rights policies approved at the most senior level as a cornerstone of their implementation of the responsibility to respect (principle 16). Most companies, particularly the large, complex financial institutions at the heart of the financial system, are very keen to demonstrate their credentials as global corporate citizens. Vikram Pandit, CEO of Citigroup, wrote in its 2011 Citizenship Report that "responsible finance is our focus—doing what's right for clients, for communities,

---

95. Financial Crisis Inquiry Report, *supra* note 7, at 393..
96. Josephine Cumbo, *Charges Cut Pension Income by a Third*, Fin. Times (Jan. 23, 2012).
97. The UK Government has looked at the issue and commissioned a report: Djuna Thurley, Business and Transport Section, Pension Scheme Charges, Standard Note SN 6209 (Dec. 19, 2012). The UK Pension Fund industry has also recently introduced a Code of Conduct to address the issue. National Association of Pension Funds, Pension Charges Made Clear (Nov. 2012). It is surprising that the issue has not been taken up as part of "sustainable finance" debates.

and for the financial system."[98] Human rights are a key part of this; Citigroup strives "to conduct [its] business in a manner that supports universal human rights."[99] JP Morgan Chase declares that it "supports fundamental principles of human rights across all our lines of business and in each region of the world in which we operate."[100] Goldman Sachs notes in its Statement on Human Rights, "[a]s a global financial institution, Goldman Sachs recognizes and takes seriously its responsibility to protect, preserve and promote human rights around the world. . . . Our respect for human rights is fundamental to and informs our business."[101] Barclays has a ten-page human rights statement, declaring that the "promotion of human rights through our business activities forms part of our broader objective to be a leader in corporate responsibility."[102] The UBS statement is more limited, setting out the UBS view that the role of private companies is to "support governments in implementing human rights," and that as part of this the company will endeavor to "promote and respect human rights standards within our sphere of influence."[103] Arguably, when your balance sheet is U.S. $1.3 trillion and spans global markets, you have a very wide sphere of influence,[104] and the UBS policy on human rights, which dates from 2006, is now somewhat outdated in light of the Guiding Principles. Businesses no longer simply play a subsidiary, supportive role for government implementation of their obligations but have their own clearly defined normative responsibilities in relation to internationally defined human rights standards.

On reading these human rights commitments and the corporate responsibility sections of major banks' Web sites and annual reports, it is easy to form a very rosy view of the banking sector's efforts to contribute positively to the human rights situation around the world and to assume that the sector is already doing much of what the Guiding Principles require. These comprehensive-sounding, voluntary statements of human rights principles and the commitment of CSR teams, which appear to be backed up by a significant

---

98. Citigroup, 2011 Global Citizenship Report 2 (2011), http://citigroup.com/citi/about/data/2011citizenship_report.pdf.

99. *Statement on Human Rights*, Citigroup (Aug. 2009), www.citigroup.com/citi/citizen/humanrights/index.htm.

100. *Corporate Responsbility: Human Rights*, JPMorgan Chase & Co, www.jpmorganchase.com/corporate/Corporate-Responsibility/human-rights.htm (last visited April 24, 2013).

101. *Statement on Human Rights*, Goldman Sachs, http://www.goldmansachs.com/investor-relations/corporate-governance/corporate-governance-documents/human-rights-statement.pdf.

102. Barclays Group, Statement on Human Rights 3 (June 2006), http://group.barclays.com/about-barclays/citizenship/policy-positions (last visited December 6, 2013).

103. *UBS Statement on Human Rights*, UBS (Mar. 14, 2013), http://www.ubs.com/global/en/about_ubs/corporate_responsibility/commitment_strategy/policies_guidelines/human_rights.html.

104. UBS, *supra* note 55. The statement does try to limit the meaning of the sphere of influence by declaring that UBS acts in accordance with human rights principles vis-a-vis its employees, that its influence with suppliers is more limited, and that "our influence with our clients is limited". Since this statement was drafted in 2006, it is now somewhat outdated given the endorsement of the *UN Guiding Principles on Business and Human Rights* and their provisions on the business responsibility to respect human rights. *See supra* note 14.

investment of corporate resources, could at first glance imply that such commitments are deeply engrained in the whole ethos of these banks, forming overarching principles of their business alongside such mainstream issues as risk appetite, quarterly returns, and corporate governance.

The difficulty, however, is that no matter how genuine these commitments are, without a developed methodology or framework to enable human rights commitments to be meaningfully applied across the complex operations of vast financial institutions, their practical operational impact is very limited. This omission is clearly evidenced by the details of the main functional areas in which these human rights commitments are applied by these banks: employee rights, including equality and diversity; financial services in areas where human rights issues are well known (such as project finance, corruption, know-your-customer legislation); supply chains (for example, responsible sourcing of products); community engagement and involvement (such as supporting charitable initiatives and affordable banking); and microfinance.[105] Citigroup reported that in 2011 it completed thirteen transactions "where our Human Rights Statement was relevant or invoked." Of these, five transactions related to resettlement, four to indigenous rights, three to security risks, and two to labor risks.[106] Although this level of transparency is admirable, it is remarkable that the Human Rights Statement was only deemed relevant to thirteen transactions across a bank with 200 million client accounts, 280,000 employees, and operations in 140 countries.

These all-encompassing statements of commitment to human rights principles should therefore be read with a far more limited frame of application in mind. Human rights have in practice been accepted as directly relevant to only a very small part of these banks' operations. Partly this is in response to human rights campaigns that have targeted these types of issues. Beyond this, there have been very few efforts on either side to untangle the complex web of interactions that link financial institutions' many types of activities to human rights enjoyment via the interface of globally integrated markets.[107] This is not necessarily only the fault of the banks themselves, given that the human rights community has also shown little interest in tackling this challenge. Banks can be forgiven for basing their understanding of human rights expectations of them on the body of work that has been done so far to clarify the human rights–financial institutions interface. And yet the Guiding Principles lay down the challenge of extending the reach of human rights within financial institutions. Principle 16 is clear that a human rights policy should be

---

105. *See, e.g.*, BARCLAYS GROUP STATEMENT ON HUMAN RIGHTS, *supra* 102. Goldman Sachs human rights commitment appears to be limited to employee issues.

106. CITIGROUP, 2011 GLOBAL CITIZENSHIP REPORT, *supra* note 98, at 48.

107. M. Dowell-Jones & D. Kinley, *Minding the Gap: Global Finance and Human Rights*, *supra* note 37.

"reflected in operational policies and procedures necessary to embed it throughout the business enterprise."

As with commitments to ethical investing, it is reasonably straightforward for banks with complex operations to make such heroic statements on human rights knowing that in practice they only require reasonably unobtrusive changes from an operational point of view—changes that will not be too costly. Human rights commitments may require more gender diversity or employees giving time to charitable causes, but currently they do not apply, for example, to key operational issues such as the size of the capital or liquidity buffers they need to hold to insulate the financial markets and human rights from the consequences of excessive risk taking in heavily leveraged financial institutions, the way risk is managed on portfolios of credit derivatives, or the way commodity derivatives are traded. Despite all the lobbying that has been going on since the crisis over the revisions to financial regulation and the capital adequacy requirements set out in the international framework for bank regulation (Basel III),[108] banks' voluntary undertakings to support and respect human rights across their operations have not been referred to by major banking groups—despite the clear link between systemic risk, financial crisis, banking operations, and global human rights enjoyment evidenced by the crisis. (It should be remembered that the Guiding Principles are clear that human rights duties and responsibilities are also relevant to the legal and regulatory architecture of business sectors, and the way this enables business enterprises to respect human rights—Principles 1 through 3, and 10). Similarly, during the run-up to the crisis, it has become clear that internal human rights policies may have applied to the provision of low-cost banking services to poor areas, but they did not apply if the bank was selling those same customers mortgages that they could not afford so the bank could package those mortgages into credit derivatives.[109] In light of the Guiding Principles' specification that human rights responsibilities apply across business operations, that businesses need to strive for coherence between "their responsibility to respect human rights and policies and procedures that govern their wider business activities and relationships" (Principle 16, commentary), and that human rights due diligence should "go beyond simply identifying and managing material risks to the company itself, to include risks to rights-holders" (Principle 17, commentary), these technical distinctions

---

108. BANK FOR INT'L SETTLEMENTS, *supra* note 13.

109. This was made manifestly clear by the account of the dealings inside the financial sector and their efforts to game the U.S. regulatory structure in the years leading up to 2007 in the FINANCIAL CRISIS INQUIRY REPORT, *supra* note 7. Another revealing document is UBS, SHAREHOLDER REPORT ON UBS's WRITE-DOWNS (2008), https://www.ubs.com/global/en/about_ubs/investor_relations/share_information/shareholderreport.html. (This details how the bank built up billions of dollars worth of credit derivatives positions linked to the U.S. housing market without conducting any due diligence on the actual state of the borrowers. Mathematical risk models were used instead and certainly none of the human rights of those affected were considered during the build up to the crisis).

in financial institutions' understanding of their human rights responsibilities arguably need to be reviewed and revised.

It is also worth noting that the banks listed at the outset of this section are all systemically important, too big to fail institutions whose malfunctioning can cause the financial system to collapse and whose bailouts imposed very heavy financial burdens on the public sector during the crisis of 2008 to 2009. Despite this, it has proven difficult to link any formal corporate responsibility for the social outcomes of the crisis generated by the banks'—and other financial institutions'—activities to them individually or to their human rights commitments. Despite their unique position at the heart of the global financial system, there has been no discussion of whether their human rights responsibilities under the Guiding Principles are more onerous than those for less systemically important financial institutions. This is nevertheless a discussion that needs to happen given the privilege conferred on big banks by their implicit taxpayer guarantee (which lowers their cost of funding), the impact on states' ability to comply with their own human rights obligations when they have had to bail out financial institutions, and the ability that systemically important financial institutions' size gives them to magnify risks to human rights in the financial markets.[110] Currently, it is difficult to link these issues by suggesting that LCFIs should have a higher level of human rights responsibility and due diligence than smaller, less systemically important financial institutions; but in light of the events of 2008 to 2009, it is clear that human rights policies in the financial sector should go deeper than they currently do.

Viewed from this angle, human rights in the financial sector are not only about the customer relationships and the exposure to human rights risks these relationships may create but also about intrinsic human rights risks embedded in balance sheets and operational strategies, and the way these impact global markets and the livelihoods of people worldwide. In light of the enormous human damage done by the crisis, it is quite surprising how limited a view of human rights still persists in the financial sector. The danger is that unless this is challenged, the opportunity offered by the Guiding Principles to improve the ethical performance of the sector will be lost because the current *acquis* may become synonymous with compliance with the principles. But the question remains whether efforts to tie human rights to the broader operations of financial institutions would prove productive. Could human rights standards, and efforts to elaborate the broader dimensions of the corporate responsibility to respect human rights, enrich debates on the regulatory architecture and internal governance of financial institutions, or are such issues too technical to be meaningfully addressed by the human rights architecture? The work of

---

110. M. Dowell-Jones & D. Kinley, *The Monster Under the Bed: Financial Services and the Ruggie Framework, supra* note 7.

scholars and legal practitioners in this area will be critical in the years ahead in defining the operational boundaries of the Guiding Principles.

Ultimately, the adoption of voluntary human rights policies by banking groups and commitments to support the Guiding Principles are a positive step forward because at the very least they establish a common acceptance that human rights are relevant to their business. Where these policies fail is in their very limited operational reach and voluntary nature, which means that banks can choose what to apply them to, and the significant diversity that currently exists in the statements and operational areas to which they apply. Whether the law could or should fill this gap is a tempting question, but at this stage it is the lack of a comprehensive template for understanding what human rights standards mean when applied across different product lines and processes within vast, complex banking (or other financial) organizations that requires dedicated scrutiny.

The *Vedanta* Case

Vedanta Resources brings together and illustrates some of the limitations of the existing piecemeal, soft law approach to embedding human rights into financial institutions that have been discussed above. It shows how even though initiatives in the project finance, ethical investing, and corporate social responsibility space now have high visibility and broad-based industry buy-in, they can fail the important test of operational relevance and be very easily circumvented by financial market reality.

Vedanta Resources is an Indian holding company that incorporates a host of mining and power generation operations, predominantly in India but also in Australia and Zambia. It is listed on the London Stock Exchange and has sufficient market capitalization to be included in the main FTSE100 index. From a human rights point of view, the company has been mired in controversy for many years. Criticism has centered around proposals to build a bauxite mine in an area of India called the Niyamgiri Hills, which is both an important ecological area and sacred to a local indigenous tribe, the Dongria Kondh. This ancient tribe enjoys special protection under Schedule V of the Constitution of India as a "primitive tribal group," and the project would significantly impact its way of life and livelihood, as well as the environment. The director of Survival International, an NGO that campaigns for indigenous rights, called this "undoubtedly the most controversial project in the world,"[111] and Amnesty International has also been vocal in highlighting the violations of human rights by the company in regard to this project.[112] The project has

---

111. Press Release, Survival International, Amnesty Slams Vedanta Resources (Feb. 11, 2010), http://www.survivalinternational.org/news/5546.

112. Amnesty International, Don't Mine Us Out of Existence: Bauxite Mine and Refinery Devastate Lives in India (2010). *See also* the campaign information on the BankTrack Web site:

been embroiled in long-running legal disputes in India dating back to 1997.[113] In 2008, the Indian government gave clearance for the project subject to conditions including full compliance with environmental laws and the protection of the rights of the indigenous tribe. However, Vedanta was found to be in violation of these conditions, and the Minister of the Environment canceled the clearance for the project in 2010.[114] In April 2013, the Indian Supreme Court upheld the rights of the Dongria Kondh by maintaining the ban on Vedanta mining the hills.[115]

In 2009, Survival International referred a complaint about the project to the UK National Contact Point (NCP) for the OECD Guidelines on Multinational Enterprises alleging systematic human rights abuses. The NCP upheld the complaint against Vedanta on the basis that it had failed "to engage [the Dongria Kondh] in adequate and timely consultation about the construction of the mine, or to use other mechanisms to assess the implications of its activities on the community such as an indigenous or human rights impact assessment."[116] As a result, the company was found to have failed to respect the rights of the Dongria Kondh in a manner consistent with India's international commitments under the International Covenant on Civil and Political Rights, the UN Convention on the Elimination of All Forms of Racial Discrimination, and the UN Declaration on the Rights of Indigenous People.[117] The UK NCP expressed particular disappointment that Vedanta refused to engage fully with the complaints process and submitted no evidence except a copy of its 2008 Sustainable Development Report.[118] The UK NCP recommended that Vedanta include a human and indigenous rights impact assessment in its project management process, directly echoing Equator Principle 2 (and Guiding Principle 19), and that Vedanta adopt "a human rights policy that is not merely aspirational but practically implemented" and applied throughout its company, subsidiaries, and supply chain[119] (echoing Guiding Principle 16). In the follow-up to the final statement, the NCP

Dodgy Deals: Bauxite Mine Niyamgiri Hills, BANKTRACK, http://www.banktrack.org/show/dodgydeals/bauxite_mine_niyamgiri_hills (last updated Aug 12, 2013).

113. *See* AMNESTY INTERNATIONAL, DON'T MINE US OUT OF EXISTENCE, *supra* note 112, at 9–16 for an overview.

114. N.C. SAXENA, ET AL., MINISTRY OF ENVIRONMENT & FORESTS, GOVERNMENT OF INDIA, REPORT OF THE FOUR MEMBER COMMITTEE FOR INVESTIGATION INTO THE PROPOSAL SUBMITTED BY THE ORISSA MINING COMPANY FOR BAUXITE MINING IN NIYAMGIRI 9 (2010), http://moef.nic.in/downloads/public-information/Saxena_Vedanta.pdf.

115. *Ban Upheld: Avatar Tribe "to Decide" Future of Vedanta Mine*, SURVIVAL INTERNATIONAL (Apr. 18, 2013), http://www.survivalinternational.org/news/9155. *See also* Survival International's resource page on the Dongria Kondh, *Tribes: The Dongria Kondh*, SURVIVAL INTERNATIONAL, http://www.survivalinternational.org/tribes/dongria (last visited Jan. 24, 2013).

116. Final Statement by the UK National Contact Point for the OECD Guidelines for Multinational Enterprises: Complaint from Survival International Against Vedanta Resources plc 1 (Sept. 25, 2009), Summary of Conclusions, *www*.bis.gov.uk/files/file53117.doc.

117. *Id.*

118. Final Statement, *supra* note 116, ¶¶ 16, 17.

119. Final Statement, *supra* note 116, ¶¶ 75, 78.

noted information from Survival International that Vedanta had not complied with the NCP's recommendations. However, as the OECD Guidelines are not legally binding, the NCP was limited to recommending that Vedanta and Survival International engage in dialogue to resolve the issue.[120]

In 2010, an enquiry committee appointed by the Indian Ministry of the Environment found the company to be in violation of several Indian laws, including the Forest Conservation Act, the Forest Rights Act, the Orissa Forest Act, and the Environmental Protection Act, and that under the circumstances to allow the project to go ahead would "shake the faith of tribal people in the laws of the land which may have serious consequences for the security and well being of the entire country."[121] Vedanta was accused of, among other things, "several deliberate attempts . . . to conceal information and falsify it in order to get the project approved"[122] and "making a mockery of the Environmental Protection Act."[123] The company was also found to be acting "in contempt of the orders of the highest authority in the country, the Honorable Supreme Court of India. This behavior is not surprising given the utter contempt with which this company has dealt with the laws of the land."[124]

Following this report, clearance for the project was withdrawn. The ministry noted that, among other things, the "blatant disregard" shown by Vedanta for the rights of the tribal people living in the area "is shocking."[125] However, as the report of the company's 2012 Annual General Meeting (AGM) shows, there continue to be significant concerns from a number of quarters about Vedanta's human rights impacts, not only in relation to the Niyamgiri Hills project but also at its other operations, which the company has largely, if not entirely, failed to address.[126]

The Disconnect

Despite all the very visible, lengthy human rights controversy attached to the project and indeed the broader company, Vedanta was able to raise significant amounts of financing and easily circumvent the strictures of the human rights and finance initiatives described in this chapter. First, even though recommendations by the UK NCP echoed provisions

---

120. Follow up to Final Statement by the UK National Contact Point for the OECD Guidelines for Multinational Enterprises (Mar. 12, 2010), http://www.bis.gov.uk/assets/biscore/business-sectors/docs/10-778-survival-international-against-vedanta-resources.pdf.

121. Report of the Four Member Committee for Investigation, *supra* note 114, at 9.

122. Report of the Four Member Committee for Investigation, *supra* note 114, at 76.

123. Report of the Four Member Committee for Investigation, *supra* note 114, at 76.

124. Report of the Four Member Committee for Investigation, *supra* note 114, at 82.

125. Ministry of Environment & Forests, Decision on Grant of Forest Clearance in Kalahandi and Rayagada Districts of Orissa for the Proposal Submitted by the Orissa Mining Corporation Ltd (OMC) for Bauxite Mining in Landjigarh Bauxite Mines Section VIII, 1 (Aug. 24 2010), http://moef.nic.in/downloads/public-information/Vedanta-24082010.pdf.

126. London Mining Network, Vedanta AGM Report (Aug. 28, 2012), http://londonminingnetwork.org/2012/08/vedanta-agm-report-2.

of the Equator Principles, project finance constraints were easily avoided. In light of the global commodities boom that had typified world markets for a decade, Vedanta had significant internal resources with which to finance the project. In the financial year 2010 to 2011, the company had revenues of U.S. $11.4 billion,[127] and in the six months to September 30, 2012, it had revenues of U.S. $7.5 billion.[128]

Banks and investors are always keen to lend to a company with a strong balance sheet, and Vedanta was able to raise a large amount of money through borrowing, including through banks that are members of the Equator Principles. Barclays, which was one of the four banks involved in developing the principles and is part of the steering group, even won awards for billion dollar Vedanta transactions; as lead manager of a U.S. $1.25 billion global bond (Best High Yield Bond, FinanceAsia Deal Awards 2008) and as a lead arranger of a U.S. $1 billion loan (Best Syndicated Loan, Asiamoney Regional Deal Awards 2008).[129] FinanceAsia commented on the bond issue.

In difficult markets, but catching the tailwind of a commodity price boom, UK-listed Vedanta launched the largest ever high-yield bond for an Asian corporate borrower. . . . The deal was coordinated by J.P. Morgan and Morgan Stanley with Barclays, Citi and Deutsche Bank joining them as bookrunners. . . . The issue attracted 150 orders worth $1.5 billion and nearly 90% was placed with asset managers.[130]

All five banks shared the award for the Best High Yield Bond. Similarly, in 2009 J. P. Morgan launched a U.S. $1.25 billion convertible bond offering for the company. In 2010, J. P. Morgan, Goldman Sachs, Morgan Stanley, and UBS coordinated the launch of another U.S. $900 million convertible bond offering. In 2011, Barclays, Citi, Credit Suisse, RBS, and Standard Chartered coordinated the launch of U.S. $1.65 billion worth of bonds, with Goldman Sachs, J. P. Morgan, and Morgan Stanley joining as bookrunners.[131] This 2011 transaction won industry awards for Best High Yield Bond, and FinanceAsia also awarded the syndicate of banks the award for Best Leveraged Finance Deal for arranging

---

127. VEDANTA RESOURCES PLC, ANNUAL REPORT 2011, KEY PERFORMANCE INDICATORS, http://ar2011 .vedantaresources.com/key-performance-indicators.html.

128. VEDANTA RESOURCES PLC: INTERIM RESULTS FOR THE SIX MONTHS ENDED 30TH SEPTEMBER 2012 (Nov. 7, 2012), http://www.vedantaresources.com/uploads/vedantafy2013interimresultsrelease_rns .pdf.

129. News Release, Barclays Capital, Asian Deals Win a Host of Awards (Jan. 23, 2009), *www*.barcap .com/About+Barclays+Capital/Press+Office/News+releases/News,1372,Asian+deals+win+a+host+of+aw ards.

130. *Id.*

131. For details of these transactions, see the prospectuses available on the company's investor relations page: *Investor Relations: Circulars and Prospectus*, VEDANTA, http://www.vedantaresources.com/ circulars-and-prospectus.aspx (last visted April 24, 2013).

U.S. \$6 billion of acquisition financing for Vedanta's purchase of Cairn India.[132] A cursory search of the 2011 Sustainability and Corporate Responsibility reports of all eight banks revealed not one mention of Vedanta, suggesting that sustainable finance and human rights due diligence are not seen as relevant to these types of transactions because they do not fall within the neat boundaries of "project finance lending" or other existing areas covered by human rights policies.[133]

Yet J.P. Morgan, Barclays, and Citi are all members of the Equator Principles and ethical investing initiatives, and all have high-sounding internal human rights policies in place. Morgan Stanley's human rights statement commits it to "conducting our business operations in ways that attempt to preserve, protect and promote the full range of human rights." It further notes that the Franchise Committee is empowered to review "potential transactions to assess . . . potential human rights issues that may warrant Morgan Stanley's further inquiry or engagement or require resolution before a potential transaction is consummated."[134] Clearly, these ethical statements were not enough to raise questions about these transactions. The Guiding Principles require nonetheless that a human rights policy statement "should be embedded from the top of the business enterprise through all its functions, which otherwise may act without awareness or regard for human rights" (Principle 16, commentary).

Given the frequent lack of joined up institutional thinking across enormous global financial institutions,[135] it is likely that people working in the bond origination and syndicated loan teams at these banks were only barely aware, if at all, of the human rights controversy surrounding Vedanta and their banks' own commitments to upholding human rights. Similarly, it is likely that the deals did not come before corporate social responsibility teams for scrutiny because they did not fall under accepted headings, such as project finance or ethical investing, where they can be benchmarked against external soft law initiatives. As has been highlighted above, the operational reach of in-house human rights policies has been defined in such a limited way that these deals would not automatically fall within their ambit and would most likely be deemed too remote from actual corporate human rights harm to trigger any human rights issues for the banks. So far, the paradigm of responsibility in the finance sector depends on an immediate and direct

---

132. Triple A Regional Deal Awards 2011, http://www.theasset.com/storage/awardpdf/2012/1325737642TheAssetTripleARegionalDealAwards2011Winners-part1.pdf; Finance Asia Achievement Awards 2011, http://www.financeasia.com/News/282850,ifinanceasiai-achievement-awards-2011.aspx/3.

133. RBS's link to the corporate social responsibility section of its corporate Web site leads to an error message..

134. Statement on Human Rights, Morgan Stanley (Nov. 2012), http://www.morganstanley.com/globalcitizen/pdf/human_rights_statement.pdf.

135. This is a well-documented failing that occurred in major banks in the run-up to the credit crisis, *see, e,g,* FINANCIAL CRISIS INQUIRY REPORT, *supra* note 7, at 260–65 for details of how it affected Citigroup in the summer and autumn of 2007.

causal relationship between financing decision and corporate human rights abuse, and transactions further down the chain (such as general funding of company activities or further acquisitions, rather than the project where human rights concerns are localized) have been beyond the net of responsibility. The Guiding Principles challenge the financial sector to rethink this approach.

Most likely, many of the asset managers who bought Vedanta's bonds also had human rights policies in place and/or were signatories to ethical investing initiatives, but none of these commitments appeared to hinder demand for these transactions. During the years of the controversy, several high-profile funds pulled their investments out of Vedanta stock because of the environmental and human rights issues highlighted, as well as a failure by Vedanta to effectively engage in meaningful dialogue over the issues with investors. The Church of England pension fund, the Norwegian government pension fund, the Joseph Rowntree Charitable Trust, and a Dutch Asset Manager, PGGM, all divested.[136] Although the share price did fall sharply during 2008 to 2009 and has subsequently underperformed its peers, the human rights controversy attached to Vedanta did not appear to completely decimate the company's market capitalization.[137]

This outcome is partly attributable to the vast global pool of liquidity that an FTSE 100 listing gives it access to, including the pool of passive investors who are well beyond the limits of ethical investing initiatives and indeed the Guiding Principles. For example, the listing means that Vedanta stock has to be held as a component of tracker products, including funds benchmarked against the FTSE 100, global mining stocks, India and/or emerging markets funds, and derivatives like exchange-traded funds. This position creates enormous demand for its equity, which effectively puts a floor under the share price, and also for its corporate bonds, irrespective of any human rights concerns. As one of the founders of the FTSE index has written,

[i]t never occurred to those of us who helped launch the FTSE 100 Index 27 years ago that one day it would be providing a cloak of respectability and lots of passive investors for companies that challenge the canons of corporate governance, such as Vedanta.[138]

---

136. Press Release, Church of England, Church of England Disinvest from Vedanta Resources plc (Feb. 5, 2010); Press Release, Norwegian Ministry of Finance, Metals and Mining Company Excluded from the Investment Universe of the Norwegian Government Pension Fund—Global (Nov. 6, 2007); Press Release, Joseph Rowntree Charitable Trust, Rowntree Sells £1.9m Vedanta Shares Over Human Rights (Feb. 18, 2010); Press Release, PGGM, PGGM Disinvests from Vedanta Resources (June 30, 2010).

137. *Cf., e.g.,* the five-year share price chart for Vedanta and Kazakhmys, another FTSE 100 listed mining company. Charts available at LONDON STOCK EXCHANGE (2013), www.londonstockexchange.com (last visited April 24, 2013).

138. R. Lambert, *supra* note 57.

Market dynamics, unfortunately, do not conform to the aspirations of those behind the value arguments for including human rights criteria in the stock selection process, nor do they neatly dovetail with the human rights policy/due diligence approach embedded in the Guiding Principles.

The case of Vedanta highlights the ethical leakage that occurs across financial entities—the fact that human rights commitments undertaken under one product heading do not transmit easily across departmental or product barriers—and the ease with which companies can circumvent or ignore human rights commitments embedded in soft law initiatives such as the Equator Principles or UNPRI. Such initiatives are an effective yet atomized attempt to address some of the functional amorality of finance because there is no impetus or incentive for banks themselves to apply the principles creatively across all their product lines and commercial relationships. Sets of soft law principles that are framed for a specific problem (financing big mining and infrastructure projects) are not readily transferable, either from lack of will or because the mechanics of applying human rights standards to different types of financial instruments may be very different. Therefore, no matter how extensive the buy-in from industry, it should not give one the impression that the buy-in signifies a full commitment. Soft law initiatives offer, in practice, no real solution to embedding ethical and human rights values right across complex financial institutions and global financial markets.

Financial Institutions and the Guiding Principles

Although the UN Guiding Principles on Business and Human Rights mark a watershed in understanding the responsibility of businesses in relation to internationally recognized human rights, as far as the financial sector is concerned, they signal the beginning of what is likely to be a long process of defining what those responsibilities actually are at the operational level. So far, as this chapter has outlined, embedding human rights into financial institutions has made progress in certain niche areas but has largely ignored or failed to tackle the vast majority of daily financial activity, and existing initiatives are easily circumvented. There are also many gaps in coherence across product lines—so a bank can be held accountable for funding a large mining project where a very precise type of funding arrangement is used but would escape accountability if it was linked to the project via a syndicated bond launch or IPO instead, or if it funded a specialized vehicle such as a private equity company that was heavily involved in the project. Such inconsistencies will need to be addressed systemically for the full implementation of the Guiding Principles.

The financial industry has a noticeable tendency to deflect accountability and scrutiny for negative human rights and social impacts by calling in aid product complexity, long chains of intermediation, and diffuse causality—as is so typified by the social and economic damage done by credit derivatives. Although there are degrees of separation between business activity and human rights impacts, which rightly raise legal issues around the ability to impute direct responsibility to a company, the reality in the financial sector is that the majority of its activities will involve degrees of separation to direct human rights impacts because of the nature of the financial business and what banks do on a daily basis. The basic fact that finance does not work the same way that other corporate sectors do should not give banks a blank check to create social damage behind the veil of complexity. There is also the problem that negative human rights impacts can be cumulative across the linked actions of many different financial institutions, as they were during the credit crisis. To limit financial institutions' responsibilities under the Guiding Principles purely to those areas with immediate and direct negative impacts on human rights will produce an atrophied model of responsibility for ethical and human rights respecting behavior that will undermine the ethos of the Guiding Principles and the needs of a socially sustainable globalization. It will largely let financial institutions off the hook for unethical and reckless behavior that can damage lives, economies, and states, and have long-term negative social impacts that are not easily remediated. In light of the damage done by the financial sector over the last five years or so, it is incongruous to argue that financial institutions' responsibilities to respect human rights can be limited to a few areas such as project finance, ethical screening of potential long-only equity investments, and CSR issues such as gender diversity and supply-chain management. The fact that many areas of finance have not yet been examined in detail from a human rights perspective does not mean that there is nothing to find from a responsibility-to-respect point of view—it just means that there is a lot of work to be done to fully flesh this out.

The challenge in implementing the Guiding Principles in the financial sector, then, is that although they provide a normative framework for understanding the nature and breadth of corporate human rights responsibilities at the level of principle, they do not in and of themselves provide normative or legal certainty from an operational point of view. The principles were deliberately framed to apply right across the business landscape. They were designed to be a coherent framework of principle for all corporate sectors, and so the details of how they would apply to any given industry or what the responsibility to respect requires in any particular context was deliberately not addressed in the development of the mandate. As has been highlighted above, the adoption of the Guiding Principles in 2011 coincided with a range of existing issue-specific initiatives in the financial sector, which in practice do not cover many parts of financial activity. There is also a noticeable diversity of practice across financial institutions themselves, which, it can be expected, would be significantly magnified if one were to survey banks and financial institutions from around the world. Furthermore, a whole range of specialized financial actors with portfolios that run into the billions of dollars have barely been touched by human rights analysis. The real challenge, then, is to define what the responsibility to respect human rights means for all the different products, services, processes, and corporate structures that make up today's financial sector, and also to examine the regulatory architecture of the global financial system from the perspective of the state duty to protect human rights. Although this is an enormous agenda of work, it is to be hoped that the Guiding Principles will provide the impetus and will not languish as a normative token that merely cements the status quo.

An essential corollary to this work will be efforts to clarify effective, robust governance mechanisms for the monitoring of human rights issues within financial institutions. As the analysis above implies, current governance arrangements at financial institutions are not effectively policing adverse human rights impacts across the balance sheet, and more can be done to streamline the monitoring of human rights issues right throughout their operations. The Guiding Principles pay particular attention to the issue of governance, devoting eight principles (17 to 24) to human rights due diligence, and it is clear that a human rights policy statement, coupled with a small team of CSR professionals to oversee it, is not enough to satisfy this due diligence requirement. The issues within financial institutions, and particularly the large, complex financial institutions, are far too extensive and technical to be dealt with in this way.

In light of this, governance and monitoring arrangements need to be proactive rather than reactive—that is, not just a committee that waits for transactions to be referred to it for scrutiny by the teams or managers involved in the deal. These teams and managers need to be equipped with the right technical expertise to identify any potential human rights issues lurking in complex products and transactions, and managers need to be equipped with the proper authority to hold people to account or override commercial decisions where necessary. The right people need to be embedded within the right operational structures and given the right level of authority within the management structure. Key features of effective governance arrangements could include the following:

- An oversight team tasked with the power to scrutinize decisions and to request information on transactions (rather than passively waiting for a few transactions to be referred to them).
- A team with the power to recommend and/or mandate changes to products, processes, strategies, or policies when they are deemed necessary to avoid human rights and/or reputational risks.
- A team equipped with the right skills to carry out this function, meaning a thorough understanding of international human rights law and issues and a solid background in financial services, as well as an understanding of how the two collide. Cursory research suggests that many staff members of CSR teams do not have extensive backgrounds

in financial services but tend instead to be human rights or CSR specialists.[139] This background would not give them the right technical abilities to wade through complex deal structures, balance sheets, and risk profiles of trading books at LCFIs to understand how human rights issues may be intermingled with the details. It is to be hoped that as the importance of good governance of ethical and human rights issues within financial institutions grows in stature, people with long track records in frontline operations (such as traders, deal makers, and market or credit risk managers) could be persuaded to move across to this new function. It would arguably be far easier to train a former trader in human rights issues than a human rights lawyer in systemic risk and market dynamics and developments.[140]

- A team that meets regularly, has appropriate committee and executive support and institutional influence, and has a clear line for the escalation of concerns. Although at the moment it seems that CSR heads can meet with CEOs, it is questionable how effective this is given the wide gap in the understanding between human rights issues and broader commercial and risk issues.

Taken together, it is possible that human rights issues could be made part of the mandate of internal, or even external, audit. This method would provide the right level of ongoing scrutiny and assurance at a firm-wide level that human rights risks are being systematically identified and managed, and it would reaffirm the institutional importance of these issues. From a regulatory point of view, there is also scope to house human rights under the operational-risk pillar of the Basel framework on international capital adequacy regulation (this could also harmonize pillar I and pillar II of the Guiding Principles). This classification currently encompasses reputational risk (where human rights could sit), and it functions as a catch-all category for residual risks that may threaten the viability or continuity of the business. Human rights would then also be subject to regulatory scrutiny and reporting requirements.

---

139. Survey by the author of profiles of CSR team members on financial institution Web sites and private conversations with CSR team members.

140. This idea may not be as far-fetched as it may appear, as this type of transition has happened in the risk management arena. The financial crisis of 2007–09 drove home to senior management the crucial importance of effective risk management, which led to higher pay and status for risk managers. This began to attract former traders to move across to what had previously been seen in some quarters as "regulatory plumbing" and a break on deal making. As the scale of global finance has grown, and with it the scale of financial crises and social damage from the interaction of finance with global poverty, the importance of ethical and human rights issues will hopefully rise in importance within financial institutions as key management priorities.

Conclusion

The globalization of the financial sector has powered ahead over the last two decades, underpinned by advances in IT, the liberalization of legal controls on financial transactions, and the use of statistical theories in modeling financial data, which has opened up whole new areas of products and forms. As a result, the financial system has grown to such a size that it now dwarfs the underlying real economy and reaches deep into the socioeconomic fabric of most corners of the globe. As has been so clearly demonstrated by the events of the last five years, the potential human rights harm that can be generated by this system is enormous. However, the expansion of the financial sector has not been accompanied by the development of an overarching ethical/human rights framework for the system as a whole. The mapping of human rights accountability into financial institutions has so far followed a piecemeal, soft law approach built largely around a subsidiarity model of risk that has only effectively reached a few corners of the financial markets. Under this model, financial institutions can be held accountable or responsible for negative human rights impacts that are predominantly generated by their commercial relationships with corporate customers in other sectors who themselves directly infringe human rights. There has been little attention paid to mapping the direct impact that global financial institutions have on the enjoyment of human rights and how this would affect the conduct of their operations, or on developing a comprehensive template that would effectively embed the respect for human rights across the operations of today's vast financial institutions. As the events of the financial crisis have shown, it is difficult to argue that current human rights policies are in practice anything more than peripheral to the way financial institutions are currently run, regulated, or supervised.

This view of human rights as tangential to financial operations raises a significant challenge for the implementation of the Guiding Principles in the financial sector because the existing reach of human rights is shallow and easily circumvented. Many issues remain unaddressed, and a consistent approach across the disparate product lines and processes of modern finance is lacking. It will be a tragedy for the aspirations embedded in human rights law, the hopes and aims attached to the Guiding Principles, and the people who are increasingly vulnerable to machinations in the financial markets if this status quo is not challenged by the implementation of the Guiding Principles.

To embed the responsibility to respect across the financial system, the subsidiarity model of human rights risk that has currently been used in the sector must be complemented by comprehensive, systemic work to investigate how the whole range of products and services offered by the financial sector interacts with human rights enjoyment. This effort needs to investigate linkages and also operational responses to those risks, setting out procedural methodologies for how those impacts can be managed. It will also need to look at how the overarching legal and regulatory architecture of financial markets interacts with human rights (for example, how procedures mandated by regulation may increase fragility in the financial sector and so help to generate human rights harms). Again, such work needs to investigate how such problems can be remedied by legal and procedural changes, as well as oversight procedures. The starting point for meaningful dialogue on this must be a recognition of the enormity of the global financial system and its *sui generis* nature; financial institutions are not just another commercial subsector of the global economy that comes into contact with human rights through its commercial relationships with other sectors. Instead, specific, idiosyncratic risks to human rights are embedded in the wide range of financial institutions' activities, and the full implementation of the Guiding Principles in financial institutions will only take effect once these risks are properly analyzed, assessed, and managed.

Once this foundation is in place, efforts can then be directed at amending the legal and governance architecture of international finance and understanding how human rights standards can be woven into this. What is needed is effective law and governance that can be used by financial institutions at a strategic and operational level. It is simply not practical to argue that human rights criteria should be taken into account, for example, in assessing the risks of derivatives or liquidity risk without supporting work that demonstrates how this can be done. Such statements, even if embedded in law, would be virtually meaningless from an operational point of view (or they would lead to more problems). This agenda is a challenge aimed squarely at those working in the business and human rights field because it will require cooperative efforts between bankers/financiers and human rights specialists over the coming years to fully embed the Guiding Principles into the diverse workings of today's financial institutions.

Chapter 15

B Corporations: Redefining Success in Business

Andrew Kassoy and Nathan Gilbert

Introduction

We live in a time of growing economic instability and wealth inequality, failing political institutions, and rising social unrest. Though addressing many of these problems requires shifts in cultural values, the root problems are systemic. Government and the nonprofit sector are necessary but alone, they simply lack the capacity to address these problems at scale. The private sector—business—has become the most powerful man-made force on the planet. Therefore, we must harness the power of business to create value for society, not just for shareholders. At its best, business should do no harm and benefit all. But business is not set up today to do anything like this at scale; in fact, the existing system of standards and laws for the private sector ensures that business will not meet these objectives. Systemic problems require systemic solutions. For business to be harnessed as a force for good, there is a need for greater infrastructure—standards, corporate forms, incentives—that will allow for growth of a beneficial business economy.

From a human rights point of view, these systemic issues are particularly important. In contrast to many countries in which human rights are delineated as a series of positive rights to things that are provided by government, in the United States human rights are generally conceived as negative rights that government is supposed to protect. As a result, even the most vulnerable in our society increasingly rely on the private sector to provide, on commercial terms, goods and services, employment, and the community and environmental framework in which they live. So the role of business as a primary human rights actor matters.

Over the past thirty years, a paradigm has emerged in which entrepreneurs, investors, policy makers, consumers, and workers are using the power of business to address our greatest social and environmental problems. This movement has accelerated into a substantial market[1] composed of social entrepreneurs who are finding innovative and beneficial ways of doing business, consumers who are demanding not just better products and services but better companies from which to buy them,[2] and investors who seek to support the growth and expansion of these businesses.[3] However, a market is not a marketplace. The growth of this new sector of the economy is challenged by the absence of systemic infrastructure; a lack of transparent standards makes it difficult for stakeholders to identify and support *good companies*, and the legal concept of shareholder primacy makes it difficult for corporations to consider employee, community, and environmental interests when making decisions.

In other words, these entrepreneurs are working to build a twenty-first-century economy with twentieth-century rules. As a result, plenty of businesses and their stakeholders are trying to conduct business ethically.

For-profit companies pursuing a social mission face great difficulty as they scale their businesses. As officers and directors of these entities raise capital to grow or seek liquidity, the default position favors the traditional fiduciary responsibility to maximize returns to shareholders over the company's social mission. Many leaders of early and growth-stage mission-driven businesses fear being pressured to change business practices or pursue strategic alternatives to independent growth

---

1.   *See Mission*, AMERICAN SUSTAINABLE BUSINESS COUNCIL, http://asbcouncil.org/mission-history (last visited Nov. 25, 2013) (we can begin to identify a *social enterprise* market by aggregating the collective revenues and number of companies that belong to sustainable business networks. The American Sustainable Business Council, an umbrella advocacy organization for social enterprise and sustainable business, counts over 150,000 among its member organizations); *see also Become a Member*, NET IMPACT, http://netimpact.org/join-the-community (last visited Nov. 25, 2013) (top business school programs are establishing centers or certificates in social enterprise, building a pipeline of future for-profit social entrepreneurs. Net Impact, a network of young professionals and business school students, has reached a membership of over 30,000 in 125 chapters. There are numerous additional companies that do not self-identify as *socially responsible* but nevertheless behave that way, and there are other sectors of the economy such as health care, education, housing, food, agriculture, and consumer products with concentrations of high-impact businesses).

2.   *See* CONE LLC., CONE CAUSE EVOLUTION STUDY 2010 (2010), http://ppqty.com/2010_Cone _Study.pdf ("85% of consumers have a more positive image of a product or company when it supports a cause they care about."); *see also* BBMG, UNLEASHED: HOW NEW CONSUMERS WILL REVOLUTIONIZE BRANDS AND SCALE SUSTAINABILITY (2011), http://www.bbmg.com/how/new-consumer-download/ (A New York City–based branding and marketing firm highlighted that 70 million Americans (30% of the population) "are values-aspirational, practical purchasers, who are constantly looking to align their actions with their ideals.").

3.   *See* INVESTOR'S CIRCLE, http://www.investorscircle.net/# (last visited Nov. 25, 2013) Investors' Circle is a network of over 150 angel investors, professional venture capitalists, foundations, and family offices that are using private capital to promote the transition to a sustainable economy. Over $150 million has been invested in 250 social enterprises and funds); *see also* SLOW MONEY, http://slowmoney .org/about (The Slow Money network has been redefining how to think about investment in regional economies and local agriculture).

by investors whose financial interests often diverge over time from the social mis-sion of the company. Whatever the letter of the law, these fears, combined with both prevailing business culture and advice of counsel about the risk of litigation if one fails to maximize shareholder value, have a chilling effect on corporate behavior as it relates to pursuit of a social mission. These fears are exacerbated by cautionary tales of investor-led board takeovers of private companies and stories like the iconic forced sale of Ben & Jerry's to Unilever.[4]

Reflecting on the sale of many companies like Ben & Jerry's and on their own experi-ences as investors and operators of companies, the idea behind the B corp (the *B* stands for *benefit*) was to find a way for a company to scale a business, take on outside capital, maintain mission, and even protect mission through changes in management and owner-ship. It seemed that if this idea could be applied not as a one-off innovation business by business but at a systems level by developing market infrastructure to allow the entire private sector to act as if people and place mattered, the private sector could meet the demands of its stakeholders to redefine success in business. As a result, individuals may enjoy greater economic opportunity, business may have a direct effect on preventing and alleviating poverty, workers and other individuals affected by business will be protected from harm, and society may address its challenging environmental problems.

B Lab

B Lab, a 501(c)(3) nonprofit, is dedicated to using the power of business to solve the world's most pressing issues by empowering entrepreneurs who seek to use business as a force for good. It is working to build a business community and the legal infrastructure necessary to create a new sector of the economy that will redefine the role of business in society and foster a new, holistic way to do business. B Lab works to accomplish this by advancing concrete, integrated solutions to systemic problems through three interrelated initiatives: (1) building a community of certified B Corporations that allow all stakehold-ers to distinguish between good businesses and just good marketing; (2) driving growth

---

4.   William H. Clark & Larry Vranka, The Need and Rationale for the Benefit Corpora-tion, at 6 (Benefit Corp., 2013) http://benefitcorp.net/forattorneys/benefit-corp-white-paper; *see also* Jill Bamburg, Jill, Getting to Scale: Growing Your Business Without Selling Out 53 (Elissa Rabel-lion et al. eds., 2006) (In 2000, the Vermont-based Ice Cream Company, Ben & Jerry's, was acquired by Unilever. The sale went against the wishes of co-founders Ben Cohen and Jerry Greenfield. However, with fear of a lawsuit from their shareholders for not maximizing their value, Ben and Jerry felt forced to proceed with the sale. "By now, every mission-driven entrepreneur knows the sad ending to the tale of Ben & Jerry's: the forced sale of one of the country's premier socially responsible businesses to a giant multinational clearly focused on the financial bottom line.").

capital to these entrepreneurs from capital sources that want to invest for impact using its GIIRS Ratings and Analytics platform, which assesses the social and environmental impact of investment opportunities;[5] and (3) promoting public policies such as a new corporate form—the benefit corporation—and incentives that will increase the size of the socially responsible marketplace.[6]

B Lab's purpose is different from that of other ratings agencies, certification bodies, and principles-based approaches that address the social and environmental performance of business in that it has created mechanisms to shine a light on companies with corporate practices, policies, and products that ensure the livelihood, well-being, and positive outcomes of their workers, community, and environment. These other bodies tend either to ignore social impact completely or to focus on negative screening of companies. B Lab is not an activist demanding regulation or highlighting bad actors—there is a critical role for this in the market that is being addressed by other players—but rather an organization building community and a movement for those who choose to redefine success in business. Through this approach, B Lab provides a set of tools for companies to self-assess, benchmark, and improve performance over time, and for other stakeholders to choose which businesses to support.

Certified B Corporations and Their Legal Implications

The emergence of the B Corporation certification[7] is a result of the recognized need to create a set of standards that can be used by consumers, investors, and policy makers to identify *good businesses*. By November of 2013, over 865 companies had been certified

---

5.   *See About Us*, Global Impact Investing Network, http://www.thegiin.org/cgi-bin/iowa/aboutus /index.html (last visited Nov. 25, 2013) (Impact investments aim to solve social or environmental challenges while generating financial profit. Impact investing includes investments that range from producing a return of principal capital (capital preservation) to offering market-rate or even market-beating financial returns. Although impact investing could be categorized as a type of *socially responsible investing*, it contrasts with negative screening, which focuses primarily on avoiding investments in *bad* or *harmful* companies—impact investors actively seek to place capital in businesses and funds that can harness the positive power of enterprise).

6.   Benefit Corporations are a new class of corporation that (1) creates a material positive impact on society and the environment; (2) expands fiduciary duty to require consideration of nonfinancial interests when making decisions; and (3) reports on its overall social and environmental performance using recognized third-party standards.

7.   *See* B Corp., http://www.bcorporation.net (last visited Nov. 25, 2013) (Certified B Corporations are a new type of corporation that uses the power of business to solve social and environmental problems. B Lab, a nonprofit organization, certifies B Corporations the same way TransFair certifies Fair Trade coffee or U.S.GBC certifies LEED buildings. B Corps, unlike traditional businesses, meet social and environmental performance standards, meet higher legal accountability standards, and build business constituency for public policies that support sustainable business. Through a company's public B Impact Report, anyone can access performance data about social and environmental practices regarding their products).

by achieving a minimum score of 80 on the B Impact Ratings System.[8] This community stretches across twenty-nine countries and represents more than sixty different industries and collective revenues over $6.5 billion. These companies range from small social enterprises with business models intended to bring resources to an underserved community to large manufacturing and consumer products companies with innovative products, services, and employment and environmental practices.

B-Corp Legal Requirement

Certified B corps must *legally expand their corporate responsibilities* to include consideration of the interests of workers, community, and the environment. *This legal structure is the differentiating characteristic of B Corporation certification from all other certifications.* The certification goes beyond principles or measuring impact to create the legal freedom and protection for entrepreneurs and investors to scale businesses with purpose, not just profit, at their core. The reason B corps are structured this way is to rebuild public trust in free market capitalism by expanding corporate accountability to require consideration of the impact of decisions not only on shareholders but also on workers, communities, and the environment.

The B Corporation certification process requires a company to implement an amendment to its articles of incorporation or other organizational documents to the maximum extent available under current corporate law. The B Corporation legal framework bakes a company's values into the DNA of the company so they can better survive new management, new investors, or even new ownership. The objective is to expand the responsibilities of the corporation to include consideration of the interests of employees, consumers, the community, and the environment; give legal permission and protection to officers and directors to consider all stakeholders, not just shareholders; create additional rights for shareholders to hold directors and officers accountable to these interests; and limit these expanded rights to shareholders exclusively—non-shareholders are explicitly not empowered with a new right of action.

To achieve this objective under existing law, the B Corporation legal framework uses "constituency statutes"[9] in thirty-one states as enabling legislation. These constituency stat-

---

8. The B Impact Rating System is a free self-assessment of corporate governance, worker practices, community engagement, and environmental management. A verification process is required to become certified. More discussion on this later in the chapter.

9. *See* CLARK JR. & VRANKA, *supra* note 14 at 9 ("The directors of companies incorporated in constituency states are expressly permitted by statute to consider persons other than shareholders in the discharge of their fiduciary duties. Constituency statutes generally provide that in fulfilling their fiduciary duties, directors may consider the effects of a decision not only on shareholders, but also on a list of other *constituency* groups. These permissible constituency groups vary state by state, but they usually include

utes are permissive—they give permission to directors to consider broader interests—and were created in reaction to the hostile-takeover era in corporate finance.[10] B corps use the permissive *may* language in the statutes in these states to add *shall* language to their own corporate articles, thus obligating themselves to a higher standard of consideration. There are nineteen states without constituency statutes[11]—including Delaware, the home of U.S. corporate law—so for companies becoming B corps in those states, there is limited protection for their mission under existing law. In nonconstituency states, B corps put the stakeholder consideration into their term sheet for B Corporation certification; that is the best that can be done for now.[12]

"While it is clear that directors of mission-driven companies incorporated in constituency statute jurisdictions may take into consideration the interests of various constituencies when exercising their business judgment, the lack of case law interpreting constituency statutes, coupled with the context in which many of these statutes were enacted, makes it difficult for directors to know exactly how, when and to what extent they can consider those interests. For example, neither the constituency statutes themselves nor state case law address questions such as how directors should decide which parties fall within a protected constituency category, what weight the directors should assign to shareholder and nonshareholder interests and what standards a court should use in reviewing directors' decisions to consider (or not to consider) nonshareholder interests. Based on the limited case law available, courts seem reluctant to wade into these issues and often fall back on shareholder primacy."[13]

The combination of lack of clarity in constituency-statute states and an inability to consider stakeholders in the other nineteen states has driven B Lab to pursue a longer-term

---

employees, creditors, suppliers, consumers, and the community at large. Thirty-three states now have some version of a constituency statute. Conspicuously absent from the list of states adopting constituency statutes is Delaware, where more than 900,000 business entities have their legal home, including more than 50% of all U.S. publiclytraded companies and 63% of the Fortune 500. Most states, including those with constituency statutes, will at a minimum consider Delaware law when interpreting local corporate law.").

10.   Clark Jr. & Vranka, *supra* note 4.

11.   *See* Clark Jr. & Vranka, *supra* note 4 (in non-constituency states, including Delaware, consideration of a public mission is even more problematic, because under the corporate laws of those states the directors are not expressly permitted to consider the interests of stakeholders or constituents other than shareholders in the discharge of their duties).

12.   *See* Clark Jr. & Vranka, *supra* note 4.

13.   Clark Jr. & Vranka, *supra* note 4, at 10; *see, e.g.*, Baron v. Strawbridge & Clothier, 646 F. Supp. 690, 697 (E.D. Pa. 1986) (stating that while it was proper for directors facing takeover attempts to consider corporation's employees, customers and community, their fiduciary duty was still "to act in the best interests of the corporation's shareholders."). Also, it is either expressly provided or generally understood that these nonshareholder constituencies do not have standing to sue on the basis that the directors failed to consider their interests, making it less likely that directors will be concerned about them.

solution to the need for corporate law to accommodate higher standards of fiduciary duty for those companies and investors who want it.

Need for a New Corporate Form: The Legal Impetus

The prevailing legal view is that corporations are required by law to maximize shareholder returns, often to the exclusion and at the expense of employees, community, and environment.[14] Directors have a fiduciary duty to these shareholders, leaving them with little flexibility to consider the interests of stakeholders, other than shareholders, beyond minimum legal standards. This problem makes it difficult for profitable, high-impact businesses to scale and create liquidity without compromising their values.[15] A few companies like Patagonia, which has a visionary founder who retains 100 percent ownership, require no outside capital and have maintained organic growth for decades, enabling them to avoid this conflict. However, very few companies like Patagonia exist. They take too long to scale given the challenges society faces, and most industries today require outside capital for a start-up business to compete and grow.

The Sustainability Dilemma

Furthermore, companies like Patagonia[16] only solve this problem for one generation, leaving behind significant succession issues. Companies that are unable or unwilling to follow this organic growth model find it increasingly difficult to lead and manage a company that considers stakeholder interests as it scales. As the number of employees and investors grows, and as the company experiences management turnover or strategic change, it becomes more difficult to operate counter to prevailing legal and cultural norms. During down cycles in the business or critical negotiations about investments, mergers, or liquidity events, the default position of directors and officers will most likely be their basic fiduciary responsibility to maximize return to shareholders. There are simply very few road maps for a different approach that gives directors and officers the legal permission and protection to consider non-shareholder interests.

We believe the doctrine of shareholder primacy results in a lack of mission-aligned growth and liquidity options for high-impact companies. In recent years, the result has been the sale of many of the highest-profile sustainable businesses to multinationals:

---

14. *See* Clark Jr. & Vranka, *supra* note 4.

15. *See* Kevin Jones, *Selling vs. Selling Out*, Stanford Social Innovation Rev. (Feb. 27, 2009), http://www.ssireview.org/blog/entry/selling_vs_selling_out (Ben & Jerry's faced this dilemma as Unilever diminished the company's social and environmental objectives after its acquisition).

16. Jennifer Rapp, *Patagonia Earns B Corporation Certification*, Snews (Jan. 17, 2012), http://www.snewsnet.com/cgi-bin/snews/24054.html (Patagonia became a Certified B Corporation and Benefit Corp in California on the first day the legislation took effect, January 3, 2012).

- Ben & Jerry's to Unilever (April 2000)[17]
- Odwalla to Coca-Cola (October 2001)[18]
- Stonyfield Farm to Group Danone (January 2004)[19]
- Body Shop to L'Oreal (March 2006)[20]
- Tom's of Maine to Colgate-Palmolive (March 2006)[21]
- Burt's Bees to Clorox (November 2007)[22]

Without fundamentally expanding the responsibilities of officers and directors, it is merely optional to consider the impact of a company's decisions on its employees, community, and environment.[23] In critical situations, such as a sale of the company, *optional* most often means *nonexistent*.[24] Furthermore, apart from comforting words of buyers and sellers in these situations, there is no way to know whether the values and practices of these companies continue to exist, let alone improve, after the sale. This explains the sense of abandonment felt by many consumers after these companies have been acquired.

Benefit Corporations

In addition to addressing these legal limitations, legal recognition of a new corporate entity—the benefit corporation—creates legitimacy for and accelerates the growth of this

---

17. Constance L. Hays, *Ben & Jerry's to Unilever, with Attitude*, N.Y. TIMES, (Apr. 13, 2000), http://www.nytimes.com/2000/04/13/business/ben-jerry-s-to-unilever-with-attitude.html.

18. *Coke buys Odwalla*, CNN MONEY (Oct. 30, 2001), http://money.cnn.com/2001/10/30/deals/coke_odwalla/.

19. *Company News: Group Danone Increases Stake in Stonyfield Farm to 80%*, N.Y. TIMES (Jan. 13, 2004), http://www.nytimes.com/2004/01/13/business/company-news-group-danone-increases-stake-in-stonyfield-farm-to-80.html.

20. *L'Oreal Buys Body Shop for £652m*, INDEPENDENT (Mar. 17, 2006), http://www.independent.co.uk/news/business/news/loreal-buys-body-shop-for-pound652m-470244.html.

21. Chris Reidy, *Colgate Will Buy Tom's of Maine*, BOSTON GLOBE (Mar. 22, 2006), http://www.boston.com/business/articles/2006/03/22/colgate_will_buy_toms_of_maine/.

22. *Clorox to Acquire Burt's Bees; Expands into Fast-Growing Natural Personal Care*, CLOROX (Oct. 31, 2007), http://investors.thecloroxcompany.com/releasedetail.cfm?releaseid=272197.

23. *See* CLARK JR. & VRANKA, *supra* note 4 at 10; ("Permissive constituency statutes only create the option (and not the requirement) for directors to consider interests of constituencies other than shareholders. Thus, directors have the permission not to consider interests other than shareholder maximization of value. Mission-driven executives and investors are often in minority shareholder positions and would prefer that directors and officers be required to consider these expanded interests when making decisions, with a shareholder right of action providing the "teeth" to enforce such consideration. This is particularly true in situations where a company is considering strategic alternatives and directors' discretion in making business decisions is more limited by traditional principles requiring shareholder value maximization.").

24. *See, e.g.*, Revlon, Inc. v. MacAndrews & Forbes Holdings, Inc., 506 A.2d 173, 182 (Del. 1986) (stating that directors, faced with a hostile takeover bid for a corporation, may only consider various nonshareholder constituencies if "there are rationally related benefits accruing to the stockholders"); *see also* CLARK JR. & VRANKA, *supra* note 4.

emerging marketplace by making it easier for the next generation of entrepreneurs and investors to build businesses that seek to create value for both shareholders and society.[25] The new benefit corporation form facilitates greater recognition of these businesses from consumers, investors, and policy makers by establishing a higher bar of corporate governance without requiring certification by a third party for a fee[26] and without prescribing specific corporate activities. All of these factors call for the creation of a legal framework for a new class of corporations that are designed to create benefit for all stakeholders, not just shareholders.[27]

B Lab has overseen the development of a model corporate code in partnership with national law firm Drinker Biddle & Reath, co-authors of the white paper on which this chapter is based. Unlike traditional corporations, benefit corporations must create a material positive impact on society and the environment; consider how decisions affect workers, community, and the environment; and publicly report their social and environmental performance using established third-party standards.[28] Twelve states have passed benefit corporation legislation. In Spring 2010, Maryland and Vermont became the first states to sign benefit corporation legislation and it was subsequently passed in Hawaii, Virginia, New Jersey, California, New York, South Carolina, Louisiana, Illinois, Massachusetts, and Pennsylvania, as well as the District of Columbia.[29] On April 18, 2013, Governor Jack Markell and members of the Delaware General Assembly introduced public benefit

---

25. *See* Clark Jr. & Vranka, *supra* note 4 (There are other legal structures that are designed to promote socially responsible businesses, such as flexible purpose corporations and L3C corporations, but these structures meet a different purpose. The L3C (short for low-profit limited liability company) as an organizational form in which to conduct business in that it provides significant flexibility in structuring governance provisions, provides legal protections to owners and managers, and can attract private capital investment. However, unlike a corporation or most traditional LLCs, an L3C expressly recognizes that its social mission takes priority over its profit objective. Currently 8 U.S. states have passed L3C legislation. Another form is the Flexible Purpose Corporation (FPC), which has passed only in California. This form requires a company to specify a "special purpose" that is intended to create public benefit. Both of these forms create a more narrow view of the purpose of the corporation compared with the benefit corporation, which is designed to produce general public benefit.).

26. Certified B Corporation is a certification conferred by the nonprofit B Lab. *Benefit corporation* is a legal status administered by the state. Benefit corporations do *not* need to be certified. Certified B Corporations have been certified as having met a high standard of overall social and environmental performance, and as a result they have access to a portfolio of services and support that benefit corporations do not.

27. A director of a benefit corporation has a duty to ensure that the benefit corporation meets its statutory obligations to make publically available an annual benefit report that assesses the overall social and environmental performance of the benefit corporation against a third party standard that meets the criteria listed in the Model Legislation (i.e. the third party standard is comprehensive, credible, independent, and transparent).

28. *See List of Standards*, Benefit Corp Info. Ctr., http://benefitcorp.net/selecting-a-third-party-standard/list-of-standards (last visited Nov. 25, 2013) (Benefit corporation legislation does not require a benefit corporation to use any particular third-party standard to prepare its annual benefit report. Nor are they required to have that report certified or audited by a third party.).

29. *See State by State Legislative Status*, Benefit Corp Info. Ctr., http://benefitcorp.net/state-by-state-legislative-status (last visited Nov. 25, 2013).

corporation legislation. B Lab is working with additional states to pass benefit corporation legislation in 2013. This introduction signifies a seismic shift in U.S. corporate law. [30]

Benefit Corporation Legislation

"There are three major provisions in benefit corporation legislation that are consistent from state to state. These provisions address *corporate purpose, accountability and transparency*. They state that a benefit corporation has: (1) a corporate purpose to create a material positive impact on society and the environment; (2) expanded fiduciary duties of directors that require consideration of non-financial interests; and (3) an obligation to report on its overall social and environmental performance as assessed against a comprehensive, credible, independent, and transparent third-party standard." [31] These requirements create a change in fiduciary obligations relative to existing corporate law; for benefit corporations, the pursuit of general public benefit has been elevated to the same status as financial value creation as being in the best interests of the corporation and its shareholders, thus both freeing and obligating the directors to balance these interests when making decisions.

Though this legal structure creates protection and accountability to consider non-financial interests, over time institutional investors will need to become willing to invest in these kinds of entities. There are already venture capital firms and institutions invested in many B Corporations, so they have already come to terms with the different legal structure. Because benefit corporations do not limit the financial returns of these entities, investors can maintain their own fiduciary duties while putting capital to work in benefit corporations. Some institutions that are governed by U.S. Employee Retirement Income Security Act (ERISA) laws have additional fiduciary constraints: they must ensure that these opportunities "match benchmarks on a risk-adjusted financial basis and are acceptable exclusively on their merits as financial investments, apart from any collateral benefits." [32] There will be an education process for these institutions to become comfortable that they are meeting their ERISA obligations when investing in benefit corporations.

Over time, other parties, including government policy makers and investors, could look to treat these benefit corporations differently based on their higher obligations to act in the public interest. For example, the board of supervisors in San Francisco passed legislation to provide bid preferences for benefit corporations in city contracting. [33]

---

30. *See Delaware Unveils Public Benefit Corporation Legislation*, NEWS.DELAWARE.GOV. WEB. (Apr. 18, 2013), http://news.delaware.gov/2013/04/18/delaware-unveils-public-benefit-corporation-legislation /.

31. CLARK JR. & VRANKA, *supra* note 41, at 15.

32. DAVID WOOD, BEN THORNLEY, & KATIE GRACE, IMPACT AT SCALE 13 (2012), http://www .pacificcommunityventures.org/uploads/research/pdf/ImpactReport_FINAL2.10.12.pdf.

33. *See* Press Release, City and County of San Francisco, Board of Supervisors Unanimously Approves

Driving Capital to Impact

Though building a community of certified B corps will help the marketplace identify good companies, and providing new legal infrastructure that enables companies to pursue mission as well as profit will allow a framework for long-term mission-aligned growth, this growing sector of the economy relies on increasing the flow of capital to high-impact businesses through the emerging impact-investing industry. After thirty years of committing over $2.5 trillion of investment capital to socially responsible investing (SRI), more and more investors want to put their capital to work in businesses that not only do no harm but actively seek to solve major social and environmental problems. Impact investments aim to solve social or environmental challenges while generating financial profit. They include investments that range from producing a return of principal capital (capital preservation) to offering market-rate or even market-beating financial returns. Although impact investing could be categorized as a type of socially responsible investing, it contrasts with negative screening, which focuses primarily on avoiding investments in *bad* or *harmful* companies—impact investors actively seek to place capital in businesses and funds that can harness the positive power of enterprise.

Impact Investing

A November 2010 report by J. P. Morgan titled *Impact Investments: An Emerging Asset Class* estimates the size of this market opportunity at between $400 billion and $1 trillion.[34] This amount included only investment opportunities in emerging markets across five sectors: housing, rural water delivery, maternal health, primary education, and financial services. J. P. Morgan estimated the ten-year profit potential from these opportunities alone ranged between $183 billion and $667 billion.[35] Approaching it from the demand side of the equation, and focused only on U.S. individual investors, a June 2010 *Money for Good* report from Hope Consulting estimated a demand for impact investments among U.S. high networth individuals at $120 billion.[36]

City Incentives for New Type of Socially Responsible Corporations (Apr. 18, 2012), http://www.sfbos.org/Modules/ShowDocument.aspx?documentid=41406.

34. J. P. MORGAN GLOBAL RESEARCH, IMPACT INVESTMENTS: AN EMERGING ASSET CLASS (2010), *available at* http://www.rockefellerfoundation.org/uploads/files/2b053b2b-8feb-46ea-adbd-f890 68d59785-impact.pdf; Nicholas Timmons, *Impact Investment: A Burgeoning Asset Class*, FIN. TIMES (Nov. 28, 2010), http://www.ft.com/intl/cms/s/0/e875dda6-fae6-11df-b576-00144feab49a.html?ftcamp=rss #axzz1XUogcz2a.>

35. J.P. Morgan Global Research, Impact Investments an Emerging Asset Class (2010), *available at* http://www.rockefellerfoundation.org/uploads/files/2b053b2b-8feb-46ea-adbd-f89068d59785-impact .pdf.

36. *Strategies for Social Change: Money For Good Report*, HOPE CONSULTING, (2009), http://www .hopeconsulting.us/money-for-good.

Transparency Barriers

Like consumers, investors lack the comprehensive tools to understand the complete picture of a company's performance across the full range of social and environmental measures. Likewise, businesses may have a hard time attracting investors by distinguishing themselves among the sea of companies that claim to be *socially responsible*. Furthermore, the current trend, particularly in the public capital markets and among policy makers and large public corporations serious about sustainability, is to encourage integrated sustainability reporting using credible third-party standards. According to Institutional Shareholder Services (ISS), the largest shareholder proxy advisory organization in the world, this trend is also true for institutional investors who "appear to be increasingly incorporating social and environmental considerations into their proxy voting decisions, as demonstrated by voting trends and institutional investor initiatives."[37]

The Securities and Exchange Commission (SEC) is known to be reviewing environmental, social, and corporate governance (ESG) reporting regulations, but it is too early to tell what they might require. However, given the SEC's mandate, to protect investors, regulation is likely to focus on reporting ESG risks to financial returns for shareholders rather than on ESG impacts in and of themselves. Though any additional ESG reporting requirements for public companies are a step forward, the outcome is unlikely to produce the kind of information that impact investors will seek (analysis of the positive impact of the business on society and the environment, not simply disclosure of ESG risks to short- or long-term financial value). Furthermore, none of this regulatory effort is focused on altering standards of fiduciary duty. As discussed earlier, under most corporate laws, particularly Delaware, where most public companies incorporate, these ESG issues can only be considered in relation to risks to shareholder value maximization, not to positive social impact. So impact investors continue to operate in a gray area when putting capital to work; the benefit corporation legal structure provides a measure of clarity to investors, but it will take time for it to become accepted among mainstream investors.

Global Impact Investment Rating System Ratings and Analytics

The impact-investing industry is driving capital to investments that actively create positive social and environmental impact. Researchers estimate that between $500 billion and $1 trillion in assets under management will be directed toward impact investing by 2020.[38]

---

37. CAROLYN MATHIASEN & ERIK MELL, CORPORATE SOCIAL ISSUES: A 2011 PROXY SEASON PREVIEW: UNITED STATES (Institutional Shareholder Serv., 2011).

38. *See* J. P. MORGAN GLOBAL RESEARCH *supra* note 34, at 6; *see also* MONITOR INSTITUTE, INVESTING FOR SOCIAL & ENVIRONMENTAL IMPACT: A DESIGN FOR CATALYZING AN INDUSTRY 8 (2009), http://www.monitorinstitute.com/downloads/what-we-think/impact-investing/Impact_Investing.pdf.

In order for the impact-investing space to reach this scale, the sector requires improved infrastructure. According to a Monitor study, this infrastructure includes third-party standards and ratings for defining, measuring, and comparing positive social and environmental impact.[39] Without standards, there are significant barriers to scale, including a fragmented market where each investor defines impact differently and there are high due diligence and transaction costs, limited understanding by investors of how to manage for impact, and a weak policy environment due to a dearth of information. To address these issues, B Lab has created Global Impact Investment Rating System (GIIRS) Ratings and Analytics.

GIIRS Ratings and Analytics provide a suite of impact standards, assessments, ratings, and analytics tools to facilitate a scalable and transparent marketplace that can channel capital from institutional investors and financial-services intermediaries to companies seeking mission-aligned growth capital. GIIRS assesses the social and environmental impact and practices (but not the financial performance) of companies and funds using a ratings methodology that has now been used by more than 7,000 companies. GIIRS Ratings are analogous to Morningstar investment ratings or S&P credit-risk ratings, providing third-party ratings of social and environmental performance for impact investment in the private markets, particularly private equity and debt investments in companies and funds.

GIIRS Analytics uses the data from GIIRS Ratings on both companies and funds to provide investors with current and historical analyses of impact performance, benchmarking, and reporting. It is a powerful tool that allows impact investors to make better decisions during due diligence, monitor performance of their investments, and help their portfolio investments improve their impact performance. If GIIRS does its job, more capital will flow to the highest impact businesses, and impact performance will become a standard component of the investment process.

The Need for Standards

The work at B Lab—B Corporation certification, benefit corporation legal structures, GIIRS Ratings and Analytics—relies on transparent, comprehensive, and comparable standards for social and environmental impact. Certifications are meaningless without standards; a corporate form accountable for creating social impact is pointless if the corporations do not have to provide evidence of impact using independent standards; and capital markets rely on clear standards (such as FASB and GAAP). Entrepreneurs who are *sustainable, green,* or *socially responsible* may find that it is hard to distinguish themselves from other companies that make similar claims but do not actually behave as they

---

39. *See* Monitor Institute *supra* note 41.

advertise. Consumers are increasingly likely to align their purchases with their values, and many more have become conscious of the issue.

> Approximately 68 million U.S. consumers have stated a preference for making purchasing decisions based upon their sense of social and environmental responsibility.[40] Some consumers use their purchasing power to punish companies for negative corporate behavior,[41] and many other consumers would like to use their purchasing power to reward companies that positively address a social or environmental issue. For example, surveys have shown that 49% of Americans say they would boycott companies whose behavior they perceive is not in the best interest of society.[42] Meanwhile, recent research has also indicated that where price and quality are equal, 86% of consumers say they would switch from their current brand to a brand that is socially responsible.[43] These consumer behaviors apply not just to purchases related to popular consumer products but also to many other industries including telecommunications, banking, and professional services (e.g., law firms). [44]

It should be acknowledged that some critics suggest that consumers often fall short in their actual behavior relative to their stated preference for good companies. Nevertheless, these studies make it clear that consumers are focused on ethical consumerism, and the performance of many of B Corporations suggests that they are successfully attracting consumers based on their ability to convey positively and transparently their social impact.

As consumer demand for socially responsible products and companies is increasing, consumer trust in corporations is decreasing.[45] Marketers use the terms "green," "responsible," "sustainable," "charitable," and similar words on a daily basis to describe their products or their companies. However, the more these terms are used, the less meaning they have because there are no standards to back up the claims.[46] This problem,

---

40. *Eco-officiency: Benefits of Becoming a Sustainable Business*, NATURAL MARKETING INST., http://www.eco-officiency.com/benefits_becoming_sustainable_business.html (last visited Feb. 14, 2013).

41. *See, e.g.*, LAWRENCE GLICKMAN, BUYING POWER: A HISTORY OF CONSUMER ACTIVISM IN AMERICA (University of Chicago Press, 1st ed. 2009); *see also, e.g.*, Steven Levingston, *Whole Foods Boycott: The Long View*, WASH. POST (Sep. 02, 2009), http://voices.washingtonpost.com/short-stack/2009/09/whole_foods_boycott_the_long_v.html?hpid=news-col-blog.

42. Shiela M. J. Bonini, Kerrin McKillop, & Lenny Mendonca, *The Trust Gap Between Consumers and Corporations*, 10, McKINSEY Q. (2007).

43. CONE COMMC'N., CONE CAUSE EVOLUTION & ENVIRONMENT SURVEY 8 (2007).

44. CLARK JR. & VRANKA, *supra* note 4, at 2. *See also* CONE COMMC'N, 2010 CONE CAUSE EVOLUTION STUDY 10 (2010).

45. EDELMAN, TRUST BAROMETER 2013 GLOBAL ANNUAL REPORT (2013), http://www.edelman.com /trust-downloads/global-results-2/ (According to the Edelman Trust Barometer report, trust in the business sector in the United States is in decline and there is increasing expectation for businesses to invest in society.).

46. *See* Christopher Hellman, *ExxonMobile: Green Company of the Year*, FORBES MAGAZINE (Aug. 24, 2009), http://www.forbes.com/forbes/2009/0824/energy-oil-exxonmobil-green-company-of-year.html

often referred to as "greenwashing," is misleading for consumers and frustrating for businesses that try to distinguish themselves based on their social and environmental business practices. Consumers are less likely to trust a company's claims as compared to consumer reports or third party certifications.[47] As a result, various voluntary certifications, such as "Organic," "Fair Trade," "Energy Star," "Green Seal," "LEED," and "Forest Stewardship Council" have emerged to provide insight into particular aspects of a company's social or environmental performance.[48] Although there has been a proliferation of narrow product or practice specific standards like those mentioned, there are fewer standards that provide a comprehensive understanding of a company's performance as a whole. The lack of comprehensive and transparent standards is making it difficult for a consumer to tell the difference between a "good company" and just good marketing.[49]

A company can highlight its organic or fair-trade products, or its Leadership in Energy and Environmental Design (LEED) Platinum headquarters while engaging in bad labor or environmental practices. Though government regulators are loath to endorse private certifications, they do fall into a similar pattern, addressing very specific policy mandates. It is easier for a regulator to use a minimum specific standard, which is why there are many standards to measure parts per billion of a chemical in drinking water. For now, standards for overall public benefit, such as those called for in the benefit corporation legislation, are going to be voluntary—not government mandated—but the hope is that the evidence will show over time that these standards lead to better results. In any case, government does not have to pick the winners, but it can use standards, at a minimum— as with the benefit corporation—to create incentives by providing particular benefits to companies that meet high overall standards of public benefit. However, it is important for government to mandate the level of independence, transparency, comprehensiveness, and credibility that goes into creating and governing those standards.

(For example, ExxonMobile was named "Green Company of the Year" by Forbes Magazine in 2009 for its focus on natural gas [as opposed to coal.]). *See also* Josh Harkinson, *ExxonMobil: Green Company of the Year?* MOTHER JONES (Apr. 27, 2009), http://www.motherjones.com/blue-marble/2009/08/exxonmobil-green-company-year-0 (However, the Forbes article failed to assess its performance on other environmental issues, such as its lobbying against climate change or even the negative effects of natural gas on the environment. In the UK, Exxon advertisements claiming to be *eco-friendly* for its natural gas projects were banned as misleading in 2008.).

47.   *See* BBMG, THE CONSCIOUS CONSUMERS REPORT: REDEFINING VALUE IN A NEW ECONOMY 16 (2009).

48.   Matty Byloos, *Guide to Green Symbols*, EASY WAYS TO GO GREEN (Apr. 27, 2008), http://www.easywaystogogreen.com/green-guides/guide-to-green-symbols/ (for a description of these and other symbols).

49.   CLARK JR. & VRANKA, *supra* note 4, at 3.

The B Impact Rating System

B Lab is one of several organizations that have developed comprehensive standards for measuring social and environmental impact. It uses the same standard for certifying B Corporations and for providing GIIRS ratings. In the case of certified B Corporations, the model has gone beyond performance standards by also integrating legal standards. Furthermore, within the benefit corporation legal structure, there is a new corporate form that requires a set of standards to evaluate the entire social and environmental performance of a company, not just a specific product or practice attribute. A company will be granted a legal license to operate based on its pursuit of social and environmental performance in addition to financial value, as measured against a third-party standard; this flips the mainstream paradigm of incorporation on its head.

The Assessment Process

The idea behind this approach is that with transparent, comprehensive, and comparable impact metrics there will be greater clarity in differentiating impact among companies across industry and size. The B Impact Ratings System is designed by B Lab to be easy to complete for the entrepreneur while still being rigorous in its approach.

The primary characteristics of the assessment include the following:

- *Transparency*—the assessment is accessible to anyone for free for internal assessment purposes, and only scores of certified B corps are posted on B Lab's Web site.
- *Ease of use*—it takes entrepreneurs 60 to 120 minutes to complete the assessment.
- *Scalability*—the tool is designed for small to mid-sized enterprises (larger versions for companies 1,000 to 10,000 employees are in development).
- *Dynamism*[50]—a new version is developed every two years in to improve the standards and raise the bar.
- *Comparability*—the assessment allows for benchmarking across company geography, size, and industry.[51]
- *Independent Governance*.[52]

---

50. A new version of the B Impact Rating System is released once every two years. The first version (V1.0) of the Developed Markets (DM) assessment was released on October 19, 2007, and V2.0 followed in January 2010 with two addenda focused on the green building and financial services industries. V3.0 was introduced in July 2011 and includes an assessment designed for companies in Emerging Markets (EM). Prior to the release of each new version of the assessment, B Lab conducts both a private and public beta to ensure that B Lab's stakeholders are being recognized in the standards development process.

51. To improve comparability of the assessment there are forty different versions of the survey based on the size, sector, and geographic location of the company. For example, a manufacturing company in the United States with fifty or more workers will have a different version than a service company with five workers operating in Kenya.

52. Oversight of the B Impact Ratings System is the responsibility of B Lab's Standards Advisory Councils (SACs), independent committees of nine to eleven members, each respected in the field for their

The survey is composed of approximately 160 questions divided into four categories: governance, workers, community, and environment. In addition, there is a section that evaluates whether a business is structured with one or more socially and environmentally focused business models, essentially going beyond the business's practices to its underlying reason for existing.

The B Impact Rating System is built to measure positive social and environmental performance, with neither *prescriptives* nor *prohibitives*. Companies are not penalized for failing to answer a question in the affirmative or for not having any of the policies and practices in place that are asked about in the assessment. Companies are rather rewarded for what they currently are doing. In this, B Lab's effort is to promote community and create a culture for business improvement, motivation, and inspiration. For example, there are questions that ask if a company has a whistle-blower policy, an employee representative or ombudsman who can manage complaints, or a process for engaging with external stakeholders. Certification as a B Corporation requires that a company receive a minimum score on the rating system, so there is a minimum level of aggregate performance required to achieve certification.

This is not a wholly uncontroversial approach. By choosing not to prohibit or prescribe specific practices, some practitioners feel that the B Corporation model fails to take a stand on those specific practices. However, our judgment has been that the slippery slope would create an endless list that would negate the appeal of B Corp's work in the first place. If a company is unable to answer these questions, it is at a minimum exposed to the policies and practices that in spirit highlight best-practice standards surrounding a full range of stakeholder issues, including human rights, environmental justice, social inclusion, and other important issues. The act of going through the assessment, and the transparency of the scoring for stakeholders, provides companies with the information they need to improve performance. Also, as a result of transparency, investors and consumers have the ability to choose whether to invest or to buy from a company that scores low on specific areas that the consumer cares about. Furthermore, to better address this issue, the newest version of the assessment now asks a series of disclosure questions that, while not included in the rating, provide additional information to stakeholders about perceived negative practices such as child-labor issues or environmental infractions.

---

wisdom and each with deep industry or stakeholder expertise. Different working groups with experts in various areas, such as employee health and safety, work in conjunction with the SACs. Affiliations include: *Developed Markets*: Duke University, CASE, Skoll Foundation, *Risk Metrics, Bridge Ventures, Monitor Institure, Seventh Generation*, SJF Advisory Services, Pacific Community Ventures, Workplace Dynamics, B Lab; *Emerging Markets*, current members: *Aspen Network of Development Entrepreneurs (ANDE)*, Dalberg Global Advisors, Grassroots Business Fund, U.S. Agency for International Development (U.S.AID), B Lab, *Sistema B, Liberty & Justice, Impact Reporting and Investment Standards (IRIS), Lien Centre for Social Innovation, Ashoka Singapore Advisory Council, Trade for Sustainable Development, The International Trade Center (ITC)*.

Below are some examples of issues and indicators that the assessment evaluates.

Impact Area: Governance		
Topics	Rationale	Indicators (Key Questions in Topic)
Anticorruption	Internal financial controls, a code of conduct, and policies to manage complaints/conflicts can help companies avoid corruption and fraud.	• Segregation of A/R and A/P, segregation of check writing and signing, and other financial controls • Written code of business conduct and ethics, whistle-blower policy, procedure for managing conflicts of interest within the board or board and staff
Transparency	Transparent financials and communication with customers and workers promote accountability and reduce fraud.	• Financial statements produced in accordance with local or international standards and reviewed or audited • Policy for sharing financials and ownership info with workers • Customer/client-protection policies

Impact Area: Workers		
Topics	Rationale	Indicators (Key Questions in Topic)
Compensation and Wages	Fair wages and performance-based bonuses, along with training for career advancement, improve the livelihoods of workers.	• All workers paid living wage • % paid above living or minimum wage • Inflation or performance-based bonuses awarded to workers • Ratio of highest-compensated to lowest-compensated worker
Worker Benefits	Offering benefits can increase employee satisfaction, improve worker health, and improve living standards.	• % health-insurance premiums paid by company for individual and family coverage • Weeks of paid maternity and paternity leave
Human Rights & Labor Policy (Emerging Markets Only)	Respecting and promoting fundamental principles is essential for the dignity of work (ILO).	• Policies on nondiscrimination, collective bargaining, freedom of association, and prohibited child labor • Third-party–certified labor practices
Occupational Health & Safety	Safe and healthy work environments protect workers and prevent work-related injuries, accidents, and diseases.	• Injury/accident/lost days/absentee days measured and transparent • Written policies and practices to minimize on-the-job employee accidents

Impact Area: Community		
Topics	Rationale	Indicators (Key Questions in Topic)
Global Code of Conduct	Routine verification of supplier practices is important to ensure that suppliers meet expectations; code-of-conduct policies hold suppliers accountable for safe and fair worker environments.	• % of overseas suppliers visited on site • Member of labor/fair-trade association • Supplier code of conduct holds suppliers accountable for social and environmental performance and is third-party verified, transparent to public, assessed annually, etc.
Diversity	Promoting diversity fosters equality and engages members from underrepresented backgrounds, including women, minorities, previously excluded populations, people with disabilities, and/or individuals living in low-income communities.	• % of management, % of the members of board of directors or advisory board, and % of company owned from underrepresented populations • % of company owned by nonaccredited investors • Policies favoring women- or minority-owned suppliers

Impact Area: Environment		
Topics	Rationale	Indicators (Key Questions in Topic)
Land, Office, Plant	Companies can greatly improve their environmental impact through decisions on management, facilities, and purchasing. For some companies, facilities have the largest environmental footprint; thus, policies and efforts aiming to reduce this impact are important to capture.	• Presence of an environmental management system • Environmental review conducted • Company's facilities compliant with green building standards (LEED or equivalent) • Office-wide recovery and recycling program • Chemical-reduction methods • Public transportation incentives/accessibility • Corporate-travel reduction policies

Impact Area: Environment		
Topics	Rationale	Indicators (Key Questions in Topic)
Inputs	Inputs include energy, water, and raw input materials used in company operations. Monitoring resource usage over time and using sustainable inputs and materials enable companies to reduce natural resource consumption and improve overall environmental impact.	• Sustainability factors integrated into design process • % of revenues from products with a life-cycle assessment • % of recycled, biodegradable, or sustainable materials in product • % of nontoxic materials • Active reclamation project for end products • Energy and water usage monitored, goals set, and reductions achieved • % of energy reduction achieved • % of energy used from renewable sources • % of recycled, biodegradable, or environmentally preferred materials used in products • % increase in water harvested or recycled • Water conservation methods • Company assessment of all materials used and material toxicity • Product source reduction achieved
Outputs	Outputs include various types of waste and emissions a company produces. Monitoring and recording outputs enable companies to assess the amount and degree of negative impact of their operations on the environment with the goal of reducing waste and emissions, especially those that are most harmful to the environment.	• Methods of monitoring and recording greenhouse gas emissions • Purchase of carbon offsets • % of greenhouse gas emissions reduction • Nonhazardous waste, hazardous waste, and universal waste production monitored, goals set, and reductions achieved • Hazardous waste disposed of responsibly • Company testing and treatment of wastewater • Active reclamation project to recycle or reuse end products

Impact Area: Environment		
Topics	Rationale	Indicators (Key Questions in Topic)
Transportation, Distribution, & Suppliers	Efforts to reduce pollution and emissions from transportation and distribution of supplies and products reduce companies' environmental footprint. Companies can also improve their overall environmental impact beyond their own practices by assessing or requiring certain environmental criteria of suppliers and making preferential purchases based on environmental criteria.	• % of clean/low-emission company or outsource fleet vehicles • Techniques for minimizing environmental impacts in distribution and supply chain • Policies that increase the % of inbound freight/shipping via lower-impact transportation • % of significant suppliers using renewable energy, recycling water, and/or water-recovery system • % of significant suppliers monitoring and implementing initiatives to reduce harmful emissions and/or waste production

Education and Management Tool

In addition to providing a third-party rating of social and environmental performance of a company or fund, B Lab has embedded into the ratings system educational and management tools. B Lab has written a range of Best Practices Guides to inform companies about how to implement the positive policies and practices included in the assessment. Sample Best Practices Guides include *How to Write an Employee Handbook*, *How to Write and Implement a Whistle-Blowing Policy*, and *Creating a Supplier Code of Conduct*. Companies that have participated in the ratings process also report increased knowledge and awareness of their company decisions and the impacts on stakeholders.[53] Many companies choose to set annual goals based on their score and use the assessment as a guideline of proactive actions to take. We have found that providing companies the necessary improvement tools creates a clearer path for businesses to approach issues surrounding better business practices and makes the improvement process easier and more accessible.

Finally, and perhaps most importantly, because B Corp is collecting comparable data on thousands of companies globally, it is able to provide analytical tools to companies, academics, and stakeholders, allowing them to benchmark performance, improve performance, and report on performance to all stakeholders. These analytics allow a level of comparability and transparency, and they will allow B Lab over time to improve performance as well as improve the content of the assessment itself.

---

53.   B Lab has received anecdotal reflections from meeting with entrepreneurs who are going through the ratings process.

Small and Medium-Sized Enterprises (SMEs)

For many small and medium-sized companies, particularly those operating in emerging markets, it is difficult to approach the issue of human rights without the necessary resources and capacity to manage any issues that might arise within the company. The B Impact Assessment provides those companies an entry point to begin to address human rights. These assessments are for the companies that do not have the financial resources to attend major human rights conferences and set up departments to manage compliance in their supply chain. By introducing certain policies and practices through the assessment and providing companies with the tools to implement those practices and improve performance, over time the companies will be in a more sustainable position to succeed through business growth based on appropriate human rights standards.

Case Studies
Greyston Bakery
Greyston Bakery, a certified B corp, has been baking gourmet brownies in Yonkers, New York since 1982. The $8.4 million for-profit bakery is most famous for its long-standing status as the brownie supplier for Ben & Jerry's and for having an open hiring policy that provides the people of Yonkers with employment opportunity regardless of work history. The company tag line is: "[w]e don't hire people to bake brownies, we bake brownies to hire people." Committed to a double bottom line, Greyston Bakery continues to be a pioneer in the world of social enterprise.

Cascade Engineering
Another example is Cascade Engineering, a manufacturer and marketer of products and services supporting a variety of industries, including renewable energy, automotive, commercial truck and bus, solid waste and recycling, material compounding, furniture, radio-frequency identification technology, and material handling. The Cascade Engineering Family of Companies is a global company based in Michigan with more than a thousand employees and fourteen businesses. The company's world-class engineering, technology, and manufacturing allow it to provide leading-edge solutions while maintaining a strong commitment to lean manufacturing and environmental stewardship, guaranteeing higher efficiency and less waste. Additionally, Cascade has made a commitment to developing its corporate culture and improving the livelihoods of its workers through worker-improvement programs in more economically depressed parts of the country. Cascade's business model is rooted in diversification and innovation and a commitment to creating sustainable products and services that contribute to the triple bottom line.

Both of these companies have shown leadership in their respective industries and have set precedents for better ways to do business. In some cases there are trade-offs between the social mission and long-term financial value of social enterprises (the Freelancers

Insurance Company intentionally manages to a lower net margin to provide higher-quality health insurance benefits more broadly to its customers). In other cases, the focus on social and environmental impact is a competitive advantage, allowing for greater financial value over the long term (Cascade and Method Home Products has found this to be the case).

In the early days of building the community of certified B Corporations, the companies pursuing certification were, like Greyston and Cascade, already leaders with a social purpose built into their businesses. For them, becoming a B Corporation started with a desire for a platform to speak louder than they could through their own business. But even these businesses, in the process of becoming a part of the B Corporation community, found that there were numerous areas where they could improve their own performance. King Arthur Flour, a nationally recognized flour company and also an Employee Share Ownership Plan (ESOP), is one such business. King Arthur Flour has had tremendous growth over the past twenty years, all the while providing greater opportunities to its workers and local community. As a B Corporation, King Arthur Flour's primary area of excellence is with workers. However, King Arthur Flour President and CEO Steve Voigt says the company's B Corporation certification is not only a validation that the company is on the right track with corporate social and environmental responsibility, but also "a great tool and impetus in helping us continue to move in that direction." King Arthur Flour also recently became a Vermont benefit corporation.[54] Dansko, another certified B corp and producer of clogs and other footwear, has a company-wide volunteering program, allowing full-time employees to participate in sixteen hours of paid volunteer work per year. For every volunteer hour worked by an employee, the company also donates the equivalent of his or her salary to that charity.

Conclusion

Government and the nonprofit sector are necessary but insufficient to address society's greatest challenges. A large and accelerating movement of social entrepreneurs is constrained by unsupportive corporate law and a lack of tools to help consumers, investors, workers, and policy makers identify and support their high-impact businesses, and this community is growing quickly. B Lab has recently established a partnership in Latin America to expand the certification in those markets and is looking to expand to other regions based on interest in B Corporation certification from entrepreneurs around the globe. As the community of B corps grows internationally, it will be required to perform

---

54. Terry Rosenstock, *King Arthur Flour Becomes a Vermont Benefit Corporation*, CORP. SOCIAL RESPONSIBILITY NEWSWIRE (Mar. 20, 2012), http://www.csrwire.com/press_releases/33904-King-Arthur-Flour-Becomes-a-Vermont-Benefit-Corporation.

legal analyses to determine the ability of companies to consider stakeholder interests as comparable with their U.S. counterparts.

The goal with the B Corporation legal structure is to create the freedom and legal protection for entrepreneurs and investors to scale businesses with purpose, not just profit, at their core, as well as to rebuild public trust in free market capitalism by expanding corporate accountability to require consideration of the impact of decisions not only on shareholders but also on workers, communities, and the environment.

B Corporations' social and environmental performance tools enable consumers to support businesses that align with their values, private and public investors to drive capital to higher-impact investments, and governments and multinational corporations to implement sustainable practices because of their intrinsic commitment to create benefits for society.

These innovations combined have created an opportunity for businesses to address great challenges and to alter their relationship with stakeholders, who have often been hurt by or excluded from private-sector activity. As a result, a more inclusive and sustainable economy can help to protect human rights, alleviate or prevent poverty, restore the environment, and create inclusive opportunities for safe and fulfilling work environments even while fulfilling business profit motives.

Chapter 16

An Attorney's Perspective on Corporate Social Responsibility and Corporate Philanthropy

Sarah A. Altschuller

Corporate Social Responsibility Practice

Foley Hoag LLP

Introduction

As an attorney advising clients on corporate social responsibility (CSR), I am often asked about the nature of my role. What kind of advice do I provide? Do I advise companies on human rights or philanthropy? Corporate governance or sustainability? Why would a corporate client hire an attorney to advise it on CSR? Who is my "client within the client"? Someone in the general counsel's office or someone with CSR included in his or her title? In navigating these conversations, I find myself confronting persistent misconceptions about the nature of CSR and its attendant expectations for companies.

When discussing the role of an attorney in the field of CSR, I hear from those who largely echo Milton Friedman ("there is one and only one social responsibility of business . . . to increase its profits"),[1] as well as those who endorse the concept of CSR but see it as something *extra* that companies do to burnish their public image without alignment to a broader business strategy. These misconceptions provide the opportunity to engage people about the ways contemporary CSR addresses a dynamic set of stakeholder expectations and standards that define a set of normative roles and responsibilities for companies.

---

1. Milton Friedman, *Social Responsibility of Business*, N.Y. Times (Sept. 13, 1970), at 32.

In these discussions, explicitly and implicitly, I am describing some of the fundamental roles of any attorney: I help my clients understand and respond to the expectations that society has established for their behavior, whether those expectations are expressed through national legislation, international legal conventions, or voluntary standards and guidelines.

One of those most enduring sources of misperception regarding CSR is its relationship to corporate philanthropy. The terms are used interchangeably in the popular media and in business publications; most frequently, specific instances of corporate philanthropy are deemed to be representative of a company's broader CSR efforts. Generally, I believe that corporate philanthropy can certainly be indicative of a company's social commitment and reflective of its values, but I do not consider it to be sufficiently representative of a company's approach to CSR.

As an attorney, I am cognizant of the dangers inherent in imprecise terminology, and I am concerned when I see the terms *CSR* and *corporate philanthropy* used without distinction. My fear is that the failure to understand the differences between the two may leave companies ill prepared to understand the demands of the stakeholders who are increasingly pushing companies to manage the social and environmental impacts of their operations. It is these expectations, and their expression through a growing number of normative, legislative, and institutional standards, that define contemporary CSR. It is especially important for companies to understand the human rights–related aspects of contemporary CSR and the increasing linkages between societal expectations and international human rights law. These linkages reflect the substantial evolution of CSR in recent decades and the corollary expansion of the responsibilities and accountabilities that drive my work in the field.

This chapter is divided into two parts. The first part provides an overview of contemporary definitions of CSR and corporate philanthropy as well as a historical overview of the recent evolution of these two concepts; and the second part addresses the roles and responsibilities of an attorney advising clients in a world where the line between CSR and corporate philanthropy is often blurred.

CSR and Corporate Philanthropy: The Evolution of a Distinction

Contemporary Definitions

An analysis that begins with an expression of concern about the blurred definitions between terms should surely begin with a clear definition (or two). One of my preferred definitions of CSR[2] is the one used by the Corporate Social Responsibility Initiative at Harvard University's Kennedy School of Government:

---

2.   One of the professional hazards of working in the field of CSR is the multitude of definitions.

Corporate social responsibility encompasses not only what companies do with their profits, but also how they make them. It goes beyond philanthropy and compliance and addresses how companies manage their economic, social, and environmental impacts, as well as their relationships in all key spheres of influence: the workplace, the marketplace, the supply chain, the community, and the public policy realm.[3]

Another contemporary definition emphasizes the importance of stakeholder expectations in framing CSR: "The social responsibility of business encompasses the economic, legal, ethical, and discretionary expectations that society has of organizations at a given point in time."[4]

These definitions both address the *external* orientation of CSR: it is responsive to external values, impacts, and expectations. Definitions of corporate philanthropy reflect more of an *internal* orientation: philanthropy is a voluntary exercise that addresses external causes but is not driven by external values to the same extent as CSR. One recent definition of corporate philanthropy states that it is "the practice of companies of all sizes and sectors making charitable contributions to address a variety of social, economic and other issues as part of their overall corporate citizenship strategy."[5] An alternative definition states that corporate philanthropy consists of "those activities that companies voluntarily undertake to have a positive impact on society, including cash contributions, contributions of products and services, volunteerism, and other business transactions to advance a cause, issue or nonprofit organization."[6]

Notably, definitions of both CSR and corporate philanthropy reflect a fundamental connection between companies and society. CSR, however, is tied to a set of expectations that companies should manage their operations in a way that accounts for their impacts on society. CSR sets up a dynamic relationship between companies and their stakeholders: to truly assess and understand the impacts of their operations, companies need to engage their stakeholders to understand and identify those impacts. Corporate philanthropy is an endeavor that is voluntarily undertaken and more unilaterally driven. Ultimately, CSR is a

---

See, e.g., Alexander Dahlsrud, *How Corporate Social Responsibility Is Defined: An Analysis of 37 Definitions,* Corporate Social Responsibility and Environmental Management 1 (2006).

3. *The Initiative Defining Corporate Social Responsibility,* Harvard Kennedy School Corporate Social Responsibility Initiative, http://www.hks.harvard.edu/m-rcbg/CSRI/init_define.html (last visited April 9, 2012).

4. Archie B. Carroll, *A History of Corporate Social Responsibility: Concepts and Practices,* in The Oxford Handbook of Corporate Social Responsibility 19, 33 (Andrew Crane et al. eds., 2008).

5. *Corporate Giving FAQs,* Council on Foundations, http://www.cof.org/templates/41.cfm ?ItemNumber=17748&navItemNumber=14850 (last visited April 9, 2012) (citing Business for Social Responsibility, www.bsr.org).

6. *Id.*

strategic approach to stakeholder expectations that defines how companies are managed, not how they choose to allocate certain profits through acts of philanthropy.[7]

The Evolution of CSR

The current distinctions between CSR and corporate philanthropy have historical underpinnings that shed light on both contemporary understandings and misperceptions. The rapid evolution of CSR in the last few decades provides insight into the nature of the current expectations that companies are confronted with when engaging with diverse sets of stakeholders.

Early Incarnations of CSR

In its earliest incarnations, CSR was largely understood as reflective of corporate willingness to make voluntary contributions. Companies operated as social benefactors, offering financial and in-kind support to a wide range of social causes. In the late 1800s, communities began to look to business leaders as patrons of the arts, churches, and local educational institutions.[8] These efforts were, in fact, largely philanthropic, and thus the earliest forms of CSR were largely indistinct from contemporary corporate philanthropy. At the same time, this giving was largely individualized philanthropy by corporate leaders, and the companies themselves were not perceived as being social benefactors. In the United States, business leaders like Andrew Carnegie, John D. Rockefeller, and Cornelius Vanderbilt earned reputations as both *robber barons* and unparalleled philanthropists; their charitable largesse may have been, in part, an effort to counter negative reactions to the increasing size and scale of the companies that emerged during a period of rapid industrialization.[9] During this period, the legality of corporate, as opposed to individual, philanthropy was often in question. With boards of directors exercising limited charter

---

7.   This is not to say that corporate philanthropy itself is not a strategic and valuable endeavor. Philanthropy allows companies to invest in human potential in a way that benefits both communities and the company. *See, e.g.*, Michael Porter & Mark Kramer, *Challenging Assumptions*, in EBF on Corporate Social Responsibility 3 (Summer 2004), http://www.johnelkington.com/ebf_CSR_report.pdf. Around the world, corporate philanthropic support for education, technology, health, social services, and infrastructure is wide-ranging, and the positive social impacts of these investments should not be underestimated.

8.   Carroll, *supra* note 4, at 21. This history focuses primarily on developments in the United States and Europe.

9.   *See, e.g.*, Myrna Wulfson, *The Ethics of Corporate Social Responsibility and Philanthropic Ventures*, J. Bus. Ethics 135, 135 (2001) ("In the early 1900's corporations were criticized for being too big, too powerful, and guilty of antisocial and anticompetitive practices. . . . To improve their public image[,] many business leaders gave donations to charitable institutions. Andrew Carnegie founded the Carnegie Corporation of New York to fund education, the Carnegie Endowment for International Peace, the Carnegie Foundation for the Advancement of Teaching, and the Carnegie Institution of Washington, which conducts scientific research. Over 2,500 libraries were built with $56 million of Carnegie's charitable funds.").

powers, some courts precluded corporate community giving, especially if there was no immediate and direct benefit to the company.[10]

In the 1940s and 1950s, corporate philanthropy, "or corporate contributions as manifestations of CSR," began to gain traction during a period of "innovation and legalization."[11] During this period, corporate philanthropy was a way for corporate executives to strengthen their ties to local communities. In addition, corporate donations were often based on the discretionary choices of corporation managers, often in response to requests from specific beneficiaries. Corporate social responsibility and corporate philanthropy remained largely one and the same: CSR represented the voluntary commitments of companies to provide support to social causes, and those efforts were largely philanthropic.

In the later part of the last century, social perceptions and expectations of companies began to shift. An early indicator of this transition was the activities of social advocates who began to turn to companies in pushing specific policy agendas, especially when more traditional public-policy recourses proved ineffective. Examples include sit-in campaigns at Woolworth lunch counters and community organizing against Eastman Kodak to force minority hiring in the 1960s, and the movement for corporate reform and divestment from South Africa in the 1970s and 1980s.[12] As one observer noted:

> The idea in each instance was that, if they lacked the resources to force governments to change public policy directly, the advocates of these causes could nevertheless achieve their objectives by motivating private institutions to change their private policies and behaviors on such a large scale as to constitute a *de facto* change in public policy.[13]

In the subsequent decades, the emergence of multinational companies with global markets and supply chains both reflected the weakening of ties between individual companies and specific local communities and provoked advocacy seeking to counter the magnitude of corporate power.[14] Corporate stakeholders, including advocacy organizations, consumers, and shareholders, called for systems that could hold companies accountable, or responsible, for capacity to bring about both positive and negative economic and

---

10. CARROLL, *supra* note 4, at 21.

11. CARROLL, *supra* note 4, at 26, citing Sophia A. Muirhead, *Corporate Contributions: The View from 50 Years* 15 Research Report No 1249-99-RR, The Conference Board (1999).

12. JAROL B. MANHEIM, CORPORATE CONDUCT UNBECOMING 13 (2000).

13. MANHEIM, *supra* 12, at 13.

14. *See, e.g.,* Wendy Schoener, *Non-Governmental Organizations and Global Activism: Legal and Informal Approaches,* IND. J. GLOBAL LEGAL STUD. 4, 537 (1997) ("Transnational corporations (TNCs) can strengthen or enfeeble a national economy, sometimes with a single decision."); Erin E. Macek, *Scratching the Corporate Back: Why Corporations Have No Incentive to Define Human Rights,* 11, MINN. J. GLOBAL TRADE 101, 103 (2002) ("Direct investment by TNCs in developing countries is greater than both the inflows from official aid and the net lending by international banks.").

social impacts on society. At the same time, corporate philanthropy, and a certain level of engaged responsiveness to social concerns, began to be an *expected* part of the dynamic between companies and their stakeholders: companies were increasingly seen as having social roles and obligations.[15]

1990s and Beyond: Codes of Conduct

In the early 1990s, a new set of dynamics heralded the advent of contemporary CSR. A number of high-profile corporations, predominantly in the apparel and footwear industries, began drafting corporate codes of conduct for suppliers. These companies recognized the need to preemptively respond to advocates targeting social and economic inequities inherent in their sourcing structures. Levi Strauss was the first corporation to draft such a code of conduct, putting together its Global Sourcing Guidelines in 1991 and making them available publicly in early 1992.[16] Nike followed suit and published its first code of conduct in 1992. Companies were responding to the understanding that the public expected them to *care* and be responsive, and be accountable, to concerns such as low wages and child labor in their product supply chains. The early codes that emerged from an increasing number of corporations beginning in the early and mid-1990s range in quality from brief, vague policy statements to comprehensive guidelines.

Though these early corporate codes for suppliers could have been easily dismissed as public relations mechanisms meant to assuage public concern, they ultimately reflected an inflection point in which the dynamics between companies and a broad group of stakeholders began to shift significantly. Through voluntary codes, corporate executives have sought to anticipate and respond to public concerns about the actual and potential harms associated with their operations. The act of drafting a code is one in which a company seeks to craft and benefit from a particular public persona: ideally, one in which the corporation is seen as responsive and accountable. Corporate codes made public a detailed pronouncement of corporate values and guidelines and provided the basis for a grounded debate with corporate stakeholders on obligations and standards.[17]

Notably, the commitments reflected in these codes were not made in a normative vacuum. Companies found that their *voluntary* internal initiatives were evaluated against a wide set of standards ranging from local, national, and international laws to voluntary guidelines established by groups ranging from industry associations to the United Nations.

---

15.   Carroll, *supra* note 4, at 24, citing Nicholas N. Eberstadt, *What History Tells Us about Corporate Responsibilities*, Bus. and Society Review/Innovation 76–81 (1973).

16.   Karl Schoenberger, Levi's Children: Coming to Terms with Human Rights in the Global Marketplace 62 (2000).

17.   Corporate codes of conduct for suppliers have also exposed companies to private enforcement mechanisms as the codes of their customers and partners have been incorporated into contracts, vendor guidelines, and other documents that have a range of potential remedies for breach, including contract termination.

The principles and guidelines embodied in multilateral initiatives such as the Voluntary Principles on Security and Human Rights as well as international conventions such as the core conventions of the International Labour Organization increasingly placed high-profile normative frameworks around corporate activity. The evolution of codes of conduct in just a few short years reflected a change from vague guidelines set internally to increasingly specific commitments grounded in external standards. In 1999, Bob Jeffcott and Lynda Yanz of the Maquila Solidary Network observed,

> In just a few years, we have moved from company codes of conduct with no provisions for monitoring or verification toward multi-company, industry-wide and multi-sectoral codes with elaborate systems of internal monitoring and external verification, factory and company certification, and mechanisms for NGO and labor participation in monitoring and third party complaints procedures. From company codes containing vague principles about corporate responsibility, we have moved toward negotiated codes with precise and fairly consistent language based on ILO conventions and UN declarations.[18]

In a relatively short period of time, the dynamics between companies and their stakeholders, especially in the field of human rights, transformed from a set of dialogues about the adequacy and potential of private codes of conduct to a set of articulated expectations that were informed by, and often expressly linked to, international human rights law.

As companies adopted codes linked to international law, corporate stakeholders were provided an opportunity to add substance to the meaning of international principles that are necessarily vague in their articulation. Rather than allowing corporations *to co-opt* public international standards, many corporate stakeholders began to ask companies to define what it is they are doing to respond to the social norms reflected in international conventions. What does it mean to respect the right to freedom of association? How can a company effectively monitor a commitment to respect an international prohibition against child labor? Addressing the challenges posed by these stakeholders increasingly required companies to develop management plans to effectuate their public commitments. As companies responded to pressures to be transparent about their activities, this line of questioning provided the basis for an overall shift in the social expectations of *acceptable* corporate behavior.

Corporate Accountability: Litigation in U.S. Courts

During this same period, a number of companies found themselves subject to claims in American courts under the Alien Tort Statute (ATS), which allowed plaintiffs to bring

---

18. Bob Jeffcott & Lynda Yanz, *Codes of Conduct: From Corporate Social Responsibility to Social Accountability*, Maquila Solidarity Network (September 1999).

claims against corporate defendants for violations of international human rights law. In November 1993, in the case of *Aquinda v. Texaco*,[19] approximately seventy individuals from Ecuador filed suit against Texaco alleging injuries as the result of environmental pollution stemming from the company's operations in that country. In October 1996, in the case of *Doe v. Unocal*, fourteen Burmese villages brought suit against Unocal Corporation (and others, including the French oil company Total) alleging that they and their families had been subjected to forced labor, murder, rape, torture, and other violations by the military of Burma during the construction of the Yadana pipeline project.[20] Since then, more than fifty ATS cases have been filed against corporate defendants.

In its 2004 decision in *Sosa v. Alvarez Machain*,[21] the United States Supreme Court affirmed the standing of certain customary international law norms as the basis for potential corporate liability under the ATS. In its 2013 decision in *Kiobel v. Royal Dutch Petroleum*,[22] the Supreme Court did not directly address the question of corporate liability, but the majority opinion by Chief Justice Roberts and the concurrence by Justice Breyer both explicitly contemplated continued corporate liability under the ATS.[23] In light of such decisions, litigation under both the Alien Tort Statute and general tort law against companies for violations of international human rights law is likely to continue. The potential liability of companies for violations of international human rights norms represents another shift in contemporary notions of corporate responsibility and has also necessitated new evaluations of legal and reputational risk by companies and their counsel.

Cases against companies have raised a new set of legal issues and a wide range of activities about the nature of company operations. Most of these cases do not involve allegations that corporations committed direct violations of international law. Rather, these cases have typically alleged indirect, or subsidiary, liability, whereby corporations are accused of aiding and abetting those who committed the direct violations, or of conspiring with those who committed the direct violations. The potential for liability, and the reputational harm that is associated with being named as a defendant, has forced companies

---

19.   Aguinda v. Texaco, 142 F. Supp. 2d 534, 536 (S.D.N.Y. 2001). The case was eventually dismissed on *forum non conveniens* grounds.

20.   Doe I v. Unocal Corp., 395 F.3d 932 (9th Cir. 2002). In 2005, a settlement was reached in the *Unocal* case. *See* Rachel Chambers, *The Unocal Settlement: Implications for the Developing Law on Corporate Complicity in Human Rights Abuses*, 13 HUMAN RIGHTS BRIEF 14–16 (2005).

21.   124 S. Ct. 2739 (2004).

22.   Kiobel v. Royal Dutch Petroleum Co., 133 S. Ct. 1659 (2013) (In *Kiobel*, the Supreme Court significantly limited the application of the ATS by declaring that the presumption against extraterritoriality applies to all cases brought pursuant to the statute.)

23.   *See Kiobel*, 133 S. Ct. at 1669–71. "On these facts, all the relevant conduct took place outside the United States. And even where the claims touch and concern the territory of the United States, they must do so with sufficient force to displace the presumption against extraterritorial application. Corporations are often present in many countries, and it would reach too far to say that mere corporate presence suffices." *Id.* at 1669 (internal citation omitted). "I agree with the Court that here it would 'reach too far to say' that such 'mere corporate presence suffices.'" *Id.* at 1770 (J. Breyer, concurrence).

to assess the nature and management of their operations around the world. How should companies structure their relationships with governments seen as repressive? How can companies manage the activities of public and private security forces that may commit human rights violations while undertaking operations in conjunction with a company's investment? What does it mean for a corporation to aid and abet a violation of international law? Do companies have to intend for violations to take place to be held liable for violations that occur during the operation of a project? Should, or will, companies be held liable for the activities of partially owned subsidiaries or joint-venture partners? Are corporations even proper defendants under international human rights law? All of these questions have emerged in the last two decades and have forced many companies to assess the nature of their operations in a new light.

An International Responsibility to Respect Human Rights
That Is Neither Contingent Nor Time Bound

Finally, in just the last few years, there has been another pronounced and fundamental shift in stakeholder expectations with regard to corporate responsibility to manage, mitigate, and prevent the adverse human rights impacts of their operations. The work of the UN Special Representative of the Secretary-General on business and human rights, Professor John Ruggie, has resulted in a clear statement that companies have a responsibility to respect human rights under international law.[24] This responsibility suggests that companies carry out sufficient due diligence efforts so that they are aware of—and thus able to address and prevent—any adverse human rights impacts associated with their operations. Companies must carefully consider a wide range of factors when assessing their potential accountability or liability for human rights abuses, including the specific local contexts in which they operate; the capacity and human rights commitments of the public authorities in those local contexts; and the complex ways in which company interactions with business partners, contractors, and other state and nonstate actors may contribute to human rights abuses.

In his 2008 report to the UN Human Rights Council, the Special Representative observed that the international community has been in need of a "common conceptual and policy framework" for approaching the debate about business and human rights.[25] He then set forward three core principles to help guide the debate: (1) states have a duty to protect against human rights abuses, including those committed by third parties; (2) companies

---

24. *See generally*, UN Human Rights Council, *Report of the Special Representative of the Secretary-General on Human Rights and Transnational Corporations, Guiding Principles on Business and Human Rights: Implementing the United Nations "Protect, Respect and Remedy" Framework*, A/HRC/17/31 (Mar. 21, 2011), http://www.ohchr.org/documents/issues/business/A-HRC-17-31_AEV.pdf.

25. UN Special Representative of the Secretary-General, *"Protect, Respect and Remedy": A Framework for Business and Human Rights*, ¶ 8, UN Doc. A/HRC/8/5 (Apr. 7, 2008).

have a responsibility to respect human rights; and (3) there needs to be effective access to remedies so that these obligations can be enforced. With regard to the obligation to respect human rights, the special representative declared that "to respect rights essentially means not to infringe on the rights of others—put simply, to do no harm." This is a "baseline expectation for all companies in all situations." He also observed that

> because companies can affect virtually all internationally recognized rights, they should consider the responsibility to respect in relation to all rights, although some may require greater attention in particular contexts. There are situations in which companies may have additional responsibilities—for example, where they perform certain public functions, or because they have undertaken additional commitments voluntarily.[26]

In his 2010 report, the Special Representative stated the following in a clear articulation of the contemporary distinction between CSR and corporate philanthropy:

> A number of stakeholders have asked whether companies have core human rights responsibilities beyond respecting rights. . . . *Companies may undertake additional human rights commitments for philanthropic reasons, to protect and promote their brand, or to develop new business opportunities.* Operational conditions may dictate additional responsibilities in specific circumstances, while contracts with public authorities for particular projects may require them. In other instances, such as natural disasters or public health emergencies, there may be compelling reasons for any social actor with capacity to contribute temporarily. *Such contingent and time-bound actions by some companies in certain situations may be both reasonable and desirable.*[27]

The Special Representative's process of stakeholder engagement to inform the development of his framework and his recognition of the role social expectation plays in defining corporate responsibility for human rights seem to reflect both the substantive and procedural components that CSR has come to embody. This process and standard further informed the final report of his UN mandate.

In March 2011, the Special Representative released his Guiding Principles on Business and Human Rights, in which he provides guidance to companies seeking to implement respect for human rights in the management of their business operations, and the UN

---

26. *Id.* at ¶ 24.
27. UN Special Representative of the Secretary-General, *Business and Human Rights: Further Steps Toward the Operationalization of the "Protect, Respect and Remedy" Framework,* ¶¶ 62–63, UN Doc. A/HRC/14/27 (Apr. 9, 2010) (emphasis added)

Human Rights Council formally endorsed these Guiding Principles in June 2011. In an October 2011 article published after the conclusion of his mandate, Professor Ruggie observed that the Guiding Principles are "not just another set of voluntary standards vying for attention in an increasingly crowded space" but rather represent "authoritative UN standards around which the articulated expectations of many public and private institutions have already converged."[28] This *convergence of expectations* is reflected in the fact that the Guiding Principles have informed the recent revisions of the International Finance Corporation's Sustainability Framework and associated performance standards and the OECD Guidelines for Multinational Enterprises, as well as the content of the new social responsibility standard adopted by the International Organization for Standardization, ISO 26000.[29]

Notably, consistent with the guidance provided by the Guiding Principles, stakeholders, including both legislators and shareholders, are asking companies to demonstrate that they have due diligence mechanisms in place to assess, and respond to, human rights concerns in their supply chains and operating areas. Recent legislative developments in this area include section 1502 of the U.S. Dodd-Frank financial-reform legislation. This provision requires companies using minerals originating in the Democratic Republic of Congo, or adjoining countries, to report on their "due diligence" measures regarding the source and chain of custody of those minerals.[30] Additionally, the California Transparency in Supply Chains Act of 2010 asks retailers and manufacturers operating in California to disclose their efforts to "evaluate and address" the risks of human trafficking and slavery in their product supply chains.[31]

These developments signal the emergence of a formal expectation that companies should conduct human rights due diligence to identify and manage the adverse human rights impacts associated with their operations. The formalization of expectations has posed a challenge for companies to ensure that they have the policies and oversight mechanisms necessary to address stakeholder concerns and expectations.

---

28.   John Ruggie, *Managing Human Rights Impacts in a World of Converging Expectations*, Corporate Secretary (Oct. 28, 2011), http://www.corporatesecretary.com/articles/corporate-social-responsibility/12043/managing-human-rights-impacts-world-converging-expectations.

29.   *See* International Finance Corporation, *IFC's Sustainability Framework*, http://www.ifc.org/wps/wcm/connect/Topics_Ext_Content/IFC_External_Corporate_Site/IFC+Sustainability/Sustainability+Framework; Organization for Economic Cooperation and Development, *OECD Guidelines for Multinational Enterprises 2011* (ed. 31–34, May 25, 2011), http://www.oecd.org/daf/inv/mne/48004323.pdf; International Organization for Standardization, *ISO 26000:2010—Social Responsibility*, http://www.iso.org/iso/home/standards/iso26000.htm.

30.   Dodd-Frank Wall Street Reform and Consumer Protection Act of 2010, 15 U.S.C. § 78m(p) (2012). *See also* Securities and Exchange Commission, Release No. 34-67716 (Aug. 22, 2012), http://www.sec.gov/rules/final/2012/34-67716.pdf.

31.   California Transparency in Supply Chains Act of 2010, Cal. Civ. Code § 1714.43 (2010).

CSR and Corporate Philanthropy: The Attorney's Role

What is the role of the attorney in talking to companies about CSR? A crucial role for any attorney is to help clients understand the requirements and implications of societal expectations, whether those expectations be mandatory or normative.[32] Contemporary CSR presents clients, and their counsel, with the challenge of assessing a range of legislative, regulatory, and institutional requirements, in addition to documents like the Guiding Principles and a plethora of multilateral and industry-specific voluntary standards. Attorneys can provide clients with critical assistance in evaluating the requirements and normative content of the standards by which stakeholders are evaluating their activities. In addition, CSR can also be a bellwether of the direction in which regulation is trending or areas in which heightened legal standards may be expected to emerge as a result of increased societal expectations. Attorneys can thus help clients spot trends in the law and help them develop forward-thinking strategies.

The Dangers of Internal Misperceptions

One of the challenges of being an attorney in the CSR space, however, is the misperceptions that continue to blur internal decision-making and assessments of strategic priorities. Companies cannot assess the reputational, operational, and legal risks of failing to be responsive to societal expectations if they do not understand the ways in which those expectations have transformed in recent years. What are the risks that a CSR program can help address? Strong CSR programs can reduce the risk of lawsuits, divestment actions, and boycotts. They can mitigate the risks of negative news stories and other communications that can create long-term damage to a company's reputation with key stakeholders. Companies are subject to the demands of a wide variety of stakeholders, including employees, shareholders, joint-venture partners, consumers, and the communities impacted by corporate operations. Increasingly, these stakeholders are advocating that companies manage the social and environmental impacts of their operations.

Against this backdrop, there are risks for companies that claim to have embraced CSR and then point to the glossy reports of their company foundation to demonstrate the degree of their commitment. Imagine a company that provides significant philanthropic

---

32. *See, e.g.,* Joe W. (Chip) Pitts III, *Business, Human Rights, & The Environment: The Role of the Lawyer in CSR & Ethical Globalization,* BERKELEY J. INT'L L. 26, 479, 484 (2008) ("Lawyers are on the frontline in dealing with these issues both for corporations and for the other stakeholders affected by corporate conduct. This means that no lawyer interfacing with corporations, or working within one, can afford to be ignorant of CSR's basic content, principles, and processes or the variety of existing soft and hard law instruments that can cause problems and/or offer solutions when CSR issues and dilemmas arise. Environmental and human rights issues are now increasingly standard in due diligence for mergers and acquisitions. CSR reports from public corporations are increasingly commonplace. Human rights and environmental impact assessments are being used—and should be considered for broader use—in major investment and other corporate decisions across the board.").

support to organizations that dig wells in the communities where the company operates. Undoubtedly, the wells provide community members with increased access to safe drinking water. The company may receive reputational benefits from its actions, and some observers may view the company as a good *corporate citizen*. In addition, the language of the company's environmental standards may be fully compliant with all applicable legislation and regulations and may, in fact, exceed the requirements of those standards. That same company, however, may have failed to develop the internal policies and mechanisms necessary to ensure that local managers are held accountable for following safe environmental practices. The company's lack of internal oversight and management may have left local groundwater supplies, and the communities that depend on them, vulnerable to contamination. The company itself may be exposed to the risk of future reputational damage as well as fines and other punitive costs, including the costs associated with potential litigation. Regardless of the extent of the company's philanthropic contributions, the company cannot be said to have fully incorporated CSR into the management of its operations.

In the above scenario, company managers may be tempted to respond to those who accuse the company of failing to protect local groundwater supplies with references to the company's support for local water-access initiatives. References to good deeds, however, do not mitigate against the risks associated with lack of internal commitment and oversight. Corporate philanthropic commitments do not ensure the existence of internal management capacity to manage social risk; a company with a strong internal commitment to CSR will have systems in place to manage the social and environmental risks associated with its operations.

Assessing Corporate Capacity

At the outset of an engagement, therefore, it is useful for attorneys to identify whether clients are approaching CSR, in whole or in part, through a traditional philanthropic mindset, and they should discuss with clients the risks of doing so.[33] Corporate confusion about the distinctions between CSR and corporate philanthropy may be reflected in a company's policies and CSR reporting. For example, policies that emphasize company philanthropic commitments when discussing stakeholder interactions rather than a company's community-engagement strategies do not provide much risk protection. Similarly, policies on employee relations that emphasize support for employee voluntarism rather than the company's labor standards are also a potential concern. When talking with clients, attorneys must be careful to emphasize that philanthropic commitments are distinct from the internal and external commitments that contemporary notions of CSR demand.

---

33. In these conversations, attorneys should not underestimate the degree to which corporate philanthropy is also a strategic and valuable endeavor. Many companies have well-developed philanthropic programs, and strategic philanthropy allows companies to invest in human potential in ways that benefit communities and companies alike.

To be responsive to stakeholder concerns, a company needs to develop the internal capacity to evaluate these concerns, assess potential responses, and make decisions about corporate strategy. CSR is about the core business functions of a company, and about being responsive to the ever-increasing demand from stakeholders that companies be held accountable for the social and environmental impacts of their operations. The expectations of those stakeholders are expressed in forms ranging from legislation and regulation to shareholder resolutions and disruptive protests. Failure to respond to these expectations is risky, and companies should regularly assess these expectations through a variety of channels. Proposed shareholder resolutions, comments on social-media channels, and community feedback through grievance mechanisms all provide important means for companies to assess stakeholder concerns.

Management personnel within the company should consider the concerns that are raised by stakeholders with regard to a company's social and environmental performance. Though this chapter has addressed definitions of CSR, it may be more interesting to ask not, *What is CSR?* but rather *What does CSR do?* and, *What is its function within the company?* At its core, I think CSR creates a culture of listening and provides the discipline to know when and how to respond to what is being said. Companies need to be skilled at listening to a range of stakeholders, including employees, investors, governments, and local communities. They need to develop a strong understanding of stakeholders' expectations of the company and their concerns about the impacts of corporate activity. Listening is an active process: it requires proactive engagement and an ability to seek out new perspectives, both internally and externally.

Building Strong Management Systems

If effective CSR begins with listening, it is enacted through a management system that is responsive to the information that stakeholders provide. If stakeholder concerns and expectations are not understood—and the company is seen as unresponsive—stakeholders begin to take action. Employees leave, consumers shop elsewhere, investors express concern, and communities protest. And perhaps legislation is passed and lawsuits are filed.

Companies need policies, and they need management systems to effectively implement those policies. Attorneys should develop these policies and management systems in a manner that reflects an understanding of the ways in which their clients are implementing their CSR standards. Moreover, a strong line of communication and accountability must exist between policies developed at headquarters and the actual operations of the company on the ground.

Company confusion between CSR and philanthropy may be reflected in the ways that specific management responsibilities are assigned within the company. Companies should have well-developed guidelines to ensure that their social and environmental standards are effectively implemented, and they should also ensure that the dedicated personnel capacity exists to implement those guidelines. Corporate philanthropic officers should not be tasked with managing the social and environmental risks of a company's operations. In setting such clear functional distinctions between those responsible for corporate philanthropy and those responsible for CSR, managers and employees will gain greater clarity about their individual areas of responsibility and accountability.

When considering a company's capacity to distinguish between CSR and corporate philanthropy in practice, attorneys should also be aware of the company's existing processes for responding to community grievances. Companies may have developed strong community-engagement processes that establish grievance mechanisms, but local managers may still be inclined to respond to community protests through the allocation of philanthropic dollars. In some contexts, philanthropic commitments may forestall immediate community protests, but they do not ultimately mitigate the risks of poor community-engagement policies and a failure to operate in a socially responsible way. Attorneys should help clients understand the longer-term legal and reputational risks of social and environmental mismanagement.

Ultimately, attorneys should work with clients to ensure that the commitments made to CSR standards are not subject to short-term, discretionary decision-making; companies cannot choose to put resources behind these commitments one year and not the next, as they might with specific philanthropic endeavors. Companies should not wait until moments of crisis to determine whether key management personnel understand that voluntary standards must translate into mandatory internal accountability to be effective. Attorneys can also assist clients in developing policies, standards, and contracts that reflect a company's true commitments, as well as in formulating implementation guidelines that reflect actual issues that come up in its business operations. Attorneys can help clients understand the distinctions between corporate philanthropy and CSR, as well as the nature and scope of specific CSR commitments, to ensure that the companies develop standards that can be implemented effectively, rather than adopting standards that represent empty and discretionary commitments to boilerplate language.

Conclusion

One of the definitions for CSR referenced at the beginning of this chapter states that "the social responsibility of business encompasses the economic, legal, ethical, and discretionary expectations that society has of organizations *at a given point in time*" (emphasis added). This definition assumes that societal expectations with regard to the roles and responsibilities of companies will change over time, and this assumption is certainly supported by the developments of the last several decades.

These shifts have associated legal, reputational, and operational implications for companies, and attorneys have an important role to play in helping companies understand both the substantive content of current expectations and the trends that are likely to define future requirements. They also have an important role to play in working with clients to develop tools, such as codes of conduct and sourcing contracts, that foster positive social and environmental outcomes for all stakeholders affected by a business venture or relationship. Helping clients understand the distinctions between CSR and corporate philanthropy, as well as the ways in which this distinction is defined, at least in part, by linkages between CSR and international human rights law, is an important part of the advice that attorneys can provide. This advice can help to ensure that clients have dedicated the proper resources to manage their operations in a way that is sufficiently responsive to both voluntary guidelines and mandatory legal and regulatory requirements, especially as the latter become more prominent in CSR.

Index